Nissan Bluebird Owners Workshop Manual

A K Legg T Eng (CEI), AMIMI

Models covered
Nissan Bluebird 1.8 DX & 1.8 Maxima Saloon; 1809 cc
Nissan Bluebird 1.8 Turbo ZX Saloon; 1809 cc
Nissan Bluebird 2.0 GL & 2.0 SGL Saloon & Estate; 1973 cc
Does not cover T12 range introduced March 1986

(1223-12M1)

ABCDE
FGHIJ
KLMNO
PQRS

Haynes Publishing Group
Sparkford Nr Yeovil
Somerset BA22 7JJ England

Haynes Publications, Inc
861 Lawrence Drive
Newbury Park
California 91320 USA

Acknowledgements

Thanks are due to the Champion Sparking Plug Company Limited who supplied the illustrations showing the spark plug conditions. Certain other illustrations are the copyright of the Nissan Motor Company Limited of Japan, and are used with their permission. Thanks are also due to Sykes-Pickavant who supplied some of the workshop tools, and all the staff at Sparkford who assisted in the production of this manual.

A book in the **Haynes Owners Workshop Manual Series**

Printed by J. H. Haynes & Co. Ltd, Sparkford, Nr Yeovil, Somerset BA22 7JJ, England

ISBN 1 85010 223 6

British Library Cataloguing in Publication Data
Legg, A. K.
Nissan Bluebird owners workshop manual. –
(Owner's Workshop Manuals)
1. Bluebird automobile
I. Title II. Series
629.28'722 TL215.B56
ISBN 1-85010-223-6

Contents

Nissan Bluebird 1.8 Turbo ZX

Nissan Bluebird 2.0 SGL

About this manual

Its aim

The aim of this manual is to help you get the best value from your vehicle. It can do so in several ways. It can help you decide what work must be done (even should you choose to get it done by a garage), provide information on routine maintenance and servicing, and give a logical course of action and diagnosis when random faults occur. However, it is hoped that you will use the manual by tackling the work yourself. On simpler jobs it may even be quicker than booking the car into a garage and going there twice, to leave and collect it. Perhaps most important, a lot of money can be saved by avoiding the costs a garage must charge to cover its labour and overheads.

The manual has drawings and descriptions to show the function of the various components so that their layout can be understood. Then the tasks are described and photographed in a step-by-step sequence so that even a novice can do the work.

Its arrangement

The manual is divided into twelve Chapters, each covering a logical sub-division of the vehicle. The Chapters are each divided into Sections, numbered with single figures, eg 5; and the Sections into paragraphs (or sub-sections), with decimal numbers following on from the Section they are in, eg 5.1, 5.2, 5.3 etc.

It is freely illustrated, especially in those parts where there is a detailed sequence of operations to be carried out. There are two forms of illustration: figures and photographs. The figures are numbered in sequence with decimal numbers, according to their position in the Chapter – eg Fig. 6.4 is the fourth drawing/illustration in Chapter 6. Photographs carry the same number (either individually or in related groups) as the Section or sub-section to which they relate.

There is an alphabetical index at the back of the manual as well as a contents list at the front. Each Chapter is also preceded by its own individual contents list.

References to the 'left' or 'right' of the vehicle are in the sense of a person in the driver's seat facing forwards.

Unless otherwise stated, nuts and bolts are removed by turning anti-clockwise, and tightened by turning clockwise.

Vehicle manufacturers continually make changes to specifications and recommendations, and these, when notified, are incorporated into our manuals at the earliest opportunity.

Whilst every care is taken to ensure that the information in this manual is correct, no liability can be accepted by the authors or publishers for loss, damage or injury caused by any errors in, or omissions from, the information given.

Introduction to the Nissan Bluebird (FWD)

The front wheel drive Nissan Bluebird was first introduced in early 1984 and is powered by a transversely-mounted engine and transmission similar to that fitted to the Nissan Stanza. 1.8 and 2.0 litre engines are available, and also a 1.8 litre Turbo version. The five-speed manual transmission incorporates overdrive fourth and fifth ratios. The automatic transmission incorporates three main ratios and an overdrive ratio which is switch-operated. The torque converter includes a lock-up facility which eliminates slip during cruising, and this provides maximum fuel economy.

The front suspension incorporates MacPherson struts, and the rear suspension includes telescopic struts, radius arms and parallel links. Front and rear anti-roll bars are fitted.

Working on the Bluebird is well within the scope of the DIY home mechanic. The mechanical design is not too complicated and does not incorporate some of the complexities found in early transversely-mounted engines.

Nissan Bluebird 2.0 Estate

General dimensions, weights and capacities

Dimensions

Overall length:		
Saloon	4500 mm (177.2 in)	
Estate	4585 mm (180.5 in)	
Overall width	1705 mm (67.1 in)	
Overall height:		
Saloon	1400 mm (55.1 in)	
Estate	1425 mm (56.1 in)	
Wheelbase	2550 mm (100.4 in)	
Track:	**Front**	**Rear**
Saloon	1460 mm (57.5 in)	1450 mm (57.1 in)
Estate	1455 mm (57.3 in)	1445 mm (56.9 in)
Minimum ground clearance	185.0 mm (7.3 in)	

Weights

Kerb weight:	
CA18 Saloon (manual)	1080 kg (2380 lb)
CA18ET Saloon (manual)	1140 kg (2515 lb)
CA18ET Saloon (automatic)	1175 kg (2590 lb)
CA20 Saloon (manual)	1110 kg (2450 lb)
CA20 Saloon (automatic)	1155 kg (2545 lb)
CA20 Estate (manual)	1155 kg (2545 lb)
CA20 Estate (automatic)	1200 kg (2645 lb)

Capacities

Fuel tank	60.0 litre (13.2 gals)	
Engine oil:		
With filter change	3.8 litre (6.7 pints)	
Without filter change	3.5 litre (6.2 pints)	
Manual transmission:		
Non-Turbo models	2.7 litre (4.8 pints)	
Turbo models	4.7 litre (8.3 pints)	
Automatic transmission	6.5 litre (11.4 pints)	
Cooling system:	**With heater**	**Without heater**
Non-Turbo models	6.5 litre (11.4 pints)	5.9 litre (10.4 pints)
Turbo models	7.0 litre (12.3 pints)	6.4 litre (11.3 pints)
Power steering	0.8 litre (1.6 pints)	

Jacking, wheel changing and towing

Jacking

Use the jack supplied with the vehicle only for wheel changing during roadside emergencies (photo). Chock the wheel diagonally opposite the one being removed.

When raising the vehicle for repair or maintenance, preferably use a trolley jack with a wooden block as an insulator to prevent damage to the underbody.

Locate the jack only under the points indicated and once the vehicle is raised, place safety stands under the side members as shown.

To avoid repetition, the procedure for raising the vehicle in order to carry out work under it is not included before each relevant operation described in this manual.

It is to be preferred and certainly recommended that the vehicle is positioned over an inspection pit or raised on a lift. Where such equipment is not available, use ramps or jack up the vehicle as previously described, but always supplement the lifting device with axle stands.

Towing

Towing hooks are welded to the front and the rear of the vehicle and should only be used in an emergency, as their designed function is as lash-down hooks, for use during transportion (photos).

When towing vehicles equipped with automatic transmission, restrict the distance towed to 20 miles (30 km) and the towing speed

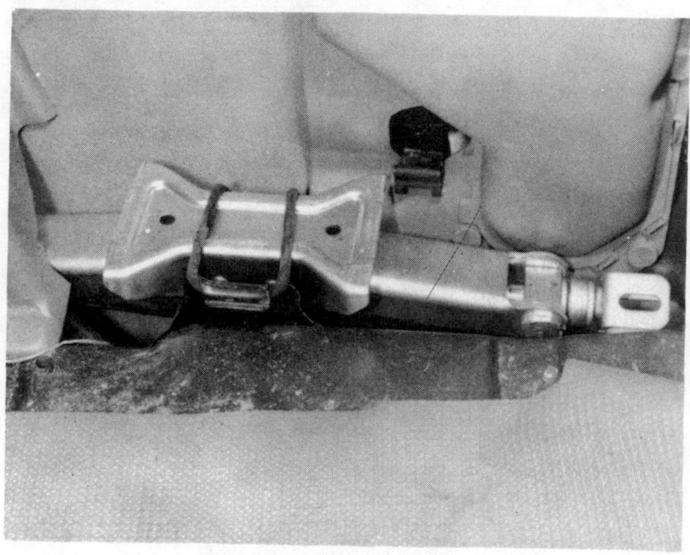

Jack supplied with car

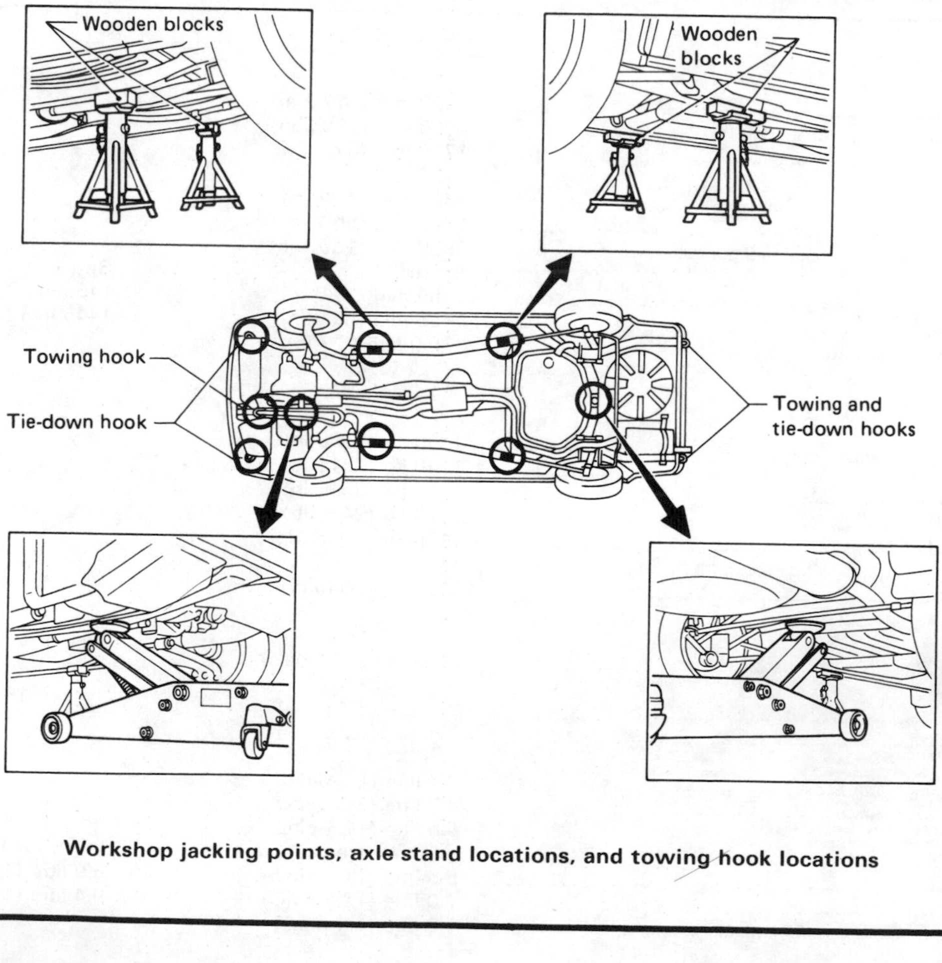

Wooden blocks

Wooden blocks

Towing hook

Tie-down hook

Towing and tie-down hooks

Workshop jacking points, axle stand locations, and towing hook locations

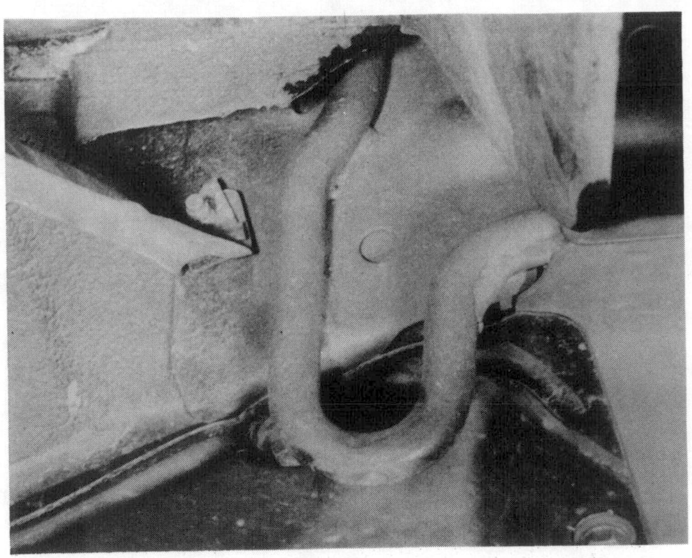

Front towing hook

Rear towing hook

to 20 mph (30 kmh). If these conditions are likely to be exceeded, then the front wheels will have to be raised off the road.

When being towed, remember to insert the ignition key and turn it to Position 1. Expect to apply greater pressure to the footbrake, as servo assistance will not be available after the first few brake applications.

Wheel changing

To change a roadwheel, first remove the wheel cap where fitted.

If the car is fairly new, the roadwheels and tyres will have been balanced on the vehicle during production. In order to maintain this balance then the position of the roadwheel in relation to the mounting hub must be marked before removing the wheel.

Release but do not remove each roadwheel bolt, and then raise the vehicle with the jack. Remove the bolts and take off the wheel.

Fit the wheel and screw in the bolts. Finally tighten the bolts after the vehicle has been lowered to the ground.

Tyre pressures are shown on a placard on the rear edge of the driver's door.

Buying spare parts and vehicle identification numbers

Buying spare parts

Spare parts are available from many sources, for example: Nissan/Datsun garages, other garages and accessory shops, and motor factors. Our advice regarding spare part sources is as follows:

Officially appointed Nissan/Datsun garages – This is the best source of parts which are peculiar to your vehicle and are otherwise not generally available (eg complete cylinder heads, internal gearbox components, badges, interior trim etc). It is also the only place at which you should buy parts if your vehicle is still under warranty: non Nissan/Datsun components may invalidate the warranty. To be sure of obtaining the correct parts it will always be necessary to give the storeman your vehicle's engine and chassis number, and if possible, to take the 'old' parts along for positive identification. Remember that some parts are available on a factory exhange scheme – any parts returned should always be clean! It obviously makes good sense to go straight to the specialists on your vehicle for this type of part for they are best equipped to supply you.

Other garages and accessory shops – These are often good places to buy materials and components needed for the maintenance of your vehicle (eg spark plugs, bulbs, drivebelts, oils and greases, touch-up paint, filler paste, etc). They also sell general accessories, usually have convenient opening hours, charge lower prices and can often be found not far from home.

Motor factors – Good factors will stock all of the more important components which wear out relatively quickly (eg clutch components, pistons, valves, exhaust systems, brake cylinders/pipes/hoses/seals/shoes and pads etc). Motor factors will often provide new or reconditioned components on a part exchange basis – this can save a considerable amount of money.

Vehicle identification numbers

The *Vehicle Identification Number* is located inside the engine compartment on the rear bulkhead (photo).

The *engine number is stamped on the side of the cylinder block at the transmission end (photo).*

The transmission number is stamped on the clutch release arm or upper surface of the unit.

Vehicle identification plate

Engine number location

General repair procedures

Whenever servicing, repair or overhaul work is carried out on the car or its components, it is necessary to observe the following procedures and instructions. This will assist in carrying out the operation efficiently and to a professional standard of workmanship.

Joint mating faces and gaskets

Where a gasket is used between the mating faces of two components, ensure that it is renewed on reassembly, and fit it dry unless otherwise stated in the repair procedure. Make sure that the mating faces are clean and dry with all traces of old gasket removed. When cleaning a joint face, use a tool which is not likely to score or damage the face, and remove any burrs or nicks with an oilstone or fine file.

Make sure that tapped holes are cleaned with a pipe cleaner, and keep them free of jointing compound if this is being used unless specifically instructed otherwise.

Ensure that all orifices, channels or pipes are clear and blow through them, preferably using compressed air.

Oil seals

Whenever an oil seal is removed from its working location, either individually or as part of an assembly, it should be renewed.

The very fine sealing lip of the seal is easily damaged and will not seal if the surface it contacts is not completely clean and free from scratches, nicks or grooves. If the original sealing surface of the component cannot be restored, the component should be renewed.

Protect the lips of the seal from any surface which may damage them in the course of fitting. Use tape or a conical sleeve where possible. Lubricate the seal lips with oil before fitting and, on dual lipped seals, fill the space between the lips with grease.

Unless otherwise stated, oil seals must be fitted with their sealing lips toward the lubricant to be sealed.

Use a tubular drift or block of wood of the appropriate size to install the seal and, if the seal housing is shouldered, drive the seal down to the shoulder. If the seal housing is unshouldered, the seal should be fitted with its face flush with the housing top face.

Screw threads and fastenings

Always ensure that a blind tapped hole is completely free from oil, grease, water or other fluid before installing the bolt or stud. Failure to do this could cause the housing to crack due to the hydraulic action of the bolt or stud as it is screwed in.

When tightening a castellated nut to accept a split pin, tighten the nut to the specified torque, where applicable, and then tighten further to the next split pin hole. Never slacken the nut to align a split pin hole unless stated in the repair procedure.

When checking or retightening a nut or bolt to a specified torque setting, slacken the nut or bolt by a quarter of a turn, and then retighten to the specified setting.

Locknuts, locktabs and washers

Any fastening which will rotate against a component or housing in the course of tightening should always have a washer between it and the relevant component or housing.

Spring or split washers should always be renewed when they are used to lock a critical component such as a big-end bearing retaining nut or bolt.

Locktabs which are folded over to retain a nut or bolt should always be renewed.

Self-locking nuts can be reused in non-critical areas, providing resistance can be felt when the locking portion passes over the bolt or stud thread.

Split pins must always be replaced with new ones of the correct size for the hole.

Special tools

Some repair procedures in this manual entail the use of special tools such as a press, two or three-legged pullers, spring compressors etc. Wherever possible, suitable readily available alternatives to the manufacturer's special tools are described, and are shown in use. In some instances, where no alternative is possible, it has been necessary to resort to the use of a manufacturer's tool and this has been done for reasons of safety as well as the efficient completion of the repair operation. Unless you are highly skilled and have a thorough understanding of the procedure described, never attempt to bypass the use of any special tool when the procedure described specifies its use. Not only is there a very great risk of personal injury, but expensive damage could be caused to the components involved.

Tools and working facilities

Introduction

A selection of good tools is a fundamental requirement for anyone contemplating the maintenance and repair of a motor vehicle. For the owner who does not possess any, their purchase will prove a considerable expense, offsetting some of the savings made by doing-it-yourself. However, provided that the tools purchased are of good quality, they will last for many years and prove an extremely worthwhile investment.

To help the average owner to decide which tools are needed to carry out the various tasks detailed in this manual, we have compiled three lists of tools under the following headings: *Maintenance and minor repair, Repair and overhaul,* and *Special.* The newcomer to practical mechanics should start off with the *Maintenance and minor repair* tool kit and confine himself to the simpler jobs around the vehicle. Then, as his confidence and experience grow, he can undertake more difficult tasks, buying extra tools as, and when, they are needed. In this way, a *Maintenance and minor repair* tool kit can be built-up into a *Repair and overhaul* tool kit over a considerable period of time without any major cash outlays. The experienced do-it-yourselfer will have a tool kit good enough for most repair and overhaul procedures and will add tools from the *Special* category when he feels the expense is justified by the amount of use to which these tools will be put.

It is obviously not possible to cover the subject of tools fully here. For those who wish to learn more about tools and their use there is a book entitled *How to Choose and Use Car Tools* available from the publishers of this manual.

Maintenance and minor repair tool kit

The tools given in this list should be considered as a minimum requirement if routine maintenance, servicing and minor repair operations are to be undertaken. We recommend the purchase of combination spanners (ring one end, open-ended the other); although more expensive than open-ended ones, they do give the advantages of both types of spanner.

Combination spanners - 10, 11, 12, 13, 14 & 17 mm
Adjustable spanner - 9 inch
Spark plug spanner (with rubber insert)
Spark plug gap adjustment tool
Set of feeler gauges
Brake bleed nipple spanner
Screwdriver - 4 in long x 1/4 in dia (flat blade)
Screwdriver - 4 in long x 1/4 in dia (cross blade)
Combination pliers - 6 inch
Hacksaw (junior)
Tyre pump
Tyre pressure gauge
Grease gun
Oil can
Fine emery cloth (1 sheet)
Wire brush (small)
Funnel (medium size)

Repair and overhaul tool kit

These tools are virtually essential for anyone undertaking any major repairs to a motor vehicle, and are additional to those given in the *Maintenance and minor repair* list. Included in this list is a comprehensive set of sockets. Although these are expensive they will be found invaluable as they are so versatile - particularly if various drives are included in the set. We recommend the ½ in square-drive type, as this can be used with most proprietary torque wrenches. If you cannot afford a socket set, even bought piecemeal, then inexpensive tubular box spanners are a useful alternative.

The tools in this list will occasionally need to be supplemented by tools from the *Special* list.

Sockets (or box spanners) to cover range in previous list
Reversible ratchet drive (for use with sockets)
Extension piece, 10 inch (for use with sockets)
Universal joint (for use with sockets)
Torque wrench (for use with sockets)
'Mole' wrench - 8 inch
Ball pein hammer
Soft-faced hammer, plastic or rubber
Screwdriver - 6 in long x 5/16 in dia (flat blade)
Screwdriver - 2 in long x 5/16 in square (flat blade)
Screwdriver - 1 1/2 in long x 1/4 in dia (cross blade)
Screwdriver - 3 in long x 1/8 in dia (electricians)
Pliers - electricians side cutters
Pliers - needle nosed
Pliers - circlip (internal and external)
Cold chisel - 1/2 inch
Scriber
Scraper
Centre punch
Pin punch
Hacksaw
Valve grinding tool
Steel rule/straight-edge
Allen keys
Selection of files
Wire brush (large)
Axle-stands
Jack (strong trolley or hydraulic type)

Special tools

The tools in this list are those which are not used regularly, are expensive to buy, or which need to be used in accordance with their manufacturers' instructions. Unless relatively difficult mechanical jobs are undertaken frequently, it will not be economic to buy many of these tools. Where this is the case, you could consider clubbing together with friends (or joining a motorists' club) to make a joint purchase, or borrowing the tools against a deposit from a local garage or tool hire specialist.

The following list contains only those tools and instruments freely available to the public, and not those special tools produced by the vehicle manufacturer specifically for its dealer network. You will find occasional references to these manufacturers' special tools in the text of this manual. Generally, an alternative method of doing the job without the vehicle manufacturers' special tool is given. However, sometimes, there is no alternative to using them. Where this is the case and the relevant tool cannot be bought or borrowed, you will have to entrust the work to a franchised garage.

Valve spring compressor (where applicable)
Piston ring compressor
Balljoint separator
Universal hub/bearing puller
Impact screwdriver
Micrometer and/or vernier gauge
Dial gauge
Stroboscopic timing light
Dwell angle meter/tachometer
Universal electrical multi-meter
Cylinder compression gauge
Lifting tackle
Trolley jack
Light with extension lead

Buying tools

For practically all tools, a tool factor is the best source since he will have a very comprehensive range compared with the average garage or accessory shop. Having said that, accessory shops often offer excellent quality tools at discount prices, so it pays to shop around.

Remember, you don't have to buy the most expensive items on the shelf, but it is always advisable to steer clear of the very cheap tools. There are plenty of good tools around at reasonable prices, so ask the proprietor or manager of the shop for advice before making a purchase.

Care and maintenance of tools

Having purchased a reasonable tool kit, it is necessary to keep the tools in a clean serviceable condition. After use, always wipe off any dirt, grease and metal particles using a clean, dry cloth, before putting the tools away. Never leave them lying around after they have been used. A simple tool rack on the garage or workshop wall, for items such as screwdrivers and pliers is a good idea. Store all normal wrenches and sockets in a metal box. Any measuring instruments, gauges, meters, etc, must be carefully stored where they cannot be damaged or become rusty.

Take a little care when tools are used. Hammer heads inevitably become marked and screwdrivers lose the keen edge on their blades from time to time. A little timely attention with emery cloth or a file will soon restore items like this to a good serviceable finish.

Working facilities

Not to be forgotten when discussing tools, is the workshop itself. If anything more than routine maintenance is to be carried out, some form of suitable working area becomes essential.

It is appreciated that many an owner mechanic is forced by circumstances to remove an engine or similar item, without the benefit of a garage or workshop. Having done this, any repairs should always be done under the cover of a roof.

Wherever possible, any dismantling should be done on a clean, flat workbench or table at a suitable working height.

Any workbench needs a vice: one with a jaw opening of 4 in (100 mm) is suitable for most jobs. As mentioned previously, some clean dry storage space is also required for tools, as well as for lubricants, cleaning fluids, touch-up paints and so on, which become necessary.

Another item which may be required, and which has a much more general usage, is an electric drill with a chuck capacity of at least 5/16 in (8 mm). This, together with a good range of twist drills, is virtually essential for fitting accessories such as mirrors and reversing lights.

Last, but not least, always keep a supply of old newspapers and clean, lint-free rags available, and try to keep any working area as clean as possible.

Spanner jaw gap comparison table

Jaw gap (in)	Spanner size
0.250	1/4 in AF
0.276	7 mm
0.313	5/16 in AF
0.315	8 mm
0.344	11/32 in AF; 1/8 in Whitworth
0.354	9 mm
0.375	3/8 in AF
0.394	10 mm
0.433	11 mm
0.438	7/16 in AF
0.445	3/16 in Whitworth; 1/4 in BSF
0.472	12 mm
0.500	1/2 in AF
0.512	13 mm
0.525	1/4 in Whitworth; 5/16 in BSF
0.551	14 mm
0.563	9/16 in AF
0.591	15 mm
0.600	5/16 in Whitworth; 3/8 in BSF
0.625	5/8 in AF
0.630	16 mm
0.669	17 mm
0.686	11/16 in AF
0.709	18 mm
0.710	3/8 in Whitworth; 7/16 in BSF
0.748	19 mm
0.750	3/4 in AF
0.813	13/16 in AF
0.820	7/16 in Whitworth; 1/2 in BSF
0.866	22 mm
0.875	7/8 in AF
0.920	1/2 in Whitworth; 9/16 in BSF
0.938	15/16 in AF
0.945	24 mm
1.000	1 in AF
1.010	9/16 in Whitworth; 5/8 in BSF
1.024	26 mm
1.063	1 1/16 in AF; 27 mm
1.100	5/8 in Whitworth; 11/16 in BSF
1.125	1 1/8 in AF
1.181	30 mm
1.200	11/16 in Whitworth; 3/4 in BSF
1.250	1 1/4 in AF
1.260	32 mm
1.300	3/4 in Whitworth; 7/8 in BSF
1.313	1 5/16 in AF
1.390	13/16 in Whitworth; 15/16 in BSF
1.417	36 mm
1.438	1 7/16 in AF
1.480	7/8 in Whitworth; 1 in BSF
1.500	1 1/2 in AF
1.575	40 mm; 15/16 in Whitworth
1.614	41 mm
1.625	1 5/8 in AF
1.670	1 in Whitworth; 1 1/8 in BSF
1.688	1 11/16 in AF
1.811	46 mm
1.813	1 13/16 in AF
1.860	1 1/8 in Whitworth; 1 1/4 in BSF
1.875	1 7/8 in AF
1.969	50 mm
2.000	2 in AF
2.050	1 1/4 in Whitworth; 1 3/8 in BSF
2.165	55 mm
2.362	60 mm

Safety first!

Professional motor mechanics are trained in safe working procedures. However enthusiastic you may be about getting on with the job in hand, do take the time to ensure that your safety is not put at risk. A moment's lack of attention can result in an accident, as can failure to observe certain elementary precautions.

There will always be new ways of having accidents, and the following points do not pretend to be a comprehensive list of all dangers; they are intended rather to make you aware of the risks and to encourage a safety-conscious approach to all work you carry out on your vehicle.

Essential DOs and DON'Ts

DON'T rely on a single jack when working underneath the vehicle. Always use reliable additional means of support, such as axle stands, securely placed under a part of the vehicle that you know will not give way.

DON'T attempt to loosen or tighten high-torque nuts (e.g. wheel hub nuts) while the vehicle is on a jack; it may be pulled off.

DON'T start the engine without first ascertaining that the transmission is in neutral (or 'Park' where applicable) and the parking brake applied.

DON'T suddenly remove the filler cap from a hot cooling system – cover it with a cloth and release the pressure gradually first, or you may get scalded by escaping coolant.

DON'T attempt to drain oil until you are sure it has cooled sufficiently to avoid scalding you.

DON'T grasp any part of the engine, exhaust or catalytic converter without first ascertaining that it is sufficiently cool to avoid burning you.

DON'T allow brake fluid or antifreeze to contact vehicle paintwork.

DON'T syphon toxic liquids such as fuel, brake fluid or antifreeze by mouth, or allow them to remain on your skin.

DON'T inhale dust – it may be injurious to health (see *Asbestos* below).

DON'T allow any spilt oil or grease to remain on the floor – wipe it up straight away, before someone slips on it.

DON'T use ill-fitting spanners or other tools which may slip and cause injury.

DON'T attempt to lift a heavy component which may be beyond your capability – get assistance.

DON'T rush to finish a job, or take unverified short cuts.

DON'T allow children or animals in or around an unattended vehicle.

DO wear eye protection when using power tools such as drill, sander, bench grinder etc, and when working under the vehicle.

DO use a barrier cream on your hands prior to undertaking dirty jobs – it will protect your skin from infection as well as making the dirt easier to remove afterwards; but make sure your hands aren't left slippery.

DO keep loose clothing (cuffs, tie etc) and long hair well out of the way of moving mechanical parts.

DO remove rings, wristwatch etc, before working on the vehicle – especially the electrical system.

DO ensure that any lifting tackle used has a safe working load rating adequate for the job.

DO keep your work area tidy – it is only too easy to fall over articles left lying around.

DO get someone to check periodically that all is well, when working alone on the vehicle.

DO carry out work in a logical sequence and check that everything is correctly assembled and tightened afterwards.

DO remember that your vehicle's safety affects that of yourself and others. If in doubt on any point, get specialist advice.

IF, in spite of following these precautions, you are unfortunate enough to injure yourself, seek medical attention as soon as possible.

Asbestos

Certain friction, insulating, sealing, and other products – such as brake linings, brake bands, clutch linings, torque converters, gaskets, etc – contain asbestos. *Extreme care must be taken to avoid inhalation of dust from such products since it is hazardous to health.* If in doubt, assume that they *do* contain asbestos.

Fire

Remember at all times that petrol (gasoline) is highly flammable. Never smoke, or have any kind of naked flame around, when working on the vehicle. But the risk does not end there – a spark caused by an electrical short-circuit, by two metal surfaces contacting each other, by careless use of tools, or even by static electricity built up in your body under certain conditions, can ignite petrol vapour, which in a confined space is highly explosive.

Always disconnect the battery earth (ground) terminal before working on any part of the fuel or electrical system, and never risk spilling fuel on to a hot engine or exhaust.

It is recommended that a fire extinguisher of a type suitable for fuel and electrical fires is kept handy in the garage or workplace at all times. Never try to extinguish a fuel or electrical fire with water.

Fumes

Certain fumes are highly toxic and can quickly cause unconsciousness and even death if inhaled to any extent. Petrol (gasoline) vapour comes into this category, as do the vapours from certain solvents such as trichloroethylene. Any draining or pouring of such volatile fluids should be done in a well ventilated area.

When using cleaning fluids and solvents, read the instructions carefully. Never use materials from unmarked containers – they may give off poisonous vapours.

Never run the engine of a motor vehicle in an enclosed space such as a garage. Exhaust fumes contain carbon monoxide which is extremely poisonous; if you need to run the engine, always do so in the open air or at least have the rear of the vehicle outside the workplace.

If you are fortunate enough to have the use of an inspection pit, never drain or pour petrol, and never run the engine, while the vehicle is standing over it; the fumes, being heavier than air, will concentrate in the pit with possibly lethal results.

The battery

Never cause a spark, or allow a naked light, near the vehicle's battery. It will normally be giving off a certain amount of hydrogen gas, which is highly explosive.

Always disconnect the battery earth (ground) terminal before working on the fuel or electrical systems.

If possible, loosen the filler plugs or cover when charging the battery from an external source. Do not charge at an excessive rate or the battery may burst.

Take care when topping up and when carrying the battery. The acid electrolyte, even when diluted, is very corrosive and should not be allowed to contact the eyes or skin.

If you ever need to prepare electrolyte yourself, always add the acid slowly to the water, and never the other way round. Protect against splashes by wearing rubber gloves and goggles.

When jump starting a car using a booster battery, for negative earth (ground) vehicles, connect the jump leads in the following sequence: First connect one jump lead between the positive (+) terminals of the two batteries. Then connect the other jump lead first to the negative (–) terminal of the booster battery, and then to a good earthing (ground) point on the vehicle to be started, at least 18 in (45 cm) from the battery if possible. Ensure that hands and jump leads are clear of any moving parts, and that the two vehicles do not touch. Disconnect the leads in the reverse order.

Mains electricity

When using an electric power tool, inspection light etc, which works from the mains, always ensure that the appliance is correctly connected to its plug and that, where necessary, it is properly earthed (grounded). Do not use such appliances in damp conditions and, again, beware of creating a spark or applying excessive heat in the vicinity of fuel or fuel vapour.

Ignition HT voltage

A severe electric shock can result from touching certain parts of the ignition system, such as the HT leads, when the engine is running or being cranked, particularly if components are damp or the insulation is defective. Where an electronic ignition system is fitted, the HT voltage is much higher and could prove fatal.

Routine maintenance

The Routine Maintenance instructions listed are basically those recommended by the vehicle manufacturer. They are sometimes supplemented by additional maintenance tasks proven to be necessary.

The maintenance intervals recommended are those specified by the manufacturer. They are necessarily something of a compromise, since no two vehicles operate under identical conditions. The DIY mechanic, who does not have labour costs to consider, may wish to shorten the service intervals. Experience will show whether this is necessary.

Where the vehicle is under severe operating conditions (extremes of heat or cold, dusty conditions, or mainly stop-start driving), more frequent oil changes may be desirable. If in doubt consult your dealer.

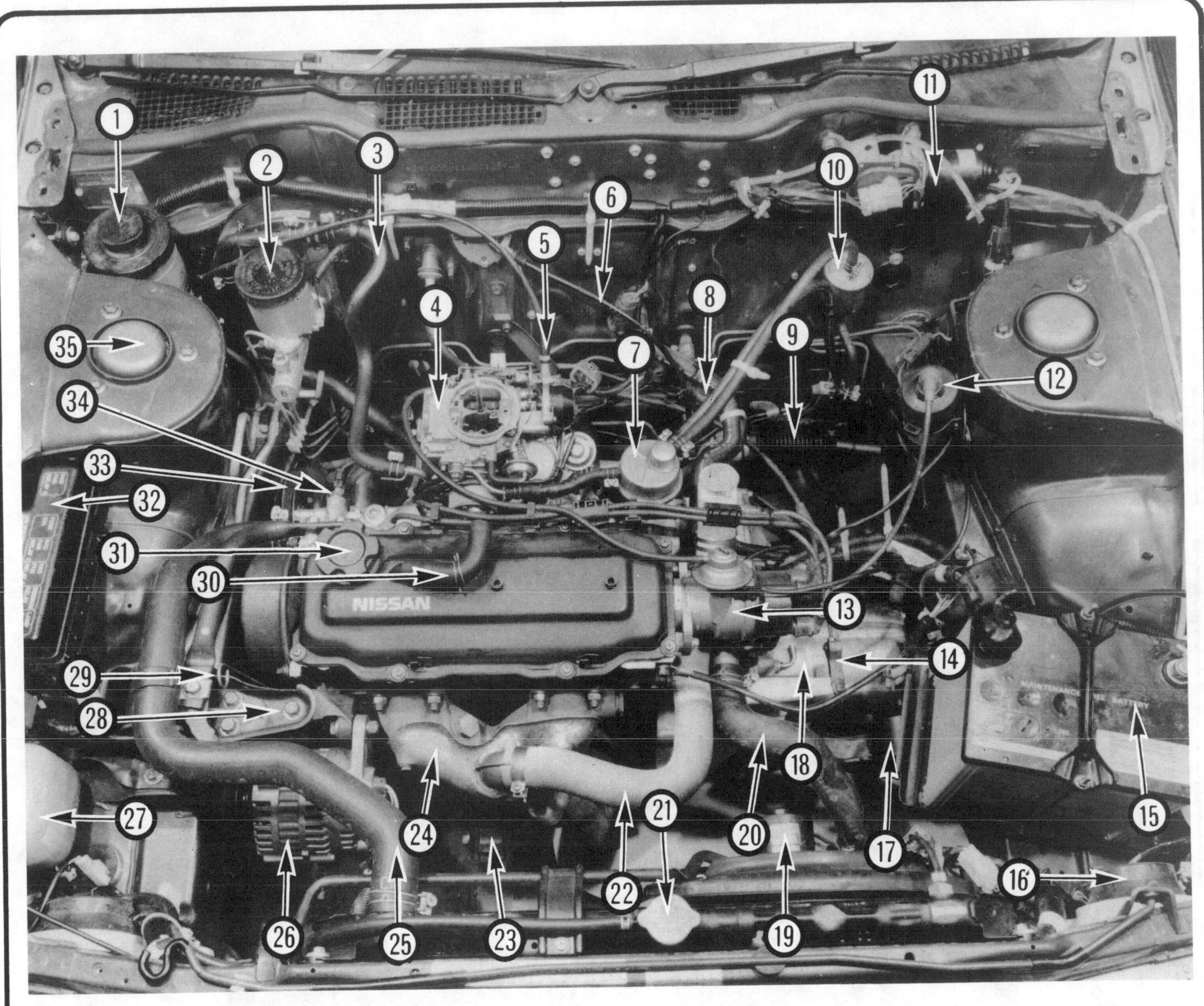

Under-bonnet view (carburettor engine)

1 *Power steering fluid reservoir*
2 *Brake fluid reservoir*
3 *Brake servo vacuum hose*
4 *Carburettor*
5 *Accelerator cable*
6 *Speedometer cable*
7 *Fuel pump*
8 *Heater hoses*
9 *Steering gear*
10 *Fuel filter*
11 *Wiper motor*
12 *Ignition coil*
13 *Distributor*
14 *Clutch cable end fitting*
15 *Battery*
16 *Headlamp unit*
17 *Engine/transmission mounting*
18 *Manual transmission*
19 *Electric cooling fan motor*
20 *Bottom hose*
21 *Radiator filler cap*
22 *Hot air hose for air cleaner*
23 *Front engine support mounting*
24 *Exhaust manifold*
25 *Top hose*
26 *Alternator*
27 *Expansion tank*
28 *Engine mounting*
29 *Engine oil level dipstick*
30 *Crankcase ventilation hose*
31 *Engine oil filler cap*
32 *Relay box*
33 *Water pump*
34 *Water temperature switch*
35 *Front suspension top mounting*

View of front underside of car

1 *Intermediate exhaust pipe and flexible section*
2 *RH driveshaft*
3 *Power steering pump drivebelt*
4 *Alternator drivebelt*
5 *Engine oil drain plug*
6 *Alternator*
7 *Engine compartment lower crossmember*
8 *Exhaust downpipe*
9 *Manual transmission*
10 *Electric cooling fan motor*
11 *LH driveshaft*
12 *Front lower suspension arm*
13 *Front suspension lower balljoint*
14 *Steering tie-rod end*
15 *Transmission support rod*
16 *Front anti-roll bar*
17 *Transmission control rod*
18 *Exhaust system mounting*

View of rear underside of car

1 *Rear anti-roll bar*
2 *Rear suspension strut*
3 *Hydraulic brake pipes and fuel lines*
4 *Handbrake cable*
5 *Fuel tank supply and return hoses*
6 *Fuel tank drain plug*
7 *Rear suspension radius arm*
8 *Fuel filler tube*
9 *Parallel link (non adjustable)*
10 *Parallel link (adjustable)*
11 *Spare wheel well*
12 *Rear brake pressure regulating valve*
13 *Rear exhaust pipe and silencer*

Weekly or before a long journey

Check engine oil level and top-up if necessary
Check coolant level in expansion tank
Check washer fluid level in reservoir(s)
Check tyre pressures, including the spare

After the first 1000 km (600 miles) – new vehicle only

Check torque wrench setting of cylinder head bolts, manifolds, exhaust, and carburettor (Chapter 1 and 3)
Adjust valve clearances (Chapter 1)
Check driveshafts for condition and tension (Chapter 2, 10 and 12)
Adjust idling speed and mixture (Chapter 3)
Check steering, suspension and driveshaft components (Chapter 10)
Check brake and clutch operation (Chapter 9 & 5)

Every 5000 km (3000 miles) or 3 months – whichever comes first

Change the engine oil on Turbo models only (Chapter 1).

Every 10 000 km (6000 miles) or 6 months – whichever comes first

Change the engine oil (Chapter 1)
Renew the oil filter (Chapter 1)
Adjust idling speed and mixture (Chapter 3)
Check and adjust ignition timing (Chapter 4)
Check and clean spark plugs (Chapter 4)
Clean air cleaner element on non-Turbo models (Chapter 3)
Check brake and clutch (where applicable) fluid level (Chapters 9 and 5)
Check automatic transmission fluid level (Chapter 7)
Check power steering fluid level and lines (Chapter 10)
Check brake, clutch, fuel and exhaust components (Chapter 9, 5 and 3)
Check manual transmission oil level (Chapter 6)
Check brake disc pads and components for wear (Chapter 9)
Lubricate locks and hinges (Chapter 11)
Check brake and clutch operation (Chapter 9 and 5)

Every 20 000 km (12 000 miles) or 12 months – whichever comes first

Adjust valve clearances (Chapter 1)
Check drivebelts for condition and tension (Chapter 2, 10 and 12)
Check cooling system components (Chapter 2)
Renew spark plugs (Chapter 4)
Check crankcase ventilation system (Chapter 1)
Check coolant, fuel and vacuum hoses (Chapters 2, 3 and 9)
Check air cleaner temperature control (Chapter 3)
Check steering, suspension and driveshaft components (Chapter 10)
Check wheel alignment and balance wheels (Chapter 10)
Check rear brake linings and drums (Chapter 9)
Check seat belts (Chapter 12)

Every 40 000 km (24 000 miles) or 24 months – whichever comes first

Renew the antifreeze solution (Chapter 2)
Check fuel system (Chapter 3)
Renew air cleaner element (Chapter 3)
Renew fuel filter (Chapter 3)
Check ignition wiring (Chapter 4)
Renew brake fluid (Chapter 9)
Check brake servo unit (Chapter 9)
Check front wheel bearing grease (Chapter 8)

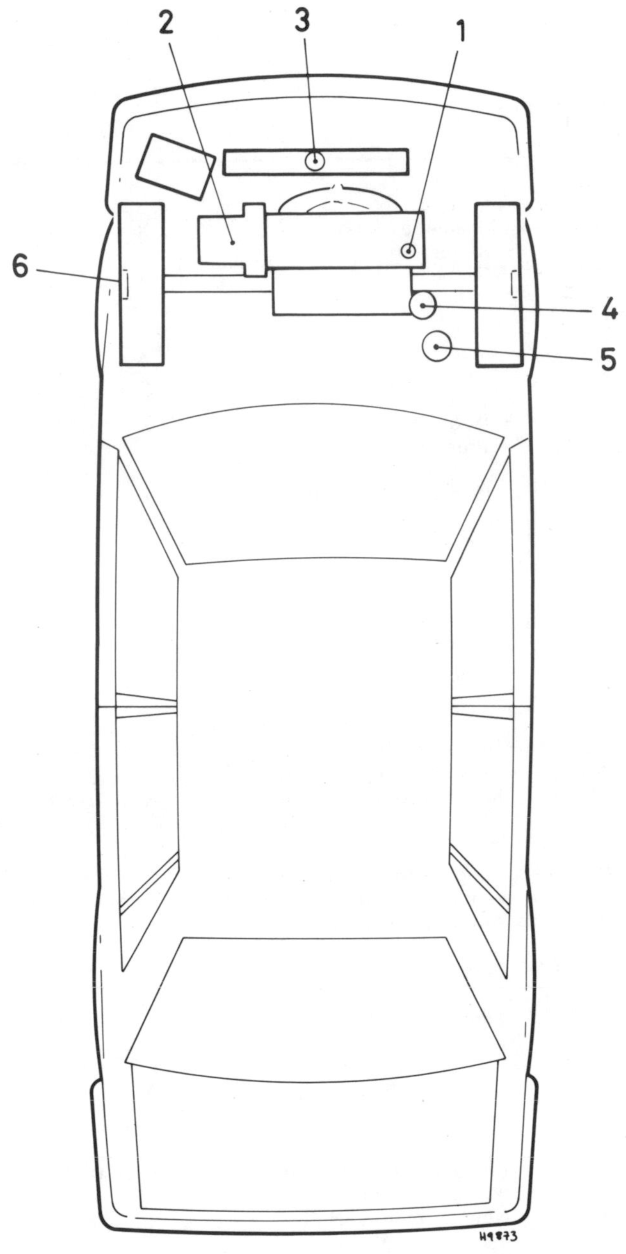

Recommended lubricants and fluids

Component or system	Lubricant type or specification
Engine (1)	Engine oil to API SE – SAE 20W/20, 20W/40 or 20W/50
Manual transmission (2)	Gear oil to API GL-4 – SAE 75W/90 or 80W/90
Automatic transmission (2)	Automatic transmission fluid to Dexron II specification
Cooling system (3)	Ethylene glycol based antifreeze mixture
Brake/clutch fluid (4)	Brake fluid to DOT 3 specification
Power steering (5)	Automatic transmission fluid to Dexron II specification
Steering gear and hub bearings (6)	Lithium based grease to NLGI No 2

Conversion factors

Length (distance)					
Inches (in)	X	25.4	= Millimetres (mm)	X	0.0394 = Inches (in)
Feet (ft)	X	0.305	= Metres (m)	X	3.281 = Feet (ft)
Miles	X	1.609	= Kilometres (km)	X	0.621 = Miles
Volume (capacity)					
Cubic inches (cu in; in^3)	X	16.387	= Cubic centimetres (cc; cm^3)	X	0.061 = Cubic inches (cu in; in^3)
Imperial pints (Imp pt)	X	0.568	= Litres (l)	X	1.76 = Imperial pints (Imp pt)
Imperial quarts (Imp qt)	X	1.137	= Litres (l)	X	0.88 = Imperial quarts (Imp qt)
Imperial quarts (Imp qt)	X	1.201	= US quarts (US qt)	X	0.833 = Imperial quarts (Imp qt)
US quarts (US qt)	X	0.946	= Litres (l)	X	1.057 = US quarts (US qt)
Imperial gallons (Imp gal)	X	4.546	= Litres (l)	X	0.22 = Imperial gallons (Imp gal)
Imperial gallons (Imp gal)	X	1.201	= US gallons (US gal)	X	0.833 = Imperial gallons (Imp gal)
US gallons (US gal)	X	3.785	= Litres (l)	X	0.264 = US gallons (US gal)
Mass (weight)					
Ounces (oz)	X	28.35	= Grams (g)	X	0.035 = Ounces (oz)
Pounds (lb)	X	0.454	= Kilograms (kg)	X	2.205 = Pounds (lb)
Force					
Ounces-force (ozf; oz)	X	0.278	= Newtons (N)	X	3.6 = Ounces-force (ozf; oz)
Pounds-force (lbf; lb)	X	4.448	= Newtons (N)	X	0.225 = Pounds-force (lbf; lb)
Newtons (N)	X	0.1	= Kilograms-force (kgf; kg)	X	9.81 = Newtons (N)
Pressure					
Pounds-force per square inch (psi; lbf/in^2; lb/in^2)	X	0.070	= Kilograms-force per square centimetre (kgf/cm^2; kg/cm^2)	X	14.223 = Pounds-force per square inch (psi; lbf/in^2; lb/in^2)
Pounds-force per square inch (psi; lbf/in^2; lb/in^2)	X	0.068	= Atmospheres (atm)	X	14.696 = Pounds-force per square inch (psi; lbf/in^2; lb/in^2)
Pounds-force per square inch (psi; lbf/in^2; lb/in^2)	X	0.069	= Bars	X	14.5 = Pounds-force per square inch (psi; lbf/in^2; lb/in^2)
Pounds-force per square inch (psi; lbf/in^2; lb/in^2)	X	6.895	= Kilopascals (kPa)	X	0.145 = Pounds-force per square inch (psi; lbf/in^2; lb/in^2)
Kilopascals (kPa)	X	0.01	= Kilograms-force per square centimetre (kgf/cm^2; kg/cm^2)	X	98.1 = Kilopascals (kPa)
Torque (moment of force)					
Pounds-force inches (lbf in; lb in)	X	1.152	= Kilograms-force centimetre (kgf cm; kg cm)	X	0.868 = Pounds-force inches (lbf in; lb in)
Pounds-force inches (lbf in; lb in)	X	0.113	= Newton metres (Nm)	X	8.85 = Pounds-force inches (lbf in; lb in)
Pounds-force inches (lbf in; lb in)	X	0.083	= Pounds-force feet (lbf ft; lb ft)	X	12 = Pounds-force inches (lbf in; lb in)
Pounds-force feet (lbf ft; lb ft)	X	0.138	= Kilograms-force metres (kgf m; kg m)	X	7.233 = Pounds-force feet (lbf ft; lb ft)
Pounds-force feet (lbf ft; lb ft)	X	1.356	= Newton metres (Nm)	X	0.738 = Pounds-force feet (lbf ft; lb ft)
Newton metres (Nm)	X	0.102	= Kilograms-force metres (kgf m; kg m)	X	9.804 = Newton metres (Nm)
Power					
Horsepower (hp)	X	745.7	= Watts (W)	X	0.0013 = Horsepower (hp)
Velocity (speed)					
Miles per hour (miles/hr; mph)	X	1.609	= Kilometres per hour (km/hr; kph)	X	0.621 = Miles per hour (miles/hr; mph)
Fuel consumption*					
Miles per gallon, Imperial (mpg)	X	0.354	= Kilometres per litre (km/l)	X	2.825 = Miles per gallon, Imperial (mpg)
Miles per gallon, US (mpg)	X	0.425	= Kilometres per litre (km/l)	X	2.352 = Miles per gallon, US (mpg)

Temperature

Degrees Fahrenheit = (°C x 1.8) + 32

Degrees Celsius (Degrees Centigrade; °C) = (°F - 32) x 0.56

**It is common practice to convert from miles per gallon (mpg) to litres/100 kilometres (l/100km), where mpg (Imperial) x l/100 km = 282 and mpg (US) x l/100 km = 235*

Fault diagnosis

Introduction

The vehicle owner who does his or her own maintenance according to the recommended schedules should not have to use this section of the manual very often. Modern component reliability is such that, provided those items subject to wear or deterioration are inspected or renewed at the specified intervals, sudden failure is comparatively rare. Faults do not usually just happen as a result of sudden failure, but develop over a period of time. Major mechanical failures in particular are usually preceded by characteristic symptoms over hundreds or even thousands of miles. Those components which do occasionally fail without warning are often small and easily carried in the vehicle.

With any fault finding, the first step is to decide where to begin investigations. Sometimes this is obvious, but on other occasions a little detective work will be necessary. The owner who makes half a dozen haphazard adjustments or replacements may be successful in curing a fault (or its symptoms), but he will be none the wiser if the fault recurs and he may well have spent more time and money than was necessary. A calm and logical approach will be found to be more satisfactory in the long run. Always take into account any warning signs or abnormalities that may have been noticed in the period preceding the fault – power loss, high or low gauge readings, unusual noises or smells, etc – and remember that failure of components such as fuses or spark plugs may only be pointers to some underlying fault.

The pages which follow here are intended to help in cases of failure to start or breakdown on the road. There is also a Fault Diagnosis Section at the end of each Chapter which should be consulted if the preliminary checks prove unfruitful. Whatever the fault, certain basic principles apply. These are as follows:

Verify the fault. This is simply a matter of being sure that you know what the symptoms are before starting work. This is particularly important if you are investigating a fault for someone else who may not have described it very accurately.

Don't overlook the obvious. For example, if the vehicle won't start, is there petrol in the tank? (Don't take anyone else's word on this particular point, and don't trust the fuel gauge either!) If an electrical fault is indicated, look for loose or broken wires before digging out the test gear.

Cure the disease, not the symptom. Substituting a flat battery with a fully charged one will get you off the hard shoulder, but if the underlying cause is not attended to, the new battery will go the same way. Similarly, changing oil-fouled spark plugs for a new set will get you moving again, but remember that the reason for the fouling (if it wasn't simply an incorrect grade of plug) will have to be established and corrected.

Don't take anything for granted. Particularly, don't forget that a 'new' component may itself be defective (especially if it's been rattling round in the boot for months), and don't leave components out of a fault diagnosis sequence just because they are new or recently fitted. When you do finally diagnose a difficult fault, you'll probably realise that all the evidence was there from the start.

Electrical faults

Electrical faults can be more puzzling than straightforward mechanical failures, but they are no less susceptible to logical analysis if the basic principles of operation are understood. Vehicle electrical wiring exists in extremely unfavourable conditions – heat, vibration and chemical attack – and the first things to look for are loose or corroded connections and broken or chafed wires, especially where the wires pass through holes in the bodywork or are subject to vibration.

All metal-bodied vehicles in current production have one pole of the battery 'earthed', ie connected to the vehicle bodywork, and in nearly all modern vehicles it is the negative (–) terminal. The various electrical components – motors, bulb holders etc – are also connected to earth, either by means of a lead or directly by their mountings. Electric current flows through the component and then back to the battery via the bodywork. If the component mounting is loose or corroded, or if a good path back to the battery is not available, the circuit will be incomplete and malfunction will result. The engine and/or gearbox are also earthed by means of flexible metal straps to the body or subframe; if these straps are loose or missing, starter motor, generator and ignition trouble may result.

Assuming the earth return to be satisfactory, electrical faults will be due either to component malfunction or to defects in the current supply. Individual components are dealt with in Chapter 12. If supply wires are broken or cracked internally this results in an open-circuit, and the easiest way to check for this is to bypass the suspect wire temporarily with a length of wire having a crocodile clip or suitable connector at each end. Alternatively, a 12V test lamp can be used to verify the presence of supply voltage at various points along the wire and the break can be thus isolated.

If a bare portion of a live wire touches the bodywork or other earthed metal part, the electricity will take the low-resistance path thus formed back to the battery: this is known as a short-circuit. Hopefully a short-circuit will blow a fuse, but otherwise it may cause burning of the insulation (and possibly further short-circuits) or even a fire. This is why it is inadvisable to bypass persistently blowing fuses with silver foil or wire.

Spares and tool kit

Most vehicles are supplied only with sufficient tools for wheel changing; the *Maintenance and minor repair* tool kit detailed in *Tools and working facilities,* with the addition of a hammer, is probably sufficient for those repairs that most motorists would consider attempting at the roadside. In addition a few items which can be fitted without too much trouble in the event of a breakdown should be

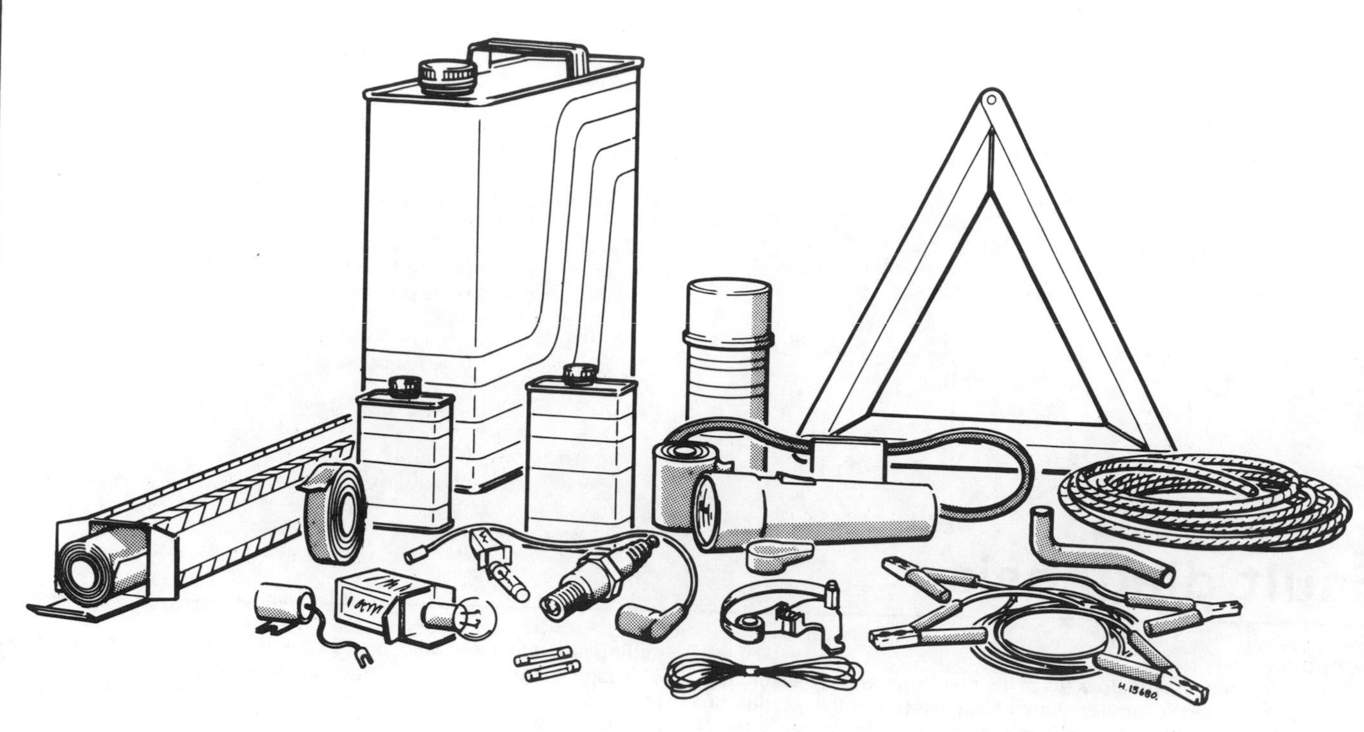

Carrying a few spares may save a long walk!

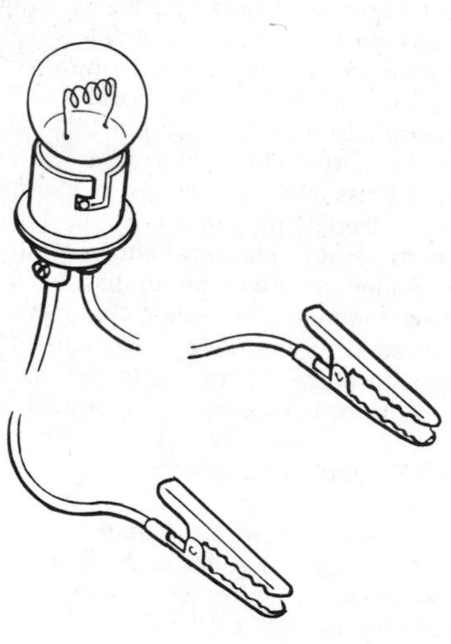

A simple test lamp is useful for checking electrical faults

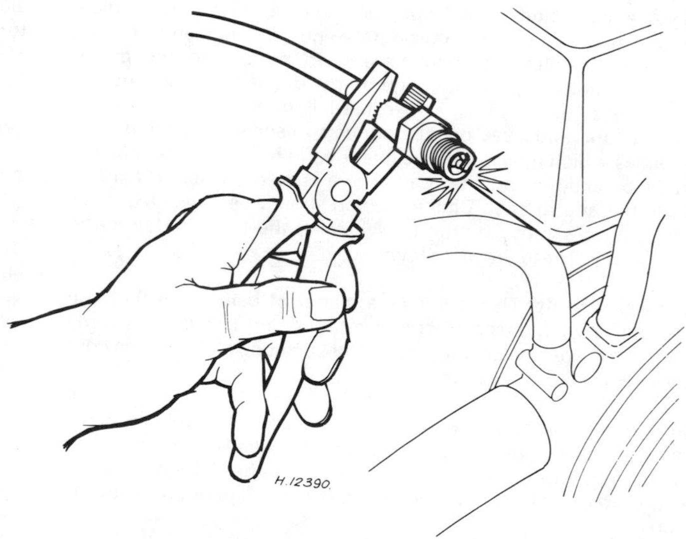

Crank engine and check for spark. Note use of insulated tool to hold plug lead

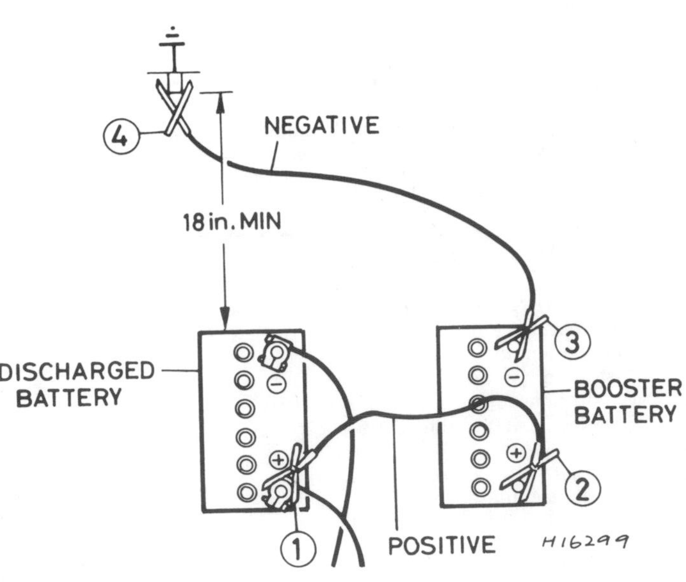

Jump start lead connections for negative earth vehicles – connect leads in order shown

carried. Experience and available space will modify the list below, but the following may save having to call on professional assistance:

Spark plugs, clean and correctly gapped
HT lead and plug cap – long enough to reach the plug furthest from the distributor
Distributor rotor, condenser and contact breaker points
Drivebelt(s) – emergency type may suffice
Spare fuses
Set of principal light bulbs
Tin of radiator sealer and hose bandage
Exhaust bandage
Roll of insulating tape
Length of soft iron wire
Length of electrical flex
Torch or inspection lamp (can double as test lamp)
Battery jump leads
Tow-rope
Ignition waterproofing aerosol
Litre of engine oil
Sealed can of hydraulic fluid
Emergency windscreen
Worm drive clips
Tube of filler paste

If spare fuel is carried, a can designed for the purpose should be used to minimise risks of leakage and collision damage. A first aid kit and a warning triangle, whilst not at present compulsory in the UK, are obviously sensible items to carry in addition to the above.

When touring abroad it may be advisable to carry additional spares which, even if you cannot fit them yourself, could save having to wait while parts are obtained. The items below may be worth considering:

Clutch and throttle cables
Cylinder head gasket
Alternator brushes
Tyre valve core

One of the motoring organisations will be able to advise on availability of fuel etc in foreign countries.

Engine will not start

Engine fails to turn when starter operated

Flat battery (recharge, use jump leads, or push start)
Battery terminals loose or corroded
Battery earth to body defective
Engine earth strap loose or broken
Starter motor (or solenoid) wiring loose or broken
Automatic transmission selector in wrong position, or inhibitor switch faulty
Ignition/starter switch faulty
Major mechanical failure (seizure)
Starter or solenoid internal fault (see Chapter 10)

Starter motor turns engine slowly

Partially discharged battery (recharge, use jump leads, or push start)
Battery terminals loose or corroded
Battery earth to body defective
Engine earth strap loose
Starter motor (or solenoid) wiring loose
Starter motor internal fault (see Chapter 10)

Engine turns normally but fails to start

Damp or dirty HT leads and distributor cap (crank engine and check for spark) (photo)
Dirty or incorrectly gapped distributor points (if applicable)
No fuel in tank (check for delivery at carburettor)
Excessive choke (hot engine) or insufficient choke (cold engine)
Fouled or incorrectly gapped spark plugs (remove, clean and regap)
Other ignition system fault (see Chapter 4)
Other fuel system fault (see Chapter 3)
Poor compression (see Chapter 1)
Major mechanical failure (eg camshaft drive)

Engine fires but will not run

Insufficient choke (cold engine)
Air leaks at carburettor or inlet manifold
Fuel starvation (see Chapter 3)
Ignition fault (see Chapter 4)

Using an old spark plug to check for HT spark

Engine cuts out and will not restart

Engine cuts out suddenly – ignition fault

Loose or disconnected LT wires
Wet HT leads or distributor cap (after traversing water splash)
Ignition fault (see Chapter 4)

Engine misfires before cutting out – fuel fault

Fuel tank empty
Fuel pump defective or filter blocked (check for delivery)
Fuel tank filler vent blocked (suction will be evident on releasing cap)

Carburettor needle valve sticking
Carburettor jets blocked (fuel contaminated)
Other fuel system fault (see Chapter 4)

Engine cuts out – other causes
Serious overheating
Major mechanical failure (eg camshaft drive)

Engine overheats

Ignition (no-charge) warning light illuminated
Slack or broken drivebelt – retension or renew (Chapter 2 or 12)

Ignition warning light not illuminated
Coolant loss due to internal or external leakage (see Chapter 2)
Thermostat defective
Low oil level
Brakes binding
Radiator clogged externally or internally
Electric cooling fan not operating correctly
Engine waterways clogged
Ignition timing incorrect or automatic advance malfunctioning
Mixture too weak

Note: *Do not add cold water to an overheated engine or damage may result*

Low engine oil pressure

Gauge reads low or warning light illuminated with engine running
Oil level low or incorrect grade
Defective gauge or sender unit
Wire to sender unit earthed
Engine overheating
Oil filter clogged or bypass valve defective
Oil pressure relief valve defective
Oil pick-up strainer clogged
Oil pump worn or mountings loose
Worn main or big-end bearings

Note: *Low oil pressure in a high-mileage engine at tickover is not necessarily a cause for concern. Sudden pressure loss at speed is far more significant. In any event, check the gauge or warning light sender before condemning the engine.*

Engine noises

Pre-ignition (pinking) on acceleration
Incorrect grade of fuel
Ignition timing incorrect
Distributor faulty or worn
Worn or maladjusted carburettor
Excessive carbon build-up in engine

Whistling or wheezing noises
Leaking vacuum hose
Leaking carburettor or manifold gasket
Blowing head gasket

Tapping or rattling
Incorrect valve clearances
Worn valve gear
Broken piston ring (ticking noise)

Knocking or thumping
Unintentional mechanical contact (eg fan blades)
Worn drivebelt
Peripheral component fault (alternator, water pump etc)
Worn big-end bearings (regular heavy knocking, perhaps less under load)
Worn main bearings (rumbling and knocking, perhaps worsening under load)
Piston slap (most noticeable when cold)

Chapter 1 Engine

Contents

Specifications

General

Engine type	Four-cylinder in-line, overhead camshaft, transversely mounted
Designation and displacement:	
CA18	1809 cc (110.39 cu in)
CA18ET (Turbo)	1809 cc (110.39 cu in)
CA20	1974 cc (120.45 cu in)
Bore:	
CA18 and CA18ET	83.00 mm (3.268 in)
CA20	84.5 mm (3.327 in)
Stroke:	
CA18 and CA18GT	83.6 mm (3.291 in)
CA20	88.0 mm (3.465 in)
Compression ratio:	
CA18	9.6:1
CA18ET	8.0:1
CA20	9.4:1
Cylinder compression pressures:	
CA18 and CA20	11.96 bar (173 lbf/in^2) at 350 rpm
CA18ET	11.77 bar (171 lbf/in^2) at 350 rpm

Cylinder block

Material	Cast iron
Bore diameter:	
CA18 and CA18ET	83.00 to 83.05 mm (3.2677 to 3.2697 in)
CA20	84.50 to 84.55 mm (3.3268 to 3.3287 in)
Permitted taper	Less than 0.01 mm (0.0004 in)
Permitted out-of-round	Less than 0.015 mm (0.0006 in)

Crankshaft

Number of main bearings	Five
Journal diameter	52.951 to 52.964 mm (2.0847 to 2.0852 in)
Crankpin diameter	44.961 to 44.974 mm (1.7701 to 1.7706 in)
Permitted taper of journal and crankpin	0.03 mm (0.0012 in) maximum
Permitted out of round of journal and crankpin	0.03 mm (0.0012 in) maximum
Crankshaft endfloat	0.3 mm (0.012 in) maximum
Main bearing running clearance (standard)	0.04 to 0.06 mm (0.0016 to 0.0024 in)
Wear limit	0.1 mm (0.004 in)
Main bearing undersizes	0.25 mm (0.0098 in) 0.50 mm (0.0197 in)

Connecting rods

Rod side clearance	0.2 to 0.3 mm (0.008 to 0.012 in)
Wear limit	0.3 mm (0.012 in)
Connecting rod big-end bearing running clearance	0.1 mm (0.004 in) maximum
Big-end bearing undersize	0.08 mm (0.0031 in), 0.12 mm (0.0047 in), 0.25 mm (0.0098 in), 0.50 mm (0.020 in)

Camshaft

Number of bearings	Five (non-renewable)
Diameter of camshaft journal	45.935 to 45.955 mm (1.8085 to 1.8092 in)
Camshaft endfloat (wear limit)	0.2 mm (0.008 in)
Cam height (inlet and exhaust):	
CA18	38.240 to 38.290 mm (1.5055 to 1.5075 in)
CA18ET	38.406 to 38.456 mm (1.5120 to 1.5140 in)
CA20	38.834 to 38.884 mm (1.5289 to 1.5309 in)
Wear limit	0.2 mm (0.008 in)

Pistons and rings

Material	Light alloy
Diameter:	
CA18 and CA18ET	82.965 to 83.015 mm (3.2663 to 3.2683 in)
CA20	84.465 to 84.515 mm (3.3254 to 3.3274 in)
Oversizes	0.50 mm (0.0197 in), 1.00 mm (0.0394 in)
Piston to cylinder bore clearance	0.025 to 0.045 mm (0.0010 to 0.0018 in)
Gudgeon pin outside diameter	19.995 to 20.000 mm (0.7872 to 0.7874 in)
Gudgeon pin to piston clearance	0.008 to 0.012 mm (0.0003 to 0.0005 in)
Interference fit of gudgeon pin in connecting rod	0.017 to 0.038 mm (0.0007 to 0.015 in)
Ring side clearance:	
Top	0.040 to 0.073 mm (0.0016 to 0.0029 in)
2nd	0.030 to 0.063 mm (0.0012 to 0.0025 in)
Wear limit	0.1 mm (0.004 in)
Ring end gap:	
Top:	
CA18 and CA20	0.25 to 0.35 mm (0.0098 to 0.0138 in)
CA18ET grades 1 and 2	0.25 to 0.32 mm (0.0098 to 0.0126 in)
CA18ET grades 3 to 5	0.19 to 0.26 mm (0.0075 to 0.0102 in)
2nd	0.15 to 0.25 mm (0.0059 to 0.0098 in)
Oil (rail)	0.20 to 0.60 mm (0.0079 to 0.0236 in)
Wear limit	1.0 mm (0.039 in)

Cylinder head

Material	Light alloy
Maximum permissible distortion of sealing face	0.1 mm (0.004 in)
Valve clearance (hot):	
Inlet and exhaust	0.30 mm (0.012 in)
Valve clearance (cold) – setting up only:	
Inlet	0.21 mm (0.008 in)
Exhaust	0.23 mm (0.009 in)
Stem-to-guide clearance:	
Inlet	0.020 to 0.053 mm (0.0008 to 0.0021 in)
Exhaust	0.040 to 0.073 mm (0.0016 to 0.0029 in)
Wear limit	0.1 mm (0.004 in)
Valve face angle	45° 15′ to 45° 45′
Valve seat angle	45°
Valve stem diameter:	
Inlet	6.965 to 6.980 mm (0.2742 to 0.2748 in)
Exhaust	6.945 to 6.960 mm (0.2734 to 0.2740 in)
Valve guide outside diameter	11.023 to 11.034 mm (0.4340 to 0.4344 in)
Interference fit of valve guide in cylinder head	0.027 to 0.059 mm (0.0011 to 0.0023 in)
Valve guide inside diameter (reamed)	7.000 to 7.018 mm (0.2756 to 0.2763 in)

Valve springs

Type	Dual
Free height:	
Outer	49.98 mm (1.9677 in)
Inner	44.10 mm (1.7362 in)

Flywheel

Permitted out of true	Less than 0.15 mm (0.0059 in)

Oil pump

Clearances:	
Inner gear to crescent	0.12 to 0.23 mm (0.0047 to 0.0091 in)
Outer gear to crescent	0.21 to 0.32 mm (0.0083 to 0.0126 in)
Outer gear to body	0.11 to 0.20 mm (0.0043 to 0.0079 in)
Gear endfloat	0.05 to 0.11 mm (0.0020 to 0.0043 in)

Torque wrench settings

	Nm	lbf ft
Timing belt tensioner	20	15
Crankshaft pulley to damper	13	10
Crankshaft pulley (damper) bolt	128	95
Timing cover	4	3
Inlet manifold	23	17

PCV valve	34	25
Exhaust manifold	25	19
Exhaust manifold cowling	5	4
Camshaft sprocket	88	65
Cylinder head bolts:		
Stage 1	29	21
Stage 2	78	58
Stage 3	Loosen all bolts completely	Loosen all bolts completely
Stage 4	29	21
Stage 5	74 to 83 *or* tighten through a further 90° to 95°	55 to 61 *or* tighten through a further 90° to 95°
Rocker shaft	20	15
Rocker cover	2	1.5
Big-end cap	34	25
Main bearing cap	49	36
Oil pump	14	10
Oil strainer	12	9
Oil pan (sump)	6	4
Oil drain plug	34	25
Driveplate or flywheel	103	76
Crankshaft rear oil seal housing	5	4
Fuel pump cam	83	61

1 General description

The engine is of four cylinder overhead cam type, mounted transversely at the front end of the vehicle.

The cylinder head is of light alloy construction and the cylinder block/crankcase is of cast iron.

The crankshaft is of five main bearing type, whilst the belt-driven camshaft runs in a similar number of non-renewable bearings in the cylinder head.

The oil pump is mounted at the timing belt end of the crankshaft and supplies pressurised oil to all moving parts after the oil has first passed through an externally mounted full-flow cartridge type filter.

The engine is available in two capacities, these being 1809 cc (CA18 and CA18ET) and 1974 cc (CA20), the larger engine displacement being obtained by increasing the bore and stroke of the smaller version.

All engines include a crankcase ventilation system, designed to return piston blow-by gases from the crankcase to the inlet manifold for further burning in the combustion chambers. A PCV (positive crankcase ventilation) valve controls the flow of gases according to inlet manifold vacuum. The crankcase is ventilated with fresh air continually to dilute the blow-by gases.

2 Routine maintenance

Carry out the following procedures at the intervals given in *'Routine Maintenance'* at the beginning of this Manual.

Adjust the valve clearances

1 Refer to Section 4 of this Chapter.

Change the engine oil

2 Apply the handbrake, then jack up the front of the car and support on axle stands.

3 If the engine is cold, run it at a fast idling speed to normal operating temperature, then switch it off.

4 Unscrew and remove the oil filler cap.

5 Position a suitable container beneath the engine and unscrew the sump drain plug, keeping the hands clear of the hot oil (photo).

6 Allow all the oil to drain, then clean the drain plug and refit it into the sump. Renew the washer if necessary.

7 If necessary, the oil filter can now be renewed as described in the next sub-section.

8 Pour the correct quantity of oil through the filler and refit the filler cap (photo).

2.5 Engine oil drain plug

2.8 Topping-up the engine oil level

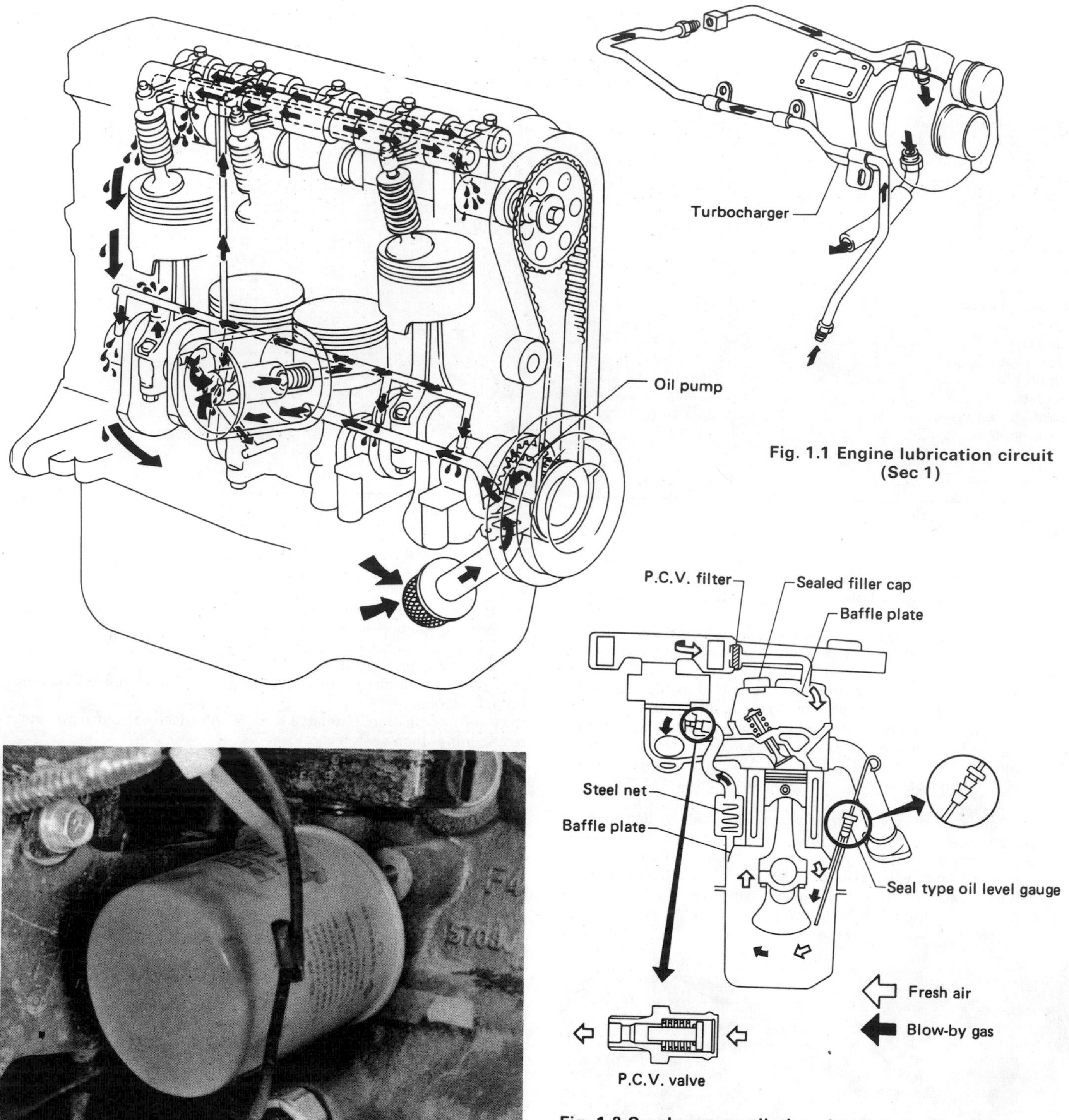

Fig. 1.1 Engine lubrication circuit (Sec 1)

Fig. 1.2 Crankcase ventilation circuit on carburettor engines (Sec 1)

2.13 Oil filter location

9 Run the engine to normal operating temperature. Stop the engine and wait two or three minutes to allow the oil to drain into the sump.
10 While waiting, lower the car to the ground.
11 Withdraw the oil level dipstick, wipe it clean, re-insert it fully, then withdraw it again. The oil level should be on the maximum (H) mark. If not, top up the level as necessary, but do not overfill.

Renew the oil filter

12 The oil filter is renewed at the same time as changing the engine oil.
13 Using a suitable oil filter wrench, unscrew the cartridge type oil filter (photo). Be prepared for some loss of oil as it is unscrewed.
14 If the old filter is found to be exceptionally tight and the wrench will not release it, drive a heavy screwdriver through the filter casing and use it as a lever to unscrew the filter.
15 Clean the filter mounting flange on the crankcase and smear a little oil on the rubber sealing ring of the oil filter.
16 Screw the filter into position as tightly as possible *using hand pressure only.*

Check crankcase ventilation system

17 The positive crankcase ventilation (PCV) valve is screwed into the inlet manifold on the carburettor mounting flange on carburettor

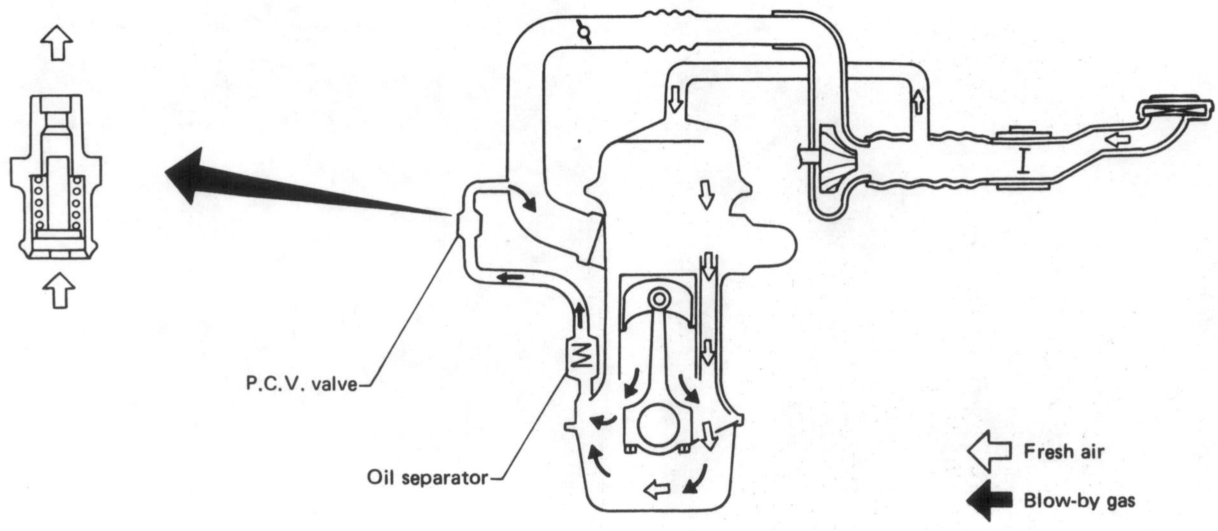

Fig. 1.3 Crankcase ventilation circuit on fuel-injection (Turbo) engines (Sec 1)

models, or is bolted onto the inlet manifold and fitted with an inlet and outlet hose on Turbo models.
18 Disconnect the hose(s) and clean out any oil or sludge then, reconnect.
19 The PCV valve can be checked by disconnecting the supply hose. With the engine idling, use a finger to check that there is little or no vacuum present at the valve inlet. Fully open the throttle momentarily and check that vacuum is then felt. Reconnect the supply hose after making the check.

3 Major operations possible without removing engine from car

The following work can be carried out without having to remove the engine:

Valve clearances – adjustment
Timing belt – removal and refitting
Cylinder head – removal and refitting
Sump pan – removal and refitting
Oil pump – removal and refitting
Pistons and big-end bearings – renewal
Engine/transmission mountings – renewal

4 Valve clearances – adjustment

1 As a routine service operation, the valve clearances should be checked and adjusted while the engine is hot. After overhaul of the engine, the valve clearances will obviously have to be set cold initially and then re-set when the engine has been run to normal operating temperature.
2 Remove the air cleaner or air ducting (Chapter 3).
3 Unclip and disconnect the spark plug leads.
4 Remove the rocker cover and disconnect the crankcase ventilation hose.
5 Turn the crankshaft until No 1 piston is at top dead centre (TDC) on its compression stroke. No. 4 cylinder valves will be 'rocking' (*ie* exhaust valve closing and inlet valve opening). To turn the engine, use a spanner on the crankshaft pulley bolt, or engage 4th gear and pull the car forwards a little at a time.
6 Adjust the clearances on valve numbers 1, 2, 4 and 6 (Fig. 1.5). To do this, insert a feeler blade between the end of the valve stem and the

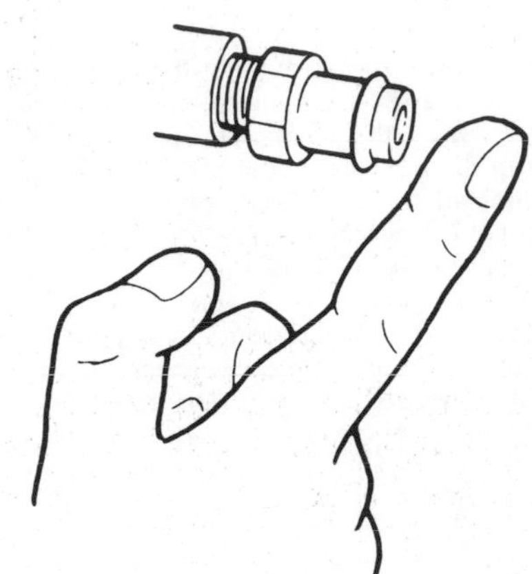

Fig. 1.4 Checking the PCV valve (Sec 2)

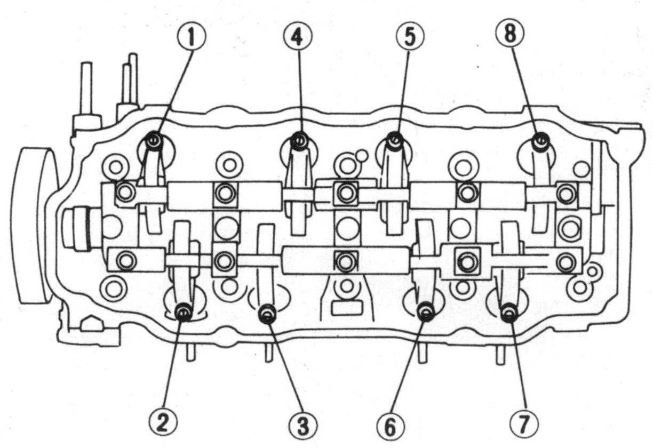

Fig. 1.5 Valve numbering (Sec 4)

4.6 Adjusting the valve clearances

4.9A Fitting the rocker cover

rocker arm. The blade should be a stiff sliding fit. If the clearance is incorrect, release the rocker arm adjuster screw locknut and turn the adjuster screw. Once the clearance is correct, tighten the locknut without altering the position of the screw (photo).

7 Having adjusted the clearances of the first four valves, turn the crankshaft until No. 4 piston is at TDC on its compression stroke. No. 1 cylinder valves will now be 'rocking'.

8 Adjust the clearances on valve numbers 3, 5, 7 and 8.

9 On completion, refit the rocker cover and crankcase ventilation hose, spark plug leads, and air cleaner or air ducting. Renew the rocker cover gasket if necessary and note that the smaller washers fit at the timing end of the rocker cover (photos).

4.9B Rocker cover small washer location

5 Timing belt – removal and refitting

1 Apply the handbrake, then jack up the front of the car and support on axle stands.

2 Remove the right-hand front roadwheel and the inner plastic shield.

3 Remove the air cleaner on carburettor models.

4 Remove No. 1 spark plug, then turn the engine clockwise until compression can be felt. Continue turning until the TDC (black) marks on the crankshaft pulley are aligned.

5 Remove the drivebelts for the alternator (Chapters 2 and 12) and power steering pump (Chapter 10) if fitted.

6 Unbolt the water pump pulley.

7 Unbolt and remove the timing belt upper and lower covers and remove the gaskets.

8 In order to unscrew the crankshaft pulley bolt, the crankshaft must be held against rotation. On manual transmission models, select a gear and have an assistant apply the footbrake hard. On automatic transmission models, the torque converter housing lower cover plate or the starter motor will have to be removed and the teeth of the driveplate ring gear jammed with a suitable blade. Slide the pulley and outer guide plate off the front of the crankshaft.

9 Check that the marks on the camshaft and crankshaft sprockets are positioned as shown in Fig. 1.7. The white lines on the timing belt may or may not be aligned with the marks on the pulleys.

10 Release the belt tensioner bolts and prise the tensioner pulley away from the belt.

11 Note the running direction of the timing belt and then remove it.

12 Fit the belt so that its running direction is correct and the marks on the belt are in alignment with the timing marks on the sprockets (photos). Where applicable the arrow on the timing belt must point outwards away from the cylinder block.

13 Check that the belt tensioner spring is hooked onto the bolt and the bracket of the tensioner, and then rotate the engine clockwise by exactly two turns. Tighten the tensioner lower bolt B followed by the upper bolt A (Fig. 1.8). The timing belt is now automatically tensioned.

14 Refit the outer guide plate and pulley to the crankshaft and tighten the bolt to the specified torque while holding the crankshaft against rotation as described in paragraph 8 (photos).

15 Refit the timing belt covers (photo). Renew the gaskets if necessary.

16 Bolt the pulley onto the water pump.

17 Refit and tension the drivebelts with reference to Chapters 2, 10 and 12.

18 Refit the No. 1 spark plug and where applicable the air cleaner.

19 Refit the plastic shield and the roadwheel, then lower the car to the ground.

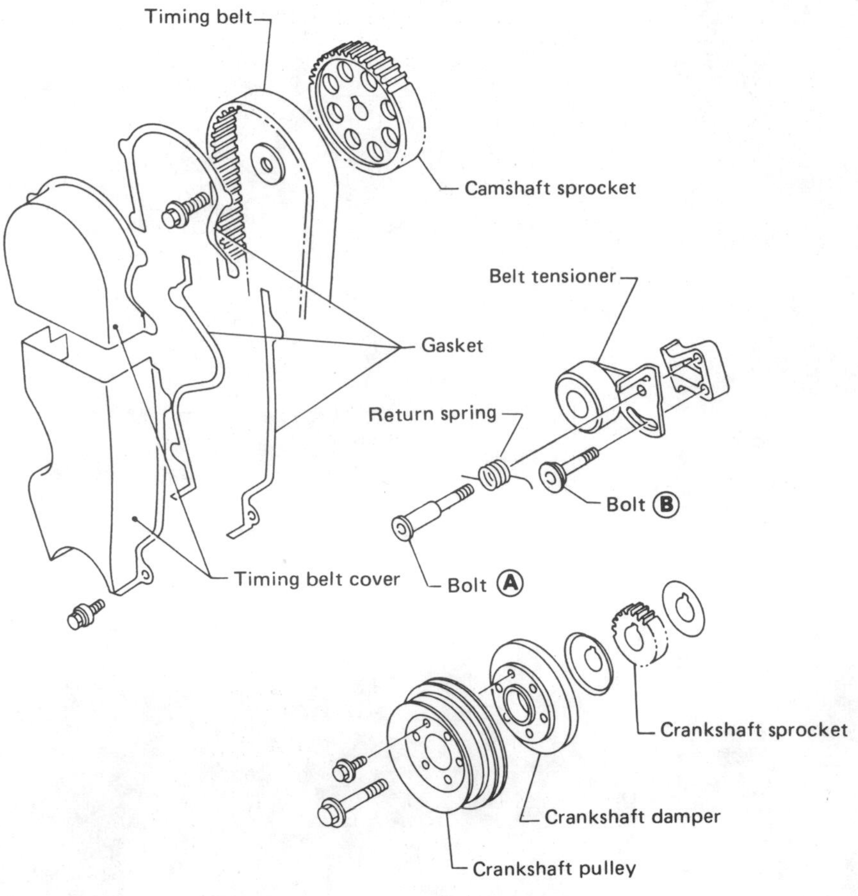

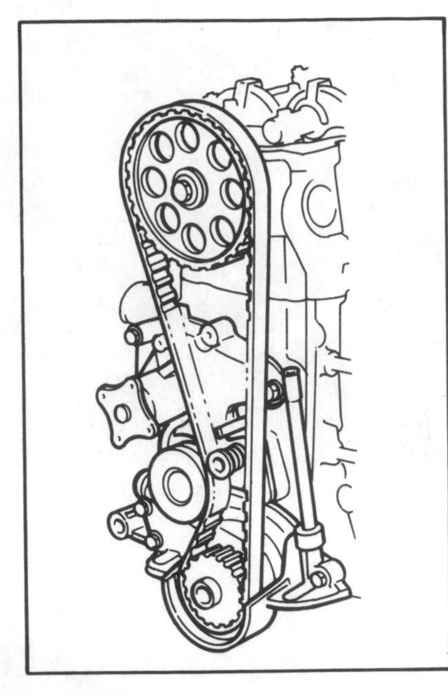

Fig. 1.6 Timing belt components (Sec 5)

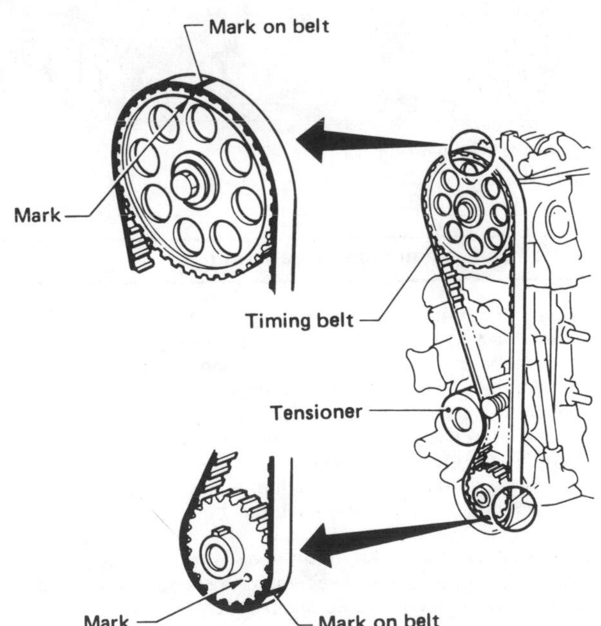

Fig. 1.7 Timing belt and sprocket alignment marks (Sec 5)

5.12A Timing belt mark at camshaft sprocket

5.12B Timing belt mark at crankshaft sprocket

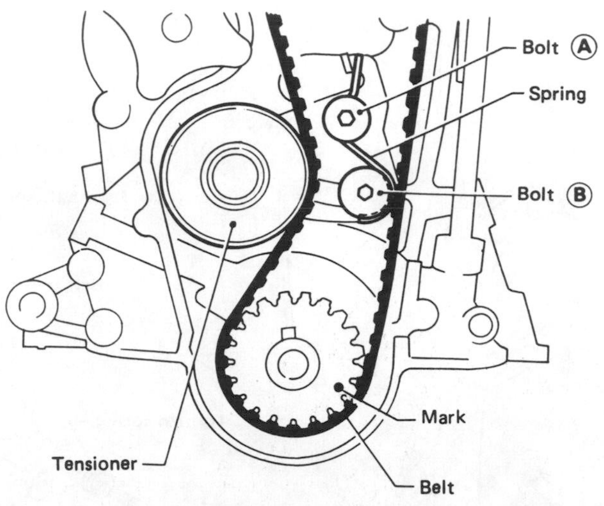

Fig. 1.8 Timing belt tensioner pivot (A) and adjustment bolts (B) (Sec 5)

5.14A Timing belt outer guide plate

5.14B Crankshaft pulley bolt

5.15 Timing belt cover screw

6 Cylinder head – removal and refitting

1 Disconnect the battery and drain the cooling system (Chapter 2).
2 Remove the air cleaner and inlet ducting according to model.
3 Disconnect the top hose from the inlet manifold.
4 Disconnect the brake servo vacuum hose from the inlet manifold.
5 Disconnect the accelerator cable (Chapter 3).
6 Unbolt the earth cable from the cylinder head (photo).
7 Remove the distributor (Chapter 4)
8 On non-Turbo models remove the fuel pump (Chapter 3).
9 On Turbo models remove the fuel-injection system components (Chapter 3).
10 Disconnect the hot air hose from the exhaust manifold.
11 Unscrew the flange nuts and separate the exhaust downpipe from the manifold or turbocharger as applicable.
12 Disconnect the wiring from the temperature sender, and the carburettor or fuel-injection equipment.
13 Remove the spark plugs and the rocker cover.
14 Remove the timing belt with reference to Section 5.
15 Remove the camshaft sprocket bolt and pull the sprocket from the camshaft. If the sprocket has two keyways, mark its position on the camshaft to ensure correct refitting.

6.6 Unbolting the earth cable

16 Loosen the cylinder head bolts in the sequence shown (Fig. 1.10), one half of a turn at a time.
17 Remove the cylinder head. If it is stuck tight, do not attempt to release it by inserting a tool in the gasket joint, but tap the sides of the head carefully with a plastic-faced hammer, or if using an ordinary hammer, use a block of hardwood as an insulator.
18 If the cylinder head is to be dismantled and decarbonised, unbolt the inlet and exhaust manifolds and refer to Section 17.
19 Before refitting the cylinder head, the mating surfaces of both head and block must be perfectly clean and free from old pieces of gasket. Take care when cleaning the cylinder head not to dig or score its surface. Clean the bolt holes in the cylinder block free from dirt and oil. Refit the manifolds together with new gaskets (photos).
20 Locate a new cylinder head gasket on the cylinder block (photo).
21 Check that No. 1 piston is still at TDC and slacken all the rocker arm adjuster screws right off.
22 Lower the cylinder head into position and screw in the lightly oiled bolts (photo). Make sure that each bolt is fitted with a washer.
23 Tighten the cylinder head bolts to the specified torque in the sequence shown (Fig. 1.11) and following the stages given in the Specifications.
24 Bolt the sprocket onto the camshaft.
25 Refit the timing belt with reference to Section 5.
26 Adjust the valve clearances as described in Section 4.

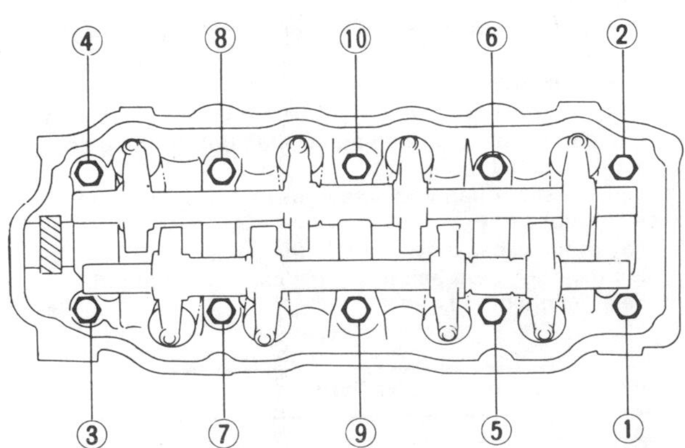

Fig. 1.10 Cylinder head bolt loosening sequence (Sec 6)

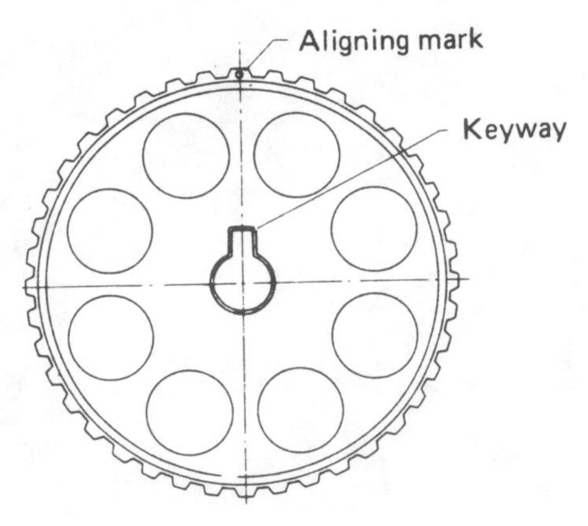

Type B

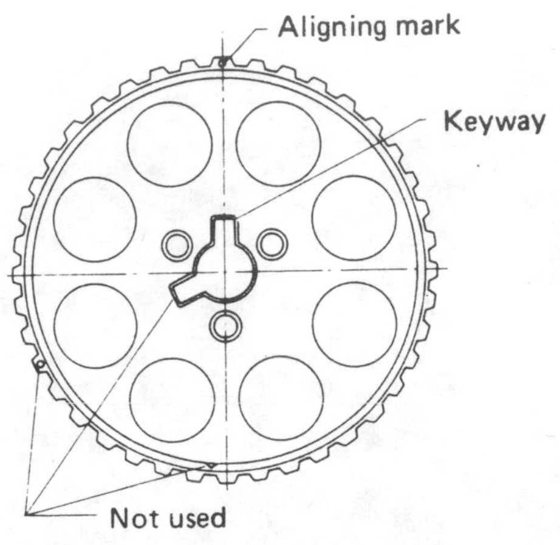

Fig. 1.9 Alternative types of camshaft sprocket (Sec 6)

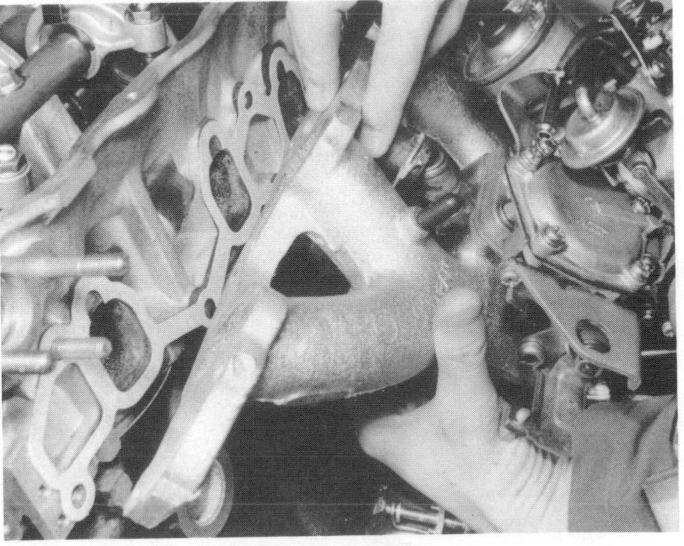

6.19A Fitting inlet manifold and carburettor

6.19B Exhaust manifold and hot air shroud

6.20 Cylinder head gasket

6.22 Fitting cylinder head

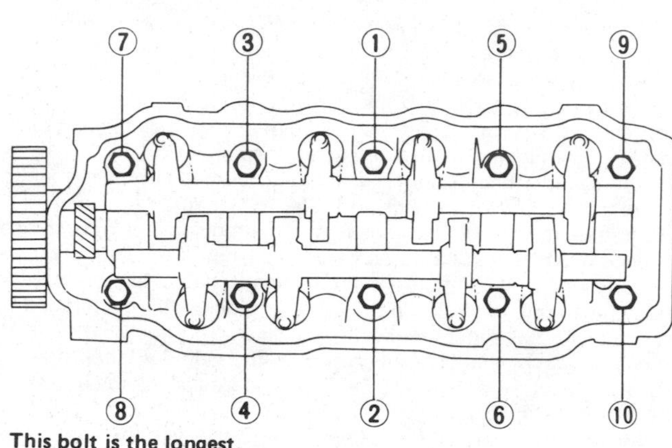

Fig. 1.11 Cylinder head bolt tightening sequence (Sec 6)

27 Refit the spark plugs.
28 Reconnect the wiring, the exhaust downpipe, and the hot air hose.
29 Refit the fuel pump or fuel-injection components (Chapter 3).
30 Refit the distributor (Chapter 4) and the earth cable.
31 Reconnect the accelerator cable (Chapter 3), the brake servo vacuum hose and the top hose.
32 Refit the air cleaner or inlet ducting.
33 Fill the cooling system (Chapter 2) and reconnect the battery.
34 Run the engine to normal operating temperature, then recheck and if necessary adjust the valve clearances.
35 After 600 miles (1000 km), the cylinder head bolts should be re-tightened with the engine cold. To do this, remove the rocker cover, then using the same sequence as for tightening the bolts, loosen each bolt half a turn and re-tighten it to the specified final torque wrench setting.

7 Sump pan – removal and refitting

1 Apply the handbrake, then jack up the front of the car and support on axle stands.
2 Remove the engine undershields.
3 Unbolt the exhaust downpipe from the manifold.
4 Release the exhaust system forward mountings and then pull the front of the system down as far as the flexible connection will allow.
5 Drain the engine oil.
6 Unscrew the sump pan retaining bolts. Pull the pan downwards and remove it.
7 Clean away the old joint gasket.
8 Stick a new gasket in position on the crankcase using a smear of jointing compound (photo), then apply additional jointing compound at the points indicated in Fig. 1.12.
9 Offer up the sump pan and screw in the bolts evenly in diagonal sequence (photo).
10 Reconnect the exhaust system and the engine undershields.
11 Tighten the drain plug and lower the car to the ground.
12 Fill the engine with oil.

8 Oil pump – removal and refitting

1 Remove the sump pan (Section 7).
2 Remove the timing belt (Section 5).
3 Unbolt and remove the oil pick-up pipe and strainer.

7.8 Fitting sump pan gasket

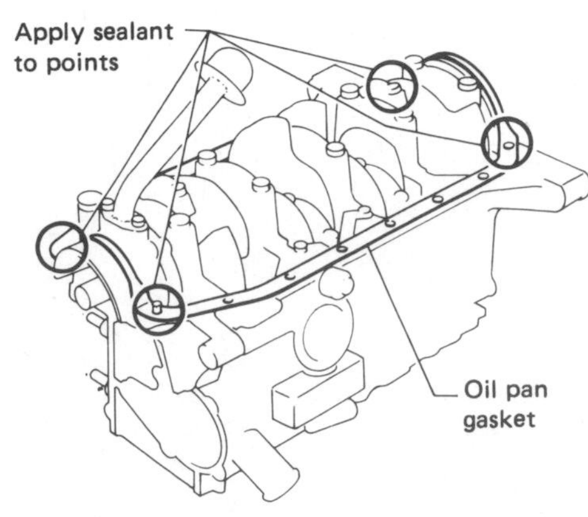

Fig. 1.12 Jointing compound application points on the sump gasket (Sec 7)

7.9 Fitting sump pan (engine removed)

4 Unbolt and remove the timing belt tensioner using an Allen key.
5 Pull off the crankshaft sprocket. Remove the Woodruff key and inner guide plate.
6 Unbolt and remove the oil pump from the front face of the crackcase. Discard the joint gasket.
7 The oil pump can be examined as described in Section 18 and renewed if worn.
8 Before refitting the oil pump, always renew the oil seal and grease the seal lips. Use a new joint gasket.
9 As the oil pump is offered into position, align the inner gear with the flats on the crankshaft. Tape the shoulder on the crankshaft to prevent damage to the oil seal lips during fitting of the pump. Remove the tape when the pump is in position (photos).
10 Fit the inner guide plate, crankshaft Woodruff key and sprocket so that its timing mark is visible (photo).
11 Apply suitable sealant to the threads of the timing belt tensioner upper bolt, then refit the tensioner leaving the bolts loose. Make sure that the spring is correctly engaged.
12 Refit the oil pick-up pipe and strainer together with a new gasket and tighten the bolts (photo).
13 Refit the timing belt (Section 5).
14 Refit the sump pan (Section 7).

8.9A Crankshaft shoulder taped

8.9B Fitting oil pump

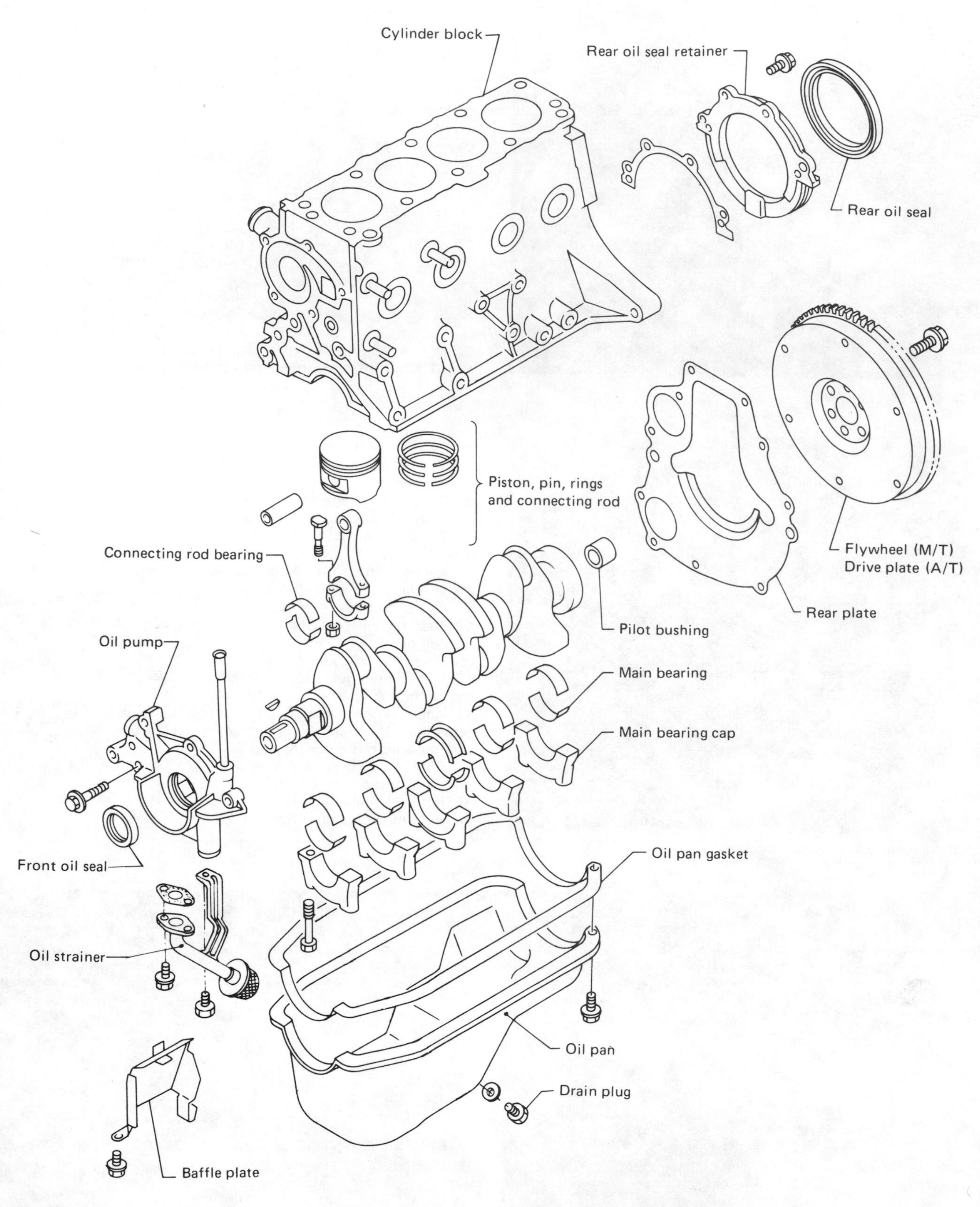

Fig. 1.13 Oil pump and crankshaft components (Secs 8, 9 and 16)

8.10A Timing belt inner guide plate

8.10B Crankshaft sprocket

9 Pistons and big-end bearings – renewal

1 Remove the cylinder head (Section 6).
2 Remove the engine sump pan (Section 7).
3 Unbolt and remove the oil pick-up pipe and strainer.
4 Note that the connecting rod big-end cap and rod are numbered at adjacent points. Number 1 is at the timing belt end of the engine (photo).
5 Feel the top of the cylinder bore for a wear ridge. If a thick one is felt then it should be removed using a ridge reamer or by careful scraping, in order to enable the piston rings to pass out of the bore during removal.
6 Unscrew the big-end cap nuts and take off the cap with shell bearing.
7 Push the piston/rod assembly out of the top of the block.
8 If the bearing shells are to be used again, tape them to their original cap or rod.
9 Repeat the operations on the three remaining assemblies.
10 If the reason for removal of the piston/rod assemblies was to fit new piston rings to reduce oil comsumption, then either standard or special proprietary rings may be fitted.
11 To remove a piston ring, slide three feeler blades behind the top ring and space them at equidistant points.
12 Remove the ring by pulling it off the top of the piston using a twisting motion.
13 Repeat on the remaining rings, always removing them from the crown of the piston.
14 Clean the piston ring grooves of carbon. A piece of broken piston ring is useful for this.
15 Make sure that the oil return holes at the base of the ring grooves are clear.
16 Push the piston rings down their cylinder bore one at a time using a piston and check the ring end gap using a feeler blade. If not as specified, carefully grind the end of the ring.
17 Check each ring in its groove for side clearance again using a feeler blade. If the clearance is too small then the piston grooves can be widened by your engine reconditioner or the ring width reduced by rubbing it on abrasive sheeting located on a very flat surface.
18 Fit the rings by reversing the removal operations. Stagger the ring gaps as shown in Fig. 1.17.
19 If new rings have been fitted, then to assist them to bed in rapidly, the hard glaze in the cylinder bores should be removed. Do this using a rotary type flap wheel in an electric drill or with fine glasspaper rubbed up and down at an angle to give a cross-hatch effect.
20 If new bearing shells are fitted, make sure that shells of the same

8.12 Fitting oil pick-up pipe and strainer

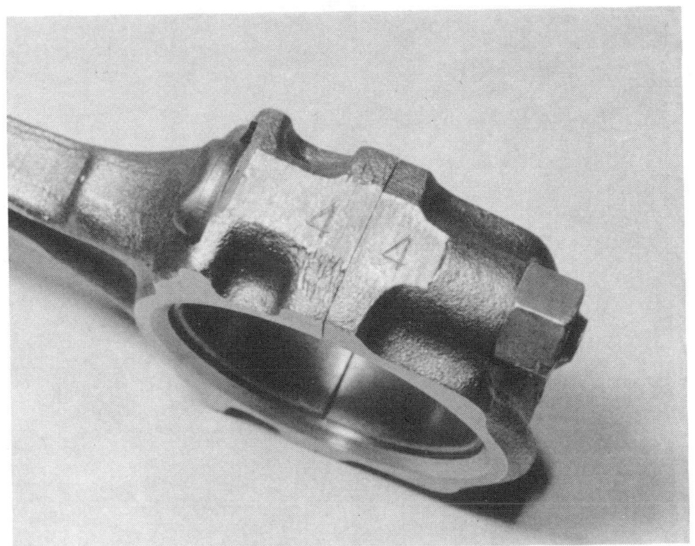

9.4 Connecting rod numbers

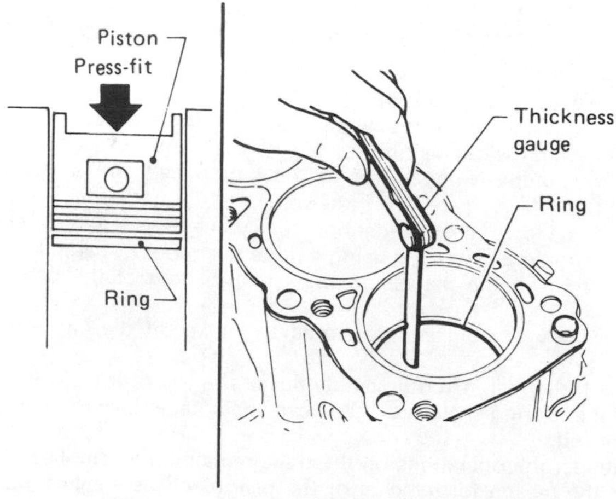

Fig. 1.14 Checking piston ring end gap (Sec 9)

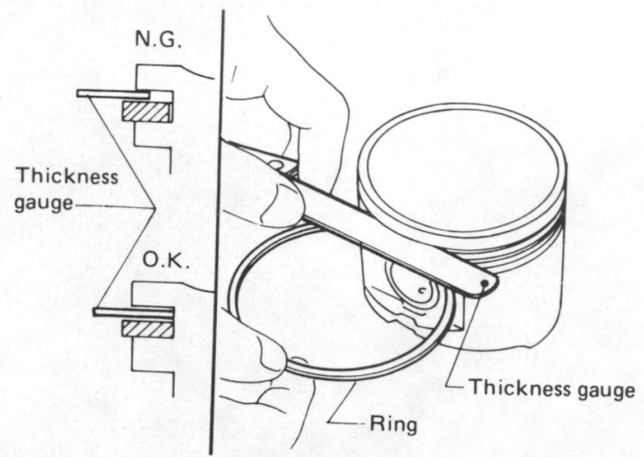

Fig. 1.15 Checking piston ring side clearance (Sec 9)

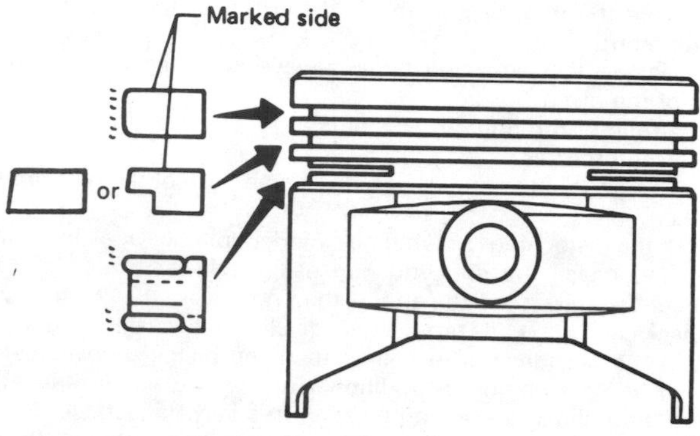

Fig. 1.16 Piston ring identification (Sec 9)

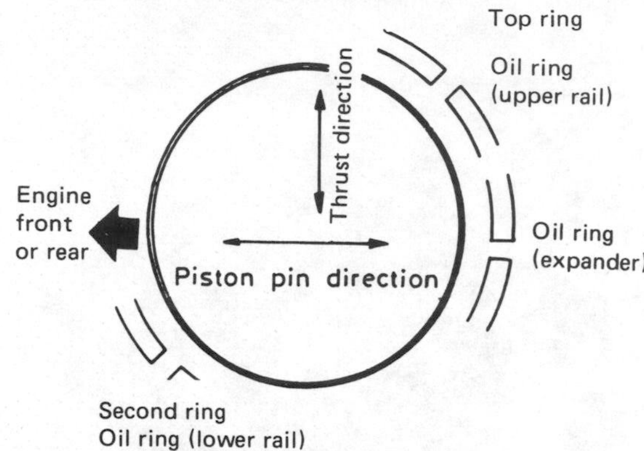

Fig. 1.17 Piston ring end gap positions (Sec 9)

size as the originals are used. The shells will be marked on their backs either standard or undersize (photo).

21 Fit the shells to caps and rods.

22 Oil the piston rings liberally and fit a piston ring compressor.

23 Lower the rod of No. 1 piston into its cylinder bore so that the compressor sits squarely on the surface of the block. Make sure that the mark on the piston crown is towards the timing belt end of the engine (photos).

24 Place the wooden handle of a hammer against the middle of the piston crown and then strike the head of the hammer with the hand to drive the piston with rings into the cylinder. The compressor will be released (photo).

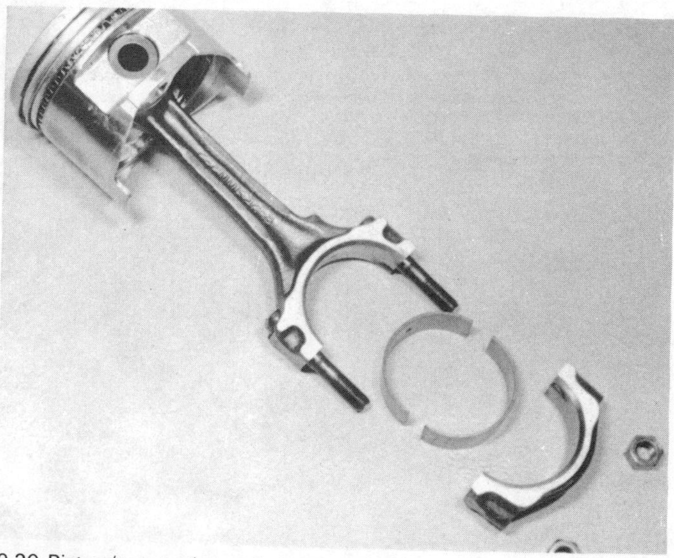

9.20 Piston/connecting rod component parts

9.23A Fitting piston with ring compressor

9.23B Piston front mark

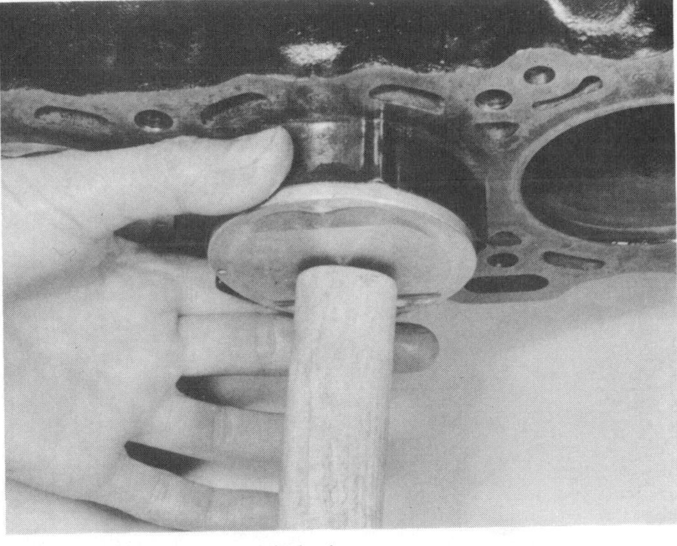

9.24 Driving piston into cylinder bore

25 Pull the rod down onto the crankshaft and fit the big-end cap (with shell) so that the matching numbers are adjacent.
26 Screw on the cap nuts and tighten to the specified torque wrench setting (photo).
27 Repeat the operations on the remaining pistons.
28 Fit the oil pick-up pipe and strainer, the sump pan and the cylinder head all as described earlier in this Chapter.
29 Fill the engine with oil.

9.26 Tightening connecting rod cap nut

10 Engine/transmission mountings – renewal

1 The mountings can be renewed provided the weight of the engine and transmission is taken on a hoist or jack (photos).
2 The component which incorporates the flexible insulator should be renewed if the rubber has become sticky or has perished or becomes deformed as the result of the weight of the power train.
3 Tighten the mountings on the crossmember last and in the order shown in Fig. 1.18.

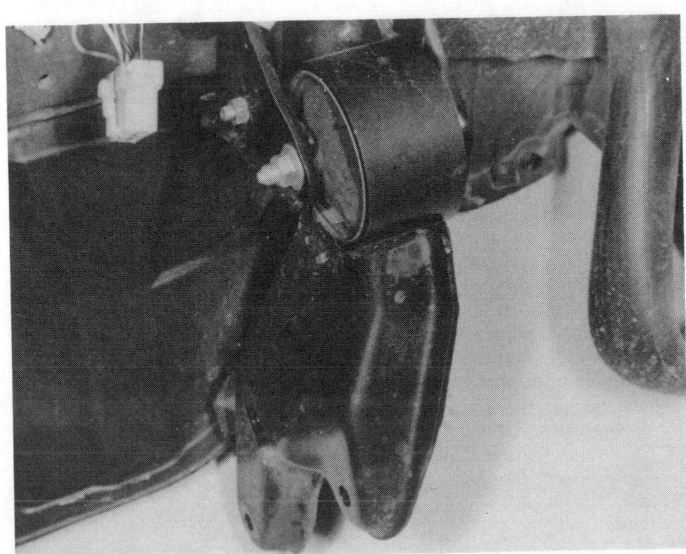

10.1A Left-hand front mounting on body bracket (engine removed)

10.1B Right-hand front mounting (engine removed)

10.1C Right-hand front mounting (engine installed)

10.1D Front mounting buffer (engine removed)

10.1E Front mounting buffer (engine installed)

10.1F Rear mounting (engine removed)

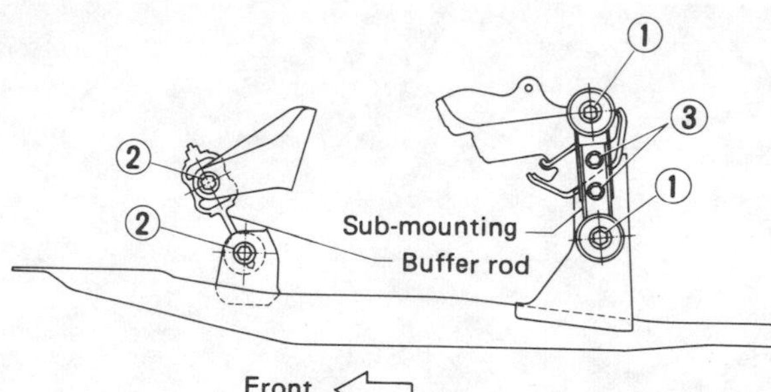

Fig. 1.18 Front and rear mounting tightening sequence (Sec 10)

11 Engine – method of removal

The engine should be removed complete with transmission by lifting it out upwards from the engine compartment.

12 Engine/manual transmission – removal and separation

1 Remove the bonnet as described in Chapter 11.
2 Remove the battery and tray (Chapter 12).
3 Drain the engine oil and coolant.
4 Remove the air cleaner and inlet ducting according to model.
5 Disconnect and remove the top and bottom hoses.
6 Disconnect the brake servo vacuum hose from the inlet manifold.
7 Disconnect the accelerator cable (Chapter 3).
8 Disconnect the clutch cable (Chapter 5).
9 Disconnect the speedometer cable (Chapter 12).
10 Unbolt the earth cable from the cylinder head and disconnect the ignition coil HT lead.
11 Note the position and routing of the wiring harness, then pull apart the multi-pin connections (photos).
12 Disconnect the fuel pump hoses or the fuel-injection components according to model.
13 Disconnect and remove the hot air hose from the exhaust manifold.
14 Disconnect the wiring from the alternator, starter motor, oil pressure switch (photo), temperature switch, and transmission switches.
15 On power steering models, remove the alternator drivebelt (Chapter 12), then remove the power steering pump with reference to

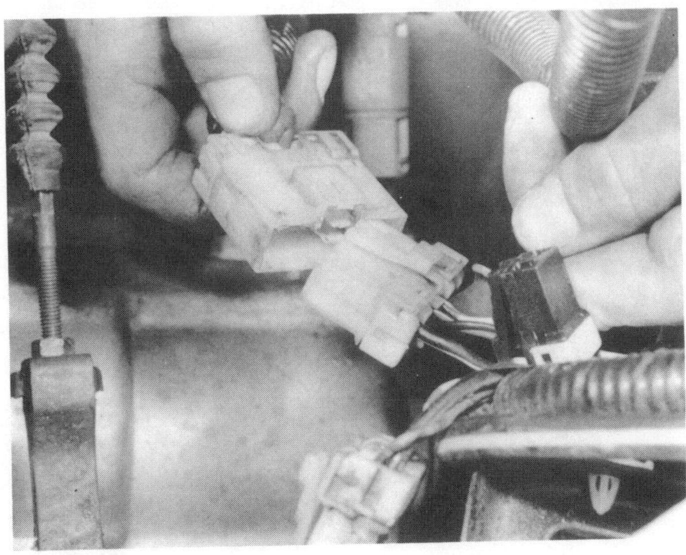
12.11A Disconnecting the wiring harness from the battery

12.11B Disconnecting the wiring harness for the carburettor

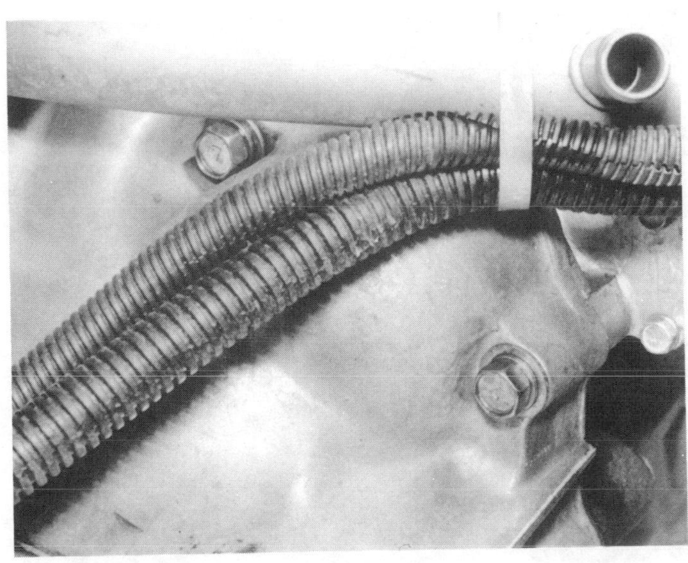
12.11C Wiring harness routing over transmission

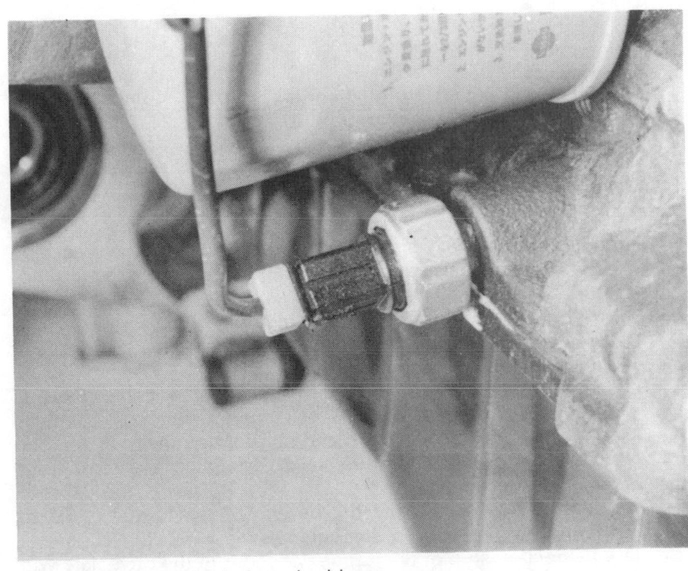
12.14 Oil pressure switch and wiring

Chapter 10, but leave the fluid hoses attached. Tie the pump to one side.

16 Disconnect the heater hoses.

17 Apply the handbrake, then jack up the front of the car and support on axle stands. Remove the splash guards.

18 Unscrew the flange nuts and separate the exhaust downpipe from the manifold or turbocharger (photo). Also unbolt the support mounting from the bottom of the gearbox.

19 Disconnect the gearchange control rod and support rod from the gearbox with reference to Chapter 6.

20 Remove both drivehafts as described in Chapter 8.

21 Connect a hoist to the engine and take its weight.

22 Unbolt the four mountings. Unbolt the left-hand mounting complete from the transmission casing.

23 Hoist the engine/transmission assembly carefully up and out of the engine compartment (photo).

24 Unbolt and remove the starter motor (Chapter 12).

25 Unscrew and remove the bolts connecting the transmission to the engine, noting the position of the engine stay.

26 Withdraw the transmission from the engine in a straight line, keeping it horizontal to prevent any damage to the clutch (photo).

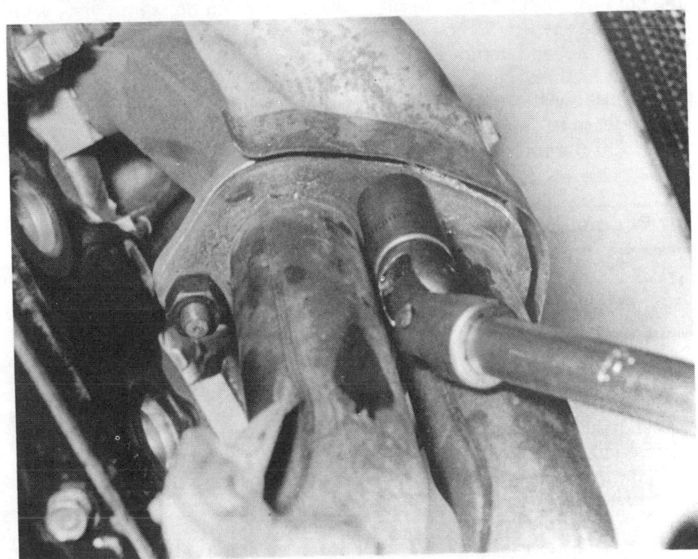
12.18 Unscrewing exhaust downpipe flange nuts

12.23 Lifting the engine/transmission assembly from the engine compartment

27 If it is required to move the car with the engine/transmission out and the driveshafts removed, preload the front wheel bearings using threaded rods, nuts and washers (photo).

13 Engine/automatic transmission – removal and separation

1 The operations are very similar to those described in the preceding Section for the manual transmission, but note the following differences.
2 Ignore the reference to the clutch cable.
3 Disconnect the wiring for the inhibitor switch, lock-up and overdrive systems from the transmission.
4 Disconnect the kickdown cable and selector lever cable (Chapter 7).
5 Disconnect the oil cooler hoses and plug or cap them.
6 With the engine/transmission removed, separate the assemblies in the following way.
7 Unbolt the cover plate from the bottom of the torque converter housing, noting the position of the engine stay.
8 Mark the relationship of the torque converter to the driveplate with quick-drying paint and then unscrew the converter-to-driveplate connecting bolts. The crankshaft will have to be turned by means of the crankshaft pulley bolt to bring the connecting bolts into view with the aperture left by removal of the cover plate.
9 Unscrew and remove the bolts connecting the torque converter housing to the engine.
10 Withdraw the transmission from the engine, but keep the torque converter in full engagement with the oil pump, otherwise the fluid will spill from the torque converter.

14 Engine – dismantling general

1 It is best to mount the engine on a dismantling stand, but if this is not available, stand the engine on a strong bench at a comfortable working height. Failing this, it will have to be stripped down on the floor, but at least place a sheet of hardboard down first.
2 Clean each component in paraffin as it is removed.
3 Never immerse parts with oilways in paraffin (eg crankshaft and camshaft). To clean these parts, wipe down carefully with a paraffin dampened rag. Oilways can be cleaned out with wire. If an air line is available, all parts can be blown dry and the oilways blown through as an added precaution.
4 Re-use of old gaskets is false economy. To avoid the possibility of trouble after the engine has been reassembled **always** use new gaskets throughout.

12.26 Separating the transmission from the engine

12.27 Using threaded rod, nuts and washers to preload the front wheel bearings

5 Do not throw away the old gaskets, as sometimes it happens that an immediate replacement cannot be found and the old gasket is then very useful as a template. Hang up the gaskets as they are removed.
6 To strip the engine, it is best to work from the top down. When the stage is reached where the crankshaft must be removed, the engine can be turned on its side and all other work carried out with it in this position.
7 Wherever possible, refit nuts, bolts and washers finger tight from wherever they were removed. This helps to avoid loss and muddle. If they cannot be fitted, then arrange them in a sequence that ensures correct reassembly.
8 Make sure that you have a valve grinding tool, a valve spring compressor and a torque wrench.

15 Engine ancillary components – removal

1 Before engine dismantling commences, remove the following ancillary components:

Alternator (Chapter 12)
Inlet manifold, carburettor and fuel pump, or fuel injection components (Chapter 3)

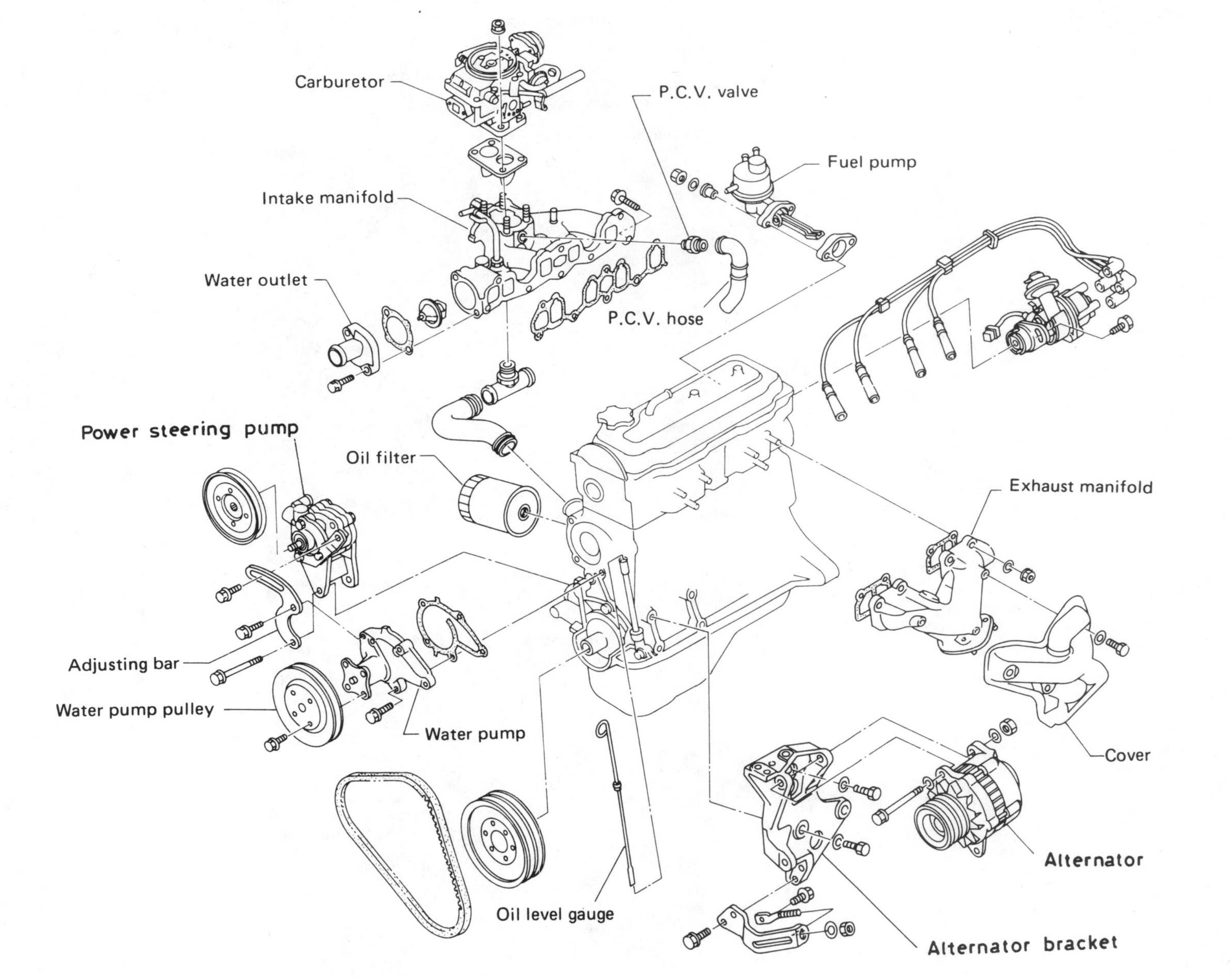

Fig. 1.19 Ancillary components on the carburettor engine (Sec 15)

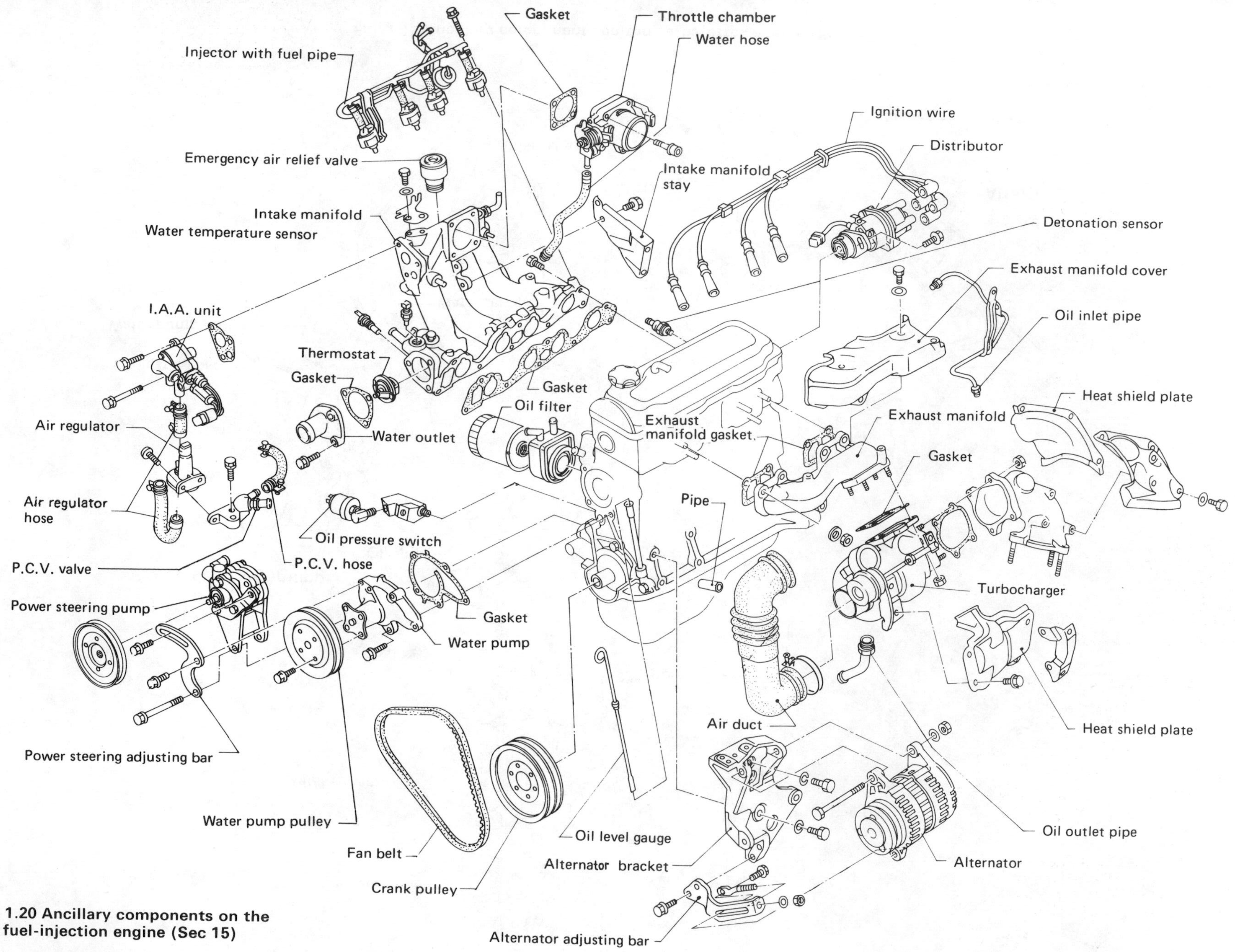

Fig. 1.20 Ancillary components on the fuel-injection engine (Sec 15)

15.1 Crankcase ventilation oil separator and hoses

15.2A Right-hand engine mounting stay bolts

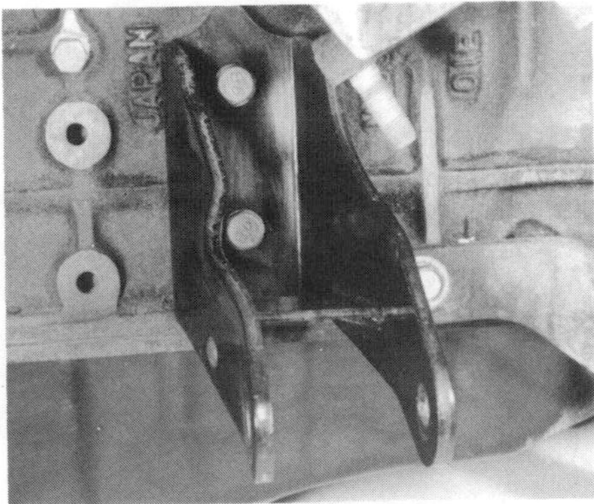
15.2B Front engine mounting bracket in cylinder block

Distributor (Chapter 4) with cap and leads
Water pump and coolant return tube (Chapter 2)
Exhaust manifold (Chapter 3)
Clutch – if applicable (Chapter 5)
Crankcase ventilation oil separator (tap it out) (photo)

2 It is also recommended that the engine mounting brackets are removed. This will make the engine easier to handle (photo).

16 Engine – complete dismantling

1 Unbolt the alternator and power steering pump adjusting links as applicable.
2 Unscrew and discard the oil filter.
3 Unscrew and remove the oil pressure switch.
4 Remove the timing belt with reference to Section 5.
5 Remove the cylinder head with reference to Section 6.
6 Turn the engine on its side.
7 Remove the sump pan and oil pump with reference to Sections 7 and 8.
8 Remove the pistons and big-end bearings with reference to Section 9.
9 Unbolt and remove the flywheel/driveplate bolts and remove the flywheel/driveplate having first marked its position in relation to the mounting flange.
10 Take off the engine rear plate.
11 Unscrew the crankshaft rear oil seal retainer bolts and remove the retainer.
12 Remove the main bearing cap bolts (Fig. 1.21).
13 Note the caps are numbered 1 to 5 from the timing end of the engine and the numbers are read from the same end (photo).
14 Remove the caps, tapping them off if necessary with a copper-faced hammer.
15 If the bearing shells are to be used again, keep them with their respective caps.
16 Lift the crankshaft from the crankcase.
17 Remove the remaining half shells from their crankcase seats and again keep them in their original sequence if they are to be refitted.
18 Unbolt and remove the baffle plate from inside the crankcase.

17 Cylinder head – dismantling and decarbonising

1 The manifolds will already have been removed from the cylinder head (see Section 15).
2 Unscrew the bolts and lift the rocker assemblies from the cylinder head. Identify which way round the assemblies are located as this will aid refitting.
3 Remove the spark plugs. Unscrew the fuel pump cam bolt. The fuel pump cam also retains the camshaft. This bolt is very tight and the camshaft must be held stationary either by using a tool on the two square projections or by jamming one of the cam lobes by inserting a length of metal strip under it. Alternatively pass a rod through one of the holes in the camshaft sprocket.

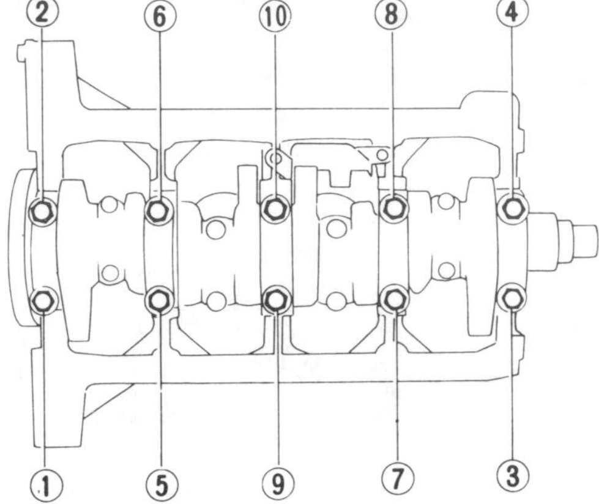

Fig. 1.21 Main bearing cap bolt loosening sequence (Sec 16)

16.13 Main bearing cap number

4 Withdraw the camshaft (sprocket previously removed during removal of the cylinder head) taking care not to damage the bearings as the cam lobes pass through.
5 The valves and their associated components should now be removed.
6 Owing to the depth of the cylinder head, a valve spring compressor having a long reach will be required.

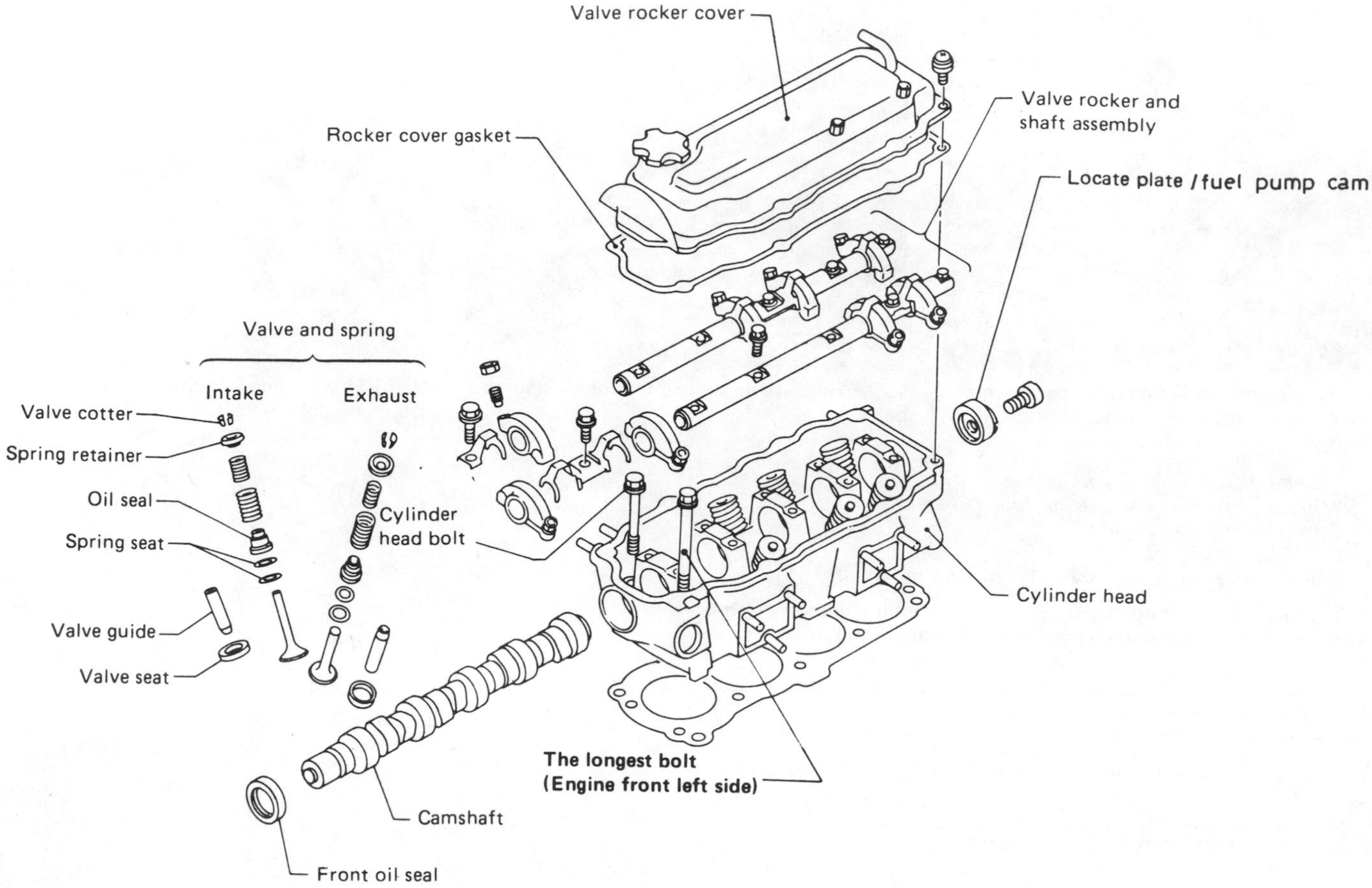

Fig. 1.22 Exploded view of the cylinder head (Sec 17)

7 If this is not available, temporarily refit the rocker shafts and then make up a lever with a fork at one end to compress the valve spring by using the underside of the shafts as a fulcrum point.
8 Compress the first valve springs, extract the split cotters. If the valve springs refuse to compress, do not apply excessive force, but remove the compressor and place the end of a piece of tubing on the valve spring retainer. Strike it a sharp blow to release the collets from the valve stem. Refit the compressor and resume operations when the collets should come out.
9 Gently release the compressor, take off the spring retaining cap, the valve springs and the spring seat.
10 Remove the valve and keep it, with its associated components, in numbered sequence so that they can be refitted in their original position. A small box with divisions is useful for this purpose.
11 Remove the remaining valves in a similar way (photo).
12 Bearing in mind that the cylinder head is of light alloy construction and is easily damaged use a blunt scraper or rotary wire brush to clean all traces of carbon deposits from the combustion spaces and the ports. The valve head, stems and valve guides should also be freed from any carbon deposits. Wash the combustion spaces and ports down with paraffin and scrape the cylinder head surface free of any foreign matter with the side of a steel rule, or a similar article.
13 If the engine is installed in the car, clean the pistons and the top of the cylinder bores. If the pistons are still in the block then it is essential that great care is taken to ensure that no carbon gets into the cylinder bores as this could scratch the cylinder walls or cause damage to the piston and rings. To ensure this does not happen, first turn the crankshaft so that two of the pistons are at the top of their bores. Stuff rag into the other two bores or seal them off with paper and masking tape. The waterways should also be covered with small pieces of masking tape to prevent particles of carbon entering the cooling system and damaging the coolant pump.

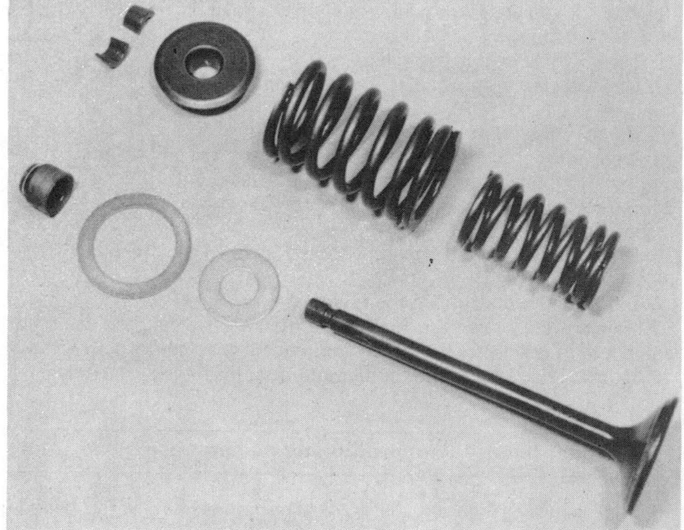

17.11 Valve components

14 Press a little grease into the gap between the cylinder walls and the two pistons which are to be worked on. With a blunt scraper carefully scrape away the carbon from the piston crown, taking great care not to scratch the aluminium. Also scrape away the carbon from the surrounding lip of the cylinder wall. When all carbon has been

removed, scrape away the grease which will now be contaminated with carbon particles, taking care not to press any into the bores. To assist prevention of carbon build-up the piston crown can be polished with a metal polish. Remove the rags or masking tape from the other two cylinders and turn the crankshaft so that the two pistons which were at the bottom are now at the top. Place rag or masking tape in the cylinders which have been decarbonised, and proceed as just described.

15 Examine the head of the valves for pitting and burning, especially the heads of the exhaust valves. The valve seatings should be examined at the same time. If the pitting on the valve and seat is very slight, the marks can be removed by grinding the seats and valves together with coarse, and then fine, valve grinding paste.

16 Where bad pitting has occurred to the valve seats it will be necessary to recut them and fit new valves. This latter job should be entrusted to the local agent or engineering works. In practice it is very seldom that the seats are so badly worn. Normally it is the valve that is too badly worn for refitting, and the owner can easily purchase a new set of valves and match them to the seats by valve grinding.

17 Valve grinding is carried out as follows. Smear a trace of coarse carborundum paste on the seat face and apply a suction grinder tool to the valve head. With a semi-rotary motion, grind the valve head to its seat, lifting the valve occasionally to redistribute the grinding paste. When a dull matt even surface is produced on both the valve seat and the valve, wipe off the paste and repeat the process with fine carborundum paste as before. A light spring placed under the valve head will greatly ease this operation. When a smooth unbroken ring of light grey matt finish is produced, on both valve and valve seat faces, the grinding operation is complete. Carefully clean away every trace of grinding compound, take great care to leave none in the ports or in the valve guides. Clean the valves and valve seats with a paraffin soaked rag, then a clean rag, and finally, if an air line is available, blow the valves, valve guides and valve ports clean.

18 Check that all valve springs are intact. If any one is broken, all should be renewed. Check the free height of the springs against new ones. If some springs are not within specifications, replace them all. Springs suffer from fatigue and it is a good idea to renew them even if they look serviceable.

19 Check that the oil supply holes in the rocker arm studs are clear.

20 The cylinder head can be checked for warping either by placing it on a piece of plate glass or using a straight-edge and feeler blades. If there is any doubt or if its block face is corroded, have it re-faced by your dealer or motor engineering works.

21 Examine the camshaft bearings for wear, scoring or pitting. If evident, then the complete cylinder head will have to be renewed as the bearings are machined directly in it.

22 The camshaft itself should show no marks or scoring on the journal cam lobe surfaces. Where evident, renew the camshaft or have it reprofiled by a specialist reconditioner.

23 Check the teeth of the camshaft sprocket, renew if chipped or worn. The fuel pump eccentric cam should not show any sign of scoring or grooving.

24 Test the valves in their guides for side to side rock. If this is anything more than almost inperceptible, new guides must be fitted. This, as with valve seal renewal, is really a job for your dealer as the cylinder head must be warmed and the oil guide driven out towards the rocker cover side. New guides should be pressed in to protrude between 10.2 and 10.4 mm (0.402 and 0.409 in) above the cylinder head and then reamed to between 7.000 and 7.018 mm (0.2756 and 0.2763 in)

25 Renew the valve stem oil seals (photo).

26 Commence reassembly by oiling the stem of the first valve and pushing it into its guide (photo).

27 Fit the spring seat, the inner and outer springs so that their closer coils are towards the cylinder head and then the spring retaining cap (photos).

28 Compress the valve springs and locate the split cotters in the valve stem cut-out (photo).

29 Gently release the compressor, checking to see that the collets are not displaced.

30 Fit the remaining valves in the same way.

31 Tap the end of each valve stem with a plastic of copper-faced hammer to settle the components.

17.25 Valve stem oil seal

17.26 Fitting valve to cylinder head

17.27A Valve spring seat

17.27B Valve springs

17.27C Valve spring cap

17.28 Compressing a valve spring (split collets arrowed)

32 Lubricate the camshaft bearings and insert the camshaft into the cylinder head (photo).

33 Fit the fuel pump cam and tighten the bolt to the specified torque. Fit a new camshaft oil seal (photos).

34 Check that the camshaft sprocket dowel is in position at the end of the camshaft and then bolt on the sprocket aligning the marks made at dismantling (photos).

35 Before refitting the rocker gear, check the shafts for wear and the rocker arms for general condition. Renew any worn components, but make sure when reassembling that they are kept in their original order (photos).

36 The inlet valve rocker shaft is marked on its end face with two lines. This end of the shaft should be at the timing belt end. The exhaust valve rocker shaft is not marked in this way.

37 The punch marks on the ends of the shafts should be uppermost These marks indicate the location of the rocker shaft oil holes.

38 The rocker arms are identical on both inlet and exhaust sides for cylinders 1 and 3 and cylinders 2 and 4, but the pairs of arms are marked 1 and 2 only.

17.32 Fitting camshaft

17.33A Fuel pump cam (incorporating distributor location plate) and bolt

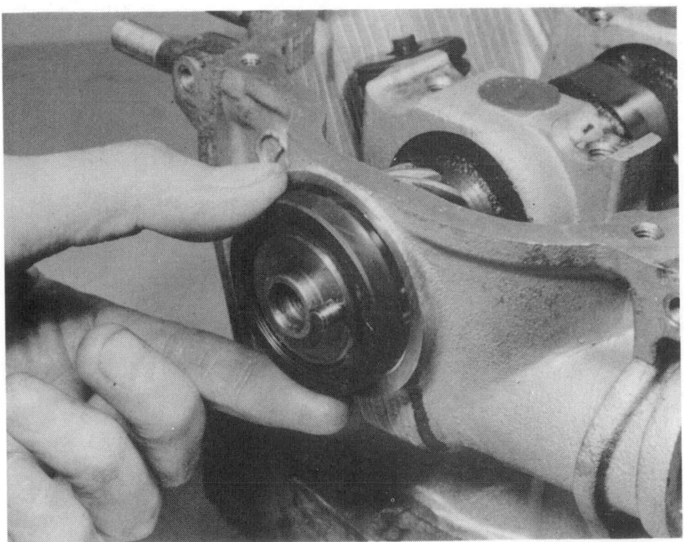
17.33B Camshaft oil seal

17.34A Camshaft sprocket (dowel arrowed)

17.34B Camshaft sprocket bolt

17.35A Rocker arm retaining springs

17.35B Rocker arms correctly located

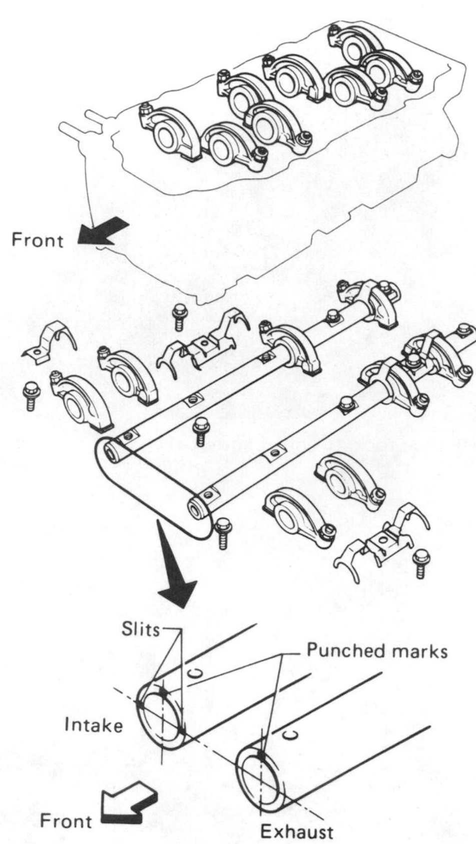

Fig. 1.23 Rocker shafts and arms showing assembly marks (Sec 17)

39 Release the rocker arm adjuster screws fully and then bolt the rocker gear onto the cylinder head. Bolt the shafts down evenly in two or three stages (Fig. 1.24) and raise the cylinder head on wooden blocks while doing it as some of the valves will be forced open by the setting of the camshaft lobes.
40 Turn the camshaft sprocket so that the camshaft lobes for No 1 cylinder are pointing towards the cylinder head.
41 Refit the spark plugs.

18 Engine – examination and renovation

1 With the engine stripped and all parts thoroughly cleaned, every component should be examined for wear. The items listed in the Sections following should receive particular attention and where necessary be renewed or renovated.
2 Many measurements of engine components require accuracies down to tenths of a thousandth of an inch. It is advisable therefore to check your micrometer against a standard gauge occasionally to ensure that the instrument zero is set correctly.
3 If in doubt as to whether or not a particular component must be renewed, take into account not only the cost of the component, but the time and effort which will be required to renew it if it subsequently fails at an early date.

Cylinder block and crankcase

4 Examine the casting carefully for cracks, especially around the bolt holes and between the cylinders.
5 The cylinder bores must be checked for taper, ovality, scoring and scratching. Start by examining the top of the cylinder bores. If they are at all worn, a ridge will be felt on the thrust side. This ridge marks the upper limit of piston ring travel. The owner will have a good indication of bore wear prior to dismantling by the quantity of oil consumed and the emission of blue smoke from the exhaust especially when the engine is cold.
6 An internal micrometer or dial gauge can be used to check bore wear and taper against Specifications, but this is a pointless operation if the engine is obviously in need of reboring as indicated by excessive oil consumption.
7 Your engine reconditioner will be abe to rebore the block for you and supply the correct oversize pistons to give the correct running clearance.
8 To rectify minor bore wear, it is possible to fit special oil control rings as described in Section 9.
9 A good way to test the condition of the engine is to have it at normal operating temperature with the spark plugs removed. Screw a compression tester (available from most motor accessory stores) into the first plug hole. Hold the throttle fully open and crank the engine on the starter motor for several revolutions. Record the reading. Zero the tester and check the remaining cylinders in the same way. All four compression figures should be approximately equal and as given in Specifications.
10 If they are all low, suspect piston ring or cylinder bore wear. If only one reading is down, suspect a valve not seating.

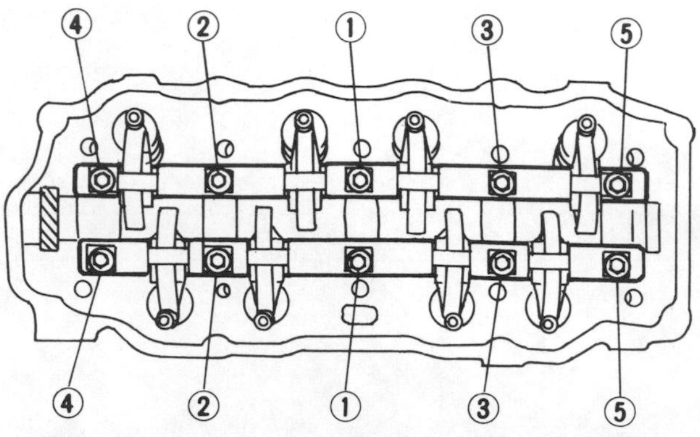

Fig. 1.24 Rocker shaft assembly bolt tightening sequence (Sec 17)

Crankshaft and bearings

11 Examine the crankpin and main journal surfaces for signs of scoring or scratches, and check the ovality and taper of the crankpins and main journals. If the bearing surface dimensions do not fall within the tolerance ranges given in the Specifications at the beginning of this Chapter, the crankpins and/or main journals will have to be reground.
12 Big-end and crankpin wear is accompanied by distinct metallic knocking, particularly noticeable when the engine is pulling from low revs, and some loss of oil pressure.
13 Main bearing and main journal wear is accompanied by severe engine vibration rumble – getting progressively worse as engine revs increase – and again by loss of oil pressure.
14 If the crankshaft requires regrinding take it to an engine reconditioning specailist, who will machine it for you and supply the correct undersize bearing shells.
15 Inspect the big-end and main bearing shells for signs of general wear, scoring, pitting and scratches. The bearings should be matt grey in colour. With lead indium bearings, should a trace of copper colour be noticed, the bearings are badly worn as the lead bearing material has worn away to expose the indium underlay. Renew the bearings if they are in this condition or if there are any signs of scoring or pitting. **You are strongly advised to renew the bearings – regardless of their condition at time of major overhaul. Refitting used bearings is a false economy.**
16 The undersizes available are designed to correspond with crankshaft regrind sizes. The bearings are in fact, slightly more than the

stated undersize as running clearances have been allowed for during their manufacture.
17 Main and big-end bearing shells can be identified as to size by the marking on the back of the shell. Standard size bearing shells are marked STD or .00, undersize shells are marked with the undersize such as 0.020 u/s (photo).

Connecting rods

18 Check the alignment of the connecting rods visually. If you suspect distortion, have them checked by your dealer or engine reconditioner on the special jig which he will have.
19 The gudgeon pin is an inteference fit in the connecting rod small-end and removal, refitting of the pin or changing a piston is a job best left to your dealer or engine reconditioner owing to the need for a press and jig and careful heating of the connecting rod.

Pistons and piston rings

20 If the engine is rebored then new oversize pistons with rings and gudgeon pins will be supplied. Have the supplier fit the new pistons to the rods making sure that the oil hole in the connecting rod is located as shown with reference to the front facing mark on the piston crown. (Fig. 1.25).
21 Removal and refitting of the piston rings is covered in Section 9.

Flywheel

22 Check the clutch mating surface of the flywheel. If it is deeply scored (owing to failure to renew a worn driven plate), then it may be possible to have it surface ground provided the thickness of the flywheel is not reduced by more than 0.3 mm (0.012 in) in thickness.
23 Where lots of tiny cracks are visible on the surface of the flywheel, then this will be due to overheating caused by slipping the clutch or riding the clutch pedal.
24 With a pre-engaged type of starter motor, it is rare to find the teeth of the flywheel starter ring gear damaged or worn, but if they are then the ring gear will have to be renewed.
25 To remove the ring gear, drill a hole between the roots of two teeth taking care not to damage the flywheel and then split the ring with a sharp cold chisel.
26 The new ring gear must be heated to between 180 and 220°C (356 and 428°F).
27 This is very hot so if you do not have facilities for obtaining these temperatures, leave the job to your dealer or engine reconditioner.

Driveplate (automatic transmission)

28 Should the starter ring gear on the driveplate require renewal, the removal and fitting procedure is the same as for the flywheel.

Timing belt and tensioner

29 Examine the belt for cracking or fraying and tooth wear. If any of these conditions is evident, or if the belt has been in service for 80 000 km (50 000 miles), it is recommended that it is renewed.
30 The tensioner should not be noisy when turned and should have a good spring action. Where these conditions are not satisfied renew the tenisioner complete (photo).

Oil pump

31 Extract the screws (impact driver), remove the cover and check the following clearances with a feeler blade and compare with the specified tolerances (photos).

Inner gear to crescent
Outer gear to crescent
Outer gear to body

32 If these clearances are satisfactory, now measure the gear endfloat using a feeler blade and a straight edge across the pump body. The endfloat must be within the specified tolerance (photo).
33 If any of the clearances are outside those specified, renew the components or complete oil pump as necessary.
34 The pressure regulator components are seldom found to be faulty, but if they are, unscrew the end plug and renew all the valve components. Renew the pump oil seal (photos).
35 While the oil filter is removed at time of renewal, it is worth checking the pressure relief valve. If there is any indication of scoring or chipping of the ball valve, prise the valve from the oil filter mounting base and tap a new one into place with a piece of tubing (photo).

18.17 Bearing shell marking

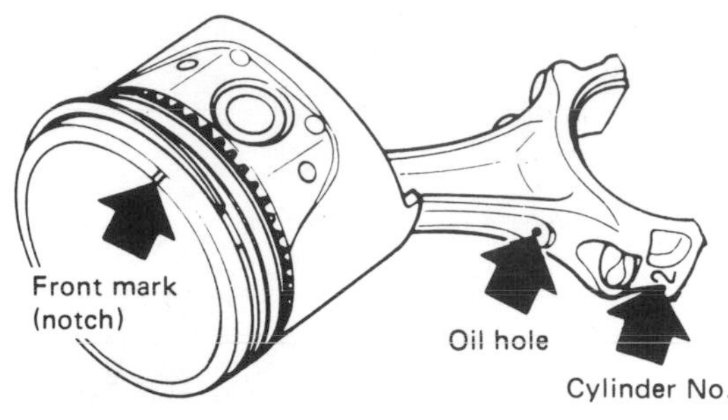

Fig. 1.25 Piston-to-connecting rod alignment (Sec 18)

18.30 Timing belt tensioner

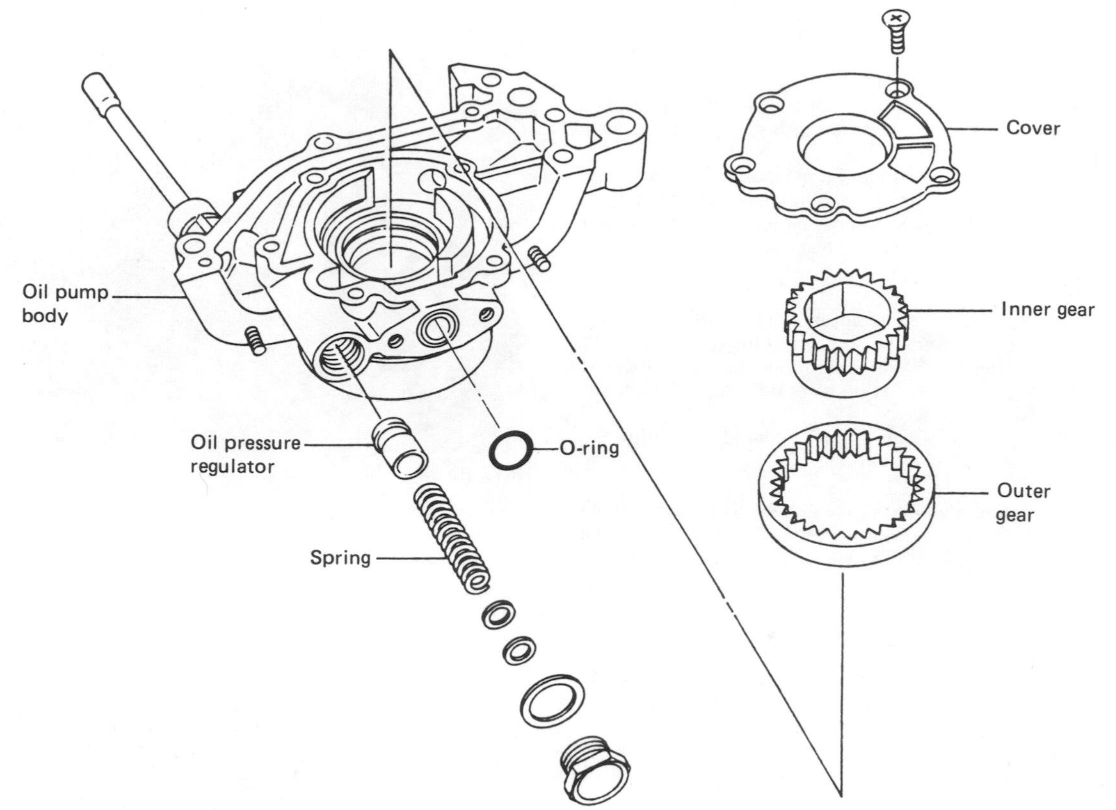

Cover
Inner gear
Oil pump body
Oil pressure regulator
O-ring
Outer gear
Spring

Fig. 1.26 Exploded view of the oil pump (Sec 18)

18.31A Oil pump cover removed

18.31B Checking inner gear-to-crescent clearance

18.31C Checking outer gear-to-crescent clearance

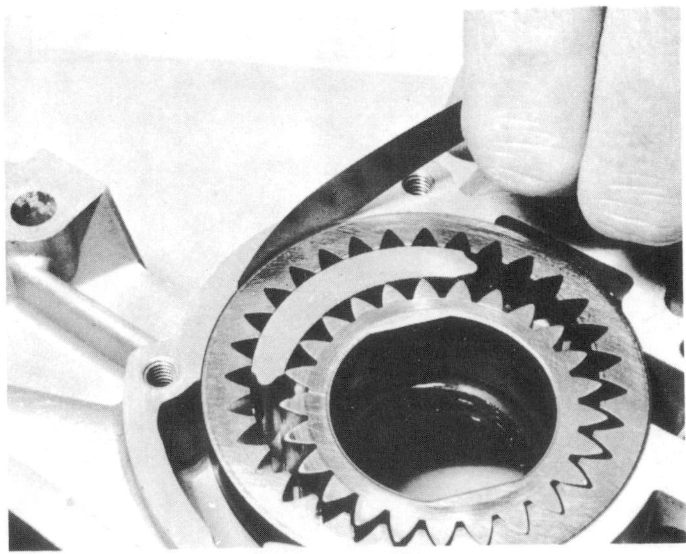
18.31D Checking outer gear-to-body clearance

18.32 Checking oil pump gear endfloat

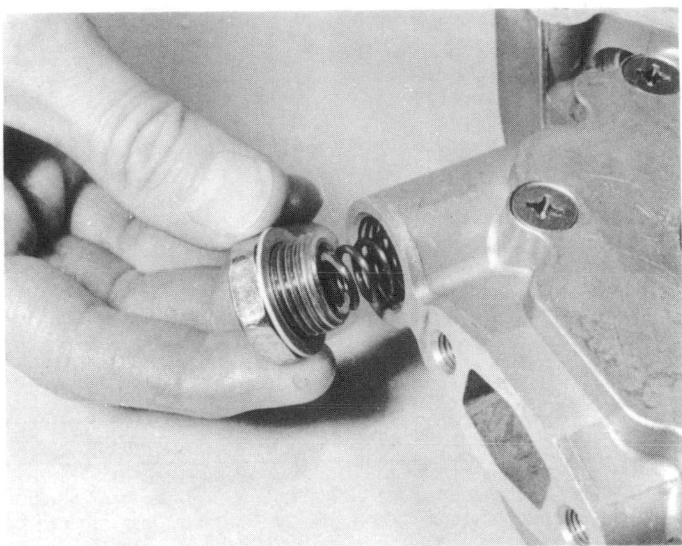
18.34A Oil pump pressure regulator cap

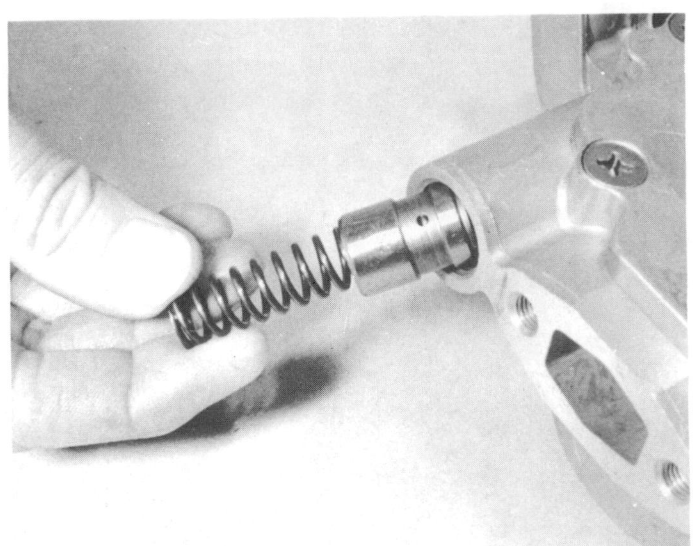
18.34B Oil pump pressure regulator plunger and spring

18.34C Prising out oil pump oil seal

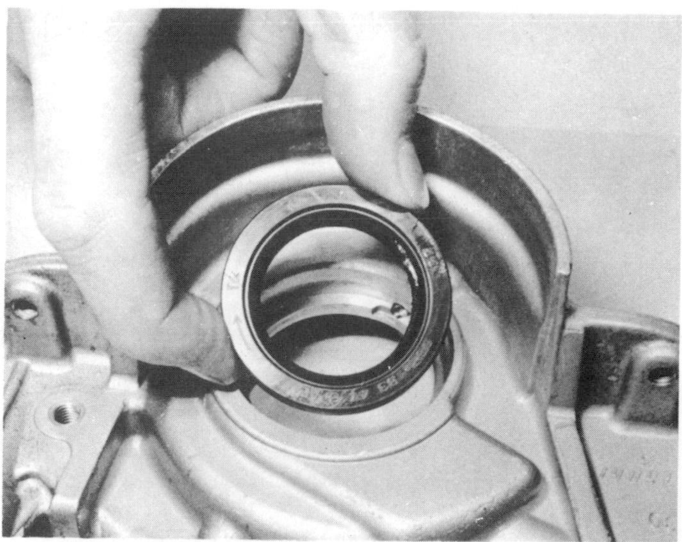

18.34D Locating oil pump oil seal

18.35 Oil pressure relief valve

Cylinder head

36 This is covered in Section 17 during dismantling and decarbonising.

Oil seals and gaskets

37 It is recommended that all gaskets and oil seals are renewed at major engine overhaul. Sockets are useful for removing and refitting oil seals. On most seals, an arrow is moulded onto the rubber lip to indicate the rotational direction of the component which it serves. Make sure that the seal is fitted the correct way round to comply with the arrow.

19 Engine – reassembly general

1 To ensure maximum life with minimum trouble from a rebuilt engine, not only must everything be correctly assembled, but everything must be spotlessly clean, all the oilways must be clear, locking washers and spring washers must always be fitted where indicated and all bearing and other working surfaces must be thoroughly lubricated during assembly.

2 Before assembly begins renew any bolts or studs, the threads of which are in any way damaged, and whenever possible use new spring washers.

20 Engine – reassembly

1 Have the block standing on a flat surface with the crankcase uppermost and thoroughly clean internally.

2 Bolt the baffle plate into the crankcase (photo).

3 Wipe out the crankcase bearing shell seats and locate the shells noting that the flanged one which controls crankshaft endfloat is the centre one (photo).

4 Oil the shells liberally and then lower the crankshaft into them (photo).

5 Wipe out the bearing shell seats in the main bearing caps and locate the shells (photo).

20.2 Crankcase oil baffle

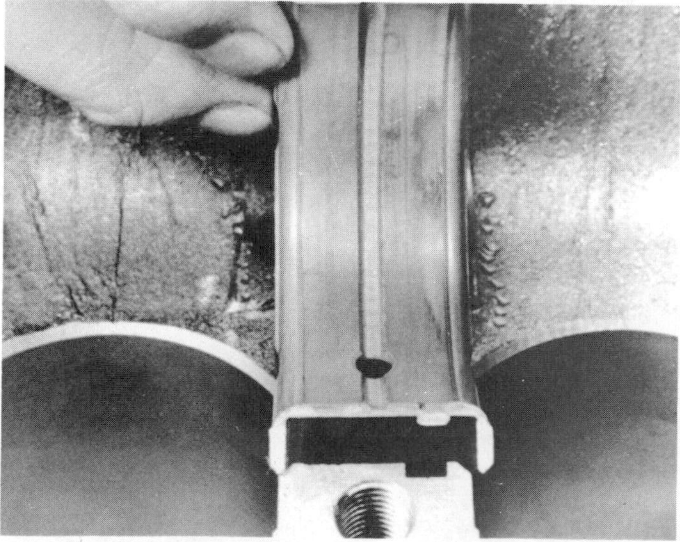

20.3 Centre main bearing shell with thrust flanges

20.4 Locating crankshaft

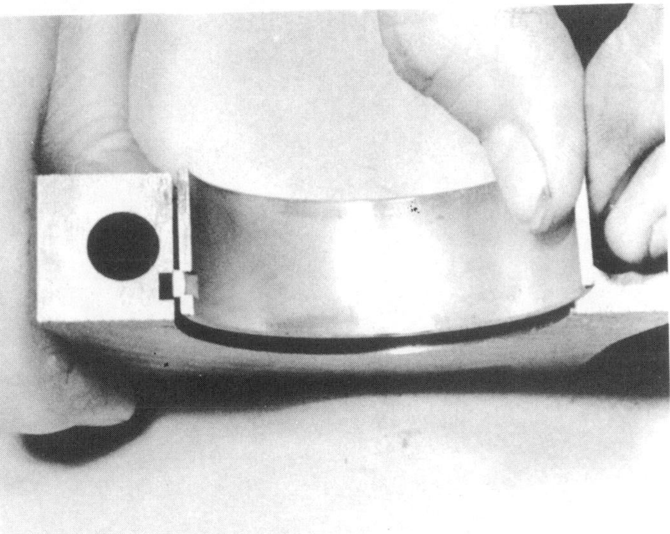
20.5 Fitting bearing shell to main bearing cap

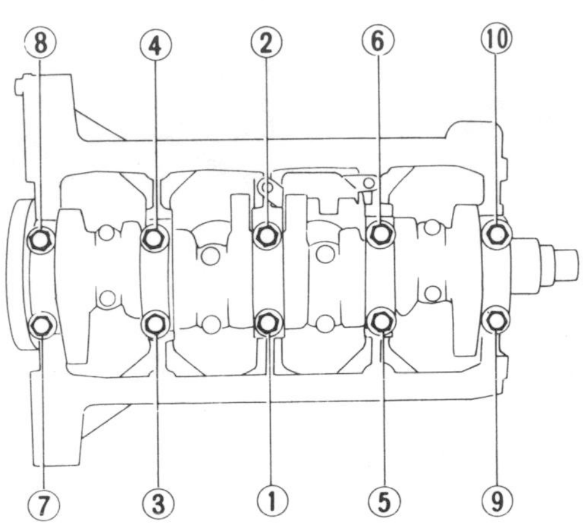

Fig. 1.27 Main bearing cap bolt tightening sequence (Sec 20)

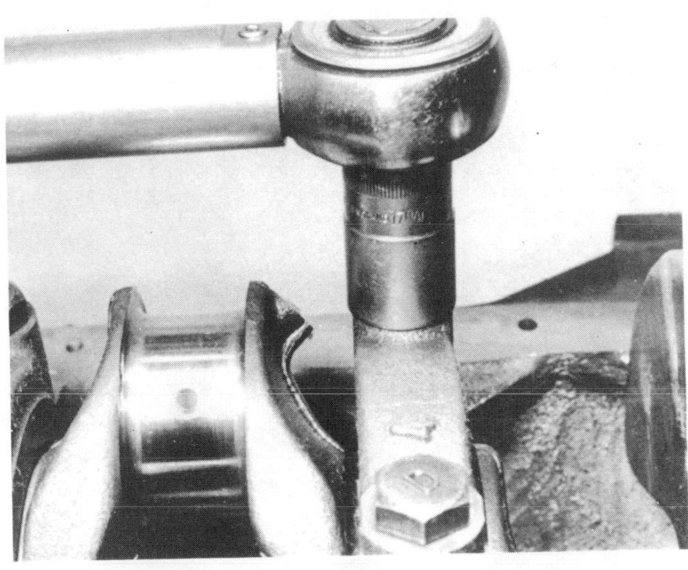
20.7 Tightening main bearing cap bolt

6 Oil the journals and fit the caps in their numbered sequence (No. 1 at timing belt end).
7 Screw in the cap bolts and tighten to the specified torque in the sequence shown in Fig. 1.27 (photo).
8 If new bearing shells have been fitted, then the crankshaft endfloat should be as specified, but it is worth checking at this stage. If the original shells are being used again then the endfloat should certainly be checked to ensure that wear on the centre bearing shell thrust flanges has not increased the crankshaft endfloat to the point where it is outside specified tolerance.
9 To check the end-float, tap the crankshaft fully in one direction and measure the gap between the thrust flange of the bearing shell and the machined face of the crankshaft (photo).
10 If the clearance is too large and new shells have been fitted, suspect a fault in re-grinding of the crankshaft.
11 Bolt the crankshaft rear oil seal retainer into position using a new oil seal and gasket (photos).
12 Locate the engine rear plate on its dowels (photo).
13 Fit the flywheel onto its mounting flange.
14 Apply thread locking fluid to the flywheel bolts, screw them in and tighten to the specified torque. Lock the flywheel teeth as shown (photos).
15 Fit the piston/connecting rods as described in Section 9.
16 Fit the oil pump and sump pan as described in Sections 8 and 7.

20.9 Checking crankshaft endfloat

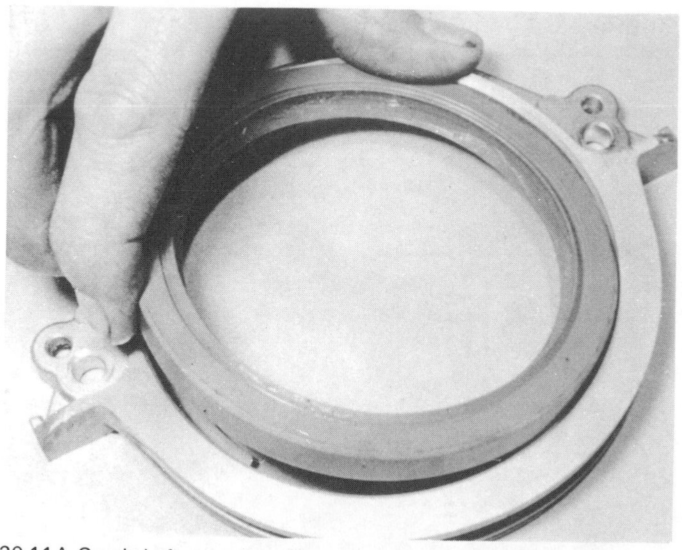
20.11A Crankshaft rear oil seal

20.11B Fitting crankshaft rear oil seal/retainer

20.12 Engine rear plate

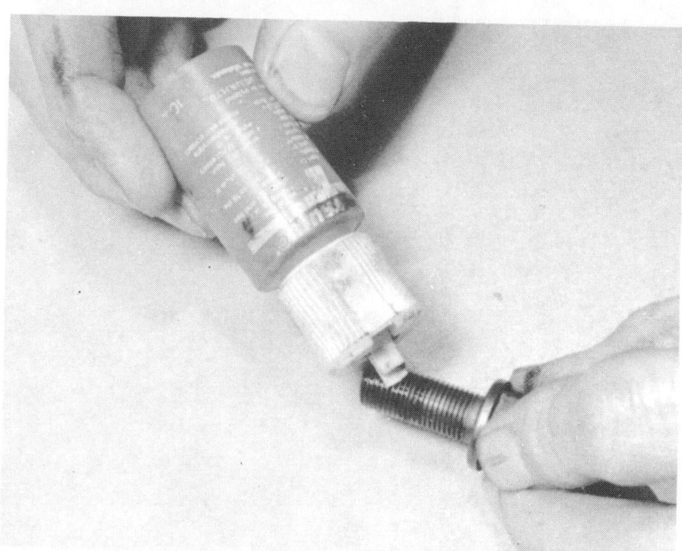
20.14A Applying thread locking fluid to flywheel bolt

20.14B Tightening a flywheel bolt

20.14C Flywheel locking device

17 Refit the cylinder head as described in Section 6.
18 Refit the timing belt as described in Section 5.
19 Screw in the oil pressure switch.
20 Fit a new oil filter with reference to Section 2.
21 Fit the alternator and power steering pump adjusting links and tighten the bolts.

21 Engine ancillary components – refitting

Reverse the procedures listed in Section 15.

22 Engine/manual transmission – reconnection and refitting

1 Reverse the procedure given in Section 12, but note the following points.
2 Tighten the engine/transmission mountings with reference to Section 10.
3 Where necessary, for adjustment procedures refer to the relevant Chapters.
4 Fill the engine with oil and coolant.

23 Engine/automatic transmission – reconnection and refitting

1 Reverse the procedure given in Section 13, but note the following points.
2 Before commencing work, check that the torque converter is correctly engaged with the oil pump with reference to Chapter 7 Section 9.
3 Apply locking fluid to the threads of the torque converter bolts and tighten them to the specified torque (Chapter 7).
4 Adjust the kickdown cable and selector lever cable as described in Chapter 7 Section 3.

24 Engine – initial start-up after overhaul

1 Make sure the battery is fully charged and that all lubricants, coolant and fuel are replenished.
2 If the fuel system has been dismantled it will require several revolutions of the engine on the starter motor to prime the system.
3 As soon as the engine fires and runs, keep it going at a fast tickover only (no faster), and bring it up to the normal working temperature.
4 As the engine warms up there will be odd smells and some smoke from parts getting hot and burning off oil deposits. The signs to look for are leaks of water or oil which will be obvious if serious. Check also the exhaust pipe and manifold connections, as these do not always 'find' exact gastight position until the warmth and vibration have acted on them, and it is almost certain that they will need tightening further. This should be done, of course, with the engine stopped.
5 When normal running temperature has been reached adjust the engine idling speed, and check the ignition timing.
6 Stop the engine and wait a few minutes to see if any lubricant or coolant is dripping out when the engine is stationary.
7 Road test the car to check that the timing is correct and that the engine is giving the necessary smoothness and power. Do not race the engine – if new bearings and/or pistons have been fitted it should be treated as a new engine and run in at a reduced speed for the first 500 miles (800 km).
8 After 600 miles (1000 km), the cylinder head bolts should be retightened with the engine cold. To do this, remove the rocker cover, then using the same sequence as for tightening the bolts, loosen each bolt half a turn and retighten it to the specified final torque wrench setting.

25 Fault diagnosis – engine

Symptom	Reason(s)
Engine will not turn over when starter switch is operated	Flat battery Loose battery connections Loose connections at solenoid switch and/or starter motor Starter motor jammed Starter motor defective
Engine turns over normally but fails to fire and run	No sparks at plugs No fuel reaching engine Too much fuel reaching engine (flooding)
Engine starts but runs unevenly and misfires	Ignition and/or fuel system fault Incorrect valve clearance Burnt out valves Blown cylinder head gasket Worn out piston rings Worn cylinder bores
Lack of power	Ignition and/or fuel system faults Incorrect valve clearance Burnt out valves Low cylinder compression
Excessive oil consumption	Oil leaks from crankshaft oil seals, camshaft oil seal, rocker cover gasket or sump gasket Worn piston rings or cylinder bores Worn valve guides and/or defective valve stem oil seals
Excessive mechanical noise from engine	Excessive valve clearances Worn crankshaft bearings Worn cylinder bores (piston slap)

Chapter 2 Cooling system

Contents

Specifications

General

System type	Pressurised, with expansion tank, front mounted radiator, electric cooling fan, water pump and thermostat
Radiator cap relief pressure	0.88 bar (13.0 lbf/in²)

Thermostat

Opening temperature	82°C (180°F)
Maximum valve lift	8.0 mm (0.31 in) at 95°C (203°F)

Cooling fan

Switch operating temperature:	
Main fan	90°C (194°F)
Sub fan (where applicable)	100°C (212°F)

Water pump

Drivebelt deflection:	New	Used
Standard models	8 to 11 mm (0.31 to 0.43 in)	10 to 13 mm (0.39 to 0.51 in)
Power steering models	4 to 6 mm (0.16 to 0.24 in)	6 to 8 mm (0.24 to 0.31 in)

Coolant

Capacity (excl. expansion tank):	With heater	Without heater
Non-Turbo models	6.5 litres (11.4 pints)	5.9 litres (10.4 pints)
Turbo models	7.0 litres (12.3 pints)	6.4 litres (11.3 pints)

Torque wrench settings

	Nm	lbf ft
Water pump	18	13
Pulley bolt	8	6
Thermostat housing cover	20	15

1 General description

The cooling system is of pressurised type incorporating an expansion tank. The radiator is front-mounted with a thermostatically-controlled electric cooling fan.

A thermostat is located in the right-hand end of the inlet manifold to prevent circulation of the coolant until the engine has warmed up, and then to maintain the engine at the correct operating temperature. Once the thermostat has opened the coolant is pumped through the radiator for cooling, and if this is insufficient, additional cooling is provided by one or two electric cooling fans according to model.

The coolant is used to heat the inlet manifold for improved fuel/air induction, and is also passed through the heater for heating the car interior.

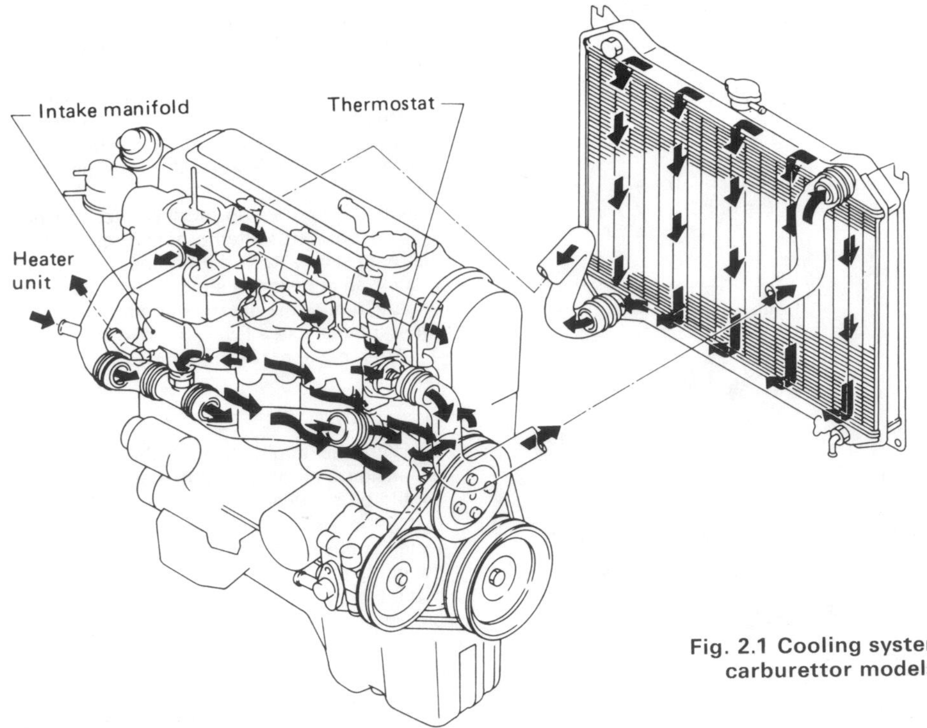

Fig. 2.1 Cooling system circuit on carburettor models (Sec 1)

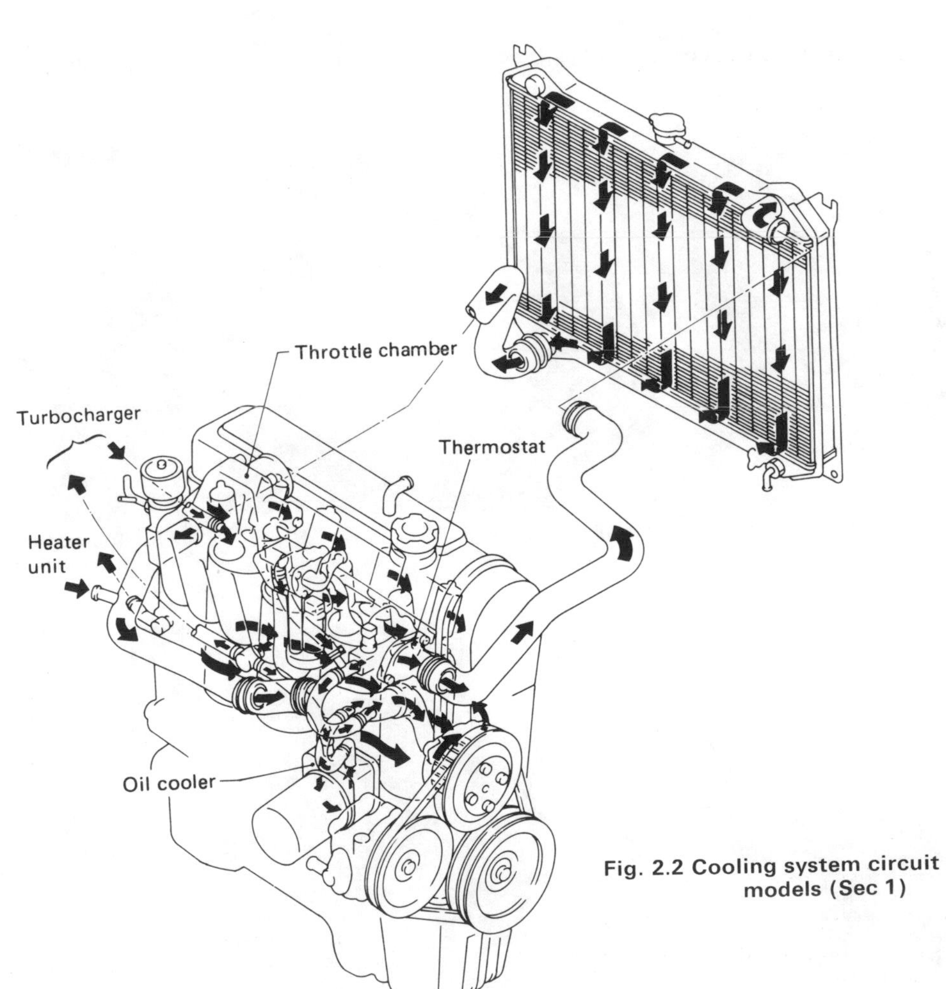

Fig. 2.2 Cooling system circuit on Turbo models (Sec 1)

2 Routine maintenance

Carry out the following procedures at the intervals given in *'Routine Maintenance'* at the beginning of the Manual.

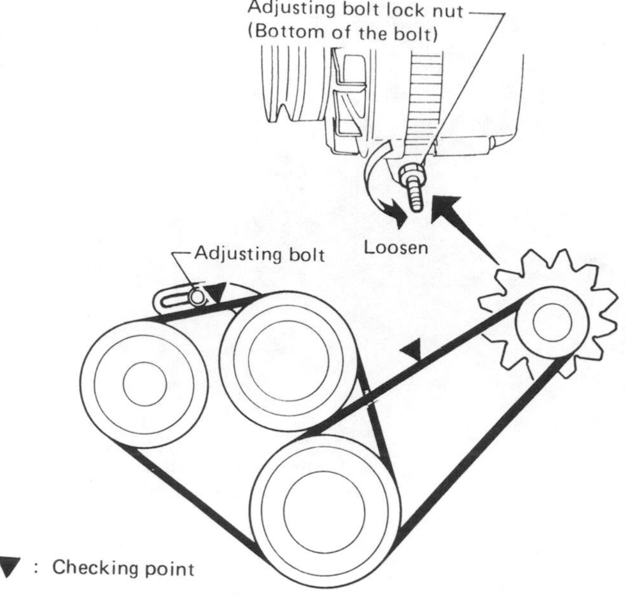

Fig. 2.3 Drivebelt layout on power steering models (Sec 2)

Water pump drivebelt

1 Examine the full length of the water pump drivebelt for cracks, fraying, deterioration and oil contamination. Renew it if necessary, but if it is in good order check and if necessary adjust its tension as follows.

2 Depress the drivebelt with moderate thumb pressure midway between the water pump and alternator or power steering pump pulleys. If the deflection is not as given in Specifications adjust the tension.

3 On power steering models refer to Chapter 10, however on other models loosen the alternator pivot and adjustment bolts and swivel the alternator away from the engine until the tension is correct. On some models an adjustment stud is provided on the bottom of the alternator, and by turning the nut the correct tension can be achieved (photo). On other models use a lever to move the alternator.

4 After making the adjustment tighten the pivot and adjustment bolts.

Coolant level

5 With the engine **cold**, check the level of the coolant in the expansion tank on the right-hand side of the engine compartment. It should be between the 'Min' and 'Max' marks. If it is below the 'Min' mark, top up to the 'Max' mark with water or preferably with a water/antifreeze solution. Should the expansion tank be empty, check the coolant level in the radiator before topping-up, and also check the complete cooling system for leaks. The system can if necessary be pressurised using a special pump to check for leaks, however this work should be carried out by a Nissan dealer (photos).

3 Cooling system – draining, flushing and refilling

1 Allow the engine to cool before draining the coolant.
2 Set the heater temperature control lever to maximum heat.
3 Unscrew and remove the radiator and expansion tank filler caps.

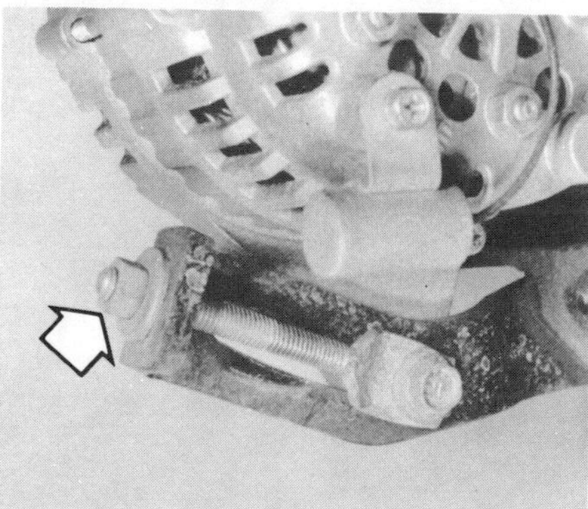

2.3 Showing adjustment stud (arrowed) for tensioning the alternator/water pump drivebelt

2.5A Expansion tank

2.5B Topping-up the coolant level in the expansion tank

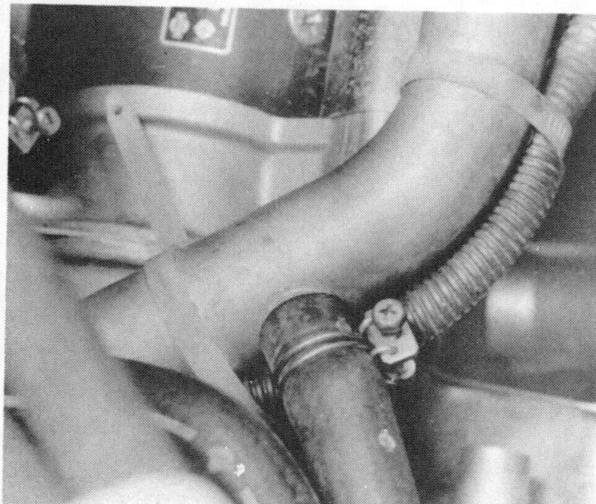

2.5C Heater return hose connected to the coolant return tube on the left-hand side of the engine

2.5D Heater feed hose connected to the cylinder block outlet elbow

2.5E Radiator bottom hose connected to the coolant return tube

4 Unscrew the drain tap on the bottom right-hand side of the radiator and drain the coolant into a suitable container.
5 If the coolant has been changed regularly there should be no evidence of rust and sediment and the system may be refilled immediately as described later in this Section.
6 If the system has been neglected, flush it through with a cold water hose until the water flows clear. In severe cases of corrosion or sediment accumulation, the radiator should be removed (Section 6) and both it and the cylinder reverse flushed. If necessary unscrew the drain plug from the front of the cylinder block (photo).
7 Allow the system to drain completely, then refit the cylinder block drain plug and tighten the radiator drain tap.
8 Fill the radiator with coolant solution made up as described in Section 4, then refit the cap (photo).
9 Fill the expansion tank with coolant to the 'Max' mark, then refit the cap.
10 Start the engine and run it at a fast idling speed to normal operating temperature.
11 Allow the engine to cool completely, then check and if necessary top up the radiator and expansion tank. Make sure that the caps are refitted correctly.

3.6 Cylinder block drain plug

4 Coolant mixture

1 It is important to use an antifreeze mixture in the system all the year round. The mixture should be made up from clean, preferably soft, tap water (or rain water) and a good quality antifreeze liquid containing corrosion inhibitor. The proportions of water to antifreeze will depend on the degree of protection required.
2 30% of antifreeze should be regarded as the minimum proportion required to maintain good anti-corrosion characteristics and to protect against freezing down to −15°C (+5°F).
3 For absolute protection, use a 50% mixture which will protect the system down to −35°C (−31°F).
4 Before filling with fresh antifreeze, drain and flush the system as described in Section 3 and check that all the hoses are in good condition and that the clips are all tight. Antifreeze has a searching action and will leak more rapidly than plain water. Pour a couple of pints of water into the system and then add the correct quantity of antifreeze fluid. Complete the refilling as described in Section 3.
5 All future topping-up should be done using mixed coolant of the correct proportions.
6 The antifreeze should be renewed every two years, as the corrosion inhibitor will then be of little use. Don't attempt to use the engine antifreeze in the windscreen wash system; it will attack the car's paintwork and will smear the windscreen. Finally remember that antifreeze is very poisonous and must be handled with due care.
7 In climates where antifreeze is not required, use a corrosion inhibitor in the cooling system water, never use plain water.

3.8 Filling the radiator with coolant

5 Thermostat – removal, testing and refitting

1 Unscrew the radiator filler cap and drain tap and draw off about 1.5 litre of coolant.
2 Disconnect the top hose from the thermostat housing cover, then unbolt and remove the cover (photos).
3 Discard the gasket and withdraw the thermostat (photo). If it is stuck tight do not lever it by its bridge piece, but cut around its edge using a sharp pointed knife.
4 The thermostat can be tested easily for correct functioning if this should be in doubt. Boil a pan of water and suspend the thermostat on a piece of cord. Lower the thermostat into the hot water and it should be seen to open on immersion. Remove the thermostat from the water and it should be seen to close. This is a simply functional test but it will identify a failed thermostat. With a thermometer you can check the correct opening temperature and maximum valve lift, see Specifications.
5 When renewing this component, make sure that the replacement item is the correct one for your car as thermostats are made for a wide range of different models and conditions. You can drive without a thermostat in an emergency, no harm will result but the engine will not warm up properly.

5.2A Top hose connected to the thermostat housing cover

5.2B Showing the thermostat housing cover and the coolant temperature switch (arrowed)

5.2C Removing the thermostat housing cover and gasket

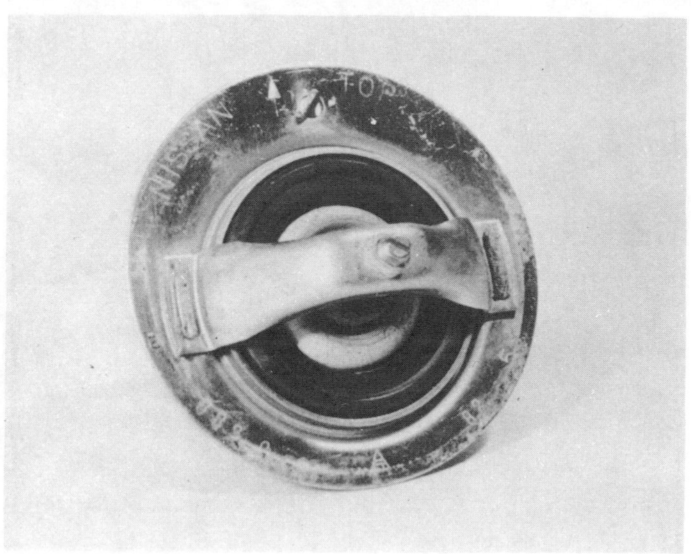

5.3 Thermostat removed

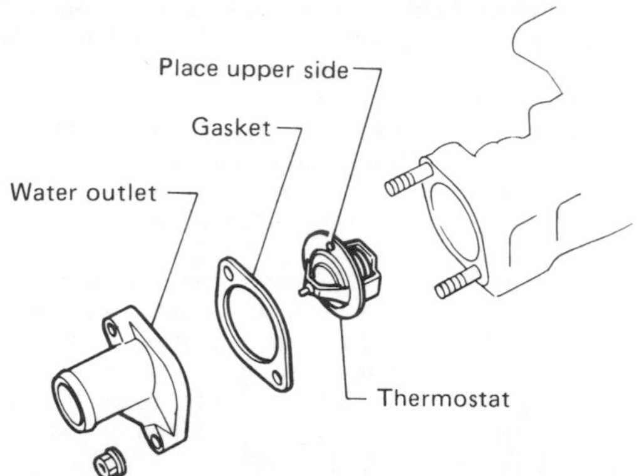

Fig. 2.4 Thermostat components (Sec 5)

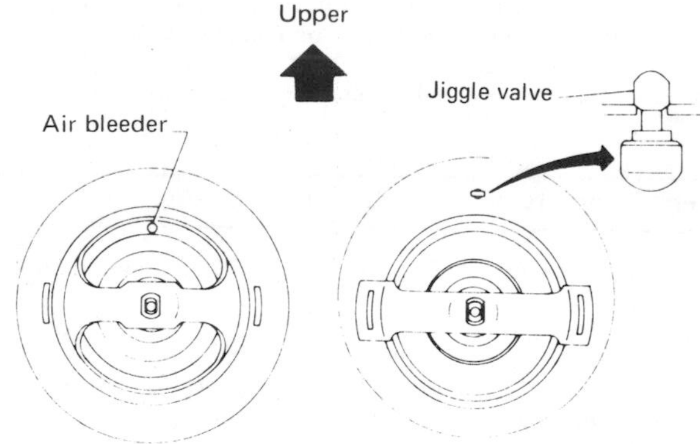

Fig. 2.6 Correct installation of thermostat (Sec 5)

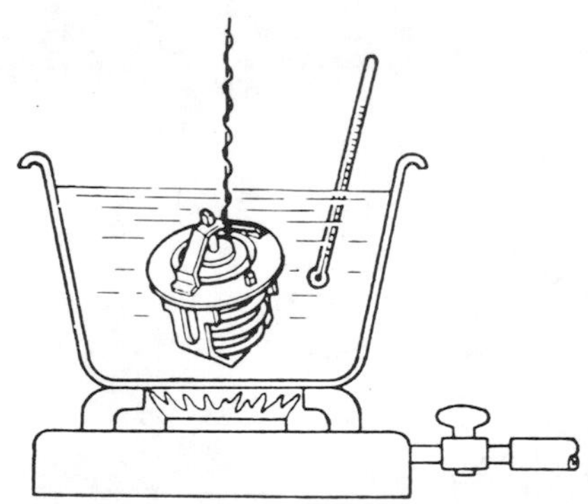

Fig. 2.5 Testing the thermostat (Sec 5)

6 Clean the mating faces of the thermostat housing and its cover and use a new gasket.

7 Locate the thermostat so that the jiggle valve is uppermost.

8 Tighten the bolts, then refit the top hose and top up the coolant in the radiator and expansion tank.

6 Radiator – removal, repair and refitting

1 Drain the cooling system as described in Section 3. Disconnect the battery negative lead.

2 Disconnect the top and bottom hoses and the expansion tank hose (photos).

3 On automatic transmission models, disconnect the oil cooler hoses from the bottom of the radiator and plug them.

6.2A Top hose connection to radiator

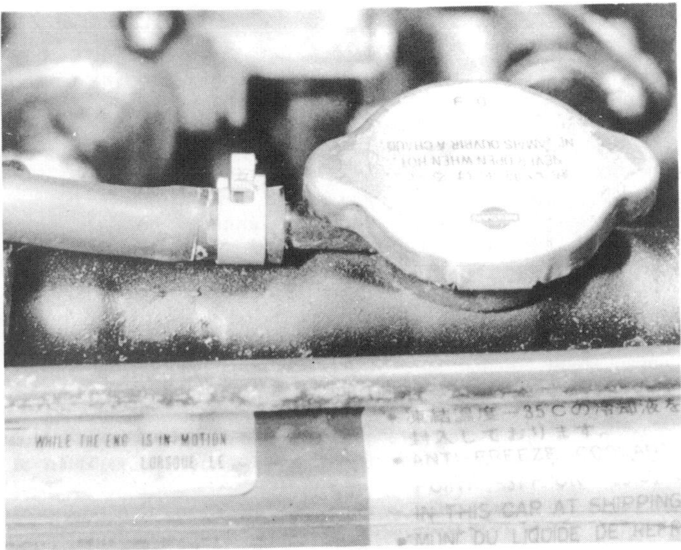

6.2B Expansion hose connection to radiator

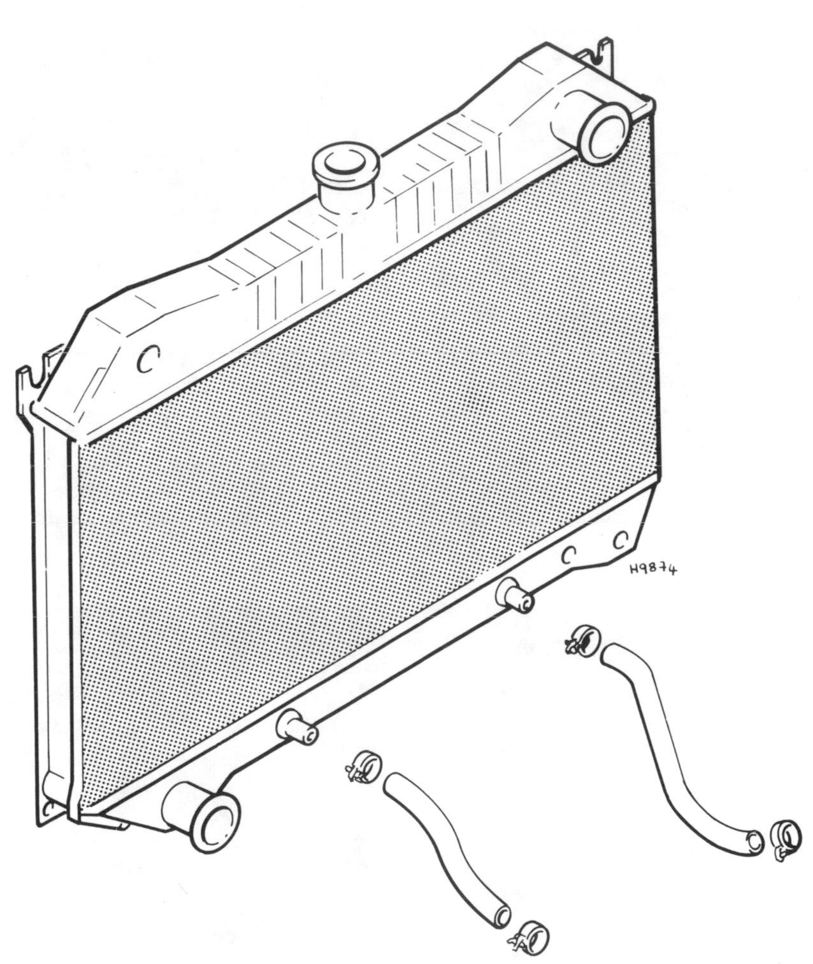

Fig. 2.7 Hoses for the automatic transmission fluid cooler located in the bottom of the radiator (Sec 6)

4 Disconnect the wiring from the radiator thermostatic switches and the cooling fan motor(s).

5 Unbolt and remove the electric cooling fan frame together with the motor(s). There are three upper and two lower mounting bolts on non-Turbo models (photos).

6 Unscrew the two radiator upper mounting bolts (photo).

7 For access to the radiator bottom mountings remove the lower shield from under the car. Unscrew the lower mounting nuts.

8 Lift the radiator from the lower mounting holes and withdraw it from the engine compartment.

9 If the radiator was removed because of clogging causing overheating then try reverse flushing or, in severe cases, use a radiator cleanser strictly in accordance with the manufacturer's instructions.

10 A leaking radiator may be sealed using one of the many products available from motor accessory stores. To make a permanent repair by soldering is a job best left to a specialist radiator repairer.

11 Check the bottom mountings (photo) and the top insulators for condition and renew them if necessary.

12 Refitting is a reversal of removal, but make sure that the upper mounting insulators are correctly located on the radiator. Refill the cooling system with reference to Section 3. On automatic transmission models, check and if necessary top up the fluid level.

6.5A Electric cooling fan frame upper mounting

6.5B Electric cooling fan frame left-hand lower mounting (arrowed), also showing radiator left-hand lower mounting

6.5C Electric cooling fan frame right-hand lower mounting and bracket

6.6 Radiator upper mounting bolt

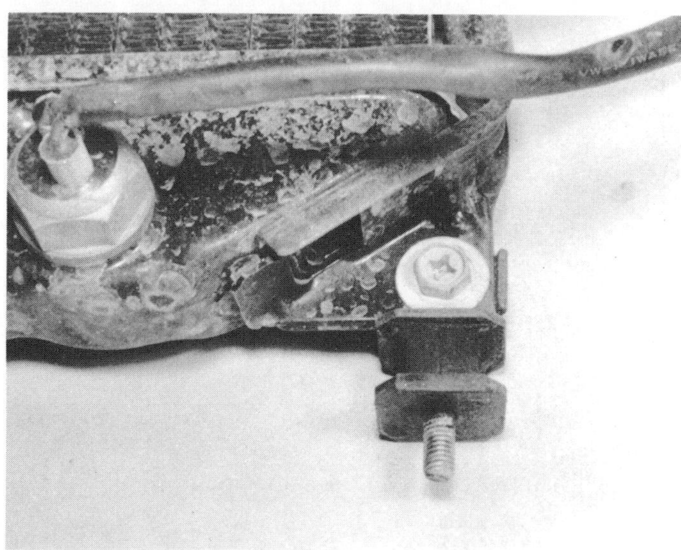

6.11 Radiator bottom mounting

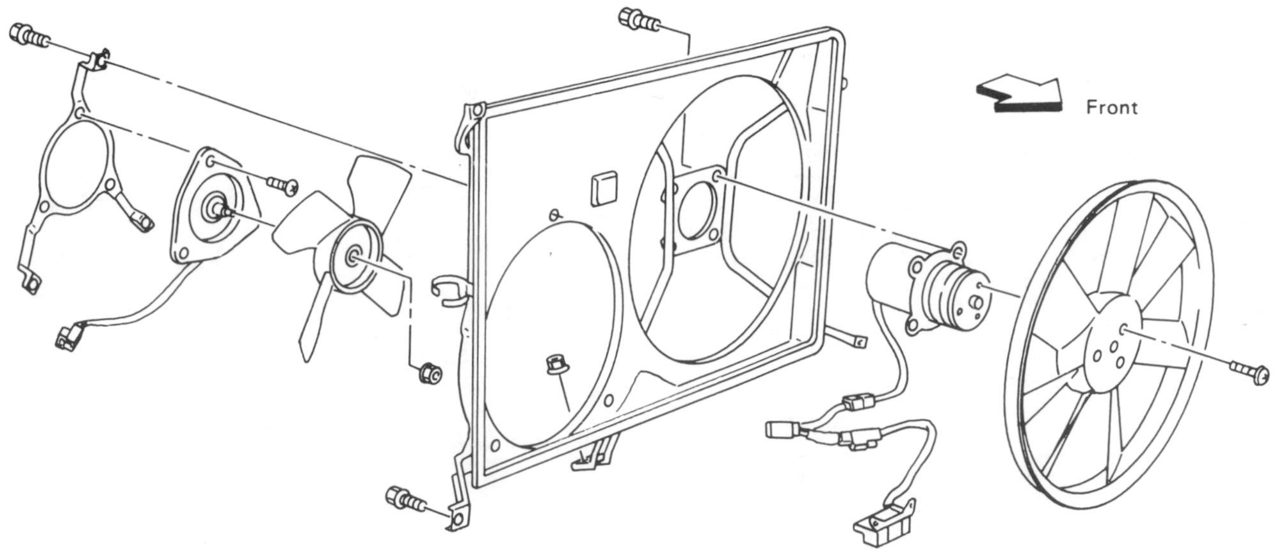

Fig. 2.8 Twin electric cooling fans and frame (Sec 7)

7 Electric cooling fan and switch – removal and refitting

1 Disconnect the battery negative lead.
2 Disconnect the wiring from the cooling fan motor(s).
3 Unbolt the cooling fan frame and withdraw it from the rear of the radiator (photo).
4 The fan can be removed from the motor shaft by unscrewing the centre bolt or nut.
5 Unbolt the motor and resistor from the frame (photos).
6 The thermostatic switch for the cooling fan is located on the top left-hand side of the radiator. Where applicable, a further switch is located on the bottom right-hand side (photos). To remove a switch, first drain the cooling system, then disconnect the wiring and unscrew the switch.
7 To test the switch, connect an ohmmeter or test lamp to it, then suspend it in water which is being heated. Check the temperature at

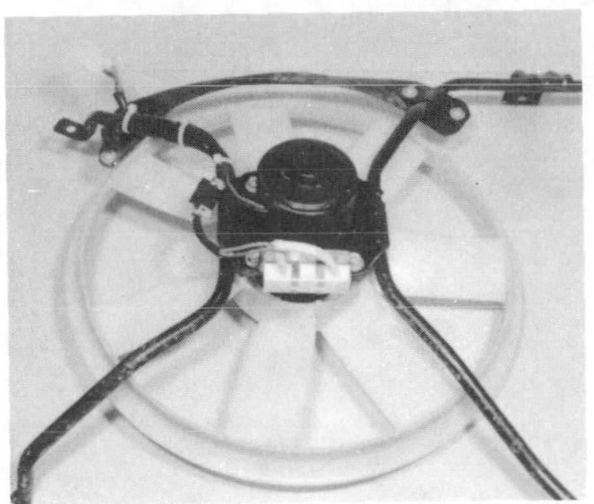

7.3 Electric cooling fan and frame

7.5A Showing electric cooling fan mounting bolts

7.5B Resistor location on the electric cooling fan motor

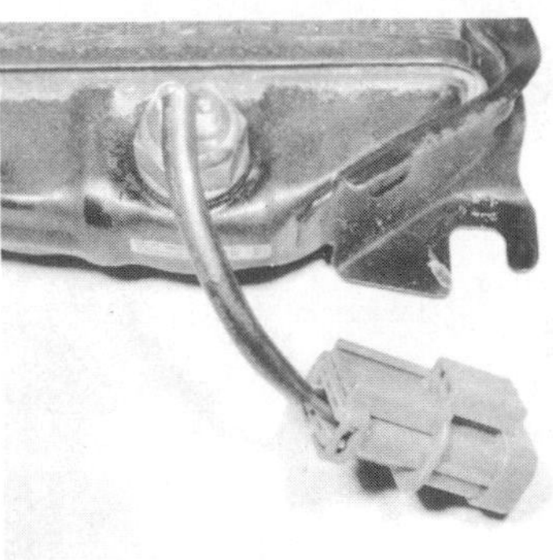

7.6A Radiator top thermostatic switch and wiring

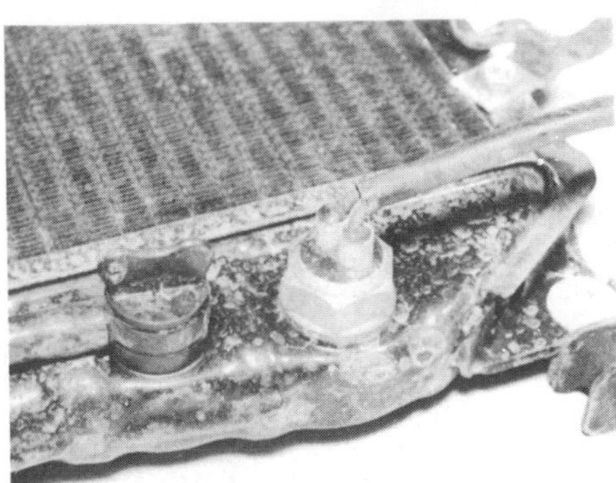

7.6B Radiator bottom thermostatic switch and wiring

which the internal contacts close, and renew the unit if this is not as given in the Specifications.
8 Refitting is a reversal of removal. Fit a new washer to the thermostatic switch and refill the cooling system with reference to Section 3.

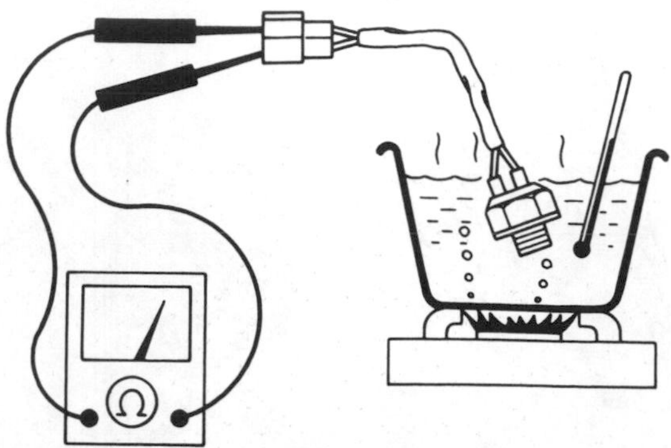

Fig. 2.9 Testing the electric cooling fan switch (Sec 7)

8 Water pump drivebelt – removal and refitting

1 On models equipped with power steering, first remove the alternator drivebelt with reference to Chapter 12, then swivel the power steering pump into the engine with reference to Chapter 10.
2 On non-power steering models, loosen the alternator pivot and adjustment bolts and swivel the alternator into the engine. Where applicable, loosen the adjustment nut on the bottom of the alternator.
3 Slip the drivebelt off of the pulleys.
4 Refitting is a reversal of removal, but adjust the drivebelt tension as described in Section 2.

9 Coolant temperature switch – removal and refitting

1 The coolant temperature switch is located on the thermostat housing on the inlet manifold.
2 If a fault develops, first check the wiring to the switch and gauge. The quickest way to check the switch is by substitution of a new unit.
3 Apply sealing compound to the threads of the new unit.
4 Disconnect the wiring, then unscrew the switch and immediately fit the new unit and tighten it into the housing. The coolant loss should be minimal. Reconnect the wiring.
5 Check the coolant level with reference to Section 2.

10 Water pump – removal and refitting

1 Remove the drivebelt as described in Section 8.
2 Drain the cooling system as described in Section 3.
3 Unbolt the pulley from the water pump flange (photo).
4 Unbolt the water pump from the cylinder block, noting the position of the power steering pump adjustment plate. Remove the gasket.
5 The pump cannot be repaired as it is a sealed unit. Renew it complete if it is leaking or the bearing is rough or noisy.
6 Refitting is a reversal of removal, but clean the mating surfaces of the pump and cylinder block and fit a new gasket. Refill the cooling system and refit the drivebelt with reference to Sections 3 and 8 respectively.

10.3 Water pump pulley

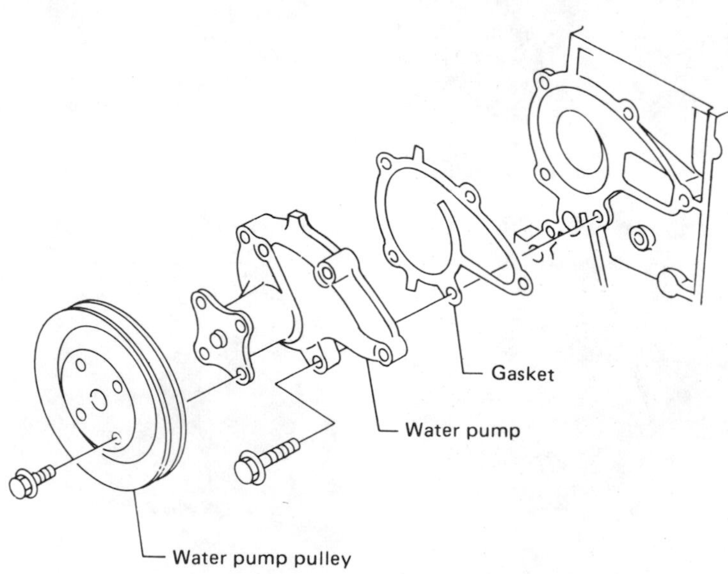

Fig. 2.10 Water pump components (Sec 10)

11 Fault diagnosis – cooling system

Symptom	Reason(s)
Overheating	Insufficient coolant in system Pump ineffective due to slack drivebelt Radiator blocked either internally or externally Kinked or collapsed hose causing coolant flow restriction Thermostat not working properly Engine out of tune Ignition timing retarded or auto advance malfunction Cylinder head gasket blown Engine not yet run-in Exhaust system partially blocked Engine oil level too low Brakes binding
Engine running too cool	Faulty, incorrect or missing thermostat
Loss of coolant	Loose hose clips Hoses perished or leaking Radiator leaking Radiator pressure cap defective Blown cylinder head gasket Cracked cylinder block or head Leak into transmission fluid (automatic transmission)

Chapter 3
Fuel, emission control and exhaust systems

Contents

Specifications

Part A: Carburettor engines

General

System type	Rear-mounted fuel tank, mechanical fuel pump, dual barrel carburettor
Fuel tank capacity	60.0 litre (13.2 Imp. gals.)
Fuel octane rating	97 (4-star)
Carburettor application:	
CA18 engine	21E series
CA20 engine	DCR series

Carburettor calibration and adjustments:

	21E series	DCR series
Primary bore	30.0 mm (1.181 in)	32.0 mm (1.260 in)
Secondary bore	34.0 mm (1.339 in)	34.0 mm (1.339 in)
Primary venturi	23.7 mm (0.933 in)	24.1 mm (0.949 in)
Secondary venturi	30.0 mm (1.181 in)	32.0 mm (1.260 in)
Primary main jet	103	111
Secondary main jet	170	155
Primary air bleed (main)	55	95
Secondary air bleed (main)	60	60
Primary slow jet	44	47
Secondary slow jet	90	115
Primary air bleed (slow)	190	170
Secondary air bleed (slow)	60	60
Power jet	50	50
Automatic choke heater resistance:		
CA18 engine with manual transmission	3.7 to 8.9 ohms	
All except CA18 engine with manual transmission	8.6 ohms	
Fast idle speed:		
CA18 engine with manual transmission	2000 to 2300 rpm	
CA18 engine with automatic transmission	2600 to 2900 rpm	
CA20 engine with manual transmission	2400 to 2700 rpm	
CA20 engine with automatic transmission	2800 to 3100 rpm	
Primary throttle valve clearance ('A'):		
CA18 engine with manual transmission	0.57 to 0.71 mm (0.0224 to 0.0280 in)	
CA18 engine with automatic transmission	0.76 to 0.90 mm (0.0299 to 0.0354 in)	
CA20 engine with manual transmission	0.66 to 0.80 mm (0.0260 to 0.0315 in)	
CA20 engine with automatic transmission	0.81 to 0.95 mm (0.0319 to 0.0374 in)	

Vacuum break choke valve clearance ('R'):	
CA18 engine	2.18 to 2.78 mm (0.0858 to 0.1094 in)
CA20 engine	3.32 to 3.92 mm (0.1307 to 0.1543 in)
Vacuum break choke valve clearance ('RA'):	
CA18 engine	1.25 to 1.55 mm (0.0492 to 0.0610 in)
CA20 engine	1.8 to 2.1 mm (0.0710 to 0.0830 in)
Choke unloader clearance ('C'):	
CA18 engine	3.16 mm (0.1244 in)
CA20 engine	2.05 to 2.85 mm (0.0807 to 0.1122 in)
Throttle interlock clearance ('G'):	
CA18 engine	6.88 to 7.88 mm (0.2709 to 0.3102 in)
CA20 engine	7.38 to 8.38 mm (0.2906 to 0.3299 in)
Dash pot touch speed	2200 rpm
Idling speed:	
Manual transmission models	750 ± 100 rpm
Automatic transmission models (in 'N' position)	850 ± 100 rpm
Idling CO%	1.0 ± 0.5

Fuel pump

Discharge pressure	0.196 to 0.265 bar (2.8 to 3.8 lbf/in²)

Accelerator pedal

Stopper bolt adjustment ('L'):	
CA18 and CA20 engines:	
Right-hand drive models	6.5 to 7.5 mm (0.256 to 0.295 in)
Left-hand drive models	10 to 11 mm (0.39 to 0.43 in)
CA18ET engine:	
Right-hand drive models	5 to 6 mm (0.20 to 0.24 in)
Left-hand drive models	8 to 9 mm (0.31 to 0.35 in)
Free play at pedal pad centre	1 to 3 mm (0.04 to 0.12 in)

Torque wrench settings

	Nm	lbf ft
Accelerator cable locknuts	7	5
Fuel tank mounting bolt	37	27
Exhaust downpipe flange	31	23
Exhaust system flange bolts	37	27
Exhaust rubber mounting bolts	10	7
Anti-dieseling solenoid	26	19
Fuel pump	12	9
Inlet manifold	20	15
Exhaust manifold	25	19

Part B: Fuel-injected turbo engine

General

System type	Rear-mounted fuel tank, electric fuel pump, computer controlled fuel-injection system
Fuel tank capacity	60.0 litre (13.2 Imp. gals.)
Fuel octane rating	97 (4-star)

Idle data

Idling speed:	
Manual transmission models	750 ± 100 rpm
Automatic transmission models (in 'N' position)	850 ± 100 rpm
Idling CO%	2.0 maximum

Fuel pressure

Regulator setting	2.50 bar (36.2 lbf/in²)
Idling pressure	2.06 bar (30.0 lbf/in²)
Accelerator pedal fully depressed	2.55 bar (37.0 lbf/in²)

Turbocharger

Turbine shaft endplay	0.013 to 0.091 mm (0.0005 to 0.0036 in)

Torque wrench settings

	Nm	lbf ft
Turbocharger	26	19
Injector	3	2
Water temperature sensor	18	13
Throttle valve switch	2	1.5
Air regulator	5	4

For items common to fuel-injected turbo and carburettor engines, see Specifications, Part A

PART A: CARBURETTOR ENGINES

1 General description

The fuel system consists of a rear-mounted fuel tank, fuel pump, mechanically operated from the camshaft, and a dual barrel carburettor incorporating an automatic choke. The inlet and exhaust manifolds are located on opposite sides of the cylinder head, and the inlet manifold is coolant heated.

The carburettor incorporates an anti-locking solenoid which shuts off the idling circuit when the ignition is switched off. A bi-metallic idle compensator is also incorporated to provide additional air during high temperature idle conditions.

The air cleaner incorporates an automatically controlled air temperature flap.

2 Routine maintenance

Carry out the following procedures at the intervals given in *'Routine Maintenance'* at the beginning of the Manual.

Check fuel system

1 Check all the fuel lines for security and damage with the car over an inspection pit or supported on axle stands.

2 Inspect the fuel tank for damage and for secure mountings.

Renew the air cleaner element

3 Refer to Section 3.

Adjust idling speed and mixture

4 Refer to Section 9.

2.5 Fuel filter clipped to the bulkhead

Fig. 3.1 Cleaning the air cleaner element (Sec 2)

Renew the fuel filter

5 The fuel filter is clipped to the left-hand side of the bulkhead. Note which way round it is fitted (photo).

6 Release the filter from the clip, then loosen the two hose clips, release the hoses and withdraw the filter.

7 Fit the new filter using a reversal of the removal procedure.

Clean air cleaner element

8 Remove the air cleaner element with reference to Section 3.

9 Tap the element to remove the loose dust, then use an air line from inside the element to remove the remaining dust.

10 Refit the element with reference to Section 3.

Check air cleaner automatic temperature control

11 Check the vacuum hoses to the sensor and motor for condition and security.

12 With the engine cold and stopped, disconnect the inlet duct and check that the internal flap is fully down and closing the warm air inlet.

13 Start the engine and check that the flap rises to open the warm air inlet.

14 Increase the engine speed momentarily and check that the flap rises slightly as the vacuum is increased.

15 As the engine warms up, check that the flap gradually lowers to close the warm air inlet.

Check fuel and exhaust system components

16 Check the fuel pump for security, condition and leaks.

17 With the car over an inspection pit or supported on axle stands, check the exhaust system and mountings for security and condition. Any signs of a leak can be confirmed by running the engine at idling speed and temporarily placing a wad of rag over the end of the exhaust tailpipe. Any leak will then be shown up by exhaust gases blowing through the hole.

3 Air cleaner element and body – removal and refitting

1 Release the spring clips, unscrew the central wing nut and lift the cover from the air cleaner (photos).

2 Lift out the element (photo).

3 Wipe clean the inside of the air cleaner body and cover.

4 To remove the body, loosen the clips and remove the flexible duct (photo).

5 Disconnect the crankcase ventilation hose and warm air hose (photo).

6 Unbolt the mounting bracket from the rocker cover (photo).

7 Withdraw the air cleaner body and disconnect the vacuum hose.

8 If required, the inlet duct can be unbolted from the left-hand side of the engine compartment (photo).

9 Refitting is a reversal of removal.

3.1A Spring clip on air cleaner cover

3.1B Central wing nut on air cleaner cover

3.2 Removing air cleaner element

3.4 Flexible duct and clip

3.5 Air cleaner warm air hose (arrowed)

3.6 Air cleaner mounting bracket

3.8 Inlet duct on left-hand side of the engine compartment

4 Air temperature vacuum motor – testing

1 With the engine cold and idling, disconnect the vacuum hose from the vacuum motor (photo) and check that there is vacuum at the end of the hose. If not, the sensor or hoses are faulty. Stop the engine.
2 Connect a tube to the motor and apply vacuum. The internal flap should rise from the hot air inlet. If not, the motor or flap is faulty.
3 Reconnect the vacuum hose.

4.1 Air temperature vacuum motor (arrowed)

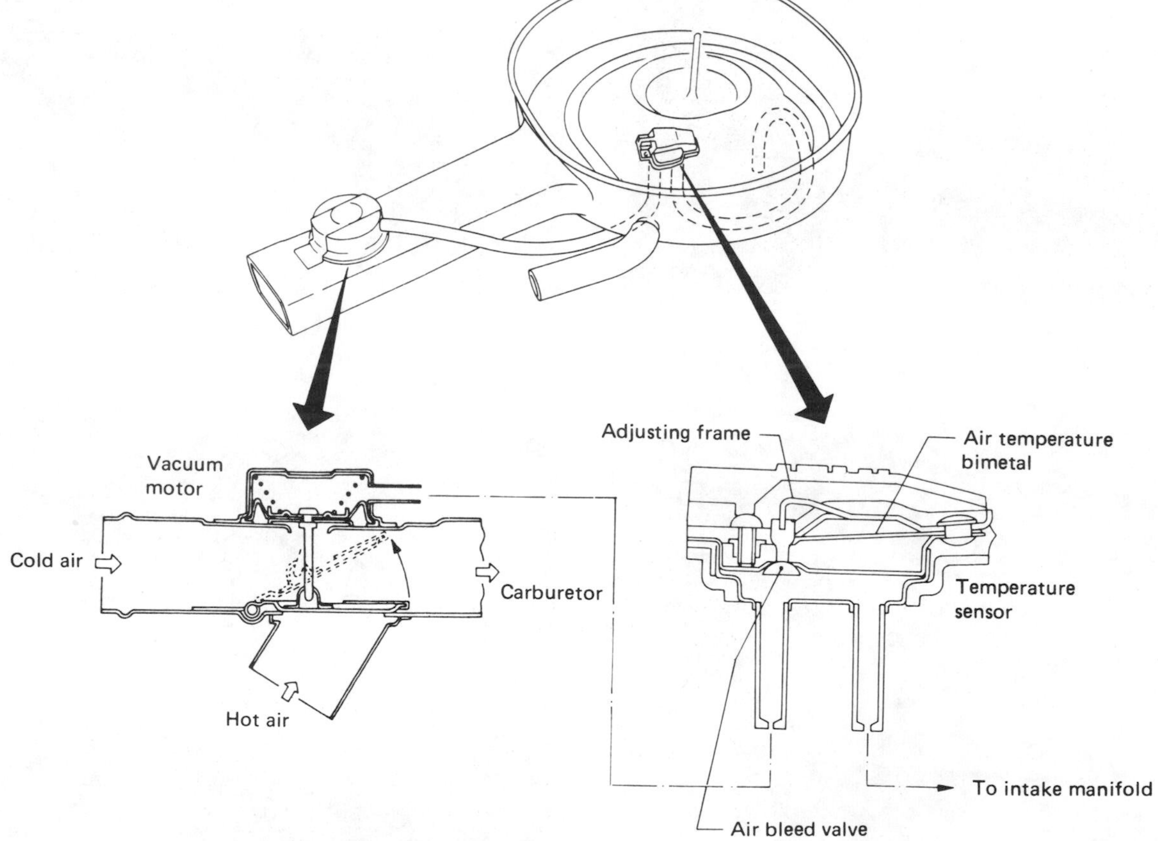

5 Fuel pump – removal and refitting

1 The fuel pump is of sealed type, no provision being made for cleaning.
2 To remove the pump, first remove the air cleaner complete (Section 3).
3 Note the location of the inlet, outlet and return hoses, then disconnect and plug them (photo).
4 Unbolt the pump from the cylinder head and remove the gasket (photo).
5 The pump can be checked for operation by blocking the outlet and return ports with a finger and thumb, then operating the rocker arm.

Vacuum motor
Cold air
Carburetor
Hot air
Adjusting frame
Air temperature bimetal
Temperature sensor
To intake manifold
Air bleed valve

Fig. 3.2 Air cleaner air temperature control components (Sec 4)

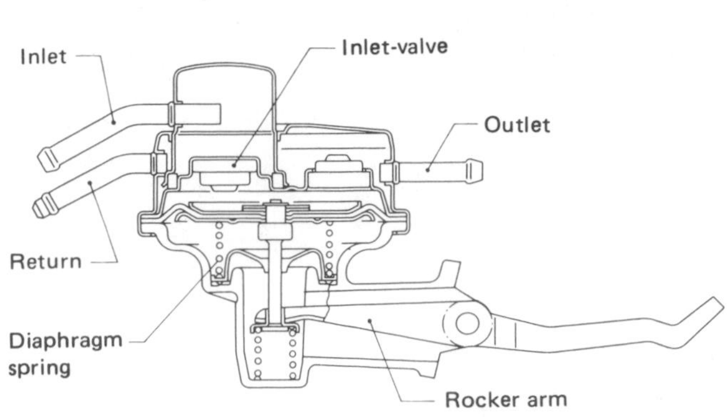

Fig. 3.3 Cross section of the fuel pump (Sec 5)

5.3 Fuel pump and hoses

1 Return *2 Inlet* *3 Outlet*

5.4 Fuel pump showing mounting nut

The air pressure built up should remain for two or three seconds.

6 Refitting is a reversal of removal, but clean the mating faces and fit a new gasket.

6 Fuel level sender – removal and refitting

1 Disconnect the battery negative lead.

2 Remove the rear seat cushion and backrest (Chapter 11).

3 Extract the four screws and remove the cover plate, taking care not to damage the wiring (photos).

4 Disconnect the wiring harness.

5 Using two screwdrivers or a piece of flat metal as a lever, rotate the transmitter cover plate until it releases.

6 Carefully withdraw the sender unit; taking care not to bend the float or float arm.

7 Refitting is a reversal of removal, but use a new O-ring.

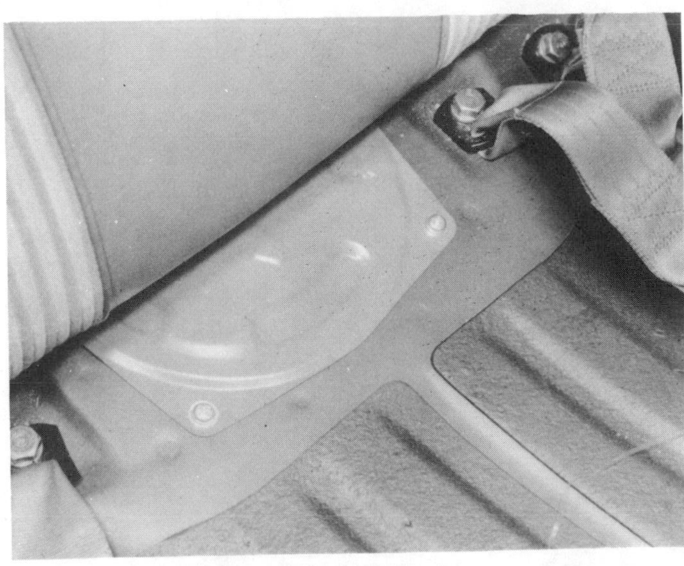

6.3A Front view of fuel level sender cover plate

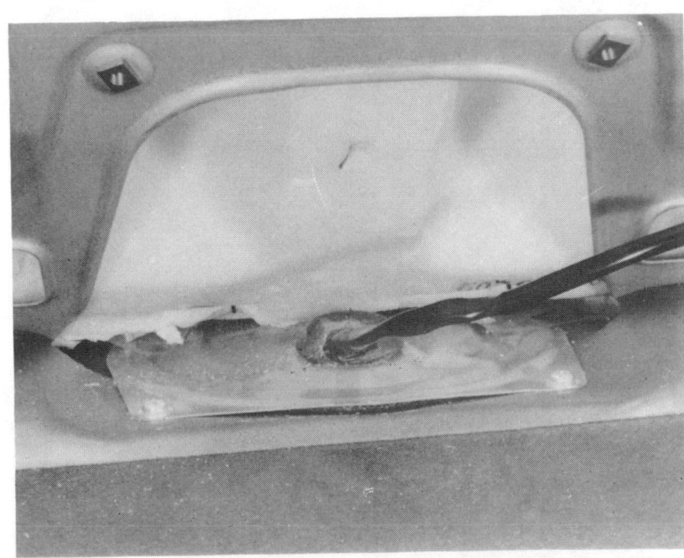

6.3B Rear view of fuel level sender cover plate

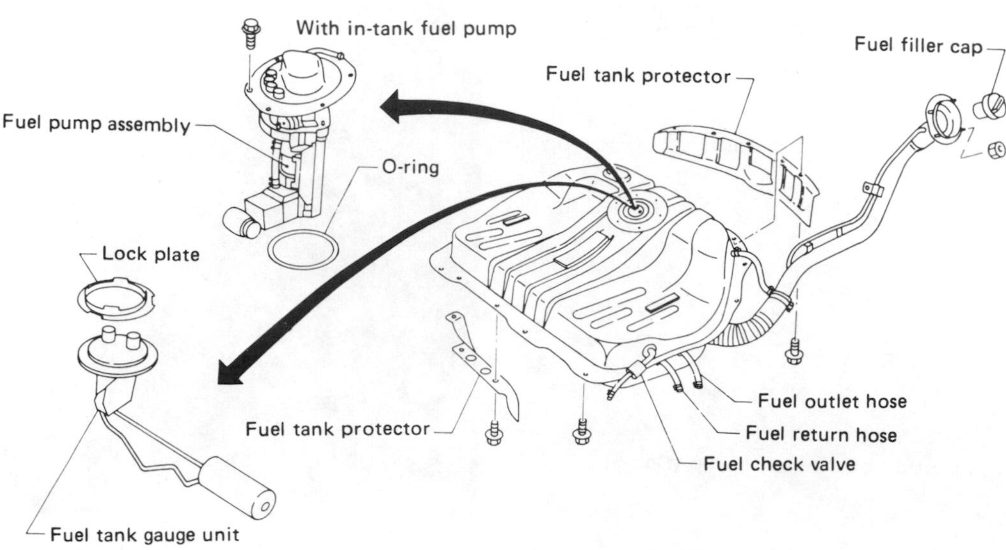

Fig. 3.4 Fuel tank components (Sec 5)

7 Fuel tank – removal, repair and refitting

1 Disconnect the battery negative lead.
2 Chock the front wheels, then jack up the rear of the car and support on axle stands.
3 Remove the fuel tank filler cap, then unscrew the drain plug and drain the fuel into a sealed container (photo). Refit the drain plug.
4 Loosen the clips, then disconnect and plug the supply and return hoses (photo).
5 Loosen the clip and disconnect the convoluted filler tube.
6 Remove the fuel level sender as described in Section 6.
7 Support the weight of the fuel tank with a jack and interposed block of wood.
8 Unscrew the mounting bolts (photo) and lower the fuel tank until the breather tubes can be disconnected. Lower the tank to the floor.
9 Note the location of the protector plates, then extract the screws and remove them from the tank.
10 If necessary, the filler neck and tubes can be removed from the body (photos).
11 If the tank contains sediment, swill it out with fuel or have it steam cleaned. Any repairs should be left to a specialist. Do not under any circumstances attempt to solder or weld a fuel tank.
12 Refitting is a reversal of removal, but make sure that the hoses are connected correctly.

8 Carburettor – description

The carburettor is of dual barrel, downdraught, progressive type. Initial throttle opening is made by the primary throttle valve, but after this is approximately two thirds open, further movement opens the secondary throttle valve as well.

The carburettor incorporates the following devices:

Anti-dieseling solenoid
Bi-metallic idle compensator
Electrically heated automatic choke
Accelerator pump
Choke valve break diaphragm
Boost controlled deceleration device (not all models)

7.3 Fuel tank drain plug

7.4 Fuel tank supply and return hoses

7.8 A fuel tank mounting bolt

7.10A Flexible tube connecting bottom of filler neck tube to fuel tank

7.10B Filler neck tube mounting

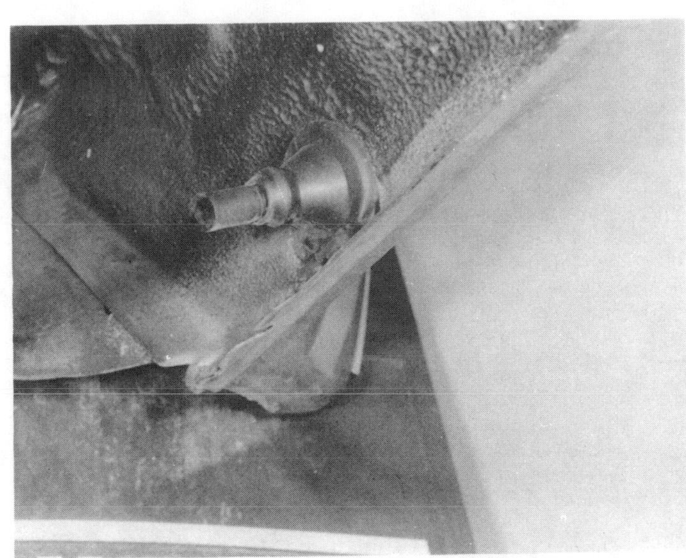

7.10C Breather tube outlet

9 Carburettor – idle speed and mixture adjustment

1 The idle mixture is set during production and therefore it is normally only the idle speed which requires adjustment.
2 Have the engine at normal operating temperature with the valve clearances and ignition timing correctly set. On models without a tachometer, connect one to the engine in accordance with the maker's instructions.
3 Allow the engine to idle for two minutes.
4 Race the engine at between 2000 and 3000 rpm two or three times, then allow it to idle.
5 Check that all electrical components are switched off, including the electric cooling fan.
6 Check that the idling speed is as given in the Specifications. If not, adjust the throttle adjusting screw to correct (photo).
7 If the mixture must be adjusted due to a change in engine characteristics (carbon build up, bore wear etc), or after major overhaul of the carburettor, the engine must be at normal operating temperature and idling at specified speed with an exhaust gas analyser (if available) connected in accordance with the maker's instructions. After a carburettor overhaul, set the mixture adjusting screw two turns out from the fully closed position. Note that the screw is of tamperproof type and a special screwdriver is required to turn it (Fig. 3.6) (photo).
8 With the engine idling, turn the mixture adjusting screw until the specified CO% is obtained (using the exhaust gas analyser), or the engine runs smoothly at the highest possible speed (without the exhaust gas analyser).
9 If the idling speed has increased, re-adjust it to the correct setting.
10 Disconnect the exhaust gas analyser and tachometer.

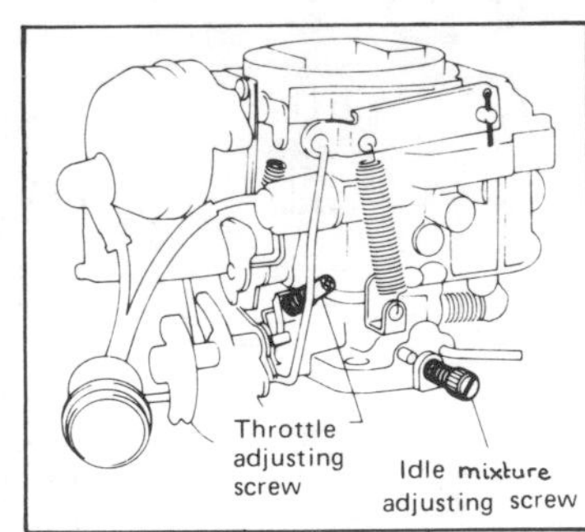

Fig. 3.5 Carburettor adjusting screws (Sec 9)

9.6 Throttle adjusting screw (arrowed)

9.7 Mixture adjusting screw (arrowed)

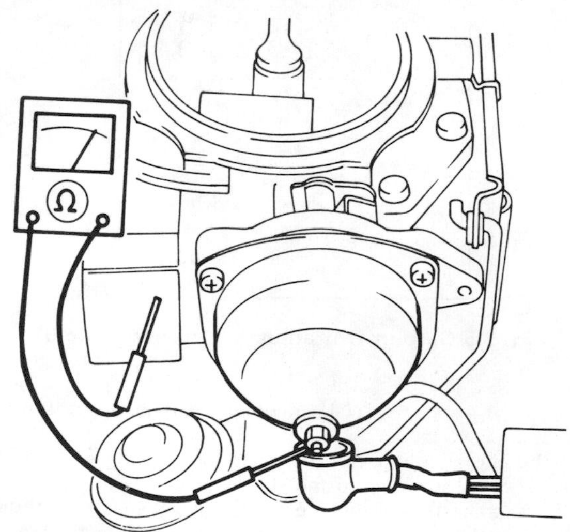

Fig. 3.7 Checking the automatic choke heater resistance (Sec 10)

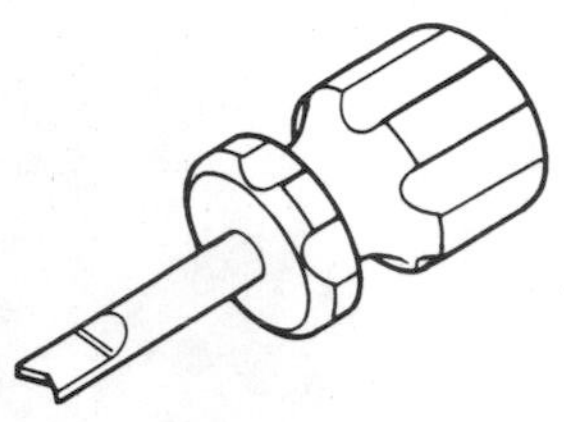

Fig. 3.6 Special screwdriver for adjusting mixture screw (Sec 9)

10 Carburettor – in-car adjustments and checks

1 The following procedures can be carried out without having to remove the carburettor from the engine.

Automatic choke

2 Remove the air cleaner, then connect an ohmmeter between the terminal on the automatic choke and the carburettor body.

3 Renew the bi-metal cover if the heater resistance is not as given in the Specifications. If the reading is correct, but the automatic choke is inoperative, check the relay in the relay box (Fig. 3.8).

Fast idle

4 With the engine warm, remove the air cleaner.

5 Mark the position of the automatic choke bi-metal cover in relation to the carburettor body, then extract the screws and remove the clamp and cover.

6 Set the fast idle screw on the second step of the fast idle cam.

7 Connect a tachometer, then run the engine and check that the fast idle speed is as given in the Specifications. If not, turn the fast idle screw as necessary and tighten the locknut.

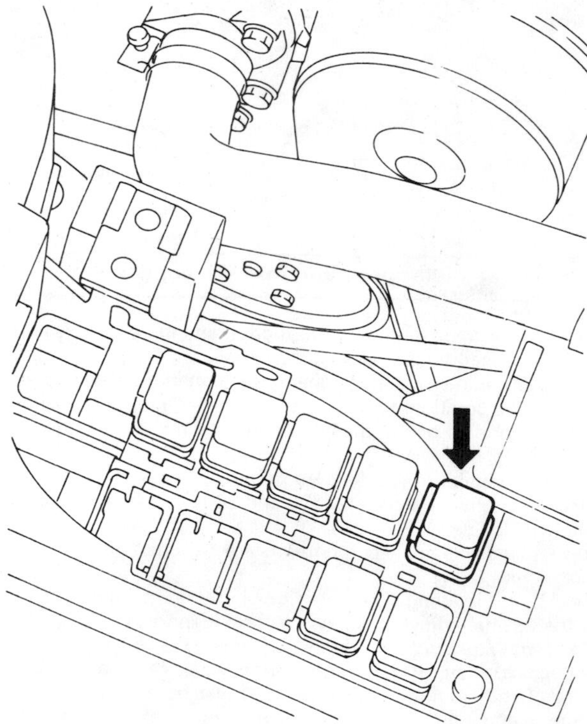

Fig. 3.8 Automatic choke relay location (Sec 10)

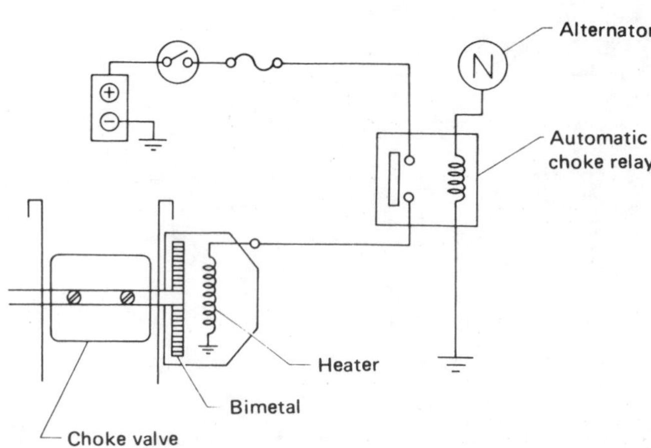

Fig. 3.9 Automatic choke wiring diagram (Sec 10)

Vacuum break

8 With the engine cold, remove the air cleaner.

9 Mark the position of the automatic choke bi-metal cover in relation to the carburettor body, then extract the screws and remove the clamp and cover.

10 Hold the choke valve fully shut using a rubber band as shown in Fig. 3.10.

11 Refer to Fig. 3.10A, and push the connecting rod until contact is made with the vacuum break diaphragm. Using feeler blades, check that the clearance between the choke valve and carburettor body ('R') is as given in the Specifications.

12 Refer to Fig. 3.10B, and with the connecting rod positioned as shown, check that the clearance between the choke valve and carburettor body ('RA') is as given in the Specifications.

Choke unloader

13 Set the choke valve as described previously for the vacuum break.

14 Turn the throttle lever until the primary throttle valve is fully open, then using a twist drill check that the clearance 'C' (Fig. 3.11) between the choke valve and carburettor body is as given in the Specifications. If not, bend the tongue at the throttle end of the linkage until the correct clearance is obtained.

Accelerator pump

15 With the engine stopped, remove the air cleaner.

16 Fully open the throttle lever and check that the pump injector injects fuel into the primary bore smoothly.

Dashpot

17 Connect a tachometer to the engine.

18 With the engine at normal operating temperature and idling,

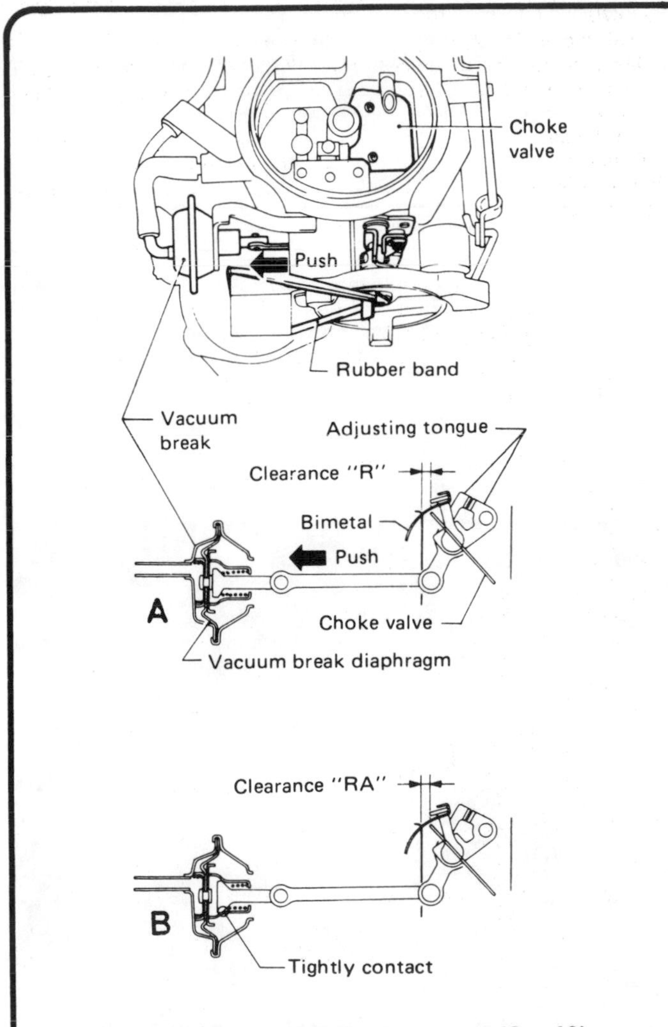

Fig. 3.10 Vacuum break adjustment (Sec 10)

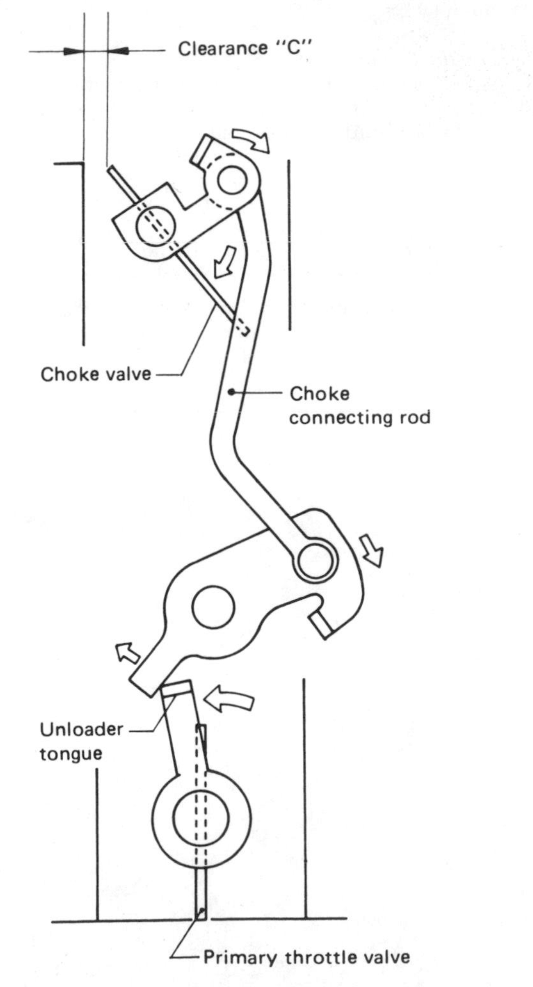

Fig. 3.11 Choke unloader adjustment (Sec 10)

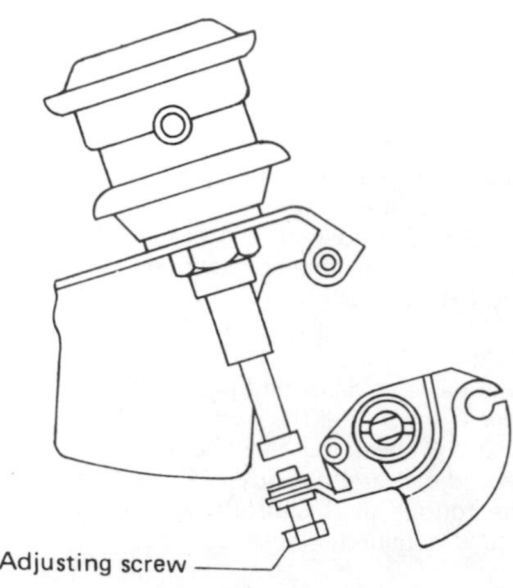

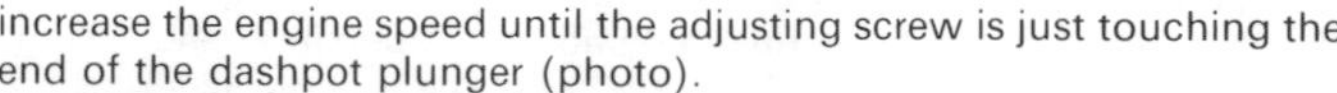
Fig. 3.12 Dashpot and adjusting screw (Sec 10)

10.18 Dashpot location (arrowed)

increase the engine speed until the adjusting screw is just touching the end of the dashpot plunger (photo).

19 Check that the engine speed is as given in the Specifications. If not, turn the adjusting screw as necessary.

20 On completion release the throttle and check that the engine speed drops smoothly.

Anti-dieseling solenoid

21 With the engine idling, disconnect the anti-dieseling solenoid wiring (photo). The engine should stop immediately and the internal valve should be heard to close audibly. Renew the solenoid if it is faulty.

11 Carburettor – removal and refitting

1 Remove the air cleaner as described in Section 3 (photo).
2 Disconnect the fuel hoses and plug them.
3 Disconnect the accelerator cable.
4 Disconnect the electrical leads from the anti-dieseling solenoid and the automatic choke on the carburettor.
5 Disconnect the distributor vacuum hose.
6 Unscrew the four mounting nuts and remove the carburettor from the intake manifold.
7 Refitting is a reversal of removal, but use a new mounting flange gasket.

12 Carburettor – overhaul

1 It is rare for the carburettor to require complete dismantling; indeed, where this is required, then it would probably be more economical to renew the complete unit. Normally it will be sufficient to remove the choke chamber (carburettor cover) and clean the float chamber and jets.

10.21 Anti-dieseling solenoid (arrowed)

11.1 View of carburettor with air cleaner removed

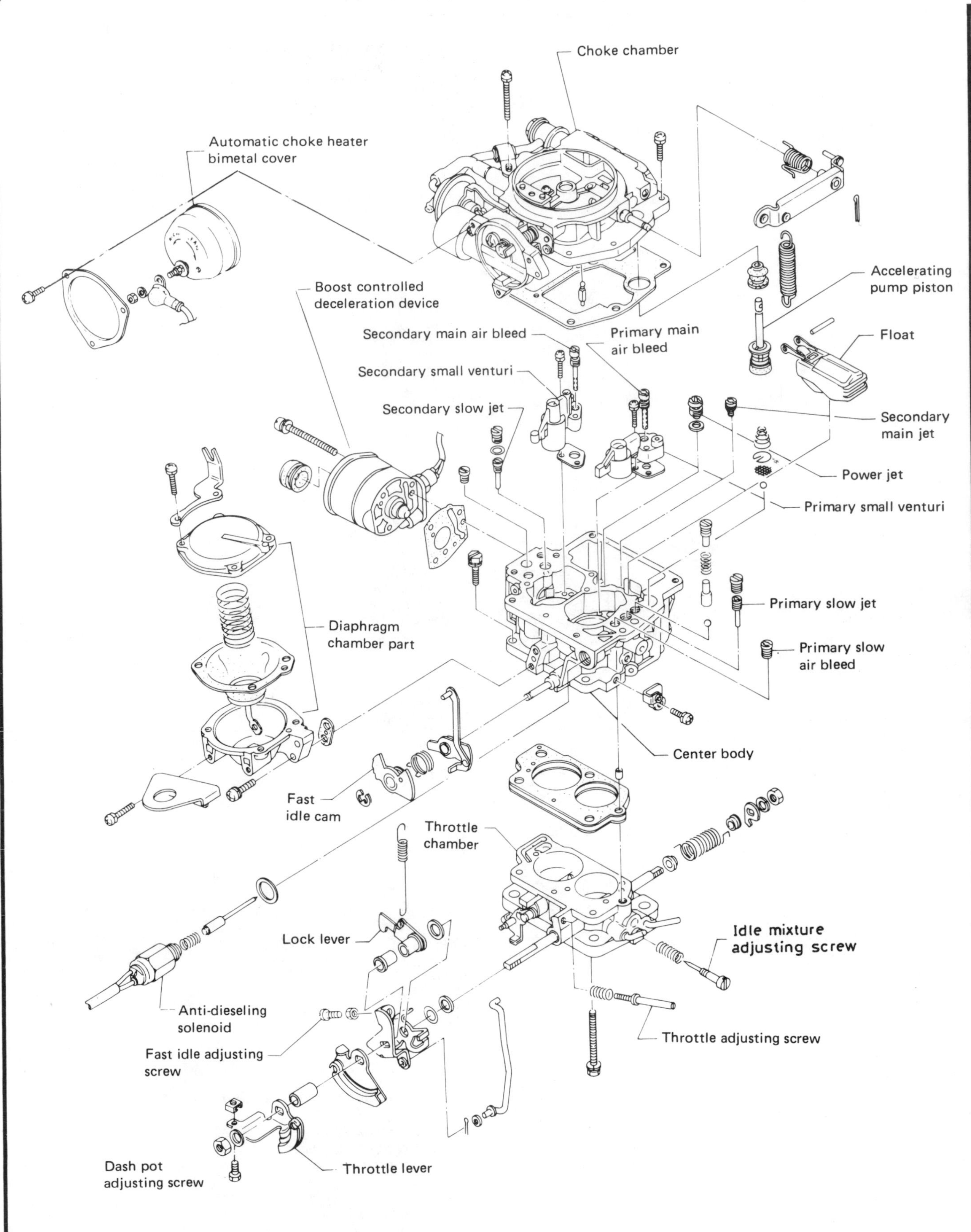

Fig. 3.13 Exploded view of the 21E type carburettor fitted to the CA18 engine (Sec 12)

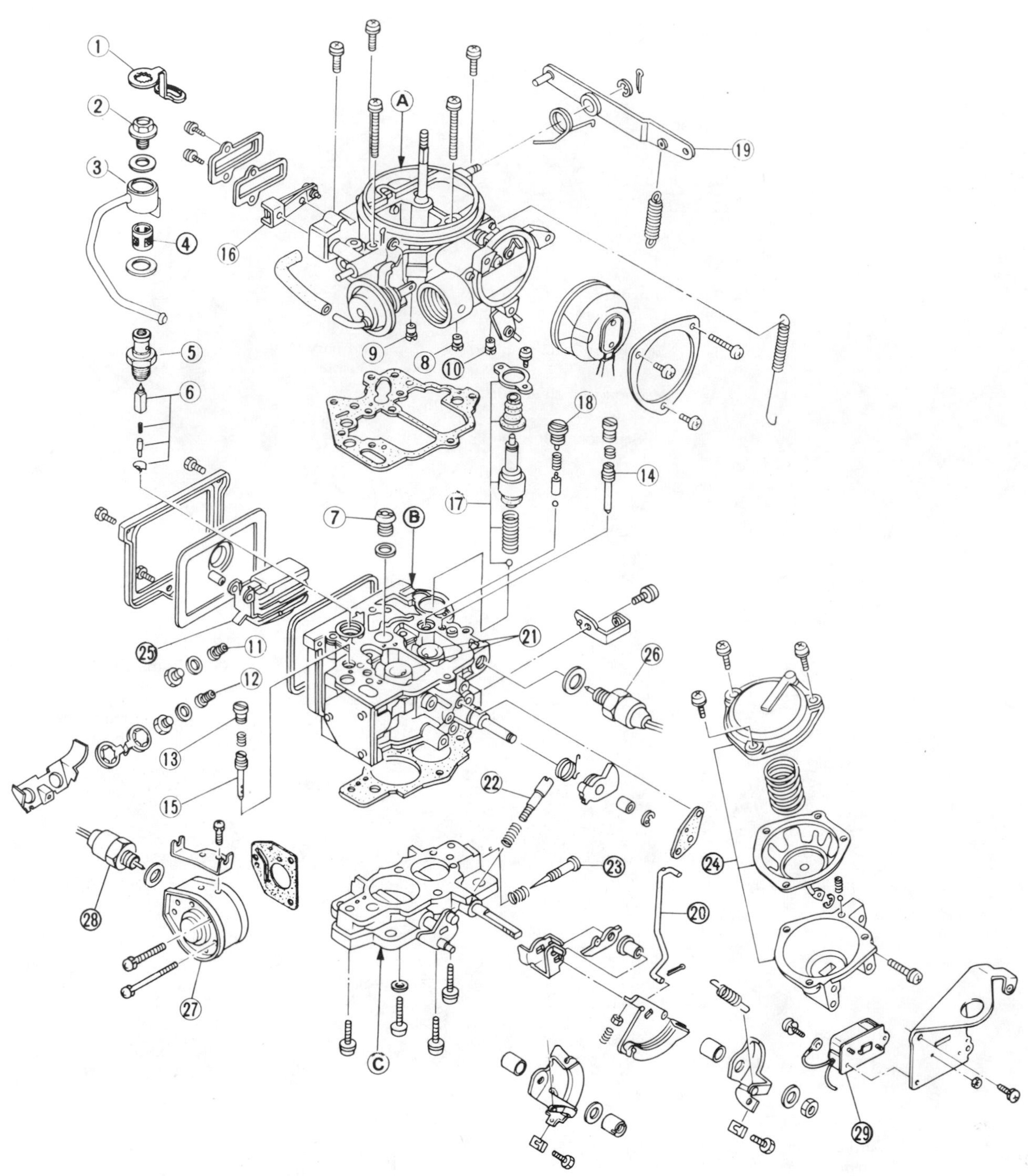

Fig. 3.14 Exploded view of the DCR type carburettor fitted to the CA20 engine (Sec 12)

A Choke chamber
B Carburettor body
C Throttle chamber
1 Lock lever
2 Filter set screw
3 Fuel nipple
4 Fuel filter
5 Needle valve body
6 Needle valve
7 Power valve
8 Primary main air bleed
9 Secondary main air bleed
10 Primary slow air bleed
11 Primary main jet
12 Secondary main jet
13 Secondary slow air bleed
14 Primary slow jet
15 Secondary slow jet
16 Idle compensator
17 Accelerating pump parts
18 Plug for accelerating mechanism
19 Accelerating pump lever
20 Accelerating pump connecting rod
21 Primary and secondary small venturi
22 Throttle adjusting screw
23 Idle adjusting screw
24 Diaphragm chamber parts
25 Float
26 Anti-dieseling solenoid valve
27 BCDD
28 BCDD control solenoid valve
29 Throttle valve switch

12.2 Fuel level sight glass (arrowed)

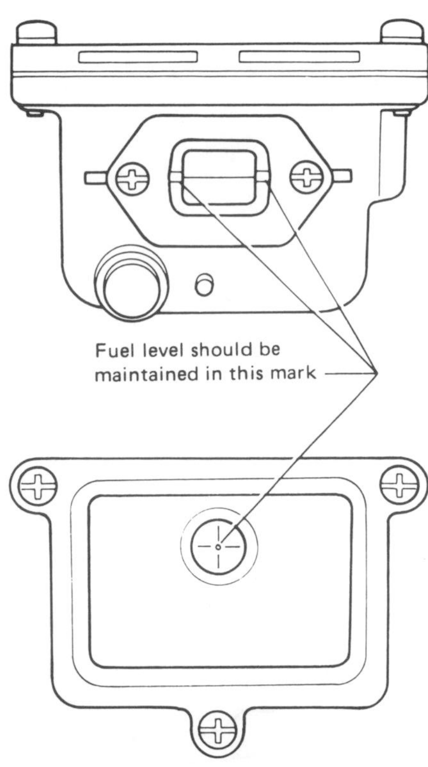

Fig. 3.15 Float level marks on the carburettor sight glass (Sec 12)

2 Before removing the carburettor, check that the fuel level, viewed through the sight glass corresponds with Fig. 3.15 (photo). If not, it will be necessary to adjust the float seat with the carburettor dismantled.
3 With the carburettor removed, clean away external dirt.
4 Disconnect the accelerator pump and choke fast idle linkages and disconnect the return springs (photo).
5 Extract the screws and lift the choke chamber from the carburettor body. Remove the gasket.
6 On the DCR carburettor, extract the screws and remove the sight glass, surround, and float.
7 Unscrew and remove the jets with reference to Figs. 3.16, 3.17 and 3.18, noting the location of each jet.
8 Clean the jets with air from a tyre pump – on no account probe them with wire, or their calibration will be ruined. Check the float and the inlet needle valve for damage and wear. If necessary, extract the screws and detach the throttle chamber from the main body.
9 With the carburettor dismantled and worn parts renewed, obtain a repair kit which will contain all the necessary new gaskets and other renewable items.

12.4 Accelerator pump linkage (A) and return spring (B)

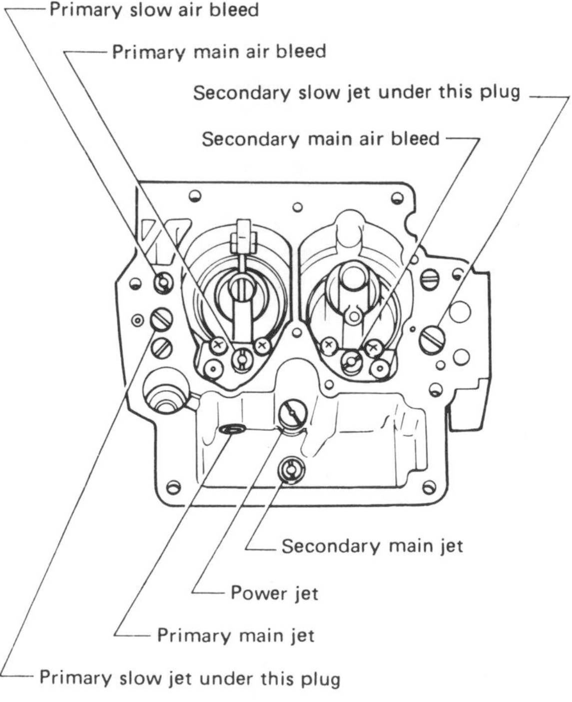

Fig. 3.16 Jet location on the 21E type carburettor (Sec 12)

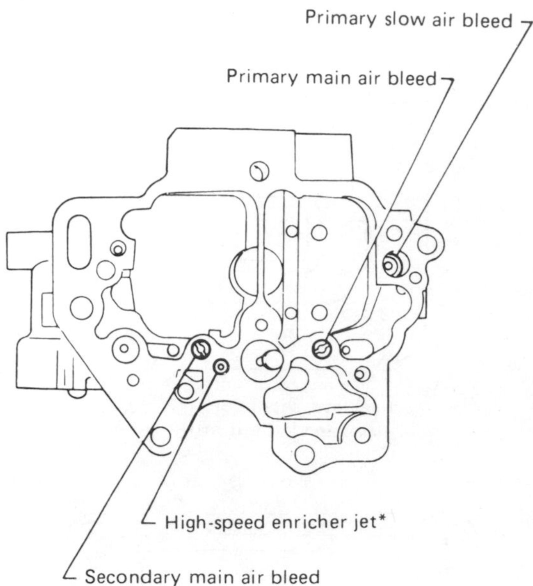

Fig. 3.17 Jet location on the DCR type carburettor choke chamber (Sec 12)

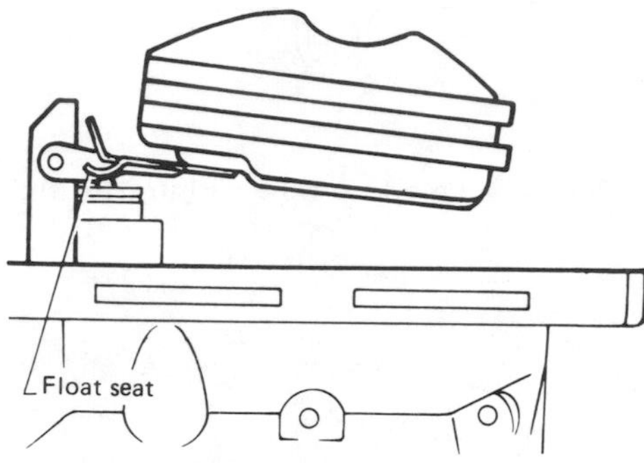

Fig. 3.19 Float seat for float level adjustment on the 21E type carburettor (Sec 12)

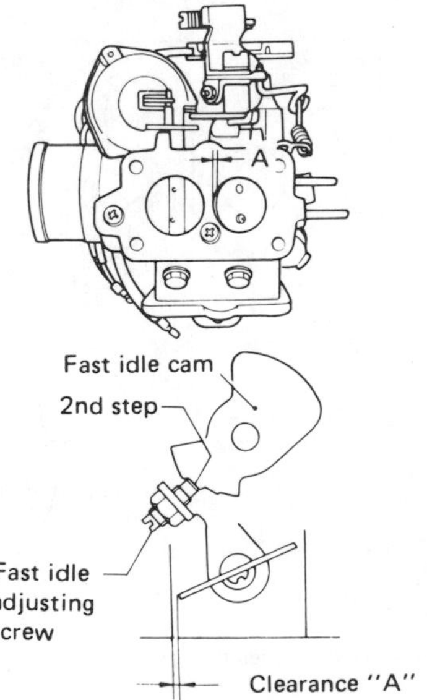

Fig. 3.21 Fast idle adjustment (Sec 12)

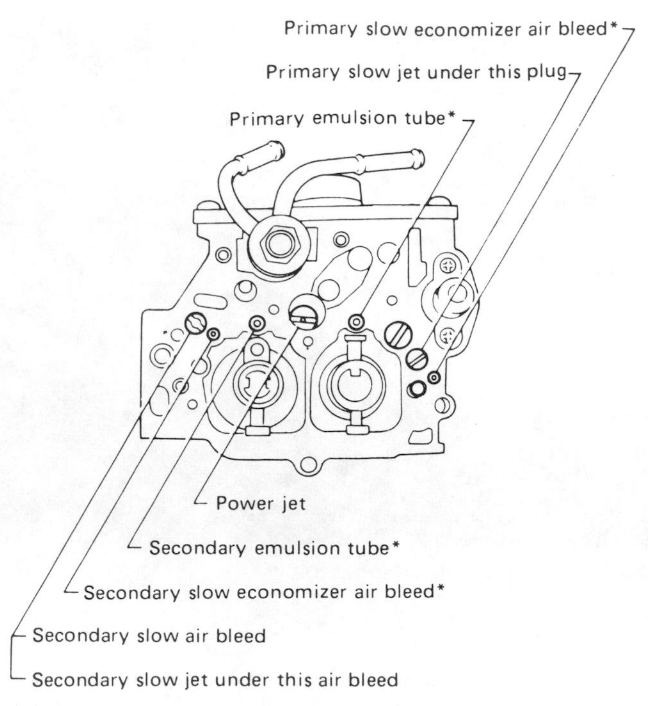

Fig. 3.18 Jet location on the DCR type carburettor main body (Sec 12)

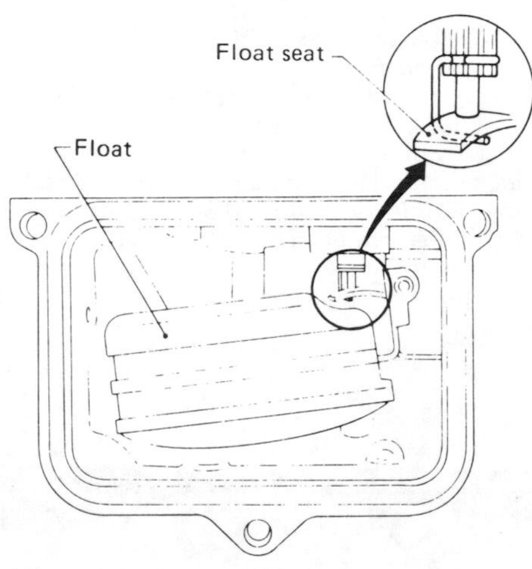

Fig. 3.20 Float seat for float level adjustment on the DCR type carburettor (Sec 12)

10 Reassembly is a reversal of dismantling, however if the float level needs adjustment, this can be checked during the course of reassembly. Refer to Figs. 3.19 or 3.20 and bend the float seat as required. On completion the following adjustments should be made.

11 Position the fast idle adjustment screw on the second step of the fast idle cam, then using feeler blades check that the clearance 'A' (Fig. 3.21) between the primary throttle valve and the carburettor body is as given in the Specifications. If not, turn the adjustment screw as necessary.

12 Open the throttle lever to the point where the secondary throttle valve lever is contacted – the primary throttle valve will then be open 50°. Refer to Fig. 3.22 and check that dimension 'G' is as given in the Specifications using a twist drill. If not, check the linkage for wear or damage.

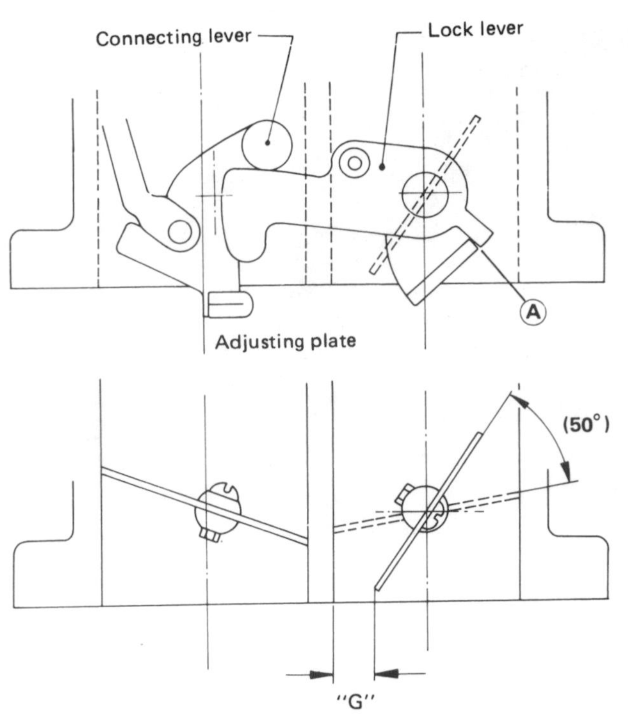

Fig. 3.22 Throttle interlock adjustment (Sec 12)

13 Accelerator cable and pedal – removal, refitting and adjustment

1 Remove the air cleaner (Section 3).
2 Release the wiring from the clip at the carburettor end of the cable.
3 Unscrew the locknuts and remove the outer cable from the bracket (photo).
4 Release the inner cable from the throttle segment.
5 Working inside the car, unhook the inner cable from the top of the pedal.
6 Remove the split plastic washer and withdraw the cable from the bulkhead into the engine compartment (photo).
7 Unbolt the pedal bracket from the bulkhead (photo).
8 If necessary, extract the 'E' ring and separate the pedal from the bracket. Recover the spring.
9 Refitting is a reversal of removal, but apply a little grease to the cable end fittings and pedal shaft. Carry out the following adjustments.
10 Position the pedal stopper bolt so that the threaded end is protruding by the amount given in the Specifications (Fig. 3.24).
11 Adjust the outer cable position on the bracket so that with the accelerator pedal fully released, the free play at the end of the pedal is between 1.0 and 3.0 mm (0.04 and 0.12 in). Tighten both locknuts on completion.

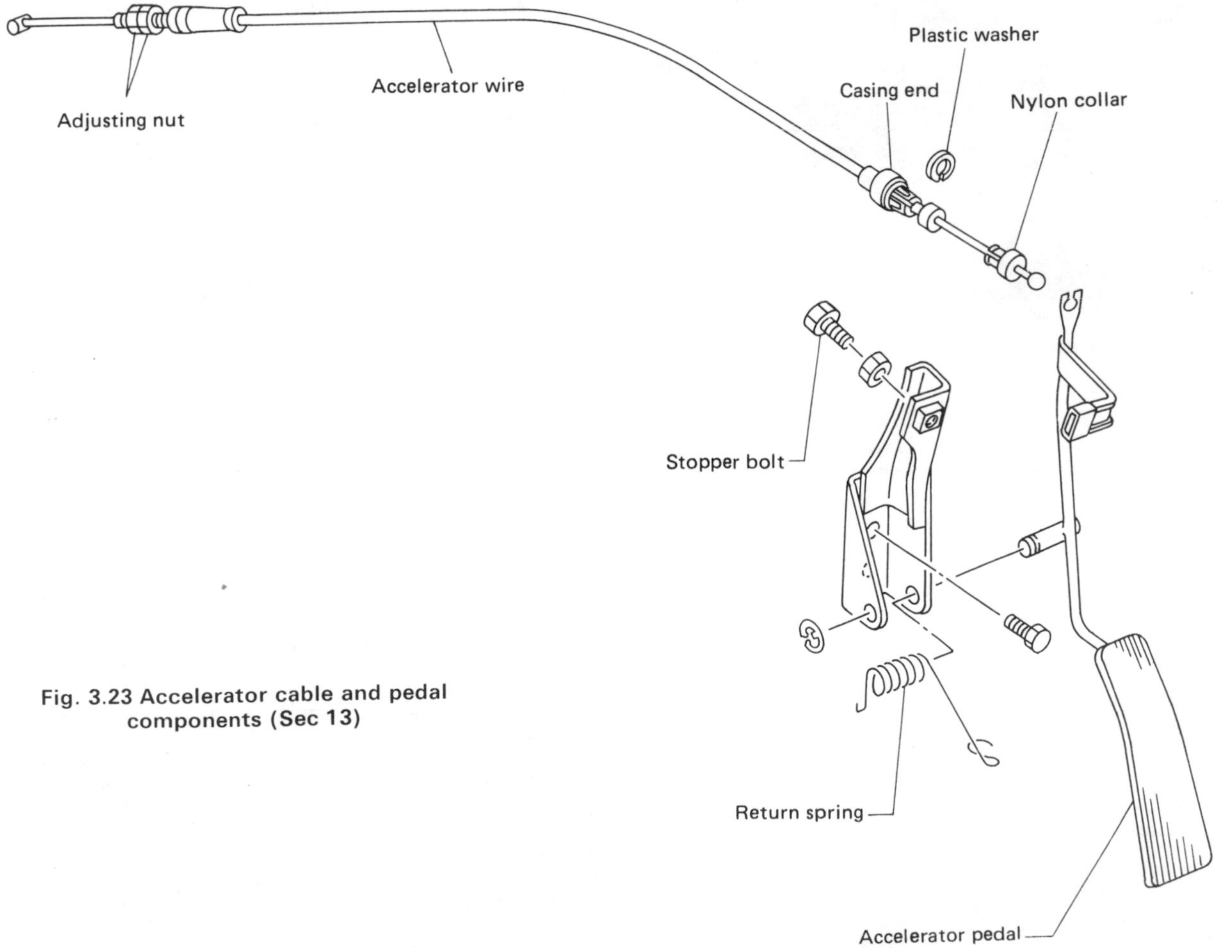

Adjusting nut
Accelerator wire
Plastic washer
Casing end
Nylon collar
Stopper bolt
Return spring
Accelerator pedal

Fig. 3.23 Accelerator cable and pedal components (Sec 13)

13.3 Accelerator cable adjustment ferrule and locknuts

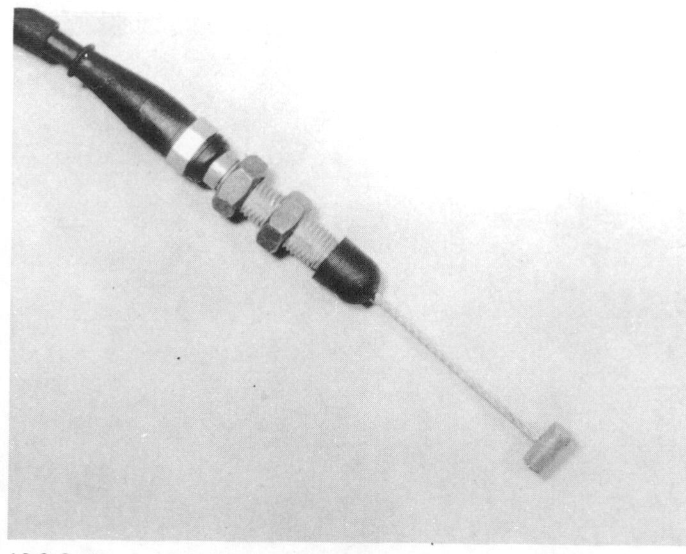

13.6 Carburettor end of accelerator cable

13.7 Accelerator pedal and mounting bracket

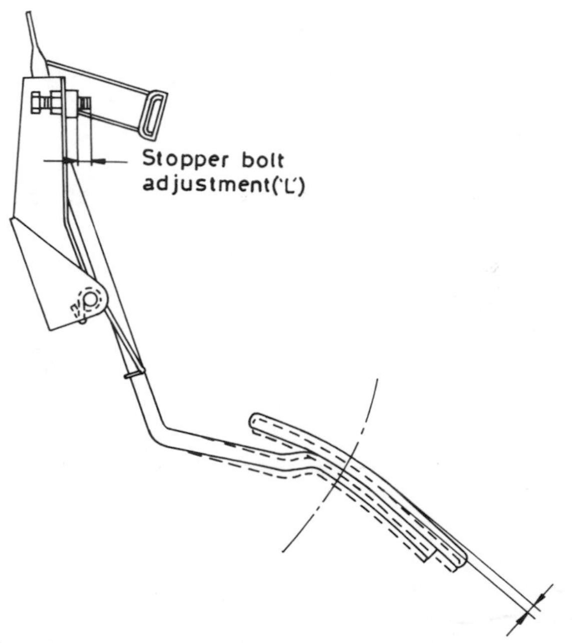

Fig. 3.24 Accelerator pedal and cable adjustment (Sec 13)

14 Boost controlled deceleration device (BCDD) – description

1 This device may be fitted to some engines with manual transmission. It is designed to reduce the emission of HC (hydrocarbon) and engine oil vapour during deceleration on the overrun with the throttle valve closed. During the period of high intake manifold vacuum, the system operates to admit additional mixture to ensure complete combustion.

2 If the device develops a fault, it should be checked by a Nissan dealer. Its location is shown in Figs. 3.13 and 3.14.

15 Manifolds and exhaust system – general

1 The intake and exhaust manifolds are located on opposite sides of the cylinder head as it is of crossflow design.

2 The intake manifold is coolant heated and before the manifold can be removed, the cooling system must be partially drained.

3 The exhaust manifold has the hot air collector plate attached to it which is the source of warm air for the temperature-controlled air cleaner (photo).

4 When removing or refitting a manifold, always use a new gasket and tighten nuts and bolts to the specified torque.

5 The exhaust system is in three sections with a braided flexible joint beneath the rear of the engine. The sections are connected by flange joints with gaskets.

6 To remove the exhaust system, position the car over an inspection pit or jack it up and support on axle stands. Unscrew the nuts and separate the downpipe from the exhaust manifold. Unbolt the sections, then release the mounting rubbers and remove the system (photos).

7 When fitting the exhaust, renew the flange gaskets and mounting rubbers as necessary. Make sure that no component of the system is

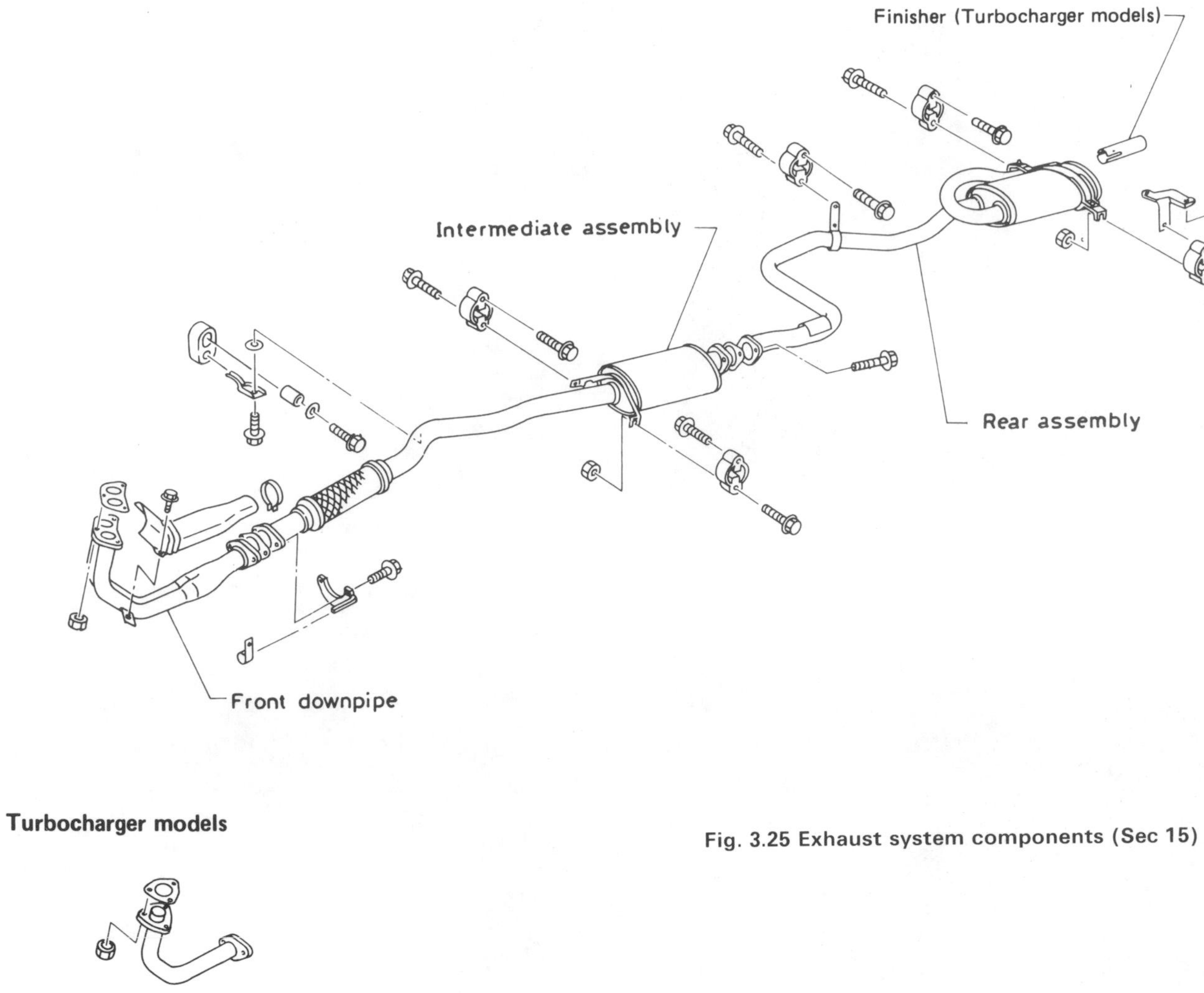

Finisher (Turbocharger models)

Intermediate assembly

Rear assembly

Front downpipe

Turbocharger models

Fig. 3.25 Exhaust system components (Sec 15)

15.3 Exhaust manifold and hot air collector plate

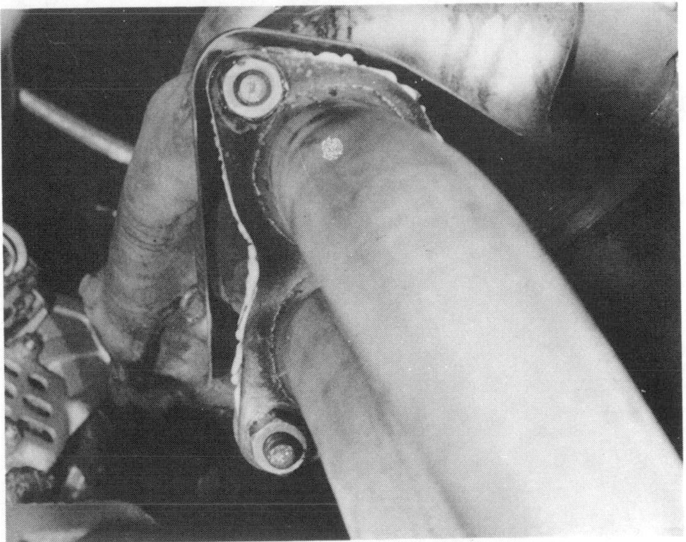

15.6A View of exhaust manifold-to-downpipe flange joint

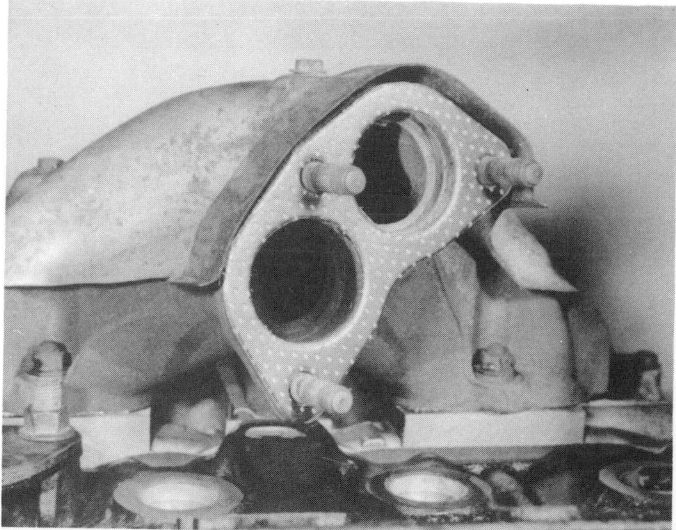

15.6B Downpipe flange gasket on the exhaust manifold

15.6C Downpipe-to-intermediate exhaust pipe flange joint and mounting

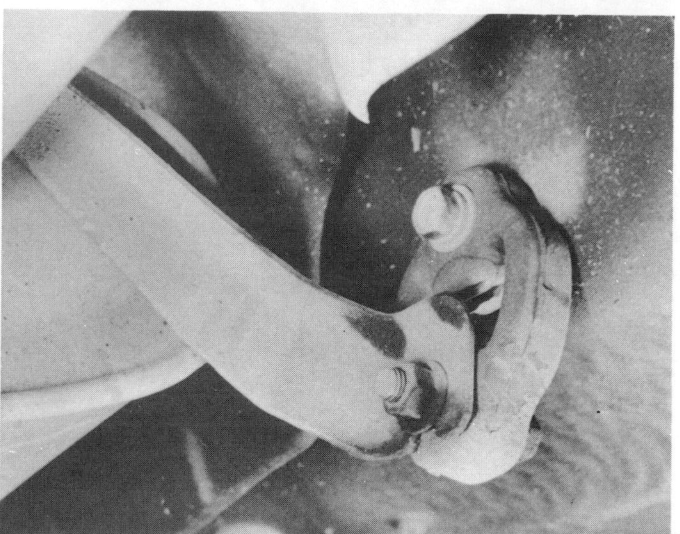

15.6D Rubber mounting at intermediate silencer

15.6E Rubber mounting at rear silencer

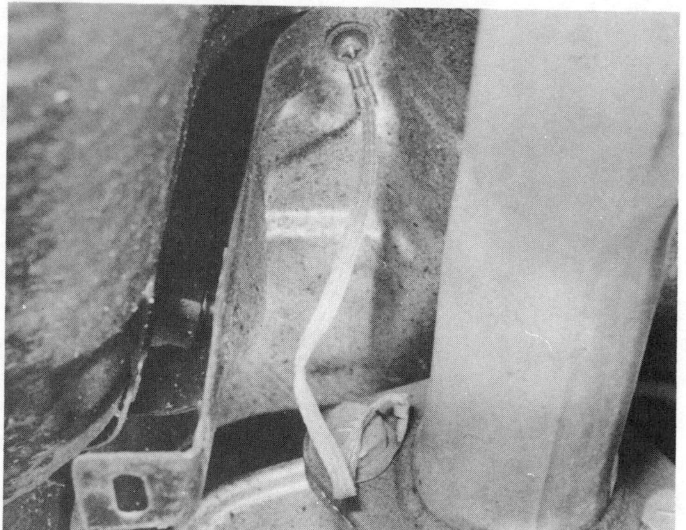

15.7 Earth strap located on the exhaust system central flange bolt

likely to touch adjacent parts of the bodyframe or suspension when deflected within the full extent of movement of its flexible mounting. Note the location of the earth strap on the central flange bolt (photo).

PART B: FUEL-INJECTED TURBO ENGINE

16 General description and precautions

Fuel-injection system

The fuel-injection system consists of a rear-mounted fuel tank, electric fuel pump mounted in the fuel tank, and fuel-injection components. The components are shown in Figs. 3.26 and 3.27.

The roller type electric pump feeds fuel through the filter to the injectors. The computerised ECCS control unit monitors engine speed, load and temperature, together with running conditions, and determines the injector opening period. The fuel pressure is automatically controlled in conjunction with the vacuum in the inlet manifold. For cold starting, additional fuel is provided and to compensate for this, additional air is provided by the air regulator.

In order to prevent damage to the electrical components, do not

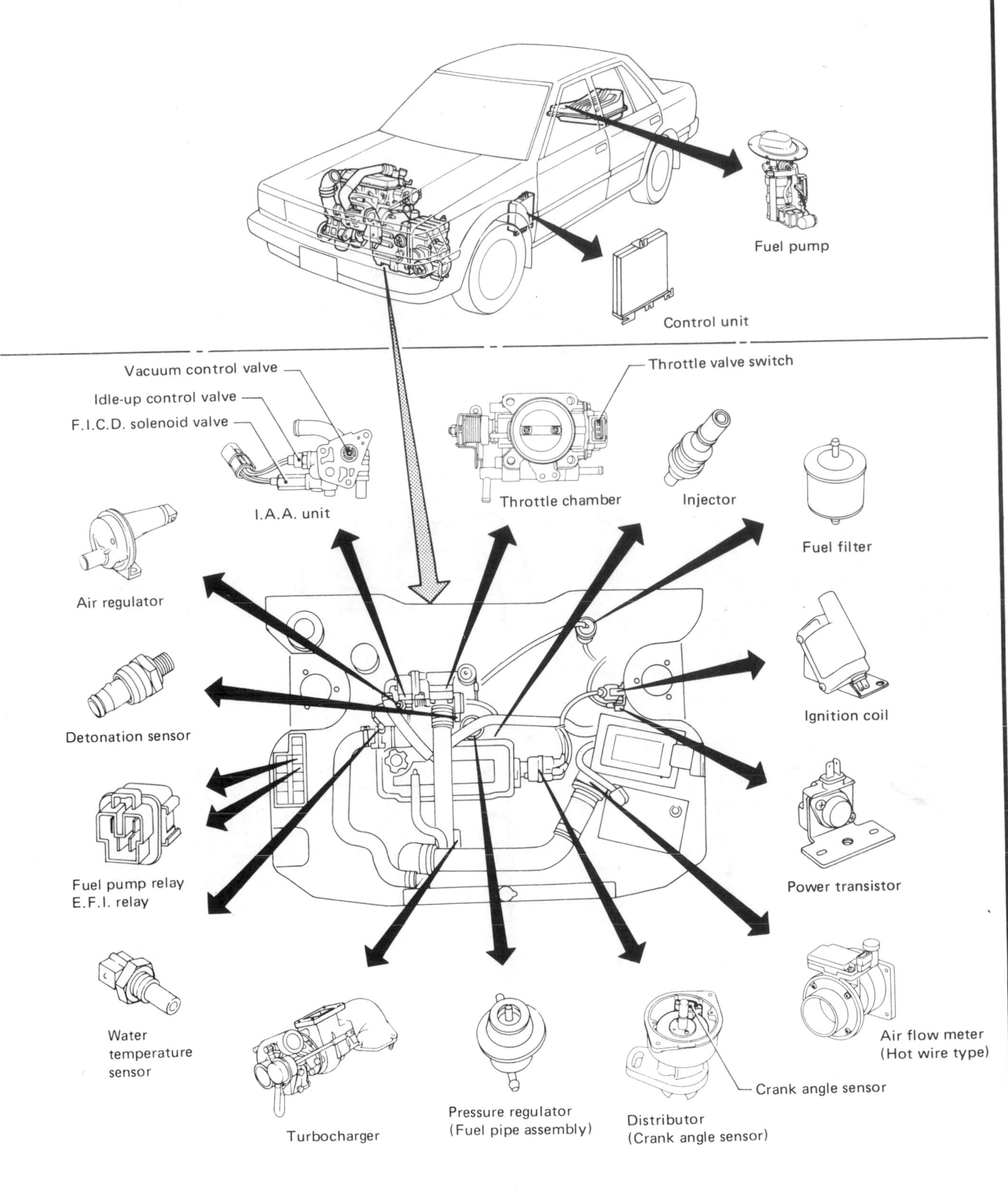

Fig. 3.26 Fuel-injection component locations (Sec 16)

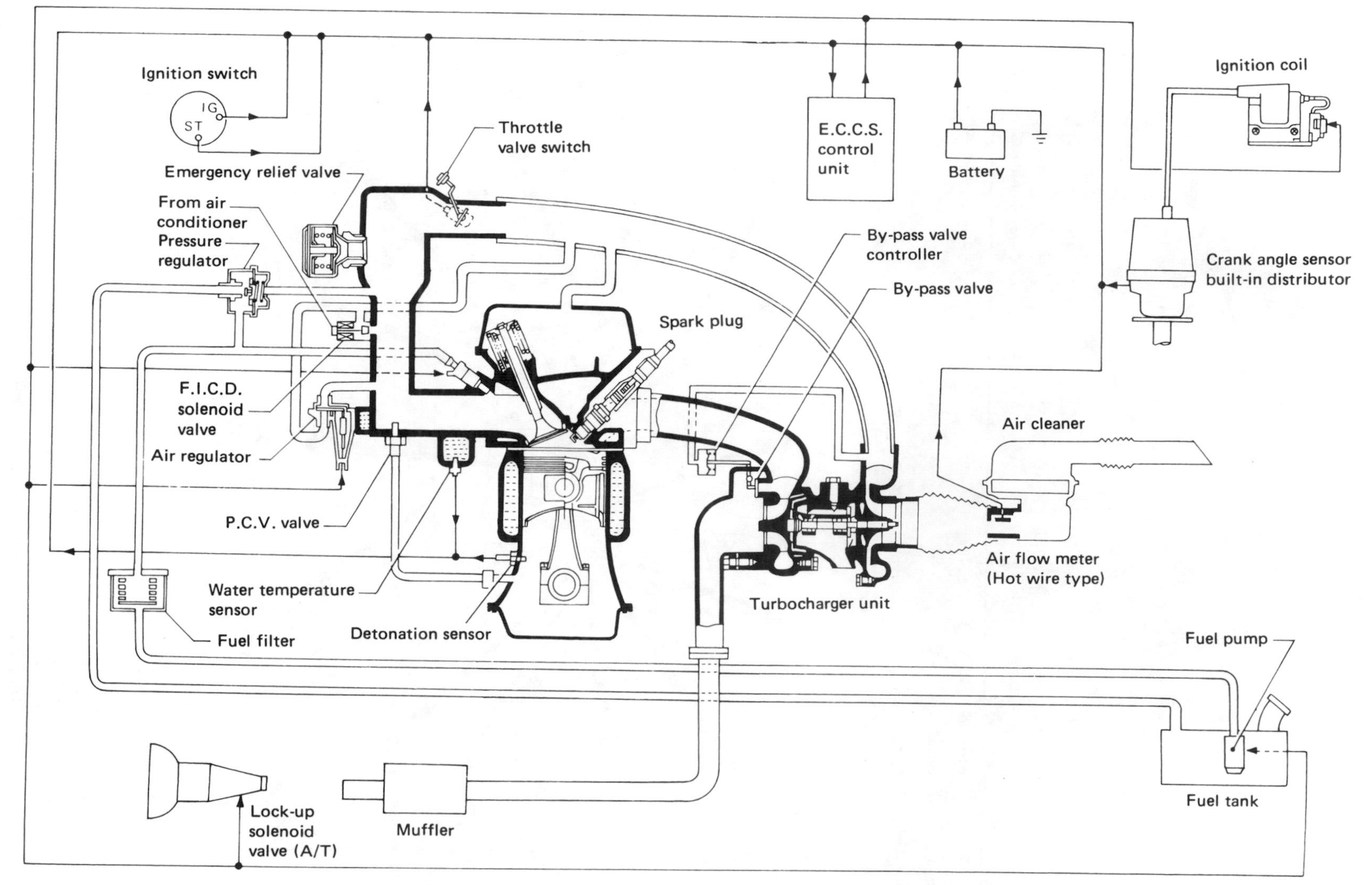

Fig. 3.27 Diagram of the fuel-injection and turbocharger systems (Sec 16)

disconnect the battery with the engine running. Do not apply battery voltage to the injectors. Do not operate the electric fuel pump with no fuel in the lines.

Turbocharger

The turbocharger utilises the flow of exhaust gases to turn a compressor in the inlet system. The pressurized air increases the charging efficiency and increases the engine output. A by-pass valve is incorporated to control the speed of the turbine shaft and in addition, an emergency relief valve is provided.

To prevent possible damage to the turbine shaft the engine should be allowed to idle for a short period after starting to enable the oil pressure to be re-established. Before switching off the engine it should also be allowed to idle for a short period.

17 Routine maintenance

Carry out the following procedures at the intervals given in *'Routine Maintenance'* at the beginning of the Manual.

Check fuel system

1 Refer to Part A, Section 2 of this Chapter.

Renew the air cleaner element

2 Refer to Section 18.

Adjust idling speed and mixture

3 Refer to Section 21.

Renew the fuel filter

4 The fuel filter is clipped to the left-hand side of the bulkhead. Note which way round it is fitted.

5 Before removing the fuel filter carry out the following procedure to reduce the fuel pressure. Start the engine, then remove the fuel pump relay from the relay box (Fig. 3.28). When the engine stalls, spin the engine two or three times on the starter, then switch off the ignition. Refit the relay.

6 Release the filter from the clip, then loosen the two hose clips, release the hoses and withdraw the filter.

7 Fit the new filter using a reversal of the removal procedure.

Check fuel and exhaust system components

8 Check all fuel-injection components for security, condition and leaks.

9 With the car over an inspection pit or supported on axle stands, check the exhaust system and mountings for security and condition. Any sign of a leak can be confirmed by running the engine at idling speed and temporarily placing a wad of rag over the end of the exhaust tailpipe. Any leak will then be shown up by exhaust gasses blowing through the hole.

18 Air cleaner element and body – removal and refitting

1 Unscrew the bolts from the air cleaner cover.
2 Lift the cover and withdraw the element.
3 Wipe clean the inside of the air cleaner body and cover.
4 To remove the body, disconnect the hose from the flowmeter and unbolt the unit from the left-hand front wheel arch.
5 If necessary, unbolt the flowmeter and remove the gasket.
6 Refitting is a reversal of removal, but fit a new flowmeter gasket where necessary.

19 Fuel pump and level sender – removal and refitting

1 The fuel pump is located in the fuel tank and incorporates the fuel level sender.

2 Release the fuel pressure by starting the engine, then removing the fuel pump relay. When the engine stalls switch off the ignition, then refit the relay.

3 Disconnect the battery negative lead.

4 Remove the rear seat cushion and backrest (Chapter 11).

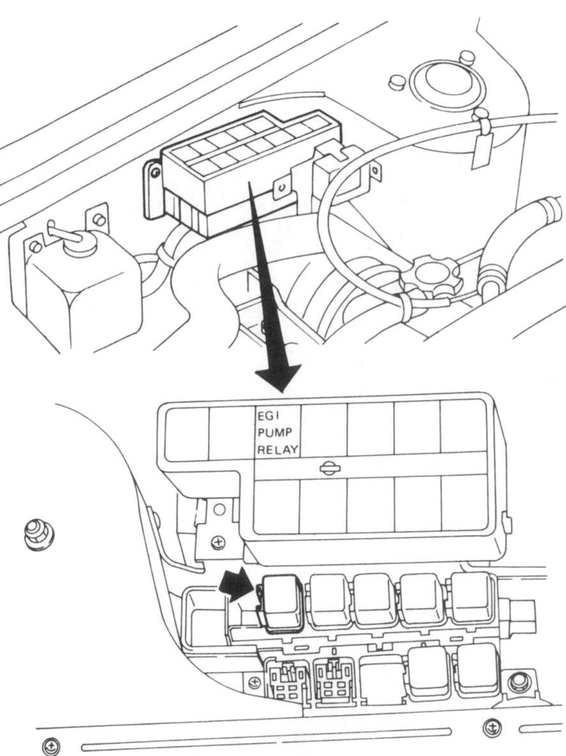

Fig. 3.28 Location of the fuel pump relay (Sec 17)

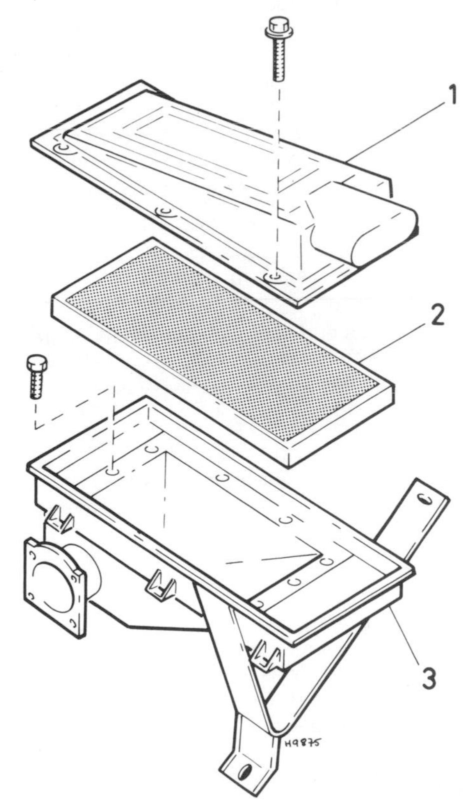

Fig. 3.29 Exploded view of the air cleaner (Sec 18)

1 Cover
2 Element
3 Body

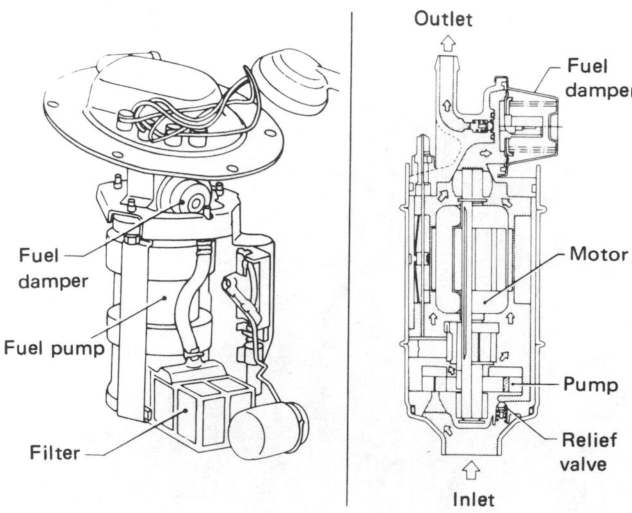

Fig. 3.30 Fuel pump components (Sec 19)

5 Extract the four screws and remove the cover plate, taking care not to damage the wiring.
6 Disconnect the wiring and the fuel hose.
7 Unbolt the unit from the fuel tank and remove the O-ring seal. Take care not to damage the float or float arm.
8 Refitting is a reversal of removal, but use a new O-ring.

20 Fuel tank – removal, repair and refitting

1 Before commencing work, release the fuel pressure by starting the engine, then removing the fuel pump relay. When the engine stalls switch off the ignition, then refit the relay.
2 Follow the procedure described in Part A, Section 7 of this Chapter, but remove the fuel pump and level sender as described in Section 19 instead of the level sender described in Section 6.

21 Idle speed and mixture – adjustment

1 The idle mixture is set during production and therefore it is normally only the idle speed which requires adjustment. The mixture adjustment screw is fitted with a tamperproof cap which must be removed in order to make an adjustment.

Idle speed

2 Run the engine to normal operating temperature.
3 With the engine stopped, disconnect the idle control valve wiring (Fig. 3.31).
4 Make up a wiring adaptor as shown in Chapter 4, Fig. 4.15, or obtain one from a Nissan dealer, then connect it as shown. Connect a tachometer.
5 Race the engine at between 2000 and 3000 rpm two or three times, then allow it to idle for one minute.
6 With all electrical components including the cooling fan switched off, check that the idling speed is as given in the Specifications. If not, turn the idle speed adjusting screw on the side of the IAA unit (Figs. 3.32 and 3.33).

Idle mixture

7 If the mixture must be adjusted due to a change in engine characteristics (carbon build up, bore wear etc), adjust the idle speed first, then stop the engine.
8 If an exhaust gas analyser is available, connect it to the engine, repeat paragraph 5, then check that the CO% is as given in Specifications. If it is correct proceed to paragraph 13.

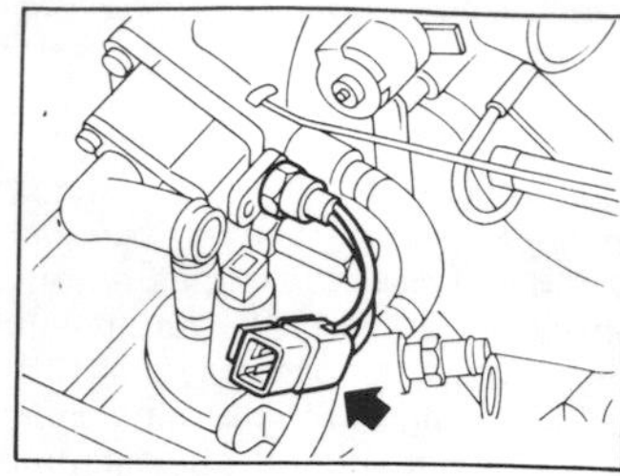

Fig. 3.31 Idle control valve wiring disconnected (Sec 21)

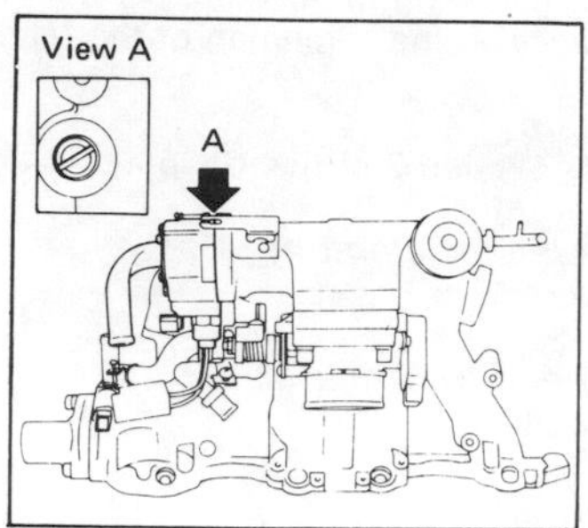

Fig. 3.32 Location of the idle speed adjusting screw (Sec 21)

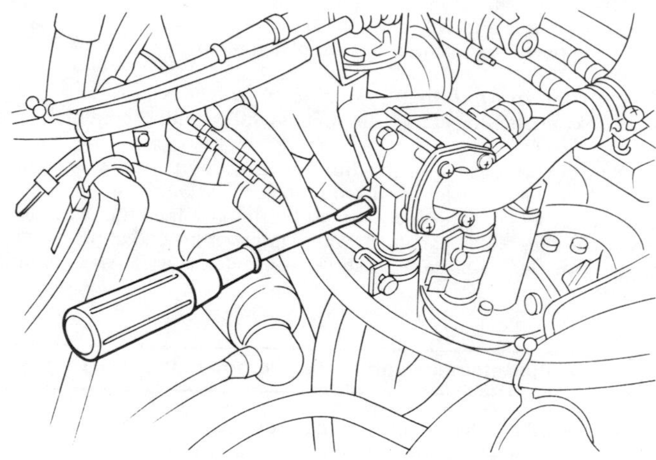

Fig. 3.33 Adjusting the idling speed (Sec 21)

9 Remove the rubber cap from the mixture adjustment screw, then carefully drill a small hole in the aluminium plug and prise it out (Fig. 3.34).
10 Disconnect the water temperature sensor wiring and connect a 2500 ohm resistor across the connector terminals (Fig. 3.35).
11 With the engine at its normal operating temperature, repeat paragraph 5.
12 Turn the mixture adjustment screw to obtain the maximum engine speed or, if using an exhaust gas analyser, to obtain the specified CO%.
13 Stop the engine, then reconnect the water temperature sensor wiring and disconnect the exhaust gas analyser. Reconnect the idle control valve wiring.

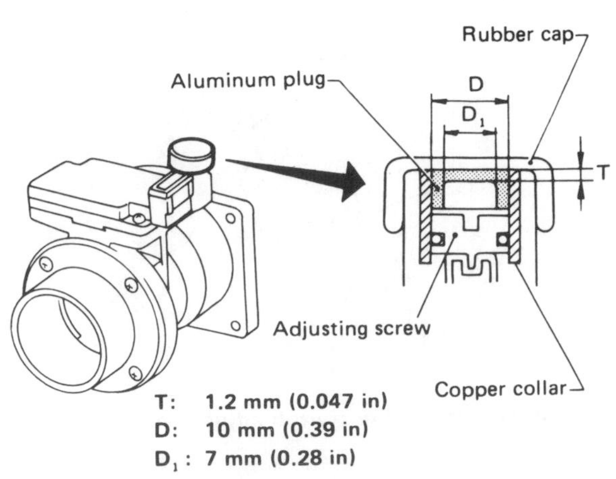

Fig. 3.34 Mixture adjustment screw tamperproof cap detail (Sec 21)

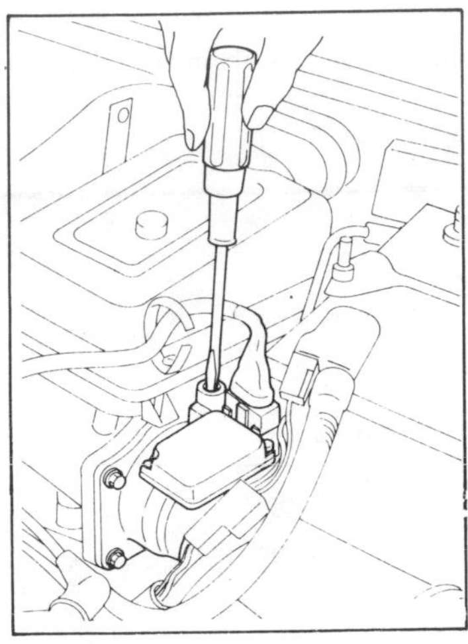

Fig. 3.36 Adjusting the idling mixture (Sec 21)

22 Injector – removal and refitting

1 Before commencing work, release the fuel pressure by starting the engine then removing the fuel pump relay. When the engine stalls, switch off the ignition then refit the relay.
2 Loosen the clips and remove the air intake hose from the throttle chamber.
3 Disconnect the wiring harness from the injectors.
4 Disconnect the spark plug HT leads.
5 Disconnect the accelerator cable from the throttle chamber.
6 Disconnect the fuel hoses and the pressure regulator vacuum hose.
7 Unbolt the fuel supply tube.
8 Unbolt the holders, then withdraw the injectors complete with the fuel supply tube.
9 Disconnect the hoses and remove the injectors.
10 The hoses are a tight fit on the injectors and to remove them it will be necessary to use a soldering iron to cut into the braided reinforcement (Fig. 3.38).
11 Refitting is a reversal of removal, but new hoses must be fitted using the following procedure. Clean the injector extension, then dip the end of the hose in fuel and push the hose fully onto the injector.

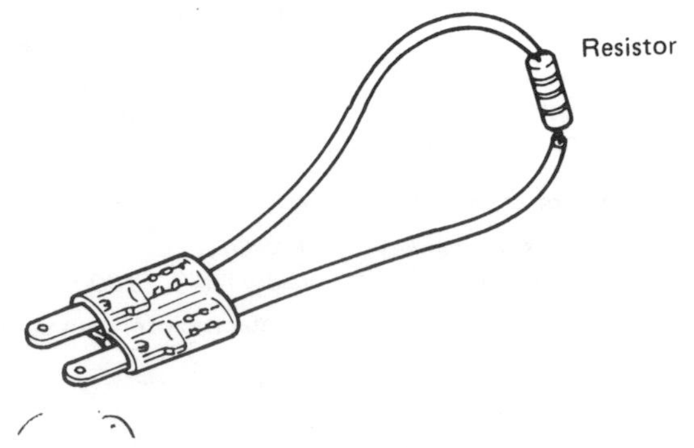

Fig. 3.35 Resistor and lead required when adjusting idling mixture (Sec 21)

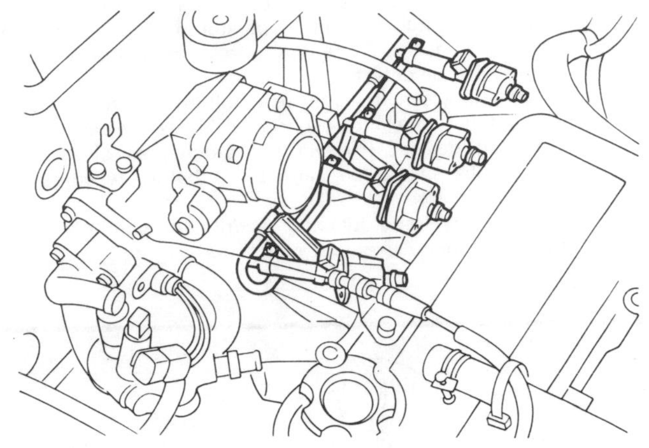

Fig. 3.37 Injection and fuel supply tube (Sec 22)

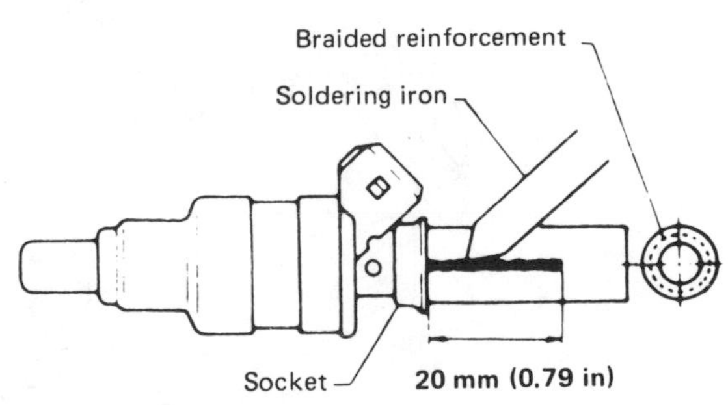

Fig. 3.38 Method of removing hose from injector (Sec 22)

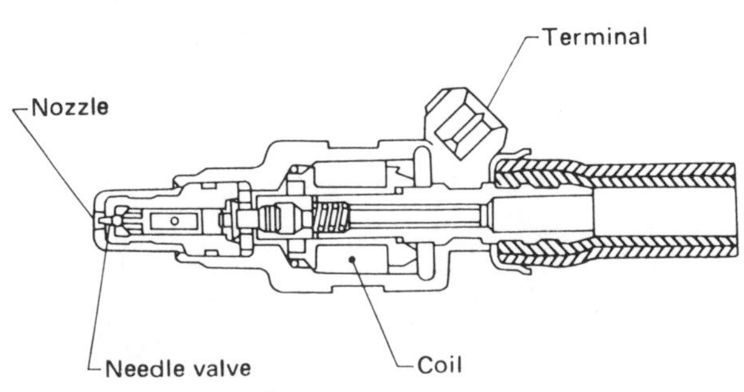

Fig. 3.39 Cross-section of injector (Sec 22)

23 Throttle valve switch – adjustment

1 The throttle valve switch is located on the side of the throttle chamber. To adjust it first connect a tachometer to the engine.
2 Loosen the bolts holding the throttle valve switch to the throttle chamber.
3 Hold the engine at the following speed:

Manual transmission models – 900 ± 50 rpm
Automatic transmission models (position 'N') – 1000 ± 50 rpm

4 Rotate the switch until the internal contacts close, then tighten the bolts.
5 Stop the engine and disconnect the tachometer.

24 Fuel-injection components – fault diagnosis procedure

1 The ECCS control unit located on the left-hand side of the passenger's footwell incorporates a self-diagnosis system. The system uses a red and green light to inform the operator of a faulty component by means of coded flashes. A memory is also incorporated so that intermittent faults can be detected.
2 The procedure necessary to diagnose a fault is not within the scope of this manual and therefore in the event of problems, the car should be taken to a Nissan dealer. However the procedures given in the following paragraphs should be carried out before resorting to a complete diagnosis check.
3 Check the inlet hoses and ducts for security and condition.
4 Check the air cleaner element for clogging.

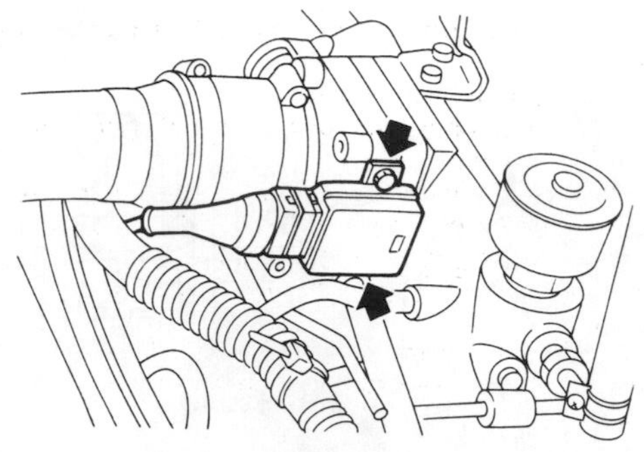

Fig. 3.40 Throttle valve switch adjusting bolts (Sec 23)

5 Check all wiring for security and condition.
6 Check and if necessary adjust the ignition timing, idle speed and idle mixture.
7 Check that the injectors are clean.

25 Turbocharger – removal and refitting

1 Disconnect and remove the air inlet and outlet hoses from the turbocharger.

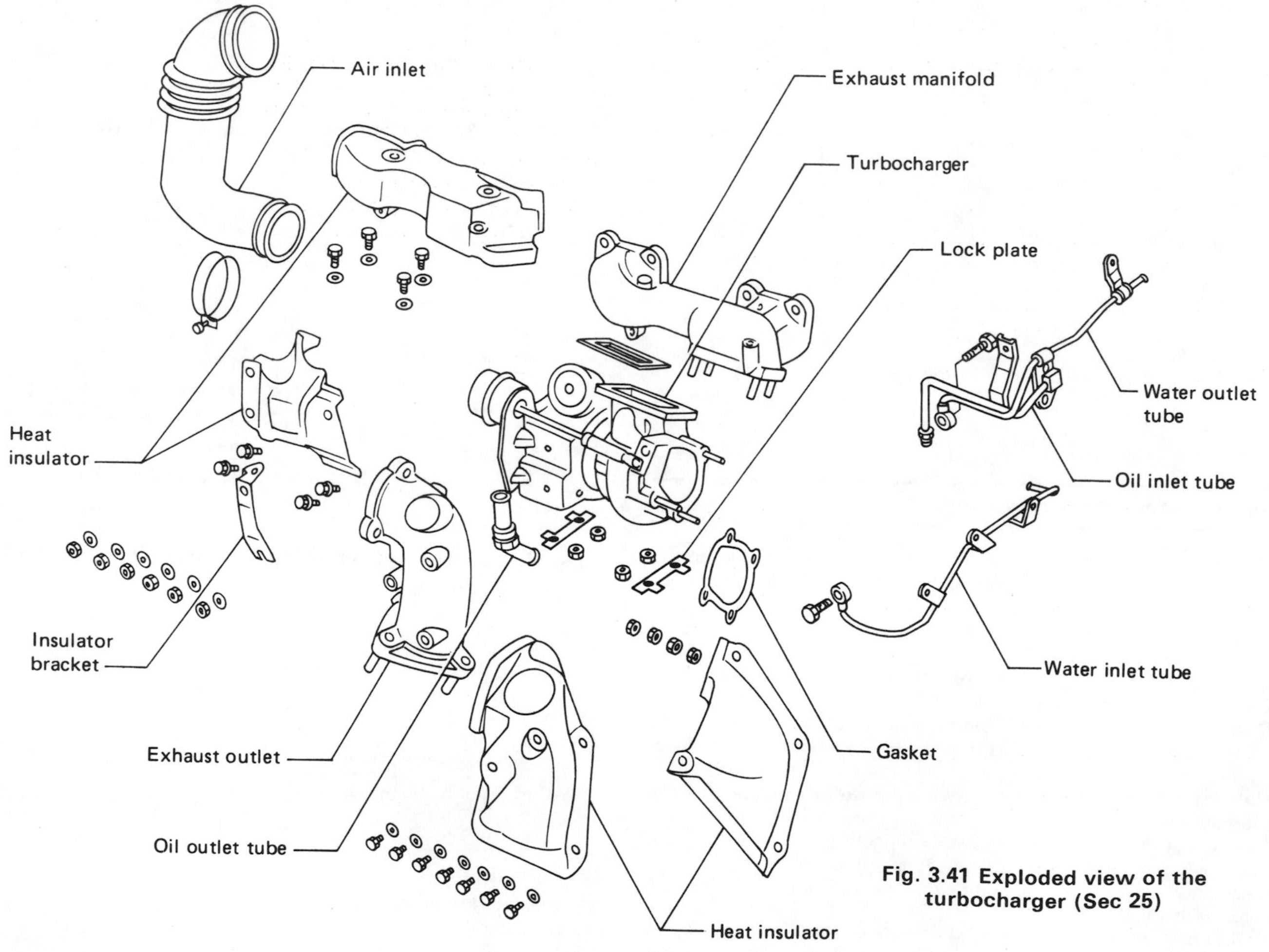

Fig. 3.41 Exploded view of the turbocharger (Sec 25)

2 Apply the handbrake, then jack up the front of the car and support on axle stands.
3 Unscrew the flange nuts holding the exhaust downpipe to the turbocharger.
4 Unbolt and remove the heat shields.
5 Unscrew the union bolts and disconnect the coolant inlet and outlet tubes. Plug the tubes.
6 Unscrew the union nuts and disconnect the oil supply inlet and outlet tubes. Plug the tubes.
7 Unscrew the mounting nuts from the exhaust manifold.
8 Withdraw the turbocharger and remove the downpipe and manifold gaskets.
9 Refitting is a reversal of removal, but allow the engine to idle for several minutes in order to re-establish the oil supply.

26 Accelerator cable and pedal – removal, refitting and adjustment

The procedure is basically as described in Part A, Section 13 of this Chapter, except for the removal of surrounding components.

27 Manifolds and exhaust system – general

Refer to Part A, Section 15 of this Chapter. The exhaust system differs only in the downpipe which is a single pipe (see Fig. 3.25).

PART C: FAULT DIAGNOSIS (ALL ENGINES)

28 Fault diagnosis – fuel, emission and exhaust systems

Symptom	Reason(s)
Difficulty starting from cold	Faulty automatic choke (carburettor) Fuel pump fault Blocked fuel line or filter Needle valve sticking (carburettor) Supplementary air device fault (fuel-injection) Water temperature sensor faulty (fuel-injection)
Difficult starting when hot	Choked air cleaner element Faulty automatic choke (carburettor) Fuel pump fault
Excessive fuel consumption	Mixture setting incorrect Excessive fuel pressure (fuel-injection) Faulty water temperature sensor (fuel-injection) Faulty automatic choke (carburettor)
Uneven idling	Mixture setting incorrect Air leak in intake system Throttle switch out of adjustment (fuel-injection)

Chapter 4 Ignition system

Contents

Specifications

System type

Non-Turbo models	Electronic, transistorized unit integral with distributor, remote ignition coil
Turbo models	Computerised, crank angle sensor in distributor, remote ignition coil and power transistor

Distributor

Rotor rotation	Anti-clockwise
Firing order	1-3-4-2 (No 1 at timing belt end of engine)
Air gap (non-Turbo models)	0.3 to 0.5 mm (0.012 to 0.020 in)
Cap insulation	50 M ohms minimum
Rotor arm insulation	50 M ohms minimum
Carbon brush length	10.0 mm (0.39 in) minimum
HT lead resistance	30 k ohms maximum

Ignition coil

Primary resistance at 20°C (68°F):	
Non-Turbo models	1.3 to 1.7 ohms
Turbo models	0.8 to 1.0 ohms
Secondary resistance at 20°C (68°F):	
Non-Turbo models – type STC106	7.4 to 11.2 k ohm
Non-Turbo models – type CIT106	7.5 to 11.3 k ohm
Turbo models	8.0 to 12.0 k ohm

Spark plugs

Type:	
CA18 engine	NGK BPR5ES Hitachi L46PW Champion RN9YC
CA18ET (Turbo) engine	NGK BCPR 6ES11 Hitachi L45PS11 Champion RC9YC
CA20 engine	NGK BCPR6ES Hitachi L45PS Champion RC9YC

Electrode gap:	
Non-Turbo engine	0.8 to 0.9 mm (0.031 to 0.035 in)
Turbo engine	1.0 to 1.1 mm (0.039 to 0.043 in)

Ignition timing (at idle, vacuum hose disconnected)

CA18 engine	5° ± 2° BTDC
CA18ET (Turbo) engine	15° ± 2° BTDC
CA20 engine	3° ± 2° BTDC

Torque wrench settings

	Nm	lbf ft
Spark plug (new)	1/2 to 3/4 turn after touching gasket	
Spark plug (used)	25	19
Distributor clamp bolt	6	4

1 General description

Non-Turbo models

On non-Turbo models the ignition system is of electronic type, incorporating a transistorized unit within the distributor. The transistorized unit consists of a reluctor, stator, magnet, and IC module which together switch the low tension circuit of the ignition coil on and off. HT voltage is induced in the coil and fed via the rotor arm and HT leads to the spark plugs. The ignition timing is advanced according to engine speed by centrifugal weights on the distributor shaft, and retarded by a vacuum capsule connected to the carburettor.

Turbo models

On Turbo models the ignition system is of computerised type linked to the ECCS system as described in Chapter 3. The distributor incorporates a special slotted rotor plate which acts as a crank angle sensor. Impulses are fed as signals to the ECCS control unit which determines the ignition timing and switches the coil primary circuit accordingly. The coil and distributor cap components function as

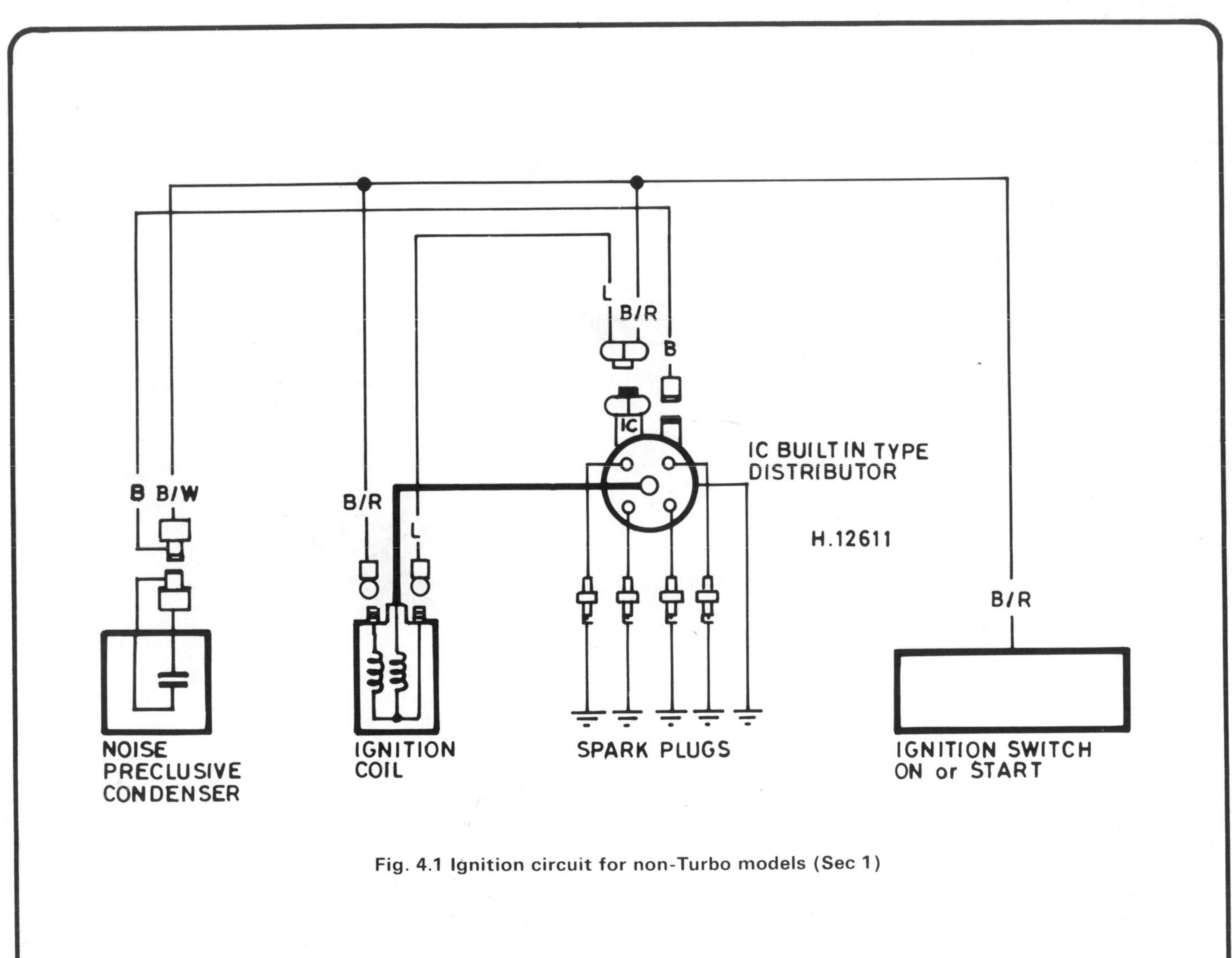

Fig. 4.1 Ignition circuit for non-Turbo models (Sec 1)

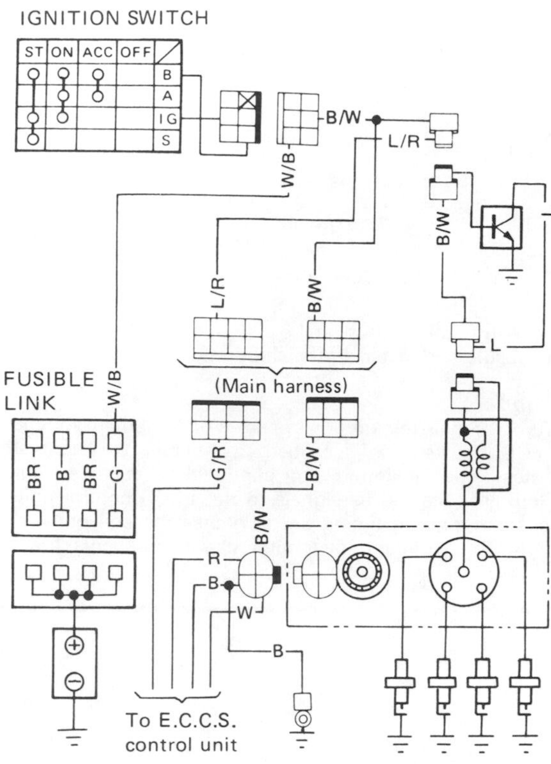

Fig. 4.2 Ignition circuit for Turbo models (Sec 1)

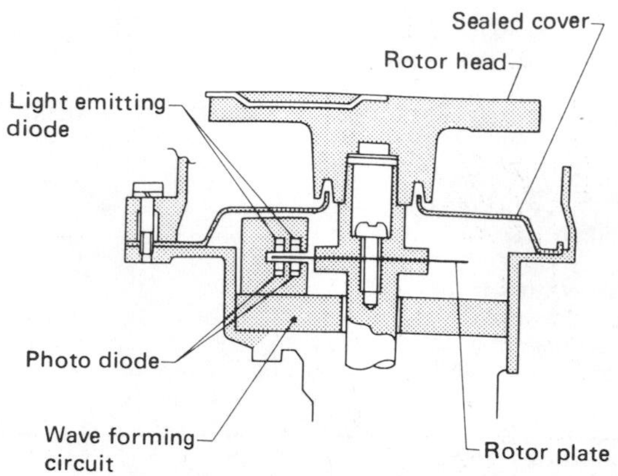

Fig. 4.3 Cross-section of the distributor for Turbo models (Sec 1)

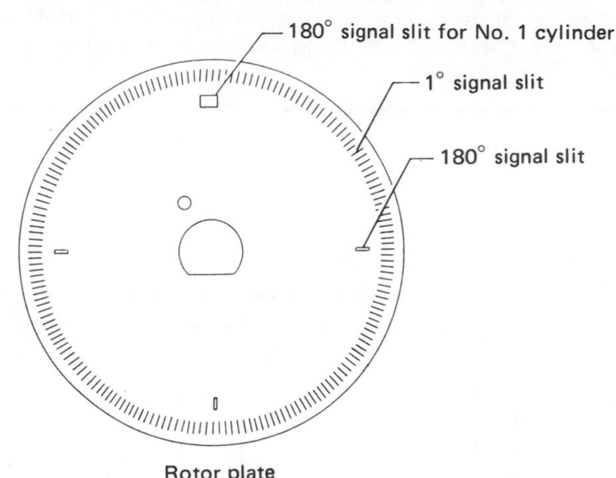

Fig. 4.4 Showing rotor plate slots in Turbo distributor (Sec 1)

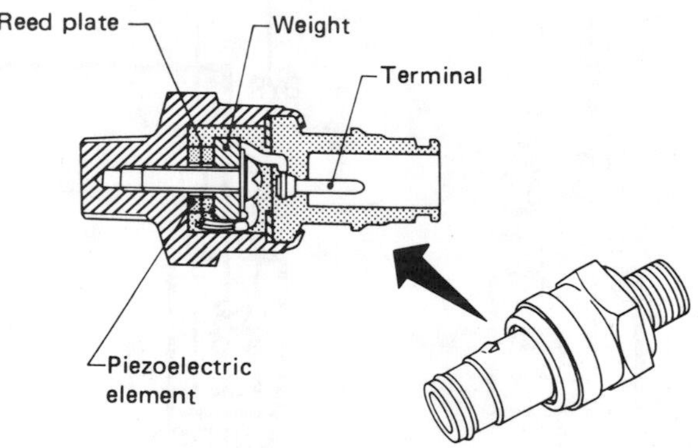

Fig. 4.5 Cross-section of the detonation sensor on Turbo models (Sec 1)

described for non-Turbo models. The ignition circuit includes a detonation sensor which retards the ignition timing by five degrees if combustion knocking occurs at engine speeds in excess of 2000 rpm. **Note:** *When working on the ignition system remember that the high tension voltage can be considerably higher than on a conventional system, and in certain circumstances could prove fatal.*

2 Routine maintenance

Carry out the following procedures at the intervals given in *'Routine Maintenance'* at the beginning of the Manual.

Check and adjust the ignition timing

1 Refer to Section 7.

Clean or renew spark plugs

2 Remove the air cleaner or inlet ducting from the carburettor (Chapter 3).

3 Identify the HT leads for position, then disconnect them from the spark plugs by pulling on the connectors, not the leads.

4 Brush any accumulated dirt from the recess in the cylinder head.

5 Unscrew and remove the spark plugs using a deep socket or box spanner (photo). Do not allow the tool to tilt, otherwise the ceramic insulator may be cracked or broken.

6 Before cleaning a spark plug, wash it in petrol to remove oily deposits.

7 Although a wire brush can be used to clean the electrode end of the spark plug, this method can cause metal conductance paths across the nose of the insulator and it is therefore to be preferred that an abrasive powder cleaning machine is used. Such machines are available quite cheaply from motor accessory stores or you may prefer to take the plugs to your dealer who will not only be able to clean them, but also check the sparking efficiency of each plug under compression.

8 The spark plug gap is of considerable importance, as, if it is too large or too small, the size of the spark and its efficiency will be seriously impaired. For the best results the spark plug gap should be set in accordance with the Specifications at the beginning of this Chapter.

9 To set it, measure the gap with a feeler gauge, and then bend open, or close the outer plug electrode until the correct gap is achieved. The centre electrode should never be bent as this may crack the insulation and cause plug failure if nothing worse.

10 Special spark plug electrode gap adjusting tools are available from most motor accessory stores.

11 Before fitting the spark plugs, wash each one thoroughly again in

2.5 Using a deep socket to remove a spark plug

2.15A Remove the screws ...

2.15B ... and withdraw the distributor cap

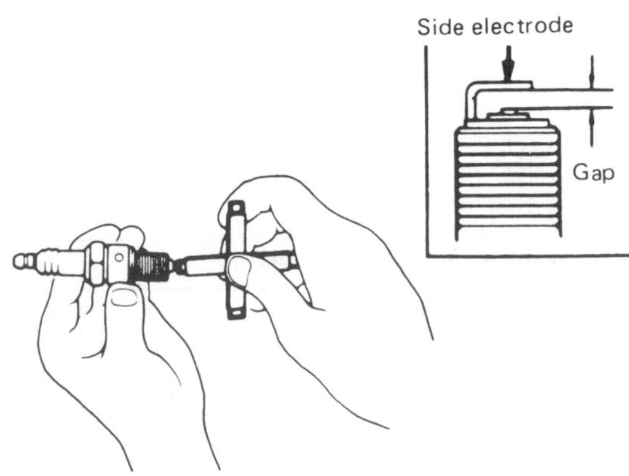

Fig. 4.6 Adjusting the spark plug electrode gap (Sec 2)

fuel in order to remove all trace of abrasive powder and then apply a trace of grease to the plug threads.

12 Screw each plug in by hand. This will make sure that there is no chance of cross-threading.

13 Tighten to the specified torque. If a torque wrench is not available, just nip up each plug. It is better to slightly undertighten rather than over do it and strip the threads from the light alloy cylinder head.

14 When reconnecting the spark plug leads, make sure that they are refitted in their correct order, 1-3-4-2. No.1 cylinder being at the timing belt end of the engine, and the distributor rotor turning anti-clockwise when viewed from the left-hand side of the engine compartment.

Distributor cap and HT leads

15 Remove the screws and lift the distributor cap from the distributor (photo). Disconnect the main HT lead from the ignition coil.

16 Wipe clean the HT leads and the distributor cap.

17 Using an ohmmeter, check for continuity between the segments inside the distributor cap and the spark plug or coil ends of the leads. If a reading in excess of 30 kohm is obtained, clean the distributor cap outer terminals and check again. If there is no improvement renew the HT lead.

3 Distributor (non-Turbo models) – air gap adjustment

1 This should only require adjustment if an engine fault indicates the need after reference to Section 10.

2 Remove the distributor cap (two screws) and pull off the rotor arm.

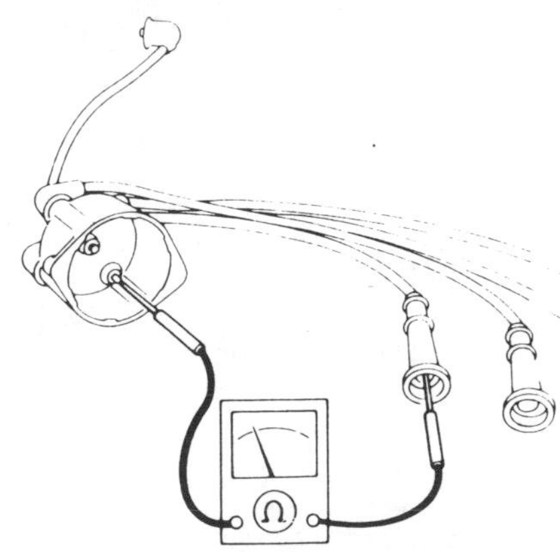

Fig. 4.7 Testing the HT leads and distributor cap with an ohmmeter (Sec 2)

3 If necessary, turn the engine until two opposite peaks on the reluctor are aligned with the two stator posts.
4 Using a feeler blade check that the air gap between the peaks and posts in between 0.3 and 0.5 mm (0.012 and 0.020 in).
5 If adjustment is necessary, loosen the two stator screws, reposition the stator, then re-tighten the screws.
6 Refit the rotor arm and distributor cap.

4 Distributor – removal and refitting

1 For better access, remove the air cleaner or inlet ducting with reference to Chapter 3.
2 Remove the distributor cap (two screws).
3 Turn the engine until the rotor arm is pointing to the location of the No.1 HT lead segment of the distributor cap. If necessary, mark the location on the distributor body before removing the cap.
4 On non-Turbo models, turn the engine as required until the reluctor peaks are aligned with the stator posts. The correct ignition timing mark on the crankshaft pulley should now be aligned with the pointer.
5 Mark the distributor body in relation to the cylinder head using a centre punch.
6 Disconnect the hose from the vacuum capsule on non-Turbo models (photo).
7 Disconnect the wiring from the earth terminal (photo).
8 Disconnect the distributor wiring at the multi-pin connector.
9 Unscrew and remove the clamp bolt, then withdraw the distributor from the cylinder head (photos).
10 Before fitting the distributor on non-Turbo models check that the ignition timing marks are still aligned. If the engine position has been disturbed, remove No.1 spark plug (timing belt end of the engine), then rotate the engine clockwise until compression can be felt with a finger over the spark plug hole. Continue turning until the ignition timing marks are aligned.
11 Align the marks on the drive dog and base of the distributor where applicable, then insert the distributor in the cylinder head and turn the rotor arm until the offset legs enter the slots in the camshaft locating plate (photo).
12 Turn the distributor body until the previously made marks are aligned. If a **new** distributor is being fitted on non-Turbo models, locate the cut-out over the clamp bolt hole, then turn the body as required to align the reluctor peaks with the stator posts.
13 Tighten the clamp bolt.
14 Reconnect the wiring and vacuum hose (if applicable).
15 Refit the distributor cap.
16 Check and adjust the ignition timing as described in Section 7.

5 Distributor (non-Turbo models) – overhaul

1 With the distributor removed as described in Section 4, pull the rotor arm from the top of the shaft.

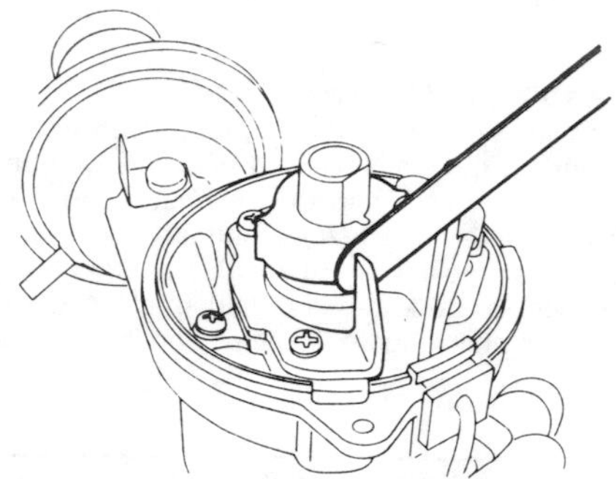

Fig. 4.8 Checking the air gap on the non-Turbo distributor (Sec 3)

4.6 Distributor vacuum capsule and hose

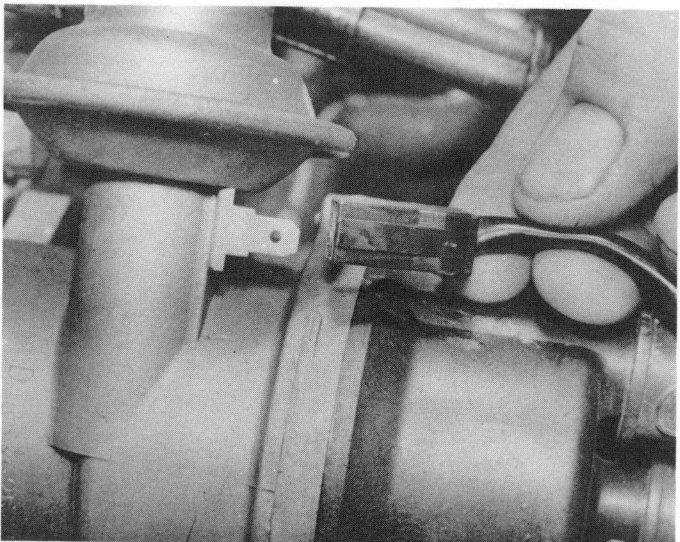

4.7 Distributor earth terminal and wire

4.9A Unscrew the clamp bolt ...

4.9B ... and withdraw the distributor from the cylinder head

4.11 Distributor drive locating plate (arrowed) on the end of the camshaft

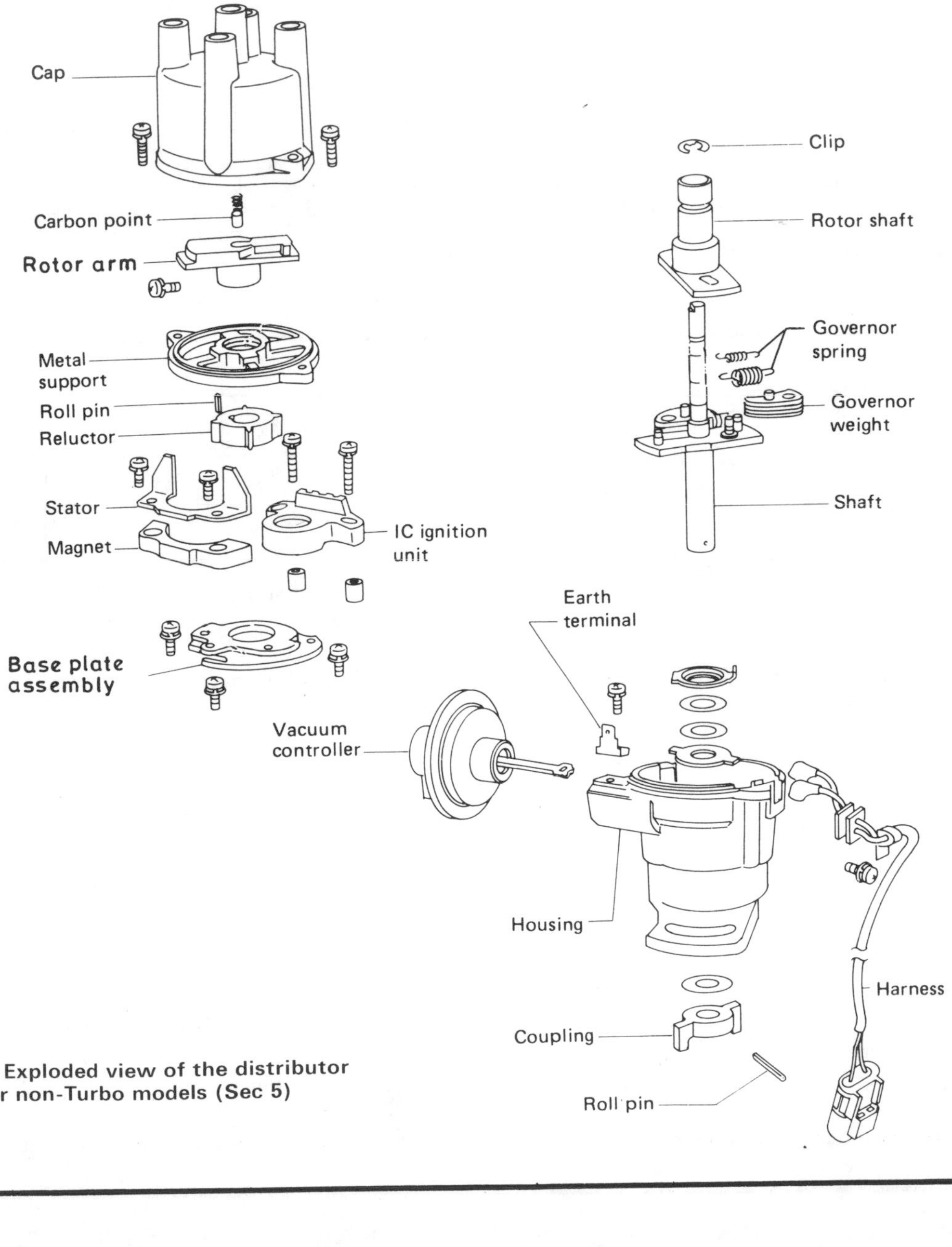

Fig. 4.9 Exploded view of the distributor for non-Turbo models (Sec 5)

2 Remove the support plate.
3 Note the fitted position of the reluctor, then extract the roll pin and withdraw the reluctor from the shaft.
4 Remove the two screws and withdraw the stator and magnet.
5 Remove the wiring harness support screw from the distributor body (photo). Idenfity the wires for position, disconnect them from the IC ignition unit, then release the rubber grommet and withdraw the harness.
6 Remove the two screws and lift out the IC ignition unit. Recover the spacers.
7 Remove the three screws and lift out the base plate assembly while disconnecting the vacuum controller arm.
8 Mark the coupling in relation to the shaft.
9 Drive out the roll pin and remove the coupling and thrust washer.
10 Slide the shaft from the body, noting the position of the thrust washers.
11 Remove the screw and withdraw the vacuum controller, noting the location of the earth terminal.
12 Mark the rotor shaft in relation to the main shaft, then extract the upper circlip and withdraw the rotor shaft, governer weight and springs.
13 Clean and examine all components and renew any that are worn or damaged.
14 Reassembly is a reversal of dismantling, but observe the following points.
15 Apply high melting point grease to the governor weight pivots, governor springs, rotor shaft, base plate assembly, vacuum controller arm, and support plate bearing surface.
16 When fitting the governer weights, attach the small springs first then the large springs.
17 Fit the rotor shaft to the main shaft with the cut-outs as shown in Fig. 4.11.
18 Fit the base plate with the matching marks (Fig. 4.12) aligned.
19 When fitting the reluctor to the rotor shaft, position the roll pin cut-out as shown in Fig. 4.13.
20 Adjust the air gap as described in Section 3.

5.5 Wiring harness and support screw

6 Distributor (Turbo models) – overhaul

1 There is very little work possible on the distributor for Turbo models, and it is not possible to obtain the internal electronic components separately. However the following procedure may prove useful to anyone transferring components from one distributor to another.

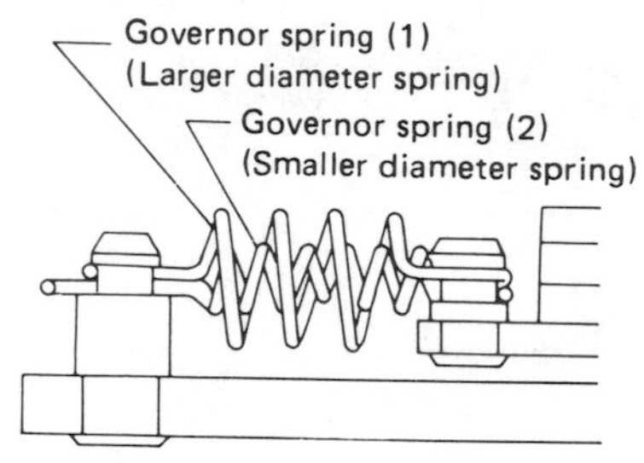

Fig. 4.10 Installation of centrifugal governor weight springs (Sec 5)

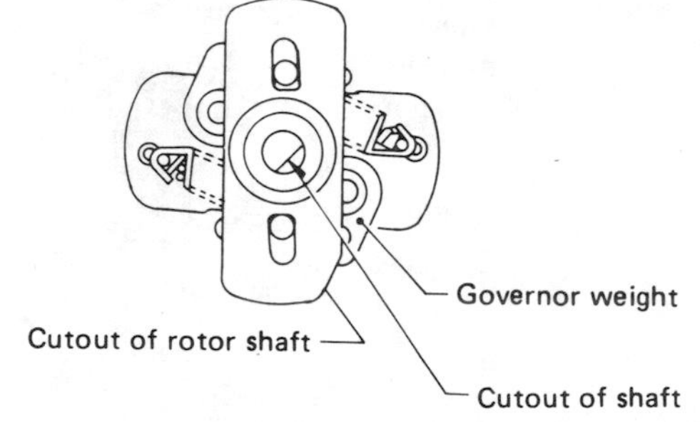

Fig. 4.11 Correct assembly of distributor shafts (Sec 5)

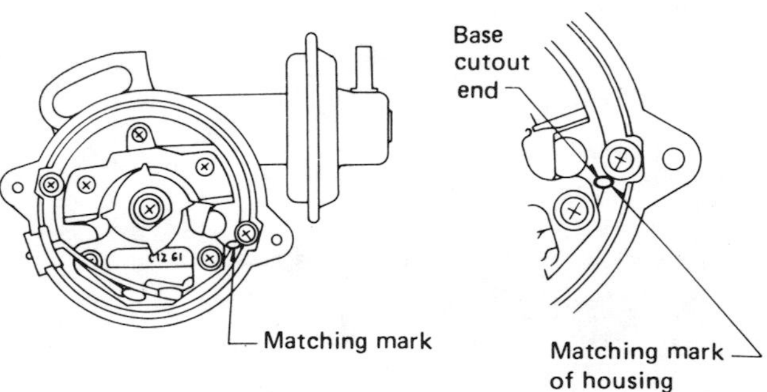

Fig. 4.12 Distributor base plate matching marks (Sec 5)

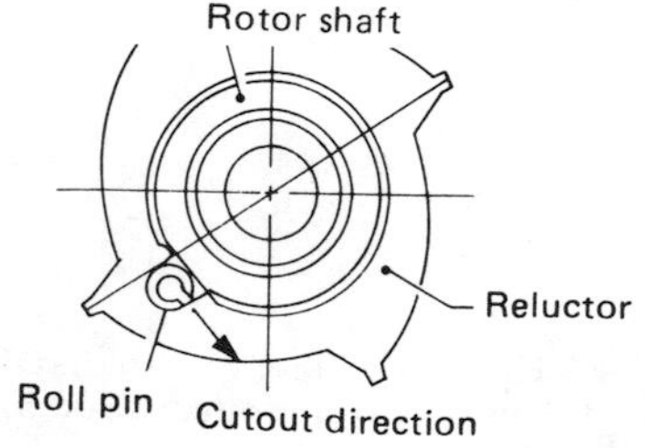

Fig. 4.13 Correct assembly of reluctor (Sec 5)

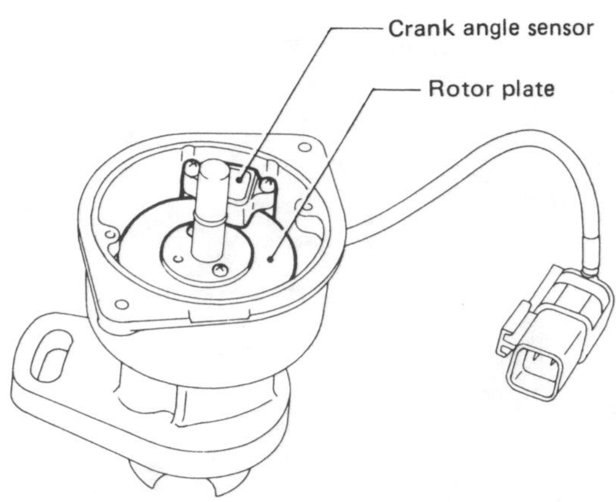

Fig. 4.14 Distributor components on Turbo models (Sec 6)

2 With the distributor removed as described in Section 4, pull the rotor arm from the top of the shaft.
3 Remove the support plate and/or the sealed cover.
4 Remove the centre screw and lift off the rotor shaft.
5 Remove the crank angle sensor securing screws, then withdraw the sensor and rotor plate together with the wiring.
6 Reassembly is a reversal of dismantling.

7 Ignition timing

1 Start the engine and run at a fast idling speed until it reaches normal operating temperature, as shown on the temperature gauge. Stop the engine.
2 On Turbo models, disconnect the idle control valve harness (Chapter 3), then fit adaptor wiring between the ignition coil and the tachometer (Fig. 4.15). The wiring can be made using connectors, or alternatively can be obtained from a Nissan dealer.
3 Connect a timing light to the engine in accordance with the maker's instructions.
4 Run the engine at idling speed. On non-Turbo models, disconnect the hose for the distributor vacuum advance unit at the inlet manifold and plug the outlet.
5 Point the timing light at the crankshaft pulley and check that the correct ignition timing mark, according to model, appears in line with the pointer on the timing cover. The black mark indicates TDC and the white marks are in increments of five degrees, as shown in Fig. 4.16 (photo).
6 If adjustment is required, loosen the distributor clamp bolt and turn the distributor body clockwise to advance the ignition, or anti-clockwise to retard it. Tighten the bolt when the setting is correct.
7 Increase the engine speed and check that the timing mark advances from the pointer. On non-Turbo models this indicates that the centrifugal advance mechanism is operating. On Turbo models the advance is controlled electronically.
8 On non-Turbo models run the engine at a fast idling speed, then reconnect the vacuum advance hose. The ignition timing should advance as the hose is connected, indicating that the vacuum capsule is functioning.

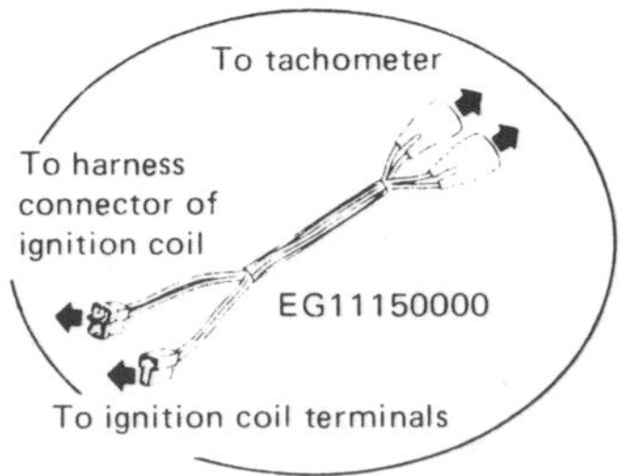

Fig. 4.15 Adaptor wiring to be fitted to Turbo models when checking the ignition timing (Sec 7)

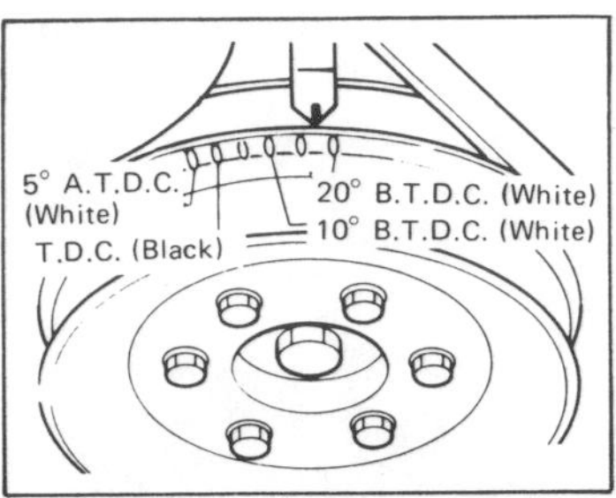

Fig. 4.16 Ignition timing marks (Sec 7)

7.5 Ignition timing marks on the crankshaft pulley

8 Ignition coil – general

1 The ignition coil changes low tension (LT) voltage to high tension (HT) voltage to provide a spark at the sparking plug. Maintenance is mininal and consists of cleaning the outer surfaces, particularly around the HT lead terminal. The high voltages generated can easily leak to earth over its surface and prevent the spark plugs functioning correctly. Water repellant sprays are now available to prevent dampness causing this type of malfunction.
2 The coil is mounted on the left-hand side of the engine compartment (photo). On Turbo models the ignition power transistor is mounted next to it.
3 Testing of the coil consists of checking the primary and secondary windings for continuity using an ohmmeter or low wattage test lamp. Using the ohmmeter the resistance of each circuit can be checked and compared with the information given in the Specifications. Note that the resistance will vary according to the ambient temperature.

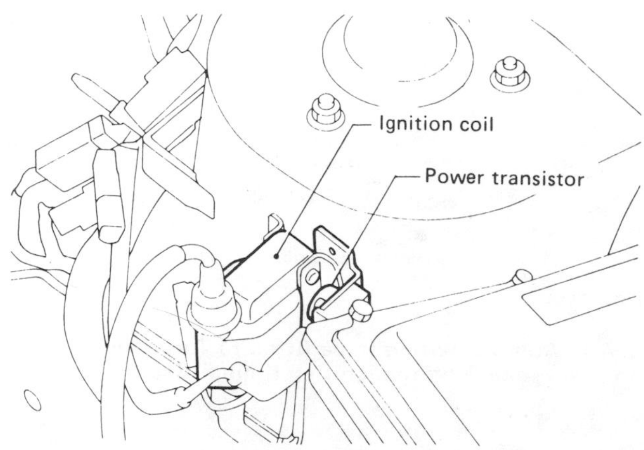

Fig. 4.17 Ignition coil location on Turbo models (Sec 8)

8.2 The ignition coil on non-Turbo models

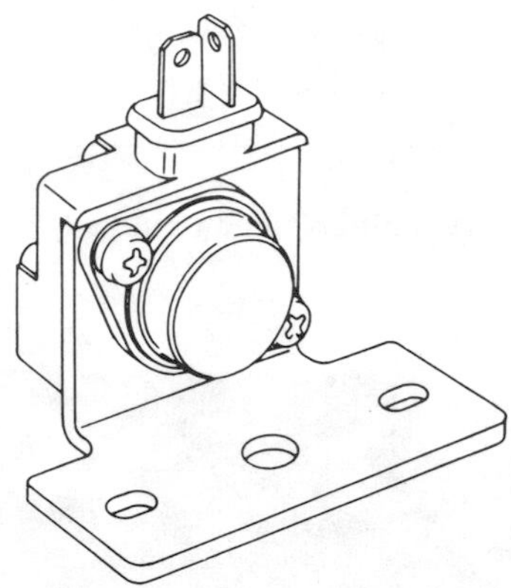

Fig. 4.18 Ignition power transistor on Turbo models (Sec 8)

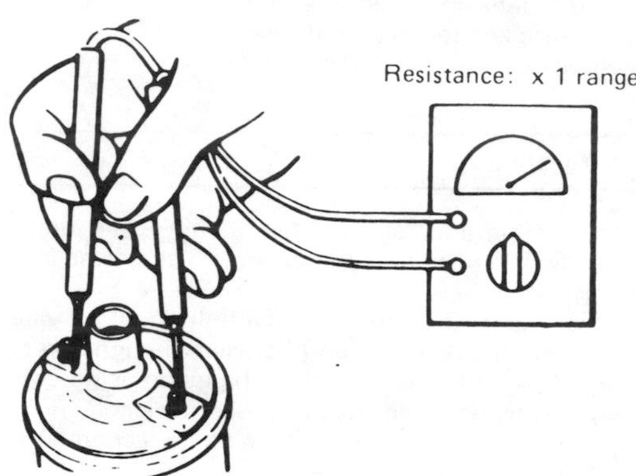

Fig. 4.19 Checking the coil primary resistance on non-Turbo models (Sec 8)

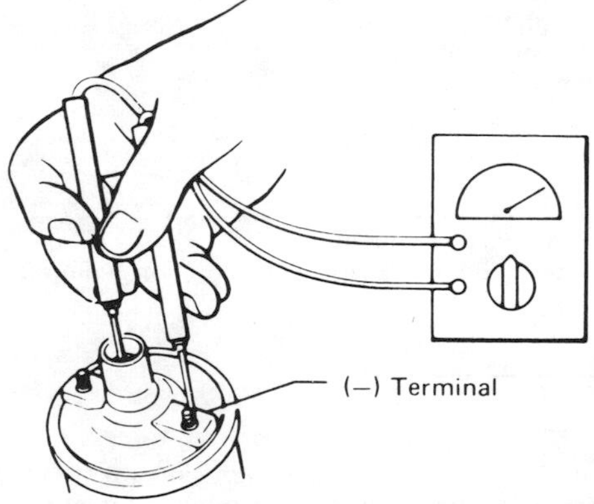

Fig. 4.20 Checking the coil secondary resistance on non-Turbo models (Sec 8)

Measuring plug gap. A feeler gauge of the correct size (see ignition system specifications) should have a slight 'drag' when slid between the electrodes. Adjust gap if necessary

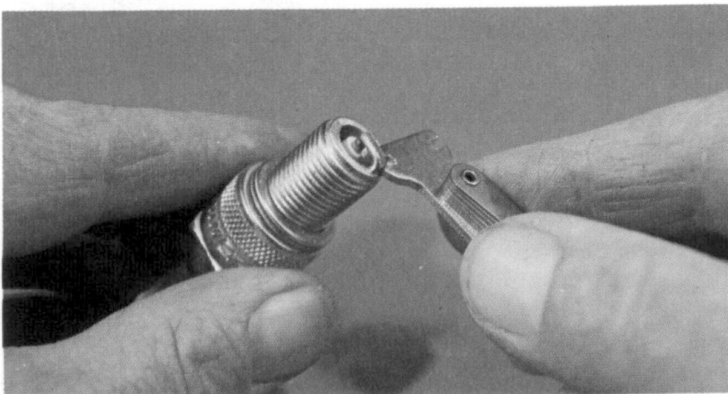

Adjusting plug gap. The plug gap is adjusted by bending the earth electrode inwards, or outwards, as necessary until the correct clearance is obtained. Note the use of the correct tool

Normal. Grey-brown deposits, lightly coated core nose. Gap increasing by around 0.001 in (0.025 mm) per 1000 miles (1600 km). Plugs ideally suited to engine, and engine in good condition

Carbon fouling. Dry, black, sooty deposits. Will cause weak spark and eventually misfire. Fault: over-rich fuel mixture. Check: carburettor mixture settings, float level and jet sizes; choke operation and cleanliness of air filter. Plugs can be re-used after cleaning

Oil fouling. Wet, oily deposits. Will cause weak spark and eventually misfire. Fault: worn bores/piston rings or valve guides; sometimes occurs (temporarily) during running-in period. Plugs can be re-used after thorough cleaning

Overheating. Electrodes have glazed appearance, core nose very white – few deposits. Fault: plug overheating. Check: plug value, ignition timing, fuel octane rating (too low) and fuel mixture (too weak). Discard plugs and cure fault immediately

Electrode damage. Electrodes burned away; core nose has burned, glazed appearance. Fault: pre-ignition. Check: as for 'Overheating' but may be more severe. Discard plugs and remedy fault before piston or valve damage occurs

Split core nose (may appear initially as a crack). Damage is self-evident, but cracks will only show after cleaning. Fault: pre-ignition or wrong gap-setting technique. Check: ignition timing, cooling system, fuel octane rating (too low) and fuel mixture (too weak). Discard plugs, rectify fault immediately

9 Spark plugs and distributor cap – general

1 The correct functioning of the spark plugs is vital for the correct running and efficiency of the engine. If after reference to Section 10 faulty spark plugs are indicated, remove them with reference to Section 2, then examine them as follows to determine the source of the fault.
2 If the insulator nose of the spark plug is clean and white with no deposits, this is indicative of a weak mixture, or too hot a plug (a hot plug transfers heat away from the electrode slowly, a cold plug transfers heat away quickly).
3 The plugs fitted as standard are specified at the beginning of this Chapter. If the top and insulator nose are covered with hard black-looking deposits, then this is indicative that the mixture is too rich. Should the plug be black and oily, then it is likely that the engine is fairly worn, as well as the mixture being too rich.
4 If the insulator nose is covered with light tan to greyish brown deposits, then the mixture is correct and it is likely that the engine is in good condition.
5 If there are any traces of long brown tapering stains on the outside of the white portion of the plug, then the plug will have to be renewed, as this shows that there is a faulty joint between the plug body and the insulator, and compression is being allowed to leak away.
6 If the distributor cap is indicated as being faulty after reference to Section 10, thoroughly clean it, then check between the HT terminal segments for fine black lines which would indicate conductance tracks. If evident, renew the cap.
7 If a suitable insulation tester is available, check that the resistance between any two terminal segments is a minimum of 50 Mohm.

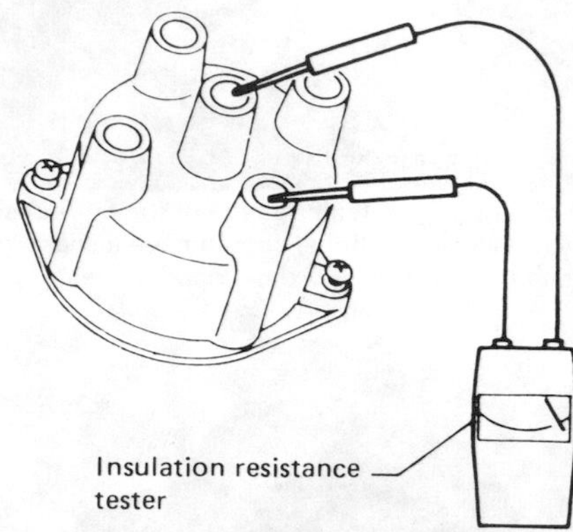

Fig. 4.21 Testing the distributor cap for insulation resistance (Sec 9)

10 Fault diagnosis – ignition system

Symptom	Reason(s)
Engine fails to start but turns over at normal speed	Disconnected coil HT lead Disconnected LT lead Ignition lead short-circuited Faulty power transistor or ECCS control unit (Turbo models)
Engine starts and runs but misfires	Faulty spark plug Cracked distributor cap Cracked rotor arm Incorrect spark plug gaps Faulty coil Intermittent open circuit Incorrect air gap adjustment (non-Turbo models)
Engine overheats	Ignition timing incorrect (retarded) Cracked vacuum advance hose (where applicable)
Engine 'pinks'	Ignition timing incorrect (advanced) Broken or weak centrifugal weight springs (where applicable)

Chapter 5 Clutch

Contents

Specifications

General

Type	Single dry plate with diaphragm spring pressure plate
Actuation:	
Carburettor models	Cable
Fuel-injection models	Hydraulic

Driven plate

Driven plate diameter:	
Carburettor models	200.0 mm (7.87 in)
Fuel-injection models	225.0 mm (8.86 in)
Driven plate run-out (maximum)	1.0 mm (0.039 in)

Clutch pedal

Clutch pedal height:	
Right-hand drive models	190.0 to 200.0 mm (7.48 to 7.87 in)
Left-hand drive models	171.0 to 181.0 mm (6.73 to 7.13 in)
Clutch pedal free play:	
Cable-operated	13.0 to 20.0 mm (0.51 to 0.79 in)
Hydraulically-operated	1.0 to 3.0 mm (0.04 to 0.12 in)

Torque wrench settings

Torque wrench settings	Nm	lbf ft
Master cylinder	10	7
Hydraulic union nut	17	13
Bleed screw	8	6
Slave cylinder	35	26
Flexible hose	19	14
Cable locknut	4	3
Cable bracket	10	7
Clutch cover bolts	26	19

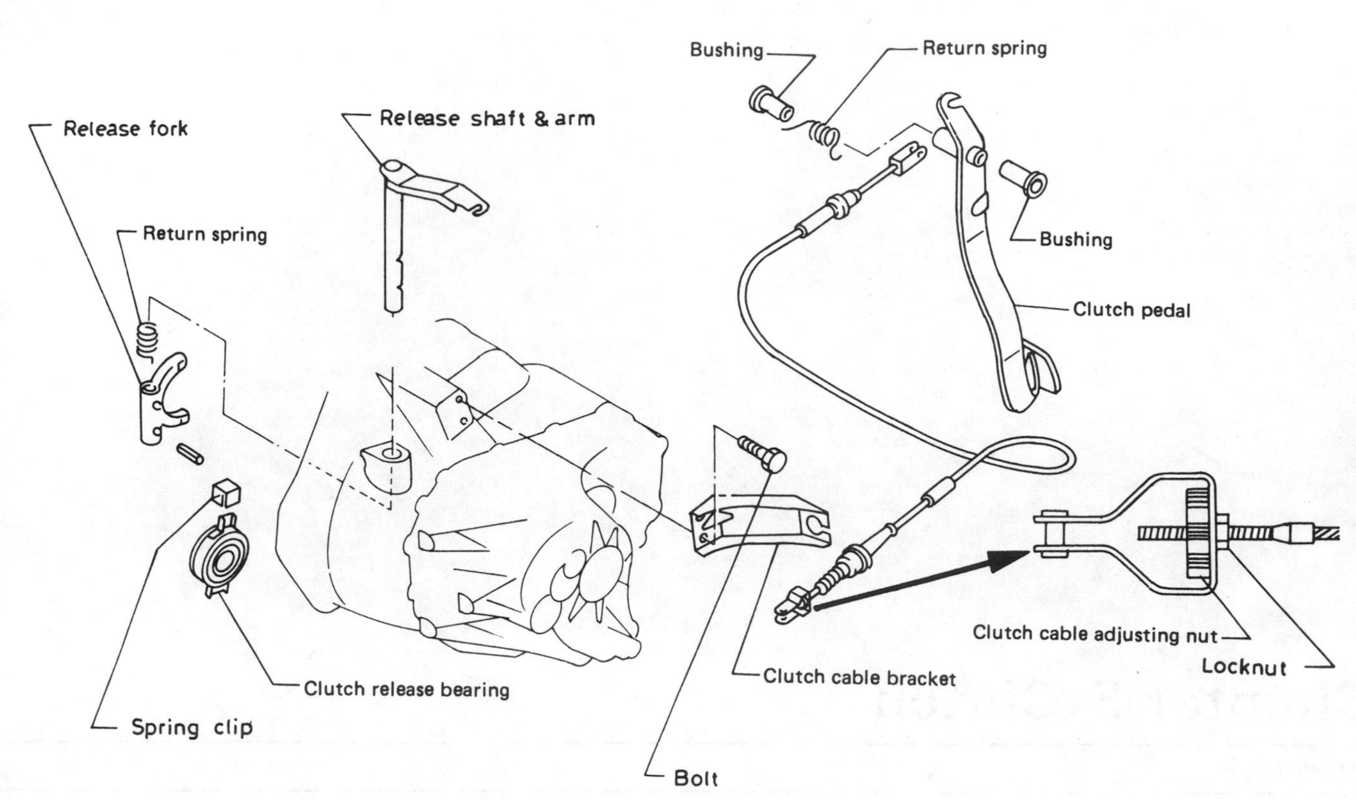

Fig. 5.1 Cable-operated clutch components (Sec 1)

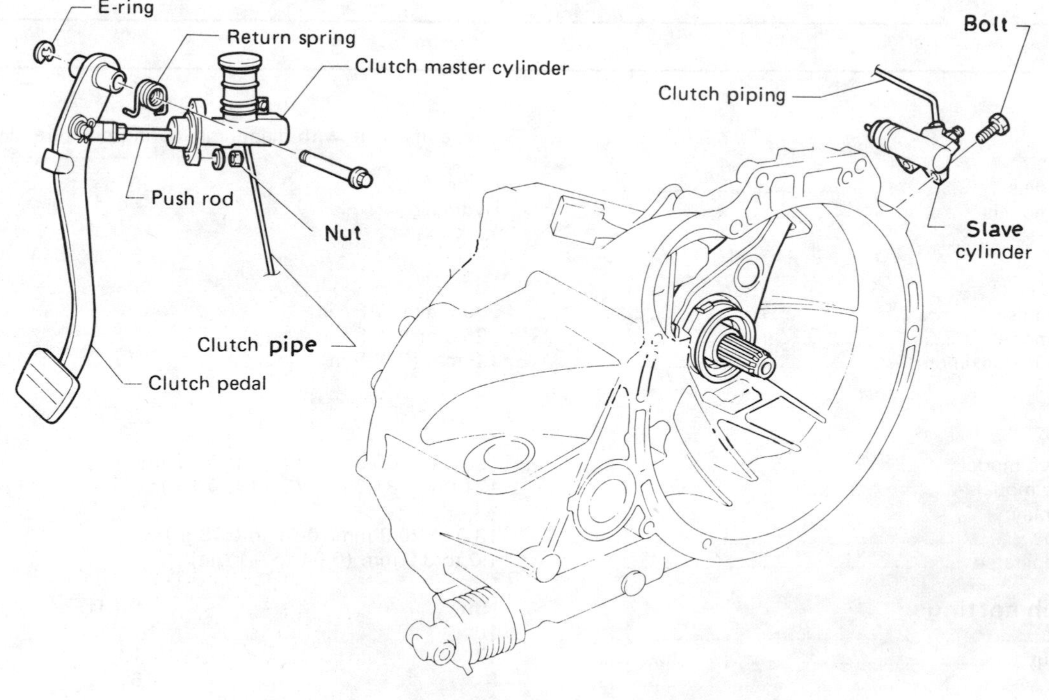

Fig. 5.2 Hydraulically-operated clutch components (Sec 1)

1 General description

The clutch is of single dry plate type with a diaphragm spring pressure plate. On all carburettor models the clutch is cable-operated, however on fuel-injection models it is hydraulically-operated. The clutch release bearing is of sealed ball type.

The clutch driven plate is located between the flywheel and the clutch pressure plate and it can slide on splines on the gearbox input shaft. When the clutch is engaged, the diaphragm spring forces the pressure plate to grip the driven plate against the flywheel and drive is transmitted from the crankshaft through the driven plate to the gearbox input shaft. On disengaging the clutch the pressure plate is lifted to release the driven plate with the result that the drive to the gearbox is disconnected.

The clutch is operated by a pendant foot pedal, connected to the release lever on the clutch bellhousing by either a cable or a hydraulic line with master and slave cylinders. Depressing the pedal causes the release lever to move the thrust bearing against the release fingers of the diaphragm spring in the pressure plate assembly. The spring is sandwiched between two rings which act as fulcrums. As the centre of the spring is moved in, the periphery moves out to lift the pressure plate and disengage the clutch. The reverse takes place when the pedal is released.

As wear of the clutch driven plate linings takes place, the pressure plate moves nearer the flywheel resulting in a corresponding movement of the release lever. On the cable-operated clutch, periodic adjustment is necessary to compensate for the wear, however on the hydraulic clutch automatic adjustment occurs at the master cylinder.

2 Routine maintenance

Carry out the following procedures at the intervals given in *'Routine Maintenance'* at the beginning of the Manual.

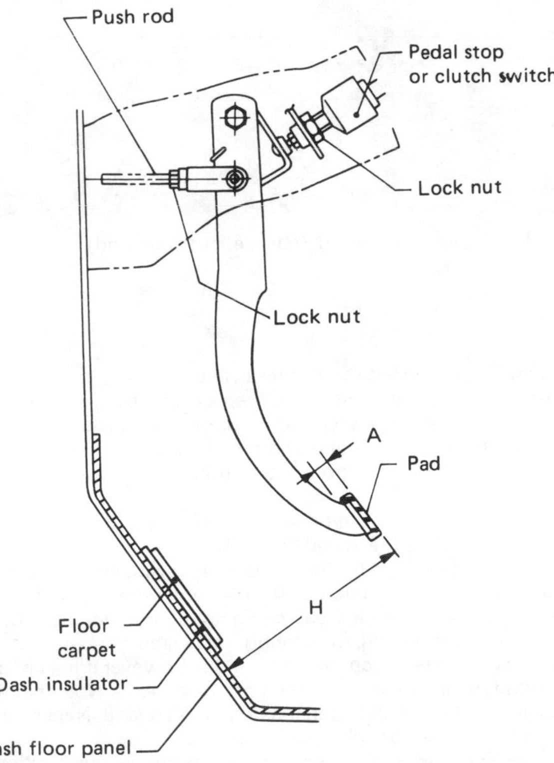

Fig. 5.3 Clutch pedal free height (H) and free play (A) dimensions. Hydraulic clutch pedal shown (Sec 2)

Hydraulic fluid level (fuel-injection models)

1 Check that the level of hydraulic fluid in the reservoir on the master cylinder is between the 'Min' and 'Max' marks. Note that the level will drop as the driven plate linings wear, however if the level drops below the 'Min' mark, or if constant topping-up is required, the complete hydraulic system should be checked for leaks. Use only new hydraulic fluid for topping-up purposes.

Clutch operation

2 Check that the clutch operation is smooth with no tendency to judder or slip. If necessary lubricate the clutch pedal pivot and the clutch cable where fitted.

3 With the clutch pedal released, check the free height dimension with reference to Fig. 5.3 and Specifications. Now depress the pedal to the point where resistance is felt and check that the free play dimension is also as given in Specifications. If adjustment is necessary, follow the procedure given later in this Section.

4 At the same time as checking the clutch operation, check as applicable the cable and bracket, clutch pedal, hydraulic lines, and master and slave cylinders for security, damage and deterioration.

Clutch adjustment

5 If the clutch pedal height as checked in paragraph 3 is incorrect, loosen the locknut and adjust the position of the stop bolt or switch as applicable. Tighten the locknut afterwards.

6 If the clutch pedal free play is incorrect proceed as follows.

7 On the cable-operated clutch loosen the locknut, then turn the knurled adjustment nut at the release lever arm end of the cable as required. The correct pedal free play is equivalent to 2.0 to 3.5 mm (0.079 to 0.138 in) play at the release lever arm, therefore the cable can be adjusted within the latter limits first, then the free play subsequently checked at the pedal. Tighten the locknut afterwards.

8 On the hydraulically-operated clutch, the free play is adjusted at the master cylinder pushrod attached to the clutch pedal. The pushrod is threaded into the clevis on the pedal and can be adjusted after loosening the locknut. Tighten the locknut afterwards.

3 Clutch cable – renewal

1 Turn the release lever arm on the transmission and unhook the cable clevis. If necessary, back off or remove the knurled adjustment nut to provide sufficient clearance (photos).

2 Working inside the car, reach up and disconnect the cable clevis from the top of the clutch pedal. Remove the small facia panel if necessary.

3 Release the cable from the bracket on the gearbox, then withdraw

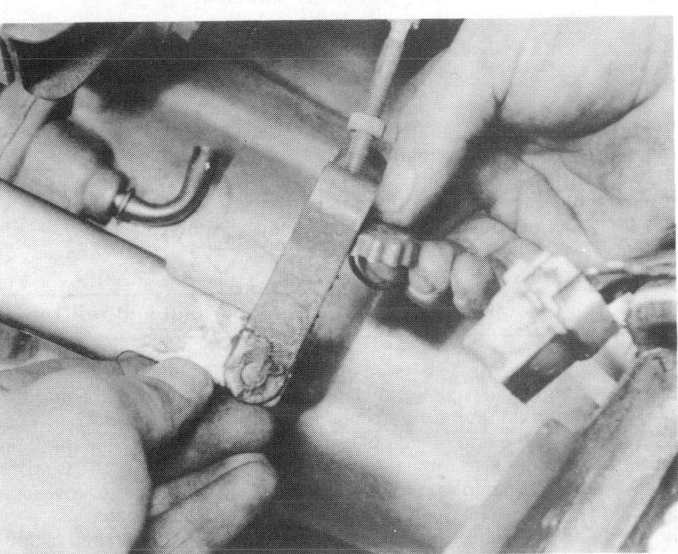

3.1A Removing the knurled adjustment nut

3.1B Release lever arm on the transmission with cable removed

3.3A Clutch cable bulkhead bracket (arrowed)

3.3B Clutch cable and support bracket on bulkhead

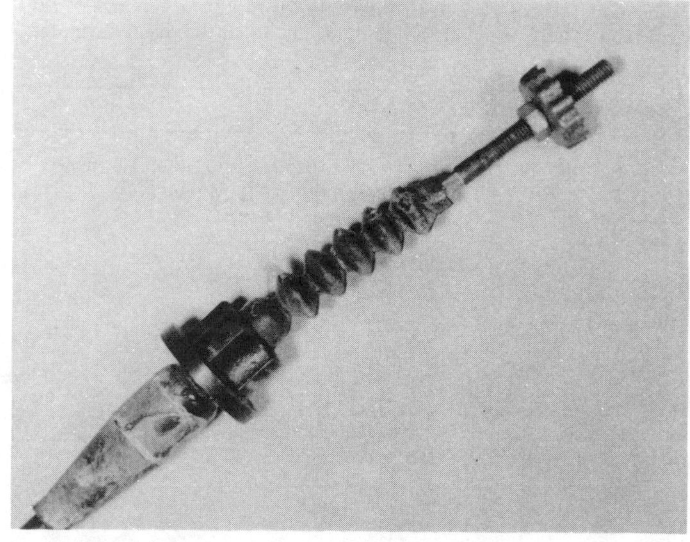

3.3C Clutch cable end fitting (release lever arm end)

the opposite end through the bulkhead bracket. Release the cable from the support bracket (photos).
4 Fit the new cable using a reversal of the removal procedure, but lubricate the end fittings with a little grease.
5 Finally adjust the cable with reference to Section 2.

4 Clutch master cylinder – removal, overhaul and refitting

1 Working inside the car, reach up under the facia and disconnect the clutch master cylinder pushrod clevis from the pedal, by extracting the spring clip and removing the clevis pin.
2 Working in the engine compartment, remove the cap from the fluid reservoir on the clutch master cylinder, and syphon out the fluid or soak it up with a clean rag. Do not spill the fluid on the car paintwork – if accidentally spilled, clean off immediately with cold water.
3 Place a container or rag beneath the master cylinder, then unscrew the union nut and disconnect the hydraulic outlet pipe.
4 Unscrew the mounting nuts, remove the washers and withdraw the master cylinder from the bulkhead.
5 Clean the exterior of the master cylinder.
6 Prise off the rubber dust cover, then extract the spring clip from the mouth of the master cylinder and withdraw the pushrod complete.
7 Loosen the retaining band and remove the fluid reservoir.
8 Unscrew the stop pin from the bottom of the master cylinder and recover the washers.
9 Extract the piston assembly and return spring, if necessary tapping the master cylinder on a wooden block.
10 With the master cylinder completely dismantled, clean all the components with methylated spirit or clean hydraulic fluid, then wipe dry and examine them for wear, damage and deterioration. Check the cylinder bore and piston for scoring, wear and corrosion. If evident, renew the complete clutch master cylinder, however if the components are in good order, obtain a repair kit of rubber seals. Note that there are two types of master cylinder, namely Tokico and Nabco, and it is important to fit the correct type of repair kit.
11 Prise the rubber seals from the piston, noting the position of the sealing lips, then dip the new seals in clean hydraulic fluid and fit them to the piston using the fingers only to manipulate them into position.
12 Remove the clevis from the pushrod, fit the new rubber dust cover, then refit the clevis in the same position.

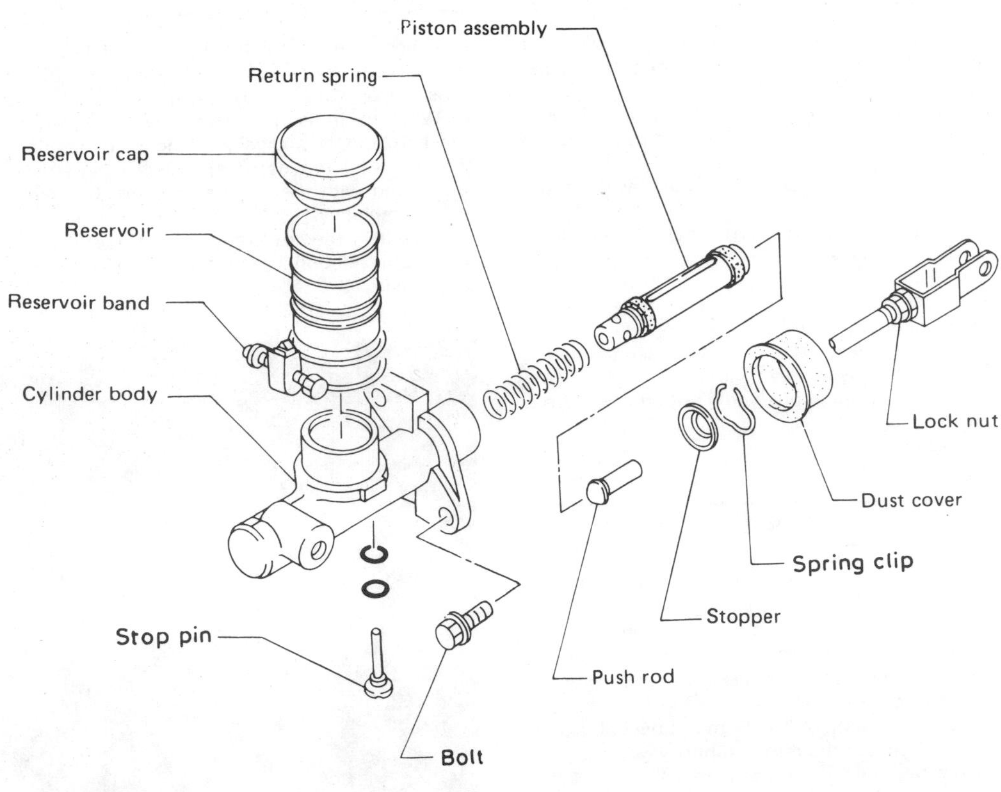

Fig. 5.4 Exploded view of the clutch master cylinder (Sec 4)

13 Locate the return spring on the piston, then insert both items in the master cylinder bore, making sure that the stop pin slot in the piston is aligned with the hole in the cylinder. As the seals enter the bore make sure that the lips are not damaged or deformed.
14 Hold the piston depressed, then refit the stop pin and washers.
15 Refit the fluid reservoir and tighten the retaining band.
16 Insert the pushrod assembly, then refit the spring clip and rubber dust cover.
17 Refitting is a reversal of removal, but lubricate the pushrod clevis pin with a little grease. Finally bleed the hydraulic system as described in Section 6, and adjust the clutch pedal height and free play as described in Section 2.

5 Clutch slave cylinder – removal, overhaul and refitting

1 Remove the cap from the hydraulic fluid reservoir on the clutch master cylinder, then tighten it down onto a piece of polythene. This will reduce the loss of fluid in subsequent operations. Alternatively, a hose clamp can be fitted to the flexible hose near the gearbox.
2 Place some rag under the slave cylinder, then unscrew the union nut and disconnect the rigid hydraulic line.
3 Unscrew the mounting nuts and remove the guard plate where fitted. Withdraw the slave cylinder from the transmission, taking care not to spill hydraulic fluid on the car paintwork.
4 Clean the exterior of the slave cylinder.
5 Prise off the rubber dust cover, then extract the pushrod followed by the piston and seal and the return spring.
6 With the slave cylinder completely dismantled clean all the components with methylated spirit or clean hydraulic fluid, then wipe dry and examine them for wear, damage and deterioration. Check the cylinder bore and piston for scoring, wear and corrosion. If evident, renew the complete clutch slave cylinder, however if the components are in good order obtain a repair kit of rubber seals.
7 Prise the rubber seal from the piston, noting the position of the sealing lip, then dip the new seal in clean hydraulic fluid and fit it to the piston using the fingers only to manipulate it into position.
8 Locate the return spring on the piston, then insert both items into the slave cylinder bore. Make sure that the seal is not damaged as it enters the bore.
9 Fit the new dust cover to the pushrod, then locate the pushrod in the piston and ease the dust cover into the groove on the slave cylinder.
10 Refitting is a reversal of removal, but lubricate the end of the pushrod with a little grease. Finally bleed the hydraulic system as described in Section 6.

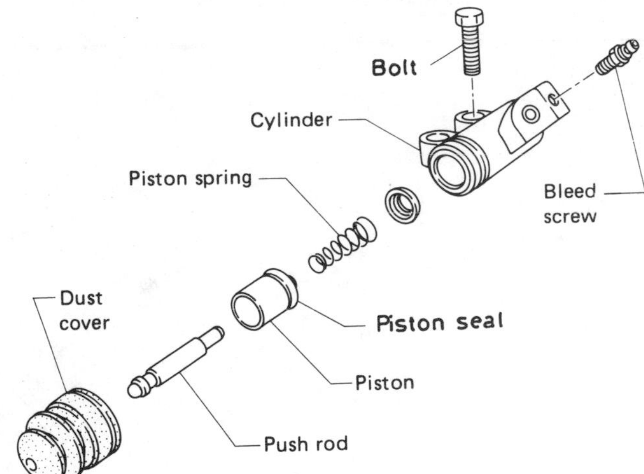

Fig. 5.5 Exploded view of the clutch slave cylinder (Sec 5)

6 Clutch hydraulic system – bleeding

Note: *Refer to Chapter 9 for details of the equipment required for bleeding the brake hydraulic system as it is identical for bleeding the clutch hydraulic system.*

1 Top up the hydraulic fluid reservoir. During the bleeding procedure the level must not be allowed to drop below the 'Min' mark on the reservoir.

2 Connect the bleed tube to the bleed screw on the slave cylinder with its free end in a suitable container.

3 Have an assistant fully depress the clutch pedal several times, keeping it depressed on the final stroke.

4 Unscrew the bleed screw and allow the trapped air and fluid to flow into the container. The assistant should continue to depress the clutch pedal, finally holding it against the floor.

5 Tighten the bleed screw, then have the assistant release the pedal. Top up the hydraulic fluid level as necessary.

6 Repeat the procedure given in paragraphs 3 to 5 until the fluid from the slave cylinder is free of air bubbles.

7 Disconnect the bleed tube.

7 Clutch pedal – removal and refitting

1 On the cable-operated clutch, disconnect the cable from the top of the clutch pedal with reference to Section 3.

2 On the hydraulically-operated clutch, reach up under the facia and disconnect the clutch master cylinder pushrod clevis from the pedal, by extracting the spring clip and removing the clevis pin.

3 Unhook the return spring from the pedal.

4 Unscrew the nut and remove the pivot bolt from the pedal bracket, then lower the clutch pedal. Remove the return spring.

5 Remove the brakes from the pedal.

6 Clean the bushes and pivot bolt and check them for wear and damage. Check the return spring for tension. Renew the components as necessary.

7 Refitting is a reversal of removal, however lubricate the bushes, pivot bolt, and clevis pin with a little grease, and finally adjust the clutch pedal height and free play as described in Section 2.

8 Clutch – removal

1 Unless the complete engine/transmission is being removed for major overhaul, access to the clutch is obtained by removing the transmission (Chapter 6) leaving the engine in place.

2 With the transmission removed, unscrew the clutch cover bolts, one half turn at a time working in diametrically opposite sequence (photo). As soon as the point is reached where the bolts can be unscrewed with the fingers, support the cover and then remove the bolts completely.

3 Withdraw the cover and catch the driven plate. There is only need to mark the relationship of the cover to the flywheel if the cover is to be used again.

8.2 View of clutch cover showing splined hub of driven plate through centre

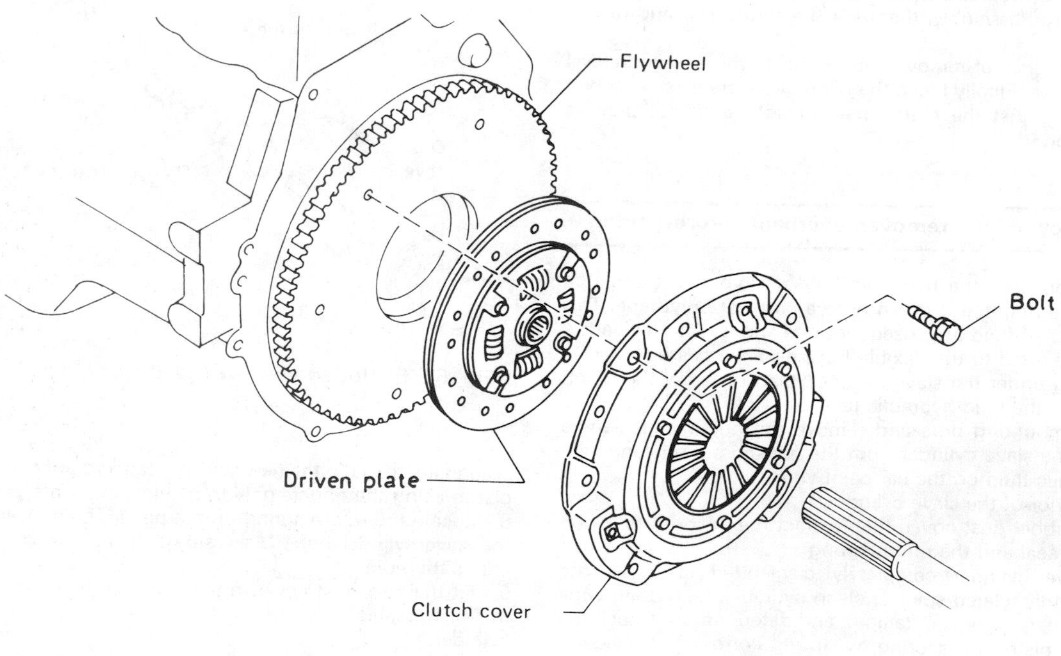

Fig. 5.6 Exploded view of the clutch driven plate and cover (Sec 8)

9 Clutch – inspection

1 Check the driven plate linings for wear or oil contamination. If the distance from the lining surface to any one of the rivet heads is less than 0.3 mm (0.012 in), the plate should be renewed. Also check the condition of the centre hub and torsion springs. If the linings are contaminated with oil, renew the faulty engine or transmission oil seal before fitting the new plate.
2 Check the pressure plate cover assembly for wear. Shake the assembly and listen for loose components indicating excessive wear. Also check the machined faces of the pressure plate and flywheel for scoring, cracks and discolouration. The latter can sometimes be removed with emery paper. Renew the cover assembly and flywheel as necessary.
3 With the clutch removed, check the release bearing in the bellhousing by spinning it. If any noise or roughness is apparent, renew the bearing as described in Section 10.

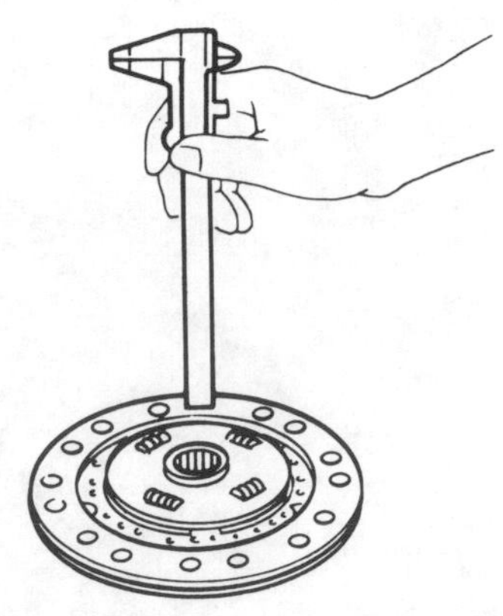

Fig. 5.7 Using a vernier gauge to check the rivet head depth on the driven plate (Sec 9)

10 Clutch release bearing – renewal

Cable-operated clutch

1 Prise the spring clip over the release fork arms, then slide the release bearing off of the guide sleeve (photo).
2 Clean the guide sleeve.
3 Pull the spring clips from the bearing and fit them to the new bearing.
4 Apply a *small* amount of molybdenum disulphide grease to the surfaces of the bearing which contact the guide sleeve and diaphragm spring fingers.
5 Locate the release bearing on the guide sleeve, then press the spring clips over the release fork arms.

Hydraulically-operated clutch

6 The procedure is similar to that for the cable-operated clutch, however due to the different release fork, the bearing retaining springs are also different.

10.1 Clutch release bearing and retaining clips

11 Clutch release fork – removal and refitting

1 Remove the release bearing as previously described.

Cable-operated clutch

2 Turn the release shaft until the fork retaining pins can be driven out into the small recesses in the face of the clutch housing. Drive out the pins. On early models the fork retaining roll pins are of the double type, whereas on later models they are single (photos).

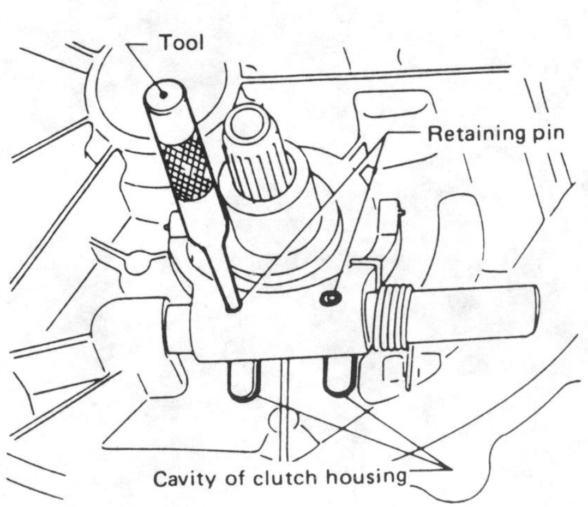

Fig. 5.8 Driving out the release fork retaining pins on the cable-operated clutch (Sec 11)

11.2A Clutch release fork outer roll pin ...

11.2B ... and inner roll pin (early models only)

11.3 Removing the release lever arm and shaft

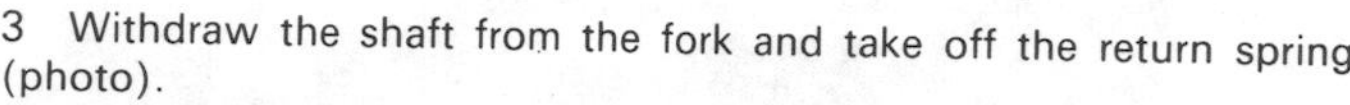

3 Withdraw the shaft from the fork and take off the return spring (photo).

4 Refitting of the components is a reversal of removal. Apply grease to the cross-shaft bushes and make sure that the return spring is correctly located.

Hydraulically-operated clutch

5 Insert the fingers behind the fork and over the retaining spring, then pull the fork from the ball-stud.

6 Withdraw the fork from inside the bellhousing. If necessary prise the rubber grommet from the aperture in the bellhousing.

7 Refitting the release fork is a reversal of removal, but apply a little grease to the ball-stud and the slave cylinder pushrod contact point.

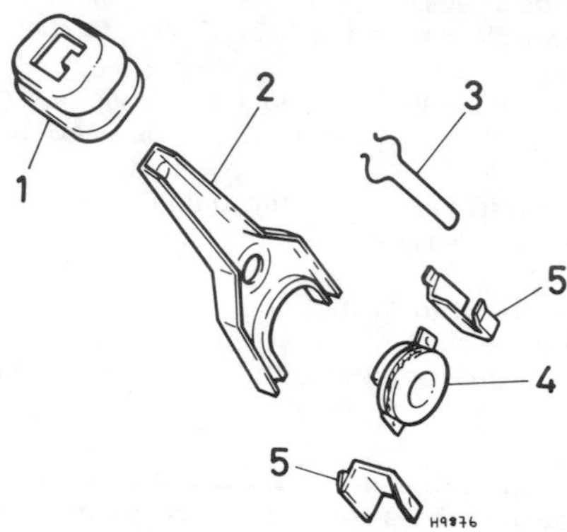

Fig. 5.9 Release fork components on the hydraulically-operated clutch (Sec 11)

1 Rubber grommet
2 Release fork
3 Retaining spring
4 Release bearing
5 Spring clips

12 Clutch – refitting

1 Make sure that the friction faces of the flywheel and pressure plate are clean. Use solvent to remove any protective grease.

2 Hold the driven plate against the flywheel so that the greater projecting boss is towards the flywheel, and the spring hub assembly faces away from the flywheel.

3 Offer up the clutch cover and locate it on its dowels.

4 Screw in the clutch cover screws evenly, but only finger tight at this stage.

5 The clutch driven plate must now be centralised in order that the transmission input shaft will be able to pass through the splined hub of the plate when the transmission is being connected to the engine.

6 Although the front end of the gearbox input shaft is not supported in the bush in the centre of the flywheel mounting flange, the bush can be used to engage a clutch alignment tool (photo). Pass the clutch alignment tool through the splined hub of the driven plate and engage the end of the tool in the pilot bearing in the end of the crankshaft flange. This will have the effect of sliding the driven plate sideways and so centralising it so that the transmission input shaft will pass through it without obstruction. Clutch alignment tools can be purchased from motor accessory stores or one can be made up from a length of dowelling or rod using tape wound around it to match the diameter of the splined hole in the hub of the driven plate.

7 Once the alignment tool is an easy sliding fit in the hub, tighten the clutch cover bolts to the specified torque. Remove the tool.

8 Apply a *small* amount of grease to the splines of the input shaft, then refit the transmission as described in Chapter 6.

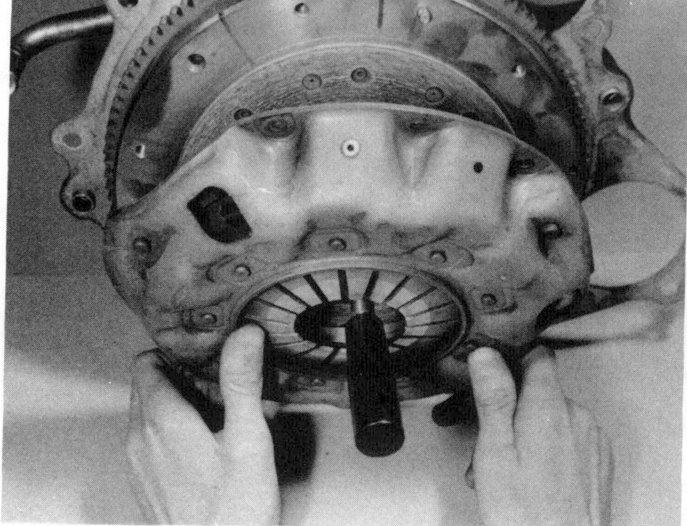

12.6 Fitting the clutch cover, showing the alignment tool fitted to the driven plate

13 Fault diagnosis – clutch

Symptom	Reason(s)
Judder when taking up drive	Loose engine or transmission mountings Badly worn or oil contaminated friction linings Worn splines on transmission input shaft or driven plate hub
Clutch drag (failure to disengage – gears cannot be meshed)	Incorrect cable adjustment Loss of hydraulic fluid or air in system Rust on transmission input shaft splines or driven plate splines Incorrect clutch pedal adjustment Damaged or misaligned pressure plate assembly
Clutch slip (increase in engine speed does not result in increase in road speed – particularly on gradients)	Incorrect cable adjustment Incorrect clutch pedal adjustment Friction linings worn out or contaminated with oil
Noise evident on depressing clutch pedal	Dry, worn or damaged release bearing Excessive play between driven plate splines and input shaft splines Loose driven plate torsion springs
Noise evident as clutch pedal released	Distorted driven plate Damaged driven plate linings

Chapter 6 Manual transmission

Contents

Specifications

General

Type	Transversely-mounted on left-hand side of engine compartment. Five forward speeds and reverse. Synchromesh on all forward gears. Floor-mounted gearchange
Designation:	
Non-Turbo models	RS5F31A
Turbo models	RS5F50A

Ratios

	RS5F31A	RS5F50A
1st	3.063:1	3.400:1
2nd	1.826:1	1.955:1
3rd	1.207:1	1.272:1
4th	0.902:1	0.911:1
5th	0.733:1	0.740:1
Reverse	3.417:1	3.428:1
Final drive ratio:		
1.8 (Non-Turbo)	4.056:1	
2.0 and Turbo	3.895:1	

Oil capacity

RS5F31A	2.7 litres (4.8 pints)
RS5F50A	4.7 litres (8.3 pints)

Torque wrench settings

	Nm	lbf ft
Transmission to engine:		
RS5F31A	35	26
RS5F50A	51	38
Speedometer pinion	5	4
Control rod	18	13
Support rod	31	23
Clutch housing to transmission casing	19	14
Reverse lever assembly	19	14
Detent plugs	19	14
Final gear crownwheel	81	60
Drain plug and filler plug	25	19
Position switch	5	4
Reversing lamp switch	25	19

PART A: ALL MODELS

1 General description

The manual transmission is of five-speed type mounted transversely on the left-hand side of the engine. Both the 4th and 5th speeds are overdrive ratios.

Synchromesh is provided on all forward gears and gear selection is by means of a floor-mounted gear lever.

Power is transmitted from the clutch through the input shaft and mainshaft to the final drive/differential which is an integral part of the transmission.

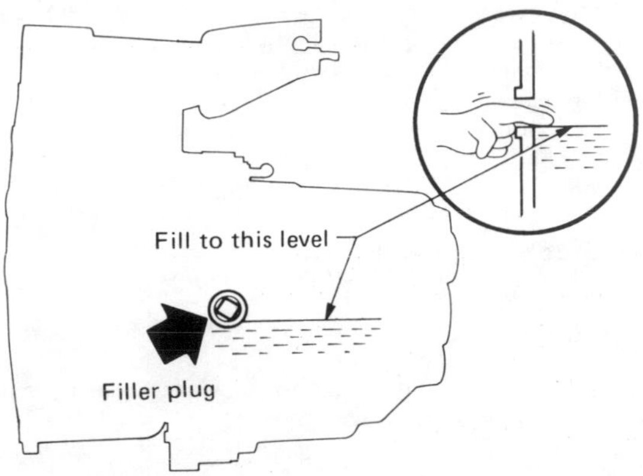

Fig. 6.1 Oil level check on non-Turbo models (Sec 2)

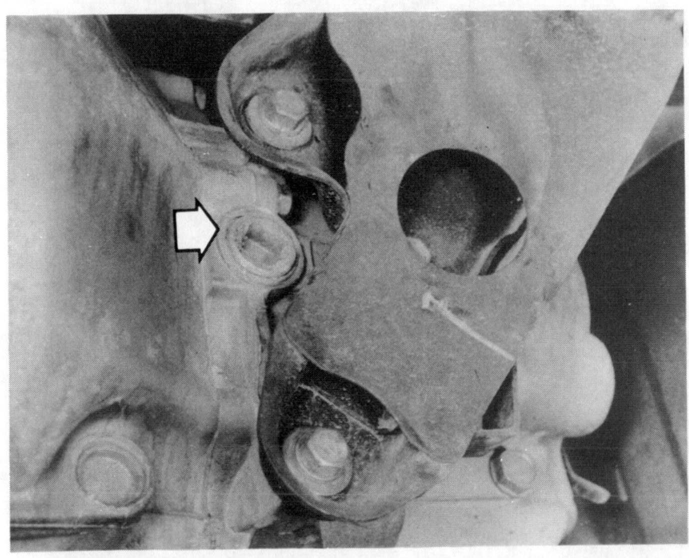

2.2 Filler plug location (RS5F31A)

2 Routine maintenance

Carry out the following procedures at the intervals given in *'Routine Maintenance'* at the beginning of the Manual.

Oil level check

1 For ease of checking and topping-up, position the car over an inspection pit or on ramps, but ensure that it is level.

2 **On non-Turbo models** use a square key to unscrew the filler plug from the front of the transmission (photo). Using a finger, check that the oil level is up to the bottom of the filler plug hole. If not, top up with the correct oil as necessary, then refit and tighten the plug.

3 **On Turbo models** disconnect the speedometer cable from the transmission (Chapter 12), then unscrew the bolt and withdraw the pinion assembly from the right-hand rear of the transmission. Refer to Fig. 6.3 and check that the oil level is between the minimum and maximum limits. If not, top up with the correct oil as necessary, then refit the pinion assembly and reconnect the speedometer cable.

4 At the same time check the transmission casing and joints for any sign of oil leakage.

Oil change

5 Position the car over an inspection pit or on ramps. Place a suitable container beneath the transmission.

6 **On non-Turbo models** use a square key to unscrew the drain plug from the bottom left-hand side of the transmission (photo).

7 **On Turbo models** unscrew the drain plug bolt from the bottom right-hand side of the transmission.

8 Allow all of the oil to drain, then wipe clean the drain plug and tighten it in the transmission casing.

9 Refer to paragraphs 1 to 4 and fill the transmission with the correct grade and quantity of oil.

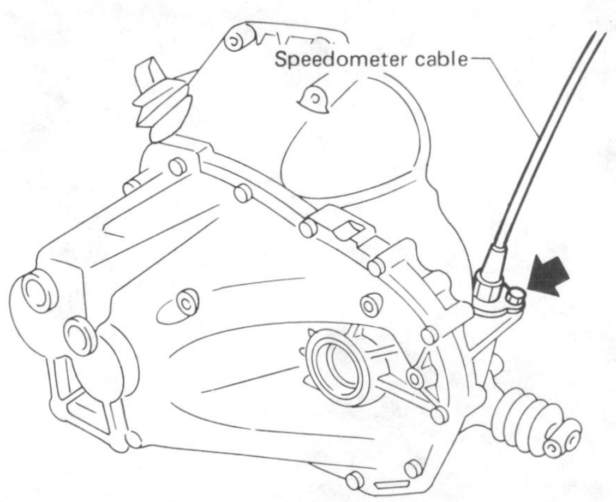

Fig. 6.2 Remove the speedometer pinion assembly to check the oil level on Turbo models (Sec 2)

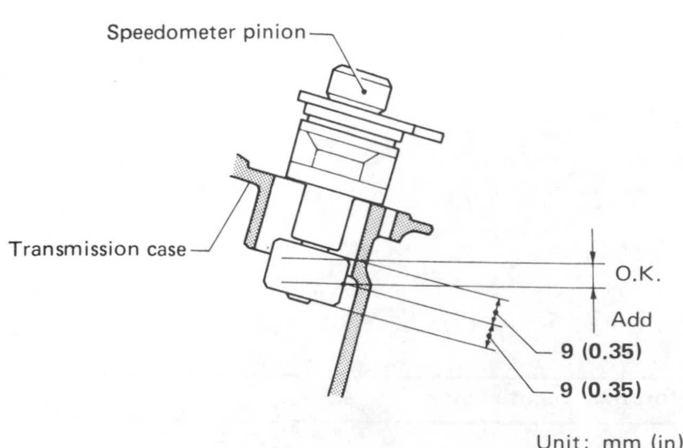

Fig. 6.3 Oil level check on Turbo models (Sec 2)

Fig. 6.4 Drain plug location on Turbo models (Sec 2)

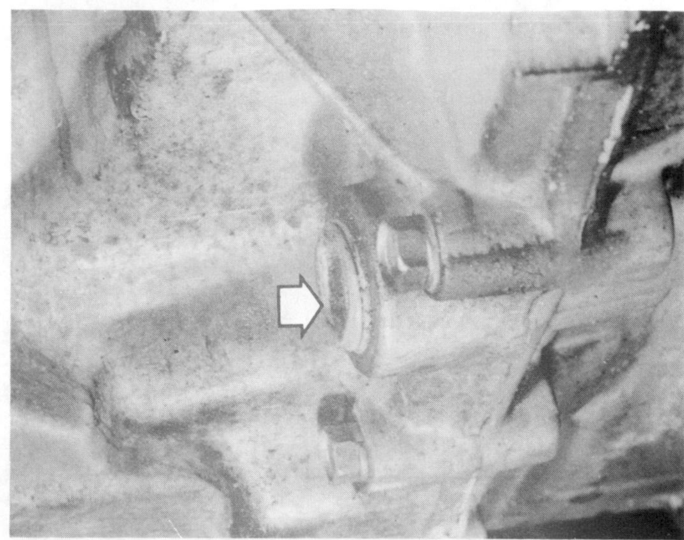

2.6 Drain plug location (RS5F31A)

3 Gearchange lever and linkage – removal and refitting

1 Apply the handbrake, then jack up the front of the car and support on axle stands.
2 Remove the centre console as described in Chapter 11. Unscrew the gear lever knob in order to remove the gaiter.
3 Remove the exhaust system as described in Chapter 3.
4 Unbolt the exhaust heat shield from the underbody.
5 Disconnect both the control rod and support rod from the transmission (Fig. 6.5) (photo).
6 Unscrew the pivot bolt from the gear lever end of the control rod, then disconnect the return spring and remove the rod (photo).
7 Prise the gear lever boot from the underbody (photo).
8 Unbolt the gear lever holder, then withdraw the gear lever and support rod from under the car.
9 Unscrew the nuts to separate the socket from the support rod and remove the gear lever components.
10 Refitting is a reversal of removal, but apply a little grease to the gear lever, socket and control rod pivot bolts.

3.5A Control rod and yoke at the transmission end (RS5F31A)

3.5B Support rod mounting at the transmission end (RS5F31A)

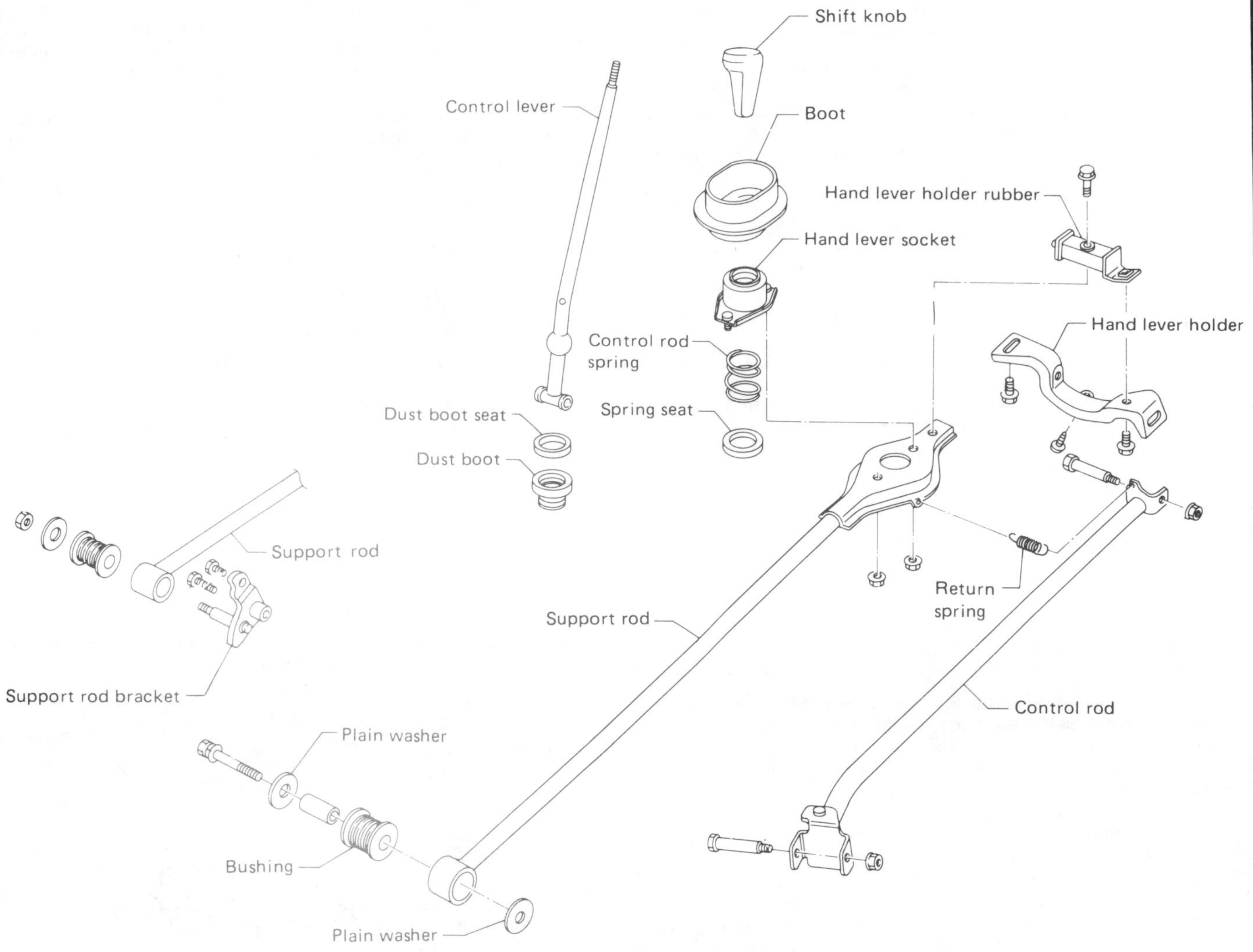

Shift knob
Control lever
Boot
Hand lever holder rubber
Hand lever socket
Hand lever holder
Control rod spring
Spring seat
Dust boot seat
Dust boot
Support rod
Return spring
Support rod
Support rod bracket
Control rod
Plain washer
Bushing
Plain washer

Fig. 6.5 Gearchange components (Sec 3)

3.6 View of gear lever linkages from under the car

3.7 Gear lever and boot

4 Differential side oil seals – removal

1 The differential side oil seals can be renewed without removing the transmission. First remove the driveshaft as described in Chapter 8.
2 Prise out the oil seal. If difficulty is experienced, use a claw-type extractor as shown in Fig. 6.6. Clean the oil seal seating.
3 Dip the new oil seal in gear oil, then drive it squarely into the transmission casing using a piece of tubing.
4 Refit the driveshaft with reference to Chapter 8.

5 Selector rod oil seal – renewal

1 Apply the handbrake, then jack up the front of the car and support on axle stands.
2 Disconnect the gearchange control rod from the selector rod by unscrewing the pivot bolt.
3 Using a suitable pin punch, drive out the roll pin securing the yoke to the end of the selector rod. Pull off the yoke.
4 Prise the oil seal from the transmission casing, or if necessary use a suitable drift to remove it.
5 Wipe clean the oil seal seating.
6 Dip the new oil seal in gear oil, then drive it squarely into the transmission casing using a piece of tubing.
7 Refit the yoke and gearchange control rod using a reversal of the removal procedure, but apply a little grease to the pivot bolt.

6 Transmission – removal and refitting

1 Remove the battery (Chapter 12) and unbolt the battery tray.
2 Remove both drivehsafts as described in Chapter 8.
3 Remove the engine compartment undershield.
4 Drain the transmission oil with reference to Section 2. Clean and refit the drain plug when complete.
5 Disconnect the clutch cable or hydraulic sleeve cylinder with reference to Chapter 5.
6 Disconnect the gearchange control and support rods from the transmission by removing the pivot bolts.
7 Disconnect the speedometer cable (Chapter 12).
8 Disconnect the wiring from the position switch, reversing lamp switch, and overdrive switch as applicable (photo). Remove the starter motor (Chapter 12).
9 Unbolt the shield from the inner side of the left-hand front wing.
10 Support the weight of the transmission either with a trolley jack or hoist. To prevent damage to the engine mountings, support the engine on a jack placed under the sump pan using an interposed wooden block.

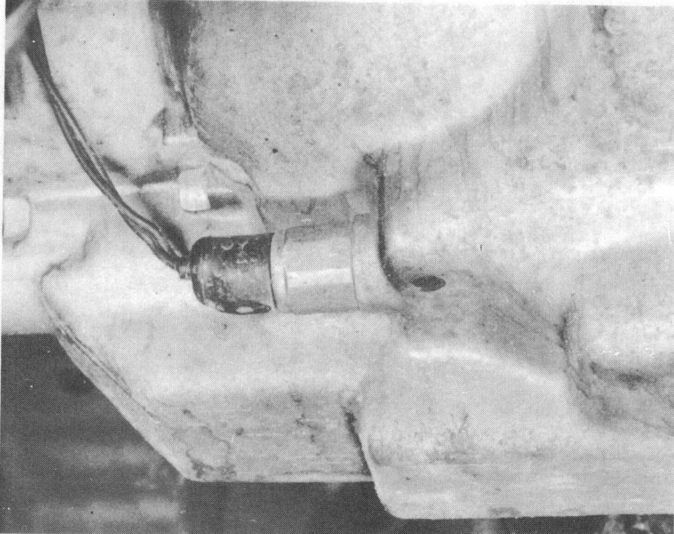

6.8 Reversing lamp switch location (RS5F31A)

11 Unbolt the front transmission mounting from the front panel, then unbolt the mounting and bracket from the front of the transmission.
12 Unscrew and remove the bolts connecting the transmission to the engine, noting the position of the engine stay and exhaust support bracket.
13 Withdraw the transmission from the engine, keeping it horizontal to prevent any damage to the clutch. When clear of the engine, lower the transmission to the ground.

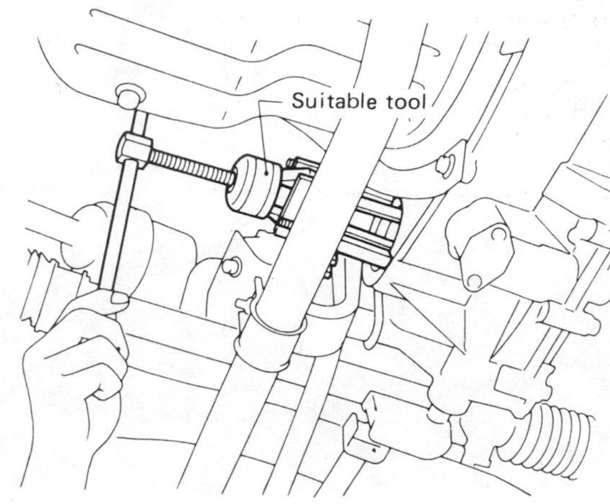

Fig. 6.6 Using an extractor to remove a differential side oil seal (Sec 4)

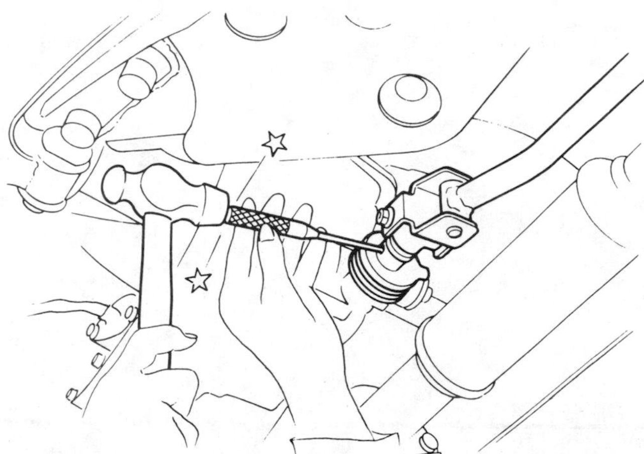

Fig. 6.7 Driving out the selector rod yoke roll pin (Sec 5)

Fig. 6.8 Removing the transmission (Sec 6)

14 Refitting is a reversal of removal. If the clutch has been removed, it must be correctly refitted and centralised as described in Chapter 5. Fill the transmission with the correct grade and quantity of oil. Adjust the clutch cable as described in Chapter 5.

PART B: NON-TURBO MODELS

7 Transmission (RS5F31A) – dismantling

1 With the transmission removed from the vehicle, clean away external dirt using a water-soluble solvent or paraffin and a stiff brush.
2 Drain the transmission oil if not drained previously.
3 With the unit standing on the flange of the clutch bellhousing, unscrew the casing-to-bellhousing bolts and withdraw the casing from the bellhousing. Tilt the casing slightly as it is withdrawn, to prevent the selector fork jamming inside the casing. If the casing is stuck, tap it off carefully, to break the joint, using a plastic hammer.

Transmission casing

4 Unscrew and remove the reverse lamp, and if fitted the overdrive switches.
5 Remove the oil trough.
6 If the input shaft rear bearing is to be renewed, remove the very small welch plug from the transmission casing. Do this by drilling a hole in the plug and then screw in a self-tapping screw. The screw will probably force out the plug or its head can be used to lever it out (photos).

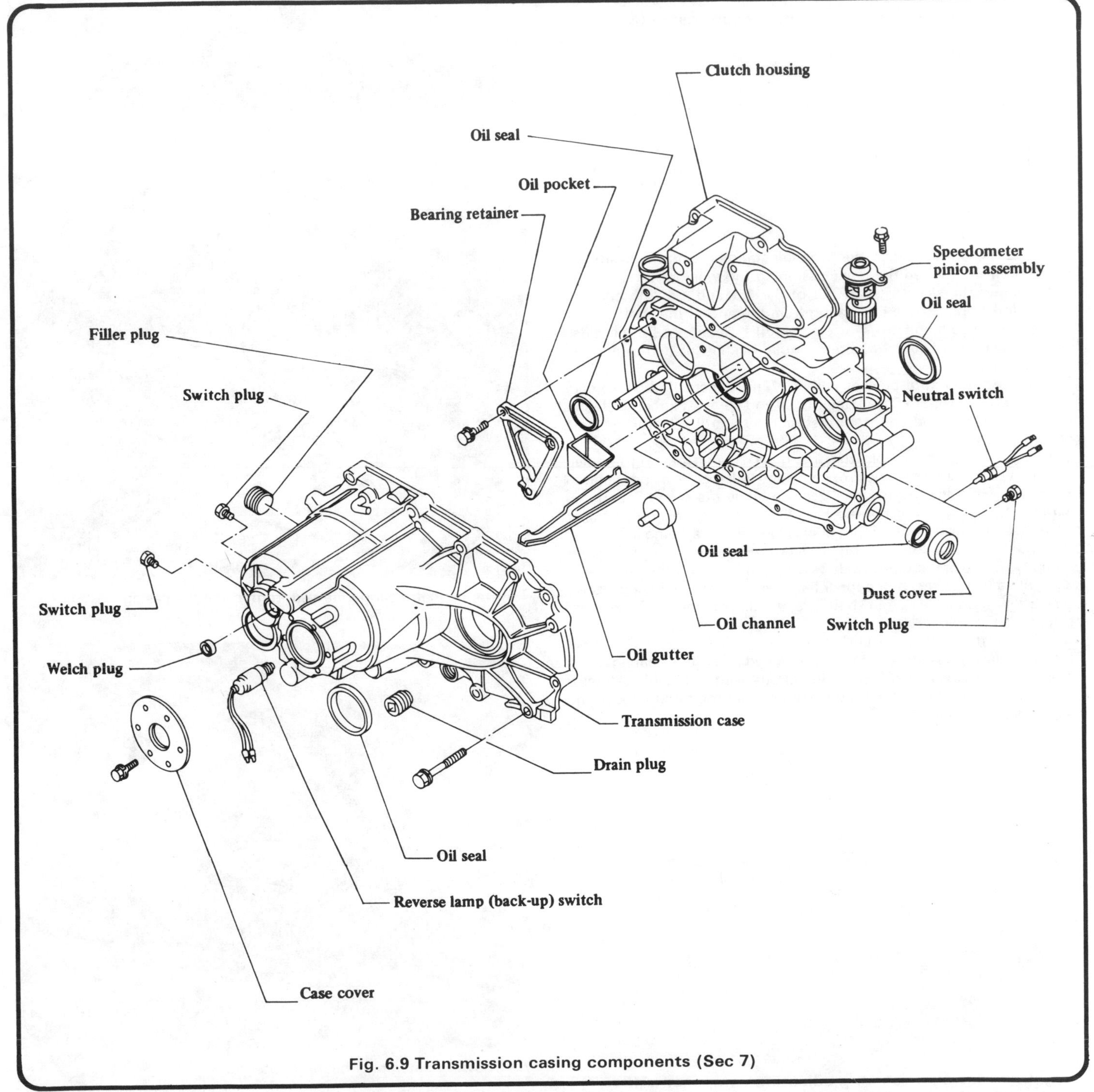

Fig. 6.9 Transmission casing components (Sec 7)

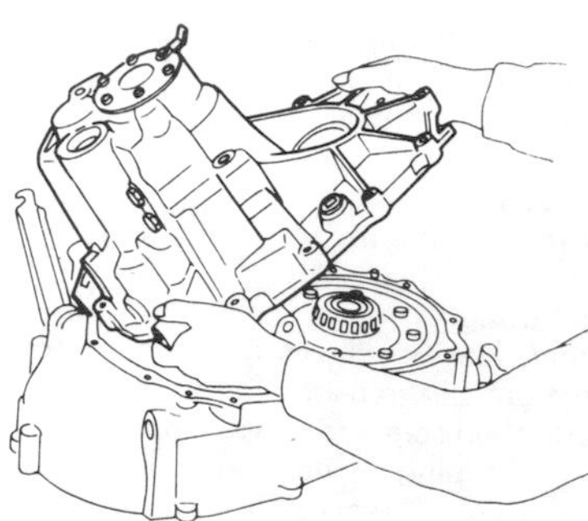

Fig. 6.10 Withdrawing the transmission casing (Sec 7)

7 Unbolt the circular cover from the casing and take out the spacer and the mainshaft bearing adjusting shim. If the mainshaft bearing is to be renewed, drive out the old outer track and fit the new one.
8 If the differential side bearings are to be renewed, drive the bearing outer track from the transmission casing. A new oil seal will be required (photo).

Clutch housing

9 The clutch housing will have been left standing with the geartrains projecting from it when the transmission casing was drawn off.
10 Withdraw the selector shaft out of the 1st/2nd, 3rd/4th and 5th selector forks. Extract the coil spring from the end of the shaft.
11 Remove the 5th and 3rd/4th selector forks. Retain the plastic slides from the forks. Do not lose the rectangular bushes located in the fork arm cut-outs.
12 Remove the control bracket with 1st/2nd selector fork. Take care not to lose the small 5th speed detent ball and spring. Extract the larger coil spring, sleeve and ball from the remote control selector rod hole (photo).
13 Remove the screws from the triangular-shaped bearing retainer. One of these screws may be of Torx type and will require a special bit to unscrew it. Hold the reverse idler gear up while the screw is undone. Remove the spacer from the reverse idler shaft. The bearing retainer can only be removed if the input shaft bearing is first removed.
14 Turn the clutch housing on its side and remove the mainshaft assembly. Remove the input shaft assembly by tapping the end of the shaft with a plastic-faced or copper hammer. The reverse idler gear will come off its shaft as the input shaft is released. Note the tooth leads are at the top.
15 Take out the final drive/differential.
16 If the plastic oil pocket must be removed, then the bearing outer track which retains it must first be drawn out using a suitable extractor which has thin claws. Extract the small retaining bolt and remove the speedometer drivegear.

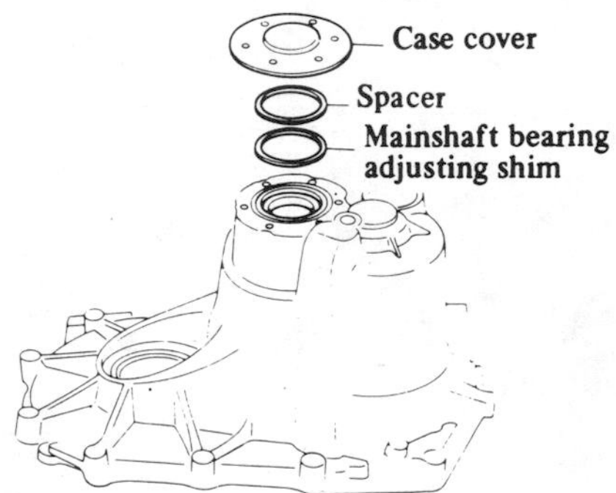

Fig. 6.11 Mainshaft bearing adjusting components (Sec 7)

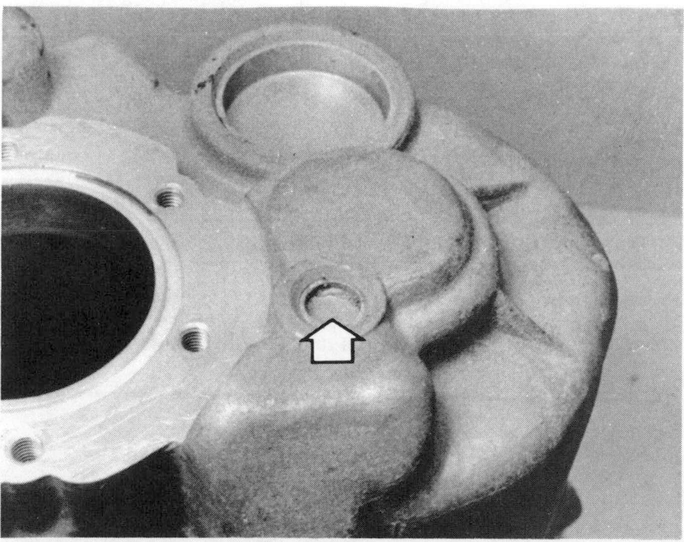

7.6A Input shaft rear bearing welch plug

7.6B Input shaft bearing viewed from inside the casing

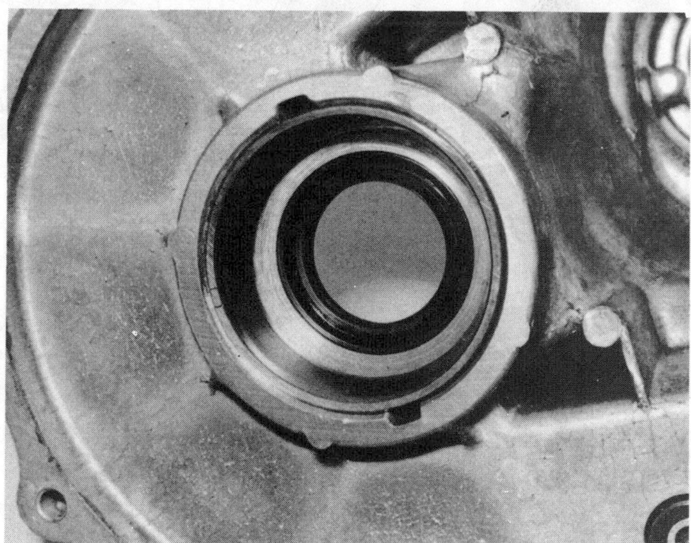

7.8 Showing differential bearing outer track

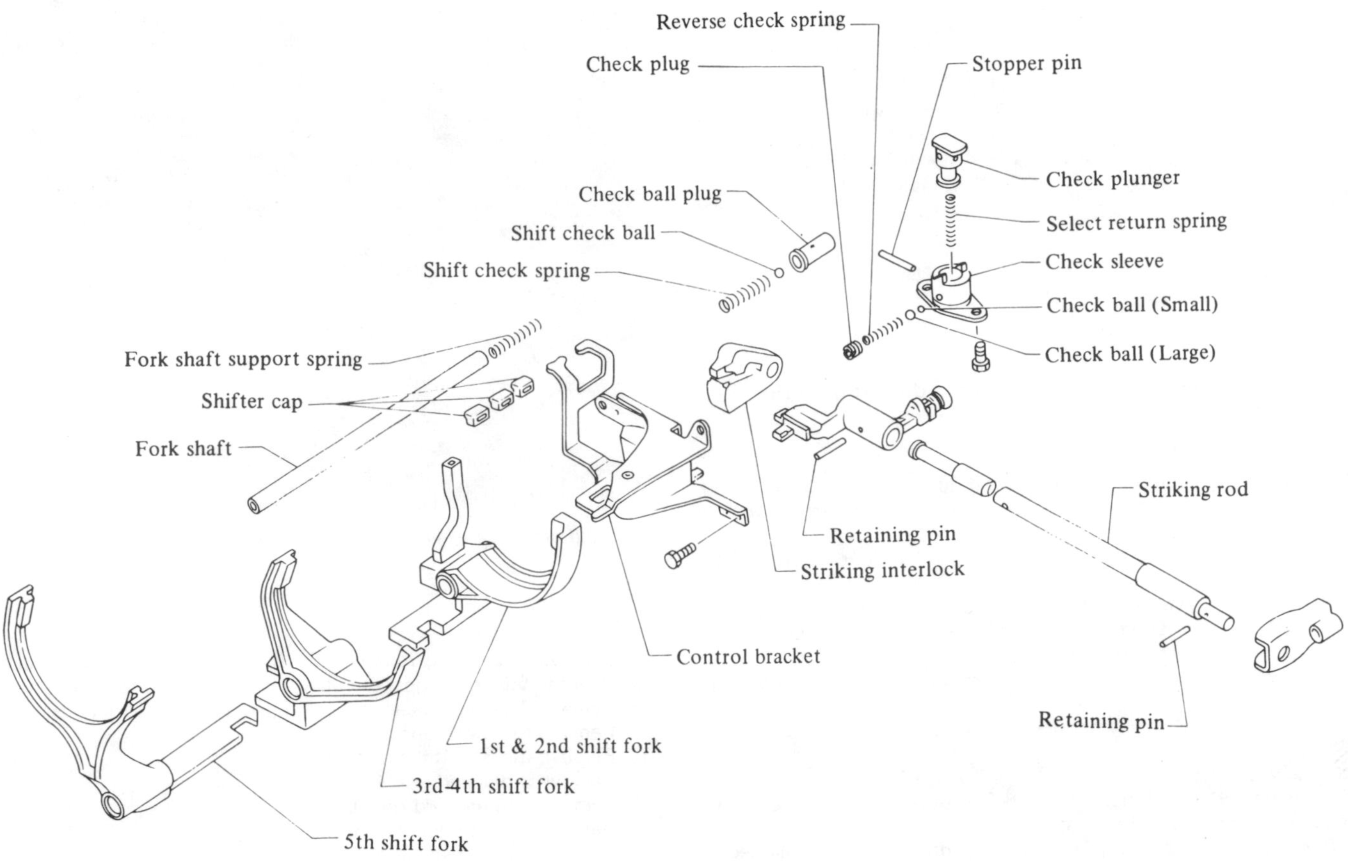

Reverse check spring
Check plug
Stopper pin
Check plunger
Check ball plug
Select return spring
Shift check ball
Check sleeve
Shift check spring
Check ball (Small)
Check ball (Large)
Fork shaft support spring
Shifter cap
Fork shaft
Striking rod
Retaining pin
Striking interlock
Control bracket
Retaining pin
1st & 2nd shift fork
3rd-4th shift fork
5th shift fork

Fig. 6.12 Selector components (Sec 7)

5th shift fork
3rd & 4th shift fork
Shifter caps

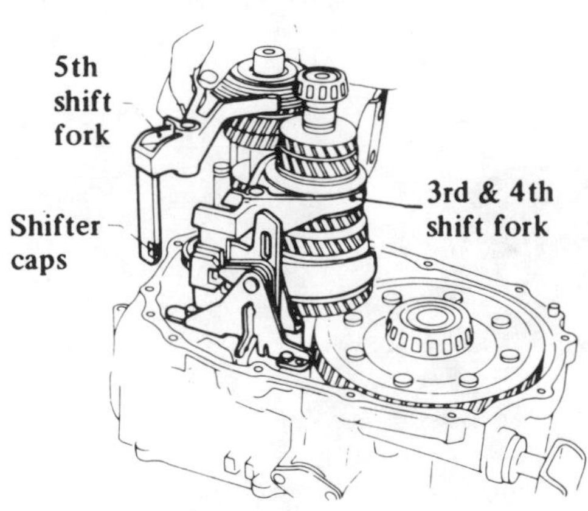

Fig. 6.13 Removing the 5th and 3rd/4th selector forks (Sec 7)

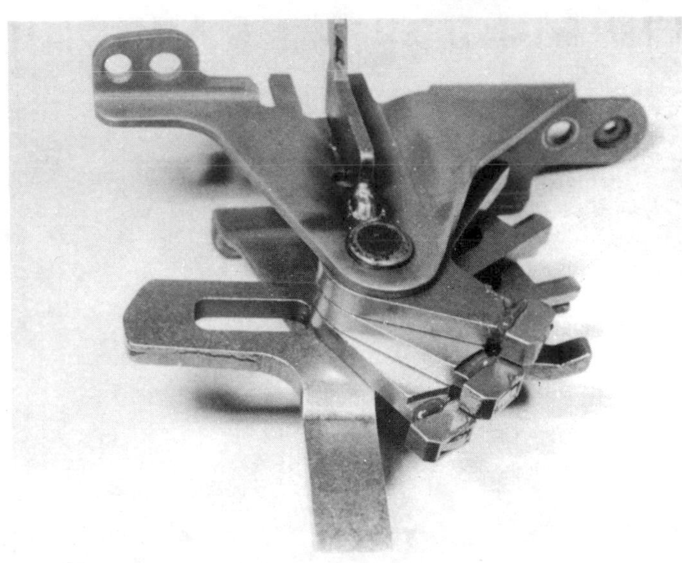

7.12 Control bracket

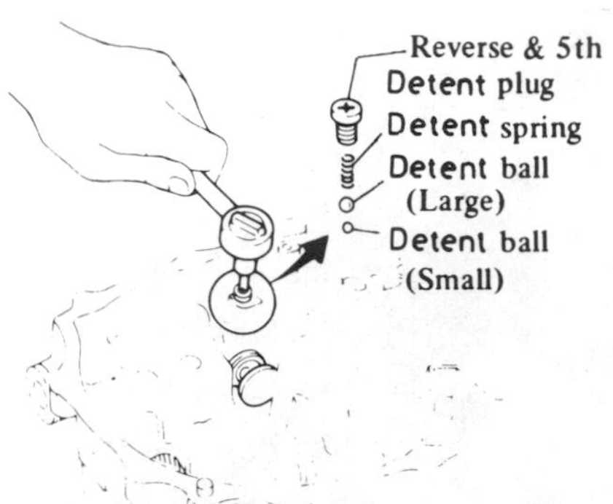

Fig. 6.14 Unscrewing the 5th/reverse detent plug (Sec 7)

7.19 Extracting 5th/reverse baulk plunger screw

17 Drive the roll pin from the selector rod dog, then withdraw the rod, dog and interlock. When removing the rod, take care not to damage the oil seal lips.
18 Unscrew 5th/reverse detent plug which will require a Torx type bit and then extract the spring and ball.
19 Remove 5th/reverse baulk plunger assembly, the screws again being of Torx type. Extract the smaller detent ball. The O-ring seal should be renewed at reassembly (photo).
20 Remove the clutch release shaft, bearing and lever as described in Chapter 5.
21 Remove the plastic oil channel from the transmission casing.

Input shaft

22 Measure and record the input shaft 5th speed gear endfloat. Extract the circlip and 5th speed gear stop plate.
23 Remove the 5th speed gear with synchroniser and the split needle bearing from inside the gear.
24 The input shaft cannot be dismantled further except to draw off the front bearing after having first extracted the retaining circlip and taken off the spacer. If a bearing puller is not available, support the bearing and drive the shaft from it (photos).

Mainshaft

25 Before dismantling the mainshaft, check and record the endfloat of the gears.
26 Remove the bearing inner races from the front and rear ends of the shaft. Use either a two-legged puller or press the shaft out of the bearings.
27 Remove the C-ring retainer, the C-rings and the thrust washer. Remove the 5th speed gear, a puller will be required for this (photo).
28 Remove 4th speed gear, the gear bush and steel locking ball.
29 Remove the baulk ring.
30 Remove the 3rd/4th synchro unit.
31 Remove 3rd speed gear.
32 Remove 2nd and 3rd gear bush.
33 Remove the steel locking ball.
34 Remove the 2nd speed gear.
35 Remove the baulk ring.
36 Remove 1st/2nd synchro unit with reverse gear (straight cut teeth on synchro sleeve) together with 1st speed gear as an assembly. The synchro hub is tight on the shaft and the best way to remove the assembly is to support under 1st speed gear and drive the shaft downward using a copper-faced hammer (photo).
37 Remove 1st speed gear split needle bearing (photo).

Differential/final drive

38 Unbolt the crownwheel from the differential case.
39 Using a punch, drive out the pinion shaft lock pin and withdraw the shaft.

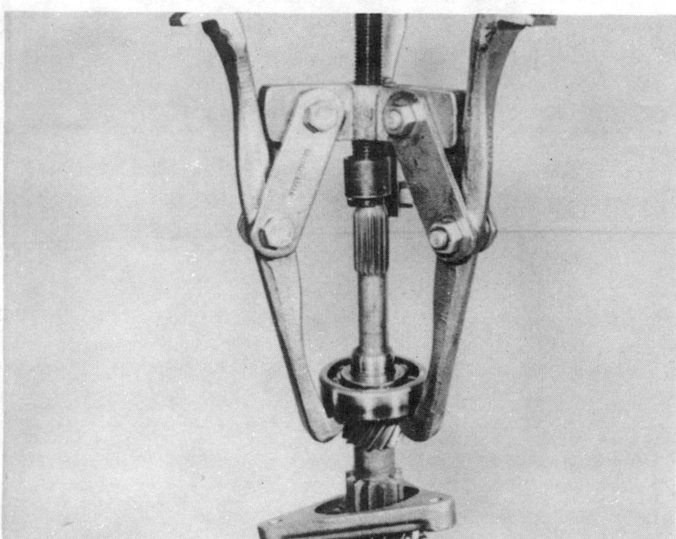

7.24A Drawing off input shaft front bearing

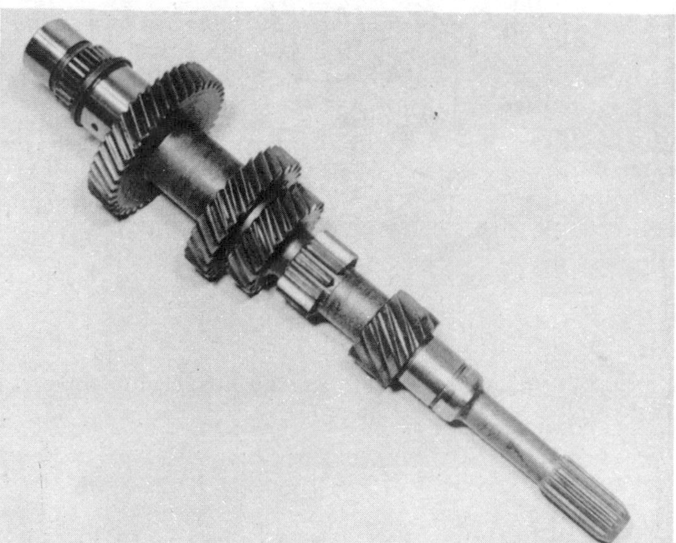

7.24B Input shaft stripped

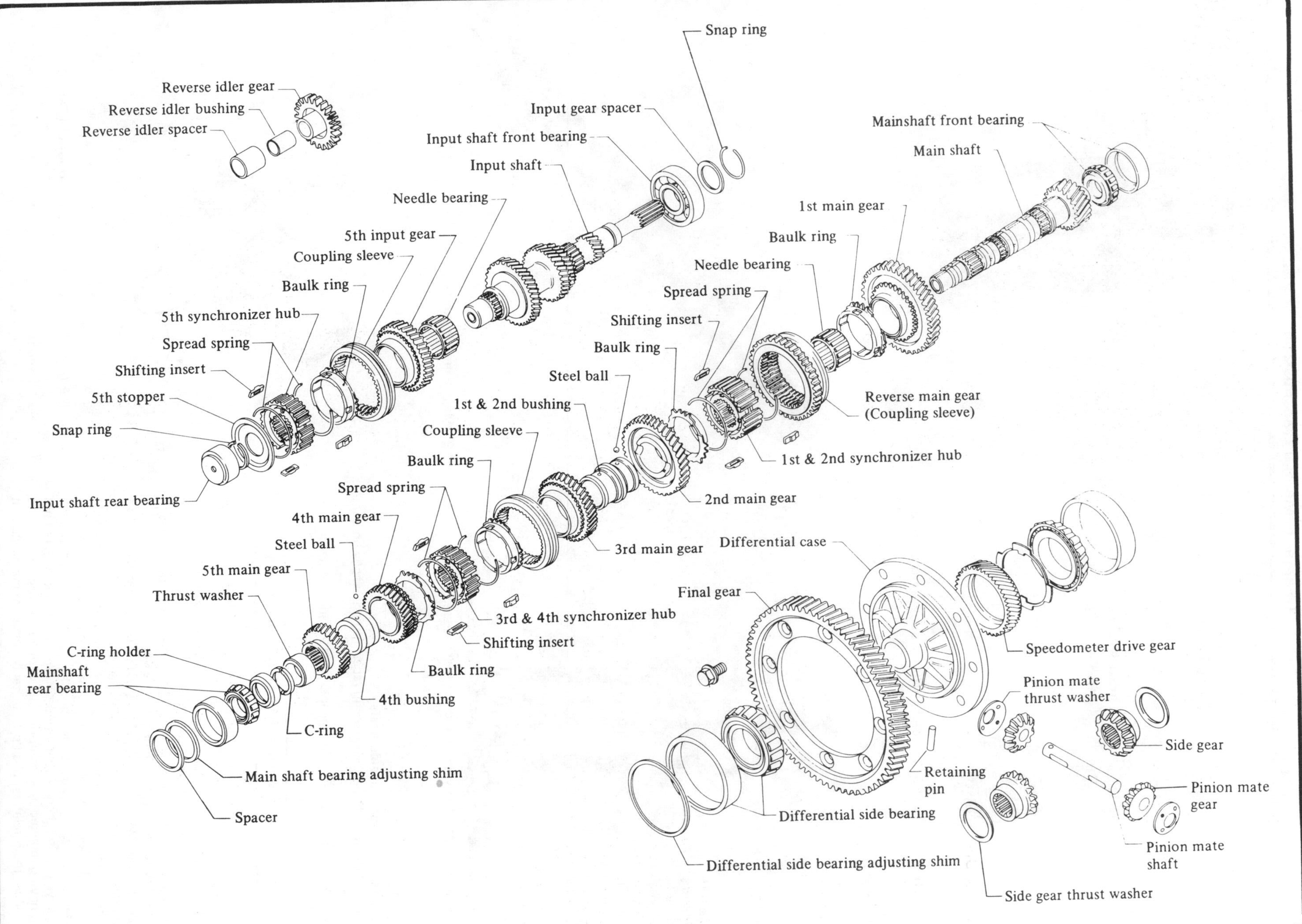

Fig. 6.15 Geartrain components (Sec 7)

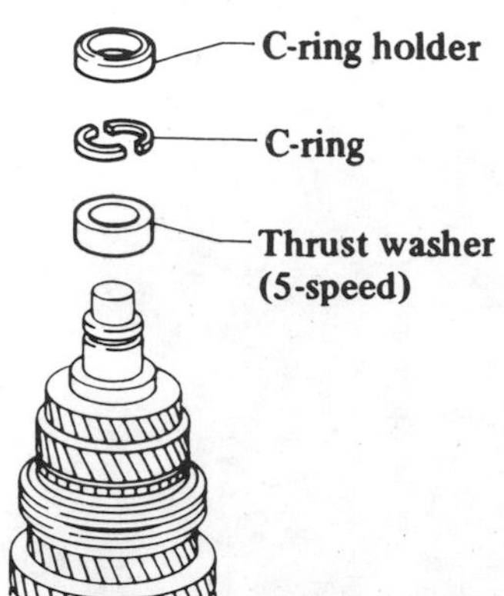

Fig. 6.16 Mainshaft 5th speed thrust washer and C-rings (Sec 7)

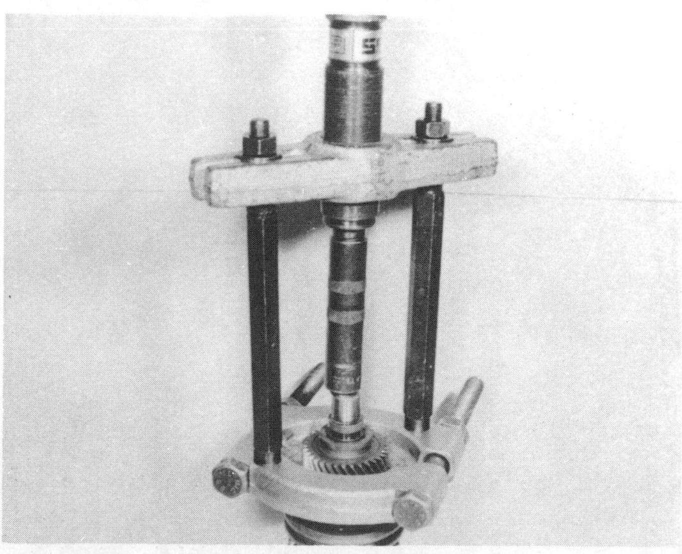

7.27 Removing mainshaft 5th speed gear

7.36 Removing 1st/2nd synchro and 1st speed gear

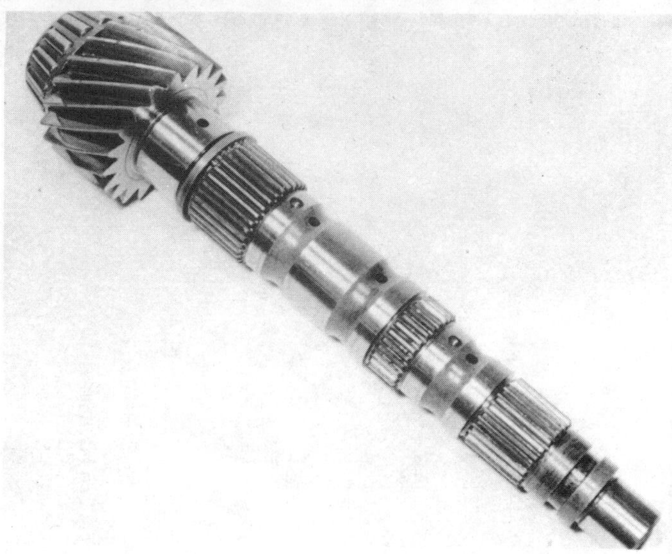

7.37 Mainshaft stripped

40 Remove the pinion and side gears.
41 Draw off the differential side bearing races, noting exactly how the taper of the rollers is set.
42 Remove the speedometer drivegear stop plate and the gear.

8 Transmission components (RS5F31A) – inspection

1 With the transmission completely dismantled, clean all components and inspect them for wear of damage.
2 Check the gears for chipped teeth and their bushes for wear.
3 Check the shafts for scoring or grooving.
4 Check the bearings for wear by spinning them with the fingers. If they shake or rattle then they must be renewed.
5 Wear in the synchronisers will usually be suspected before dismantling as a result of noisy gear changing.
6 Even if the synchro is operating quietly, it is worthwhile checking the units in the following way at time of major overhaul.
7 Refer to Fig. 6.17. Extract the spreader springs (1), remove the sliding keys (2) and then push the hub (4) from the sleeve (3), but not before having marked the components with quick drying paint to ensure that their relative position to each other is maintained at reassembly.

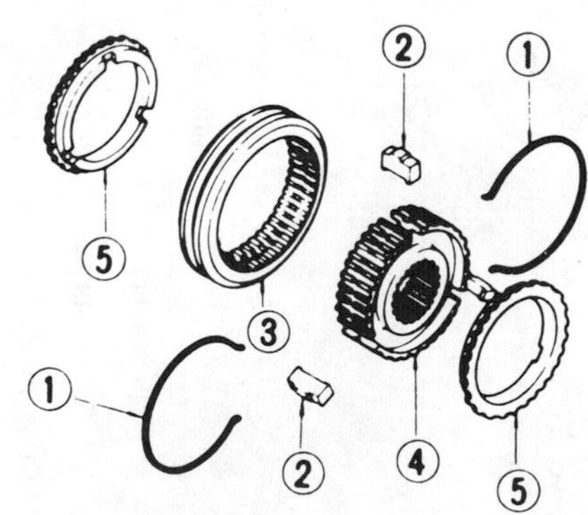

Fig. 6.17 Synchroniser components (Sec 8)

1 *Spring*
2 *Sliding key*
3 *Sleeve*
4 *Hub*
5 *Baulk ring*

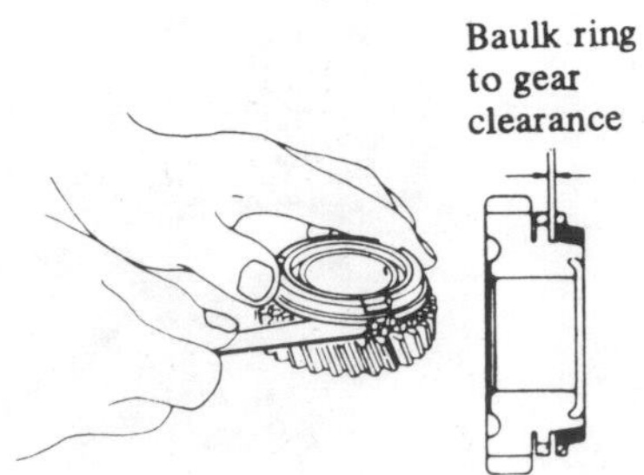

Fig. 6.18 Checking baulk ring wear (Sec 8)

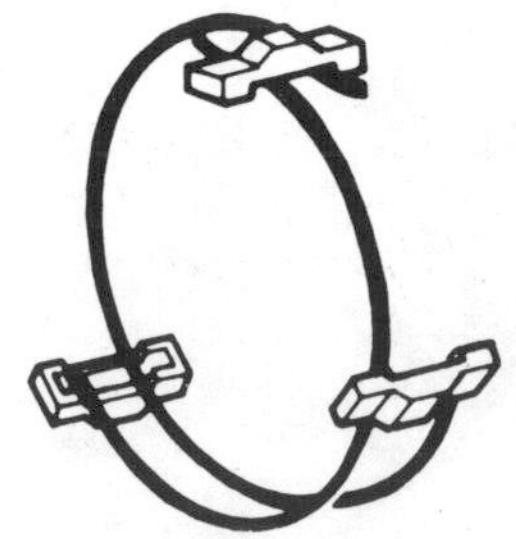

Fig. 6.19 Fitted direction of synchro springs (Sec 8)

8.11 Gearchange remote control oil seal

8 Check the synchro components for wear or deformation. Place the baulk ring on its cone and twist it to ensure good contact between the surfaces. Using a feeler blade, check that the gap between gear and baulk ring is not less than 0.7 mm (0.028 in). If it is, renew the baulk ring.

9 When reassembling the synchro units, make sure that the spreader springs run in opposite directions when viewed from each side of the synchro and that the spring ends do not engage in the same sliding key.

10 It is recommended that all oil seals are renewed at time of major overhaul. These include those for the clutch cross-shaft, differential side bearings, gearchange remote control rod and the input shaft.

11 The oil seals for the differential side bearings and the gearchange remote control rod can be renewed without having to remove the transmission from the vehicle, should anything more than the slightest seepage of oil be observed during normal operation of the vehicle (photo).

9 Transmission (RS5F31A) – reassembly

Differential/final drive

1 Fit the speedometer worm drivegear and its stop plate to the differential case.
2 Press on the differential bearing inner races (photo).
3 Into the differential case fit the pinion and side gears with thrust washers and the pinion shaft.
4 Drive in a new pinion shaft roll pin, making sure that it is flush with the differential case.
5 Clean the threads of the crownwheel bolts and apply thread locking fluid, then screw them in and tighten to the specified torque.

Mainshaft

6 Oil all components liberally as they are reassembled.
7 Fit 1st speed gear needle bearing (photo).
8 Fit 1st speed gear (photo).
9 Fit 1st speed gear baulk ring (photo).
10 Fit 1st/2nd synchro unit with reverse. Tap the synchro hub down the mainshaft using a piece of tubing, but hold the synchro together with the hand in case the vibration makes it fall apart (photo).
11 Locate the steel lock ball in its hole in the shaft. On no account place the ball in the hole in the shaft groove (photo).
12 Fit 2nd speed gear baulk ring.
13 Fit 2nd speed gear.
14 Fit 2nd/3rd speed gear bush, turning it slowly to engage its cut-out with the lockball (photo).
15 Fit 3rd speed gear (photo).
16 Fit the baulk ring (photo).
17 Fit 3rd/4th synchro unit so that the engraved dashes on the sleeve are visible (photo).

9.2 Differential bearing inner race

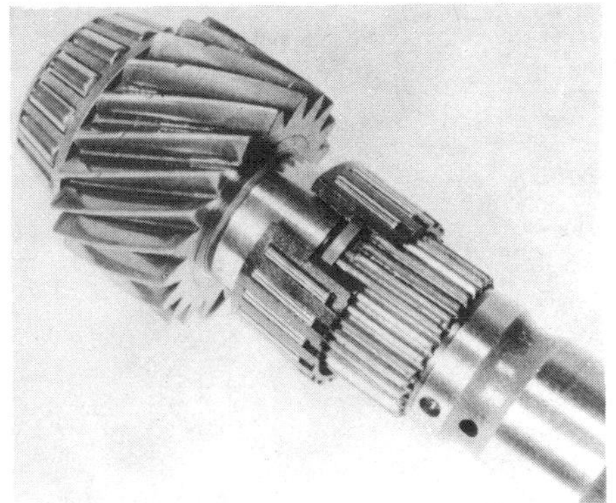

9.7 Mainshaft 1st speed gear split needle bearing

9.8 1st speed gear fitted to mainshaft

9.9 Mainshaft 1st speed gear baulk ring

9.10 1st/2nd synchro, with reverse fitted to mainshaft

9.11 Gear bush locking ball

9.14 2nd speed gear and bush being fitted to mainshaft

9.15 Fitting 3rd speed gear to mainshaft

9.16 3rd speed gear baulk ring fitted to mainshaft

18 Using thick grease, stick the second (4th gear bush) lock ball in its shaft hole (not the hole in the shaft groove) (photo).
19 Fit the baulk ring.
20 Fit 4th speed gear bush, turning it slowly to engage its cut-out with the lock ball (photo).
21 Fit 4th speed gear (photo).
22 Fit 5th speed gear. Drive it carefully onto the mainshaft using a piece of tubing (photo).
23 Fit the 5th speed gear thrust washer (photo).
24 Fit the C-rings. These are supplied in various thicknesses to correct gear endfloat (photo).
25 Fit the C-ring retainer (photo).
26 Press on new bearing inner races to both ends of the mainshaft (photo).
27 Using a feeler blade, check that the gear endfloat is as recorded at dismantling or within the following tolerances (photo).

1st speed gear	*0.18 to 0.31 mm (0.0071 to 0.0122 in)*
2nd, 3rd, 4th speed gear	*0.20 to 0.40 mm (0.079 to 0.0157 in)*

Input shaft

28 Fit the split type needle roller bearing (photo).
29 Fit 5th speed gear (photo).
30 Fit the baulk ring (photo).
31 Fit the synchro unit so that the engraved 'dashes' on the sleeve are visible (photo).

9.17 3rd/4th synchro fitted to mainshaft

9.18 4th speed gear locking ball fitted to mainshaft

9.20 Fitting 4th speed gear bush

9.21 Fitting 4th speed gear

9.22 Fitting 5th speed gear

9.23 Fitting thrust washer to 5th speed gear

9.24 C-rings

9.25 C-ring retainer

9.26 Mainshaft bearing inner race

9.27 Checking gear endfloat

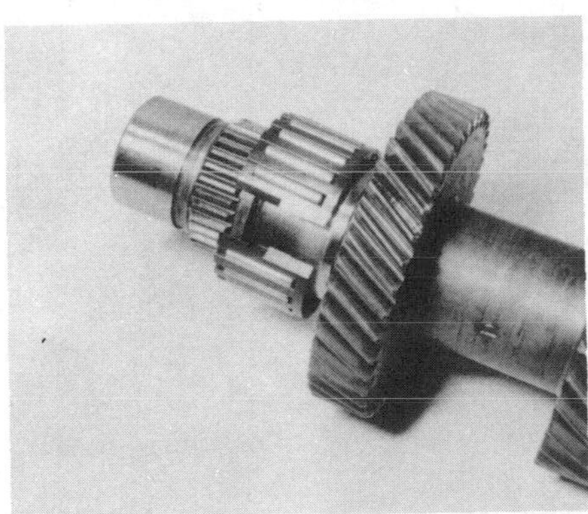

9.28 Input shaft split needle roller bearing

9.29 Fitting input shaft 5th speed gear

9.30 Input shaft 5th speed gear baulk ring

9.31 Input shaft 5th speed gear synchro

9.32A Input shaft synchro stop plate

9.32B Input shaft circlip

9.33A Input shaft bearing and retainer

9.33B Input shaft bearing and circlip

32 To the synchro unit fit the stop plate and the circlip. The circlips are available in various thicknesses to eliminate endfloat (photos).

33 Using a feeler blade, check that the 5th speed gear endfloat is as recorded at dismantling, or between 0.18 and 0.41 mm (0.0071 and 0.0161 in). Finally, locate the triangular bearing retainer on the shaft, then press on a new shaft front bearing, fit the spacer and use a new circlip (photos).

Clutch housing

34 Fit a new oil channel so that its relieved area is towards the oil pocket when installed (photos).

35 Press or drive in the differential and mainshaft bearing outer tracks into their seats. Fit new differential bearing oil seals (photos).

36 Remember that the mainshaft bearing outer track retains the oil pocket, so align the pocket correctly before fitting the bearing track.

9.34A Oil channel (arrowed)

9.34B Oil pocket

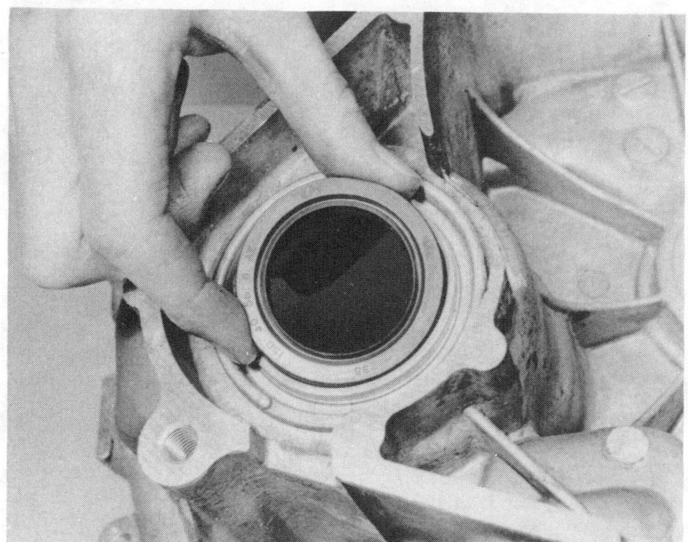

9.35A Differential bearing oil seal

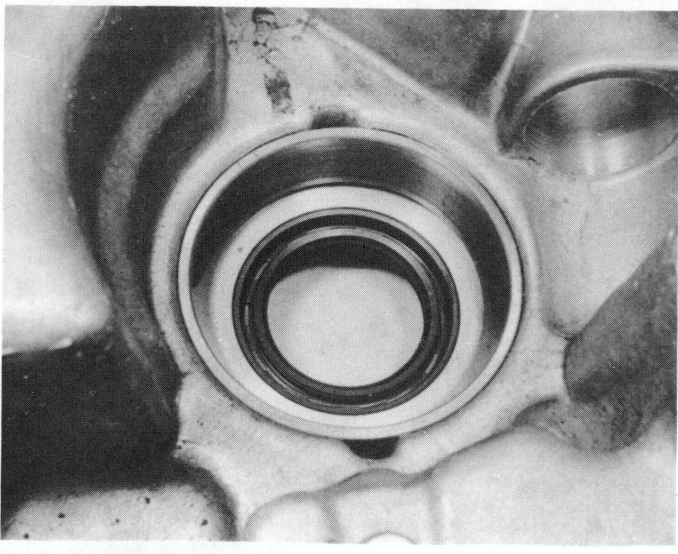

9.35B Differential bearing outer track and oil seal

37 Fit the 5th/reverse baulk assembly and tighten the Torx type fixing screws. A new O-ring should be used (photo).
38 Fit reverse/5th baulk plunger balls (small one first), the spring and the plug (photos).
39 The force of the reverse baulk plunger should now be checked using a spring balance. the pull should be between 10.3 and 12.7 Nm (91.0 and 113.0 lbf in) measured as a torque; *eg:* 9.1 lbs at 10 in radius from shaft centre (see Fig. 6.21).

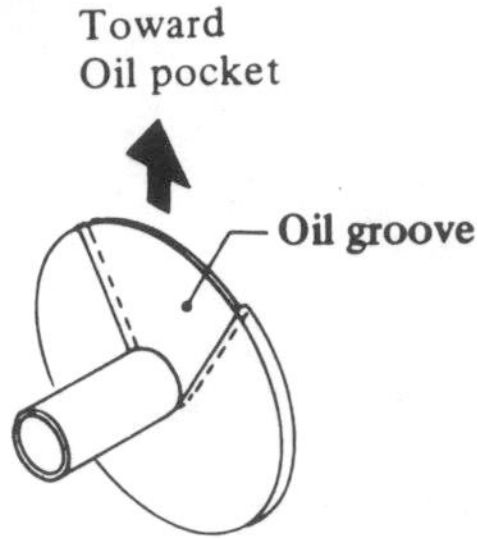

Fig. 6.20 Oil channel (Sec 9)

9.37 5th/reverse baulk plunger with O-ring

9.38A 5th/reverse baulk plunger balls and spring

9.38B 5th/reverse baulk plunger screw plug

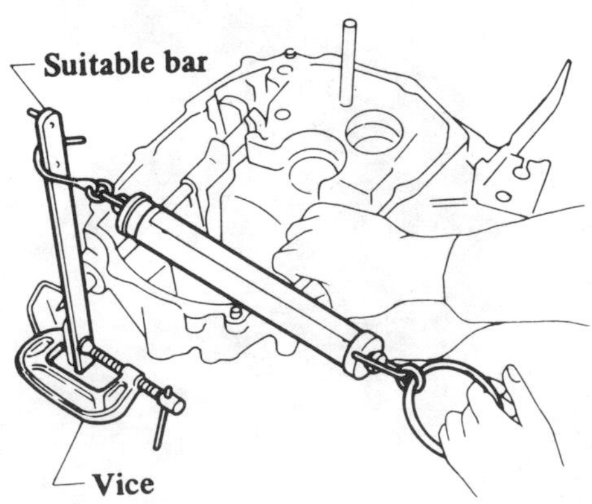

Fig. 6.21 Checking reverse detent torque (Sec 9)

40 The detent force may be increased by changing the detent plug for one of greater length. When correct, apply locking fluid to the threads of the detent plug and tighten it.
41 Using new double roll pins, refit the remote control rod so that the detent notch is downward. Fit the striking lever and interlock (photos).
42 Refit the speedometer drivegear and then screw in the lockbolt (photos).
43 Where the differential incorporates curved side gears which can be removed leaving the pinion gears in position, use length of wooden dowel rod to retain the gears (photos).
44 Lower the differential/final drive into positon (photo).
45 Fit the input shaft and reverse idler gear simultaneously. the idler gear (marked before removal) should be refitted in its original position. Use a plastic-faced or copper hammer to tap the input shaft fully home in the clutch housing (photo).
46 Fit the spacer to the reverse idler shaft.
47 Fit the triangular-shaped bearing retainer. Apply thread locking fluid to the screw threads and tighten them (photo).
48 Fit the mainshaft, carefully meshing the gear teeth with those of the input shaft. As the operation proceeds, push both synchro sleeves down and hold the reverse idler gear up (photo).

9.41 A Remote control rod outer roll pin

9.41 B Remote control rod inner roll pin

9.41 C Striking lever and interlock

9.42A Speedometer drivegear pinion

9.42B Speedometer pinion lockbolt

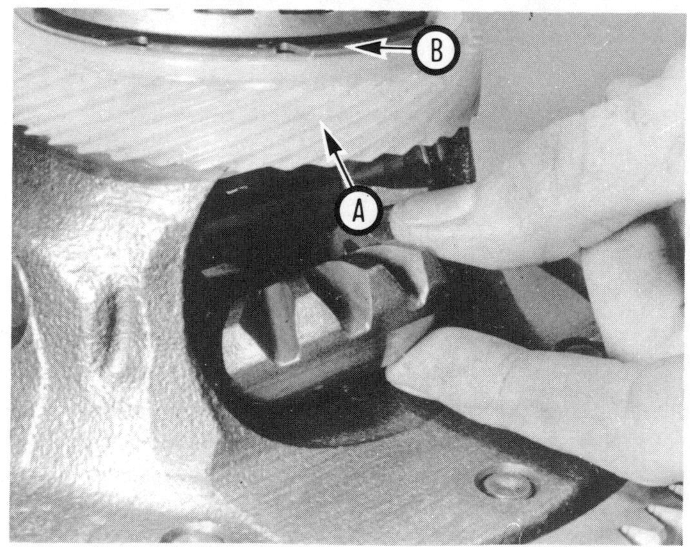

9.43A Fitting differential side gear

A Speedometer worm gear *B Lockplate*

9.43B Side gear retainer with dowel

9.44 Differential/final drive installed

9.45 Fitting input shaft and reverse idler gear

9.47 Bearing retainer (arrowed)

9.48 Fitting mainshaft assembly

49 Fit the bush, the ball and the large coil spring to the hole in the remote control rod housing (photos).
50 Locate 1st/2nd selector fork under the control bracket which itself incorporates reverse selector fork. As the control bracket is bolted into place, make sure that 5th speed detent spring and ball are in the hole in the remote control interlock (photos).
51 Locate the remaining selector forks. The 2nd/3rd fork is the lower one and the 4th/5th fork the upper one. Make sure that the plastic slides are in position in the fork arm cut-outs, also the rectangular shaped metal bushes are in the selector dog cut-outs (photos).
52 Pass the selector shaft through the forks making sure that the coil spring is located in the recess at the lower end of the shaft (photos).

Transmission casing

53 If the differential side bearings were renewed, fit the new bearing outer track now with a new oil seal.
54 If the mainshaft bearing was renewed, fit the new track into the casing now.
55 If the input shaft rear bearing was renewed, tap a new small welch plug into the hole in the casing, having coated the outer surface with sealing compound.

9.49A Remote control rod housing bush

9.49B Remote control rod detent spring and ball

9.50A 1st/2nd selector fork

9.50B Control bracket located

9.50C 5th speed detent spring and ball

9.50D Control bracket selector fork on reverse idler gear

9.50E 5th speed detent ball (arrowed) held by control bracket

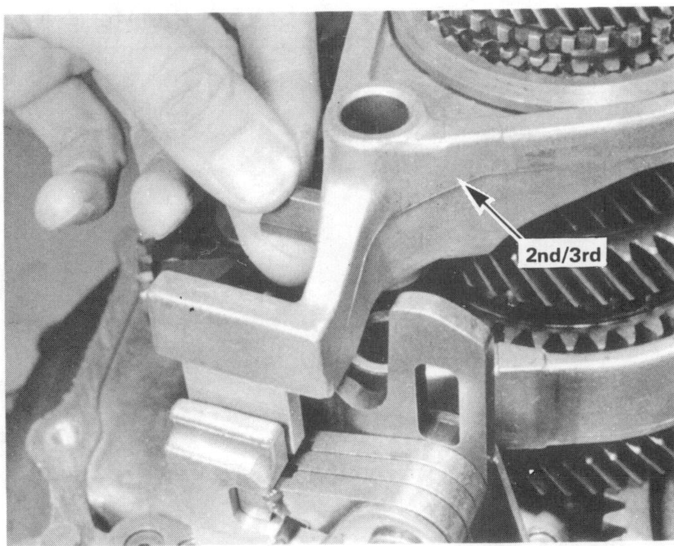

9.51A 2nd/3rd selector fork

9.51B 4th/5th selector fork

9.51C Selector fork arm cut-outs and plastic slides

9.52A Selector shaft and coil spring

9.52B Selector shaft installed

9.56 Plastic oil trough in transmission casing

9.59 Lowering transmission casing into position

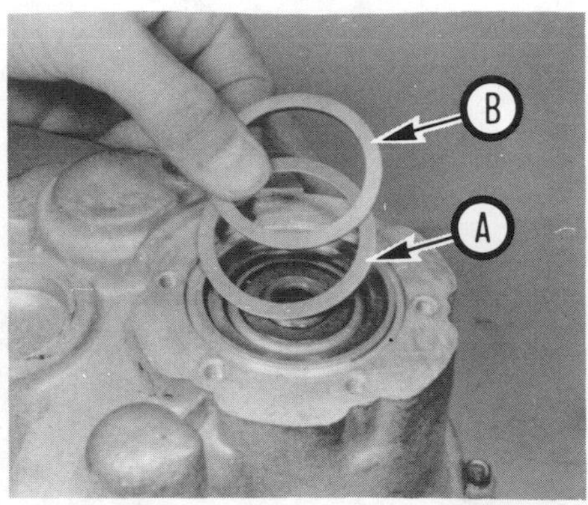

9.61 Mainshaft adjusting shim (A) and spacer (B)

56 Fit the plastic oil trough (photo).
57 Screw in the reverse lamp switch and if fitted the overdrive switch.
58 With the clutch housing standing on the bench with the geartrains vertical, apply jointing compound to the mating faces of the transmission casing and clutch housing.
59 Lower the casing into position cver the geartrains. Tilt the casing as necessary to clear the selector fork (photo).
60 Fit the connecting bolts and tighten to specified torque.
61 If the mainshaft bearing has not been changed, fit the original adjusting shim and the spacer. If a new bearing has been fitted, refer to Section 11 for details of mainshaft bearing preload adjustment (photo).
62 Apply jointing compound to the edges of the circular cover and bolt it into position on the transmission casing (photo).

9.62 Refitting transmission casing circular cover

10 Final drive (RS5F31A) – adjustment

1 If any of the following components of the transmission have been renewed during overhaul, then you have to take the assembly to your dealer for the final drive to be adjusted to ensure correct crownwheel to pinion meshing and specified bearing preload.

Differential case
Differential side bearing
Clutch housing
Transmission casing

Owing to the need for special tools, this work is not within the scope of the home mechanic.

11 Mainshaft bearing preload (RS5F31A) – adjustment

1 If any of the following components have been renewed during overhaul, then the mainshaft bearing preload must be checked and adjusted.

Mainshaft
Mainshaft bearings
Clutch housing
Transmission casing

2 Remove the circular cover from the transmission. To carry out the adjustment, measure between the machined face of the transmission casing and the surface of the spacer. A shim should now be selected which is 0.2 mm (0.008 in) thicker than the dimension just taken.
3 Fit the spacer, the selected shim and the cover and check that the input shaft turns smoothly with 4th gear selected. A special tool is available at Datsun/Nissan dealers (KV38105900) which engages in the side gears and gives a torque reading for rotation of the final drive when 4th gear is selected.
4 The correct turning torque should be between 7.4 and 10.8 Nm (65 to 95 lbf in).

PART C: TURBO MODELS

12 Transmission (RS5F50A) – dismantling

1 Clean away all external dirt from the transmission exterior. Drain the oil.
2 Stand the transmission on the flange of the clutch housing.

Transmission casing and clutch housing

3 Unscrew the 1st/2nd and 3rd/4th detent plugs and extract the springs and balls.
4 Unbolt the position switch, speedometer pinion, and the reverse idler shaft bolt (Fig. 6.24).
5 Unscrew the bolts and lift off the transmission casing. If necessary break the joint by tapping the casing with a mallet. Recover the shims for the input shaft rear bearing.
6 If necessary drive out the position switch from the inside of the transmission casing.
7 Select 4th gear, then pull out the reverse idler shaft and remove the reverse idler gear from the selector assembly.
8 Pull out the retaining pin and extract the reverse arm shaft.
9 Unbolt and remove the reverse lever assembly.
10 Unscrew the 5th/reverse detent plug and extract the spring and ball.

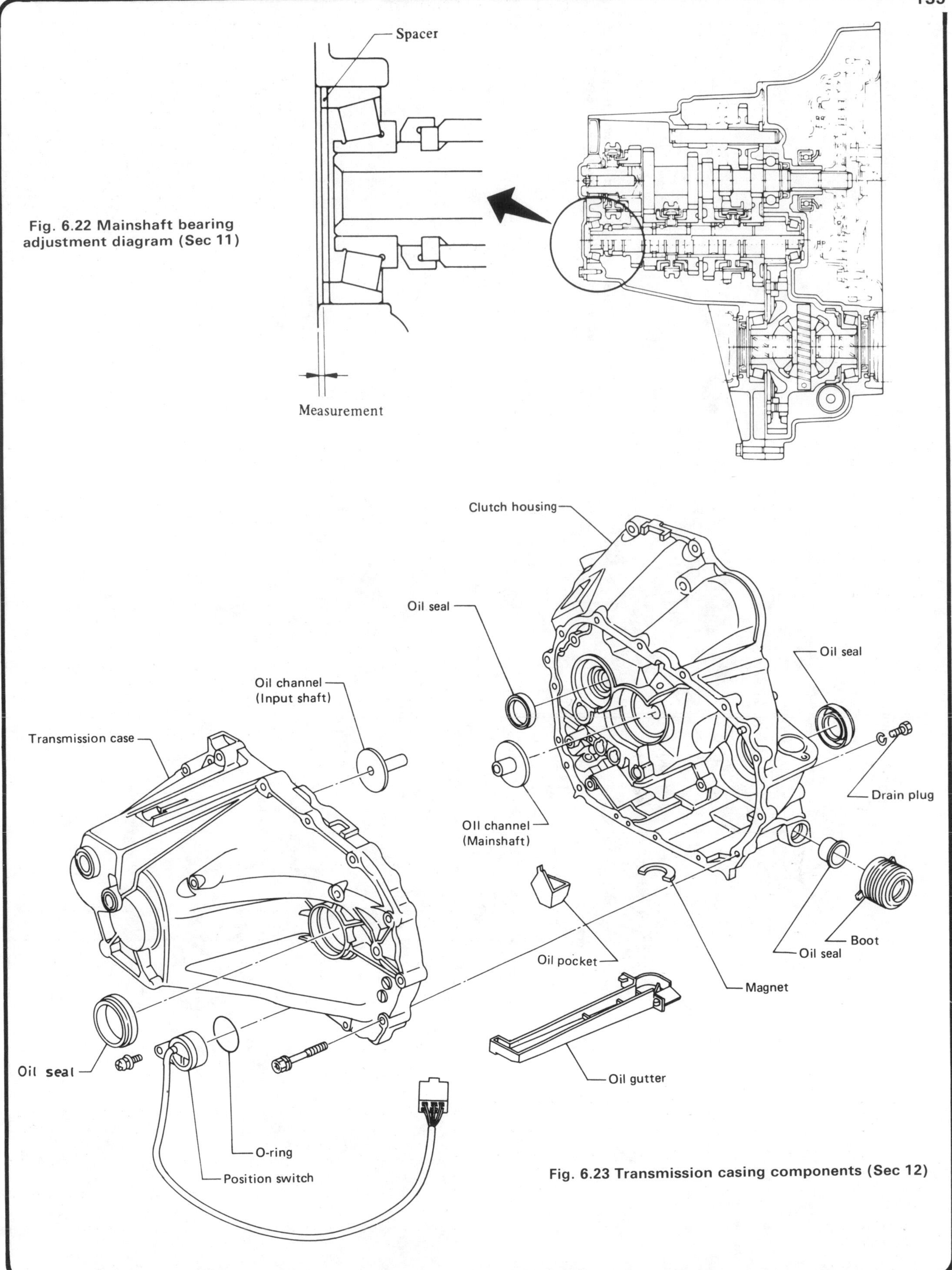

Fig. 6.22 Mainshaft bearing adjustment diagram (Sec 11)

Fig. 6.23 Transmission casing components (Sec 12)

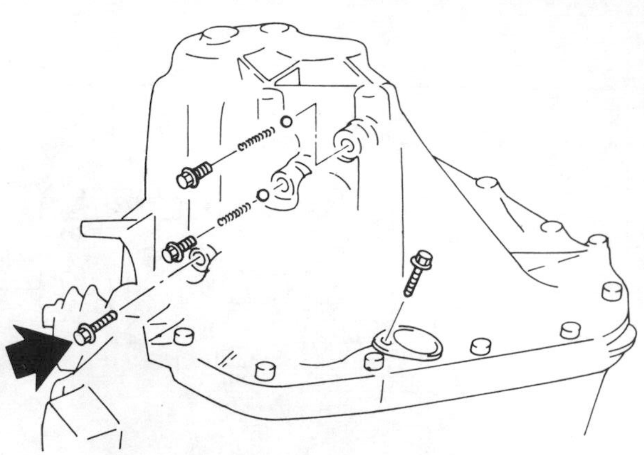

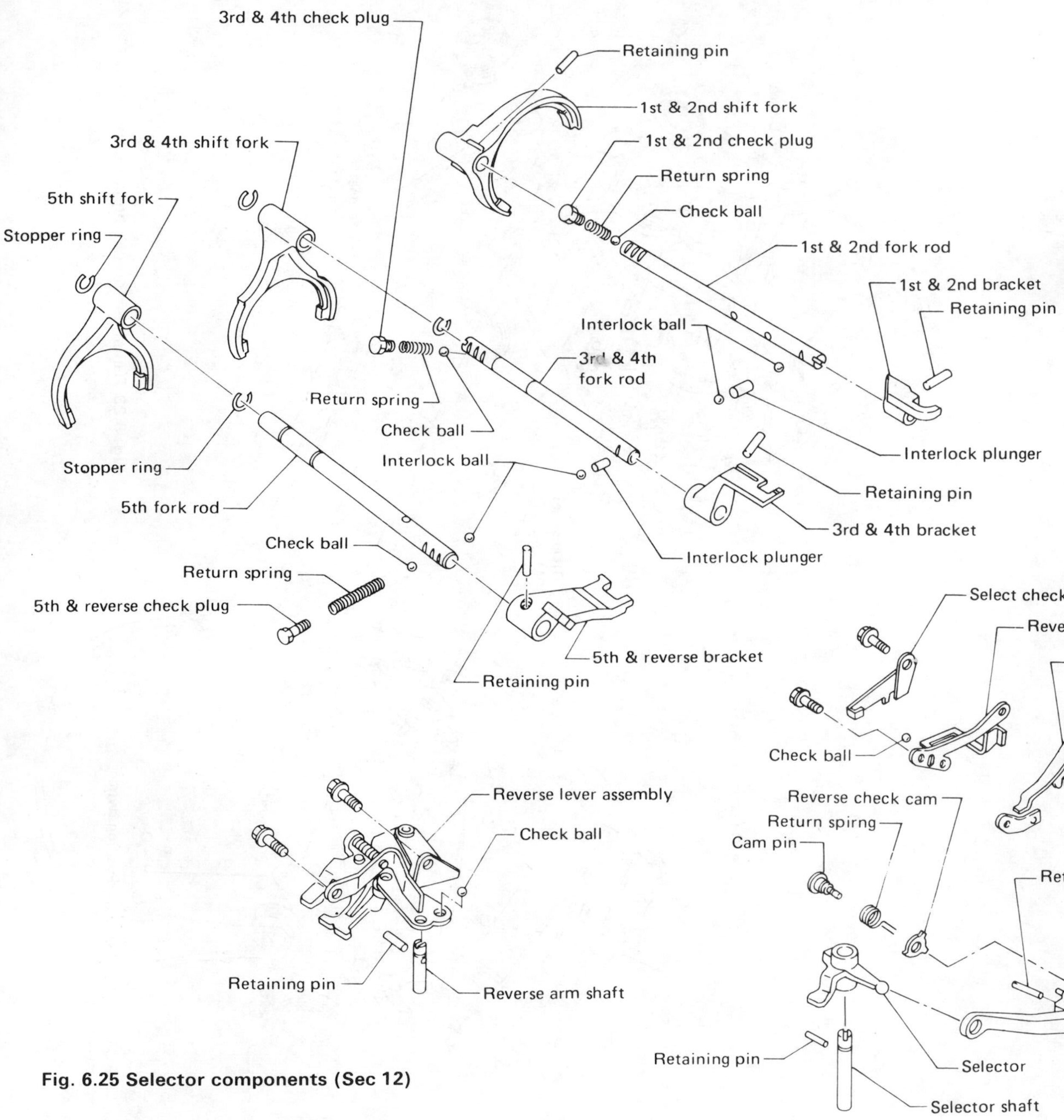

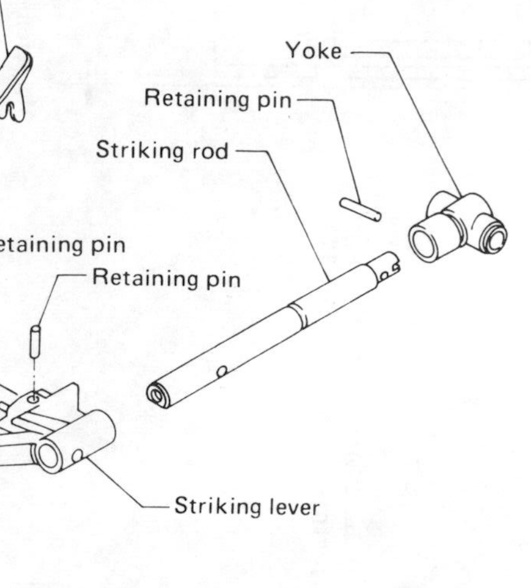

Fig. 6.25 Selector components (Sec 12)

Fig. 6.24 Detent plugs, position switch bolt, and reverse idler shaft bolt (arrowed) (Sec 12)

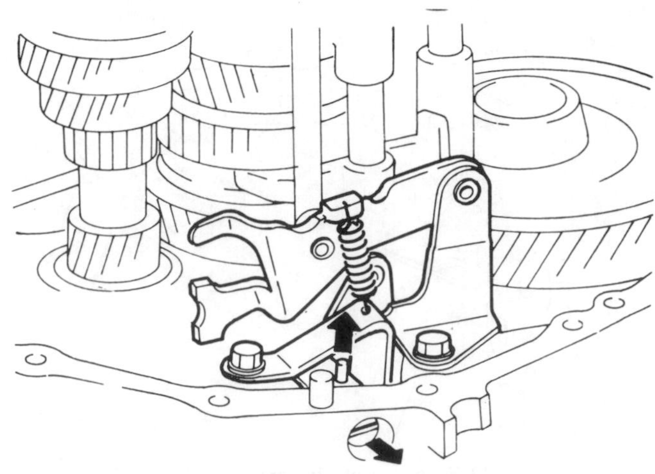

Fig. 6.26 Reverse arm shaft withdrawal (Sec 12)

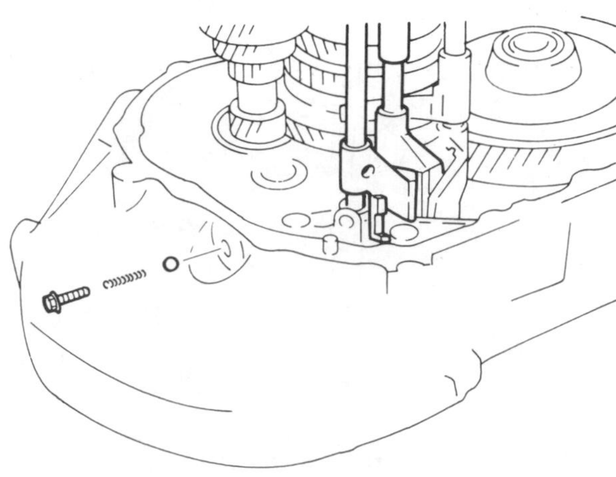

Fig. 6.27 5th/reverse detent plug removal (Sec 12)

Fig. 6.28 5th/reverse and 3rd/4th selector rod removal (Sec 12)

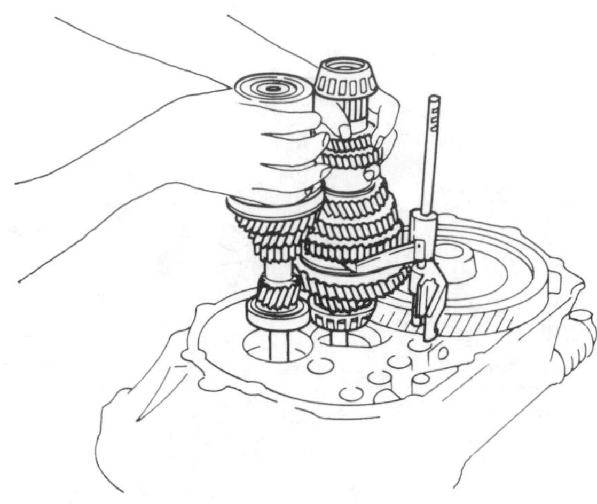

Fig. 6.29 Removing the input shaft and mainshaft assemblies together with the 1st/2nd selector fork and rod (Sec 12)

11 Extract the circlips from the lower ends of the 5th/reverse and 3rd/4th selector forks.
12 Drive out the roll pins securing the selector dog brackets to the 5th/reverse and 3rd/4th selector rods.
13 Pull out the 5th/reverse and 3rd/4th selector rods, then remove the selector forks and dog brackets.
14 Grip the input shaft and mainshaft assemblies and lift them from the clutch housing, together with the 1st/2nd selector fork and rod. Also lift out the final drive/differential assembly.
15 Recover the interlock balls and plunger from the clutch housing.
16 Unbolt the reverse check assembly.
17 Drive out the selector shaft retaining pin, then drive out the shaft using a narrow drift (Fig. 6.32) and remove the selector.
18 Unscrew the drain plug if still in position, then, from the opposite side of the housing, drive out the striking lever retaining pin.
19 Withdraw the striking rod and remove the lever.
20 Remove the clutch release fork and bearing as described in Chapter 5.
21 Drive off the clutch release shaft seal from the clutch housing. Also prise out the input shaft oil seal.
22 Remove the oil channel from the clutch housing, then extract the mainshaft bearing outer track using a suitable extractor.
23 Remove the differential side bearing outer tracks from the clutch housing and transmission casing using a suitable extractor.
24 Remove the mainshaft bearing outer track from the transmission casing using a suitable extractor.
25 Before dismantling the input shaft and mainshaft, measure and record the endfloat of each gear using feeler blades (Fig. 6.36).

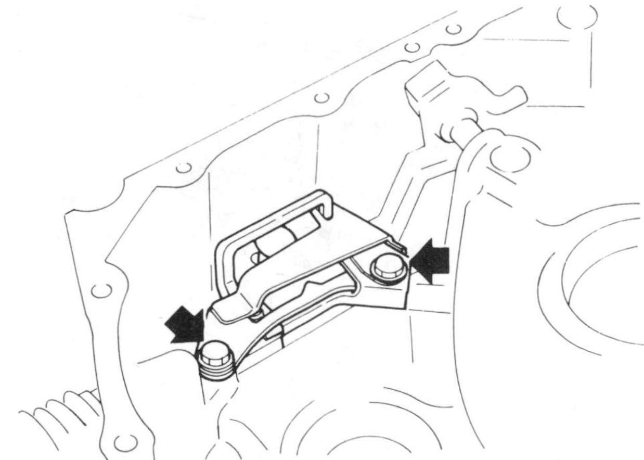

Fig. 6.30 Reverse check assembly removal (Sec 12)

Compare the results with the tolerances given in Section 14, paragraphs 16 and 27. If the endfloat is not within these tolerances, any worn components should be renewed.

Input shaft

26 Remove the rear bearing from the input shaft by supporting the bearing on a vice and driving the shaft through.

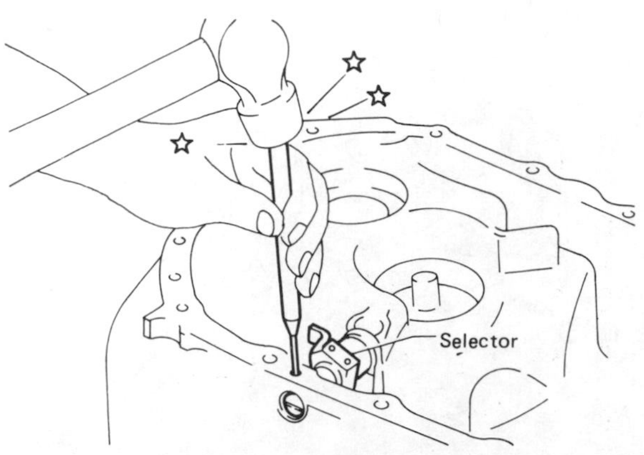

Fig. 6.31 Driving out the selector shaft retaining pin (Sec 12)

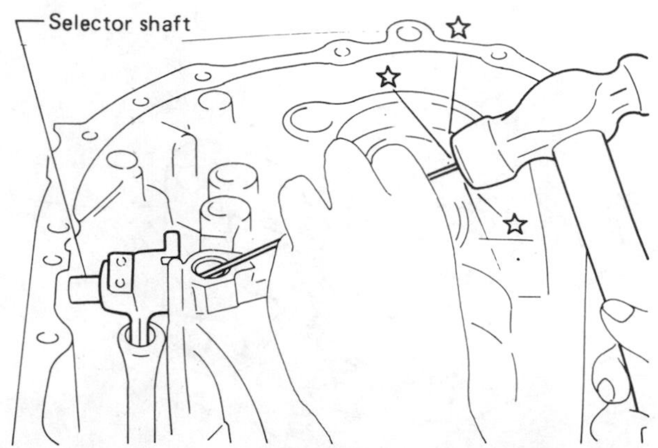

Fig. 6.32 Selector shaft removal (Sec 12)

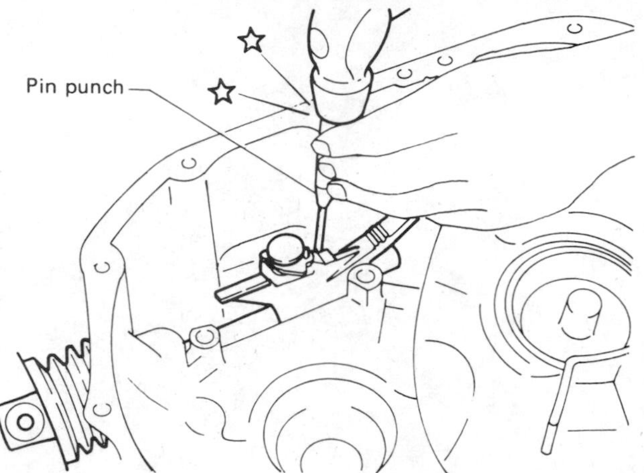

Fig. 6.33 Striking lever retaining pin removal (Sec 12)

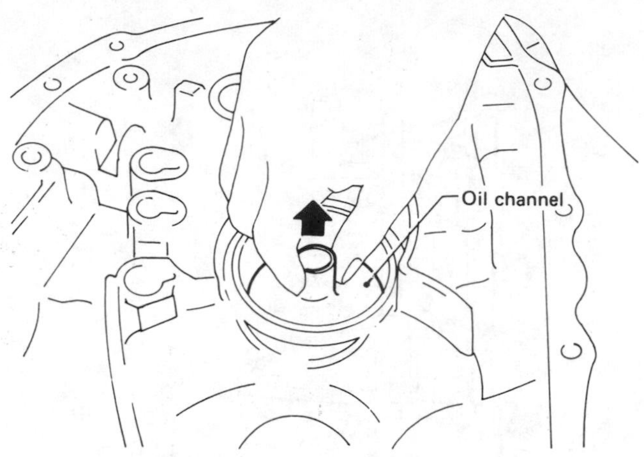

Fig. 6.34 Removing the oil channel from the clutch housing (Sec 12)

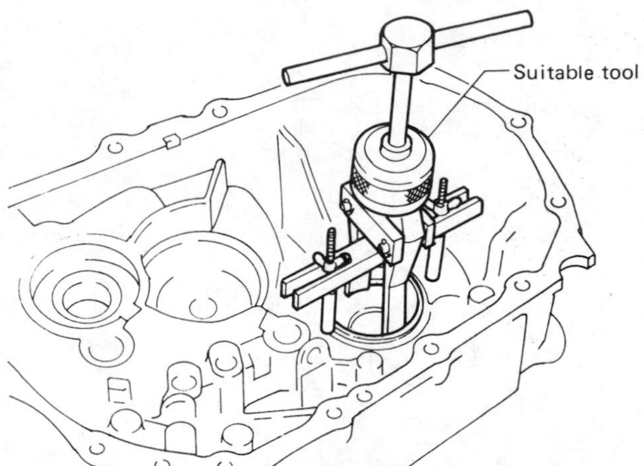

Fig. 6.35 Using an extractor to remove the differential side bearing outer track from the clutch housing (Sec 12)

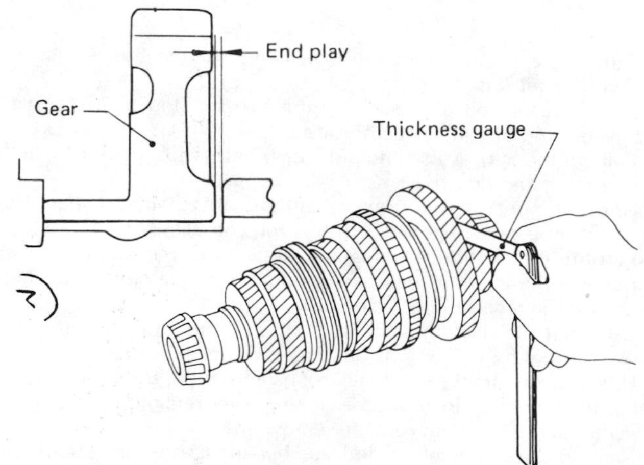

Fig. 6.36 Checking the gear endfloat (Sec 12)

27 Similarly support the 5th gear and drive the shaft through the 5th synchro unit and gear.
28 Remove the thrust washer ring and the split thrust washers.
29 Remove 4th gear.
30 Extract the circlip, then support the 3rd gear and drive the shaft through the 3rd/4th synchro unit and 3rd gear.
31 Remove the bearing from the front of the shaft by supporting the bearing on a vice and driving the shaft through.

Mainshaft

32 Support the rear bearing inner race on a vice, then drive the mainshaft through.

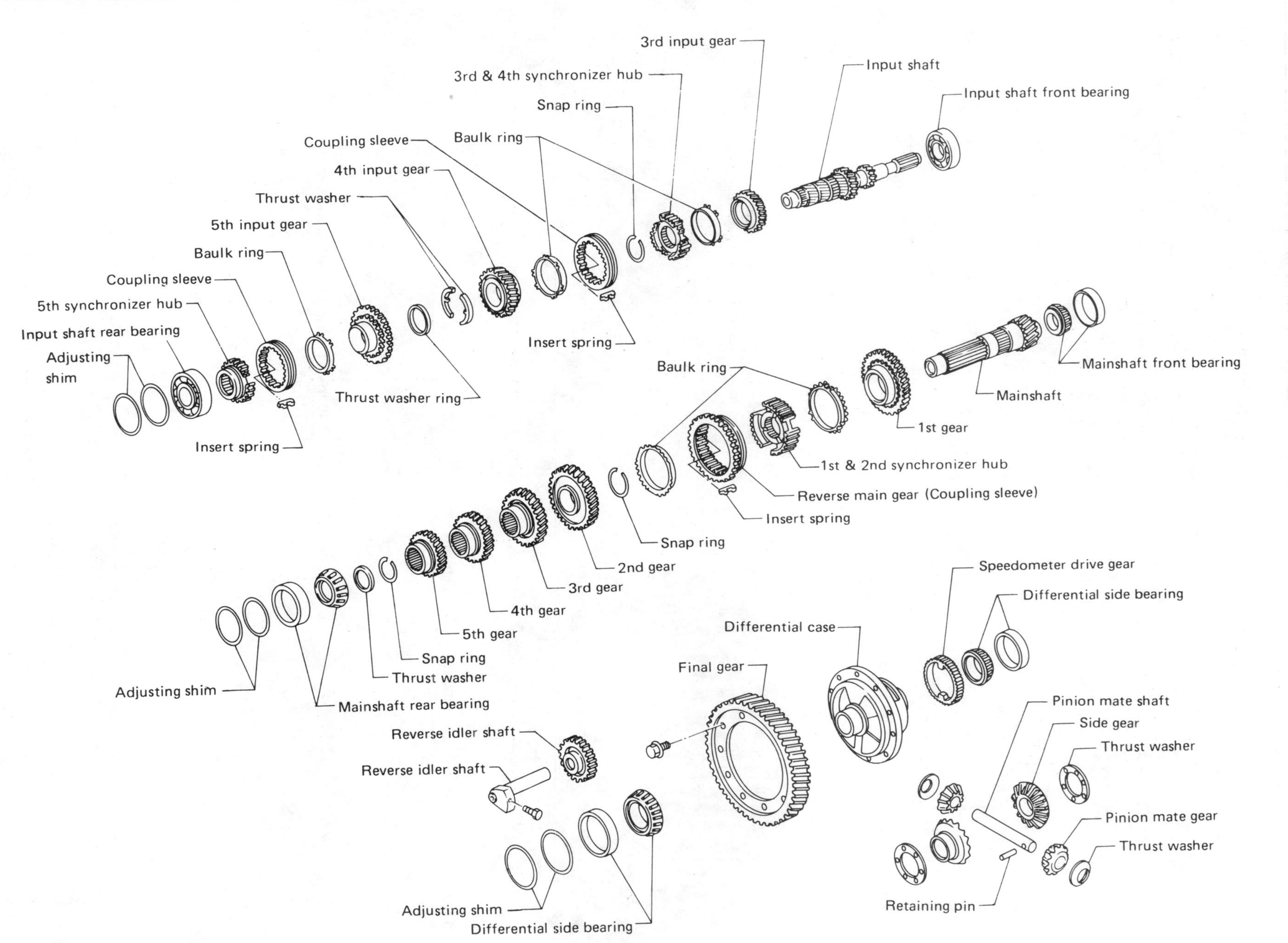

Fig. 6.37 Gear train components (Sec 12)

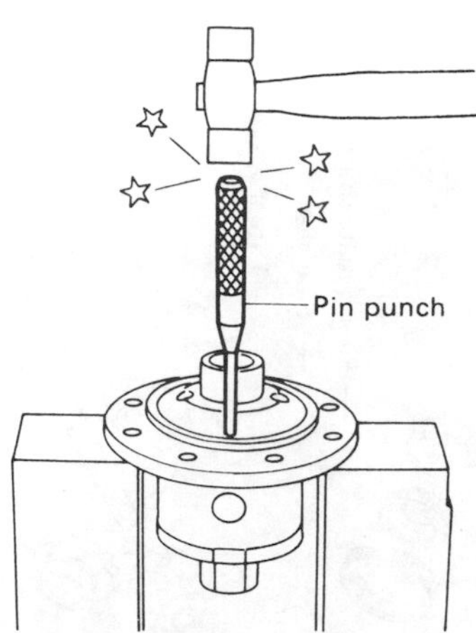

Fig. 6.38 Differential pinion shaft lock pin removal (Sec 12)

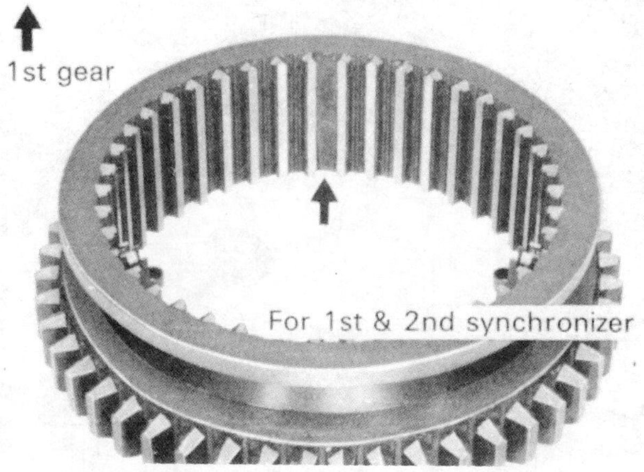

Fig. 6.39 Insert spring location on 1st/2nd synchro sleeve (Sec 13)

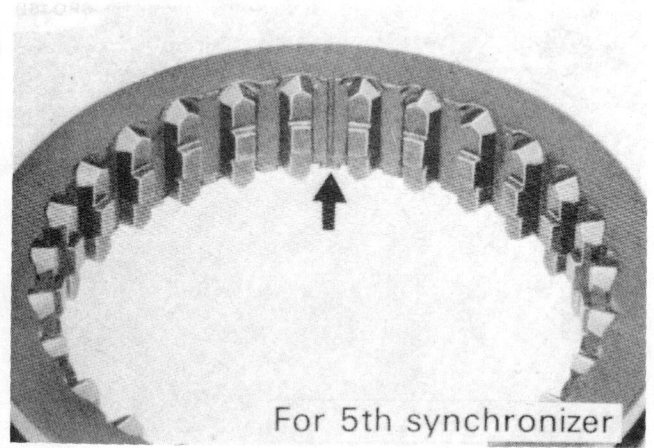

Fig. 6.41 Insert spring location on 5th synchro sleeve (Sec 13)

33 Remove the thrust washer and extract the circlip.
34 Support the 4th gear on a vice, then drive the mainshaft through to remove 5th and 4th gears together.
35 Similarly support the 2nd gear to remove 3rd and 2nd gears together.
36 Extract the circlip, then support the 1st gear and drive the mainshaft through to remove the 1st/2nd synchro unit and 1st gear.
37 Remove the bearing inner race from the front of the mainshaft by supporting it on a vice and driving the shaft through.

Differential/final drive

38 Drain off the side bearing inner races keeping them identified side for side.
39 Unbolt the crownwheel from the differential case.
40 Remove the speedometer drive gear and stop plate.
41 Using a punch, drive out the pinion shaft lock pin and withdraw the shaft.
42 Remove the pinion and side gears together with the thrust washers.

13 Transmission components (RS5F50A) – inspection

1 Refer to Part B, Section 8, but note that the synchro units are different. Instead of circular springs and keys, three insert springs are fitted. Refer to Figs. 6.39, 6.40 and 6.41.
2 Checking the synchro baulk rings is identical.
3 Mark the sleeve and hub before separating them to ensure correct reassembly.
4 When checking the mainshaft bearings, check the area shown in Fig. 6.42 which is susceptible to overheating.

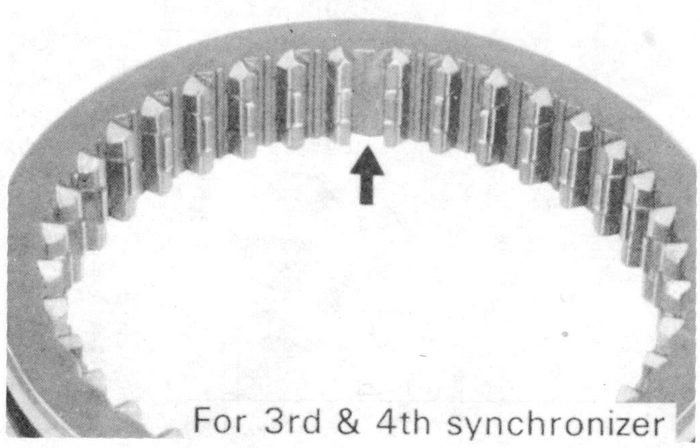

Fig. 6.40 Insert spring location on 3rd/4th synchro sleeve (Sec 13)

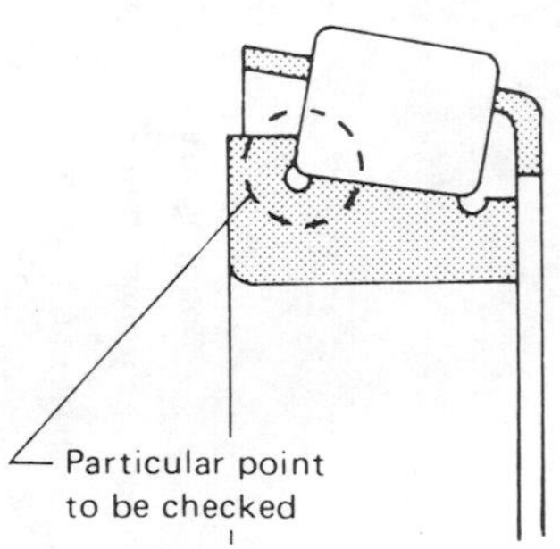

Fig. 6.42 Check the mainshaft bearings in the area shown (Sec 13)

14 Transmission (RS5F50A) – reassembly

Differential/final drive

1 Locate the side gears and thrust washers in the differential case, followed by the pinion gears and thrust washers.
2 Carefully insert the pinion shaft.
3 Drive in a new pinion shaft roll pin until flush with the differential case.
4 Clean the crownwheel bolts and apply thread locking fluid, then fit the crownwheel and tighten the bolts to the specified torque.
5 Fit the speedometer drive gear and stop plate.
6 Press on the side bearing inner races.

Mainshaft

7 Oil all components liberally as they are reassembled.
8 Press the bearing inner race on to the front of the mainshaft.
9 Fit the 1st gear and locate the baulk ring on it.
10 Press on the 1st/2nd synchro unit, making sure it is the correct way round (Fig. 6.43). Fit the 2nd baulk ring.
11 Fit the circlip. If the clearance in the groove exceeds 0.10 mm (0.0039 in) obtain a thicker circlip.
12 Locate 2nd gear on the mainshaft.
13 Press on the 3rd gear followed by the 4th and 5th gears.
14 Fit the circlip. If the clearance in the groove exceeds 0.15 mm (0.0059 in) obtain a thicker circlip.
15 Fit the thrust washer, then press on the rear bearing inner race.
16 Using a feeler blade, check that the gear endfloat is within the following tolerances.

1st gear	*0.23 to 0.43 mm (0.0091 to 0.0169 in)*
2nd gear	*0.23 to 0.58 mm (0.0091 to 0.0228 in)*

Input shaft

17 Oil all components liberally as they are reassembled.
18 Press on the front bearing using a metal tube on the inner track.
19 Locate the 3rd gear on the shaft together with the 3rd bulk ring.
20 Press on the 3rd/4th synchro unit making sure it is the correct way round (Fig. 6.44).
21 Fit the circlip. If the clearance in the groove exceeds 0.10 mm (0.0039 in) obtain a thicker circlip.
22 Fit the 4th baulk ring and 4th gear.
23 Fit the split thrust washers and ring. The thrust washers are obtainable in different thicknesses to adjust the gear endfloat.
24 Locate the 5th gear on the shaft together with the 5th baulk ring.
25 Press on the 5th synchro unit.
26 Press on the rear bearing using a metal tube on the inner track.
27 Using a feeler blade, check that the gear endfloat is within the following tolerances.

3rd gear	*0.23 to 0.43 mm (0.0091 to 0.0169 in)*
4th gear	*0.25 to 0.55 mm (0.0098 to 0.0217 in)*
5th gear	*0.23 to 0.48 mm (0.0091 to 0.0189 in)*

Transmission casing and clutch housing

28 Refer to Section 15 and if necessary carry out the bearing preload procedure in order to determine the correct shims to fit during reassembly.
29 Locate the shims in the transmission casing and drive in the mainshaft bearing outer track.
30 Drive the mainshaft bearing outer track into the clutch housing and refit the oil channel.
31 Similarly fit the differential side bearing outer tracks into the clutch housing and transmission casing.
32 Into the clutch housing, press a new input shaft oil seal and clutch release shaft seal.
33 Refit the clutch release fork and bearing with reference to Chapter 5.
34 Locate the lever in the clutch housing, then insert the striking rod. Secure the lever by driving in the retaining pin. Refit the drain plug.
35 Engage the selector with the striking lever, then insert the selector shaft and secure by driving in the retaining pin.
36 Fit the reverse check assembly and tighten the bolts.
37 Stand the clutch housing on the bench and fit the final drive/differential assembly.
38 Insert the 1st/2nd selector rod in the 1st/2nd selector fork and locate the fork on the mainshaft 1st/2nd synchro sleeve.

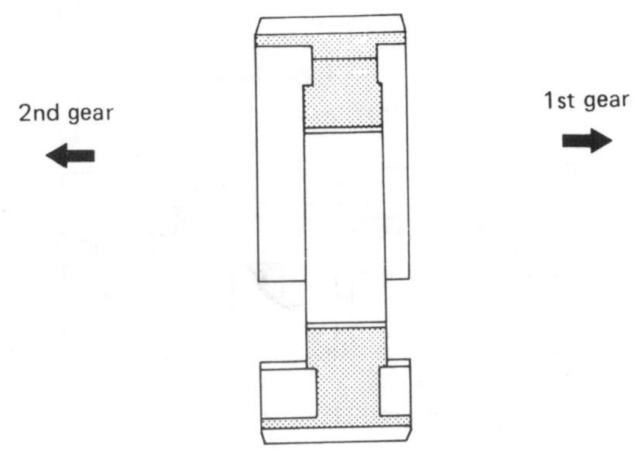

Fig. 6.43 Correct installation of 1st/2nd synchro unit (Sec 14)

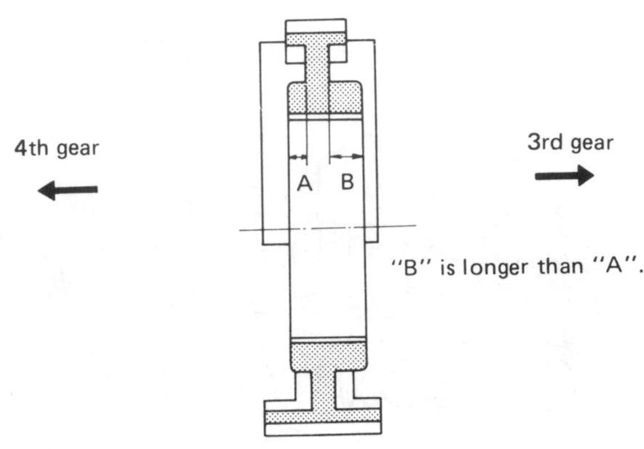

Fig. 6.44 Correct installation of 3rd/4th synchro unit (Sec 14)

39 Mesh the input shaft assembly with the mainshaft and lower them into the clutch housing, while guiding the 1st/2nd selector rod into its hole.
40 Insert the interlock ball, plunger, and further ball to lock the 1st/2nd selector rod.
41 Locate the 3rd/4th selector fork on the input shaft 3rd/4th synchro sleeve.
42 Locate the selector dog bracket and insert the 3rd/4th selector rod. Align the holes and drive in the roll pin. Fit the circlip to the lower end of the selector fork.
43 Insert the two interlock balls to lock the 3rd/4th selector rod.
44 Locate the 5th selector fork on the input shaft 5th synchro sleeve.
45 Locate the selector dog bracket and insert the 5th selector rod. Align the holes and drive in the roll pin. Fit the circlip to the lower end of the selector fork.
46 Insert the 5th/reverse detent ball and spring and tighten the detent plug.
47 Fit the reverse lever assembly and tighten the bolts.
48 Insert the reverse arm shaft and fit the retaining pin.
49 Select 4th gear. Locate the reverse idler gear, then insert the shaft. Position the shaft end fitting as shown in Fig. 6.47 so that the casing bolt will enter the threaded hole.
50 Check that the swarf magnet is located correctly in the clutch housing.
51 Grease the input shaft rear bearing shims and locate them in the transmission casing.
52 Apply jointing compound to the mating faces of the transmission casing and clutch housing.
53 Lower the transmission casing onto the clutch housing, then fit and tighten the bolts.

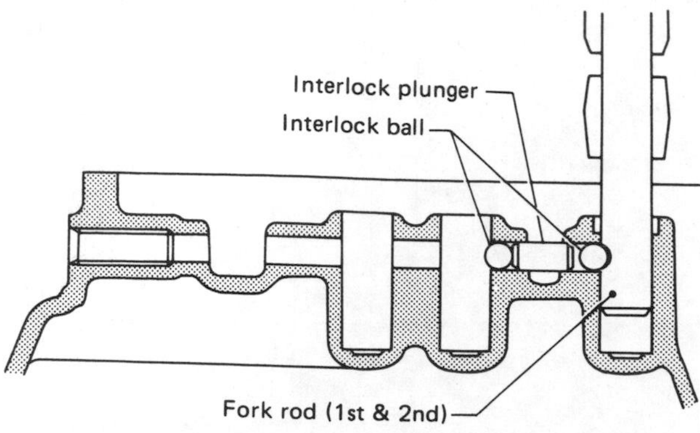

Fig. 6.45 Interlock balls and plunger refitting with 1st/2nd selector rod in place (Sec 14)

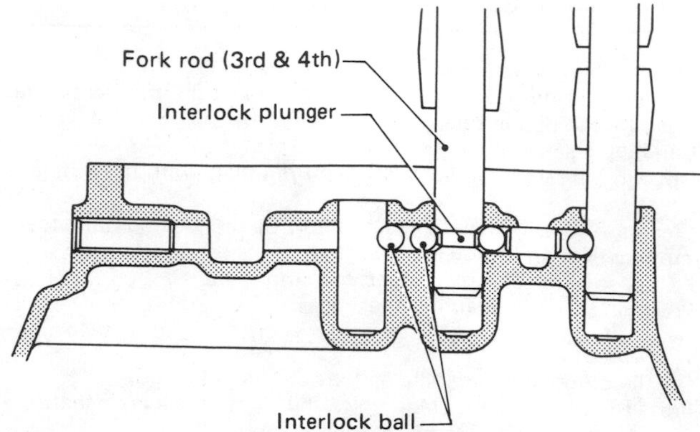

Fig. 6.46 Interlock balls refitting with 3rd/4th selector rod in place (Sec 14)

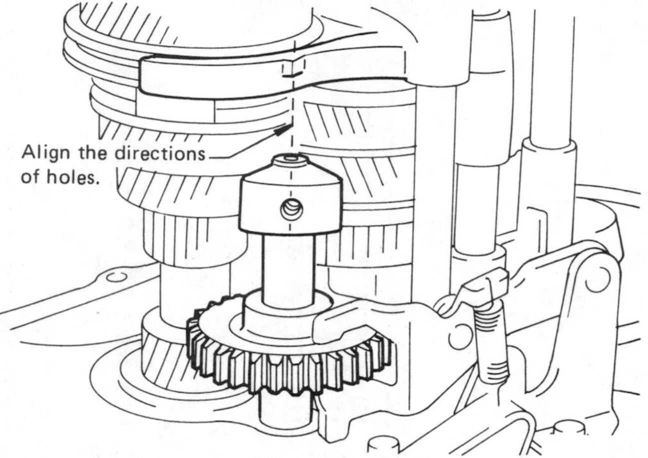

Fig. 6.47 Correct alignment of the reverse idler shaft (Sec 14)

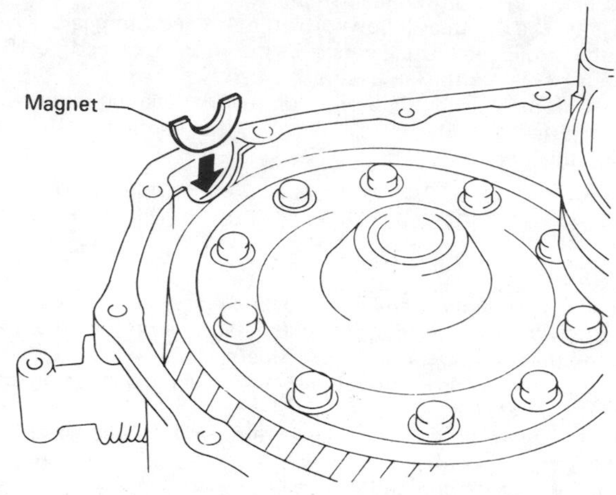

Fig. 6.48 Swarf magnet location in the clutch housing (Sec 14)

54 Insert the 1st/2nd and 3rd/4th detent balls and springs. Apply sealing compound to the the plug threads, then tighten the plugs.
55 Apply sealing compound to the bolt threads, then refit the position switch (with a new O-ring), the speedometer pinion, and the reverse idler shaft bolt.

15 Bearing preload (RS5F50A) – adjustment

1 If any of the following components have been renewed during overhaul, then the bearing preload must be checked and adjusted.

Clutch housing
Transmission casing
Input shaft
Mainshaft
Final drive/differential
Input or mainshaft bearings

2 Drive the differential side bearing outer track into the transmission casing without any shims.
3 Locate the input shaft and the final drive/differential assembly in the clutch housing.
4 Fit the transmission casing without the input shaft bearing shims and tighten the bolts.
5 Stand the unit on blocks of wood with the open end of the clutch housing upwards.
6 Attach a dial gauge to measure the movement of the final drive/differential unit, then record the end play, using a wooden dowel in the lower side gear to move the unit up and down.
7 The thickness of the shims to fit behind the differential side bearing outer track is the amount recorded in paragraph 6 **plus** a further 0.40 to 0.46 mm (0.0157 to 0.0181 in).
8 Attach a dial gauge to measure the movement of the input shaft (Fig. 6.51), then move the shaft up and down and record the end play.
9 The thickness of the shims to fit in the transmission casing is the amount recorded in paragraph 8 **less** 0 to 0.6 mm (0. to 0.0024 in).
10 Remove the transmission casing and lift out the input shaft and final drive/differential assembly.
11 Drive the mainshaft rear bearing outer track into the transmission casing without any shims.
12 Invert the transmission casing and locate the mainshaft assembly in the rear bearing outer track.
13 Locate the front bearing outer track on the mainshaft and rotate it while pressing down on it.
14 Measure the distance (A) from the joint face to the top of the outer track, using a straight edge (of known width) and a depth micrometer (Fig. 6.52).
15 Working on the clutch housing, measure the distance (B) from the joint face to the outer track seating, using a depth micrometer (Fig. 6.53).
16 Repeat the procedure in paragraphs 14 and 15 three times to arrive at two average dimensions for (A) and (B).
17 The mainshaft bearing clearance (C) is dimension (B) minus dimension (A).

$C = B - A$

18 The thickness of the shims to fit behind the mainshaft rear bearing outer track is dimension (C) **plus** 0.25 to 0.31 mm (0.0098 to 0.0122 in)

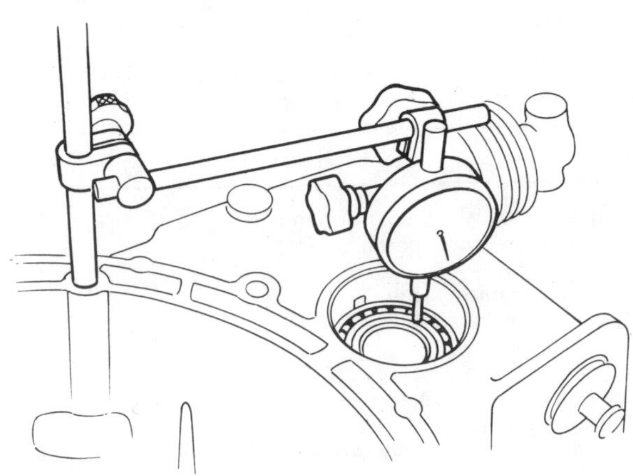
Fig. 6.49 Dial gauge location for checking the final drive/differential bearing endplay (Sec 15)

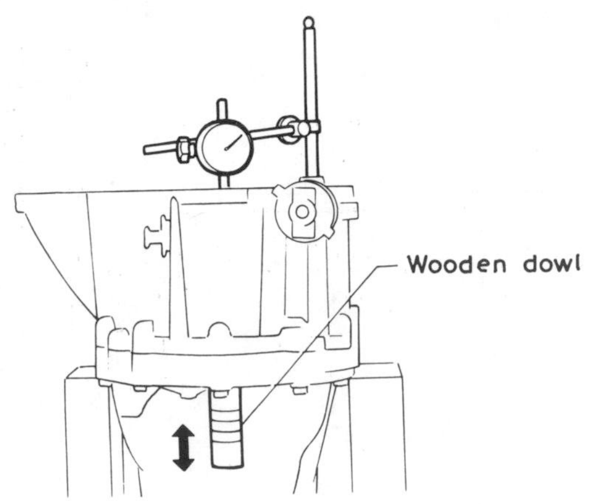

Fig. 6.50 Use a wooden dowel to move the final drive/differential (Sec 15)

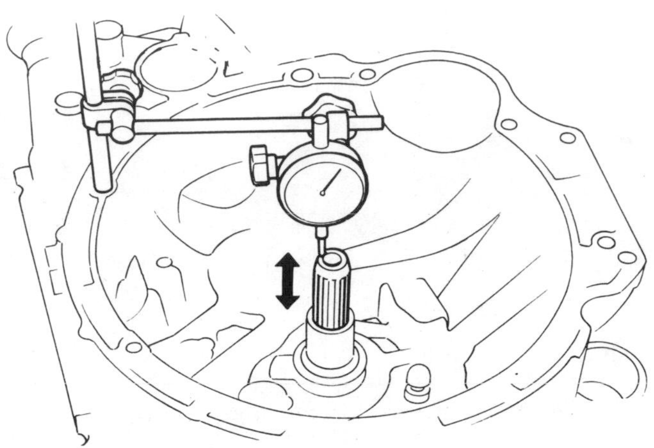
Fig. 6.51 Dial gauge location for checking the input shaft bearing endplay (Sec 15)

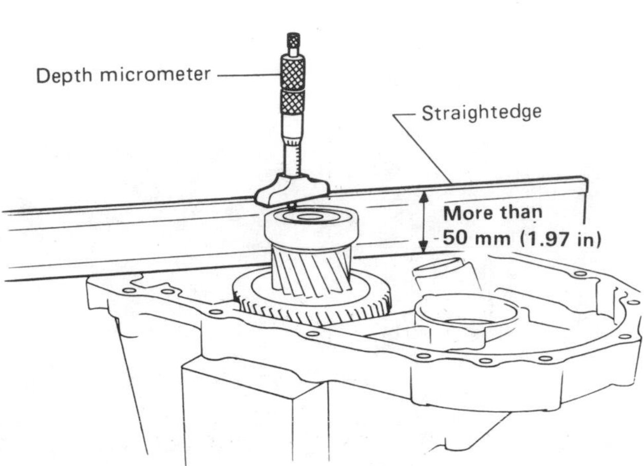

Fig. 6.52 Checking the mainshaft bearing clearance dimension (A) on the transmission casing (Sec 15)

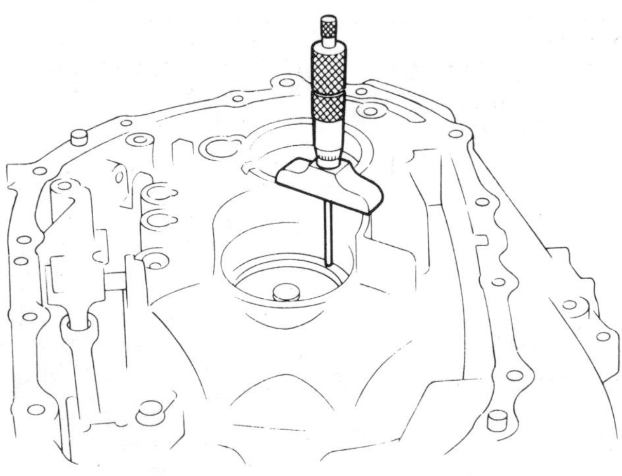
Fig. 6.53 Checking the mainshaft bearing clearance dimension (B) on the clutch housing (Sec 15)

PART D: ALL MODELS

16 Fault diagnosis – manual transmission

Symptom	Reason(s)
Weak or ineffective synchromesh	Synchro baulk rings worn, split or damaged Synchromesh units worn, or damaged
Jumps out of gear	Gearchange mechanism worn Synchromesh units badly worn Selector fork badly worn
Excessive noise	Incorrect grade of oil in gearbox or oil level too low Gearteeth excessively worn or damaged Intermediate gears or bushes worn allowing excessive end play Worn bearings
Difficulty in engaging gears	Cltuch pedal adjustment incorrect Worn selector components Worn synchromesh units

Chapter 7 Automatic transmission

Contents

Specifications

General

Type	RL4F02A, torque convertor with lock-up system, two planetary gear sets with multi-clutch and brake band, integral final drive, overdrive

Ratios

1st	2.785:1
2nd	1.545:1
3rd	1.000:1
4th (overdrive)	0.694:1
Reverse	2.272:1
Final drive	3.876:1
Fluid capacity	6.5 litre (11.4 pints)

Torque wrench settings

	Nm	lbf ft
Drive plate to torque converter	44	33
Transmission to engine	44	33
Cover plate	35	26
Dust cover	7	5
Engine stay	19	14
Valve cover	6	4
Control valve assembly	6	4
Governor cap	7	5
Speedometer fitting	7	5
Inhibitor switch	2	1.5
Control cylinder	7	5
Drain plug	18	13

1 General description

The automatic transmission comprises a torque converter, a planetary geartrain gearbox, and an integral final drive unit.

The torque converter provides a fluid coupling between the engine and transmission, and its three main components are an impeller, a turbine, and a stator. In addition, a lock-up system inside the assembly locks the impeller to the turbine during cruising to provide a more efficient torque transfer. The lock-up system is disengaged when the accelerator pedal is fully released or the engine is cold.

The planetary geartrain provides four speeds including one overdrive ratio which, like the other ratios, is engaged automatically. However an overdrive switch is provided which cuts out the overdrive ratio when in the off position.

Due to the need for special tools and equipment, work on the

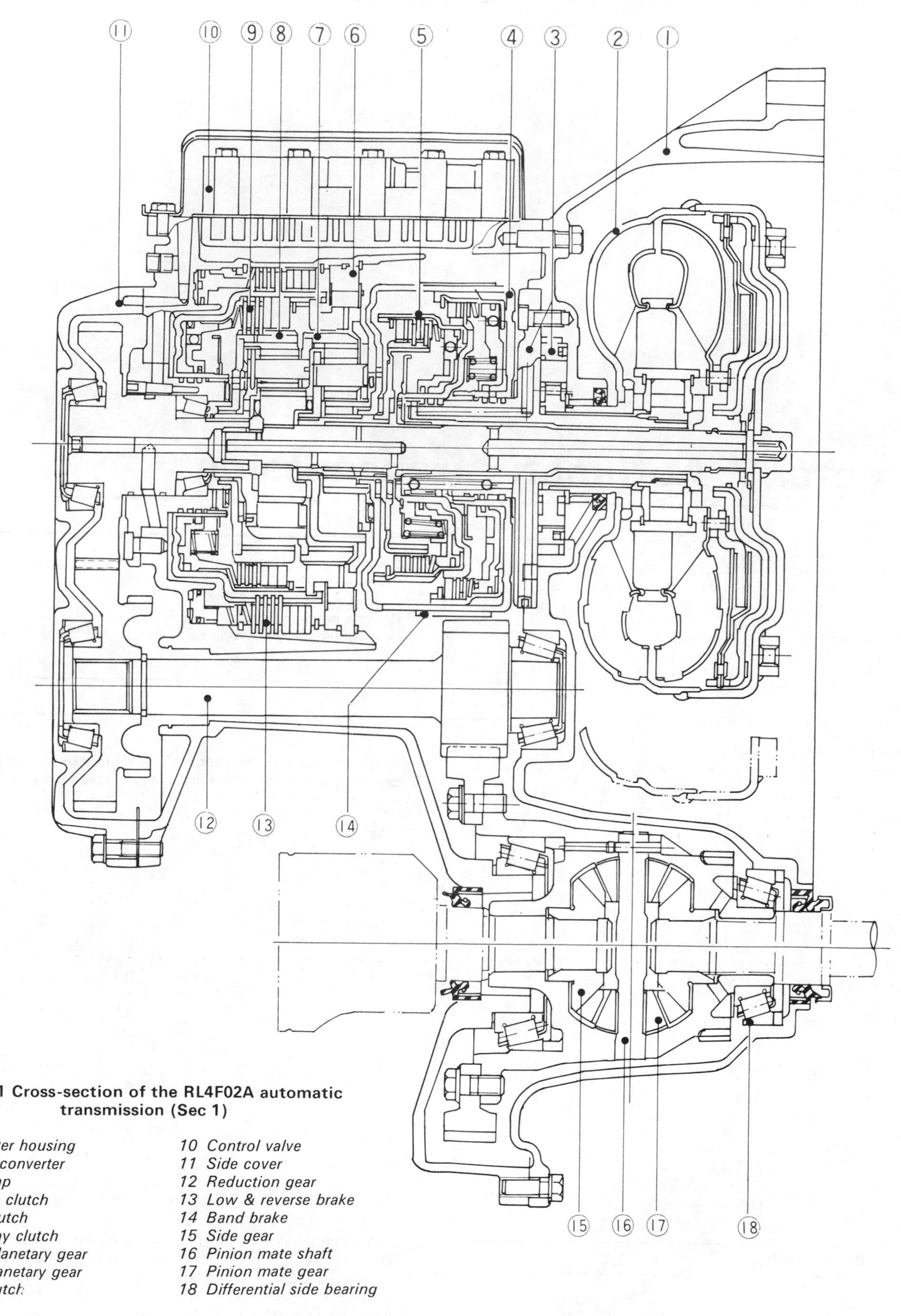

Fig. 7.1 Cross-section of the RL4F02A automatic transmission (Sec 1)

1 *Converter housing*
2 *Torque converter*
3 *Oil pump*
4 *Reverse clutch*
5 *High clutch*
6 *One-way clutch*
7 *Front planetary gear*
8 *Rear planetary gear*
9 *Low clutch*
10 *Control valve*
11 *Side cover*
12 *Reduction gear*
13 *Low & reverse brake*
14 *Band brake*
15 *Side gear*
16 *Pinion mate shaft*
17 *Pinion mate gear*
18 *Differential side bearing*

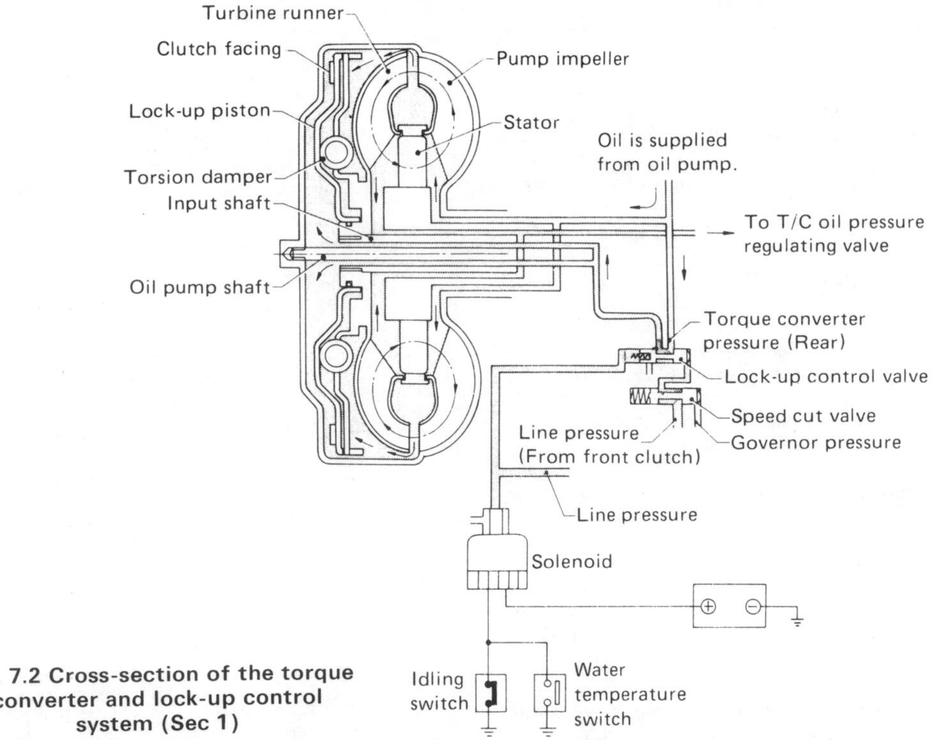

Fig. 7.2 Cross-section of the torque converter and lock-up control system (Sec 1)

automatic transmission should be limited to the procedures detailed in the following Sections. Where in-depth diagnosis is required, the car should be taken to a Nissan dealer or automatic transmission specialist.

2 Routine maintenance

Carry out the following procedures at the intervals given in *'Routine Maintenance'* at the beginning of the Manual.

Automatic transmission fluid level check

1 Although 'Cold' level marks are incorporated in the dipstick, a more accurate check is obtained with the fluid hot after at least 10 minutes driving.

2 Park the car on a level surface and apply the handbrake.

3 Run the engine at idling speed then move the selector lever slowly through each position ending in Park (P).

4 Withdraw the dipstick and wipe it clean, then reinsert it fully into the guide tube and withdraw it again.

5 The fluid level should be within the limits shown in Fig. 7.3. Note that if the car has previously been driven at high speeds, in hot city conditions, or towing a trailer, the fluid should be allowed to cool for approximately 30 minutes before checking the level.

6 If required, top up the level by pouring additional fluid through the dipstick guide tube, using a suitable funnel. Do not, however overfill the transmission otherwise serious damage can occur.

Automatic transmission fluid condition

7 Whenever the dipstick is removed, make a close examination of the fluid withdrawn. If it is very dark in appearance or smells burned, the internal clutch friction linings may be disintegrating and in need of renewal.

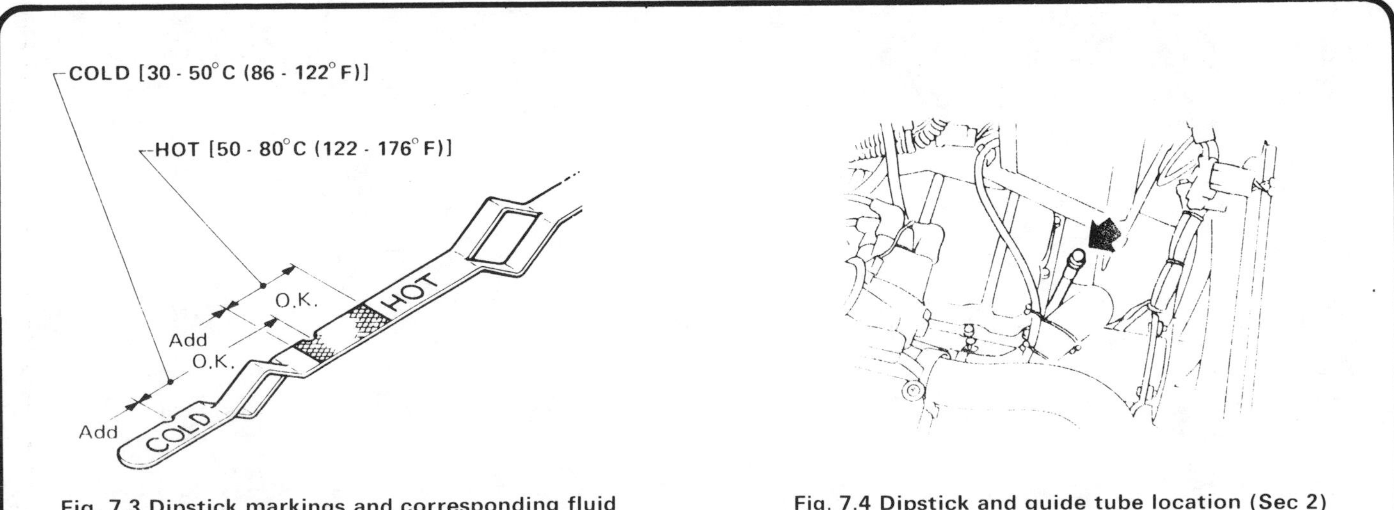

Fig. 7.3 Dipstick markings and corresponding fluid temperatures (Sec 2)

Fig. 7.4 Dipstick and guide tube location (Sec 2)

3 Automatic transmission – in car adjustment

Kickdown cable

1 Remove the air cleaner and/or inlet ducting.
2 Loosen the cable adjusting nuts at the engine bracket.
3 Move the throttle quadrant to its fully open position (P1 in Fig. 7.5), then pull the adjustment ferrule away from the quadrant (direction T in Fig. 7.5).
4 Tighten nut 'B' onto the bracket, then back it off three complete turns and tighten nut 'A'.
5 Mark the inner cable with a dab of paint, then check that the inner cable stroke is between 39.0 and 43.0 mm (1.54 and 1.69 in).
6 Failure to adjust the kickdown cable correctly will result in an incorrect shift speed range. Note that an adjustment ferrule is also provided at the transmission end of the cable, so if it is found that there is insufficient adjustment at the engine bracket end, the outer cable can be repositioned as required at the transmission end.

Selector lever cable

7 The cable should be adjusted if the cable or lever has been renewed, after refitting the transmission, or if the lever detents are not aligned with the positions on the indicator.
8 Move the selector lever to the Park (P) position.
9 Apply the handbrake, then jack up the front of the car and support on axle stands.
10 Loosen the two adjustment nuts on the inner cable end fitting, so that they are well clear of the trunnion on the bottom of the selector lever.
11 Make sure that both the selector lever and the lever at the transmission end are in the Park (P) position, then screw the adjustment nuts lightly onto the trunnion. Finally tighten the nuts.
12 Lower the car to the ground.

Inhibitor switch

13 Move the selector lever to the Neutral (N) position.
14 Loosen the crosshead screws securing the inhibitor switch to the transmission.
15 Obtain a 4.0 mm (0.160 in) diameter metal pin or twist drill, and position the inhibitor switch so that the pin can be inserted through the special holes in the lever and switch (Fig. 7.9).
16 Tighten the crosshead screws, then remove the pin.

Brake band

17 Remove the control valve assembly as described in Section 7.
18 Loosen the locknut, then tighten the brake bank end pin to 4 to 6 Nm (2.9 to 4.3 lbf ft). Back off the end pin by 4 1/2 turns exactly, then tighten the locknut while holding the end pin stationary.
19 Refit the control valve assembly with reference to Section 7.

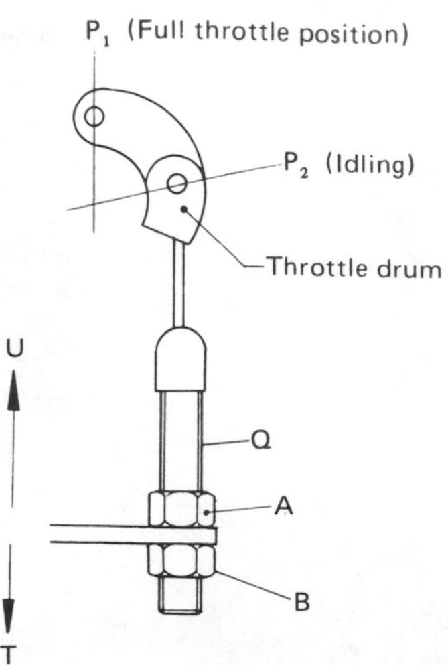

Fig. 7.5 Kickdown cable adjustment (Sec 3)

A and B Locknuts *Q Adjustment ferrule*

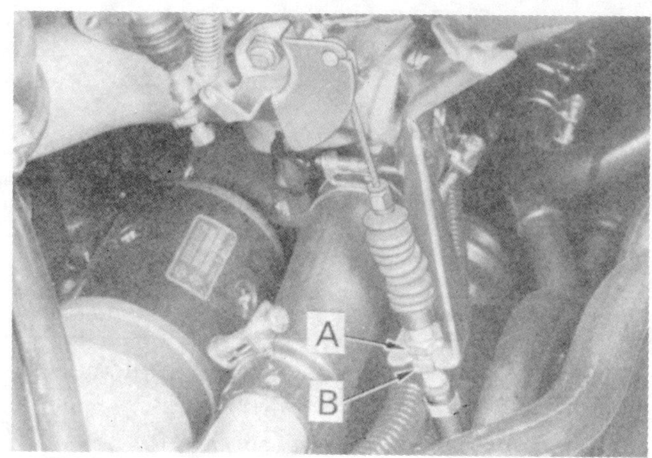

Fig. 7.6 Kickdown cable adjustment nuts A and B at the engine bracket (Sec 3)

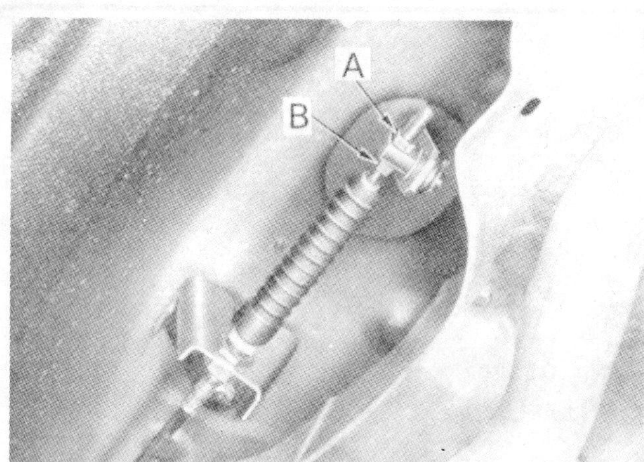

Fig. 7.7 Selector lever cable adjustment nuts (A and B) at the trunnion on the bottom of the lever (Sec 3)

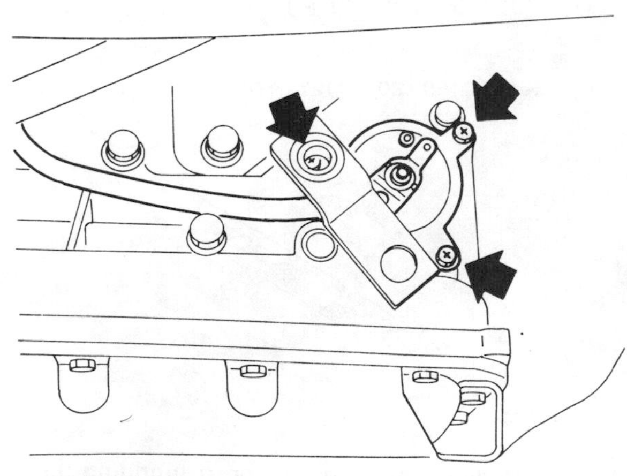

Fig. 7.8 Inhibitor switch mounting screw locations (Sec 3)

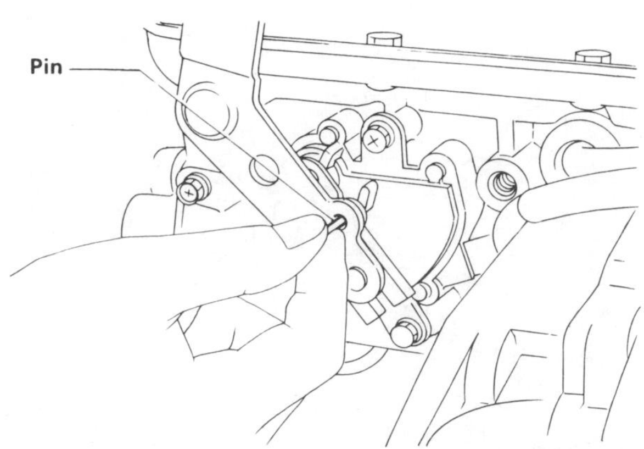

Fig. 7.9 Inhibitor switch adjustment (Sec 3)

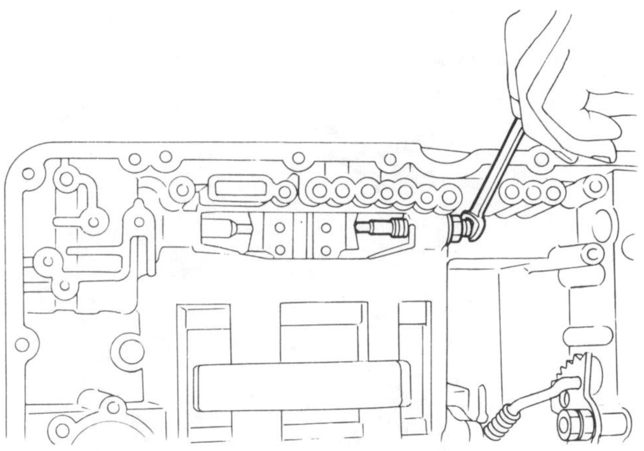

Fig. 7.10 Adjusting the brake band (Sec 3)

4 Kickdown cable – renewal

1 Remove the air cleaner and/or inlet ducting.
2 Unscrew the cable adjusting nuts at the engine bracket, then release the outer cable from the bracket and the inner cable from the throttle quadrant.
3 Similarly at the transmission end, unscrew the nuts, then release the outer cable from the cover bracket and the inner cable from the transmission lever.
4 Withdraw the cable from the engine compartment.
5 Fit the new cable using a reversal of the removal procedure, and finally adjust it with reference to Section 3.

5 Selector lever cable – renewal

1 Apply the handbrake, then jack up the front of the car and support on axle stands.
2 Unscrew the adjustment nuts and disconnect the inner cable end fitting fom the trunnion on the bottom of the selector lever.
3 Remove the boot, then unscrew the nut and disconnect the outer cable from the underbody bracket.
4 Extract the split pin and disconnect the inner cable end fitting from the selector lever on the transmission. Note the position of the plain and spring washers and the insulator.
5 Remove the boot, then unscrew the nut and disconnect the outer cable from the bracket on the transmission.
6 Release the cable from the clips and withdraw it from the car.
7 Fit the new cable using a reversal of the removal procedure, and finally adjust it with reference to Section 3.

6 Governor – removal and refitting

1 This will only be required if a fault is indicated after reference to Section 10.
2 Release the selector lever cable from the clip, then unbolt the governor cap and remove the gasket.
3 Unscrew the bolt and extract the governor pin.
4 Withdraw the governor assembly from the transmission, while disengaging it from the speedometer drive gear.
5 Refitting is a reversal of removal, but fit a new cap gasket.

7 Control valve assembly – removal and refitting

1 Remove the battery and the mounting bracket with reference to Chapter 12.
2 Disconnect the kickdown and selector lever cables from the transmission with reference to Sections 4 and 5.

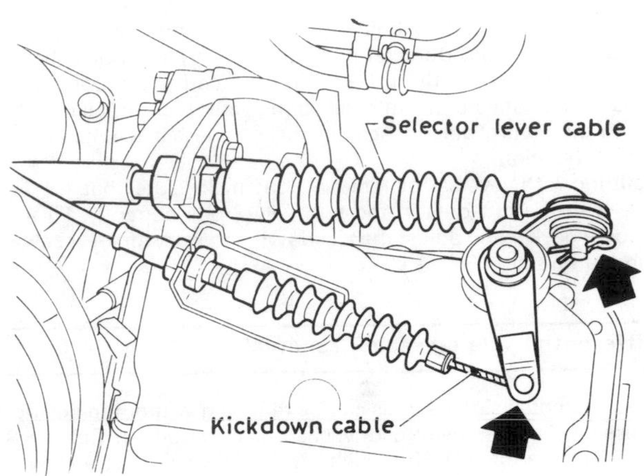

Fig. 7.11 Kickdown and selector lever cable attachment at the transmission (Secs 4 and 5)

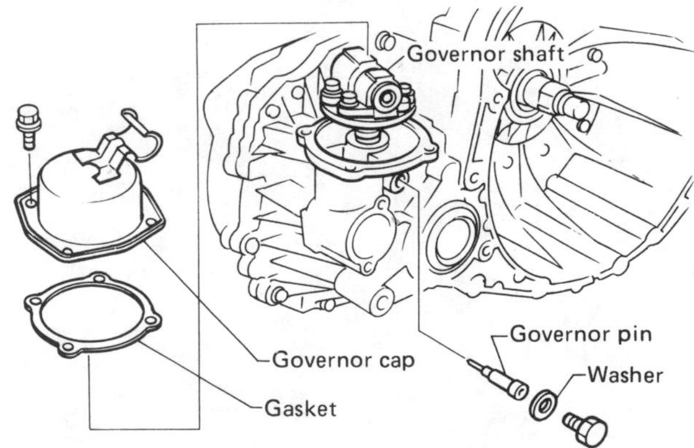

Fig. 7.12 Governor components (Sec 6)

3 Unscrew the nut and withdraw the kickdown lever from its shaft, noting which way round it is fitted.
4 Unbolt the control cylinder.
5 Unbolt the valve cover and remove it together with the gasket.
6 Note the location of the wiring harness, then disconnect it from the solenoids and terminal.

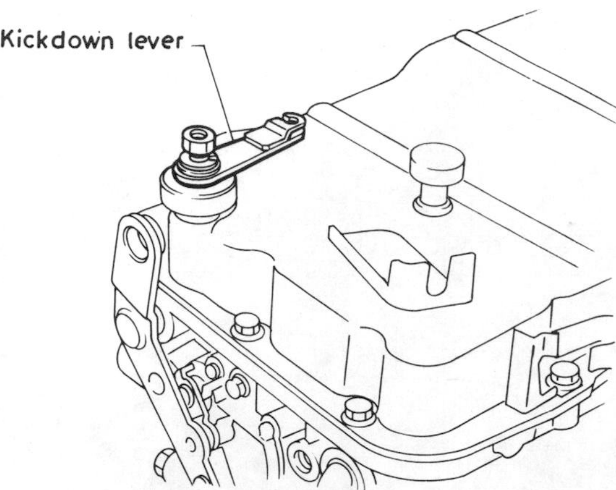

Fig. 7.13 Removing the kickdown lever from the transmission (Sec 7)

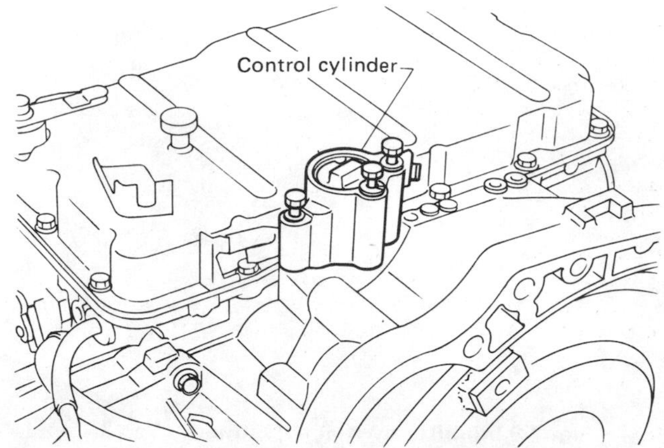

Fig. 7.14 Removing the control cylinder (Sec 7)

7 Unscrew the mounting bolts and lift the control valve assembly from the transmission. Be careful to remove only the bolts shown in Fig. 7.15 – removal of the other bolts will cause the control valve sections to separate and the internal springs and balls to fall out. When removing the control valve assembly, make sure that the manual valve remains in position.

8 Refitting is a reversal of removal, but make sure that the levers engage with the cut-outs in the two valve rods correctly. Fit a new valve cover gasket and adjust the kickdown and selector lever cables as described in Section 3.

8 Differential side oil seals – renewal

1 The differential side oil seals can be renewed without removing the transmission. First remove the driveshaft as described in Chapter 8.

2 Prise out the oil seal. If difficulty is experienced, use a claw-type extractor as shown in Fig. 7.17. Clean the oil seal seating.

3 Dip the new oil seal in automatic transmissioon fluid, then drive it squarely into the transmission casing using a piece of tubing.

4 Refit the driveshaft with reference to Chapter 8.

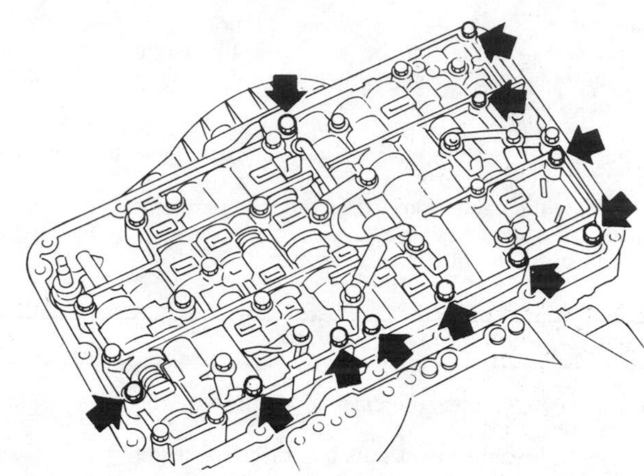

Fig. 7.15 Location of the control valve assembly mounting bolts (Sec 7)

Fig. 7.16 Showing correct engagement of levers and rods when refitting the control valve assembly (Sec 7)

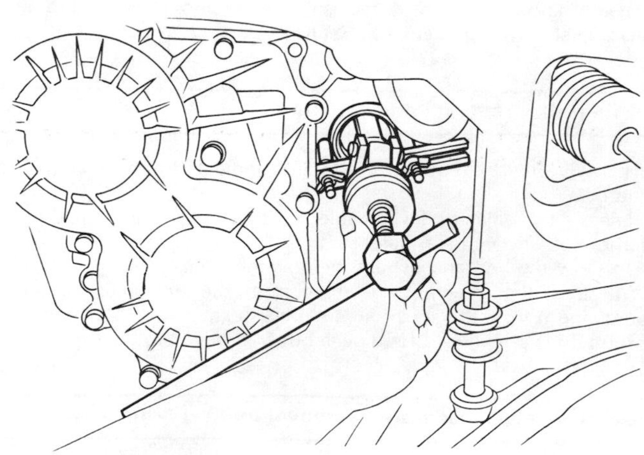

Fig. 7.17 Using a claw extractor to remove a differential side oil seal (Sec 8)

9 Automatic transmission – removal and refitting

1 Remove the battery (Chapter 12) and unbolt the battery tray.
2 Remove both driveshafts as described in Chapter 8.
3 Remove the engine compartment undershield.
4 Unscrew the drain plug from the bottom front of the transmission and drain the fluid into a suitable container. Clean and refit the plug when complete.
5 Unbolt the cover plate from the bottom of the torque converter housing, noting the positions of the engine stay and the exhaust support bracket.
6 Mark the relationship of the torque converter to the driveplate with quick-drying paint and then unscrew the converter-to-driveplate connecting bolts. The crankshaft will have to be turned by means of the crankshaft pulley bolt to bring the connecting bolts into view within the aperture left by removal of the cover plate.
7 Disconnect the speedometer drive cable and the wiring for the inhibitor switch, lock-up and overdrive systems from the transmission.
8 Disconnect the kickdown cable (Section 4) and the selector lever cable (Section 5).
9 Unbolt the shield from the inner side of the left-hand front wing.
10 Disconnect the oil cooler hoses and plug or cap them.
11 Support the weight of the transmission either with a trolley jack or hoist.
12 Unscrew and remove the bolts connecting the torque converter housing to the engine.
13 Unbolt the front transmission mounting from the front panel.
14 Withdraw the transmission from the engine, but keep the torque converter in full engagement with the oil pump, otherwise the fluid will spill from the torque converter.
15 With the transmission clear of the engine, lower it to the ground.
16 Before refitting the transmission, check that the torque converter is correctly engaged with the oil pump by using a straight edge and steel rule, as shown in Fig. 7.20, taking the measurement from one of the mounting bosses.
17 Refitting is a reversal of removal, but apply locking fluid to the threads of the torque converter bolts and tighten them to the specified torque. Refill the transmission with the correct quantity of fluid and adjust the kickdown cable and selector lever cable with reference to Section 3.

Fig. 7.19 Lowering the automatic transmission from the engine compartment with a sling (Sec 9)

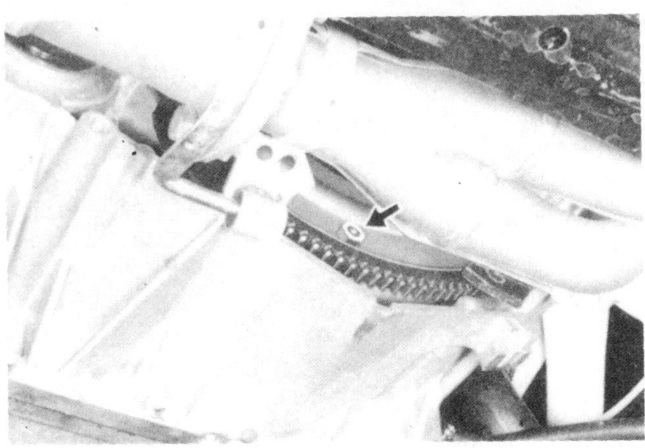

Fig. 7.18 Showing a torque converter bolt with the transmission cover plate removed (Sec 9)

Fig. 7.20 Checking full engagement of the torque converter before refitting the automatic transmission (Sec 9)

A = 19.0 mm (0.75 in) minimum

10 Fault diagnosis – automatic transmission

Symptom	Reason(s)
Starter operates in positions other than N or P	Incorrectly adjusted inhibitor switch Incorrectly adjusted selector lever cable
Noise in N and P positions	Low fluid level
Jerk when shifting from N to D positions	Engine idling speed too high Incorrectly adjusted kickdown cable
Failure to change gear	Incorrectly adjusted selector lever cable Incorrectly adjusted kickdown cable Faulty governor Poor fluid quality
Poor maximum speed and acceleration	Low fluid level Incorrectly adjusted selector lever cable
Transmission overheats	Low fluid level Poor fluid quality Faulty oil pump or torque converter

Chapter 8 Driveshaft and hubs

Contents

Specifications

Driveshafts

Type .... Open, with spider inner joint and constant velocity outer joint. RH support bearing on Turbo and 2.0 litre models

Joint grease capacity:	Inner	Outer
Non-Turbo models	230 g (8.1 oz)	165 g (5.8 oz)
Turbo models	260 g (9.2 oz)	215 g (7.6 oz)

Front hubs

Type .... Twin taper roller bearings with single outer track

Rear hubs

Type .... Two separate taper roller bearings

Torque wrench settings

	Nm	lbf ft
Driveshaft nut	235 to 314	174 to 231

1 General description

The driveshafts are of open type, with a spider type inner joint and a constant velocity outer joint. On Turbo and 2.0 litre models, the right-hand driveshaft incorporates an extension and support bearing.

The front hubs incorporate twin taper roller bearings which are not adjustable, but are pre-loaded by tightening the driveshaft nut. Note that the weight of the car must be put on the bearings without the driveshaft being fitted.

The rear hubs incorporate two taper roller bearings each, with a separate outer track. Bearing preload is adjustable with the stub axle nut.

2 Routine maintenance

Carry out the following procedures at the intervals given in *'Routine Maintenance'* at the beginning of the Manual.

Driveshaft bellows and joints

1 Jack up the front of the car and support on axle stands. Apply the handbrake. Turn each driveshaft and check the bellows for splits or damage. If evident, renew the bellows immediately, otherwise the driveshaft joint could be damaged by lack of lubrication or contamination with external dirt.

2 At the same time, check the driveshaft inner and outer joints by gripping the centre section and attempting to move it up and down.

Wheel bearings

3 Jack up the front of the car until the wheels just clear the ground. Grip the top and bottom of each wheel in turn and attempt to rock it. If any play is evident, the wheel bearings are possibly worn and should be renewed, however, make sure that the movement is not due to wear in the lower suspension balljoint.

4 Check the rear wheel bearings in the same way, but if any play exists adjust the preload. Any roughness evident in the bearing indicates excessive wear, in which case the bearings should be renewed.

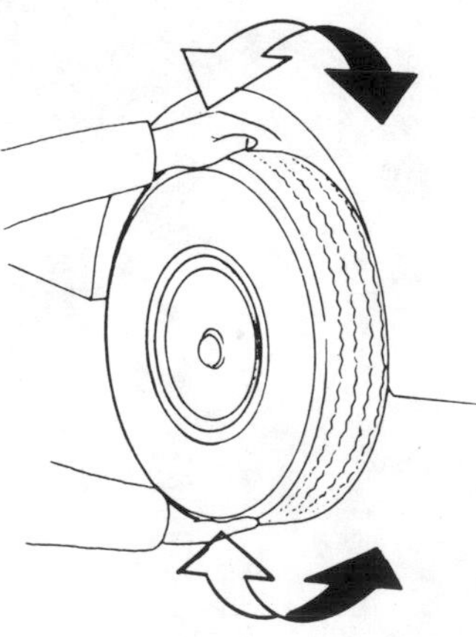

Fig. 8.1 Method of checking for wheel bearing play (Sec 2)

3 Driveshaft – removal and refitting

1 Remove the appropriate front wheel embellisher, then prise off the plastic cap and remove the split pin, locking ring and soft washer from the end of the driveshaft (photos).
2 With the handbrake applied, loosen the driveshaft nut using a socket and long extension. If preferred, the nut can be loosened after removal of the front wheel by refitting two wheel nuts and using a flat bar between two wheel studs.
3 Jack up the front of the car and support on axle stands, then remove the wheel, driveshaft nut and washer.
4 Unscrew the nut, then use a balljoint separator tool to disconnect the tie-rod end from the steering arm.
5 Unscrew the three nuts and separate the lower suspension arm from the lower balljoint.
6 Pull the hub and strut off of the driveshaft (photo). If necessary, tap the driveshaft through the hub splines using a mallet.
7 On Turbo and 2.0 litre models, the right-hand driveshaft incorporates a support bearing which is located in a bracket bolted to the cylinder block. On this driveshaft, unscrew the bolts securing the bearing housing to the bracket, then use a long rod to tap the housing

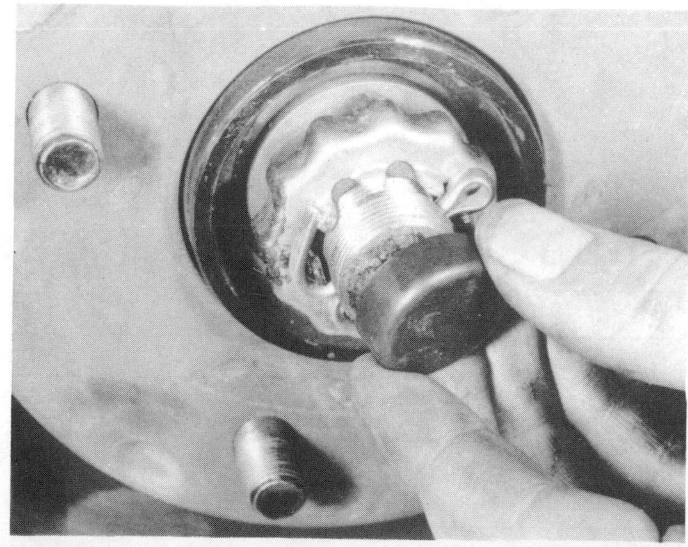
3.1A From the end of the driveshaft remove the plastic cap ...

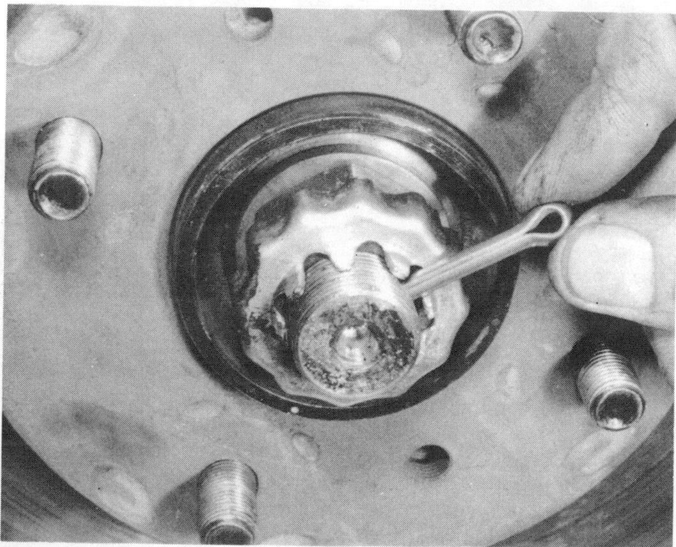
3.1B ... split pin ...

3.1C ... locking ring ...

3.1D ... and soft washer

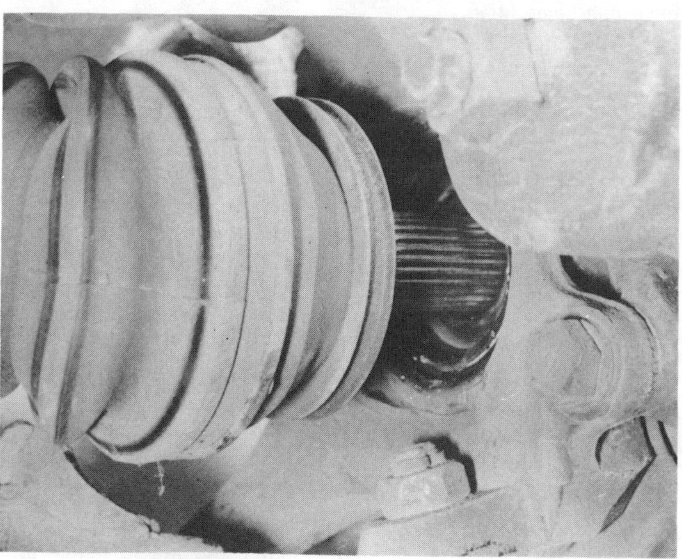
3.6 Separating the driveshaft from the hub

from the bracket, while guiding the extension shaft out of the differential side gear.
8 On all driveshafts except the type mentioned in paragraph 7, use a lever inserted between the inner joint and the transmission casing to prise out the driveshaft, so that the retaining circlip is released from the differential side gear.
9 If it is required to remove the support bearing bracket on Turbo and 2.0 litre models, first support the engine with a trolley jack and wooden block positioned under the sump, then unbolt and remove the bracket.
10 Refitting is a reversal of removal, but where applicable make sure that the driveshaft retaining circlip is fully engaged with the groove in the differential side gear, by pulling sharply on the inner joint by hand. Tighten all nuts and bolts to the specified torque and replenish any oil/fluid lost from the transmission (photo).

4 Driveshaft – overhaul

1 With the driveshaft removed, clean the exterior, then mount the centre shaft section in a vice.
2 Release the bellows clips, remove the bellows from the inner and outer joints and slide them towards the centre of the shaft (photos).
3 Mark both joint housings in relation to the centre shaft, then slide the inner joint off of the spider assembly. Make sure that the rollers remain on the spider assembly.
4 Mark the spider assembly in relation to the centre shaft.
5 Using circlip pliers extract the circlip from the inner end of the centre shaft, then slide the spider assembly from the splines.
6 Remove the inner bellows from the centre shaft, however if it is to be refitted, first cover the splines on the end of the shaft with adhesive tape to prevent damage to the bellows.
7 Remove the outer joint from the centre shaft splines by lightly tapping it with a mallet. The outer joint cannot be dismantled, but can be renewed as an assembly.
8 Remove the outer bellows from the centre shaft, however if it is to be refitted, first cover the splines on the end of the shaft with adhesive tape to prevent damage to the bellows.

3.10 Tightening the driveshaft nut

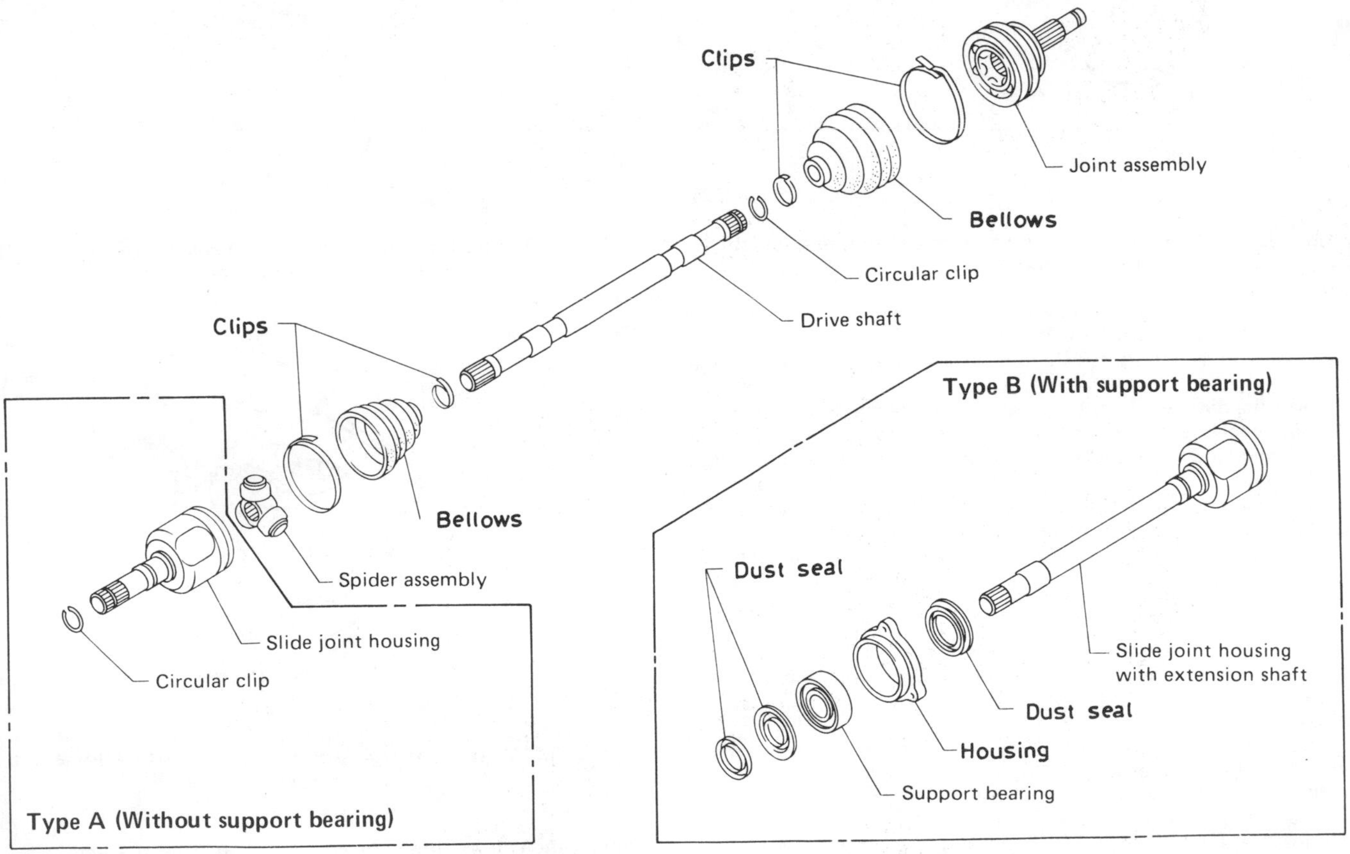

Clips
Joint assembly
Bellows
Circular clip
Drive shaft
Clips
Bellows
Spider assembly
Slide joint housing
Circular clip
Type A (Without support bearing)
Type B (With support bearing)
Dust seal
Slide joint housing with extension shaft
Dust seal
Housing
Support bearing

Fig. 8.2 Exploded view of the driveshaft (Sec 4)

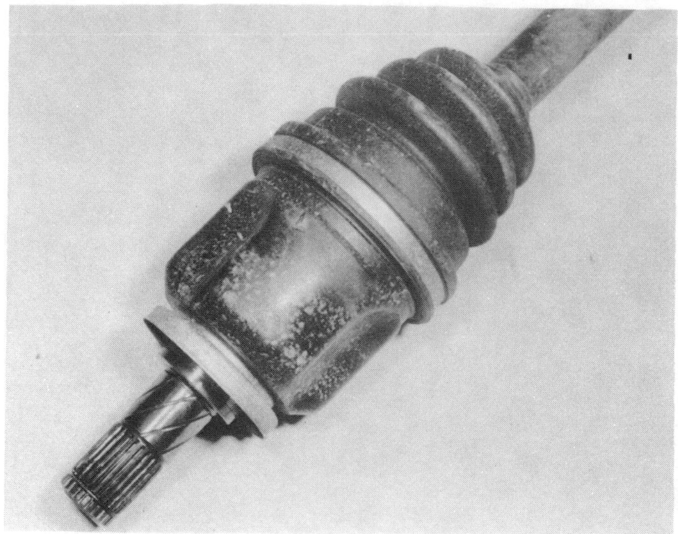

4.2A Driveshaft inner joint and bellows

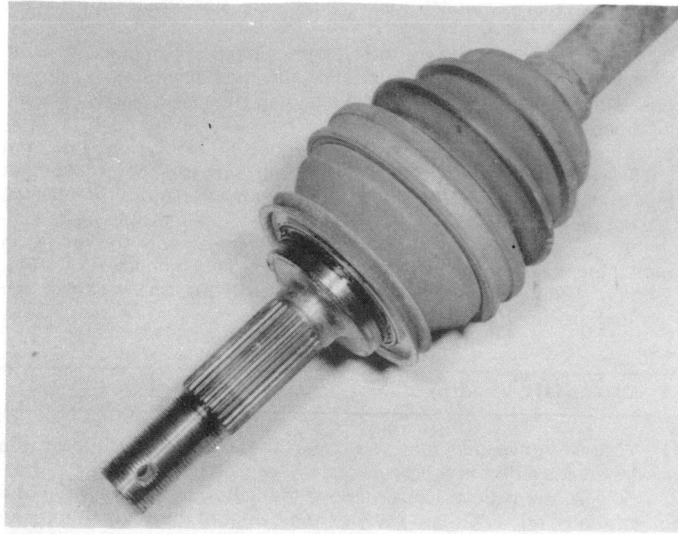

4.2B Driveshaft outer joint and bellows

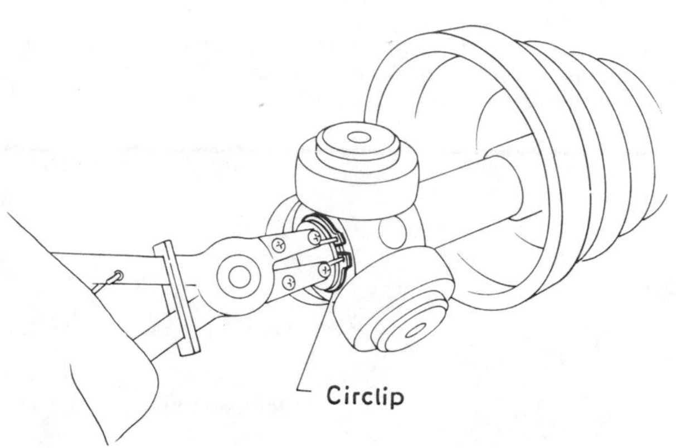

Fig. 8.3 Extract the circlip to remove the spider assembly (Sec 4)

9 On Turbo and 2.0 litre models the support bearing can be removed from the right-hand driveshaft as follows.
10 Using a suitable drift, tap the dust seal from the inner end of the extension shaft.
11 Lever the dust seal from the inner side of the support bearing.
12 Using circlip pliers, extract the circlip, then mount the bearing in a vice as shown in Fig. 8.4 and press or drive the extension shaft through the bearing.
13 Mount the bearing housing in the vice, then use a suitable metal tube to drive out the bearing and outer dust seal.
14 Clean all the components and check them for wear, damage and deterioration. Check the bellows for splits. Spin the support bearing and check it for excessive play or roughness which would indicate excessive wear.
15 Repair kits are available for both the inner and outer joints, the inner and outer bellows, and the support bearing. Note that the outer joint kit also includes the centre shaft, but not the inner spider assembly.
16 Commence reassembly by covering the splines on the centre shaft with adhesive tape to prevent damage to the bellows.
17 Fit the outer bellows to the centre shaft.
18 Fit a new circular clip to the groove in the splines, then locate the outer joint on the splines and tap it on until the circular clip engages the groove in the joint. Make sure that the previously made marks are aligned where applicable.
19 Pack the outer joint with the specified amount of grease (supplied with the kit), then locate the bellows on the joint and fit the clip.

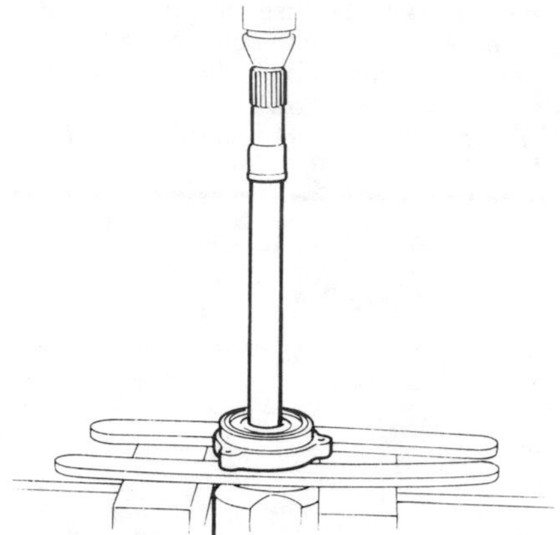

Fig. 8.4 Method of removing the extension shaft from the support bearing (Sec 4)

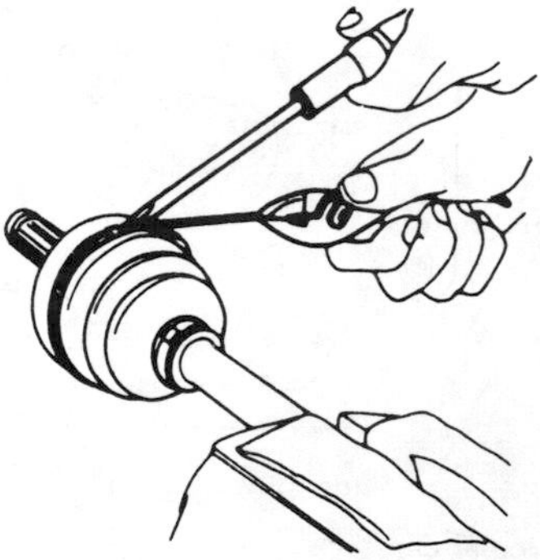

Fig. 8.5 Method of tightening a driveshaft bellows clip (Sec 4)

Tighten the clip as shown in Fig. 8.5, then bend the end back and secure with the tags.
20 Set the outer bellows to the dimension shown in Fig. 8.7 and release any trapped air.
21 Fit the inner clip using the method described in paragraph 19.

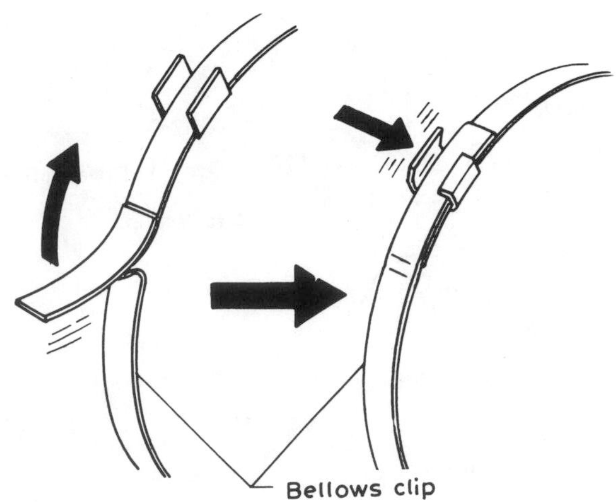

Fig. 8.6 Secure the clip by bending the end back under the tags (Sec 4)

22 Fit the inner bellows to the centre shaft.
23 Locate the spider assembly on the shaft splines, slide it fully on, then fit the circlip in the groove. Make sure that the previously made marks are aligned where applicable.
24 On Turbo and 2.0 litre models, reassemble the support bearing on the right-hand driveshaft as follows before refitting the inner joint. Where this is not applicable proceed to paragraph 30.
25 Drive the support bearing into the bearing housing using a metal tube on the outer track.
26 Press the outer dust seal into the housing using a block of wood.
27 Locate the housing on a vice, then insert the extension shaft and drive it fully into the bearing. Fit the circlip in the groove provided.
28 Press the inner dust seal into the housing.
29 Using a metal tube, press the dust seal onto the inner end of the extension shaft.
30 Locate the inner joint on the spider assembly making sure that the previously made marks are aligned where applicable.
31 Pack the inner joint with the specified amount of grease (supplied with the kit), then locate the bellows on the joint and fit the clip with reference to paragraph 19.
32 Set the inner bellows to the dimension shown in Fig. 8.8 and release any trapped air.
33 Fit the small outer clip using the method described in paragraph 19.

5 Driveshaft bellows – renewal

1 The driveshaft bellows can be renewed after removing the driveshaft, then removing the inner joint spider assembly for the inner bellows or the outer joint assembly for the outer bellows. Both procedures are covered in Section 4 of this Chapter.
2 If *both* driveshaft bellows require renewal it is only necessary to remove the components from one end of the centre shaft. Both bellows can then be removed from the same side.

6 Front hub bearings – renewal

1 Remove the front suspension stub axle carrier as described in Chapter 10.
2 Remove the brake disc from the hub.
3 Mount the stub axle carrier upside down in a vice, then use a suitable diameter metal tube inserted from the rear of the carrier to drive the hub from the bearings. The outer bearing inner race will remain on the hub and will also force out the outer seal.

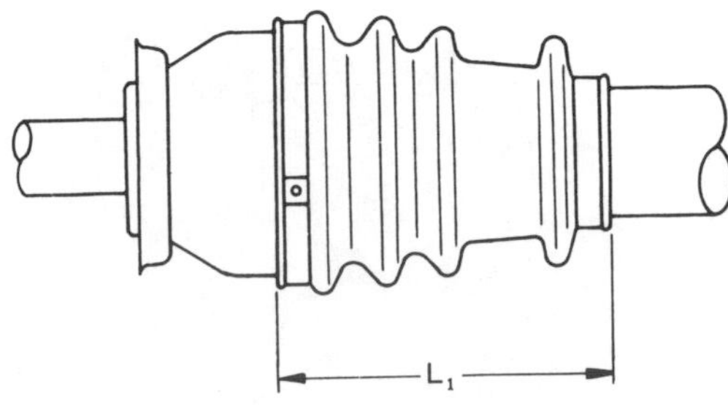

Fig. 8.7 Driveshaft outer bellows setting dimension (Sec 4)

L1 = 96.0 to 98.0 mm (3.78 to 3.86 in)

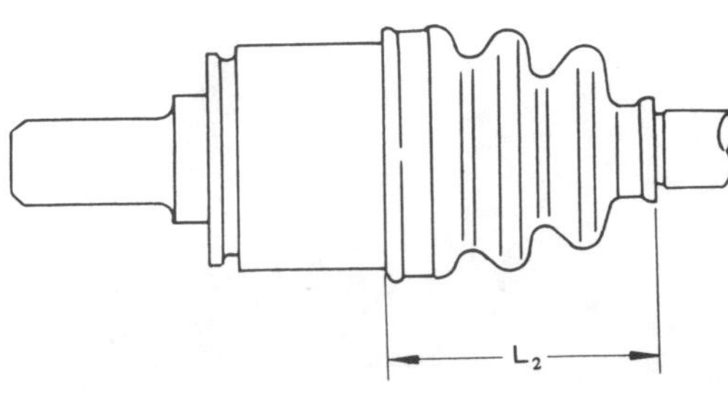

Fig. 8.8 Driveshaft inner bellows setting dimension (Sec 4)

L2 = 101.5 to 103.5 mm (4.00 to 4.07 in)

4 Using a screwdriver, prise the inner seal from the stub axle carrier and remove the inner race.
5 Extract the circular clips from each side of the bearing outer race, then use a suitable metal tube to drive the outer race from the stub axle carrier.
6 Using a puller, remove the inner race from the hub, followed by the outer seal.
7 Clean the bearing races, hub, and stub axle carrier recesses, then check them for wear and damage. The bearings must be renewed if pitting or excessive wear is evident on the tapered rollers or races.
8 Commence reassembly by fitting one circular clip to the outside of the stub axle carrier.
9 Using a metal tube, drive the bearing outer race into the carrier from the inner side until it contacts the clip, then fit the inner circular clip in the groove.
10 Pack the bearings with multi-purpose grease, insert them on either side of the outer race, then press the inner and outer seals into the carrier. Smear a little grease on the seal lips.
11 Place the hub on a block of wood, then locate the stub axle carrier over it, with the bearing inner races on the hub shank. Using a metal tube on the inner races, drive the bearings fully onto the hub.
12 At this stage it will normally be in order to refit the stub axle carrier to the car, however if a suitable spring balance is available, the turning torque of the bearings can be checked first. It will be necessary to remove the driveshaft and fit it to the hub with the driveshaft nut tightened to the correct torque.
13 Mount the driveshaft outer joint in a vice and spin the hub several times in both directions.
14 Using the spring balance as shown in Fig. 8.13 check that the *starting* turning torque is between 0.6 and 2.5 Nm (5.3 and 22.1 lbf in). With the spring balance on the wheel stud, this is equivalent to a pull of 10.8 to 45.1 N (2.4 to 10.1 lb).
15 An incorrect reading indicates faulty bearings or incorrect tightening of the driveshaft nut.
16 Finally, locate the brake disc on the hub, then refit the stub axle carrier with reference to Chapter 10.

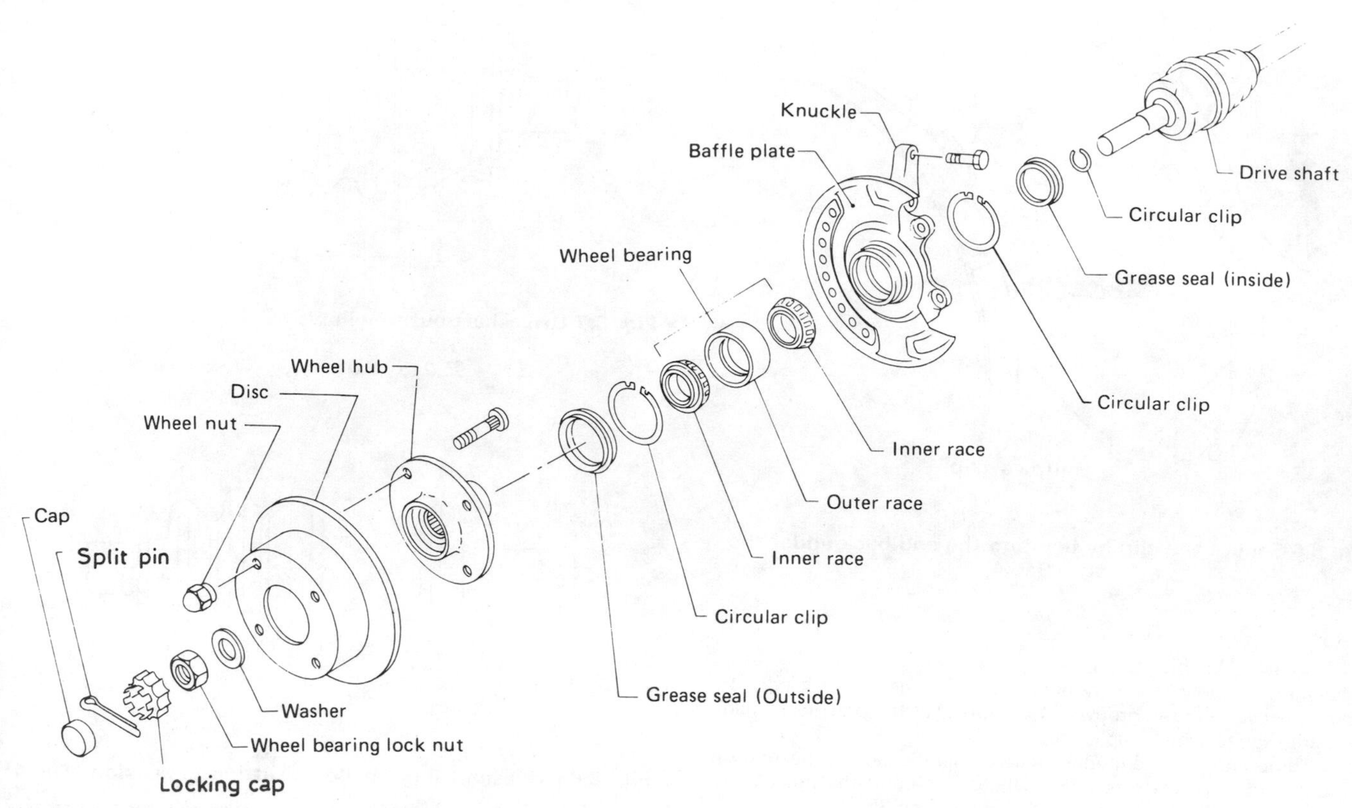

Fig. 8.9 Exploded view of the front hub and bearings (Sec 6)

Fig. 8.10 Removing the hub from the bearings (Sec 6)

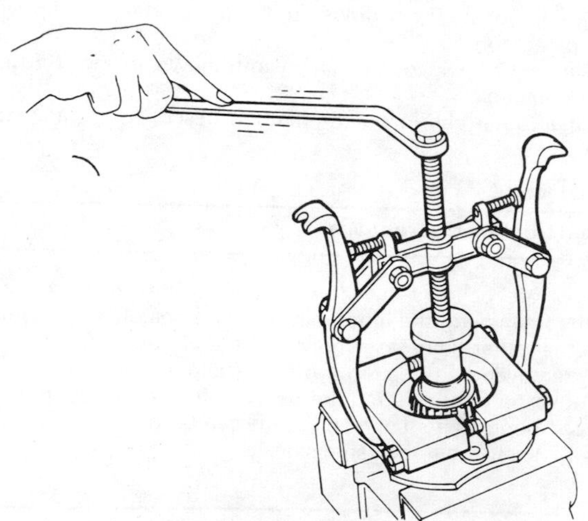

Fig. 8.11 Using a puller to remove the inner race from the hub (Sec 6)

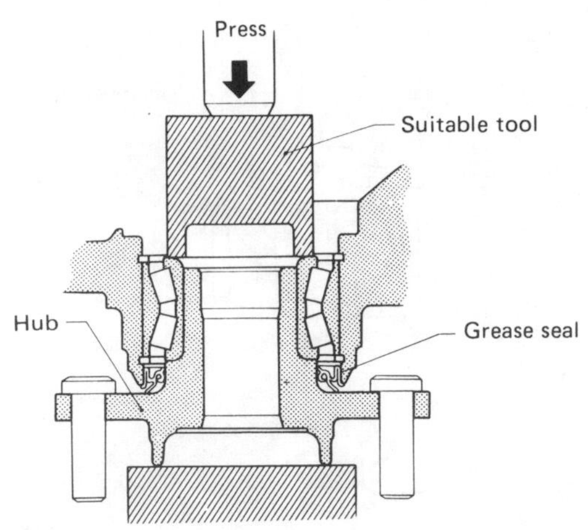

Fig. 8.12 Refitting the bearings on the hub (Sec 6)

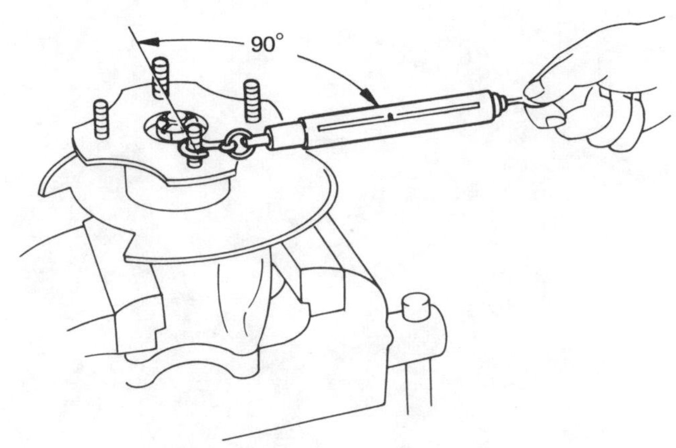

Fig. 8.13 Checking the turning torque of the front hub bearings (Sec 6)

7 Rear hub bearings – adjustment

1 Chock the front wheels, then jack up the rear of the car and support on axle stands. Remove the rear wheels and release the handbrake.
2 Prise off the grease cap and remove the split pin and locking cap.
3 Unscrew the stub axle nut and check that the stub axle threads and thrust washer are coated with grease.
4 Refit the nut, then tighten it to between 39.0 and 44.0 Nm (29.0 and 33.0 lbf ft).
5 Rotate the hub several times in both directions to settle the bearings, then check again that the nut is tightened to the torque given in paragraph 4.
6 Loosen the nut a quarter turn (90°) then locate the locking cap on the nut so that two of the cut-outs are aligned with the split pin hole. If

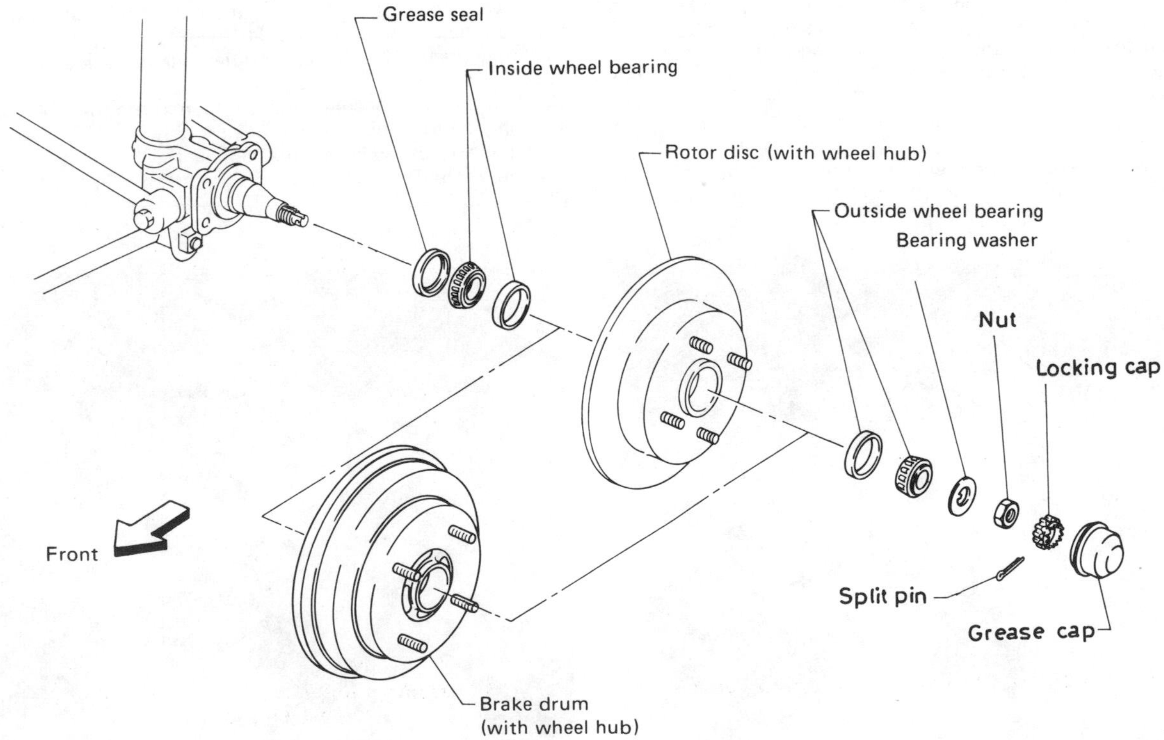

Fig. 8.14 Exploded view of the rear hub and bearings (Sec 7 and 8)

7.7 Showing correct fitting of rear hub split pin

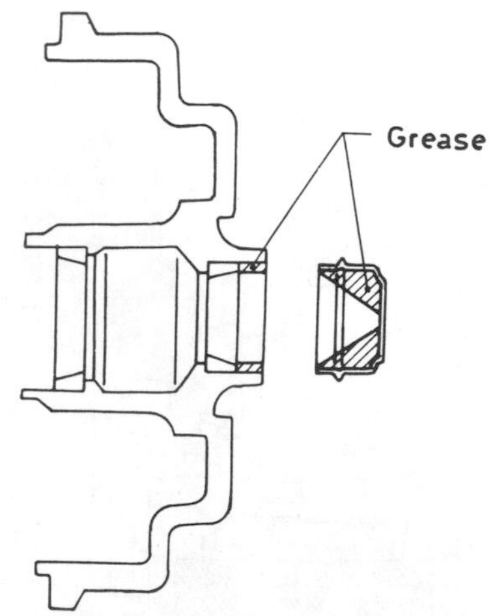

Fig. 8.15 Apply grease to the shaded area before refitting the rear hub grease cap (Sec 7)

necessary, the nut can be tightened a **maximum** of 15° in order to align the cap.

7 Insert the split pin and bend the legs back over the stub axle (photo).

8 Half fill the grease cap with grease, then tap it squarely into position.

9 Refit the rear wheels and lower the car to the ground.

8 Rear hub bearings – renewal

1 Chock the front wheels, then jack up the rear of the car and support on axle stands. Remove the rear wheel and release the handbrake.

2 On Turbo mdoels, remove the brake caliper and suspend it from the coil spring with reference to Chapter 9. Do not disconnect the hydraulic hose.

3 Prise off the grease cap and remove the split pin and locking cap (photo).

4 Unscrew the stub axle nut and remove the thrust washer (photos).

5 Withdraw the brake drum or disc assembly (as applicable) from the stub axle, taking care to retain the outer bearing (photo).

6 Prise out the hub inner seal and discard it. Remove both inner bearing races, but keep them identified for position if either is to be re-used.

7 Drive out the bearing outer tracks. Cut-outs are provided in the hub to permit use of a drift to remove them.

8 Clean the inside of the hub and then fit the new bearing tracks. It is recommended that they are pressed or drawn into position using a bolt, nut and washers rather than driving them into position, as they may crack.

9 Apply grease liberally to the inner bearing race and locate it in the hub.

10 Drive the new inner seal into the hub using a block of wood, and apply a little grease to the seal lip.

11 Apply grease liberally to the outer bearing race and locate it in the hub.

12 Hold the outer bearing in place, then locate the brake drum or disc assembly on the stub axle and push it fully on.

13 Fit the thrust washer, then adjust the bearings as described in Section 7. On Turbo models, refit the brake caliper with reference to Chapter 9.

8.3 Removing the rear hub locking cap

8.4A Removing the rear hub stub axle nut ...

8.4B ... and thrust washer

8.5 Rear hub outer bearing

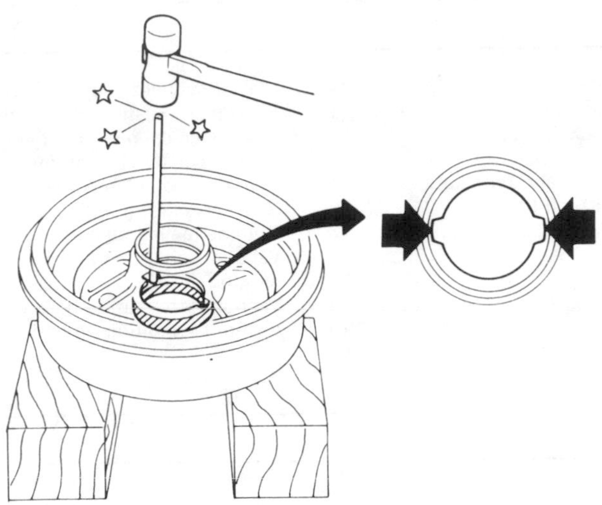

Fig. 8.16 Driving out the bearing outer tracks (Sec 8)

9 Fault diagnosis – driveshafts and hubs

Symptom	Reason(s)
Knocking noise, particularly on full lock	Worn driveshaft joints Loose driveshaft nut Worn splines on driveshaft, front hub, or differential side gears
Noise from RH driveshaft only (Turbo and 2.0 litre)	Worn support bearing for RH driveshaft
Noise from rear hubs especially when cornering	Worn rear hub bearings Incorrectly adjusted rear hub bearings

Chapter 9 Braking system

Contents

Specifications

General

System type ..... Front disc brakes, rear drum brakes (non-Turbo models) or disc brakes (Turbo models), vacuum servo unit, and pressure regulating valve. Cable-operated handbrake on rear wheels

Front disc brakes

Disc diameter ..... 250.0 mm (9.84 in)
Pad lining minimum thickness ..... 2.0 mm (0.079 in)
Disc:
  Maximum run-out ..... 0.07 mm (0.003 in)
  Minimum thickness ..... 20.0 mm (0.787 in)

Rear disc brakes

Disc diameter ..... 258.0 mm (10.16 in)
Pad lining minimum thickness ..... 2.0 mm (0.079 in)
Disc:
  Maximum run-out ..... 0.7 mm (0.03 in)
  Minimum thickness ..... 9.0 mm (0.354 in)

Rear drum brakes

Drum internal diameter ..... 228.6 mm (9.0 in)
Shoe lining minimum thickness ..... 1.5 mm (0.059 in)
Drum:
  Maximum internal diameter ..... 230.0 mm (9.06 in)
  Maximum out-of-round ..... 0.03 mm (0.0012 in)
  Maximum run-out ..... 0.05 mm (0.002 in)
  Maximum taper ..... 0.04 mm (0.0016 in)

Brake pedal

Free height (H)	190 to 200 mm (7.48 to 7.87 in)
Stop clearance (C)	0.3 to 1.0 mm (0.012 to 0.039 in)
Free play (A)	1.0 to 3.0 mm (0.04 to 0.12 in)
Depressed height (D) (force of 110 lbf/50 kg with engine running)	100.0 mm (3.94 in) minimum

Vacuum servo unit

Diaphragm diameter	228.6 (9.0 in)

Torque wrench settings

	Nm	lbf ft
Pedal bracket to body	10	7
Pedal fulcrum pin	19	14
Stoplamp switch locknut	14	10
Servo unit	10	7
Master cylinder	10	7
Hydraulic pipe union nut	17	13
Front caliper to torque member (pin bolt)	27	20
Torque member to strut axle carrier	85	63
Rear caliper to torque member (pin bolt)	19	14
Torque member to rear strut	45	33
Rear drum backplate	31	23
Rear wheel cylinder	7	5
Handbrake lever	10	7
Handbrake cable adjuster locknut	4	3
Primary cable bracket	4	3
Secondary cable mounting	10	7

1 General description

The braking system is of hydraulic type, front discs and rear drums on non-Turbo models, and discs all round on Turbo models. The handbrake is cable-operated on the rear wheels.

The dual hydraulic system incorporates two separate circuits arranged diagonally. The primary circuit comprises the left front and right rear brakes, and the secondary circuit the right front and left rear brakes. In the event of a failure of one circuit, the remaining circuit is still functional. A pressure regulating valve (or dual lead sensing valve) is fitted in the hydraulic system, to reduce hydraulic pressure to the rear brakes under heavy applications of the brake pedal, in order to prevent rear wheel lock-up. The valve incorporates an inertia ball which senses deceleration.

All models are fitted with a vacuum servo unit.

The rear brakes are of self-adjusting type.

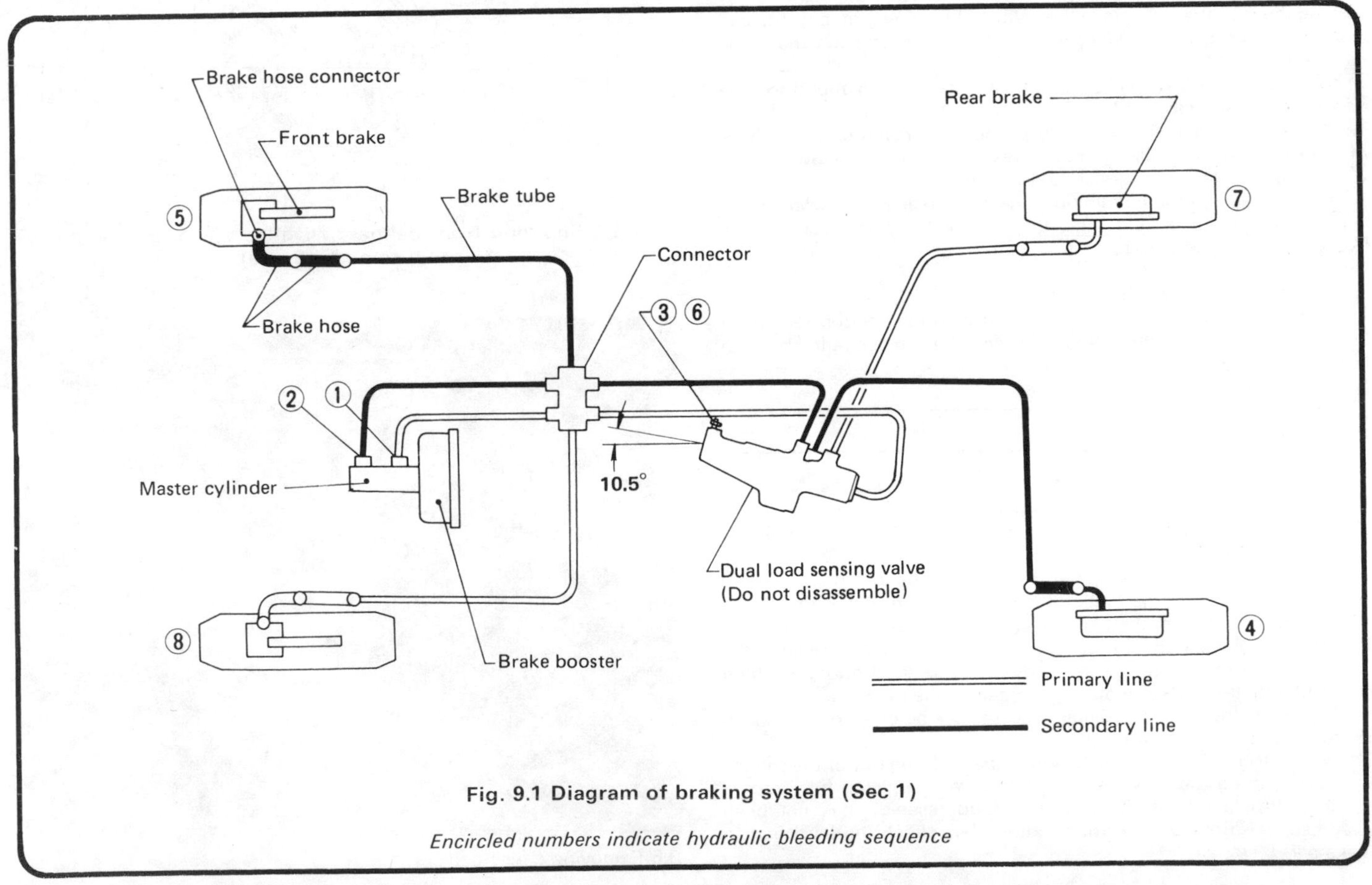

Fig. 9.1 Diagram of braking system (Sec 1)

Encircled numbers indicate hydraulic bleeding sequence

2 Routine maintenance

Carry out the following procedures at the intervals given in *'Routine Maintenance'* at the beginning of the Manual.

Hydraulic fluid level

1 Check that the level of hydraulic fluid in the reservoir on top of the master cylinder is between the 'Min' and 'Max' marks. The reservoir is translucent so there is no need to remove the filler cap. Normally the fluid should be at or near the 'Max' mark, however as the front disc pads (and rear pads on Turbo models) wear, the level will drop slightly. In this case it is not necessary to top up the level.
2 Where regular topping-up is required, the hydraulic system should be thoroughly checked for leakage.

Hydraulic fluid renewal

3 Refer to Section 12 and carry out the preliminary procedures as for bleeding the system.
4 Syphon all the fluid from the reservoir.
5 With the help of an assistant loosen each bleed screw in turn, then depress the footbrake pedal repeatedly until all the fluid is drained.
6 Pour the new fluid in the reservoir and bleed the system as described in Section 12.

Vacuum servo system check

7 Check the vacuum hoses between the inlet manifold and servo unit for splits or damage.
Make sure that the hose clips are secure.
8 Check that the vacuum servo unit is functioning correctly by first depressing the footbrake pedal repeatedly, until all the vacuum is dissipated with the engine switched off.
9 Now depress the pedal moderately, then start the engine and check that the pedal moves slightly down to the floor as the vacuum assistance is introduced. If there is no movement, the servo unit is faulty.

Brake linings and wheel cylinders

10 Remove the front wheels and check the disc pads for wear by looking through the aperture in the caliper. If the lining on any disc pad is worn below 2.0 mm (0.079 in), all the front disc pads should be renewed.
11 On Turbo models, check the rear disc pads using the procedure described in paragraph 10.
12 On models with rear drum brakes, remove the rear drums and check the shoe linings. If the lining on any rear shoe is worn below 1.5 mm (0.059 in), all the rear shoes should be renewed.
13 While checking the rear linings, check the rear wheel cylinders for leakage of hydraulic fluid, and the rear brake drums for scoring, excessive wear, and cracks.

Handbrake adjustment

14 Check that the rear wheels are locked with the handbrake applied between 7 and 9 notches. If necessary, adjust the handbrake with reference to Section 18.

3 Front disc pads – renewal

1 Jack up the front of the car and support on axle stands. Apply the handbrake and remove the front roadwheels.
2 Unscrew and remove the lower caliper pin bolt, and loosen only the upper pin bolt (photo).
3 Swivel the caliper body upwards to expose the disc pads.
4 If the thickness of the friction material has worn down to 2.0 mm (0.079 in) or less, then the pads must be renewed as an axle set.
5 Prise the pads from the caliper torque member and remove the shims from them (photo). Also remove the top and bottom retaining clips. Note that the wear indicator is fitted to the inner pad.
6 Brush the dust from the caliper recesses, taking care not to inhale it as it is dangerous to health.
7 Do not touch the brake pedal while the pads are out of the caliper.
8 Before fitting the new pads, push or lever the piston fully into its cylinder. Provided that the hydraulic fluid reservoir has not been overfilled, the fluid should not overflow, but check the level first to make sure.

3.2 Removing the lower pin bolt from the front brake caliper

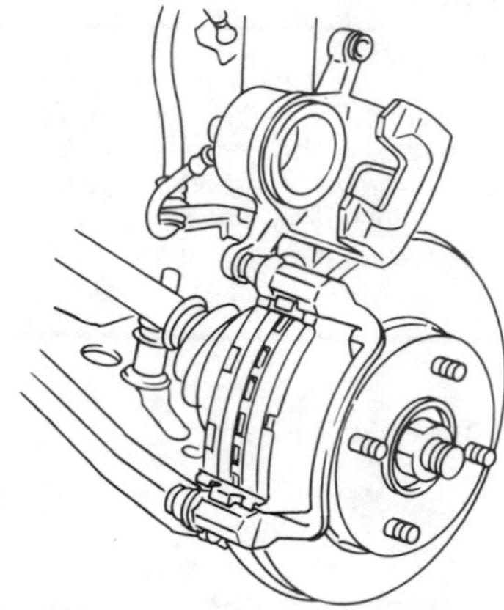

Fig. 9.2 Showing front caliper swivelled upwards to expose the disc pads (Sec 3)

3.5 Removing a disc pad

9 Apply just a smear of high melting point brake grease to the backing plates of the new disc pads, then fit them using a reversal of the removal procedure. Tighten the bolts to the specified torque.
10 Repeat the operations on the opposite side, then refit the roadwheels and lower the car to the ground.
11 Apply the footbrake hard several times to set the pads in their normal position.
12 Finally check and if necessary top up the fluid level in the reservoir.

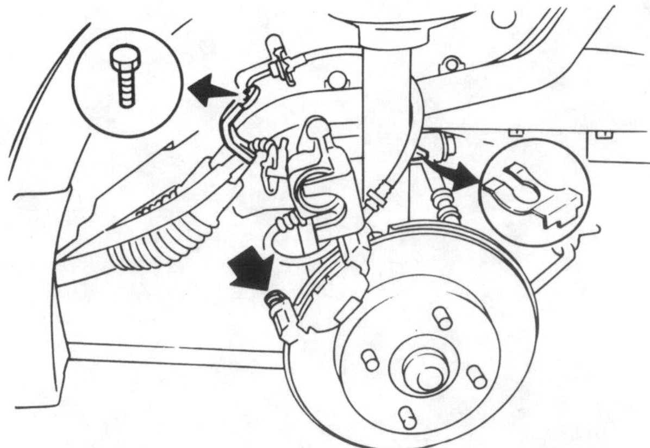

Fig. 9.3 Rear disc pad removal (Sec 4)

4 Rear disc pads – renewal

1 Chock the front wheels, then jack up the rear of the car and support on axle stands. Release the handbrake and remove the rear roadwheels.
2 Unbolt the rear handbrake cable bracket from the underbody to allow movement of the cable.
3 Pull out the spring clip and disconnect the brake hose from the bracket on the rear suspension strut. This will facilitate free movement of the caliper in subsequent operations.
4 Unscrew and remove the lower caliper pin bolt, and loosen only the upper pin bolt.
5 Swivel the caliper body upwards to expose the disc pads.
6 If the thickness of the friction material has worn down to 2.0 mm (0.079 in) or less, then the pads must be renewed as an axle set.
7 Prise the pads from the caliper torque member and remove the shims from them. Also remove the top and bottom retaining clips. Note that the wear indicator is fitted to the inner pad.
8 Brush the dust from the caliper recesses, taking care not to inhale it as it is dangerous to health.
9 Do not touch the brake pedal or handbrake while the pads are out of the caliper.
10 Before fitting the new pads, retract the piston into the cylinder by turning it clockwise using long nose pliers in the piston cut-outs. Take care not to damage the piston boot.
11 Apply just a smear of high melting point brake grease to the backing plates of the new disc pads, then fit them using a reversal of the removal procedure. Tighten the bolts to the specified torque.
12 Repeat the operations on the opposite side, then refit the roadwheels and lower the car to the ground.
13 Apply the footbrake hard several times to set the pads in their normal position, and finally check the handbrake adjustment with reference to Section 18.

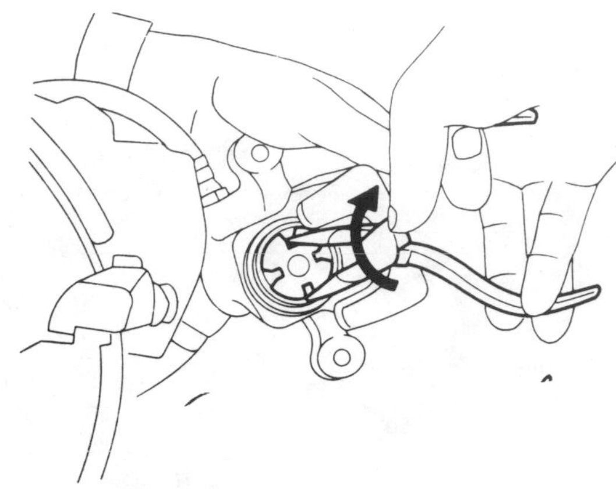

Fig. 9.4 Retracting the rear caliper piston (Sec 4)

5 Rear brake shoes – renewal

1 Chock the front wheels, then jack up the rear of the car and support on axle stands. Remove the rear wheels and release the handbrake.
2 Remove the rear brake drum and hub as described in Chapter 8 Section 8.
3 Brush the dust from the brake shoes, backplate, and drum, taking care not to inhale it as it is dangerous to health.
4 If the thickness of the friction material has worn down to 1.5 mm (0.059 in) or less, then the shoes must be renewed as an axle set.
5 Remove the anti-rattle springs with a pair of pliers by depressing the retainer and turning it through 90° (photo). Remove the retainers, springs and seats.
6 Note the position of the shoes, springs and strut adjuster to ensure correct reassembly, then lever the shoe ends from the bottom anchor and remove the bottom return spring (photo).
7 Lever the upper ends of the shoes from the wheel cylinder and remove the upper return spring, self-adjusting strut, and the leading brake shoe (photo).
8 Unhook the handbrake cable from the lever and remove the trailing brake shoe.
9 Clean the backplate and apply a smear of high melting point brake grease to the shoe contact points on the backplate, anchor, and wheel cylinder piston grooves. Apply grease sparingly to the threads of the self-adjusting strut, then turn the serrated nut to fully retract the strut.
10 Prise open the clip and transfer the handbrake lever to the new trailing shoe. Fit a new clip and squeeze it into the pivot pin groove. Make sure the spring is fitted correctly.

5.5 Rear brake shoe anti-rattle spring (arrowed)

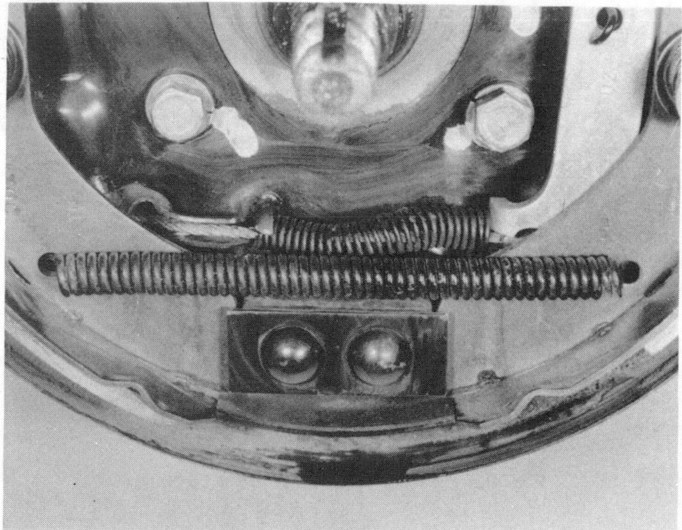

5.6 Rear brake shoe bottom anchor and return spring

5.7 Showing rear brake shoe upper ends together with the upper return spring and self-adjusting strut

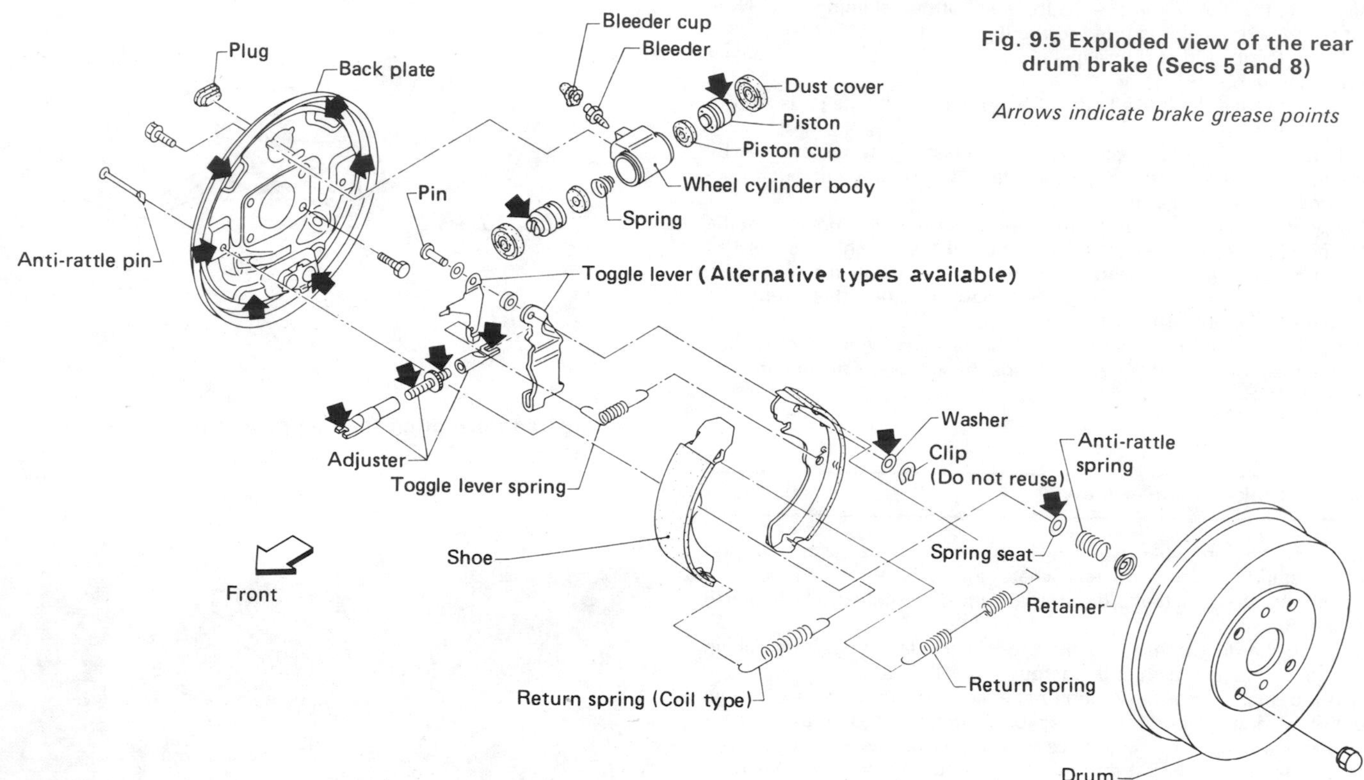

Fig. 9.5 Exploded view of the rear drum brake (Secs 5 and 8)

Arrows indicate brake grease points

11 Pull back the spring on the handbrake cable and attach the cable to the lever.

12 Locate both shoes loosely on the backplate, but not engaged with the wheel cylinder, then fit the self-adjusting strut and upper return spring.

13 Locate the upper ends of the shoes in the wheel cylinder piston grooves by moving the lower ends together.

14 Fit the bottom return spring, then lever the bottom ends of the shoes onto the bottom anchor.

15 Refit the anti-rattle springs and turn the retainers through 90° (photo).

16 Measure the inner diameter of the brake drum, then turn the serrated nut on the self-adjusting strut so that the centre diameter of the brake shoes is 0.6 mm (0.024 in) less. A plug is provided in the backplate so that the nut can be turned with a screwdriver.

17 Refit the rear brake drum and adjust the hub bearings as described in Chapter 8.

18 Refit the rear wheels and lower the car to the ground. Finally apply the handbrake several times to operate the self-adjuster and set the shoes in their normal position.

6 Front brake caliper – removal, overhaul and refitting

1 Remove the disc pads as described in Section 3.

2 Fit a brake hose clamp to the front flexible brake hose. If a clamp is not available, remove the cap from the hydraulic fluid reservoir and tighten it down onto a piece of polythene sheeting.

5.15 Rear brake shoes assembled ready for fitting of brake drum

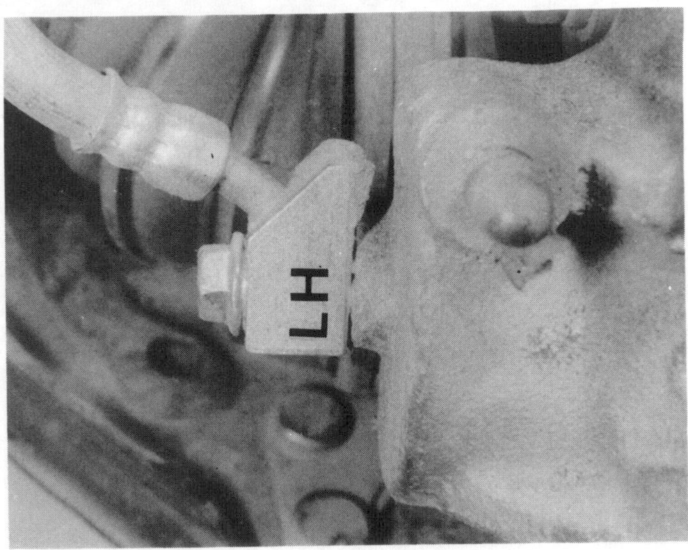

6.3 Brake hose banjo union connection to front brake caliper. Note the 'LH' inscription on the union indicating fitting to the left-hand caliper

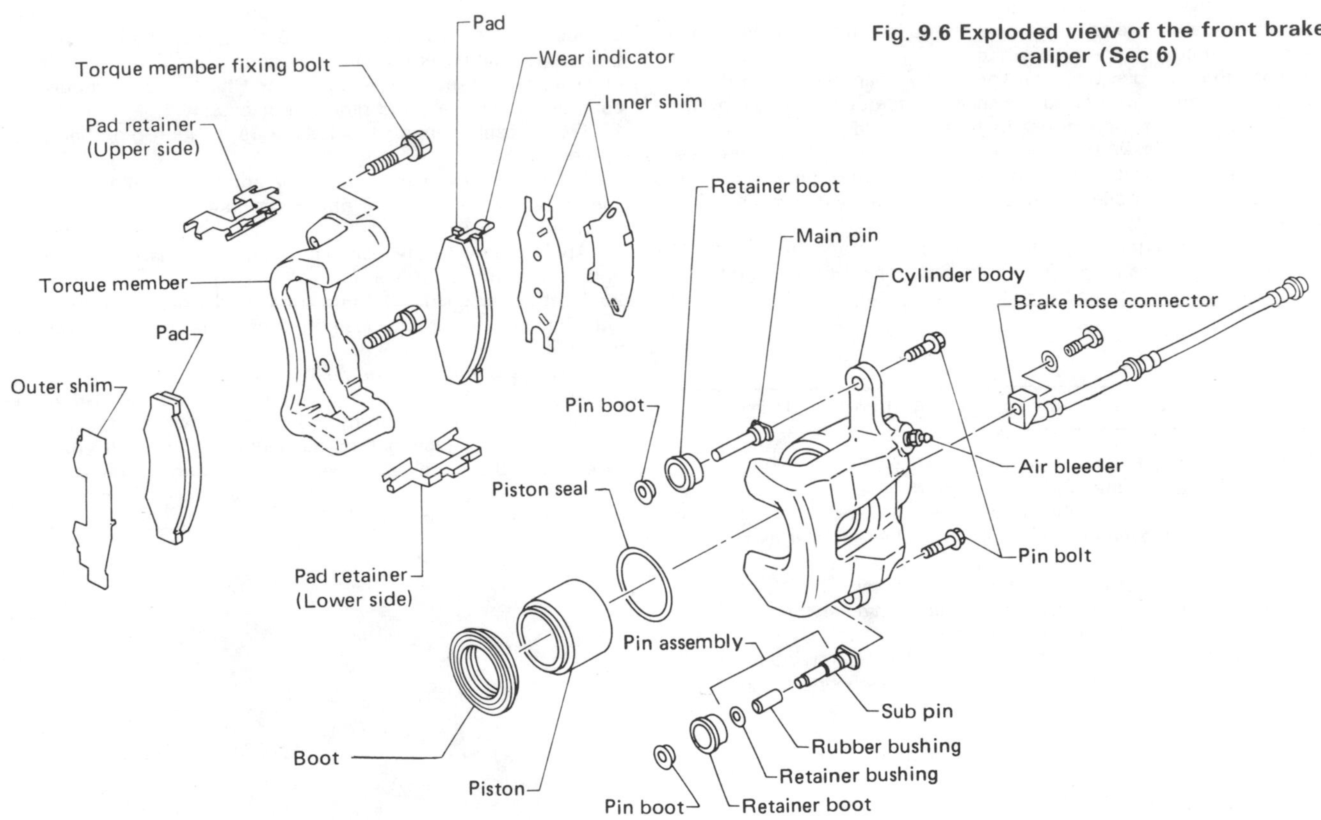

Fig. 9.6 Exploded view of the front brake caliper (Sec 6)

3 Disconnect the brake hose at the caliper by unscrewing the banjo union hollow bolt (photo). Note the sealing washer on each side of the union.

4 Unscrew the upper caliper pin bolt and withdraw the caliper cylinder body.

5 If necessary unbolt the torque member from the stub axle carrier and remove the guide pins.

6 Clean the components to remove all external dirt.

7 Place a small block of wood in the jaws of the caliper, then remove the piston by applying air pressure from a tyre pump at the fluid entry port.

8 Remove the boot from the piston, then prise the piston seal from the cylinder using a blunt instrument to prevent damage to the cylinder bore.

9 Wash the components in clean brake fluid or methylated spirit, then examine them for wear and damage. If the surfaces of the piston or cylinder bore are scored or corroded, then the complete caliper should be renewed, however if they are in good condition obtain a repair kit of seals and discard the old ones.

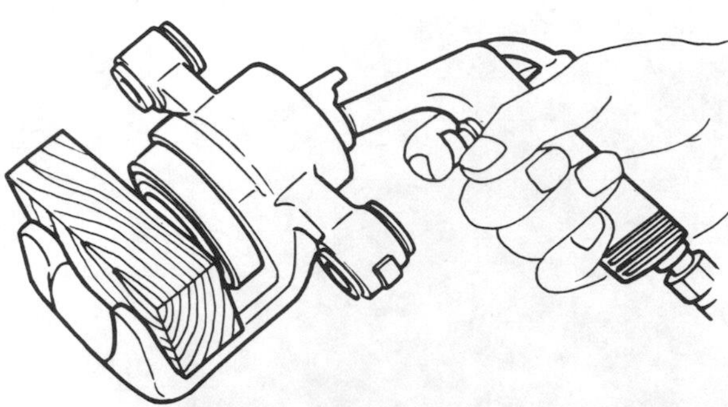

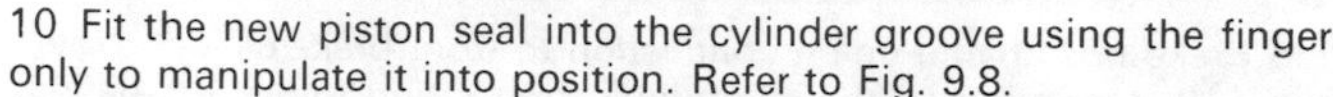

Fig. 9.7 Using air pressure to remove the piston from the caliper (Sec 6)

10 Fit the new piston seal into the cylinder groove using the fingers only to manipulate it into position. Refer to Fig. 9.8.
11 Dip the piston in clean hydraulic fluid and insert it squarely into the cylinder.
12 Fit the boot to the piston and caliper body.
13 If removed, refit the torque member to the stub axle carrier and tighten the bolts to the specified torque.
14 Apply rubber grease to the guide pins and locate them in the torque member together with the rubber boots.
15 Locate the cylinder body on the torque member, then refit the upper pin bolt and tighten it to the specified torque while holding the pin stationary with a spanner on the flats provided.
16 Reconnect the brake hose with the banjo union bolt and two new sealing washers. Tighten the bolt with the banjo union correctly located, so that the hose will not be twisted with the caliper in its normal position.
17 Remove the polythene sheeting or hose clamp as applicable.
18 Refit the disc pads with reference to Section 3, but before refitting the roadwheel bleed the appropriate hydraulic circuit, as described in Section 12.

7 Rear brake caliper – removal, overhaul and refitting

1 Remove the disc pads as described in Section 4.
2 Release the handbrake inner cable from the the lever on the caliper and withdraw the outer cable from the support bracket. If there is insufficient cable movement, back off the cable adjuster as required (see Section 18).
3 Fit a brake hose clamp to the flexible brake hose. If a clamp is not available, remove the cap from the hydraulic fluid reservoir and tighten it down onto a piece of polythene sheeting.
4 Disconnect the brake hose at the caliper by unscrewing the banjo union hollow bolt. Note the sealing washer on each side of the union.
5 Unscrew the upper caliper pin bolt and withdraw the caliper cylinder body.
6 If necessary unbolt the torque member from the rear suspension strut and remove the guide pins and rubber boots.
7 Clean the components to remove all external dirt.
8 Using long-nosed pliers in the cut-outs provided, unscrew the piston in an anti-clockwise direction and remove it from the cylinder. Remove the piston boot.
9 From inside the piston extract the circlip (ring 'A') with circlip pliers, then remove the spacers, wave washer, bearing and adjusting nut, noting the order of removal. Prise the cup seal from the adjusting nut.
10 Working on the cylinder body, extract the circlip (ring 'B') with circlip pliers, then remove the spring cover, spring, and seat.
11 Extract the circlip (ring 'C') with circlip pliers, then remove the key plate, pushrod and plunger. Prise the O-ring from the pushrod.
12 Prise the piston seal from the cylinder using a blunt instrument to prevent damage to the cylinder bore.

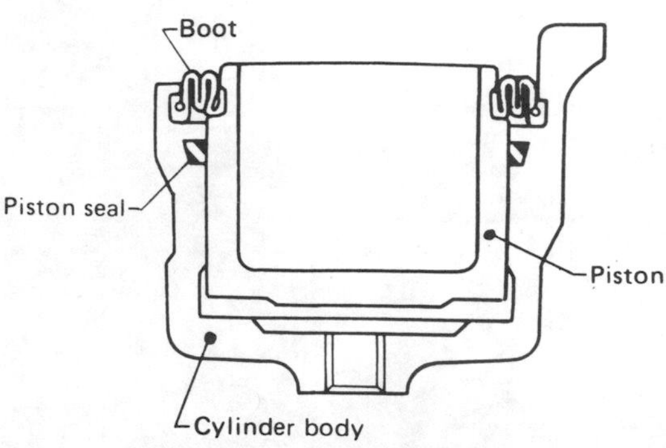

Fig. 9.8 Showing correct position of piston seal and boot in the cylinder (Sec 6)

13 Unhook the return spring from the handbrake control lever and remove the adjusting cam from the cylinder body.
14 Grip the adjusting cam in a soft-jawed vice, then unscrew the nut and remove the spring washer, lever and cam boot.
15 Unbolt and remove the cable support bracket.
16 Wash the components in clean brake fluid or methylated spirit, then examine them for wear and damge. If the surfaces of the piston or cylinder bore are scored or corroded, then the complete caliper should be renewed, however if they are in good condition, obtain a repair kit of seals and discard the old ones. Check the handbrake control components for wear and renew as necessary.
17 Fit the cable support bracket on its locating pin, then insert and tighten the bolt.
18 Locate the new cam boot on the adjusting cam, then fit the lever, spring washer and nut. Tighten the nut with the adjusting cam mounted in a vice.
19 Apply grease to the adjusting cam, then insert it in the cylinder body and fit the return spring.
20 Fit the new piston seal into the cylinder groove using the fingers only to manipulate it into position. Make sure that it is the correct way round, as shown in Fig. 9.8.
21 Ease the O-ring into the pushrod groove.
22 Apply rubber grease to the plunger, pushrod and O-ring.
23 Locate the key plate on the pushrod, so that the dot indicating the convex side will face out of the cylinder. This will ensure correct assembly of the key plate in the concave portion of the cylinder body.
24 Fit the plunger, pushrod and key plate in the cylinder body, and retain with the circlip (ring 'C').

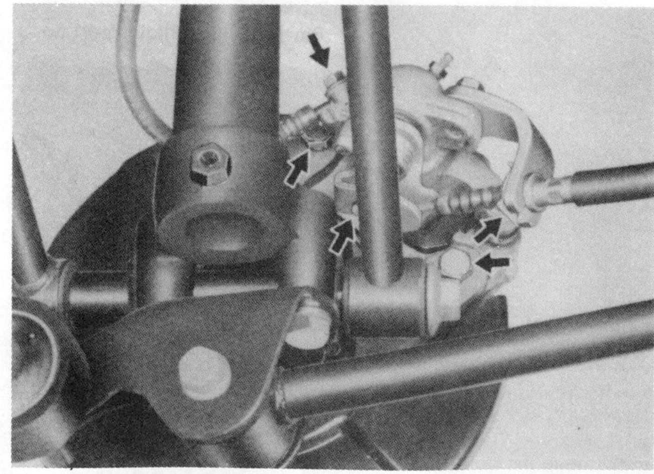

Fig. 9.9 Rear brake caliper removal (Sec 7)

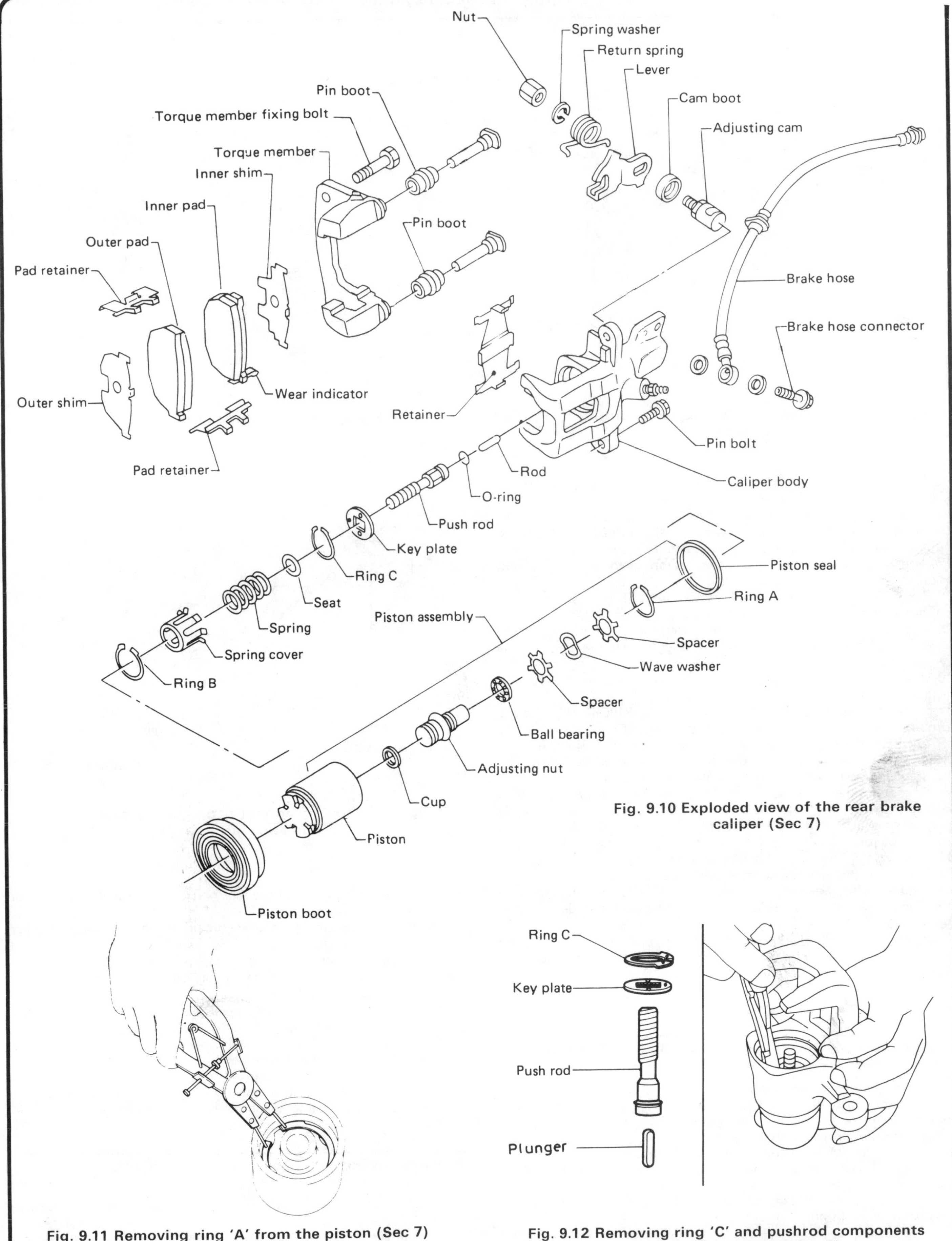

Fig. 9.10 Exploded view of the rear brake caliper (Sec 7)

Fig. 9.11 Removing ring 'A' from the piston (Sec 7)

Fig. 9.12 Removing ring 'C' and pushrod components from the cylinder body (Sec 7)

Fig. 9.13 Disconnecting the handbrake control lever return spring (Sec 7)

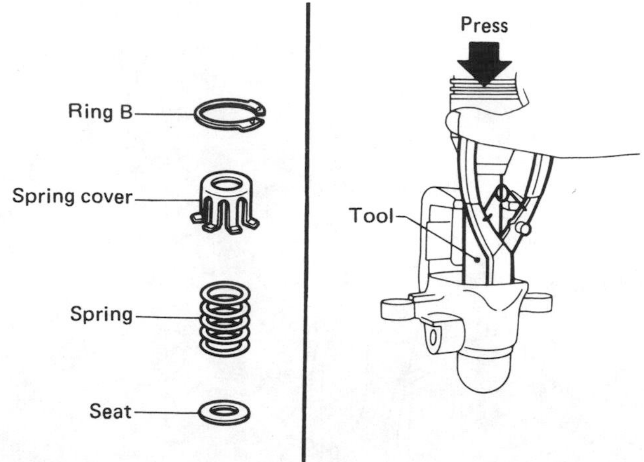

Fig. 9.14 Reassembly of ring 'B' (Sec 7)

25 Fit the spring seat, spring and cover in the cylinder body and retain with the circlip (ring 'B'). It will be necessary to compress the spring in order to engage the circlip in its groove.
26 Fit the cup seal to the adjusting nut as shown in Fig. 9.15, using the fingers only to manipulate it into position.
27 Apply rubber grease to the cap seal, piston, piston seal, and piston boot.
28 Locate in the piston the adjusting nut, bearing, spacer, wave washer, and spacer, and retain with the circlip (ring 'A').
29 Locate the boot on the piston, then insert the piston in the cylinder bore and turn it clockwise until fully entered. Fit the boot to the cylinder body.
30 If removed, refit the torque member to the rear suspension strut and tighten the bolts to the specified torque.
31 Apply rubber grease to the guide pins, and locate them in the torque member together with the rubber boots.
32 Locate the cylinder body on the torque member, then refit the upper pin bolt and tighten it to the specified torque, while holding the pin stationary with a spanner on the flats provided.
33 Reconnect the brake hose with the banjo union bolt and two new sealing washers. Tighten the bolt with the banjo union correctly located so that the hose will not be twisted with the caliper in its normal positon.
34 Remove the polythene sheeting or hose clamp as applicable.
35 Reconnect the handbrake inner and outer cables.
36 Refit the disc pads with reference to Section 4, but before refitting the roadwheel, bleed the appropriate hydraulic circuit as described in Section 12.
37 Apply the handbrake several times to operate the self-adjusting mechanism for the handbrake cable. If necessary adjust the cable end play with reference to Section 18.

8 Rear wheel cylinder – removal, overhaul and refitting

1 Remove the rear brake shoes as described in Section 5.
2 Fit a brake hose clamp to the flexible brake hose. If a clamp is not available, remove the cap from the hydraulic fluid reservoir and tighten it down onto a piece of polythene sheeting.
3 Unscrew the wheel cylinder mounting bolts from the backplate.
4 Unscrew the hydraulic line union nut, and remove the wheel cylinder from the backplate.
5 Clean away external dirt, then pull off the dust covers and extract the pistons and spring.
6 Examine the surface of the pistons and cylinder bores and if scored or corroded, the complete cylinder must be renewed.
7 If the components are in good condition however, remove and discard the seals and wash the other parts in clean hydraulic fluid or methylated spirit – nothing else.
8 Obtain a repair kit which will contain the new seals and other renewable components. It should be noted that both Nabco and Tokico wheel cylinders are fitted during production. Make sure that you obtain the correct kit for your vehicle as they are not interchangeable.
9 Fit the new seals using the fingers only to manipulate them onto the pistons. Note that the seal lips are towards the spring.
10 Dip the pistons in clean hydraulic fluid and insert them into the cylinder with the spring between them.
11 Fit the dust covers, having packed some rubber grease inside them.
12 Refitting is a reversal of removal. Refit the rear brake shoes with reference to Section 5, then bleed the hydraulic circuit as described in Section 12.

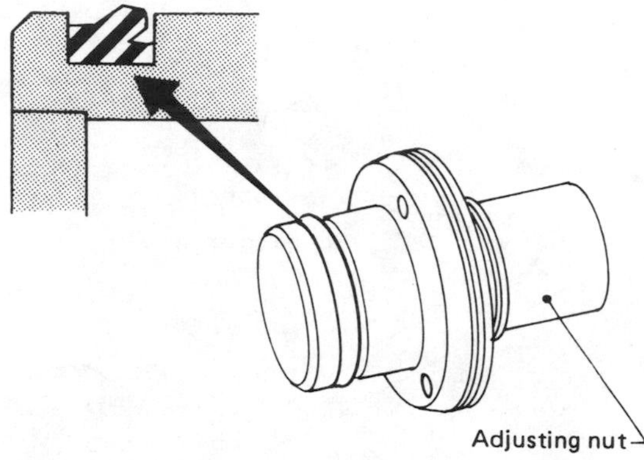

Fig. 9.15 Showing correct fitting of cup seal on the adjusting nut (Sec 7)

9 Master cylinder – removal, overhaul and refitting

1 Remove the filler cap and syphon the fluid from the reservoir (photo).
2 Disconnect the wiring multi-plug for the low level warning system from the bottom of the reservoir.
3 If necessary, remove the air cleaner for better access.

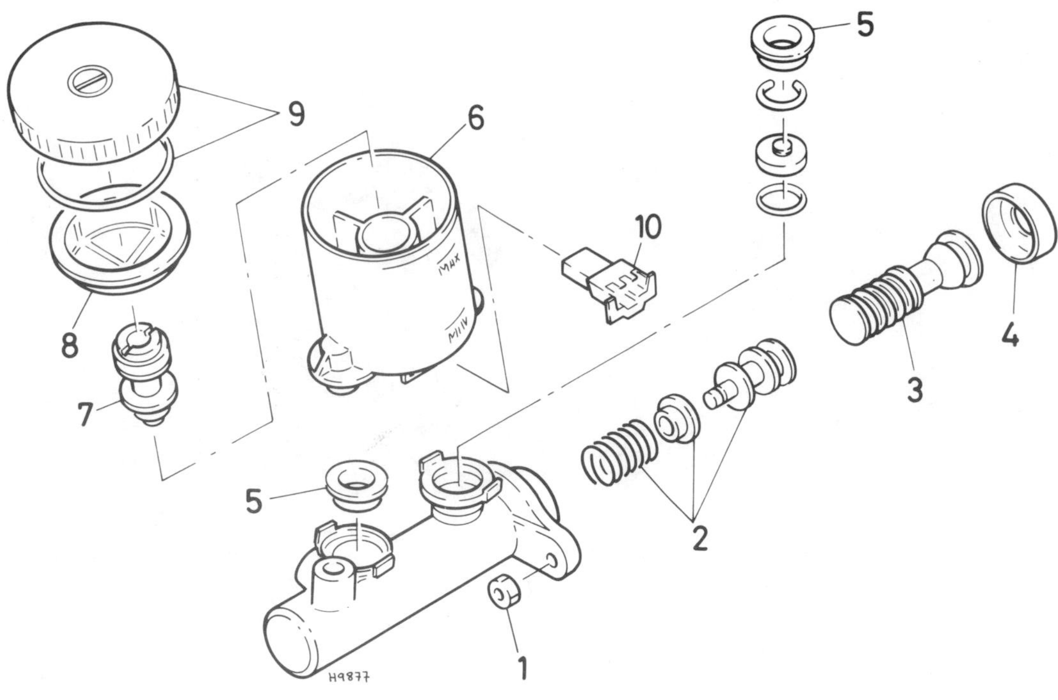

Fig. 9.16 Exploded view of the master cylinder (Sec 9)

1 Mounting nut
2 Secondary piston assembly
3 Primary piston assembly
4 Stopper cap
5 Fluid reservoir seal
6 Fluid reservoir
7 Low level warning float
8 Filter
9 Filler cap and seal
10 Low level warning indicator

9.1 View of the master cylinder on the servo unit

4 Place a suitable container or cloth beneath the master cylinder to catch spilled fluid.
5 Unscrew the union nuts and disconnect the hydraulic lines.
6 Unscrew the mounting nuts, remove the support plate, then withdraw the master cylinder from the front face of the servo unit.
7 Remove the filter and float from the reservoir, then prise it from the master cylinder and remove the two seals.
8 Clean away external dirt, then prise the stopper cap from the mouth of the master cylinder and extract the primary and secondary piston assemblies. Note the order of removal of the components.
9 Clean all the components in hydraulic fluid or methylated spirit, then inspect them for wear and damage. Examine the surfaces of the pistons and cylinder bore. If they are scored or show signs of corrosion, then the master cylinder must be renewed complete. If these items are in good condition, remove the seals, noting the direction in which the lips face, and discard them. Obtain a repair kit which will contain all the necessary new seals and other renewable items. Make sure that you obtain the correct kit for your master cylinder, two makes are used in production, Nabco and Rhythm, parts are not interchangeable.
10 Fit the new seals the correct way round on the pistons, using the fingers only to manipulate them into position.
11 Dip both piston assemblies in clean hydraulic fluid, then refit them in the master cylinder.
12 Press the stopper cap onto the mouth of the master cylinder.
13 Fit the two reservoir seals in the master cylinder, then press the reservoir into them. Locate the float and filter in the reservoir.
14 Refitting is a reversal of removal, but finally bleed the hydraulic system as described in Section 12.

10 Pressure regulating valve – removal and refitting

1 The pressure regulating or dual load sensing valve is located on the rear underbody behind the fuel tank (photo). The valve cannot be dismantled, so if it is faulty it must be renewed.
2 Chock the front wheels, then jack up the rear of the car and support on axle stands.
3 Remove the cap from the hydraulic fluid reservoir and tighten it down onto a piece of polythene sheeting. This will reduce the loss of fluid in subsequent operations.
4 Note the location of the hydraulic lines, then unscrew the union nuts and disconnect the lines from the valve.
5 Unscrew the mounting bolt and remove the valve from the underbody.
6 Refitting is a reversal of removal, but finally bleed the hydraulic system as described in Section 12.

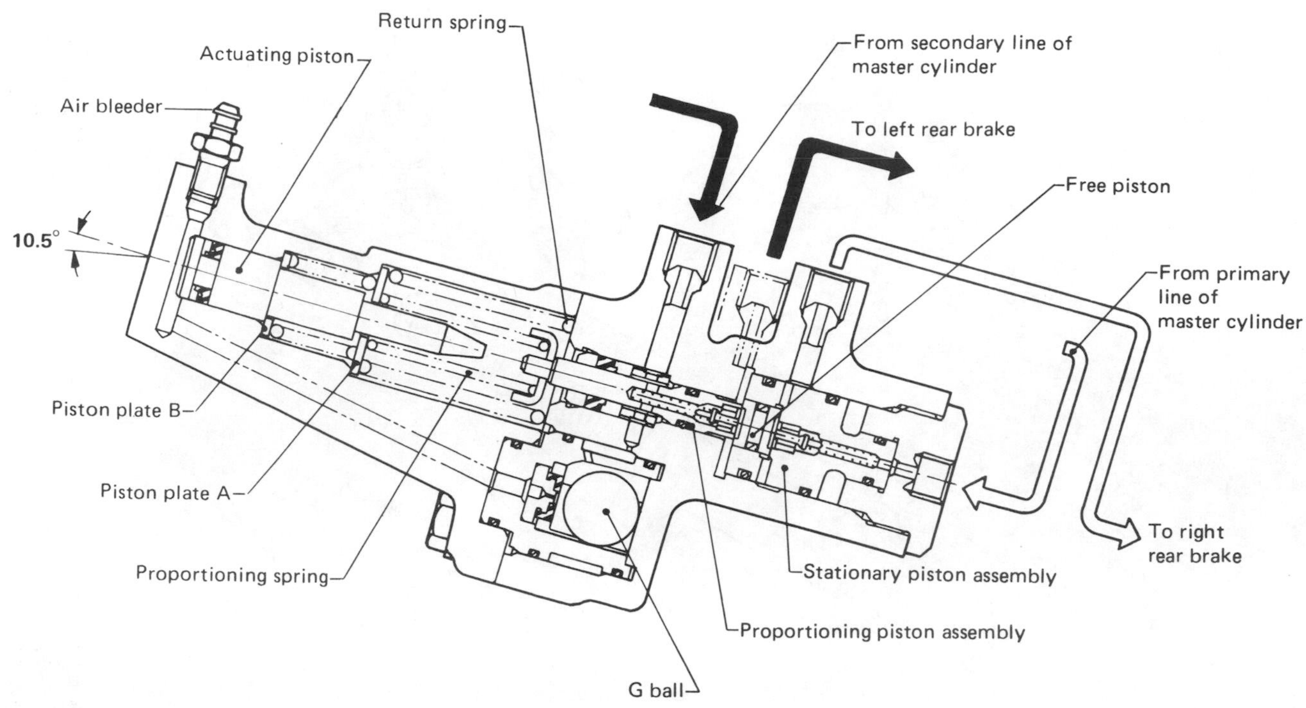

Fig. 9.17 Cross-section of the pressure regulating valve (Sec 10)

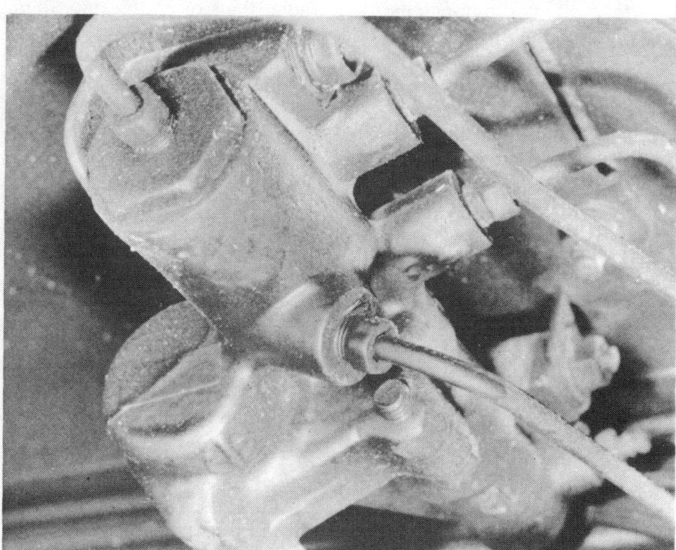

10.1 Pressure regulating valve

11 Flexible and rigid hydraulic lines – inspection and renewal

Flexible hoses

1 Periodically, inspect the condition of the flexible brake hoses. If they appear swollen, chafed, or when bent double with the fingers tiny cracks are visible, then they must be renewed.

2 Always uncouple the rigid pipe from the flexible hose first, then release the end of the flexible hose from the support bracket. To do this, pull out the lockplate using a pair of pliers. The front flexible hoses incorporate an intermediate support which is attached to the front suspension strut with the same type of lockplate (photos).

3 Where connected to disc brakes, disconnect the hose from the caliper by unscrewing the banjo union hollow bolt and removing the two sealing washers. The washers should be renewed when fitting the new hose.

4 When installation is complete, check that the flexible hose does not rub against the tyre or other adjacent components. Its attitude may be altered to overcome this by pulling out the clip at the support bracket and twisting the hose in the required direction.

5 Finally, bleed the hydraulic system as described in Section 12.

Rigid lines

6 At regular intervals wipe the steel brake pipes clean and examine them for signs of rust or denting caused by flying stones.

7 Examine the fit of the pipes in their insulated securing clips and adjust the clips if necessary to ensure a positive fit (photo).

8 Check that the pipes are not touching any adjacent components or rubbing against any part of the vehicle. Where this is observed, bend the pipe gently away to clear.

9 Any section of pipe which is rusty or chafed should be renewed. Brake pipes are available, to the correct length and fitted with end unions, from most dealers and can be made to pattern by many accessory suppliers. When installing the new pipes use the old pipes as a guide to bending and do not make any bends sharper than is necessary.

10 The system will of course have to be bled when the circuit has been reconnected.

12 Hydraulic system – bleeding

1 If the master cylinder or the pressure regulating valve have been disconnected and reconnected, then the complete system (both circuits) must be bled. If a component of one circuit has been disturbed, then only that particular circuit need be bled.

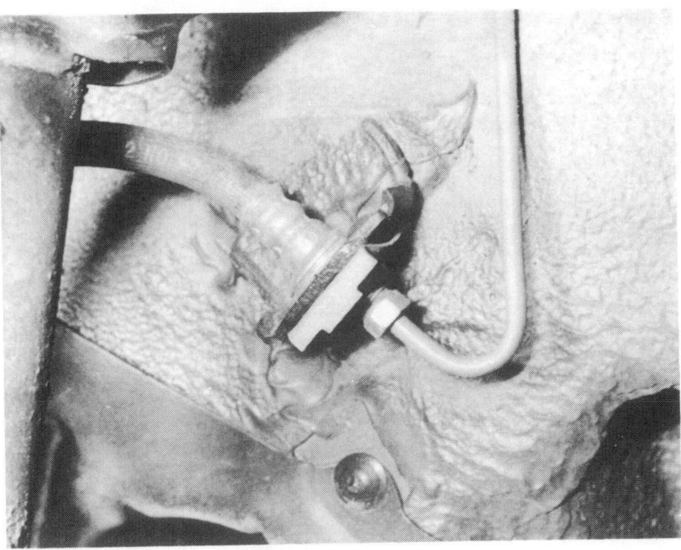
11.2A Front brake line support bracket

11.2B Rear brake line support bracket

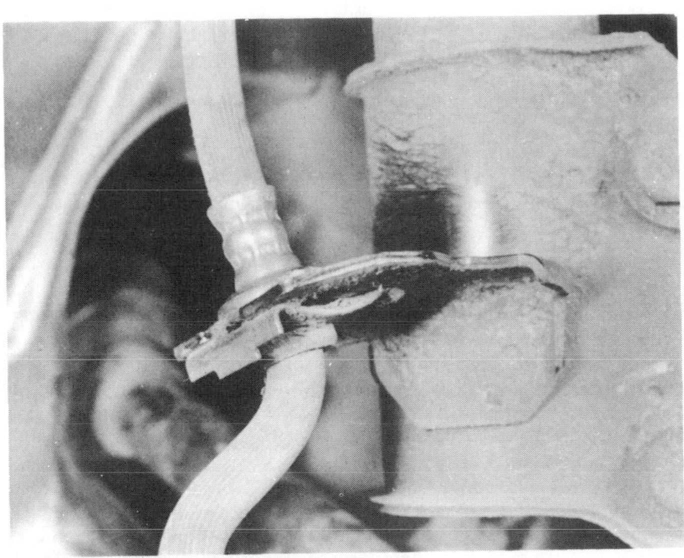
11.2C Front brake flexible hose intermediate support

11.7 Brake and fuel line securing clip

2 Bleed the system in the following order:

Left-hand rear brake
Right-hand front brake
Pressure regulating valve
Right-hand rear brake
Left-hand front brake

3 If the system is completely empty, bleed from the following points prior to those in paragraph 2:

Master cylinder primary outlet (loosen the union nut)
Master cylinder secondary outlet (loosen the union nut)
Pressure regulating valve

4 Unless the pressure bleeding method is being used, do not forget to keep the fluid level in the master cylinder reservoir topped up to prevent air from being drawn into the system which would make any work done worthless.
5 Before commencing operations, check that all system hoses and pipes are in good condition with all unions tight and free from leaks.
6 Take great care not to allow hydraulic fluid to come into contact with the vehicle paintwork as it is an effective paint stripper. Wash off any spilled fluid immediately with cold water.
7 If the system incorporates a vacuum servo, destroy the vacuum by giving several applications of the brake pedal in quick succession.

Bleeding – two man method

8 Gather together a clean glass jar and a length of rubber or plastic tubing which will be a tight fit on the brake bleed screws.
9 Engage the help of an assistant.
10 Push one end of the bleed tube onto the first bleed screw and immerse the other end in the glass jar which should contain enough hydraulic fluid to cover the end of the tube.
11 Open the bleed screw one half a turn and have your assistant depress the brake pedal fully, then slowly release it. Tighten the bleed screw at the end of each pedal downstroke to obviate any chance of air or fluid being drawn back into the system (photo).
12 Repeat this operation until clean hydraulic fluid, free from air bubbles, can be seen coming through into the jar.
13 Tighten the bleed screw at the end of a pedal downstroke and remove the bleed tube. Bleed the remaining screws in a similar way.

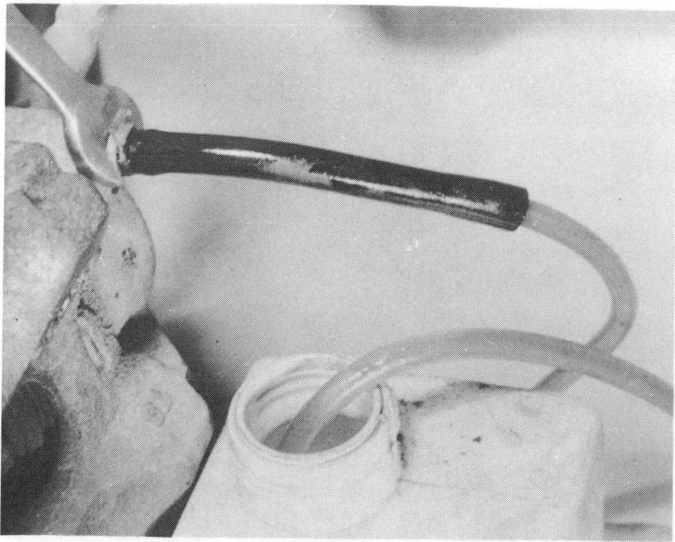

12.11 Bleeding a front brake caliper

Bleeding – using one way valve kit

14 There are a number of one-man, one-way brake bleeding kits available from motor accessory shops. It is recommended that one of these kits is used wherever possible as it will greatly simplify the bleeding operation and also reduce the risk of air or fluid being drawn back into the system, quite apart from being able to do the work without the help of an assistant.
15 To use the kit, connect the tube to the bleedscrew and open the screw one half a turn.
16 Depress the brake pedal fully and slowly release it. The one-way valve in the kit will prevent expelled air from returning at the end of each pedal downstroke. Repeat this operation several times to be sure of ejecting all air from the system. Some kits include a translucent container which can be positioned so that the air bubbles can actually be seen being ejected from the system.
17 Tighten the bleed screw, remove the tube and repeat the operations on the remaining brakes.
18 On completion, depress the brake pedal. If it still feels spongy repeat the bleeding operations, as air must still be trapped in the system.

Bleeding – using a pressure bleeding kit

19 These kits too are available from motor accessory shops and are usually operated by air pressure from the spare tyre.
20 By connecting a pressurised container to the master cylinder fluid reservoir, bleeding is then carried out by simply opening each bleed screw in turn and allowing the fluid to run out, rather like turning on a tap, until no air is visible in the expelled fluid.
21 By using this method, the large reserve of hydraulic fluid provides a safeguard against air being drawn into the master cylinder during bleeding which often occurs if the fluid level in the reservoir is not maintained.
22 Pressure bleeding is particularly effective when bleeding 'difficult' systems or when bleeding the complete system at time of routine fluid renewal.

All methods

23 When bleeding is completed, check and top up the fluid level in the master cylinder reservoir.
24 Check the feel of the brake pedal. If it feels at all spongy, air must still be present in the system and further bleeding is indicated. Failure to bleed satisfactorily after a reasonable repetition of the bleeding operation may be due to worn master cylinder seals.
25 Discard brake fluid which has been expelled. it is almost certain to be contaminated with moisture, air and dirt making it unsuitable for further use. Clean fluid should always be stored in an airtight container as it absorbs moisture readily (hygroscopic) which lowers its boiling point and coulld affect braking performance under severe conditions.

13 Disc – inspection, renovation or renewal

1 Whenever the disc pads are being inspected, check the disc for deep scoring. Light scoring is normal, but heavy scoring can only be remedied by fitting a new disc or by surface grinding the original one provided its thickness is not reduced below the minimum specified.
2 If it is suspected that the disc is distorted, it can be checked for run-out using a dial gauge or feeler blades between the disc and a fixed point while the disc is being rotated.
3 To remove a front brake disc, remove the disc pads (Section 3), then unbolt the caliper and torque member from the stub axle carrier and suspend it from the coil spring without disconnecting the hydraulic hose. The disc can then be withdrawn from the wheel studs. Refitting is a reversal of removal.
4 To remove and refit a rear brake disc, refer to Chapter 8, Section 8 for the renewal of the rear hub bearings.

14 Brake drum – inspection, renovation or renewal

1 Whenever the brake drum is removed to inspect the linings, take the opportunity to check the drum itself.
2 If it is scored internally or has been stepped or grooved by the brake shoes, it may be possible to refinish it provided the internal diameter is not increased beyond the specified limit, otherwise the drum must be renewed.
3 If as the result of reference to Fault Diagnosis, the drum is suspected of being out of round, it can be measured using an internal micrometer and if confirmed, the drum will probably require renewing.

15 Vacuum servo unit – description

1 The unit operates in series with the master cylinder to provide assistance to the driver when the brake pedal is depressed. this reduces the effort required by the driver to operate the brake under all braking conditions. The unit operates by vacuum, obtained from the intake manifold and basically consists of a booster diaphragm and control valve assembly.
2 The servo unit and hydraulic master cylinder are connected together so that the servo unit piston rod (valve rod) acts as the master cylinder pushrod. The driver's braking effort is transmitted through another pushrod, to the servo unit piston and its built-in control system. The servo unit piston is attached to a rolling diaphragm, which ensures an airtight seal between the two major parts of the servo unit casing. The forward chamber is held under vacuum conditions created in the intake manifold of the engine and during periods when the brake pedal is not in use, the controls open a passage to the rear chamber, so placing it under vacuum conditions as well. When the brake pedal is depressed, the vacuum passage to the rear chamber is cut off and the chamber opened to atmospheric pressure. The consequent pressure difference across the servo piston pushes the piston forward in the vacuum chamber and operates the main pushrod to the master cylinder.
3 The controls are designed so that assistance is given under all conditions and, when the brakes are not required, vacuum in the rear chamber is re-established when the brake pedal is released.
4 No maintenance is required except occasionally to check the security and condition of the vacuum connecting pipe and check valve.
5 Should a fault develop in the servo unit, do not attempt to overhaul it, but renew it complete.

16 Vacuum servo unit – removal and refitting

1 Remove the master cylinder as described in Section 9.
2 Disconnect the vacuum hose from the servo unit.

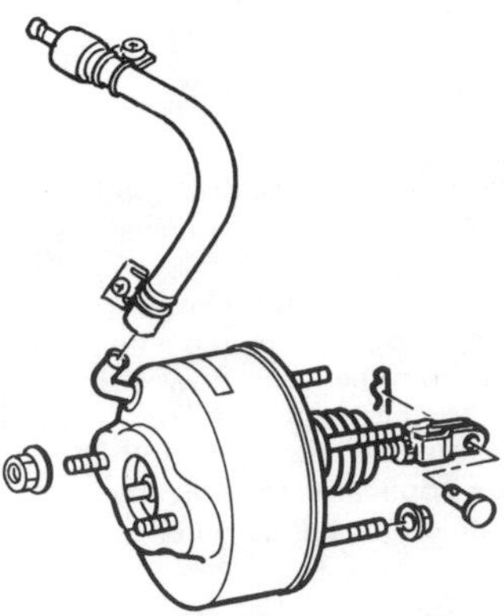

Fig. 9.18 Vacuum servo unit and hose (Sec 16)

3 Working inside the car, remove the small facia panel beneath the steering column and also the plastic air ducting, then disconnect the pushrod from the brake pedal by removing the clip and clevis pin.
4 Unscrew the mounting nuts and remove the servo unit from the engine compartment. Remove the gasket from the mounting studs.

5 Refitting is a reversal of removal, with reference also to Section 9. The servo output rod is not adjustable, but the position of the clevis on the input rod should be adjusted as described in Section 21.

17 Vacuum servo unit check valve – removal, checking and refitting

1 The vacuum check valve is located on the bracket secured by the master cylinder to the front of the vacuum servo unit. To remove it, loosen the clips and disconnect the hoses from each end of the valve.
2 Test the valve by blowing through it from the servo unit side when there should be no resistance to the flow of air. Now blow from the inlet manifold side when the valve should close and prevent any airflow. Renew the valve if it is proved faulty.
3 Refitting is a reversal of removal.

18 Handbrake – adjustment

1 Although the handbrake is self-adjusting by virtue of the automatic adjuster on the rear shoes, the cable may stretch after a high mileage. This will become evident when the handbrake lever moves over more than seven to nine notches to lock the rear wheels.

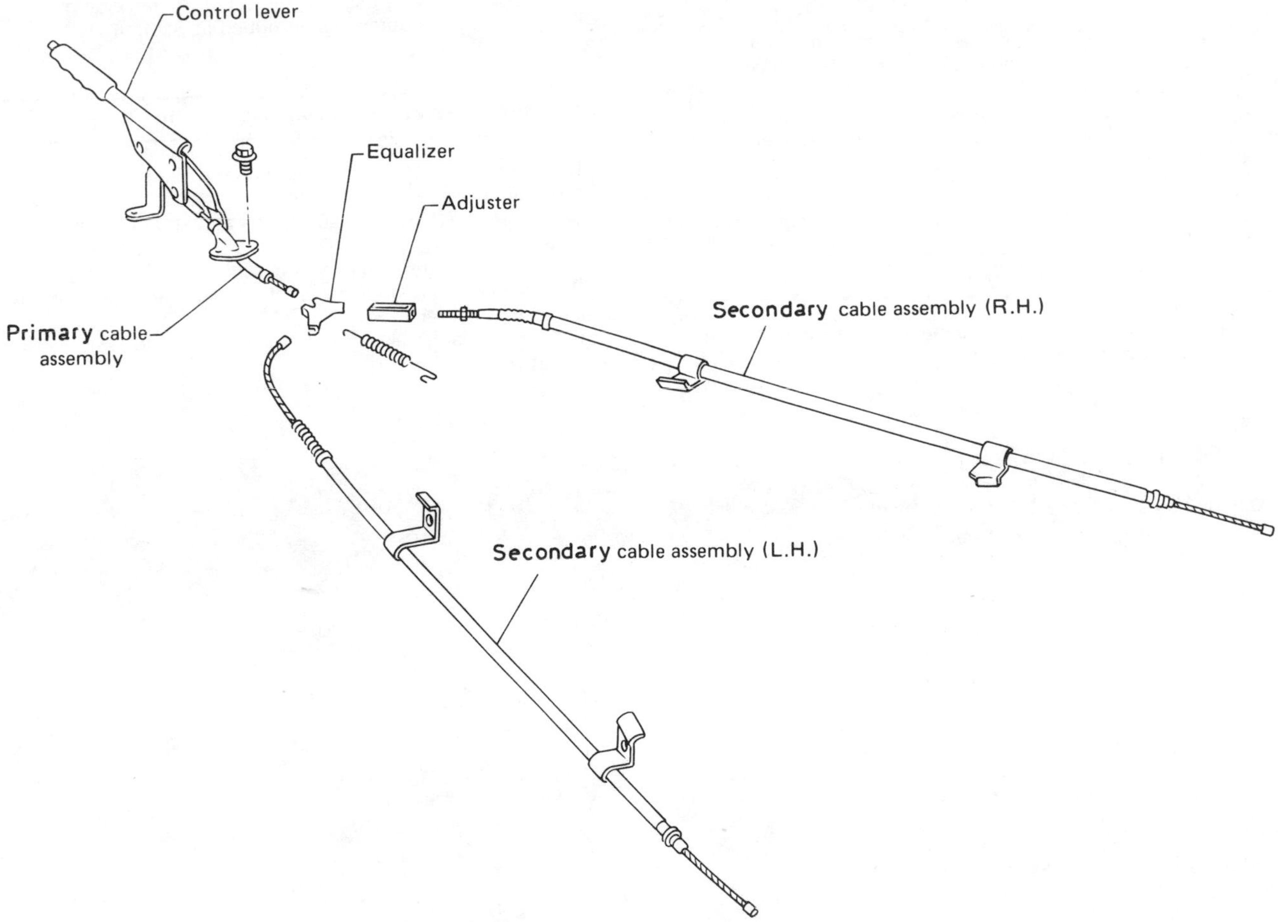

Fig. 9.19 Handbrake components (Sec 18)

18.3 Handbrake cable adjuster location

2 To adjust the handbrake, jack up the rear of the car and support on axle stands.
3 Release the locknut on the cable adjuster just forward of the fuel tank (photo), then turn the adjuster as necessary until the rear wheels are fully locked, with the handbrake lever applied between seven and nine notches.
4 Tighten the locknut on completion and lower the car to the ground.
5 Check the operation of the handbrake 'ON' warning switch. The warning lamp should come on when the handbrake lever is moved over the first notch, but go out when the lever is returned to the fully off position. If necessary, remove the centre console (Chapter 11) and bend the switch plate as required.

19 Handbrake cables – renewal

1 Chock the front wheels, then jack up the rear of the car and support on axle stands. Release the handbrake.
2 Loosen the locknut and back off the adjuster to release any tension in the cable.

Primary cable
3 Remove the centre console as described in Chapter 11.
4 Unscrew the two cable bracket bolts located behind the handbrake (photo).
5 Disconnect the cable from the handbrake lever. On new cars, the clevis pin does not incorporate a split pin and must therefore be broken in order to remove it from the lever. However when the primary cable is renewed separately the clevis pin includes a split pin.
6 Working under the car, disconnect the primary cable from the equalizer and where applicable the adjuster.
7 Withdraw the cable into the car interior.

Secondary cables
8 Disconnect the front end of the cable from the equalizer or adjuster as applicable.
9 On non-Turbo models, remove the rear brake shoes as described in Section 5, then disconnect the cable from the backplate.
10 On Turbo models, disconnect the cable from the handbrake lever on the rear caliper.
11 Pull out the clip securing the front end of the outer cable to the underbody bracket.
12 Unbolt the cable guide and support bracket from the underbody and withdraw the complete cable from the car (photo).

All cables
13 Fit the new cable(s) using a reversal of the removal procedure and finally adjust the handbrake as described in Section 18.

20 Handbrake lever – removal and refitting

1 Chock the front wheels, then jack up the rear of the car and support on axle stands. Release the handbrake.
2 Loosen the locknut and back off the adjuster to release any tension in the cables.
3 Remove the centre console as described in Chapter 11.
4 Remove the warning lamp switch from the handbrake lever, as described in Chapter 12.
5 Unbolt the handbrake lever from the floor and remove it from the car (photo).

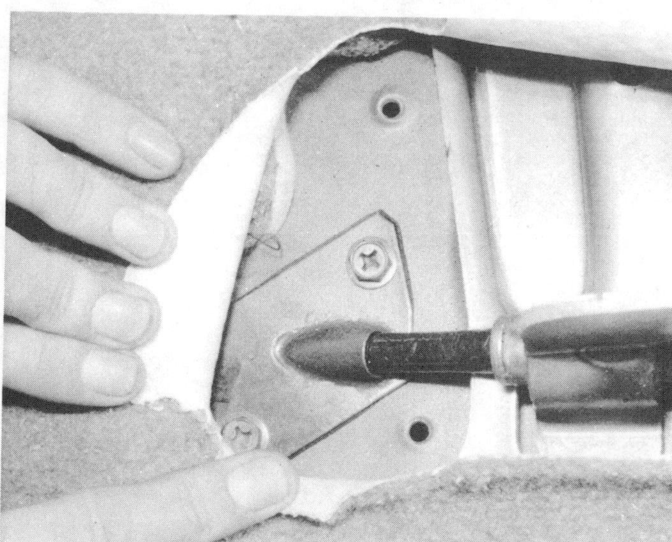
19.4 Handbrake primary cable bracket and bolts

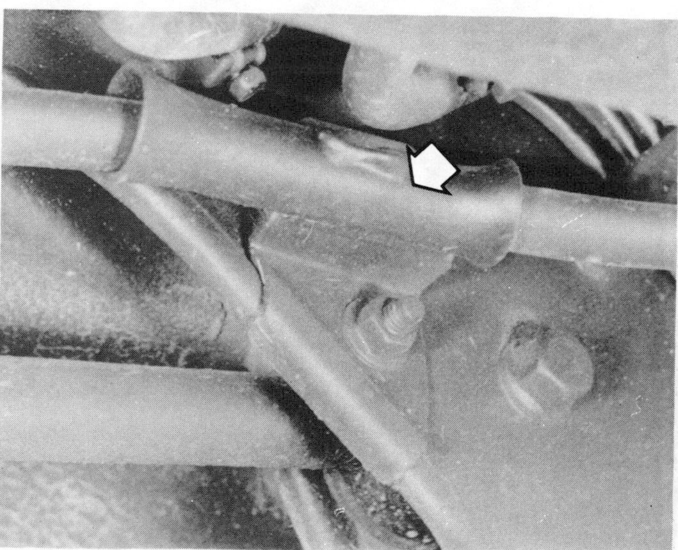
19.12 Handbrake cable guide (arrowed)

6 Refitting is a reversal of removal, but first check that the pawl and ratchet mechanism is adequately lubricated with grease. Finally adjust the handbrake as described in Section 18.

21 Brake pedal – removal, refitting and adjustment

1 Remove the small facia panel beneath the steering column and also the plastic air ducting, then disconnect the pushrod from the brake pedal by removing the clip and clevis pin.
2 Remove the clip or nut from the fulcrum pin, then pull out the pin and withdraw the pedal from the bracket.
3 Refit the pedal using a reversal of the removal procedure, but apply a little grease to the fulcrum pin, clevis pin, and return spring. Make sure that the ends of the return spring are correctly located on the pedal and bracket. On completion, adjust the pedal as follows.

Adjustment

4 Check the free height (H) of the pedal with reference to Fig. 9.21. If adjustment is necessary, loosen the locknut on the pedal pushrod clevis and turn the pushrod as required. Make sure that the end of the pushrod remains visible within the clevis (Fig. 9.22), and tighten the locknut on completion.

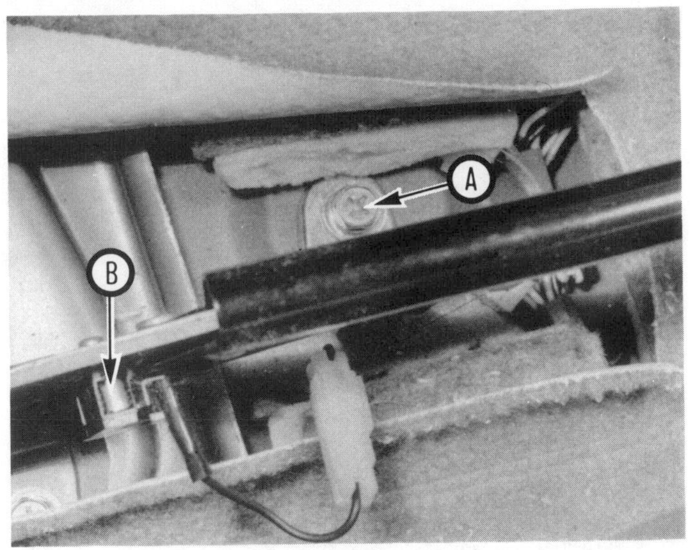

20.5 Handbrake lever mounting bolt (A) and warning lamp switch (B)

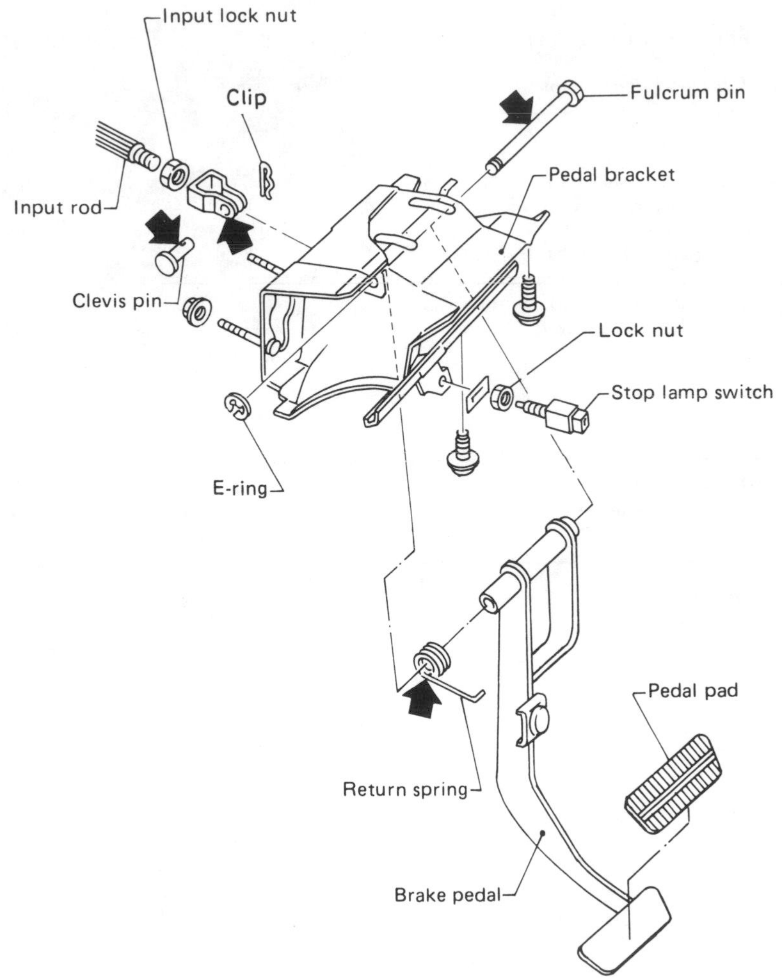

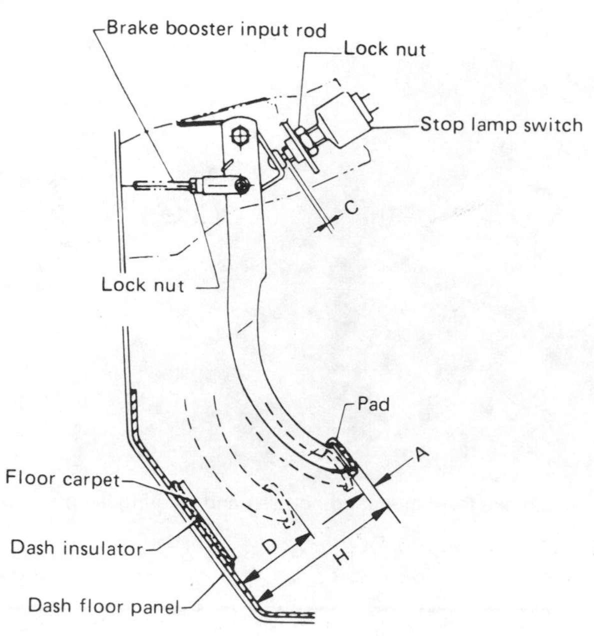

Fig. 9.21 Brake pedal adjustment (Sec 21)

Refer to Specifications for actual dimensions

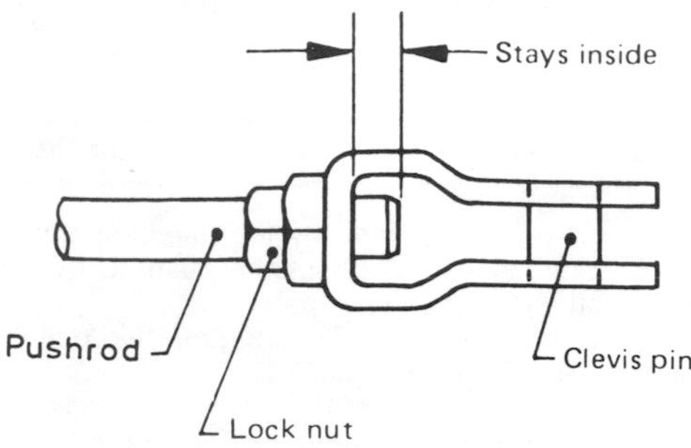

Fig. 9.22 After adjustment, the end of the pushrod must still be visible inside the clevis (Sec 21)

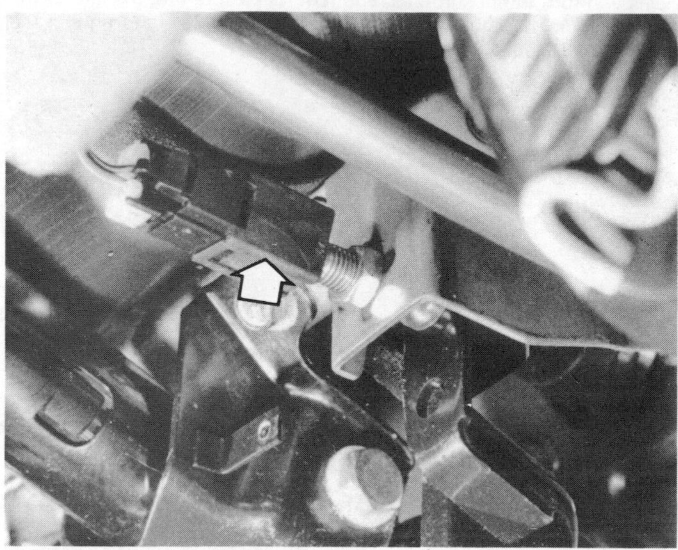

21.5 Stop lamp switch

5 Check that the correct clearance (C) exists between the stop lamp switch and the pedal stop (Fig. 9.21). If necessary, loosen the locknut, adjust the switch position, then tighten the locknut (photo).
6 Check that the pedal free play is as shown in Fig. 9.21. If excessive play is evident, wear in the clevis or fulcrum pin is indicated.
7 With the engine running, check that the depressed height is as shown in Fig. 9.21. If below the specified height, check the hydraulic system for leaks and accumulation of air.

22 Fault diagnosis – braking system

Symptom	Reason(s)
Excessive brake pedal travel	Incorrect pedal adjustment Faulty self-adjusting mechanism on rear brakes (except Turbo)
Car pulls to one side when brakes applied	Linings on one side contaminated with oil or brake fluid Partially seized caliper or wheel cylinder Brake disc distorted or excessively worn
Pedal feels spongy	Air in the hydraulic system
Pedal feels springy when brakes applied	New linings not yet bedded-in Out-of-round drums or discs with excessive run-out
Lack of servo assistance	Vacuum hose leaking Check valve inoperative Servo internal fault

Chapter 10
Suspension, steering wheels and tyres

Contents

Specifications

Front suspension

Type	Independent with MacPherson struts and coil springs, anti-roll bar	
Camber:		
Saloon	0°25′ negative to 1°5′ positive	
Estate	0°20′ negative to 1°10′ positive	
Castor	1°15′ to 2°45′	
Steering axle inclination:		
Saloon	13°45′ to 15°15′	
Estate	14°40′ to 15°10′	
Toe-in	1.0 to 3.0 mm (0.04 to 0.12 in) or 0°6′ to 0°19′	
Timing angles (full lock):	**Inside wheel**	**Outside wheel**
14 inch wheels	38° to 42°	29° to 33°
15 inch wheels	34° to 38°	27° to 31°

Rear suspension

Type	Independent with telescopic struts, coil springs, parallel links and radius arms, anti-roll bar
Camber:	
Saloon	0°30′ negative to 1°0′ positive
Estate	0°2′ negative to 1°10′ positive
Toe-in:	
Saloon	2.0 to 6.0 mm (0.08 to 0.24 in) or 0°12′ to 0°37′
Estate	3.0 to 7.0 mm (0.12 to 0.28 in) or 0°18′ to 0°43′

Rear suspension strut

Fluid capacity and type	0.33 litres (11.6 fluid oz) of Nissan strut fluid
Piston rod diameter	20.0 mm (0.79 in)
Cylinder inner diameter	30.0 to 30.1 mm (1.181 to 1,185 in)

Steering

Type	Rack and pinion with safety column, optional power-assisted steering
No. of turns lock-to-lock:	
Manual steering	4.6
Power steering	3.0
Power steering fluid capacity	0.8 litre (1.4 pints)
Power steering pump drivebelt tension deflection:	
New belt	4.0 to 6.0 mm (0.16 to 0.24 in)
Used belt	6.0 to 8.0 mm (0.24 to 0.31 in)

Roadwheels

Type:	
Non-Turbo models	Pressed steel or optional light alloy
Turbo models	Light alloy
Size:	
Non-Turbo models	5J x 14 (pressed steel) or 5½JJ x 14 (light alloy)
Turbo models	6JJ x 15 (light alloy)

Tyres

Size:	
Non-Turbo models	165SR14, 175SR14, 185/70HR14, 185/70SR14, 175HR14
Turbo models	195/60R15
Pressures	Refer to the placard affixed to the driver's side door for manufacturer's recommendations

Torque wrench settings

	Nm	lbf ft
Front suspension		
Piston rod	68	50
Strut top mounting	37	27
Strut to knuckle	118	87
Lower balljoint to arm	93	69
Lower balljoint nut	79	58
Lower arm bolt	103	76
Lower arm nut	133	98
Anti-roll bar clamp	37	27
Anti-roll bar link	19	14
Driveshaft nut	235 to 314	174 to 231
Rear suspension		
Parallel link to crossmember	103	76
Parallel link to strut	103	76
Rear parallel link locknut	88	65
Radius arm	98	72
Strut bottom bracket	69	51
Piston rod	69	51
Strut top mounting	37	27
Seal retainer	98	72
Steering		
Steering wheel	34	25
Lower joint to column	27	20
Lower joint to gear	27	20
Column mounting	12	9
Tie-rod end stud nut	34	25
Tie-rod end locknut	42	31
Tie-rod inner balljoint	88	65
Steering gear clamp	31	23
Power steering high pressure hose to pump	39	29
Power steering high pressure pipe to steering gear	20	15
Power steering pump:		
M8 bolt	16	12
M10 bolt	31	23
Roadwheels		
Wheel nut	88	65

1 General description

The front suspension is of independent type, incorporating MacPherson struts and coil springs, and an anti-roll bar.

The rear suspension is also independent, incorporating telescopic struts and coil springs, parallel links, radius arms and an anti-roll bar.

The steering gear is of rack and pinion type with a safety steering column. Power-assisted steering may be fitted as an optional extra.

2 Routine maintenance

Carry out the following procedures at the intervals given in *'Routine Maintenance'* at the beginning of the Manual.

Power steering pump drivebelt

1 Examine the full length of the power steering pump drivebelt for cracks, fraying, deterioration and oil contamination. Renew it if

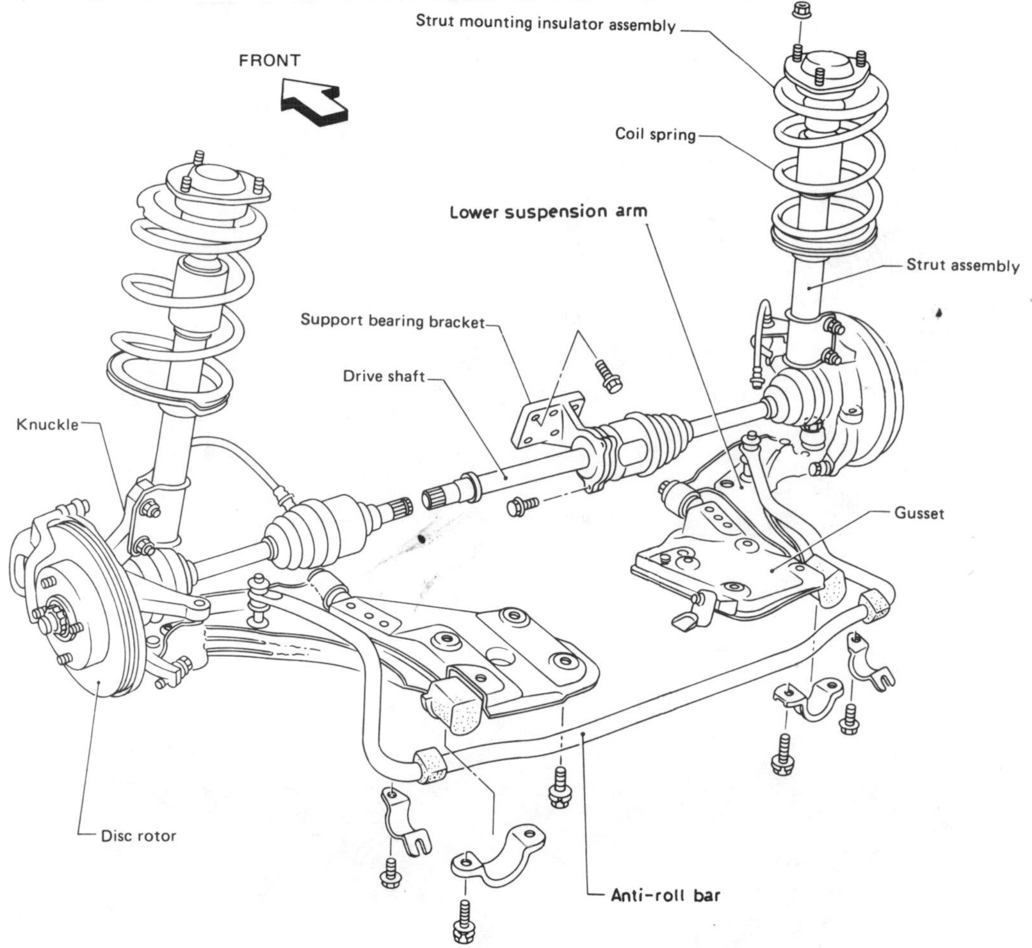

Fig. 10.1 Front suspension components (Sec 1)

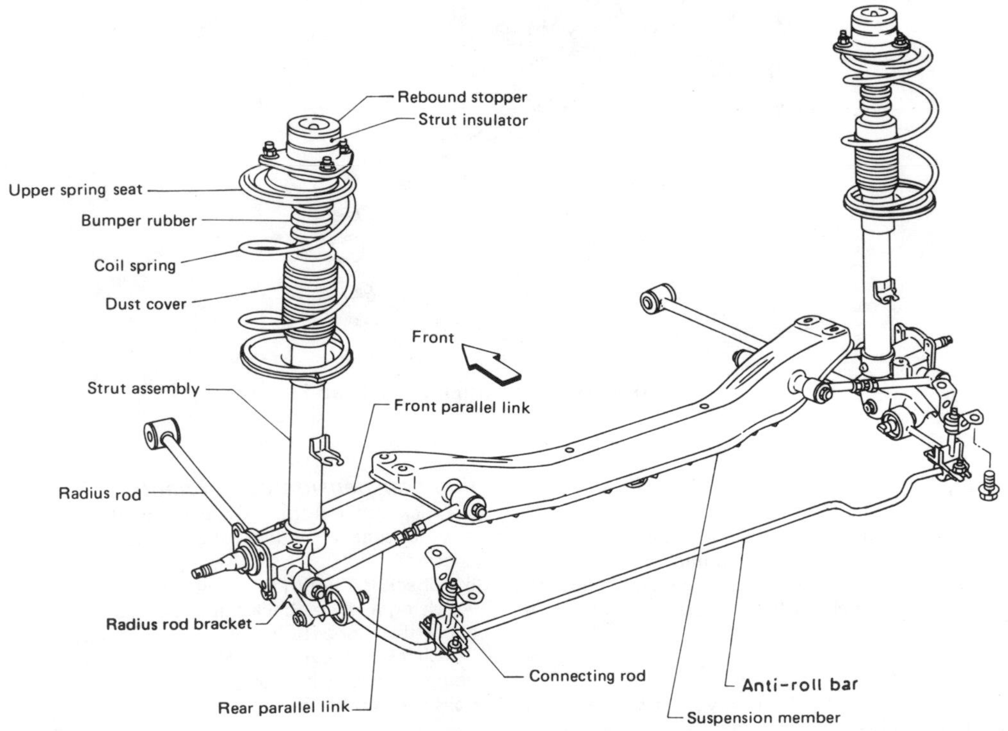

Fig. 10.2 Rear suspension components (Sec 1)

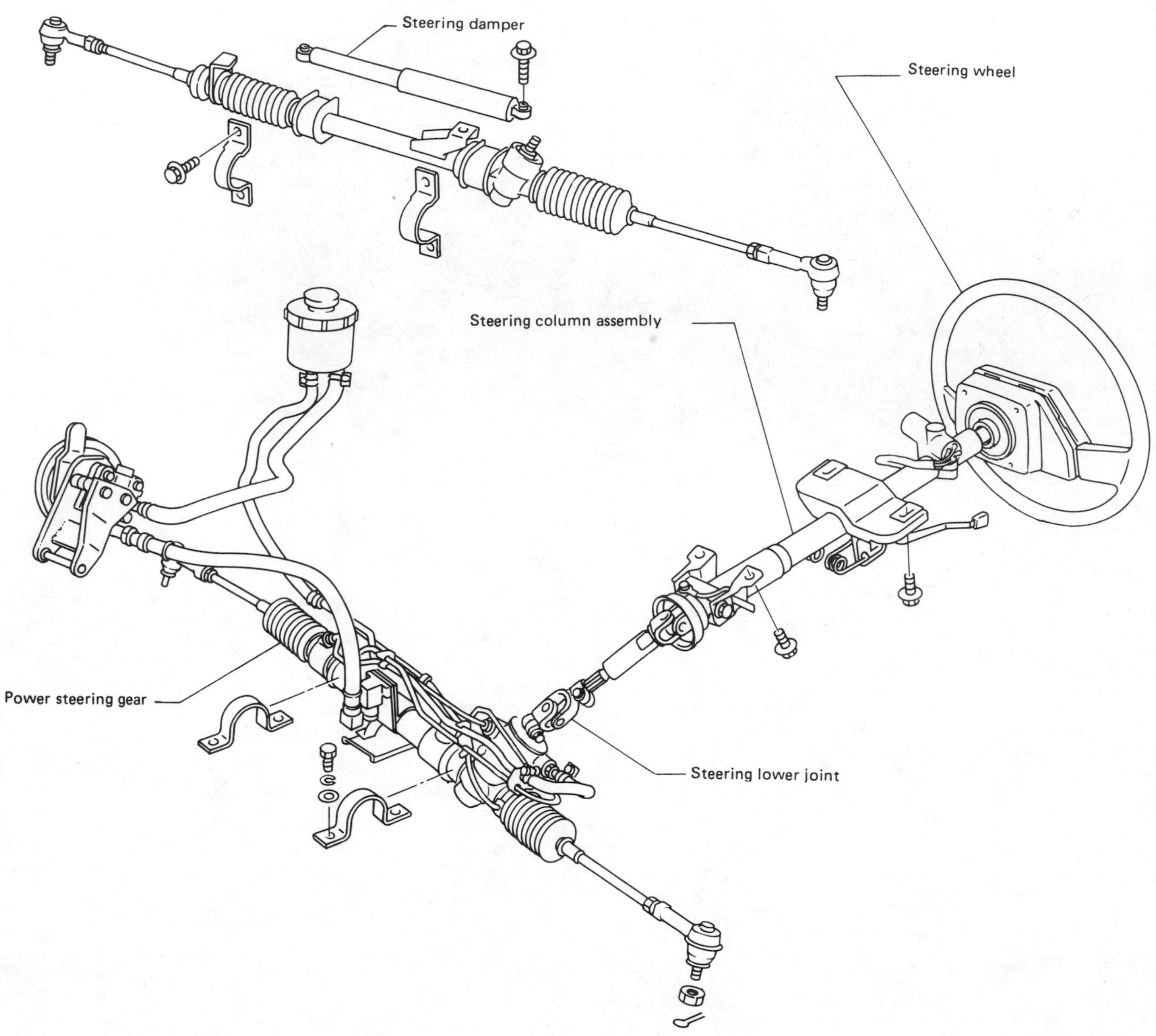

Fig. 10.3 Steering components (Sec 1)

necessary, but if it is in good order check and if necessary adjust its tension as follows.

2 Depress the drivebelt with moderate thumb pressure midway between the water pump and power steering pump pulleys. If the deflection is not as given in Specifications, loosen the adjusting bolt and if necessary the pivot bolt, swivel out the pump as required, then re-tighten the bolts.

Power steering fluid level and fluid lines

3 Check that the fluid level *(cold)* in the reservoir is between the 'Min' and 'Max' marks. If it is below the 'Min' mark, check the system for leaks as follows, then top up the level to the 'Max' mark (photo).

4 Check all the fluid lines and hoses for leaks, security and deterioration. Also check the rubber bellows on the steering gear for leaks and security.

Front suspension components

5 Jack up the front of the car and attempt to shake each front wheel. Any looseness evident should be investigated and corrected as necessary.

6 Check the tightness of all front suspension nuts and bolts.

7 Using a lever, check the lower suspension balljoints for wear. Also check the rubber bolts for damage and leaks.

8 Check the strut shock absorbers for leaks. A little dampness is permissible, but if excessive the strut should be renewed as it is not possible to overhaul it.

Rear suspension components

9 Jack up the rear of the car and attempt to shake each rear wheel. Investigate any looseness and correct it as necessary.

10 Check the tightness of all rear suspension nuts and bolts. Access to

2.3 Removing the power steering fluid reservoir filler cap for topping-up

the strut upper mounting nuts is gained by removing the rear seat backrest and rear window shelf on Saloon models.

11 Check the strut shock absorbers for leaks, and overhaul if necessary.

Steering gear and linkage

12 Check the tightness of the steering gear mounting bolts.

13 Check the steering gear rubber bellows for splits, leaks and deterioration.

14 Check the steering column intermediate shaft universal joint for wear.

15 Check the tie-rod end balljoints for wear by holding each side of the wheel and rocking it (check that play is not due to worn wheel bearings – see Chapter 8).

Tyre condition

16 Check all tyres for tread wear and general deterioration. Uneven wear indicates incorrect wheel alignment, faulty shock absorbers or worn balljoints.

Wheel alignment and balance

17 Check and if necessary adjust the front and rear wheel alignment, as described in Sections 24 and 25. Unless damage has occurred, or associated components have been renewed, it should only be necessary to check the toe-in adjustment.

18 Change the wheel positions front to rear on each side of the car (to promote more even tyre wear), and where necessary have them balanced.

3 Front suspension lower balljoint – renewal

1 Remove the appropriate front wheel embellisher. Prise off the plastic cap, then remove the split pin and locking ring.

2 With the handbrake applied, loosen the driveshaft nut using a socket and long extension.

3 Jack up the front of the car and support on axle stands, then remove the wheel, driveshaft nut and washer.

4 Unscrew the three nuts and separate the lower suspension arm from the lower balljoint (photo).

5 Unscrew the nut, then use a separator tool to disconnect the tie-rod end from the steering arm.

6 Pull the hub and strut off of the driveshaft. If necessary, tap the driveshaft through the hub splines using a mallet.

7 Extract the split pin and unscrew the nut, then use a separator tool to remove the lower balljoint from the stub axle carrier.

8 Fit the new balljoint using a reversal of the removal procedure. Tighten all nuts to the specified torque and fit new split pins where necessary. Refer to Chapter 8 when tightening the driveshaft nut. Finally, check and if necessary adjust the front wheel alignment.

4 Front suspension strut and coil spring – removal and refitting

Note: *Coil spring compressor tools are required to remove the coil spring from the strut.*

1 Jack up the front of the car and support on axle stands. Remove the roadwheel.

2 Disconnect the brake hydraulic line from the suspension strut with reference to Chapter 9.

3 Position a jack under the front lower suspension arm.

4 Unscrew the bolts securing the bottom of the strut to the stub axle carrier, noting which way they are fitted (photo).

5 Support the strut, then unscrew the top mounting nuts from within

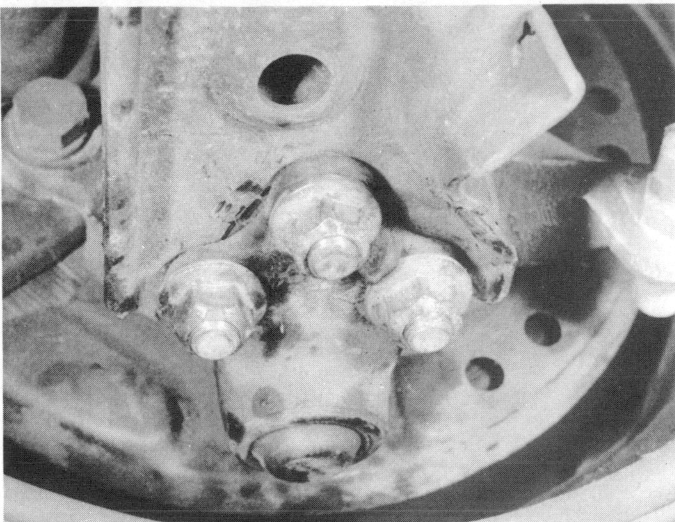

3.4 Front suspension lower balljoint nuts

4.4 Front suspension strut-to-stub axle carrier bolts

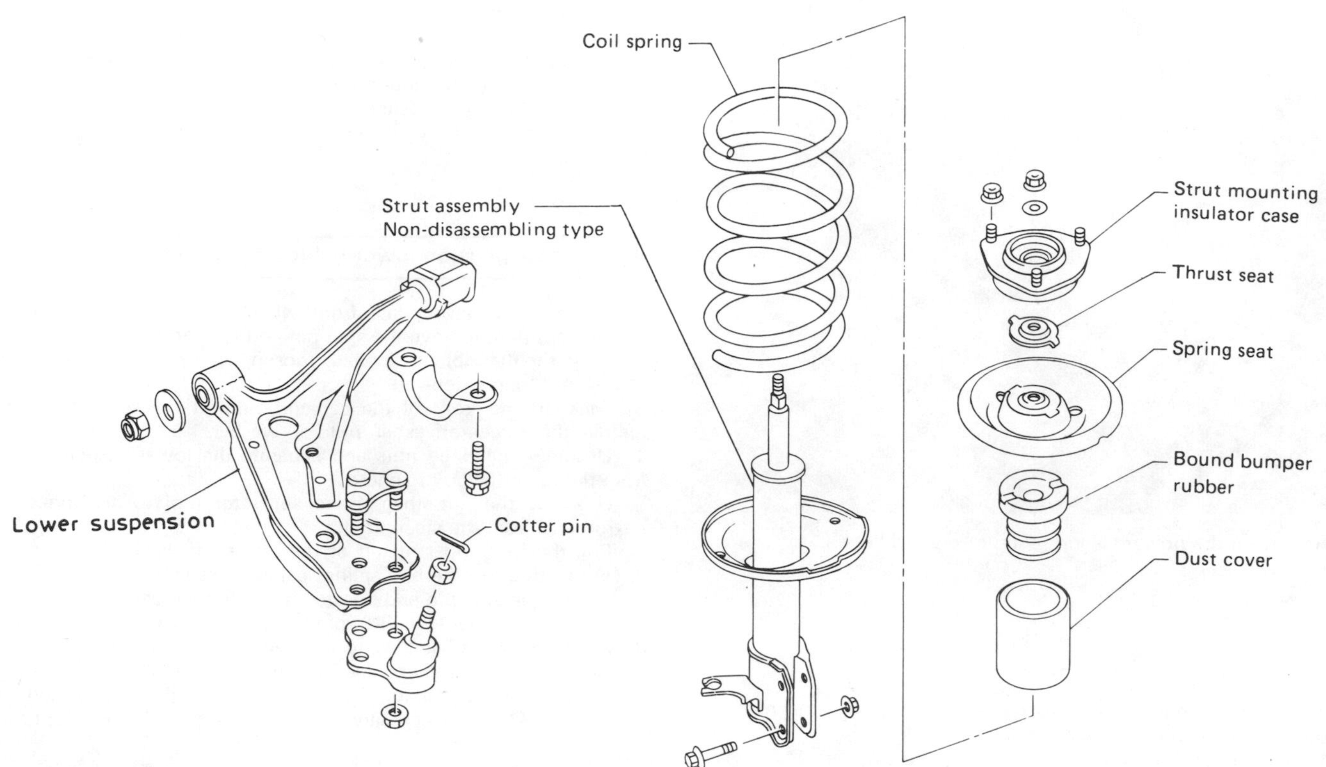

Fig. 10.4 Exploded view of the front suspension strut and lower suspension arm (Secs 4 and 5)

4.5A Front suspension strut top mounting nuts

4.5B Lower view of front suspension strut and coil spring

the engine compartment. Withdraw the strut from under the front wing (photos).

6 Loosen but do not remove the piston nut in the top mounting.

7 Fit spring compressors (available from most motor accessory shops) to the coil spring, and compress the spring until it is just clear of the top mounting.

8 Remove the piston nut and washer.

9 Remove the top mounting, thrust seat, upper spring seat and coil spring.

10 Remove the rebound rubber and dust cover from the piston rod.

11 To check the shock absorber, mount the strut upright in a vice and move the piston rod fully up and down. The resistance should be even in both directions. Check for fluid leakage where the piston rod enters the strut. It is not possible to renew the shock absorber separately, therefore if it is faulty, the complete suspension strut must be renewed.

12 Check the coil spring and top mounting components for damage and deterioration and renew them as necessary.

13 Before fitting either an old or new strut, it should be mounted

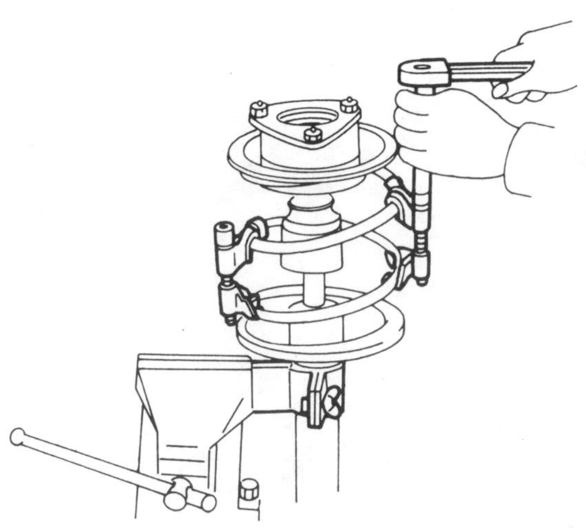

Fig. 10.5 Fitting spring compressors to the front coil spring (Sec 4)

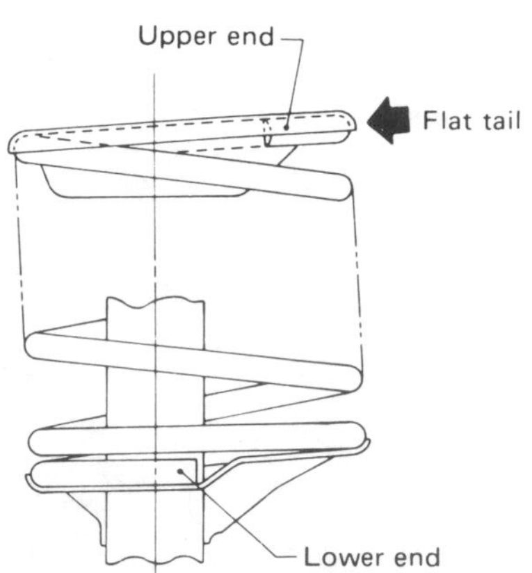

Fig. 10.6 Showing correct location of front coil spring (Sec 4)

upright in a vice and the shock absorber piston rod operated fully up and down several times.
14 Compress the coil spring with the spring compressors.
15 Refitting is a reversal of removal, but make sure that the ends of the coil spring are located correctly in the spring seats. Tighten all nuts and bolts to the specified torque. Finally, check and if necessary adjust the front wheel alignment.

5 Front lower suspension arm – removal and refitting

1 Remove the front anti-roll bar as described in Section 6.
2 Remove the roadwheel, then unscrew the three nuts and separate the lower suspension arm from the lower balljoint.
3 Unscrew the inner pivot nut and the rear clamp bolts, then remove the lower suspension arm from the support plate (photo). If necessary, the plate can be unbolted from the underbody, but the engine mounting bracket must be supported on the right-hand side.
4 Check the arm and the bushes for damage and deterioration. The flexible bushes are renewable. Press or draw the front bush out or into its seat. The rear bush can be gripped in the jaws of a vice while the control arm is twisted out of it. Use brake fluid or soapy water to ease the fitting of the new bushes.
5 Refitting is a reversal of removal, however the flexible bush mounting nut and bolts should initially be only tightened hand-tight, then fully tightened with the weight of the car on the suspension. Finally, check and if necessary adjust the front wheel alignment.

6 Front anti-roll bar – removal and refitting

1 Jack up the front of the car and support on axle stands. Apply the handbrake.
2 Remove the front roadwheels.
3 Unscrew the nuts from the top of the bolts securing the anti-roll bar to the front lower suspension arms. Remove the bolts together with the mounting rubbers, washers and spacer tubes, noting the position of each item (photos).
4 Unscrew the rear mounting clamp bolts, remove the clamps and withdraw the anti-roll bar from under the car (photo).
5 Check the anti-roll bar and mounting components for damage. In particular check the flexible rubber mountings and renew them if necessary.
6 Refitting is a reversal of removal. The mounting clamp rear bolts can be inserted several threads before lifting the anti-roll bar into position, as the rear holes of the clamps are slotted. Delay fully tightening the clamp bolts until the weight of the car is on the suspension.

5.3 Front lower suspension arm rear mounting

6.3A Front anti-roll bar mounting on the lower suspension arm

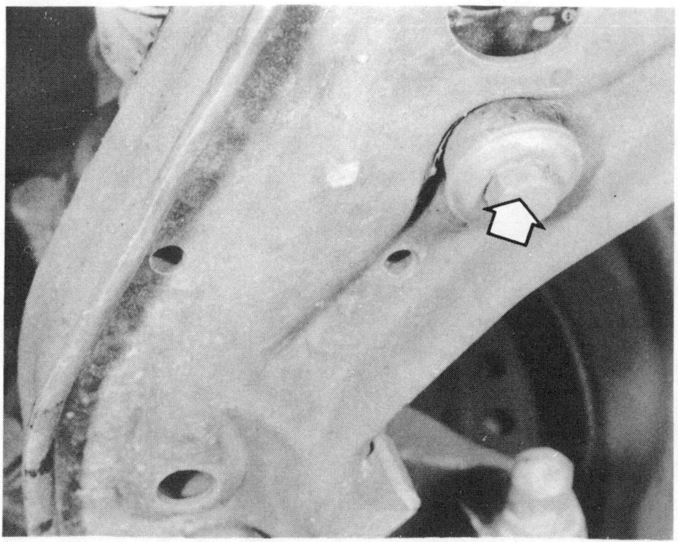

6.3B Lower view of the front anti-roll bar mounting bolt

6.4 Front anti-roll bar mounting clamp

7 Front suspension stub axle carrier – removal and refitting

1 Remove the appropriate front wheel embellisher, then prise off the plastic cap and remove the split pin and locking ring.
2 With the handbrake applied, loosen the driveshaft nut using a socket and long extension. If preferred, the nut can be loosened after removal of the front wheel, by refitting two nuts and using a bar between the two wheel studs as shown in Fig. 10.7.
3 Jack up the front of the car and support on axle stands, then remove the wheel, driveshaft nut and washer.
4 Unbolt the brake disc caliper from the stub axle carrier with reference to Chapter 9, then suspend it from the coil spring, leaving the hydraulic hose still attached.
5 Unscrew the nut, then use a separator tool to disconnect the tie-rod end from the steering arm.
6 Unscrew the three nuts and separate the lower suspension arm from the lower balljoint.
7 Pull the hub and strut off of the driveshaft. If necessary tap the driveshaft tthrough the hub splines using a mallet.
8 Extract the split pin and unscrew the nut, then use a separator tool to remove the lower balljoint from the stub axle carrier.
9 Unscrew the bolts securing the bottom of the strut to the stub axle carrier, noting which way they are fitted, then withdraw the stub axle carrier from the car.
10 Remove the brake disc and the hub and bearings with reference to Chapters 9 and 8 respectively.
11 Refitting is a reversal of removal. Refer to Chapters 8 and 9 as necessary, and tighten all nuts and bolts to the specified torque. Use a new split pin to lock the lower balljoint nut.

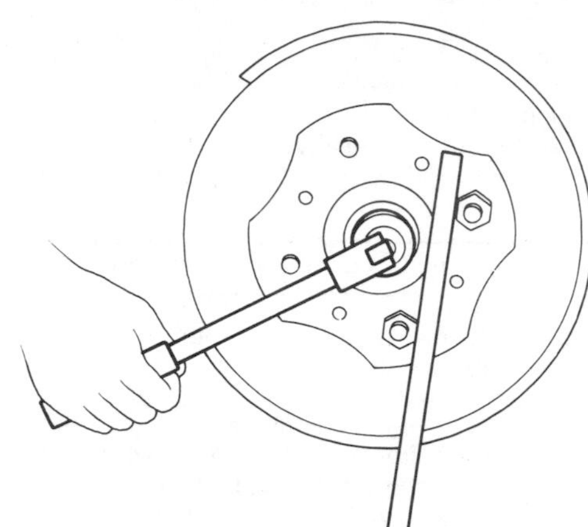

Fig. 10.7 Loosening the driveshaft nut while retaining the hub with a metal bar (Sec 7)

8 Rear radius rod – removal and refitting

1 Chock the front wheels, then jack up the rear of the car and support on axle stands. Remove the roadwheel.
2 Unscrew and remove both mounting bolts, noting that the nuts are on the outside, then remove the radius rod (photo).
3 Check the rod and bushes for wear and damage, and renew the rod complete if necessary. The bushes cannot be renewed separately.
4 Refitting is a reversal of removal, but delay fully tightening the mounting bolts until the weight of the car is on the suspension.

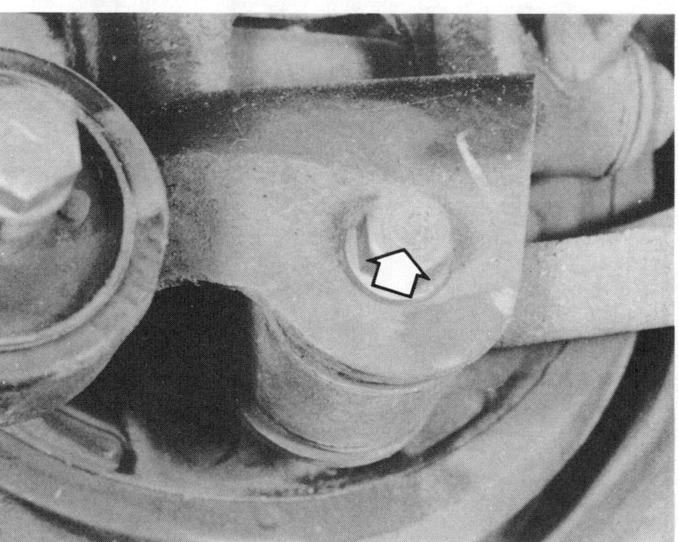

8.2 Rear radius rod mounting bolt

9 Rear parallel links – removal and refitting

1 Chock the front wheels, then jack up the rear of the car and support on axle stands. Remove the roadwheel.

Left-hand side only

2 Remove the rear exhaust system with reference to Chapter 3.
3 Unbolt the rear anti-roll bar left-hand bracket from the underbody.
4 Unbolt the rear suspension crossmember from the underbody, then support it on axle stands so that the parallel link inner bolt clears the fuel tank.

Both sides

5 Unscrew and remove the mounting through-bolts and withdraw the parallel links. Note that the bolt heads face forwards and that the adjustable link is at the rear of the crossmember (photo).
6 Check the links and bushes for wear and damage. The bushes cannot be renewed separately, so if they are worn the complete link must be renewed.
7 Refitting is a reversal of removal, but delay fully tightening the mounting through-bolts until the weight of the car is on the suspension. Finally check and if necessary adjust the rear wheel alignment.

9.5 Rear adjustable parallel link

10 Rear suspension strut and coil spring – removal, overhaul and refitting

Note: *Coil spring compressor tools are required to remove the coil spring from the strut.*

1 Jack up the rear of the car and support on axle stands. Chock the front wheels. Remove the roadwheel.
2 Disconnect the brake hydraulic line from the suspension strut with reference to Chapter 9. Do not unscrew the hydraulic unions.
3 Remove the brake components (drum or disc type) from the stub axle with reference to Chapter 9. Support the backplate or caliper as applicable on an axle stand.
4 Unscrew and remove the radius rod pivot bolt at the strut. Loosen the front pivot bolt and pull the rod down from the strut.

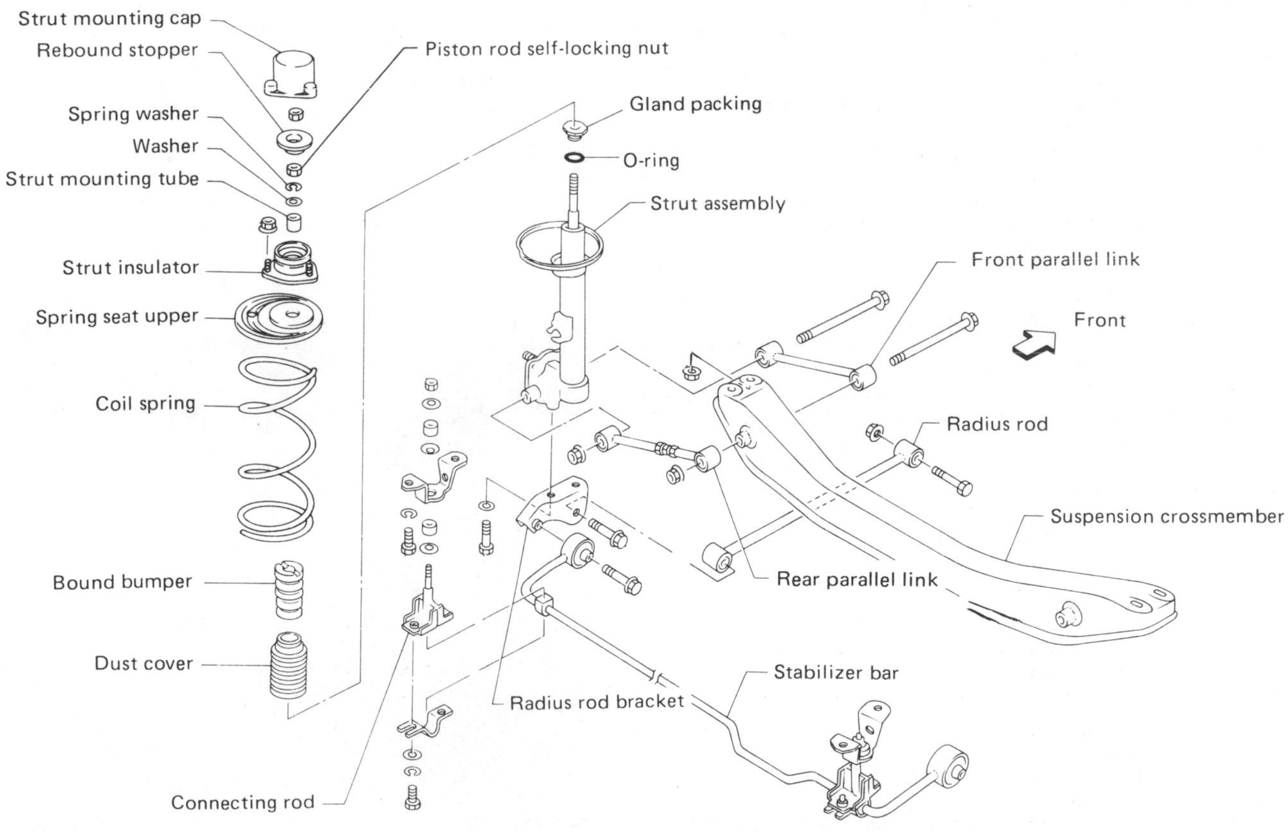

Fig. 10.8 Exploded view of the rear suspension components (Sec 10)

10.8A View of the rear suspension strut top mounting taken through the rear window

10.8B Lower view of rear suspension strut and coil spring

5 Unscrew and remove the parallel link inner pivot bolt, noting that the bolt head faces forwards.
6 Unbolt the bracket from the bottom of the strut, but leave it attached to the anti-roll bar.
7 Pull the cover from the strut top mounting. On Saloon models it is necessary to remove the rear seat backrest and rear shelf. On Estate models remove the trim panel.
8 Support the strut, then unscrew the three top mounting nuts. Withdraw the strut from under the rear wing (photos).
9 Mark the top mounting and strut in relation to each other. The left- and right-hand top mountings are located symmetrically opposite on their respective struts.
10 Fit spring compressors (available from most motor accessory shops) to the coil spring, and compress the spring until it is just clear of the top mounting.
11 Hold the top mounting with a bar between the studs, then unscrew the nut and remove the rebound stopper.
12 Unscrew the piston nut and remove the washers.
13 Remove the top mounting, upper spring seat and coil spring.
14 Remove the rebound rubber and dust cover from the piston rod.
15 Push the piston rod fully into the strut, then unscrew the retainer from the top of the strut and remove the seal.
16 Place the strut in a suitable container, then slowly withdraw the piston rod and guide. Pour out the remaining fluid and remove the cylinder.
17 Clean all the components and examine them for wear, damage and corrosion. Check the piston rod and cylinder, if possible using a dial gauge with the information given in the Specifications. If worn excessively, the shock absorber components can be renewed separately, but make a thorough check of the strut to make sure it is still serviceable.
18 Check the coil spring and top mounting components for damage and deterioration and renew them as necessary.
19 Commence reassembly by inserting the cylinder, together with the piston rod, in its fully retracted position.
20 Measure the exact quantity of recommended fluid as given in the Specifications, and pour it into the cylinder. Note that the quantity is critical for the correct performance of the shock absorber.
21 Lubricate the seal with a little grease. Where an O-ring is fitted, locate it on the cylinder, but with the other type fit the seal in the retainer and fill the space between the two lips with grease. With the latter type, cover the threads on the top of the piston rod with tape to prevent damage to the seal.
22 Fit the retainer and tighten it to the specified torque.
23 Fully operate the piston rod several times, first with the strut inverted, then with it upright.
24 Compress the coil spring with the spring compressors.
25 Refitting is a reversal of the removal procedure, but make sure that the ends of the coil spring are correctly located in the spring seats. Position the top mounting so that the previously made marks are aligned. Tighten all nuts and bolts to the specified torque, but leave the final tightening of the radius rod and parallel link pivot bolts until the weight of the car is on the suspension. Finally, check and if necessary adjust the rear wheel alignment.

11 Rear anti-roll bar – removal and refitting

1 Chock the front wheels, then jack up the rear of the car and support on axle stands. Remove both rear wheels.
2 Unscrew and remove the bolts securing the anti-roll bar to the brackets on the bottom of each strut. Note that the bolt heads face inwards (photo).
3 Unscrew the mounting clamp bolts, remove the clamps and withdraw the anti-roll bar from under the car (photo).

11.2 Rear anti-roll bar mounting on strut

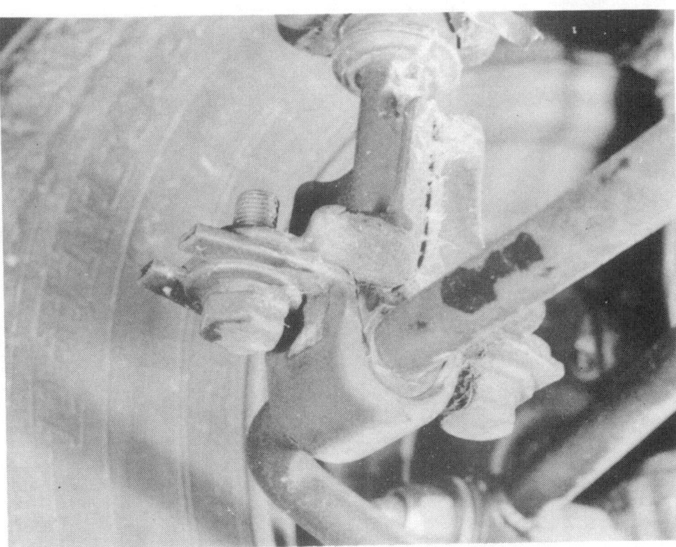
11.3 Rear anti-roll bar mounting on support bracket

4 If necessary, the two connecting rods and support brackets may be unbolted from the underbody.
5 Check the anti-roll bar and mounting components for damage. In particular check the flexible rubber mountings and renew them if necessary. The circular mountings in the ends of the anti-roll bar can be renewed using a long bolt, a short length of metal tube and suitable washers. Coat the outer surface of the new mountings with brake fluid for ease of fitting.
6 Refitting is a reversal of removal. The mounting clamp rear bolts can be inserted several threads before lifting the anti-roll bar into position, as the rear holes of the clamps are slotted. Delay fully tightening the clamp bolts and end mounting bolts until the weight of the car is on the suspension.

12 Steering rack bellows – renewal

1 Jack up the front of the car and support on axle stands. Apply the handbrake and remove the roadwheel.
2 Unscrew the nut from the tie-rod end taper pin, then use a balljoint separator tool to disconnect the end from the steering arm.
3 Loosen the locknut, then unscrew the tie-rod end from the tie-rod while counting the exact number of trims necessary to remove it.

All except left-hand bellows on models with a steering damper

4 Remove the outer clip from the tie-rod and the inner wire clip from the steering gear, then remove the bellows.

Left-hand bellows on models with a steering damper

5 Remove the tie-rod with reference to Section 21. Depending on the model, it may be necessary to remove the air cleaner and ducting for access to the tie-rod in the engine compartment.
6 Remove the outer clip, then release the bellows from the steering damper bracket. Extend the damper to move the bracket away from the rack.
7 Remove the inner clip from the steering gear, then remove the bellows.

All models

8 Replace any grease removed with the old bellows.
9 Fit the new bellows using a reversal of the removal procedure, but apply suitable sealant between the inner end and steering gear. Do not over-tighten the wire clips, otherwise the bellows may be damaged. Finally, check and if necessary adjust the front wheel alignment.

13 Tie-rod end – renewal

1 Jack up the front of the car and support on axle stands. Apply the handbrake and remove the roadwheel.
2 Loosen the locknut on the tie-rod a quarter of a turn.
3 Unscrew the nut from the tie-rod end taper pin, then use a balljoint separator tool to disconnect the end from the steering arm (photos).
4 Unscrew the tie-rod end from the tie-rod, while counting the exact number of turns necessary to remove it.
5 Screw the new tie-rod end onto the tie-rod the same number of turns as noted for removal.
6 Fit the tie-rod end to the steering arm and tighten the nut.
7 Refit the roadwheel, lower the car to the ground, then check and if necessary adjust the front wheel alignment before tightening the tie-rod end locknut.

14 Steering wheel – removal and refitting

1 Disconnect the battery negative lead.
2 Remove the horn pad from the steering wheel. On models with a single horn push, simply prise out the pad, but on models with two

13.3A Using a balljoint separator tool ...

13.3B ... to release the tie-rod end from the steering arm

14.2 Removing the horn pad and wiring on a model with two horn pushes

14.3 Showing the steering wheel alignment marks

horn pushes remove the screws from the rear of the steering wheel. Disconnect the wiring (photo).

3 Check that the steering wheel and column shaft are marked in relation to each other. They are normally marked during production with a cast arrow indicating the top of the steering wheel, and a corresponding punch mark on the shaft (photo).

4 Unscrew the steering wheel retaining nut and pull the wheel from the tapered splined shaft. If it is tight, try rocking it but on no account strike the reverse side of the wheel or the end of the shaft as the built-in safety features of the column will be damaged. Use a small puller similar to the one shown. The steering wheel hub has tapped holes provided for this purpose.

5 Refitting is a reversal of the removal, but first apply a little grease to the direction indicator cancelling poles on the underside of the steering wheel. Tighten the retaining nut to the specified torque.

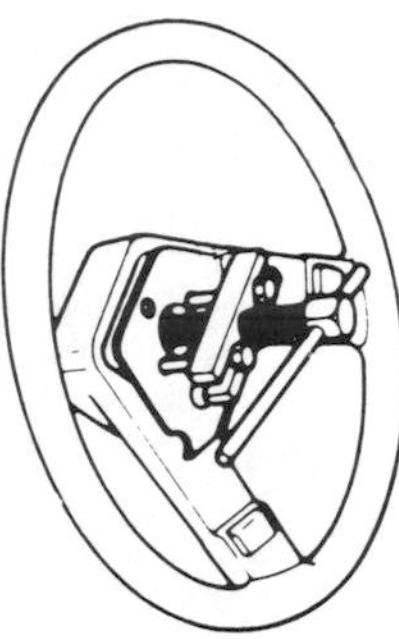

Fig. 10.9 Using a puller to remove the steering wheel (Sec 14)

15 Steering shaft lower joint – removal and refitting

1 Set the steering wheel and front roadwheels in the straight-ahead position.

2 For better access, if necessary remove the hole cover at the bottom of the steering column from the bulkhead, by unscrewing the two nuts.

3 Check that the slit in the lower part of the joint is aligned with the mark on the steering gear cap or spacer.

4 Unscrew and remove the joint pinch-bolts.

5 Pull the joint up from the steering gear pinion splines, then down from the steering shaft splines. If it is tight, prise apart the joint slits with a screwdriver.

6 Refitting is a reversal of removal, but make sure that the longer joint section is uppermost (on the steering shaft), that the lower slit is aligned with the mark (photo), and that both pinch-bolts pass freely through the cut-outs provided. Tighten the bolts to the specified torque.

15.6 Steering shaft lower joint showing correct alignment of lower section

16 Steering column (non-tilt type) – removal, inspection and refitting

1 Remove the steering wheel (Section 14).

2 Remove the steering shaft lower joint (Section 15).

3 Remove the small facia panel beneath the steering column, then remove the plastic air ducting for access to the bottom of the column (photos).

4 Remove the screws and withdraw the top and bottom shrouds from the steering column. Disconnect the wiring from the ignition switch illumination bulb in the lower shroud (photos).

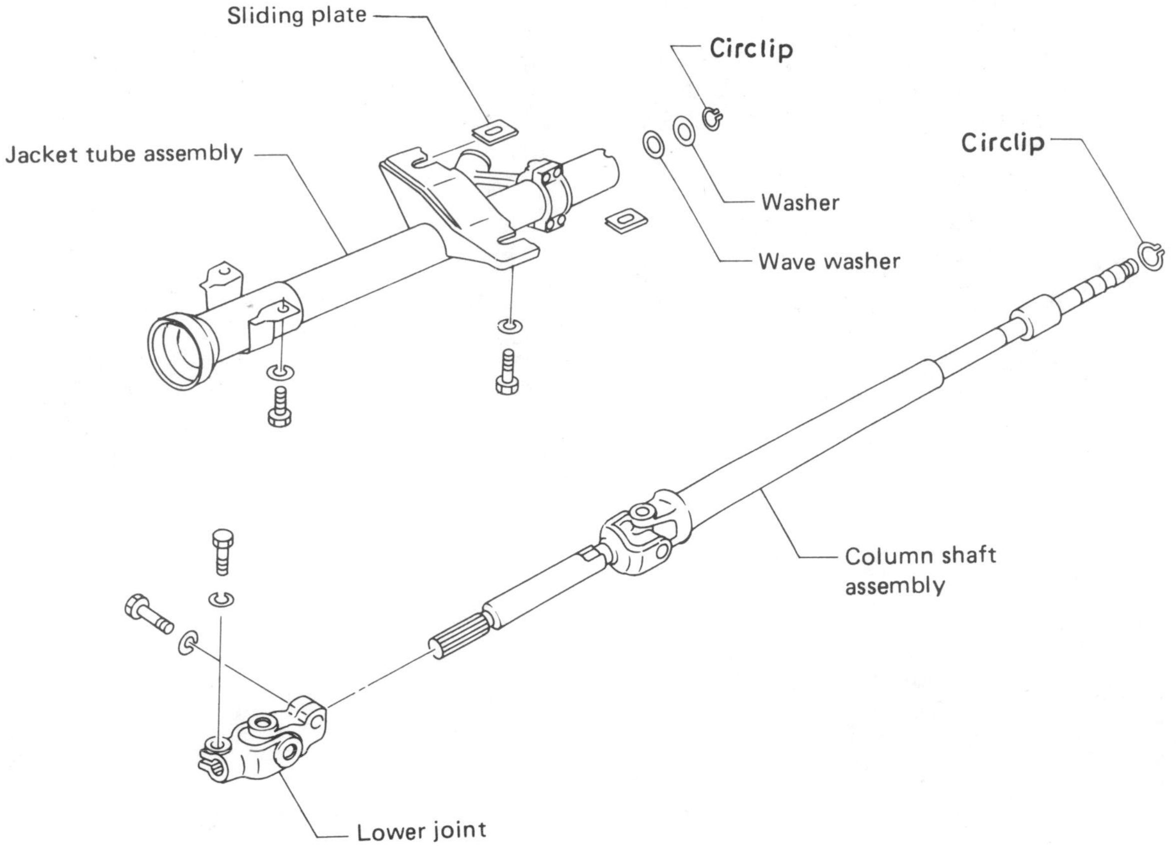

Fig. 10.10 Exploded view of non-tilt steering column (Sec 16)

16.3A Remove the small facia panel ...

16.3B ... and the air ducting

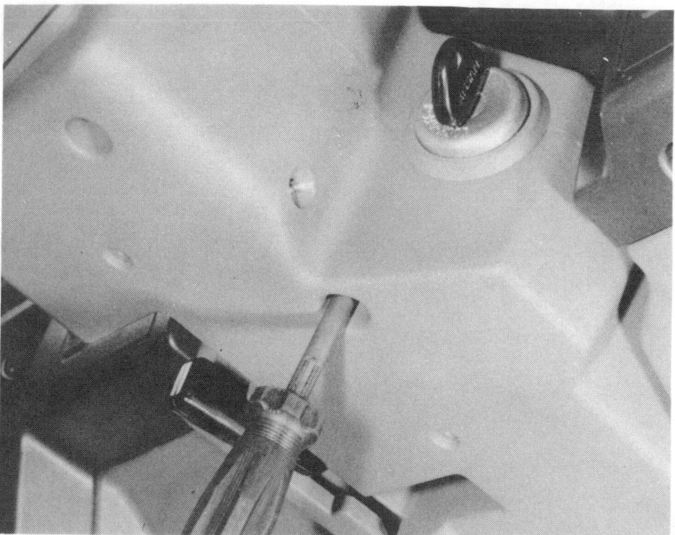

16.4A Remove the steering column shroud screws ...

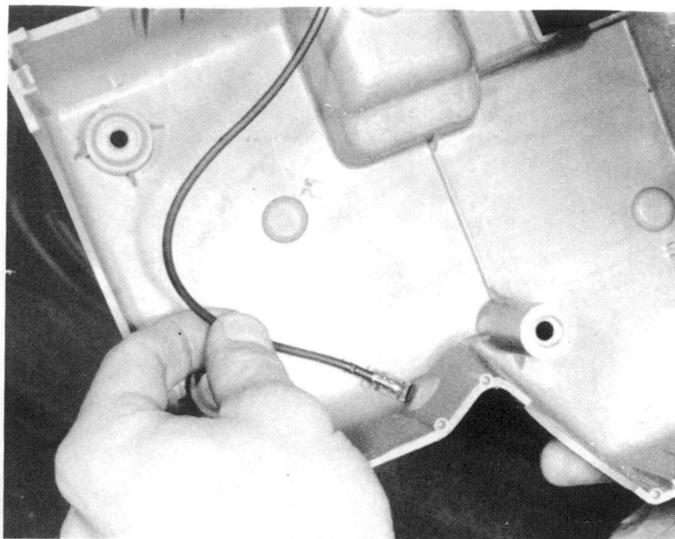

16.4B ... disconnect the wiring from the bottom shroud illumination bulb ...

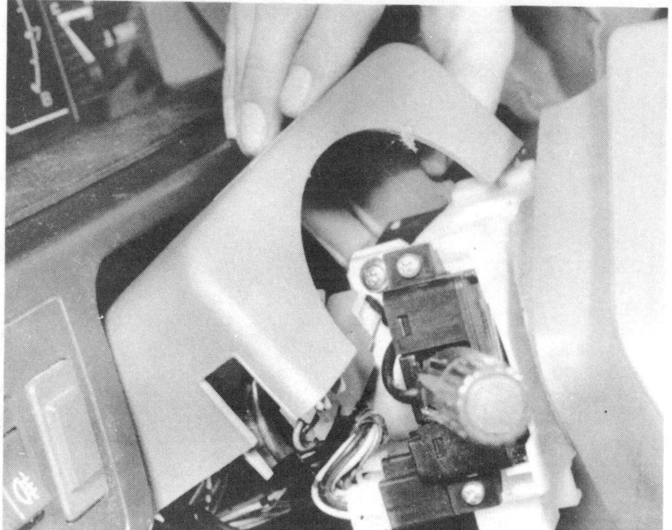

16.4C ... and remove the top shroud

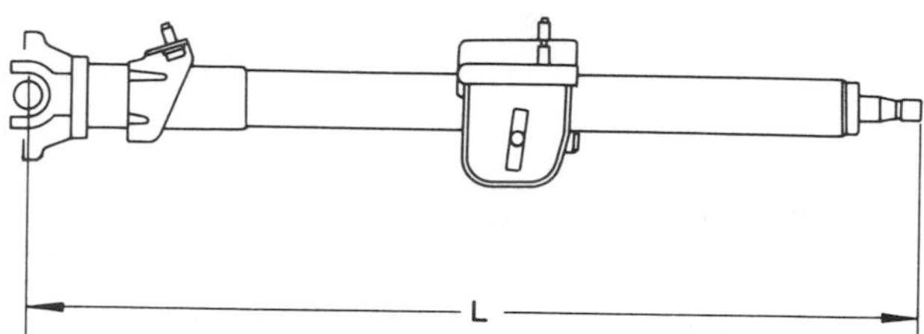

Fig. 10.11 Column length checking dimension (Sec 16)

L = 623.5 to 624.5 mm (24.55 to 24.59 in)

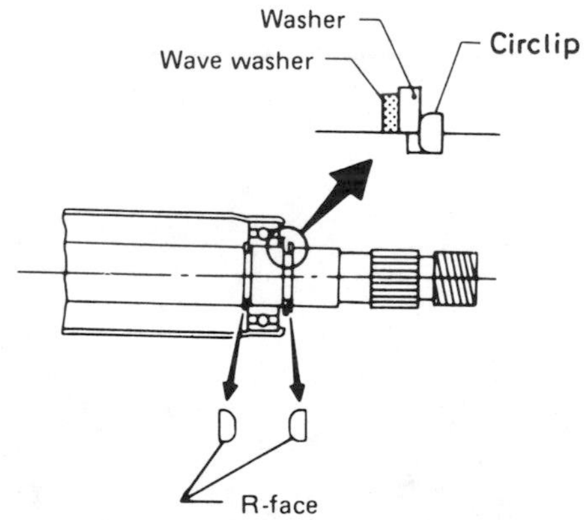

Fig. 10.12 Showing the correct fitting of the circlips on the steering column top bearing (Sec 16)

5 Remove the combination switches (Chapter 12).
6 Disconnect the wiring from the ignition switch.
7 Unscrew the two nuts and remove the hole cover from the bulkhead, if not already removed.
8 Unbolt the lower end of the column from the pedal bracket.
9 Unscrew the upper mounting bolts, noting the position of the sliding plates, then withdraw the steering column from inside the car.
10 Release the clip and remove the hole cover boot from the bottom of the column.
11 Before further dismantling, check for excessive play of the shaft upper bearing and lower bush, and for wear of the universal joint. The bearing and bush are not available separately, so if they are worn, the complete column must be renewed. Check the column length (Fig. 10.11) – if it is not within the specified limits, renew the shaft and thoroughly inspect the column tube for accident damage.
12 Release the steering lock by turning the ignition key.
13 Extract the circlip, washer and wave washer from the top of the shaft, then withdraw the shaft from the bottom of the column tube.
14 Clean all the components and check them for wear and damage.
15 Commence reassembly by lubricating the upper bearing and lower bush with multi-purpose grease.
16 Check that the upper bearing lower circlip is correctly fitted to the shaft (Fig. 10.12), then insert the shaft into the column tube and through the upper bearing.
17 Fit the wave washer, washer and circlip with its radius face towards the bearing.
18 Refitting is a reversal of removal, but insert all the column mounting bolts loosely before finally tightening them, to ensure there is no uneven stress on the column.

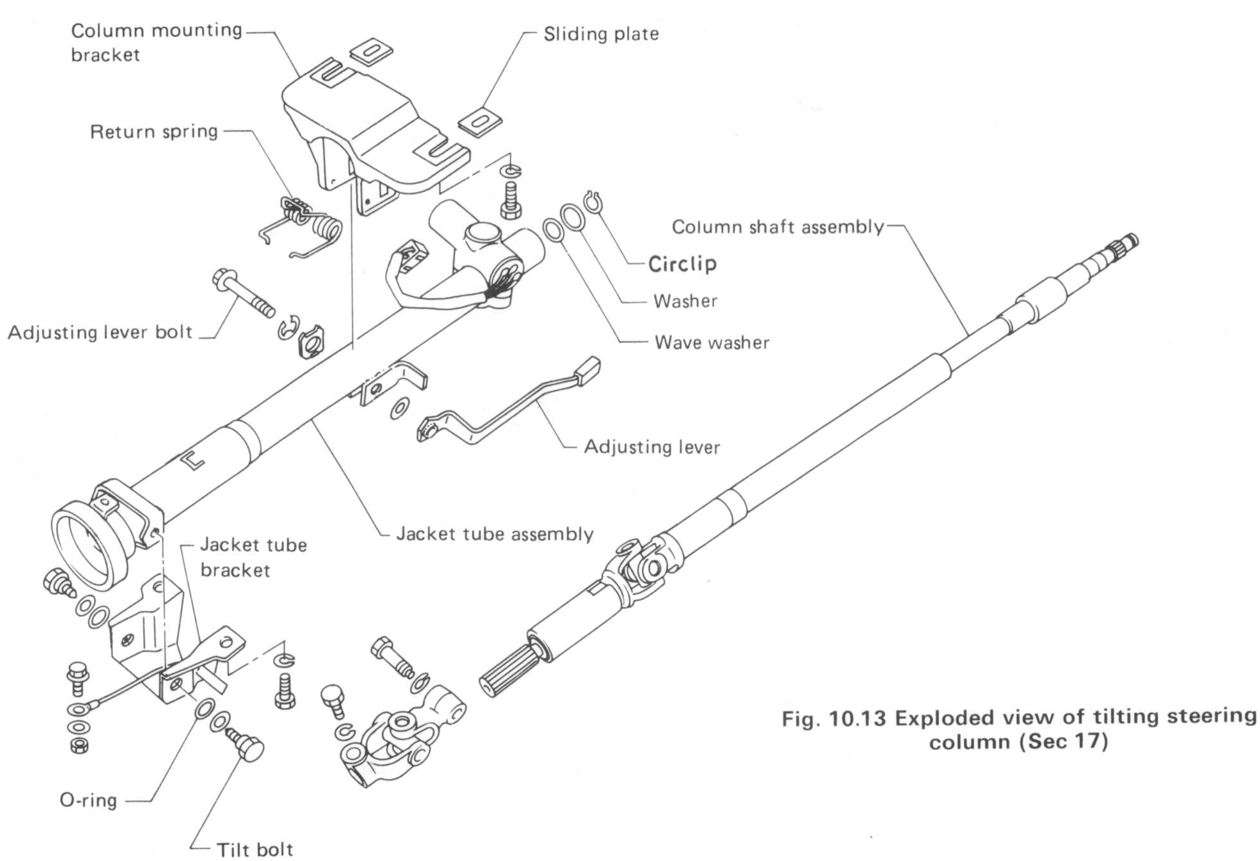

Fig. 10.13 Exploded view of tilting steering column (Sec 17)

17 Steering column (tilt type) – removal, inspection and refitting

1 The procedure is identical to that given in Section 16, but in addition, the adjustment bracket can be removed from the top of the column tube and the pivot bracket from the bottom. Refer to Fig. 10.13 for details of the component parts (photos).
2 When reassembling the tilt components, lubricate the moving parts with a little grease.

18 Steering column lock – removal and refitting

1 Remove the steering wheel (Section 14).
2 Remove the screws and withdraw the top and bottom shrouds from the steering column. Disconnect the wiring from the ignition switch illumination bulb in the lower shroud.
3 Disconnect the wiring from the ignition switch.
4 Drill out the shear-head bolts which secure the lock to the column, then remove the lock and the clamp plate.

17.1A Steering column lower pivot bracket on tilt type column

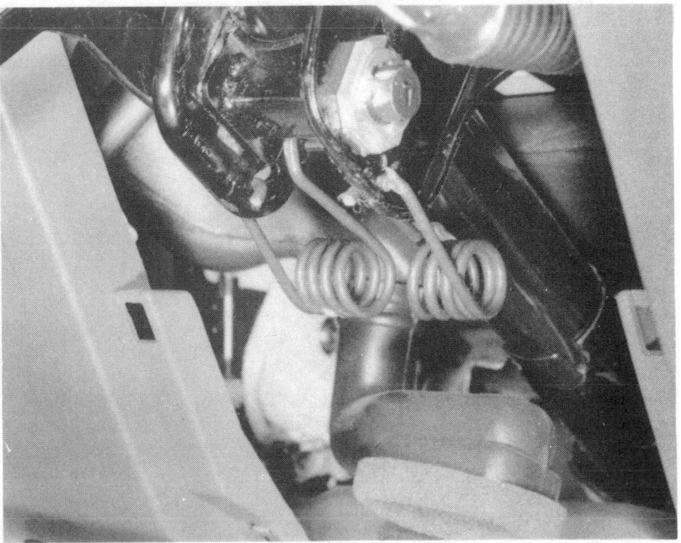

17.1B Steering column upper mounting bracket on tilt type column

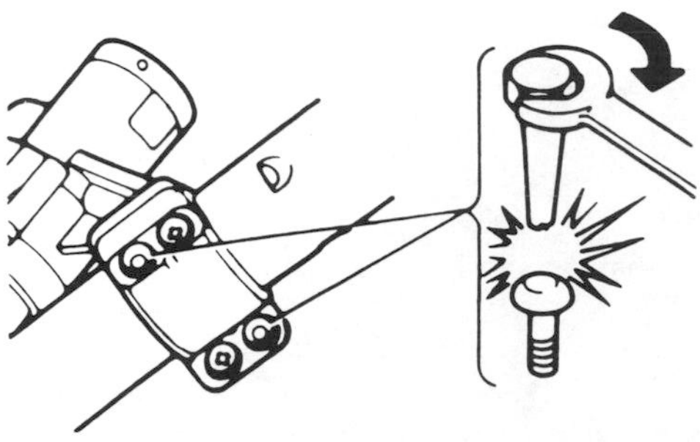

Fig. 10.14 The steering column lock is secured by shear-head bolts (Sec 18)

5 Refitting is a reversal of removal, but first obtain new shear-head bolts and initially fit them only finger-tight. Check that the lock operates correctly before finally tightening the bolt heads until they break off.

19 Steering gear (manual) – removal and refitting

1 Apply the handbrake, then jack up the front of the car and support on axle stands.
2 Unscrew the nuts, then use a separator tool to disconnect the tie-rod ends from the steering arms.
3 Remove the steering shaft lower joint as described in Section 15.
4 Unscrew the mounting clamp bolts, remove the clamps, and withdraw the steering gear from the side of the car.
5 Check the mounting rubbers for deterioration and renew them if necessary.
6 Refitting is a reversal of removal, with reference to Section 15 when refitting the steering shaft lower joint. Finally, check and if necessary adjust the front wheel alignment.

20 Steering gear (power-assisted) – removal and refitting

1 Apply the handbrake, then jack up the front of the car and support on axle stands. Remove both front roadwheels.
2 Unscrew the nuts, then use a separator tool to disconnect the tie-rod ends from the steering arms.
3 Remove the steering shaft lower joint as described in Section 15.
4 Remove the exhaust system (Chapter 3).
5 Remove the manual transmission gearchange rods (Chapter 6) or the automatic transmission downshift cable (Chapter 7).
6 Syphon the fluid from the power steering fluid reservoir, or alternatively clamp the flexible hoses to the steering gear.
7 Place a suitable container beneath the steering gear to catch any spilled fluid.
8 Disconnect the supply and return hoses from the steering gear by unscrewing the union nut and loosening the clip respectively.
9 Disconnect the wiring from the hydraulic pressure sender unit on the steering gear, where fitted (photo).
10 Unscrew the mounting clamp bolts (photo), remove the clamps, and withdraw the steering gear from the side of the car.
11 Check the mounting rubbers for deterioration and renew them if necessary.
12 Refitting is a reversal of removal, but fill and bleed the hydraulic system as described in Section 23, and finally check and if necessary adjust the front wheel alignment.

21 Steering gear – overhaul

1 Under normal conditions the steering gear should not require any attention, even after the car has covered a high mileage. If the rack bellows are damaged, they can be renewed as described in Section 12, but apart from this, renewal of the tie-rod and inner balljoint is the only other repair recommended for the home mechanic. To do this proceed as follows.
2 Remove the tie-rod end as described in Section 13.
3 Loosen the clip and release the bellows end nearest the inner balljoint.
4 Prise up the lockplate, then unscrew the balljoint with one spanner, while holding the rack stationary with a further spanner. Remove the lockplate.
5 Clean the end surfaces of the rack and balljoint.
6 Coat the threads of the inner balljoint with locking fluid, then screw it into the end of the rack together with a new lockplate, making sure that the lockplate tags enter the groove in the rack. On manual steering gears with a damper, make sure that the damper bracket is located correctly.
7 Tighten the balljoint to the specified torque, then lock it by bending the lockplate onto two flats. Remove any sharp edges with a file.
8 Refit the bellows and secure with the clip.
9 Refit the tie-rod end with reference to Section 13.

20.9 Sender unit and wiring connector on power steering gear

20.10 Power steering gear mounting clamp

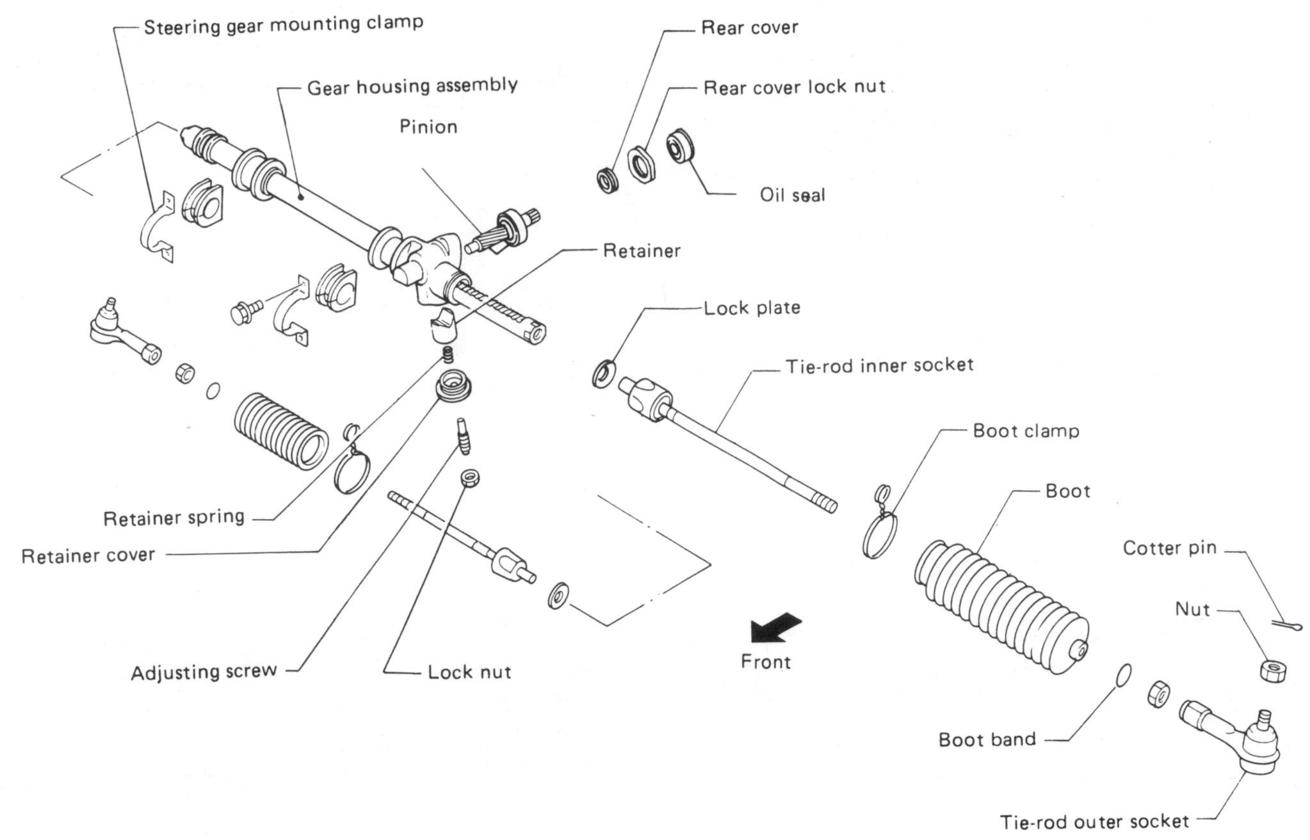

Fig. 10.15 Exploded view of the steering gear (Sec 21)

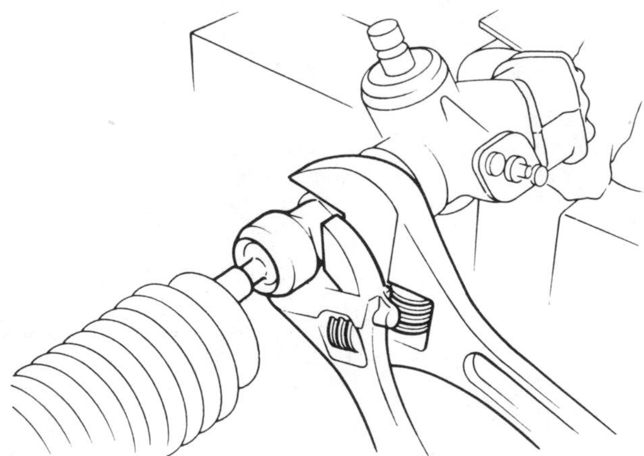

Fig. 10.16 Unscrewing the tie-rod inner balljoint (Sec 21)

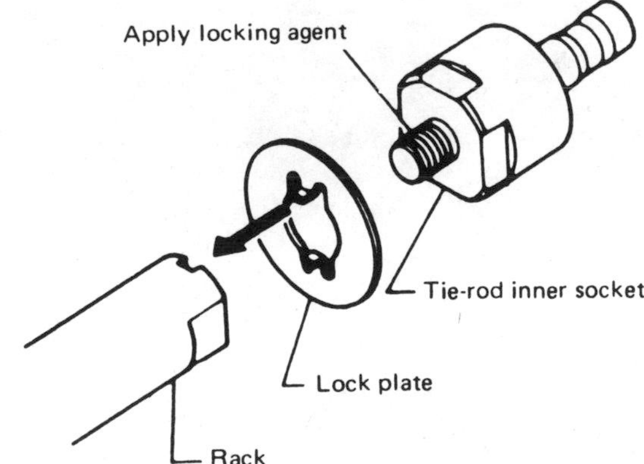

Fig. 10.17 Tie-rod inner balljoint refitting to rack (Sec 21)

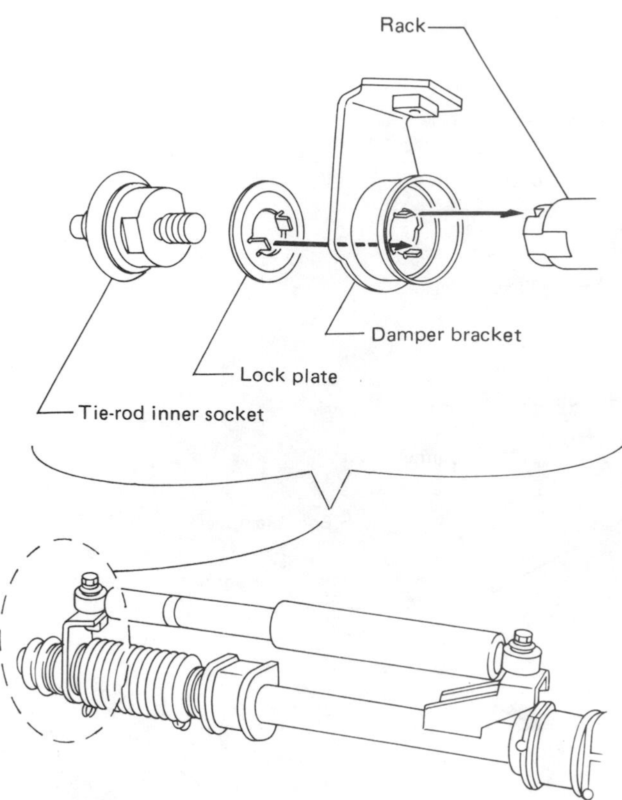

Fig. 10.18 Showing damper bracket location on the manual steering gear fitted with a damper (Sec 21)

22.4 Power steering pump

22 Power steering pump and reservoir – removal and refitting

1 Remove the air cleaner and ducting as described in Chapter 3.
2 Loosen the pivot and adjustment bolts, then swivel the power steering pump towards the engine and remove the drivebelt.
3 Disconnect the fluid hoses from the pump and plug them.
4 Remove the pivot and adjustment bolts and withdraw the pump from the engine (photo).
5 The fluid reservoir can be removed after disconnecting the fluid hoses and unbolting the bracket.
6 Refitting is a reversal of removal, but adjust the tension of the drivebelt as described in Section 2, then fill and bleed the hydraulic system as described in Section 23.

23 Power steering hydraulic system – filling and bleeding

1 Using only fluid which is clean and of the specified type, fill the system by pouring it into the reservoir until it reaches the 'FULL' mark on the dipstick.
2 Raise the front wheels clear of the floor and support the vehicle securely. Turn the steering wheel gently from lock to lock ten times.
3 Check the fluid level and top up if necessary.
4 Start and run the engine until the temperature of the fluid in the pump reaches 60 to 80°C (140 to 176°F). Test this with a contact type thermometer on the pump body.
5 Switch off and top up as necessary to the 'FULL' mark.
6 Run the engine for another five seconds, switch off and add more fluid if required.
7 Turn the steering wheel from lock to lock quickly ten times and top up again.
8 Start the engine and while it is idling, repeat the operations described in paragraphs 6 and 7.
9 Should air still be present in the system, indicated by air bubbles in the reservoir fluid or the steering wheel turning stiffly, turn the steering from lock to lock between five and ten times with the engine idling and hold the steering each time at full lock position for five seconds.
10 While holding at full lock, check for a fluid leak in a hose or pipe union.
11 On no account hold the steering in the full lock position for more than fifteen seconds at a time.

24 Steering angles and front wheel alignment

1 Accurate front wheel alignment is essential to provide good steering and roadholding characteristics and to ensure slow and even tyre wear. Before considering the steering angles, check that the tyres are correctly inflated, that the front wheels are not buckled, the hub bearings are not worn or incorrectly adjusted and that the steering linkage is in good order, without slackness or wear at the joints.
2 Wheel alignment consists of four factors:
Camber, is the angle at which the road wheels are set from the vertical when viewed from the front or rear of the vehicle. Positive camber is the angle (in degrees) that the wheels are tilted outwards at the top from the vertical.
Castor, is the angle between the steering axis and a vertical line when viewed from each side of the vehicle. Positive castor is indicated when the steering axis is inclined towards the rear of the vehicle at its upper end.
Steering axis inclination, is the angle when viewed from the front or rear of the vehicle between vertical and an imaginary line drawn between the upper and lower strut mountings.
Toe, is the amount by which the distance between the front inside edges of the roadwheel rims differs from that between the rear inside edges. If the distance between the front edges is less that that at the rear, the wheels are said to toe-in. If the distance between the front inside edges is greater than that at the rear, the wheels toe-out.
3 Camber, castor and steering axis inclination are set during production. Any deviation from specified tolerances must therefore be due to collision damage or grossly worn suspension components.
4 To check the front wheel alignment, first make sure that the length of both tie-rods are equal when the steering is in the straight-ahead position. The tie-rods can be set initially as shown in Fig. 10.19 after having released the locknuts and rotated the tie-rod.
5 Obtain a tracking gauge. These are available in various forms from accessory stores or one can be fabricated from a length of steel tubing suitably cranked to clear the sump and bellhousing and having a setscrew and locknut at one end.
6 With the gauge, measure the distance between the two wheel inner rims (at hub height) at the rear of the wheel. Push the vehicle forward to rotate the wheel through 180° (half a turn) and measure the distance between the wheel inner rims, again at hub height, at the front of the

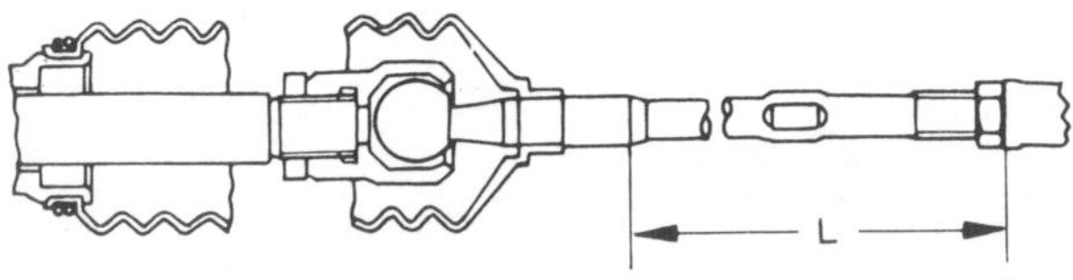

Fig. 10.19 Tie-rod basic setting (Sec 24)

RHD models	–	*RH tie-rod = 151.9 mm (5.98 in)*
	–	*LH tie-rod = 152.4 mm (6.00 in)*
LHD models	–	*RH tie-rod = 153.0 mm (6.02 in)*
	–	*LH tie-rod = 152.4 mm (6.00 in)*

wheel. This last measurement should differ from the first by the appropriate toe-in according to specifications (see Specifications Section).

7 Where the toe-in is found to be incorrect, release the tie-rod balljoint locknuts and turn the tie-rods equally. only turn them a quarter of a turn at a time before re-checking the alignment. Do not grip the threaded part of the tie-rod/balljoint during adjustment and make sure that the bellows outboard clip is free, otherwise the bellows will twist as the tie-rod is rotated. Always turn both rods in the same direction when viewed from the centre line of the vehicle otherwise the rods will become unequal in lengths. This would cause the steering wheel spoke position to alter and cause problems on turns with tyre scrubbing.

8 On completion, tighten the tie-rod end locknuts without disturbing their setting, check that the balljoint is at the centre of its arc of travel.

25 Rear suspension angles and rear wheel alignment

1 There are only two specified angles for the rear wheel alignment. The camber angle (refer to Section 24) is set during production and cannot be adjusted. Any deviation from the specified tolerances must be due to damage or excessive wear.

2 Check the toe-in as described in the preceding Section, but where adjustment is required, adjust the length of each rear parallel link as required. If necessary, the links can be set to the initial dimension shown in Fig. 10.20, then if adjustment is required the adjustment studs can be rotated by equal amounts to ensure that the links remain equal in length. When tightening the locknuts, hold the link ends stationary with a spanner on the flats provided to ensure that no strain is imposed on the link mountings.

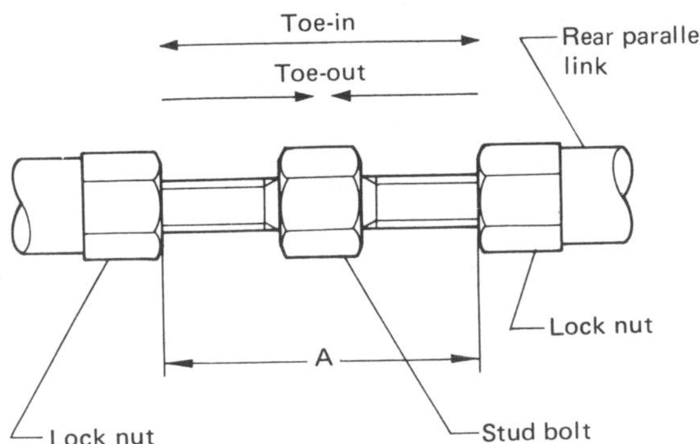

Fig. 10.20 Rear suspension rear parallel link adjustment (Sec 25)

Initial dimension A = 49.5 mm (1.949 in)

26 Wheels and tyres – general care and maintenance

Wheels and tyres should give no real problems in use provided that a close eye is kept on them with regard to excessive wear or damage. To this end, the following points should be noted.

Ensure that tyre pressures are checked regularly and maintained correctly. Checking should be carried out with the tyres cold and not immediately after the vehicle has been in use. If the pressures are checked with the tyres hot, an apparently high reading will be obtained owing to heat expansion. Under no circumstances should an attempt be made to reduce the pressures to the quoted cold reading in this instance, or effective underinflation will result.

Underinflation will cause overheating of the tyre owing to excessive flexing of the casing, and the tread will not sit correctly on the road surface. This will cause a consequent loss of adhesion and excessive wear, not to mention the danger of sudden tyre failure due to heat build-up.

Overinflation will cause rapid wear of the centre part of the tyre tread coupled with reduced adhesion, harsher ride, and the danger of shock damage occurring in the tyre casing.

Regularly check the tyres for damage in the form of cuts or bulges, especially in the sidewalls. Remove any nails or stones embedded in the tread before they penetrate the tyre to cause deflation. If removal of a nail *does* reveal that the tyre has been punctured, refit the nail so that its point of penetration is marked. Then immediately change the wheel and have the tyre repaired by a tyre dealer. Do *not* drive on a tyre in such a condition. In many cases a puncture can be simply repaired by the use of an inner tube of the correct size and type. If in any doubt as to the possible consequences of any damage found, consult your local tyre dealer for advice.

Periodically remove the wheels and clean any dirt or mud from the inside and outside surfaces. Examine the wheel rims for signs of rusting, corrosion or other damage. Light alloy wheels are easily damaged by 'kerbing' whilst parking, and similarly steel wheels may become dented or buckled. Renewal of the wheel is very often the only course of remedial action possible.

The balance of each wheel and tyre assembly should be maintained to avoid excessive wear, not only to the tyres but also to the steering and suspension components. Wheel imbalance is normally signified by vibration through the vehicle's bodyshell, although in many cases it is particularly noticeable through the steering wheel. Conversely, it should be noted that wear or damage in suspension or steering components may cause excessive tyre wear. Out-of-round or out-of-true tyres, damaged wheels and wheel bearing wear/maladjustment also fall into this category. Balancing will not usually cure vibration caused by such wear.

Wheel balancing may be carried out with the wheel either on or off the vehicle. If balanced on the vehicle, ensure that the wheel-to-hub relationship is marked in some way prior to subsequent wheel removal so that it may be refitted in its original position.

General tyre wear is influenced to a large degree by driving style – harsh braking and acceleration or fast cornering will all produce more rapid tyre wear. Interchanging of tyres may result in more even wear, but this should only be carried out where there is no mix of tyre types on the vehicle. However, it is worth bearing in mind that if this is completely effective, the added expense of replacing a complete set of tyres simultaneously is incurred, which may prove financially restrictive for many owners.

Front tyres may wear unevenly as a result of wheel misalignment. The front wheels should always be correctly aligned according to the settings specified by the vehicle manufacturer.

Legal restrictions apply to the mixing of tyre types on a vehicle. Basically this means that a vehicle must not have tyres of differing construction on the same axle. Although it is not recommended to mix tyre types between front axle and rear axle, the only legally permissible combination is crossply at the front and radial at the rear. When mixing radial ply tyres, textile braced radials must always go on the front axle, with steel braced radials at the rear. An obvious disadvantage of such mixing is the necessity to carry two spare tyres to avoid contravening the law in the event of a puncture.

In the UK, the Motor Vehicles Construction and Use Regulations apply to many aspects of tyre fitting and usage. It is suggested that a copy of these regulations is obtained from your local police if in doubt as to the current legal requirements with regard to tyre condition, minimum tread depth, etc.

27 Fault diagnosis – suspension, steering, wheels and tyres

Symptom	Reason(s)
Suspension	
Car wanders	Incorrect wheel alignment Worn front suspension lower balljoint Incorrect tyre pressures
Wheel wobble or vibration	Unbalanced wheels Damaged wheels Worn shock absorbers Worn wheel bearings
Excessive pitching or rolling	Worn shock absorbers Worn anti-roll bar mountings
Excessive tyre wear	Incorrect tyre pressures Unbalanced wheels Worn front suspension lower balljoint
Lost motion at steering wheel	Worn tie-rod end balljoints Worn steering gear
Power-assisted steering	
Lack of assistance or jerky action	Low fluid level Slipping pump drivebelt
Noisy operation	Air in system Low fluid level Worn pump

Chapter 11 Bodywork and fittings

Contents

Specifications

Torque wrench settings

	Nm	lbf ft
Bumper side mountings	11	8
Bumper main mountings	19	14
Bonnet lock	26	19
Bonnet hinge	11	8
Boot lid hinge	5	4
Boot lid lock and striker	5	4
Tailgate lock	7	5
Door lock	5	4
Window regulator	5	4
Seat runners	16	12

1 General description

The body shell is of one-piece design and is available in 4-door saloon and 5-door estate versions. The front wings are bolted to the main body for ease of removal.

The body equipment includes, according to model, power-operated windows, central locking, manual or electric sunroof, and manual or electric exterior mirrors.

2 Routine maintenance

Carry out the following procedures at the intervals given in *'Routine Maintenance'* at the beginning of the Manual.

Locks and hinges

1 Apply a little grease to the lock latches and strikers of the bonnet, bootlid or tailgate, and doors.

2 Apply a little grease to the door hinges and check links. Also grease the bonnet hinges.

Seat belts

3 Examine the full length of the seat belts for damage and wear, especially for cuts and fraying of the webbing. Check the buckles for correct operation and periodically clean them.
4 Check all anchor bolts for security, and the surrounding bodywork for any signs of weakness.

3 Maintenance – bodywork and underframe

The general condition of a vehicle's bodywork is the one thing that significantly affects its value. Maintenance is easy but needs to be regular. Neglect, particularly after minor damage, can lead quickly to further deterioration and costly repair bills. It is important also to keep watch on those parts of the vehicle not immediately visible, for instance the underside, inside all the wheel arches and the lower part of the engine compartment.

The basic maintenance routine for the bodywork is washing – preferably with a lot of water, from a hose. This will remove all the loose solids which may have stuck to the vehicle. It is important to flush these off in such a way as to prevent grit from scratching the finish. The wheel arches and underframe need washing in the same way to remove any accumulated mud which will retain moisture and tend to encourage rust. Paradoxically enough, the best time to clean the underframe and wheel arches is in wet weather when the mud is thoroughly wet and soft. In very wet weather the underframe is usually cleaned of large accumulations automatically and this is a good time for inspection.

Periodically, except on vehicles with a wax-based underbody protective coating, it is a good idea to have the whole of the underframe of the vehicle steam cleaned, engine compartment included, so that a thorough inspection can be carried out to see what minor repairs and renovations are necessary. Steam cleaning is available at many garages and is necessary for removal of the accumulation of oily grime which sometimes is allowed to become thick in certain areas. If steam cleaning facilities are not available, there are one or two excellent grease solvents available which can be brush applied. The dirt can then be simply hosed off. Note that these methods should not be used on vehicles with wax-based underbody protective coating or the coating will be removed. Such vehicles should be inspected annually, preferably just prior to winter, when the underbody should be washed down and any damage to the wax coating repaired. Ideally, a completely fresh coat should be applied. It would also be worth considering the use of such wax-based protection for injection into door panels, sills, box sections, etc, as an additional safeguard against rust damage where such protection is not provided by the vehicle manufacturer.

After washing paintwork, wipe off with a chamois leather to give an unspotted clear finish. A coat of clear protective wax polish will give added protection against chemical pollutants in the air. If the paintwork sheen has dulled or oxidised, use a cleaner/polisher combination to restore the brilliance of the shine. This requires a little effort, but such dulling is usually caused because regular washing has been neglected. Care needs to be taken with metallic paintwork, as special non-abrasive cleaner/polisher is required to avoid damage to the finish. Always check that the door and ventilator opening drain holes and pipes are completely clear so that water can be drained out. Bright work should be treated in the same way as paint work. Windscreens and windows can be kept clear of the smeary film which often appears by the use of a proprietary glass cleaner. Never use any form of wax or other body or chromium polish on glass.

4 Maintenance – upholstery and carpets

Mats and carpets should be brushed or vacuum cleaned regularly to keep them free of grit. If they are badly stained remove them from the vehicle for scrubbing or sponging and make quite sure they are dry before refitting. Seats and interior trim panels can be kept clean by wiping with a damp cloth. If they do become stained (which can be more apparent on light coloured upholstery) use a little liquid detergent and a soft nail brush to scour the grime out of the grain of the material. Do not forget to keep the headlining clean in the same way as the upholstery. When using liquid cleaners inside the vehicle do not over-wet the surfaces being cleaned. Excessive damp could get into the seams and padded interior causing stains, offensive odours or even rot. If the inside of the vehicle gets wet accidentally it is worthwhile taking some trouble to dry it out properly, particularly where carpets are involved. *Do not leave oil or electric heaters inside the vehicle for this purpose.*

5 Minor body damage – repair

The photographic sequences on pages 202 and 203 illustrate the operations detailed in the following sub-sections.
Note: *For more detailed information about bodywork repair, the Haynes Publishing Group publish a book by Lindsay Porter called The Car Bodywork Repair Manual. This incorporates information on such aspects as rust treatment, painting and glass fibre repairs, as well as details on more ambitious repairs involving welding and panel beating.*

Repair of minor scratches in bodywork

If the scratch is very superficial, and does not penetrate to the metal of the bodywork, repair is very simple. Lightly rub the area of the scratch with a paintwork renovator, or a very fine cutting paste, to remove loose paint from the scratch and to clear the surrounding bodywork of wax polish. Rinse the area with clean water.

Apply touch-up paint to the scratch using a fine paint brush; continue to apply fine layers of paint until the surface of the paint in the scratch is level with the surrounding paintwork. Allow the new paint at least two weeks to harden: then blend it into the surrounding paintwork by rubbing the scratch area with a paintwork renovator or a very fine cutting paste. Finally, apply wax polish.

Where the scratch has penetrated right through to the metal of the bodywork, causing the metal to rust, a different repair technique is required. Remove any loose rust from the bottom of the scratch with a penknife, then apply rust inhibiting paint to prevent the formation of rust in the future. Using a rubber or nylon applicator fill the scratch with bodystopper paste. If required, this paste can be mixed with cellulose thinners to provide a very thin paste which is ideal for filling narrow scratches. Before the stopper-paste in the scratch hardens, wrap a piece of smooth cotton rag around the top of a finger. Dip the finger in cellulose thinners and then quickly sweep it across the surface of the stopper-paste in the scratch; this will ensure that the surface of the stopper-paste is slightly hollowed. The scratch can now be painted over as described earlier in this Section.

Repair of dents in bodywork

When deep denting of the vehicle's bodywork has taken place, the first task is to pull the dent out, until the affected bodywork almost attains its original shape. There is little point in trying to restore the original shape completely, as the metal in the damaged area will have stretched on impact and cannot be reshaped fully to its original contour. It is better to bring the level of the dent up to a point which is about ⅛ in (3 mm) below the level of the surrounding bodywork. In cases where the dent is very shallow anyway, it is not worth trying to pull it out at all. If the underside of the dent is accessible, it can be hammered out gently from behind, using a mallet with a wooden or plastic head. Whilst doing this, hold a suitable block of wood firmly against the outside of the panel to absorb the impact from the hammer blows and thus prevent a large area of the bodywork from being 'belled-out'.

Should the dent be in a section of the bodywork which has a double skin or some other factor making it inaccessible from behind, a different technique is called for. Drill several small holes through the metal inside the area – particularly in the deeper section. Then screw long self-tapping screws into the holes just sufficiently for them to gain a good purchase in the metal. Now the dent can be pulled out by pulling on the protruding heads of the screws with a pair of pliers.

The next stage of the repair is the removal of the paint from the damaged area, and from an inch or so of the surrounding 'sound' bodywork. This is accomplished most easily by using a wire brush or abrasive pad on a power drill, although it can be done just as effectively by hand using sheets of abrasive paper. To complete the preparation for filling, score the surface of the bare metal with a screwdriver or the tang of a file, or alternatively, drill small holes in the affected area. This will provide a really good 'key' for the filler paste.

To complete the repair see the Section on filling and re-spraying.

Repair of rust holes or gashes in bodywork

Remove all paint from the affected area and from an inch or so of the surrounding 'sound' bodywork, using an abrasive pad or a wire brush on a power drill. If these are not available a few sheets of abrasive paper will do the job just as effectively. With the paint removed you will be able to gauge the severity of the corrosion and therefore decide whether to renew the whole panel (if this is possible) or to repair the affected area. New body panels are not as expensive as most people think and it is often quicker and more satisfactory to fit a new panel than to attempt to repair large areas of corrosion.

Remove all fittings from the affected area except those which will act as a guide to the original shape of the damaged bodywork (eg headlamp shells etc). Then, using tin snips or a hacksaw blade, remove all loose metal and any other metal badly affected by corrosion. Hammer the edges of the hole inwards in order to create a slight depression for the filler paste.

Wire brush the affected area to remove the powdery rust from the surface of the remaining metal. Paint the affected area with rust inhibiting paint; if the back of the rusted area is accessible treat this also.

Before filling can take place it will be necessary to block the hole in some way. This can be achieved by the use of aluminium or plastic mesh, or aluminium tape.

Aluminium or plastic mesh is probably the best material to use for a large hole. Cut a piece to the approximate size and shape of the hole to be filled, then position it in the hole so that its edges are below the level of the surrounding bodywork. It can be retained in position by several blobs of filler paste around its periphery.

Aluminium tape should be used for small or very narrow holes. Pull a piece off the roll and trim it to the approximate size and shape required, then pull off the backing paper (if used) and stick the tape over the hole; it can be overlapped if the thickness of one piece is insufficient. Burnish down the edges of the tape with the handle of a screwdriver or similar, to ensure that the tape is securely attached to the metal underneath.

Bodywork repairs – filling and re-spraying

Before using this Section, see the Sections on dent, deep scratch, rust holes and gash repairs.

Many types of bodyfiller are available, but generally speaking those proprietary kits which contain a tin of filler paste and a tube of resin hardener are best for this type of repair. A wide, flexible plastic or nylon applicator will be found invaluable for imparting a smooth and well contoured finish to the surface of the filler.

Mix up a little filler on a clean piece of card or board – measure the hardener carefully (follow the maker's instructions on the pack) otherwise the filler will set too rapidly or too slowly. Using the applicator apply the filler paste to the prepared area; draw the applicator across the surface of the filler to achieve the correct contour and to level the filler surface. As soon as a contour that approximates to the correct one is achieved, stop working the paste – if you carry on too long the paste will become sticky and begin to 'pick up' on the applicator. Continue to add thin layers of filler paste at twenty-minute intervals until the level of the filler is just proud of the surrounding bodywork.

Once the filler has hardened, excess can be removed using a metal plane or file. From then on, progressively finer grades of abrasive paper should be used, starting with a 40 grade production paper and finishing with 400 grade wet-and-dry paper. Always wrap the abrasive paper around a flat rubber, cork, or wooden block – otherwise the surface of the filler will not be completely flat. During the smoothing of the filler surface the wet-and-dry paper should be periodically rinsed in water. This will ensure that a very smooth finish is imparted to the filler at the final stage.

At this stage the 'dent' should be surrounded by a ring of bare metal, which in turn should be encircled by the finely 'feathered' edge of the good paintwork. Rinse the repair area with clean water, until all of the dust produced by the rubbing-down operation has gone.

Spray the whole repair area with a light coat of primer – this will show up any imperfections in the surface of the filler. Repair these imperfections with fresh filler paste or bodystopper, and once more smooth the surface with abrasive paper. If bodystopper is used, it can be mixed with cellulose thinners to form a really thin paste which is ideal for filling small holes. Repeat this spray and repair procedure until you are satisfied that the surface of the filler, and the feathered edge of the paintwork are perfect. Clean the repair area with clean water and allow to dry fully.

The repair area is now ready for final spraying. Paint spraying must be carried out in a warm, dry, windless and dust free atmosphere. This condition can be created artificially if you have access to a large indoor working area, but if you are forced to work in the open, you will have to pick your day very carefully. If you are working indoors, dousing the floor in the work area with water will help to settle the dust which would otherwise be in the atmosphere. If the repair area is confined to one body panel, mask off the surrounding panels; this will help to minimise the effects of a slight mis-match in paint colours. Bodywork fittings (eg chrome strips, door handles etc) will also need to be masked off. Use genuine masking tape and several thicknesses of newspaper for the masking operations.

Before commencing to spray, agitate the aerosol can thoroughly, then spray a test area (an old tin, or similar) until the technique is mastered. Cover the repair area with a thick coat of primer; the thickness should be built up using several thin layers of paint rather than one thick one. Using 400 grade wet-and-dry paper, rub down the surface of the primer until it is really smooth. While doing this, the work area should be thoroughly doused with water, and the wet-and-dry paper periodically rinsed in water. Allow to dry before spraying on more paint.

Spray on the top coat, again building up the thickness by using several thin layers of paint. Start spraying in the centre of the repair area and then, using a circular motion, work outwards until the whole repair area and about 2 inches of the surrounding original paintwork is covered. Remove all masking material 10 to 15 minutes after spraying on the final coat of paint.

Allow the new paint at least two weeks to harden, then, using a paintwork renovator or a very fine cutting paste, blend the edges of the paint into the existing paintwork. Finally, apply wax polish.

Plastic components

With the use of more and more plastic body components by the vehicle manufacturers (eg bumpers, spoilers, and in some cases major body panels), rectification of damage to such items has become a matter of either entrusting repair work to a specialist in this field, or renewing complete components. Repair by the DIY owner is not really feasible owing to the cost of the equipment and materials required for effecting such repairs. The basic technique involves making a groove along the line of the crack in the plastic using a rotary burr in a power drill. The damaged part is then welded back together by using a hot air gun to heat up and fuse a plastic filler rod into the groove. Any excess plastic is then removed and the area rubbed down to a smooth finish. It is important that a filler rod of the correct plastic is used, as body components can be made of a variety of different types (eg polycarbonate, ABS, polypropylene).

If the owner is renewing a complete component himself, he will be left with the problem of finding a suitable paint for finishing which is compatible with the type of plastic used. At one time the use of a universal paint was not possible owing to the complex range of plastics encountered in body component applications. Standard paints, generally speaking, will not bond to plastic or rubber satisfactorily. However, it is now possible to obtain a plastic body parts finishing kit which consists of a pre-primer treatment, a primer and coloured top coat. Full instructions are normally supplied with a kit, but basically the method of use is to first apply the pre-primer to the component concerned and allow it to dry for up to 30 minutes. Then the primer is applied and left to dry for about an hour before finally applying the special coloured top coat. The result is a correctly coloured component where the paint will flex with the plastic or rubber, a property that standard paint does not normally possess.

6 Major body damage – repair

The repair of collision damage or making good severe corrosion damage to major structures or suspension attachment points should be left to your dealer or body repair specialist as special jigs and gauges will be required to ensure that alignment of the structure is maintained. This is essential to good steering and roadholding.

This sequence of photographs deals with the repair of the dent and paintwork damage shown in this photo. The procedure will be similar for the repair of a hole. It should be noted that the procedures given here are simplified – more explicit instructions will be found in the text

In the case of a dent the first job – after removing surrounding trim – is to hammer out the dent where access is possible. This will minimise filling. Here, the large dent having been hammered out, the damaged area is being made slightly concave

Now all paint must be removed from the damaged area, by rubbing with coarse abrasive paper. Alternatively, a wire brush or abrasive pad can be used in a power drill. Where the repair area meets good paintwork, the edge of the paintwork should be 'feathered', using a finer grade of abrasive paper

In the case of a hole caused by rusting, all damaged sheet-metal should be cut away before proceeding to this stage. Here, the damaged area is being treated with rust remover and inhibitor before being filled

Mix the body filler according to its manufacturer's instructions. In the case of corrosion damage, it will be necessary to block off any large holes before filling – this can be done with aluminium or plastic mesh, or aluminium tape. Make sure the area is absolutely clean before ...

... applying the filler. Filler should be applied with a flexible applicator, as shown, for best results; the wooden spatula being used for confined areas. Apply thin layers of filler at 20-minute intervals, until the surface of the filler is slightly proud of the surrounding bodywork

Initial shaping can be done with a Surform plane or Dreadnought file. Then, using progressively finer grades of wet-and-dry paper, wrapped around a sanding block, and copious amounts of clean water, rub down the filler until really smooth and flat. Again, feather the edges of adjoining paintwork

The whole repair area can now be sprayed or brush-painted with primer. If spraying, ensure adjoining areas are protected from over-spray. Note that at least one inch of the surrounding sound paintwork should be coated with primer. Primer has a 'thick' consistency, so will find small imperfections

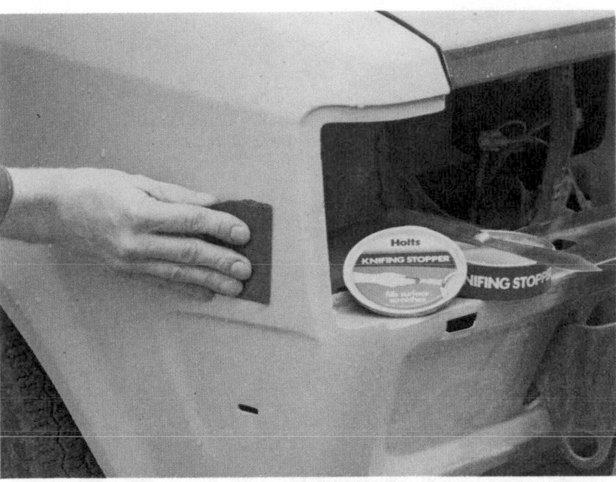

Again, using plenty of water, rub down the primer with a fine grade wet-and-dry paper (400 grade is probably best) until it is really smooth and well blended into the surrounding paintwork. Any remaining imperfections can now be filled by carefully applied knifing stopper paste

When the stopper has hardened, rub down the repair area again before applying the final coat of primer. Before rubbing down this last coat of primer, ensure the repair area is blemish-free – use more stopper if necessary. To ensure that the surface of the primer is really smooth use some finishing compound

The top coat can now be applied. When working out of doors, pick a dry, warm and wind-free day. Ensure surrounding areas are protected from over-spray. Agitate the aerosol thoroughly, then spray the centre of the repair area, working outwards with a circular motion. Apply the paint as several thin coats

After a period of about two weeks, which the paint needs to harden fully, the surface of the repaired area can be 'cut' with a mild cutting compound prior to wax polishing. When carrying out bodywork repairs, remember that the quality of the finished job is proportional to the time and effort expended

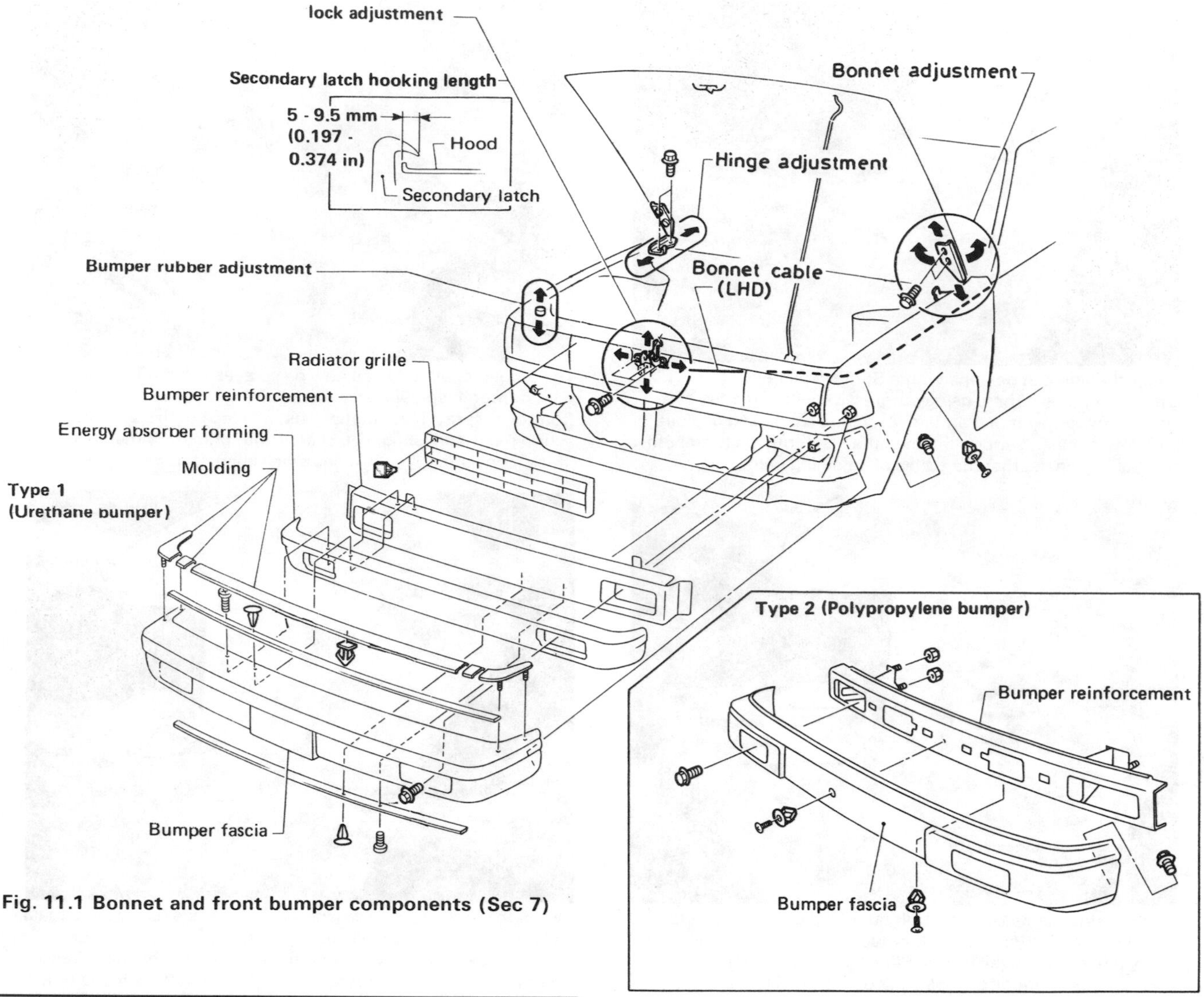

Fig. 11.1 Bonnet and front bumper components (Sec 7)

7 Bumpers – removal and refitting

Front bumper

1 Disconnect the battery negative lead and remove the front direction indicator lamps as described in Chapter 12.
2 Where applicable, remove the headlamp wash/wipe components with reference to Chapter 12.
3 Working under the front of the car, unscrew the bumper side mounting bolts.
4 Unscrew the front mounting bolts, working through the front direction indicator lamp apertures as necessary, then withdraw the bumper from the car.
5 If necessary the reinforcement plate and mouldings, where applicable, may be removed from the bumper facia (photo).
6 Refitting is a reversal of removal.

Rear bumper

7 On Estate models, disconnect the battery negative lead and remove the rear fog lights from the bumper with reference to Chapter 12.
8 Open the bootlid or tailgate and unscrew the bumper mounting nuts or bolts as applicable.
9 Where applicable, on Estate models prise out the plastic plugs and unscrew the side mounting bolts.
10 Withdraw the bumper from the car.
11 If necessary the reinforcement plate and mouldings, where applicable, may be removed from the bumper facia.
12 Refitting is a reversal of removal.

7.5 Front bumper reinforcement plate retaining screw

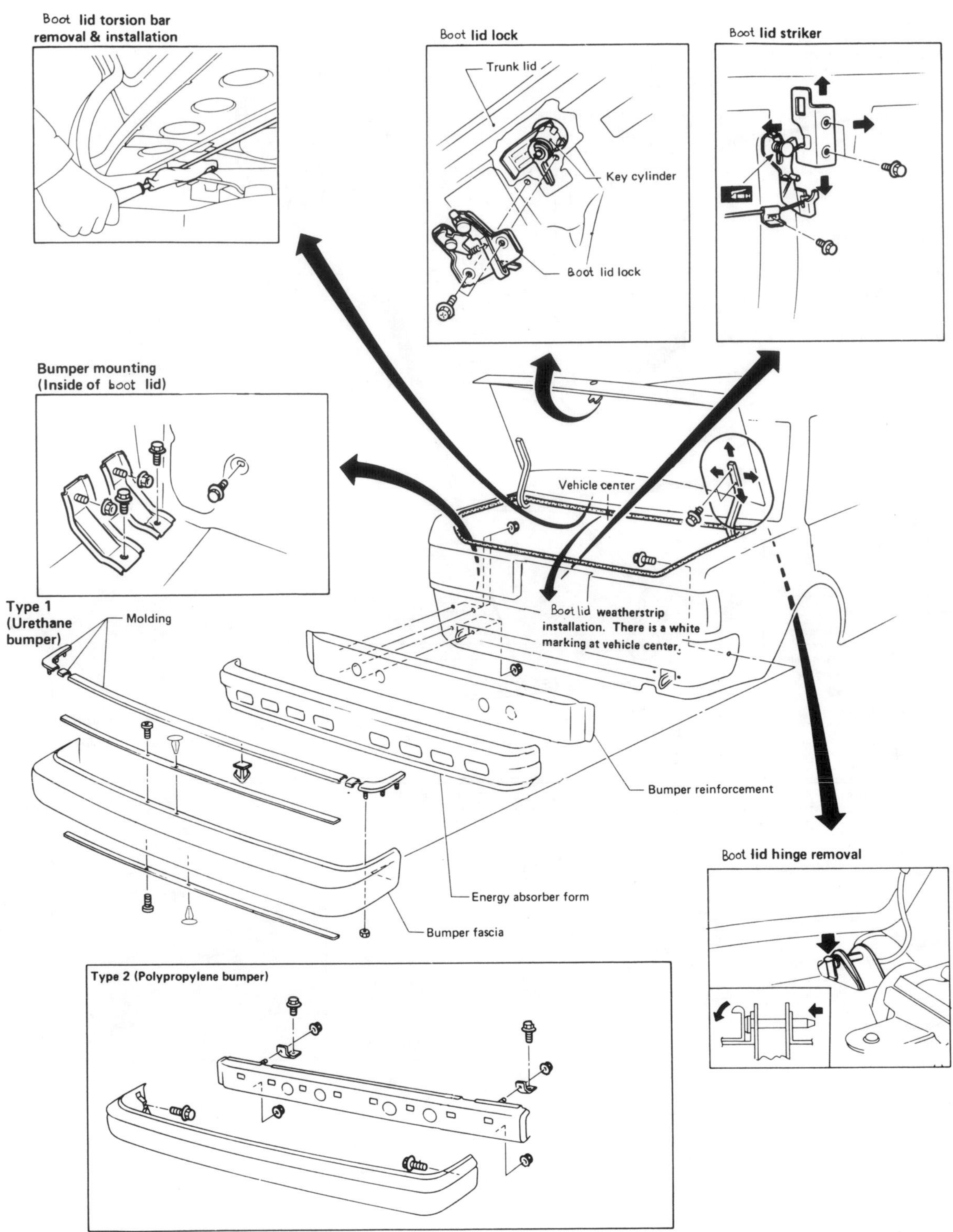

Fig. 11.2 Bootlid and rear bumper components (Sec 7)

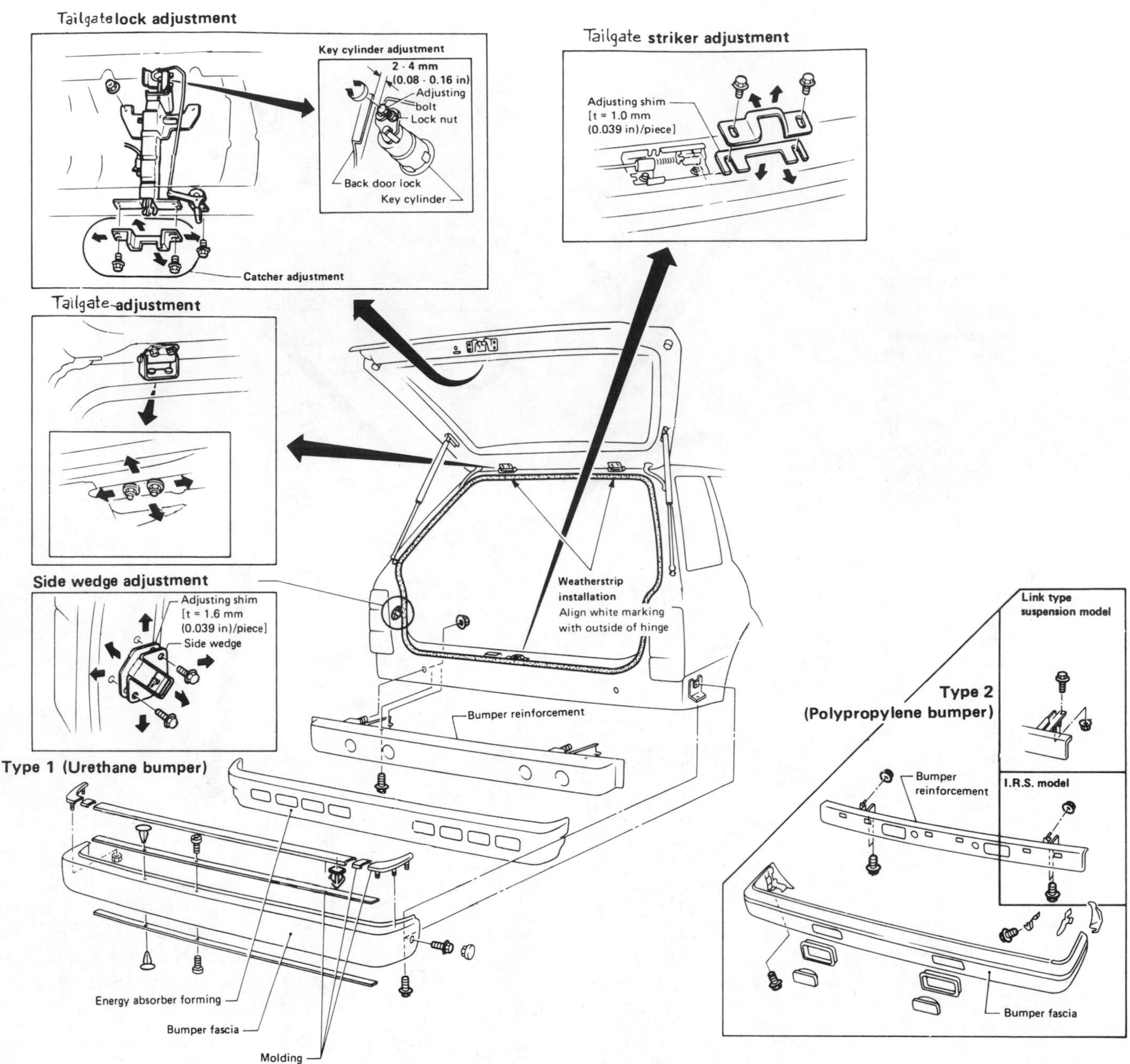

Fig. 11.3 Tailgate and rear bumper components (Sec 7)

8 Radiator grille – removal and refitting

1 The radiator grille is secured by a special clip at each corner.

2 To disengage the clips, use a screwdriver to turn the square heads 45° in either direction, then withdraw the radiator grille.

3 To remove the clips, use pliers to squeeze the plastic legs together.

4 Refitting is a reversal of removal, although it may be found easier to assemble the clips to the grille first (photo).

9 Bonnet – removal and refitting

1 The help of an assistant will be necessary for these operations. First, with the bonnet open, place a thick pad of cloth beneath each rear corner of the bonnet to protect the paintwork.

2 Unclip and disconnect the windscreen washer tubing (photo).

3 Mark around the hinge plates on the underside of the bonnet with a pencil.

Fig. 11.4 Radiator grille clip (Sec 8)

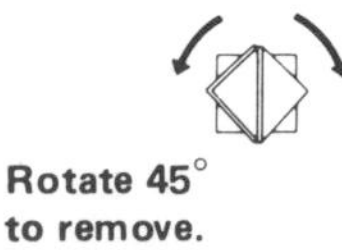

Fig. 11.5 Releasing the radiator grille clips (Sec 8)

8.4 Refitting the radiator grille with clips assembled

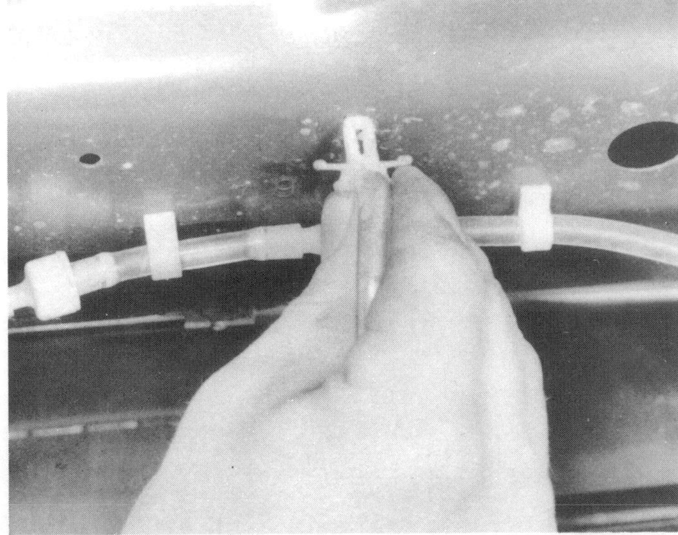

9.2A Release the clip ...

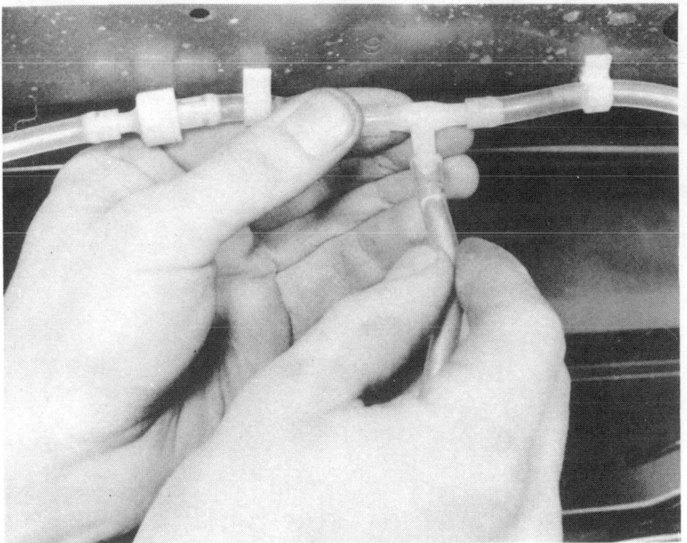

9.2B ... and disconnect the windscreen washer tube

9.5 Removing the bonnet hinge bolts

4 Support the bonnet on the shoulders and lower the stay.
5 Working with one person at each side, unscrew the hinge bolts and lift the bonnet from the vehicle (photo). It may be found that the hinge plates are stuck to the bonnet by the strong sealing compound used, in which case it will be necessary to cut the compound away before loosening the bolts.
6 Refitting is a reversal of removal, using new sealing compound. Do not fully tighten the bolts until the bonnet has been closed and checked for alignment with the surrounding bodywork. Refer to Section 10 for adjustments possible with the bonnet lock.

10 Bonnet lock and cable – removal, refitting and adjustment

1 Remove the radiator grille as described in Section 8 with the bonnet open.
2 Unbolt the lock from the crossmember, then disconnect the cable by releasing the clip (photo).
3 Working inside the car, remove the trim and the time control unit from the right-hand footwell with reference to Chapter 12.

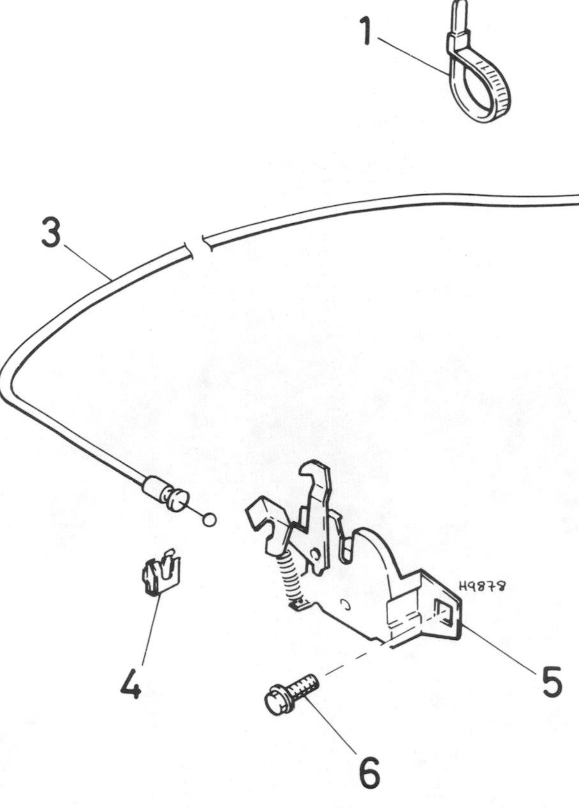

Fig. 11.6 Bonnet lock and cable (Sec 10)

1 Strap
2 Grommet
3 Cable
4 Clip
5 Lock
6 Bolt

4 Unscrew the bonnet release lever mounting screws (photo).
5 Prise out the cable grommet from the bulkhead.
6 Unclip the cable within the engine compartment, then withdraw the release lever and cable from inside the car.
7 Refitting is a reversal of removal, but the lock should be adjusted so that the bonnet striker enters the lock opening centrally (photo), and the bonnet is held flush with the surrounding bodywork when shut. The rubber buffers supporting the front corners of the bonnet should be adjusted so that their free length is approximately 13.0 mm, allowing them to deflect about 2.0 mm when the bonnet is shut (photo). Do not bend the cable acutely within the engine compartment.

10.2 Bonnet lock

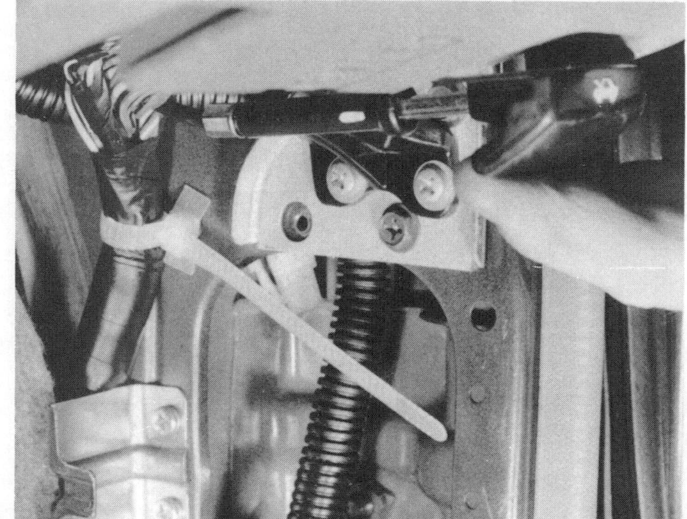

10.4 Bonnet release lever and mounting screws

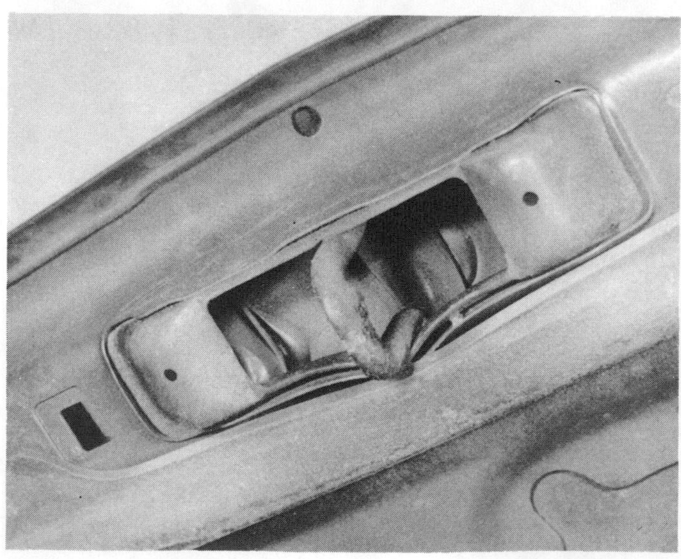

10.7A Bonnet striker

10.7B Bonnet support buffer

11.4 Front wing stay

11 Front wing – removal and refitting

1 Remove the front bumper (Section 7).
2 Raise the front of the car and remove the roadwheel.
3 Remove the clips and bolts and withdraw the under-wing protective shield.
4 Unbolt the wing stay (photo).
5 Remove the headlamp unit and side marker lamp (Chapter 12).
6 Remove the row of wing fixing bolts from the top edge and from the front and rear of the wing.
7 Cut along the mastic joints and then remove the wing.
8 Before fitting the new wing, clean the mating flanges on the body and apply a fresh bead of suitable mastic.
9 Fit the wing and tighten the screws and bolts.
10 Apply protective coating under the wing and refinish the outer surface to match the body colour.
11 Refit the remaining components using a reversal of the removal procedure.

12.3 Boot lid hinge arm

12 Boot lid – removal and refitting

1 The help of an assistant will be necessary for these operations. First, with the boot lid open, place a thick pad of cloth beneath each front corner to protect the paintwork.
2 Mark around the hinge arms on the underside of the boot lid with a pencil.
3 Have an assistant support the lid, then unbolt the hinge arms and lift the boot lid from the car (photo).
4 If necessary, the boot lid torsion bars may be removed using a hooked lever to release them. The hinge arms may also be removed by bending down the stop tabs and extracting the hinge pins, after removing the rear seat backrest and rear shelf.
5 Refitting is a reversal of removal, but apply a little grease to the hinge pins. Do not fully tighten the hinge arm bolts until the boot lid has been closed and checked for alignment with the surrounding bodywork. Refer to Section 13 for adjustments possible with the striker.

13.1 Boot lid lock

13 Boot lid lock, striker, and cable – removal, refitting and adjustment

1 To remove the lock, unscrew the two bolts and withdraw the lock from the underside of the boot lid (photo). The private lock cylinder can be removed by pulling out the spring clip.

13.3 Boot lid striker and release cable bracket

13.4 Location of the release lever mounting bolts

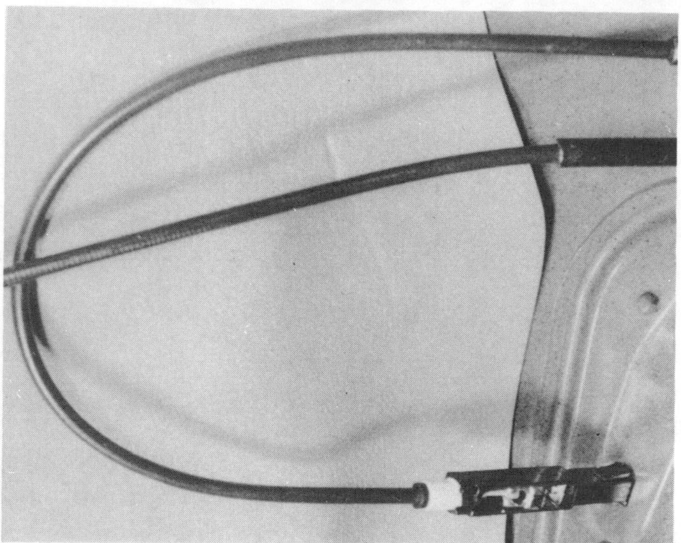
14.1 View of the fuel filler lid lock and cable with trim removed

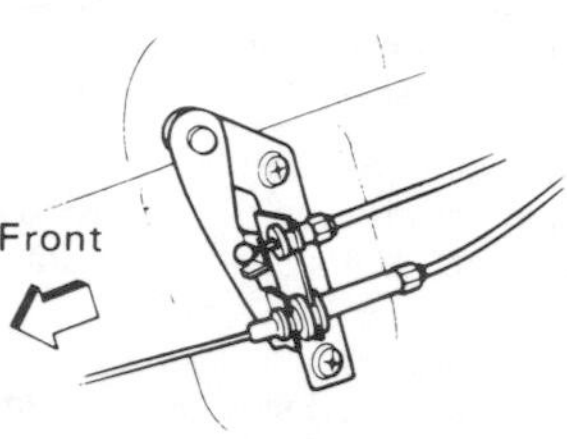

Fig. 11.7 Swing lever for the fuel filler lid cables (Sec 14)

2 The striker is located on the rear panel of the luggage compartment and incorporates a release mechanism operated by cable from the driver's seat.
3 To remove the striker, first remove the trim from the rear of the luggage compartment, then unscrew the striker mounting bolts and the outer cable bracket (photo). Disconnect the inner cable and withdraw the striker.
4 To remove the cable, remove the trim and rear seat cushion, as applicable, from inside the car, then unbolt the release lever and disconnect the cable (photo).
5 Refitting is a reversal of removal, but the striker should be adjusted so that the lock engages correctly with it, and the boot lid is held flush with the surrounding bodywork when shut. Adjust the rubber buffers on each rear corner as required. Adjust the clamp on the release lever at the front, and the outer cable bracket at the rear, so that the lever operates correctly.

14 Fuel filler lid lock and cable – removal and refitting

1 Open the boot lid or tailgate and remove the trim from the left-hand side (photo).

14.5 Fuel filler lid private lock

2 Reach round over the left-hand rear wheel arch and disconnect the cable from the swing lever.
3 Prise the outer cable from the lock bracket and the inner cable from the pullrod inside the bracket.
4 Remove the lock by depressing the plastic tags.
5 If necessary the private lock may be removed from the filler lid by pulling out the spring clip (photo).
6 Refitting is a reversal of removal.

15 Tailgate – removal and refitting

1 The help of an assistant will be necessary for these operations. First, with the tailgate open, place a thick pad of cloth on the roof of the car beneath the top corners of the tailgate.
2 Remove the trim panel and disconnect the wiring and rear washer pipe from the tailgate.
3 Support the tailgate, then unbolt the two stays.
4 Mark around the hinges on the tailgate with a pencil, then unscrew the hinge bolts and lift the tailgate from the car.
5 If required, the hinges can be removed if the roof trim and lining are detached at the rear edge to give access to the bolts.
6 Refitting is a reversal of removal, but before tightening the hinge bolts to the tailgate, close it to check for correct alignment. The tailgate may be moved within the limits of the elongated bolt holes to achieve this, but the striker will then need adjustment to ensure smooth positive closure. The height of the striker may be adjusted using 1.0 mm (0.039 in) thick shims.

16 Tailgate lock, striker and cable – removal, refitting and adjustment

1 To remove the lock, remove the tailgate trim panel then unbolt and remove the lock. The private lock cylinder can be removed by disconnecting the release rod and pulling out the spring clip.
2 The striker and adjustment shims are removed by unbolting them from the rear body panel.
3 The cable release mechanism is removed by unbolting it from the rear body panel and disconnecting the cable.
4 To remove the cable, remove the trim and rear seat cushion as applicable from inside the car, then unbolt the release lever and disconnect the cable.
5 Refitting is a reversal of removal, but adjust the lock catcher, striker, and the side wedges so that the tailgate closes correctly. Adjust the clamp on the release lever at the front and the release mechanism at the rear so that the lever operates correctly.

17 Door trim panel – removal and refitting

1 On the front door, prise out the plastic cover from the exterior mirror inner plate, then remove the screw and withdraw the plate (photos).

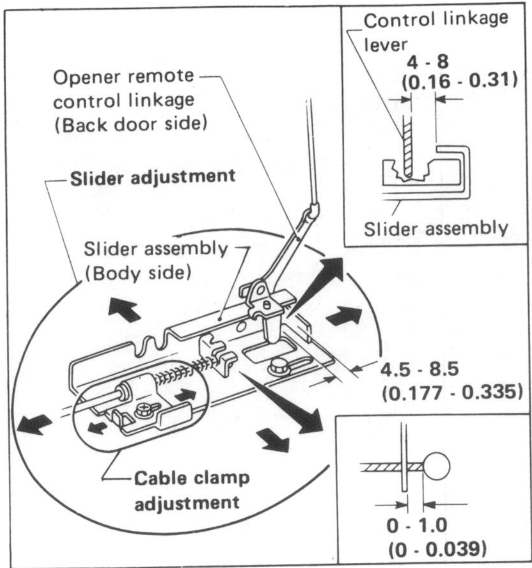

Fig. 11.8 Tailgate striker adjustment (Sec 16)

2 On manual window models, fully close the window and note the position of the regulator handle. Release the clip from behind the handle by drawing a piece of cloth along so that it pulls out the clip, then remove the handle from the splines. Remove the plastic washer (photos).
3 Prise out the interior handle surround (photo).
4 Remove the screws and withdraw the armrest (photo).
5 Using a wide blade screwdriver, prise the twin panel clips from the door, taking care not to break them.
6 Lift the panel over the locking knob, then disconnect the wiring as applicable and withdraw the panel.
7 Carefully peel away the waterproof sheet.
8 Refitting is a reversal of removal, but fit the clip to the window regulator handle before pressing the handle direct onto the splines.

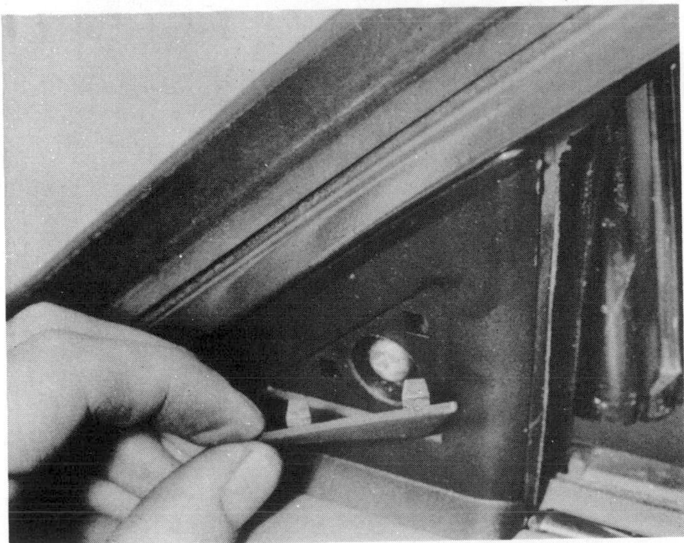

17.1A Remove the plastic cover ...

17.1B ... and the exterior mirror inner plate

17.2A Window regulator handle in the closed position

17.2B Showing the window regulator handle retaining clip

17.2C Window regulator handle plastic washer

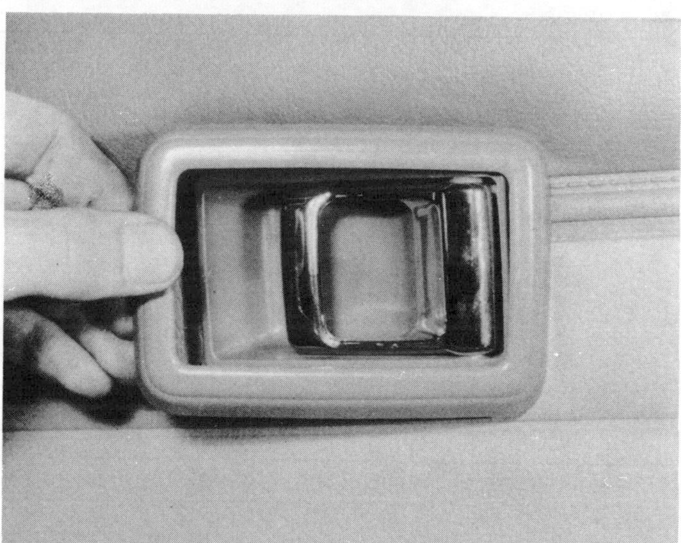
17.3 Removing the interior handle surround

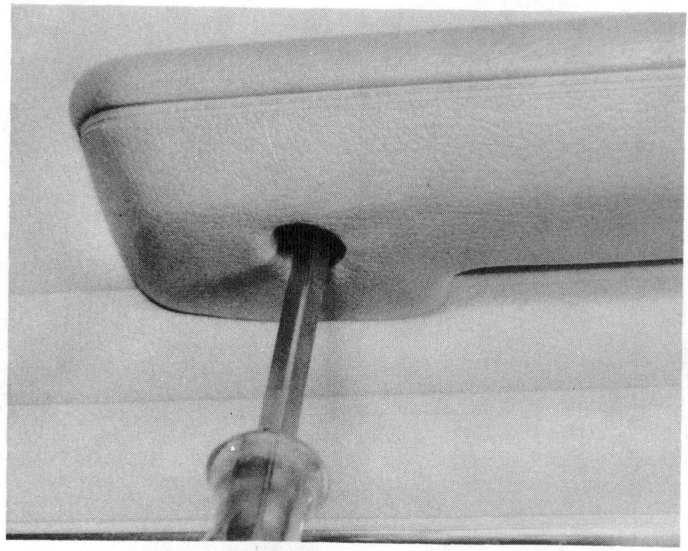
17.4 Removing the armrest screws

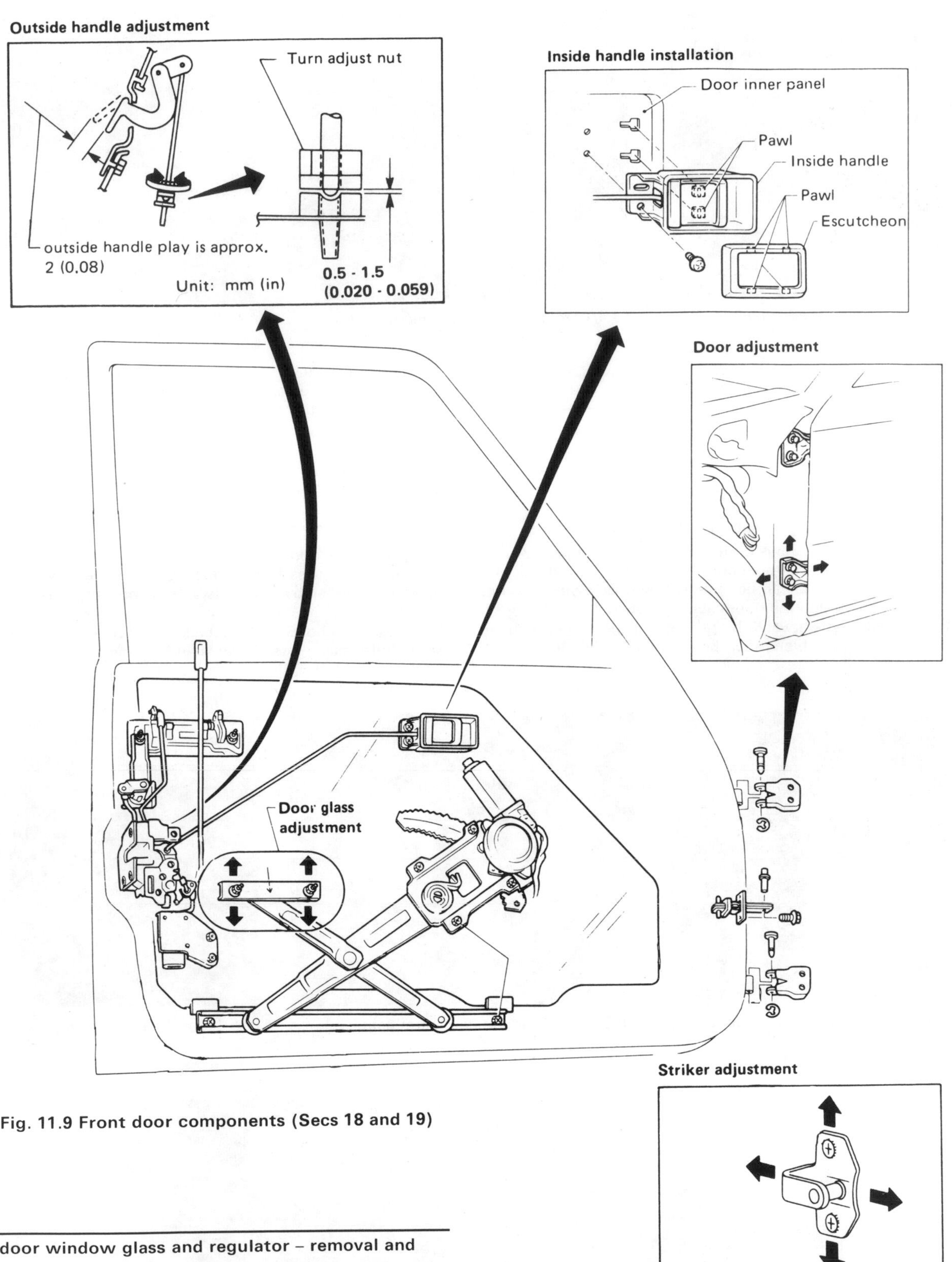

Fig. 11.9 Front door components (Secs 18 and 19)

18 Front door window glass and regulator – removal and refitting

1 Remove the door trim panel as described in Section 17.
2 Position the window so that the guide channel is visible in the door apertures (photo), then remove the nuts from the guide channel and support the glass with a block of wood.
3 Remove the weather seal strips, then pull the glass upwards and by tilting it, remove it from the door.
4 To remove the regulator, unscrew the mounting bolts and disengage it from the guide, then withdraw it through the door aperture (photos). If power windows are fitted disconnect the wiring.
5 Refitting is a reversal of removal, but adjust the guide within the elongated holes as necessary so that the glass contacts the weather strip correctly. Lubricate both guide channels and the regulator gear with a little grease.

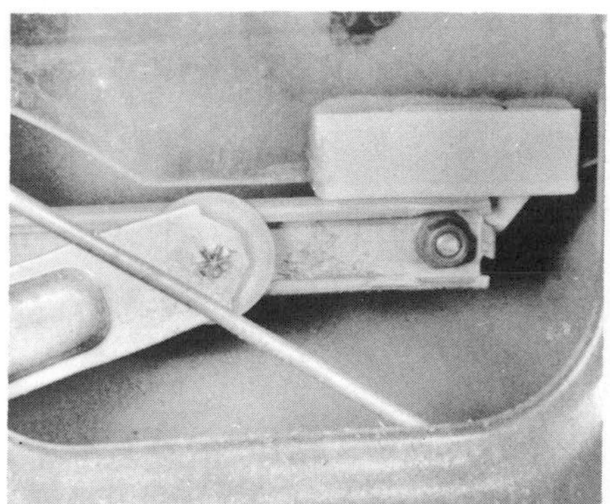
18.2 Window glass and guide channel

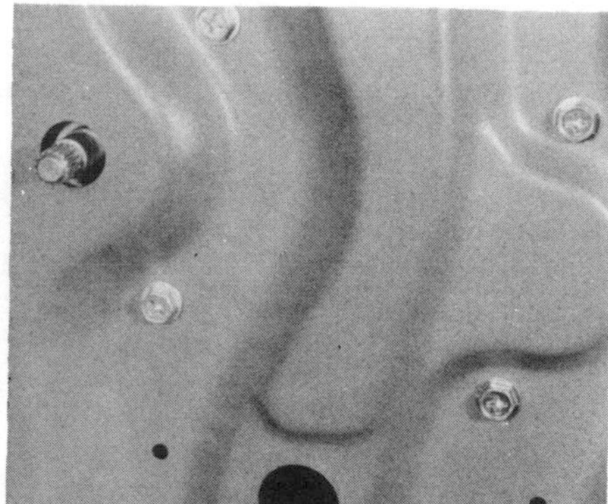
18.4A Front door window regulator bolts

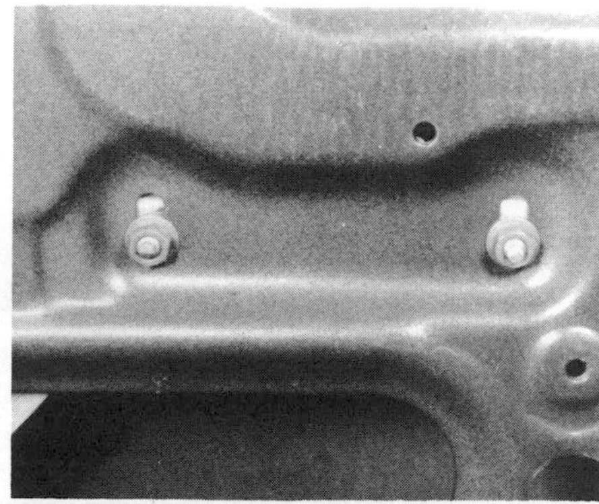
18.4B Front door window guide nuts

19 Front door lock – removal and refitting

1 Remove the door trim panel as described in Section 17.
2 Temporarily refit the window winder handle and wind the glass fully up.
3 Disconnect the rod from the lock cylinder (photo).
4 Disconnect the door lock plunger rod.
5 Extract the remote control handle screws (photo).
6 Extract the lock fixing screws from the door edge (photo).
7 Withdraw the lock and remote control assemblies from the door.
8 The door exterior handle can be removed by unscrewing the nuts which are accessible within the door cavity (photo).
9 The lock cylinder is removable by prising out the spring securing clip which again is accessible within the door cavity (photo).
10 Refitting is a reversal of removal, but lightly grease the mechanism of the lock and exterior door handle. The exterior handle pushrod should be adjusted to provide 0.5 to 1.5 mm (0.020 to 0.059 in) endplay.

20 Rear door window glass and regulator – removal and refitting

1 Remove the door trim panel as described in Section 17.
2 Lower the glass so that the bottom edge is visible in the door aperture, then remove the nuts and support the glass with a block of wood.
3 Loosen the bolt which secures the lower end of the glass divider.
4 Pull the main glass upwards and remove it.

19.3 Showing front door lock cylinder and plunger rods

19.5 Front door remote control handle

19.6 Front door lock fixing screws

19.8 Front door exterior handle and mounting nuts

19.9 Front door lock cylinder (private lock)

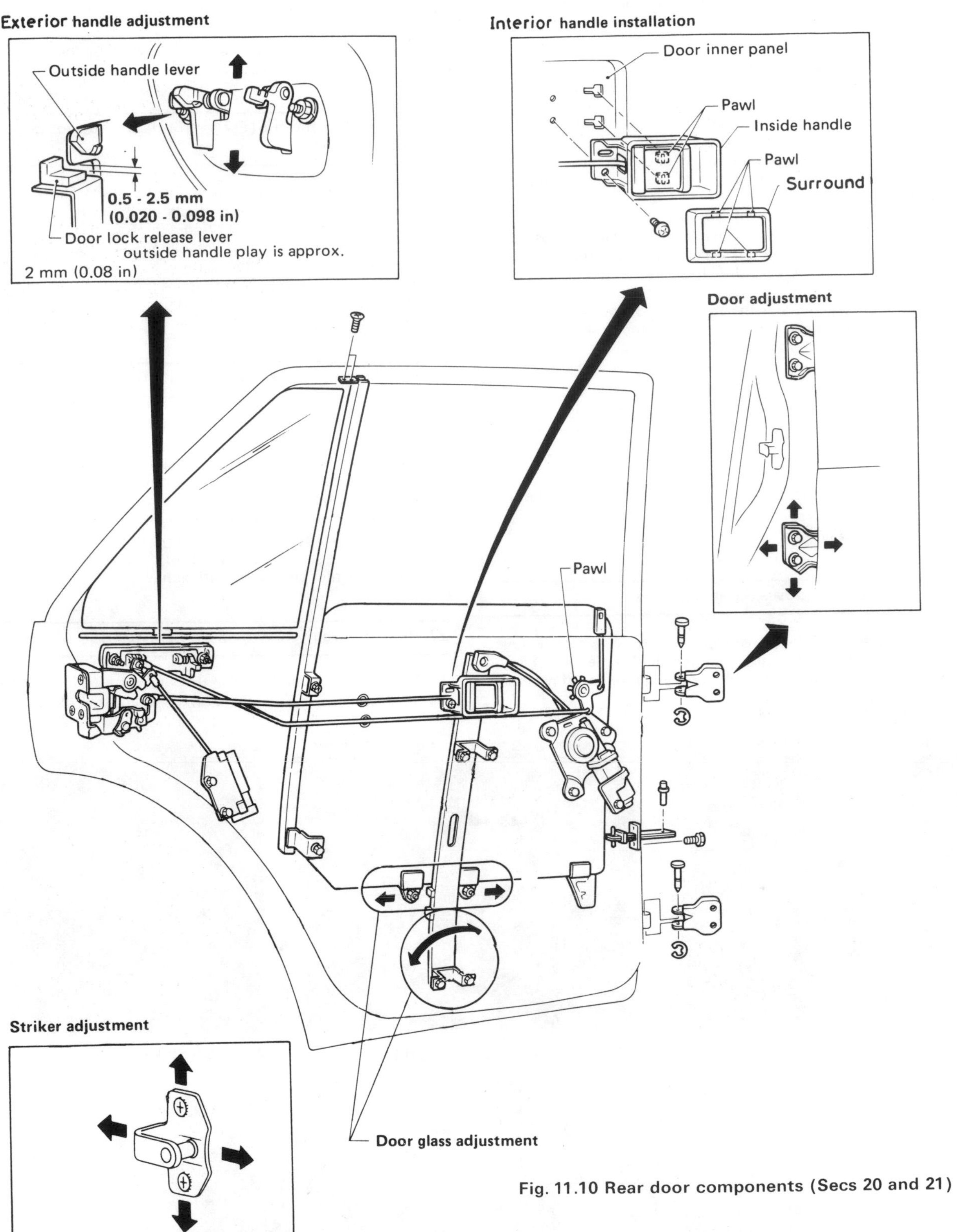

Fig. 11.10 Rear door components (Secs 20 and 21)

5 The fixed quarter glass can be removed if the divider top screw is removed and the upper end moved towards the front of the vehicle.

6 Unscrew the regulator bolts and withdraw the mechanism through the door aperture. if power windows are fitted disconnect the wiring.

7 Refitting is a reversal of removal, but position the regulator within the elongated bolt holes so that the glass moves smoothly up and down. Lubricate the regulator mechanism with a little grease.

21 Rear door lock – removal and refitting

The procedure is similar to that for the front door lock described in Section 19, however the exterior door handle should be adjusted within the elongated holes so that there is between 0.5 and 2.5 mm (0.020 and 0.098 in) clearance between the handle and lock.

22 Door – removal, refitting and adjustment

1 On the front door remove the trim panel (Section 17) and disconnect the wiring harness for the loudspeaker, power windows, and central locking as applicable.
2 Disconnect the check link by driving out the pin upwards (photo).
3 Support the door on blocks of wood.
4 Extract the circlips and drive out the hinge pins, noting that the heads face each other between the hinges (photo).
5 Lift the door from the car. If necessary the hinges may be unbolted from the door pillars.
6 Refitting is a reversal of removal, but lubricate the hinge pins and check link pin with a little grease. Check that the door is positioned centrally in the body aperture, and if necessary loosen the hinge bolts and reposition them. Check that the door lock engages the striker smoothly, and if necessary loosen the hinge bolts and reposition them. Check that the door lock engages the striker smoothly, and if necessary loosen the cross-head screws and reposition the striker within the elongated holes (photo).

23 Exterior mirror (manual) – removal and refitting

1 Prise out the plastic cover from the inner plate on the front door, then remove the screw and withdraw the plate.
2 Remove the three screws, then withdraw the mirror from the door (photos).
3 Refitting is a reversal of removal.

24 Power-operated windows – general

1 The electric motors for the power-operated windows are removed together with the window regulators as described in Sections 18 and 20. The motors can be unbolted from the regulators and if necessary renewed separately.
2 The control switches for the power windows are located on the drivers door trim panel and can be removed with reference to Chapter 12.
3 The system includes a lock facility, whereby the driver can lock all windows except the driver's by depressing the lock switch.

25 Rear side window (Estate models) – removal and refitting

1 Open the tailgate, then prise out the studs and unhook the rear pillar finisher from the small brackets on the side window.
2 Remove the two rear mounting screws from the window.
3 Support the window, then remove the front mounting screws from inside the car and lift off the window.
4 If necessary renew the lower glass moulding with reference to Fig. 11.12 and the weatherstrip with reference to Fig. 11.13.
5 Refitting is a reversal of removal.

26 Windscreen – removal and refitting

1 The windscreen is bonded into the body aperture and removal or refitting by the home mechanic is not recommended.
2 Special primers and sealant are required, together with spacers, and therefore the work is best left to a specialist.
3 It should be noted that after renewing the windscreen the car must not be driven over rough surfaces until the sealant is completely cured. The period for curing varies according to the ambient temperature and humidity, but as a general guide four days in the summer and eleven days in the winter should be sufficient.

27 Rear window – removal and refitting

1 The removal and refitting of this glass is best left to specialists but for those wishing to tackle the job, carry out the following operations.

22.2 Door check link

22.4 Door hinge and hinge pin

22.6 Door striker

23.2A Remove the screws ...

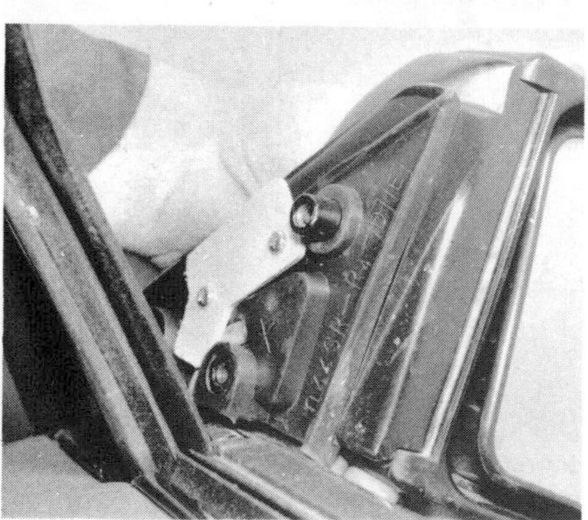
23.2B ... and withdraw the exterior mirror

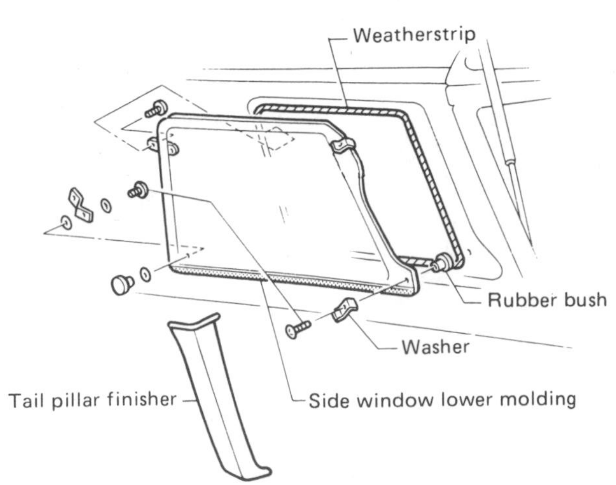

Fig. 11.11 Rear side window components on Estate models (Sec 25)

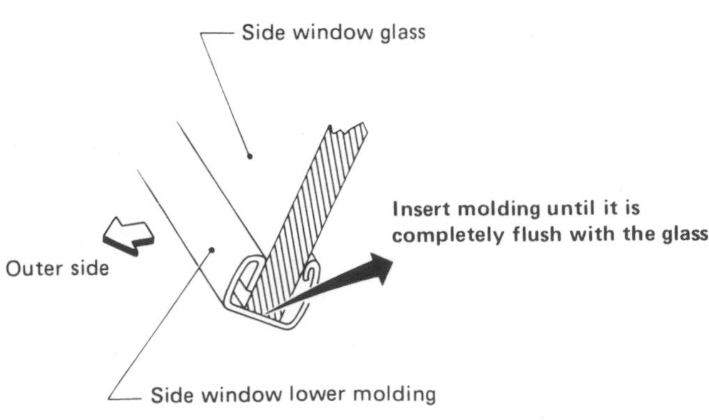

Fig. 11.12 Rear side window lower moulding renewal on Estate models (Sec 25)

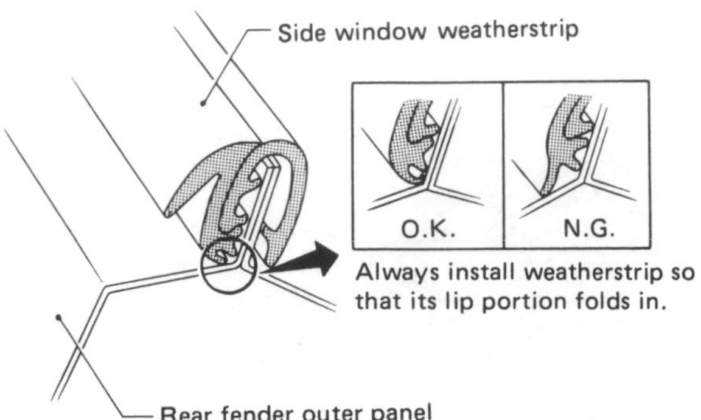

Fig. 11.13 Rear side window weatherstrip renewal on Estate models (Sec 25)

2 Release the rubber surround from the bodywork by running a blunt, small screwdriver around and under the rubber weatherstrip both inside and outside the car. This operation will break the adhesive of the sealer originally used. Take care not to damage the paintwork or catch the rubber surround with the screwdriver.

3 Disconnect the demister element wiring leads.
4 Have your assistant push the inner lip of the rubber surround off the flange of the window body aperture. Once the rubber surround starts to peel off the flange, the glass may be forced gently outward by careful hand pressure. The second person should support and remove the glass complete with rubber surround.
5 Fit a new weatherseal to the glass and ensure that all old sealant is removed from the body flange. Scrape it away and then clean it off with a fuel-soaked cloth.
6 Apply a bead of sealant to the body flange all round the window aperture.
7 Cut a piece of strong cord greater in length than the periphery of the glass and insert it into the body flange locating the channel of the rubber surround.
8 Offer the glass to the body aperture and pass the ends of the cords, previously fitted and located at bottom centre, into the vehicle interior.
9 Press the glass into place, at the same time have an assistant pull the cords to engage the lip of the rubber channel over the body flange.
10 Remove any excess sealant with a paraffin-soaked rag.

28 Sun roof – general

1 Either a manually-operated hatch-type sun roof is fitted, or an electrically-operated sliding type.
2 The manually-operated type is removed by releasing the rear catch and unhooking it from the front brackets. Both the catch and the hooks can be removed from the sun roof after removing the cross-head screws (photos).

28.2A Manually-operated sunroof catch ...

28.2B ... and hook

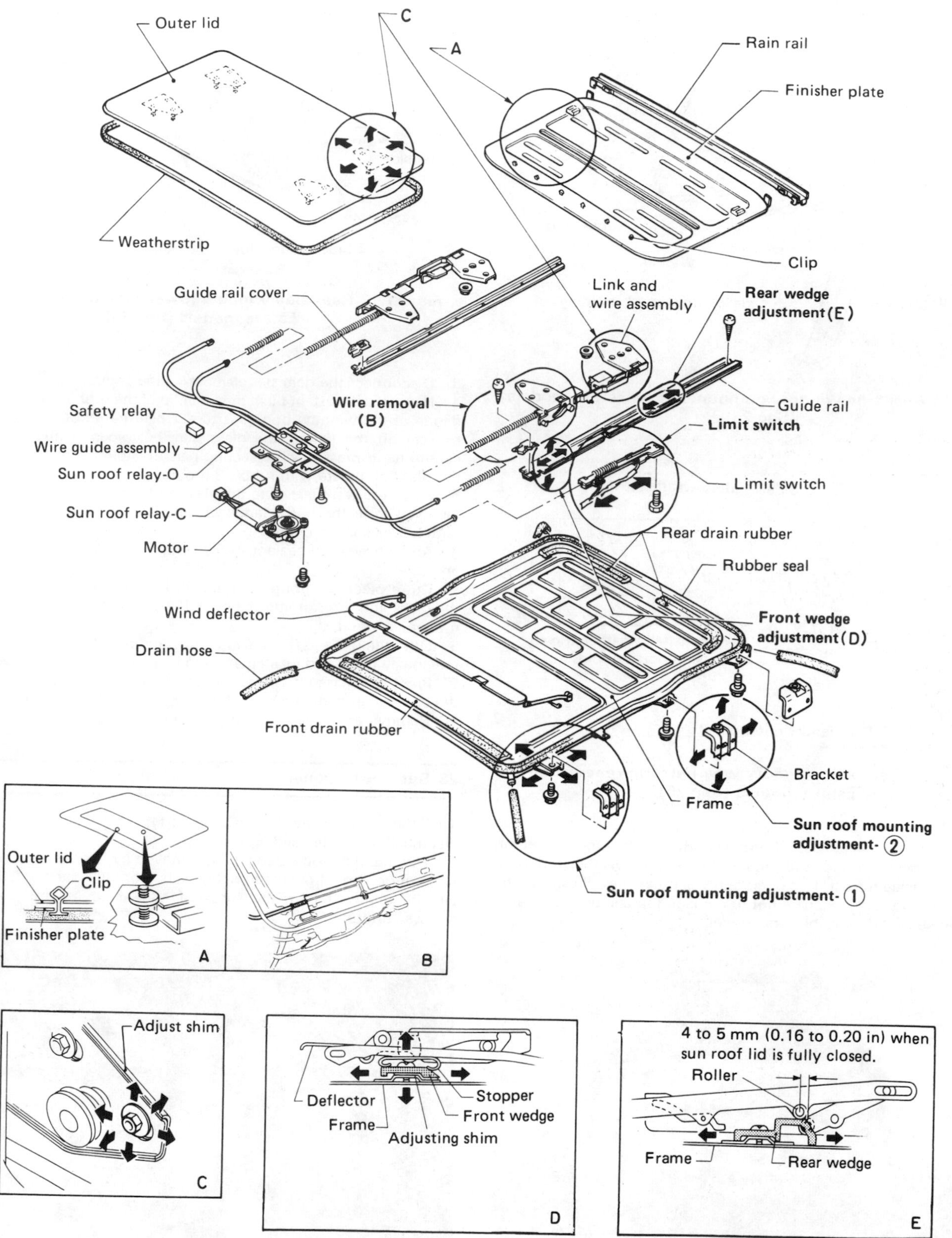

Fig. 11.14 Exploded view of the electrically-operated sun roof (Sec 28)

3 Components of the electrically-operated sun roof are shown in Fig. 11.14. Note that the finisher plate is clipped to the outer lid although the clips are not visible (see ref. 'A'). To renew the cable, remove the rail first, followed by the link and wire assembly ('B'). Adjustments are provided at the rear of the outer lid ('C') and the front of the guide rail ('D'). The rear wedge on the guide rail should be adjusted so that the roller rests on the top of the wedge with the sun roof shut (see ref. 'E'). Lightly grease the cables and guide rails when refitting them.

29 Central locking system – general

1 Some models are equipped with a central door locking system, whereby all doors are automatically locked when the driver's door is locked from the outside. Unlocking the driver's door also unlocks the other doors.
2 On the inside of the driver's door, together with the power window switches, a switch is provided to lock and unlock all doors except the driver's door.
3 The central locking motors are fitted to all the doors except the driver's door, and their location is shown in Figs. 11.9 and 11.10.
4 It is not possible to repair a motor, therefore in the event of a fault the unit must be renewed.

30 Seats – removal and refitting

Front seats

1 Operate the adjuster and move the seat fully rearwards.
2 Unscrew the bolts securing the front of the runners to the floor (photo).
3 Move the seat fully forwards, then remove the plastic covers and unscrew the rear bolts (photo).
4 Lift the seat from inside the car, and where the seat is of the heated type, disconnect the wiring.
5 Refitting is a reversal of removal.

Rear seat

6 Remove the seat cushion first. There are two types. The standard type is removed by lifting the front edge of the cushion to remove the wire legs from the retainers, then pulling the cushion forwards to release the rear legs (photo). On the alternative type on Saloon models, where the cushion and folding locknuts are reclinable, unbolt the runners from the floor and remove the cushion together with the folding backrests.
7 To remove the backrest *on Saloon models* first unbolt the non-reclinable folding backrests where fitted. Remove the bottom corner screws, and the mounting bolts on folding backrest models, then lift up the backrest to release the upper wire legs from the retainers.
8 *On Estate models,* the non-reclinable backrest is removed by unbolting the pivot brackets. To remove the reclinable backrest, first unbolt the folding backrest mounting brackets from the floor. The fixed side backrests are removed by removing the bottom mounting screws, then lifting the backrests to release the upper wire legs from the retainers.
9 Refitting the rear seat is a reversal of removal, but lubricate the reclining mechanisms with a little grease and where applicable adjust the pivot and striker brackets to ensure correct operation of the backrests.

31 Seat belts and head restraints – general

1 The front seat belt and inertia reel are mounted on the centre door pillar and can be unbolted once the trim panels have been removed.

30.2 Front seat runner front mounting bolt

30.3 Front seat runner rear mounting bolt and cover

30.6 Rear seat cushion wire leg and retainer

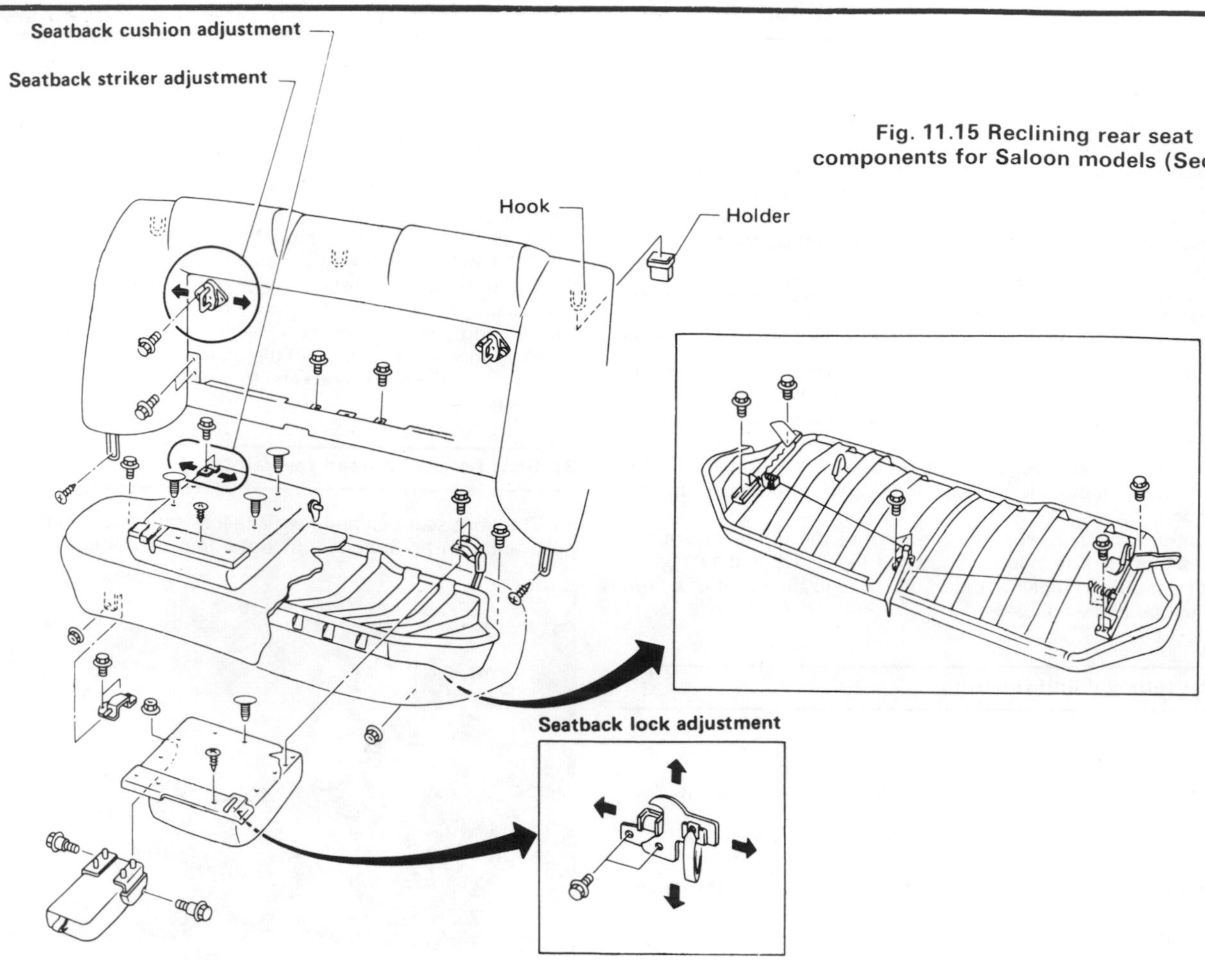

Seatback cushion adjustment

Seatback striker adjustment

Hook

Holder

Seatback lock adjustment

Fig. 11.15 Reclining rear seat components for Saloon models (Sec 30)

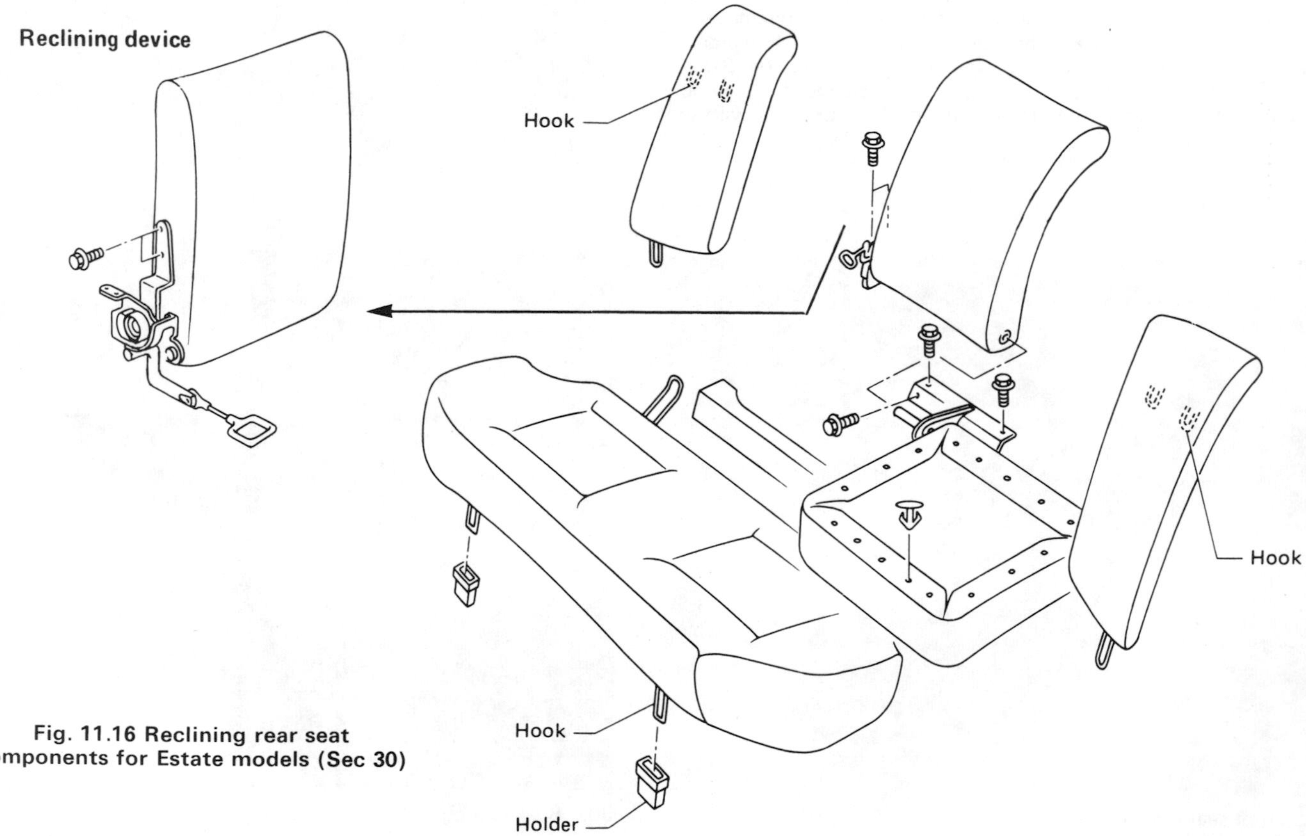

Reclining device

Hook

Hook

Hook

Holder

Fig. 11.16 Reclining rear seat components for Estate models (Sec 30)

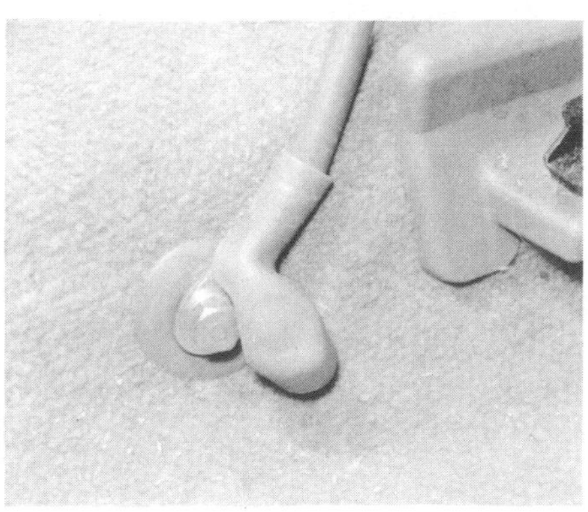

31.1 Front seat belt stalk mounting bolt

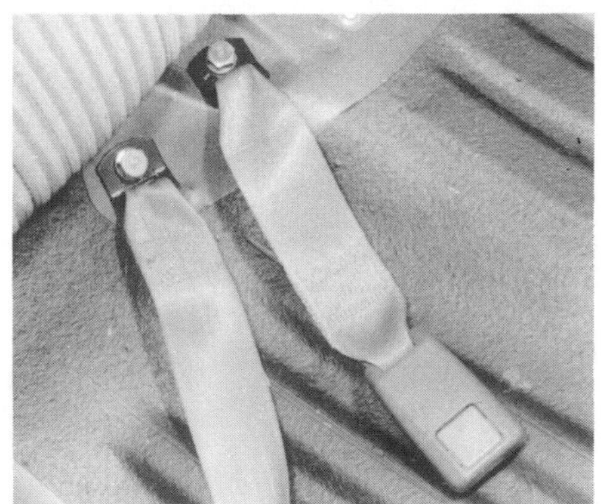
31.2A Rear seat belt straps and mountings

31.2B Rear seat belt inertia reel

The stalks are located on the centre tunnel and can be removed by prising off the plastic boot and unscrewing the mounting bolt (photo).
2 Seat belts for three persons are fitted to the rear seat. The centre belt is of lap type, but the outer belts may be either of lap or inertia type. The rear seat cushion must be removed for access to the strap mountings, and the luggage compartment trim must be removed for access to the inertia reels (photos).
3 The seat belt fabric can be cleaned with warm soapy water then wiped dry.
4 The head restraints can be removed by pulling them from the top of the seats. If necessary dismantle the restraints with reference to Fig. 11.17. The trim must be removed from the front seat in order to remove the restraint sockets.
5 When reassembling the head restraint lightly grease the ratchet mechanism.

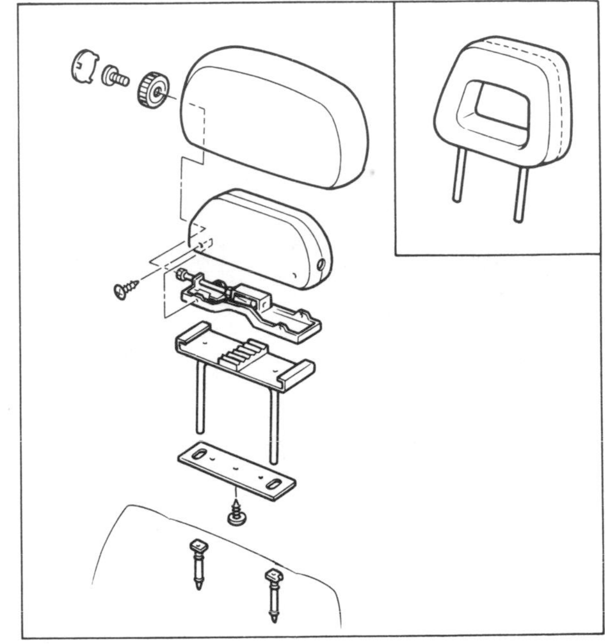
Fig. 11.17 Exploded view of the head restraint (Sec 31)

32 Centre console – removal and refitting

1 Prise out the rear cover or open the rear lid as applicable, then remove the rear mounting screws (photo).
2 Where the rear section is separate, prise out the cover, remove the central mounting screws and lift the section over the handbrake lever.
3 Remove the front and central mounting screws by prising out the plastic covers where necessary (photos).
4 Remove the gear lever boot (manual transmission) or surround (automatic transmission) by prising them from the console.
5 Lift the console over the gear lever and remove it from the car.
6 Refitting is a reversal of removal.

32.1 Removing the centre console rear cover

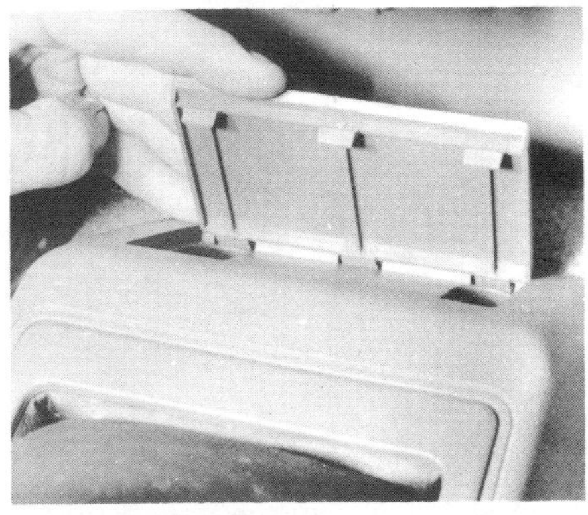
32.3A Removing the centre console front cover ...

32.3B ... and central mounting screws

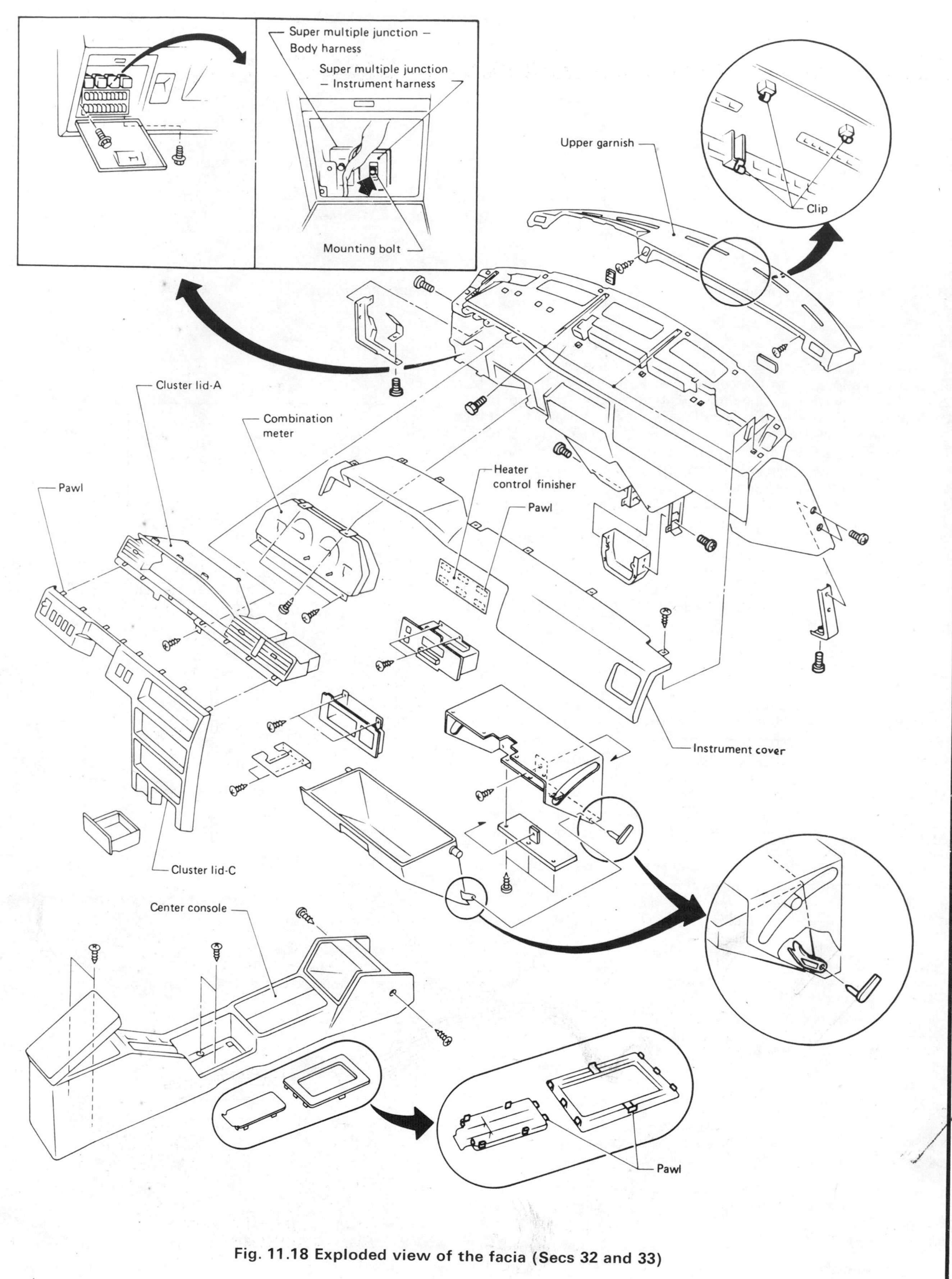

Fig. 11.18 Exploded view of the facia (Secs 32 and 33)

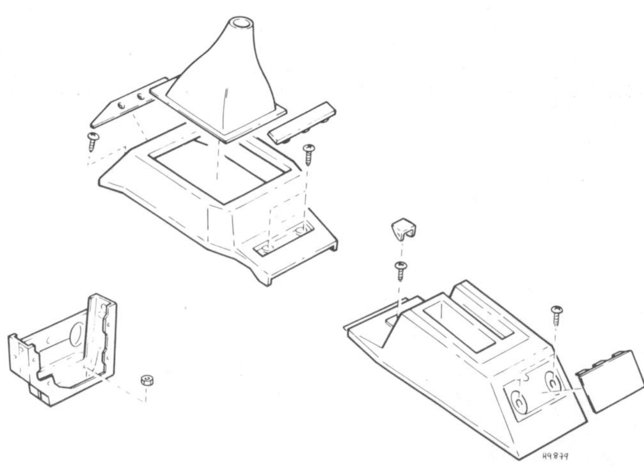

Fig. 11.19 Centre console fitted to DX models (Sec 32)

33 Facia panel – removal and refitting

1 Disconnect the battery negative lead.
2 Remove the instrument panel, fusebox, steering column combination switches, radio, clock and facia switches as described in Chapter 12.
3 Prise out the plastic covers and remove the upper garnish mounting screws (photos), then release the garnish from the clips and remove it, at the same time disconnecting the ventilation ducts.
4 Remove the centre console front section or facia centre support panel as applicable (photo).
5 Remove the heater controls as described in Section 35.
6 Remove the glovebox with reference to Fig. 11.18.
7 Remove the screws and lift out the glovebox housing (photo).
8 Remove the small facia panel beneath the steering column, then remove the plastic air ducting.
9 Remove the steering wheel (Chapter 10).
10 Remove the screws and withdraw the instrument cover (photos).
11 Unscrew all the remaining mounting screws and bolts and withdraw the facia panel from the car.
12 Refitting is a reversal of removal.

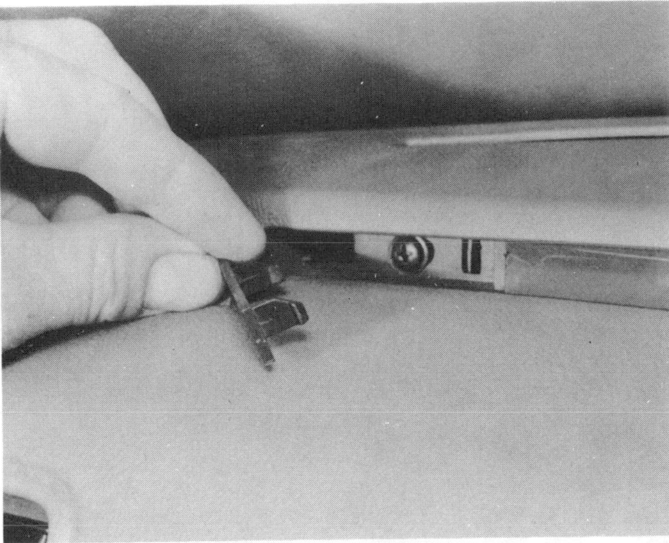

33.3A Prise the plastic covers from the upper garnish ...

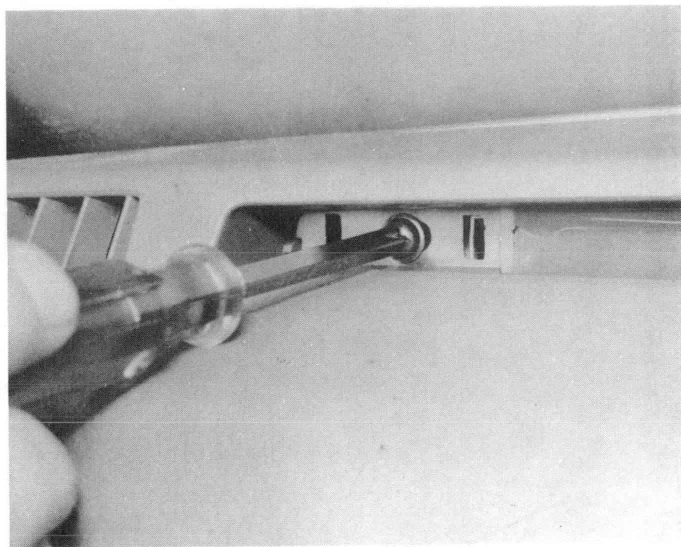

33.3B ... and remove the mounting screws

33.4 Facia centre support panel

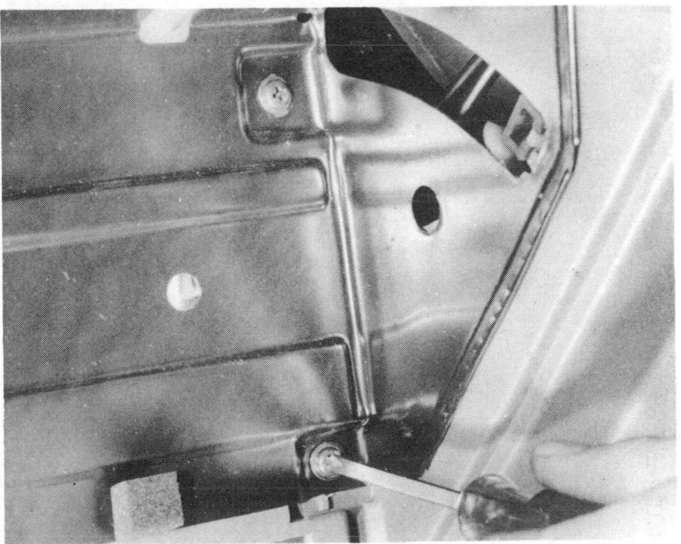

33.7 Removing the glovebox housing screws

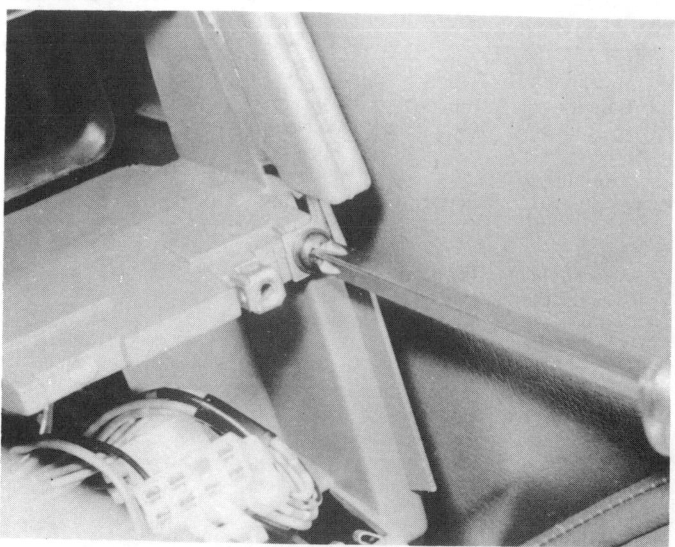

33.10A Instrument cover right-hand mounting screw

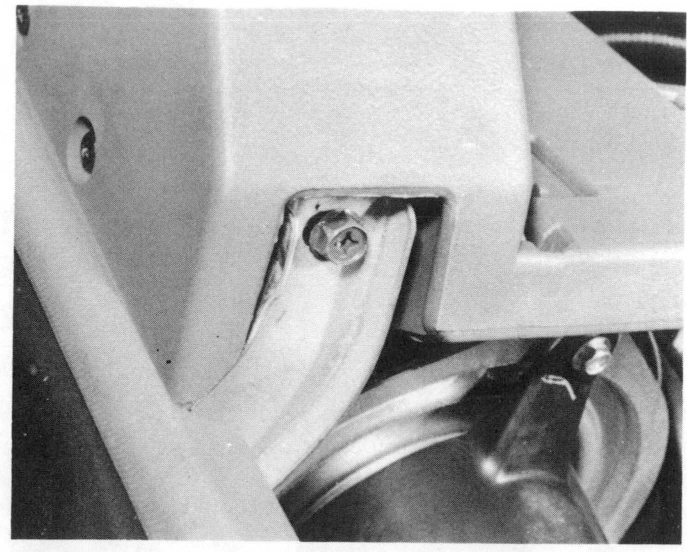

33.10B Instrument cover left-hand mounting bracket

34 Heater blower motor – removal and refitting

1 Disconnect the battery negative lead.

2 Working under the left-hand side of the facia panel, disconnect the wiring plug from the heater motor (photo).

3 Disconnect the rubber tube, then unscrew the mounting bolts and withdraw the motor from the housing (photos).

4 Remove the cover (photo).

5 If necessary, the impeller can be removed from the motor shaft by unscrewing the nut (photo).

6 Refitting is a reversal of removal.

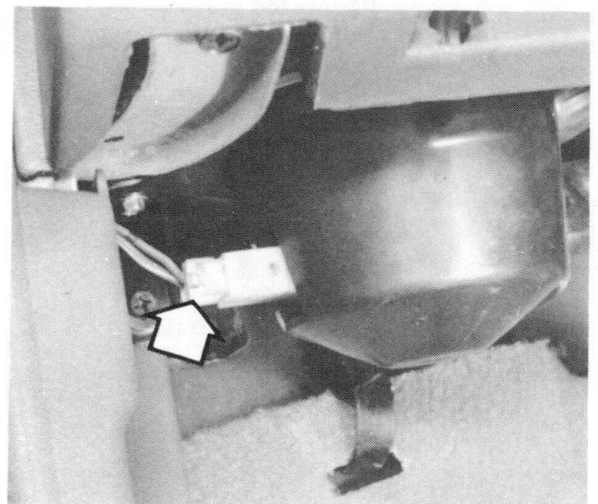

34.2 Heater blower motor wiring plug

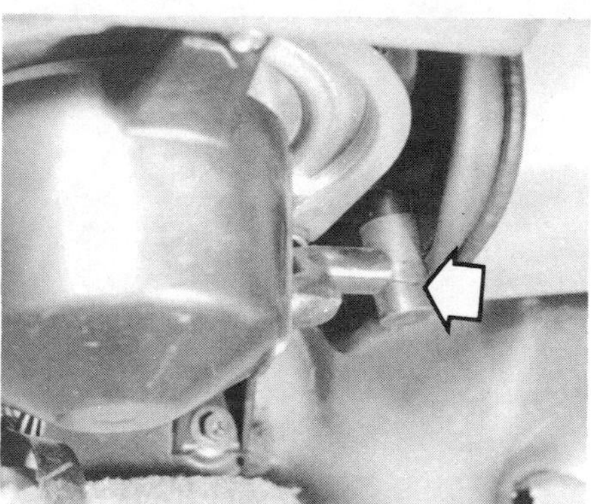

34.3A Disconnect the rubber tube ...

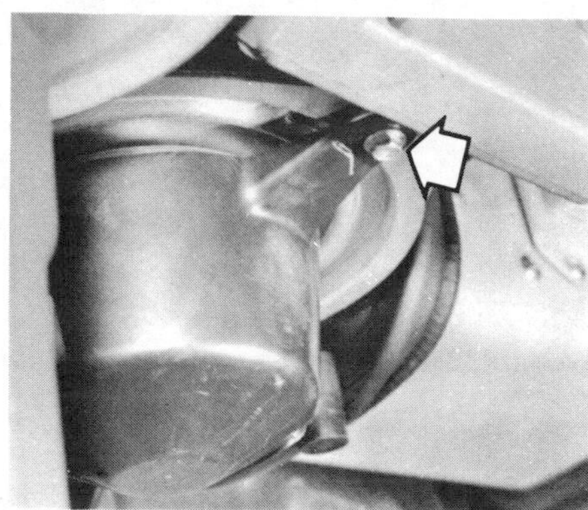

34.3B ... unscrew the mounting bolts ...

34.3C ... and withdraw the heater blower motor

34.4 Removing the cover from the heater blower motor

34.5 Heater blower motor impeller retaining nut

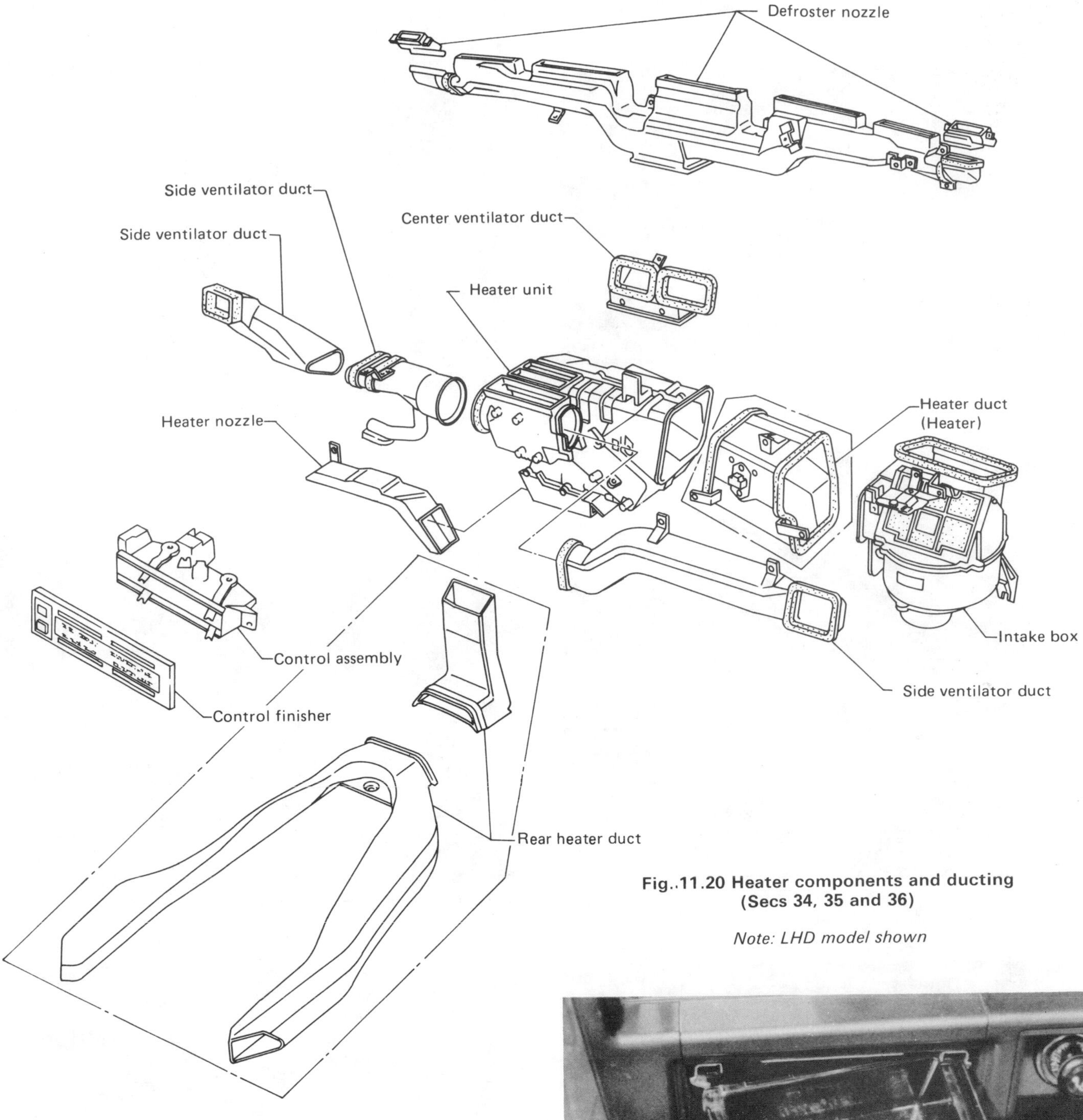

Defroster nozzle
Side ventilator duct
Side ventilator duct
Center ventilator duct
Heater unit
Heater nozzle
Heater duct (Heater)
Control assembly
Control finisher
Intake box
Side ventilator duct
Rear heater duct

Fig. 11.20 Heater components and ducting (Secs 34, 35 and 36)

Note: LHD model shown

35 Heater controls – removal, refitting and adjustment

Removal and refitting

1 Disconnect the battery negative lead.
2 Remove the ash tray (photo).
3 Remove the surround mounting screws and release the surround from the upper pawls. Withdraw the surround and disconnect the wiring from the cigar lighter and switches (photos).
4 Remove the screws above the heater control panel and the screws around the instrument panel location, then withdraw the surround and vent assembly (photos).
5 Pull the knobs from the heater control levers, then prise out the control panel plate (photos).
6 Disconnect the control cables from the heater by releasing the outer cable clips and prising the inner cable ends from the control levers.

35.2 Removing the ash tray

35.3A Facia surround upper ...

35.3B ... and lower screw removal

35.3C Surround upper pawl

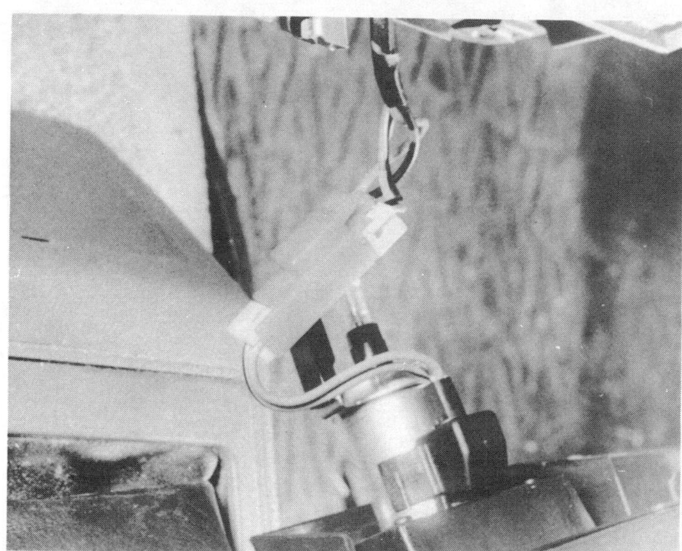

35.3D Cigar lighter wiring connector

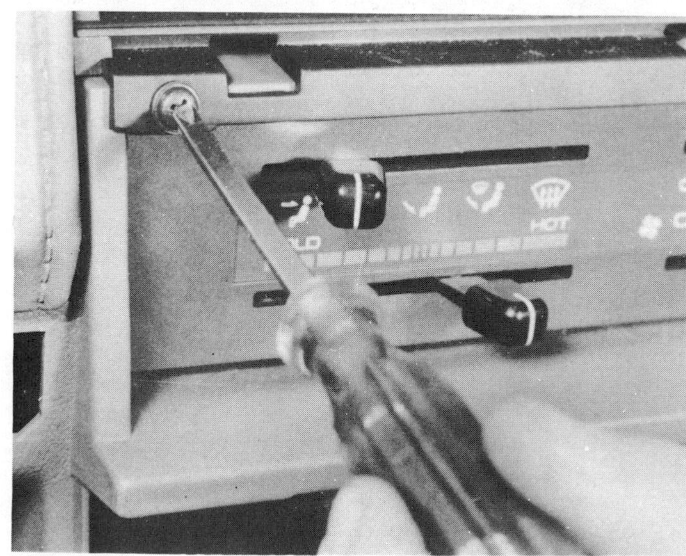

35.4A Extract the screws ...

35.4B ... and withdraw the surround and vent assembly

35.5A Pull off the knobs ...

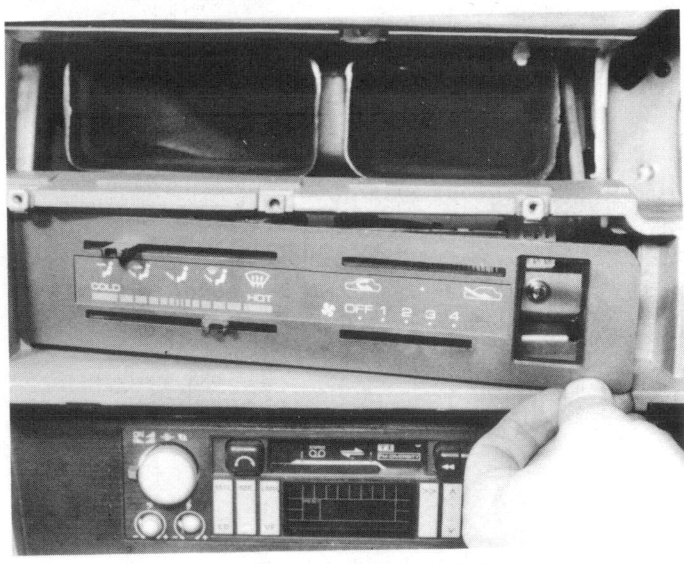
35.5B ... and prise out the heater control panel plate

7 Remove the mounting screws and withdraw the heater controls from the facia together with the cables (photo).
8 Refitting is a reversal of removal, but leave the cables disconnected from the heater at this stage.

Adjustment

9 Check the ventilator control rod adjustment on the right-hand side of the heater by first disconnecting both rods. Move the side link and levers as shown in Fig. 11.21, then reconnect the lower rod followed by the upper rod.
10 Disconnect the defroster control rod on the right-hand side of the heater. Move the side link and rod as shown in Fig. 11.22, then reconnect the rod.
11 Move the side link on the right-hand side of the heater as shown in Fig. 11.23, then connect the bi-level inner cable (photo) to the lever behind the side link. Move the outer cable as shown, then clamp it with the clip.
12 Have as assistant hold the air control knob in the centre position (ie directing air only to the feet), then connect the inner cable to the side link on the right-hand side of the heater. Move the side link and outer cable as shown in Fig. 11.24, then clamp the outer cable with the clip.
13 Have the assistant hold the temperature control knob in the maximum heat position, then connect the inner cable to the air mix

35.7 Heater control panel mounting screw

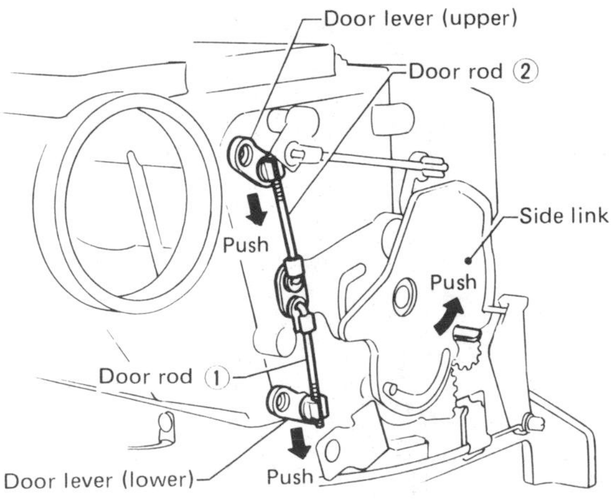

Fig. 11.21 Ventilator control rod adjustment (Sec 35)

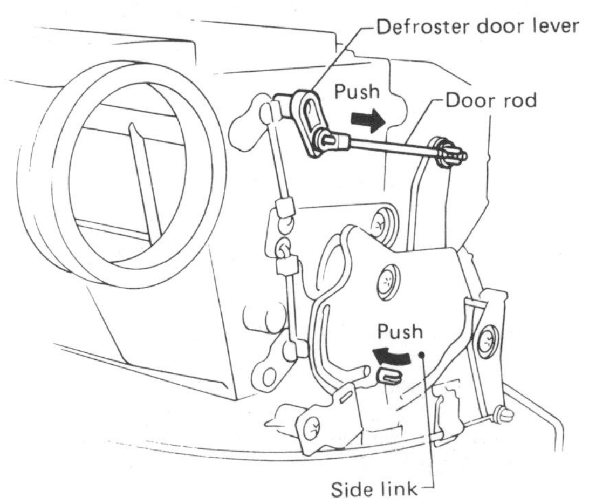

Fig. 11.22 Defroster control rod adjustment (Sec 35)

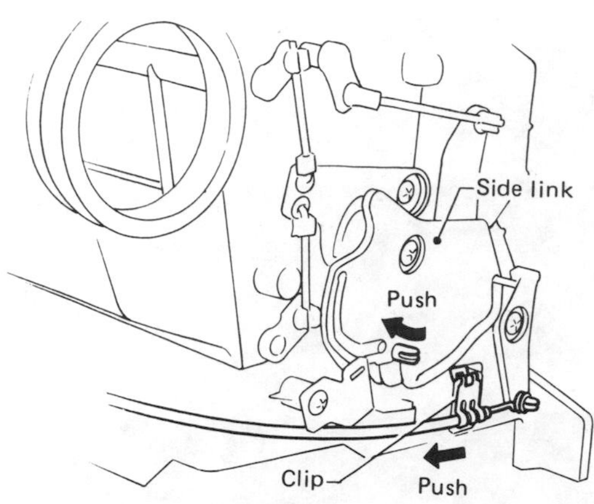

Fig. 11.23 Bi-level cable adjustment (Sec 35)

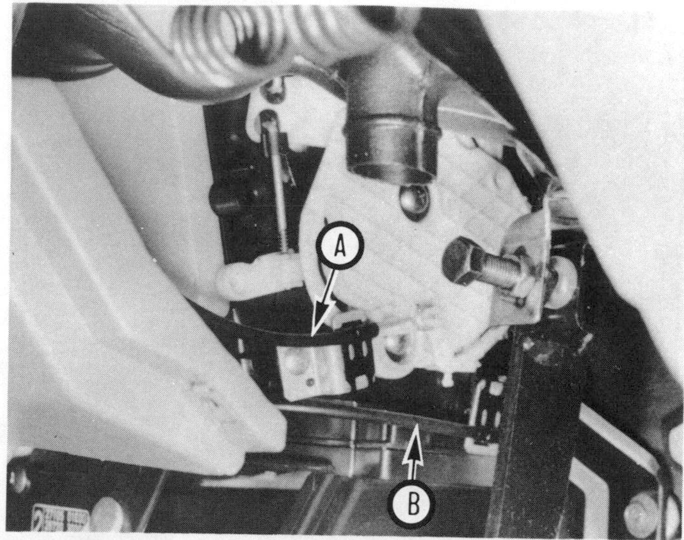

35.11 Heater air control cable (A) and bi-level control cable (B)

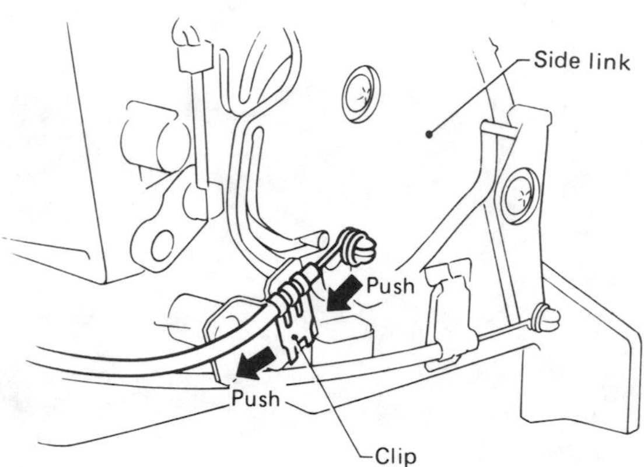

Fig. 11.24 Air control cable adjustment (Sec 35)

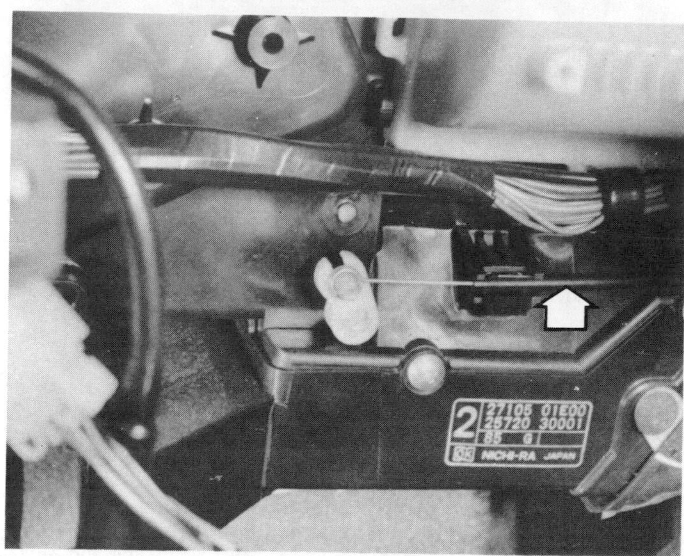

35.13 Air mix door control cable (arrowed) on front of heater

door lever on the front of the heater (photo). Move the lever and outer cable as shown in Fig. 11.25, then clamp the outer cable with the clip.
14 Have the assistant hold the air intake lever fully to the left (ie internal air only), then connect the inner cable to the intake door lever on the front of the heater (photo). Move the lever and outer cable as shown in Fig. 11.26, then clamp the outer cable with the clip.

36 Heater unit – removal and refitting

1 Remove the facia panel as described in Section 33.
2 Drain the cooling system (Chapter 2).
3 Disconnect the heater hoses on the bulkhead within the engine compartment. Remove the air cleaner or inlet ducting as necessary for better access (Chapter 3).
4 Remove the ducting from the heater unit.
5 Unscrew the mounting nuts and bolts and withdraw the heater unit from inside the car (photo).
6 Before refitting the heater unit, adjust the water cock control rod as follows. Refer to Fig. 11.27 and disconnect rod (1), Move the air mix door lever as shown, then push rod (1) until it just contacts rod (2). At this point, the spring should be compressed by 2.0 mm (0.08 in). Now connect rod (1) to the air mix door lever.
7 Refitting is a reversal of removal. Fill the cooling system with reference to Chapter 2.

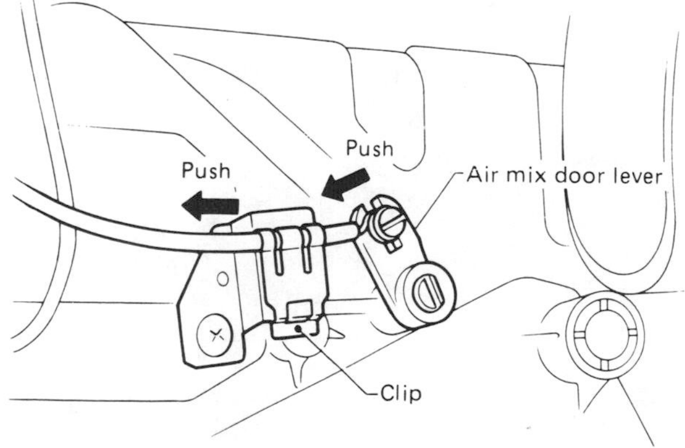

Fig. 11.25 Temperature control cable adjustment (Sec 35)

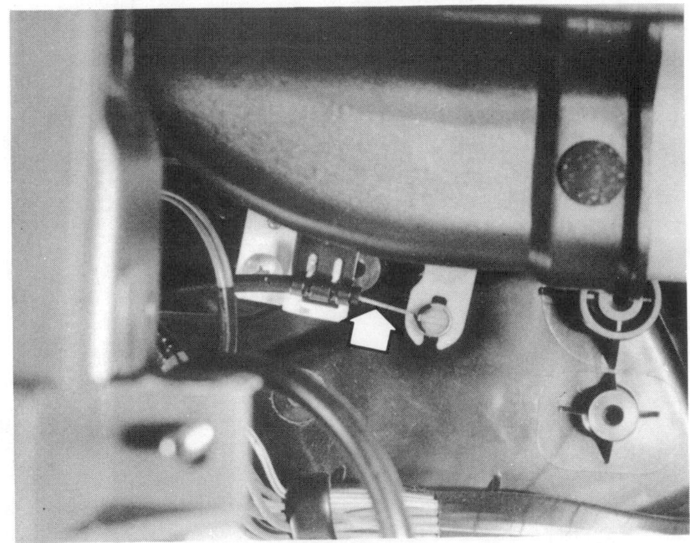

35.14 Air intake door control cable (arrowed) on front of heater

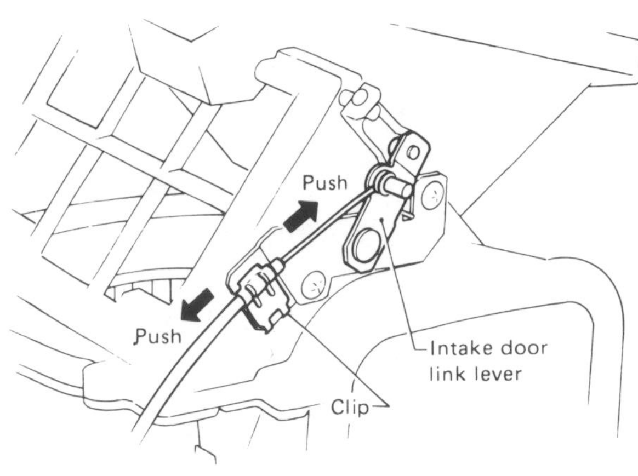

Fig. 11.26 Air intake control cable adjustment (Sec 35)

36.5 Heater unit mounting bolt

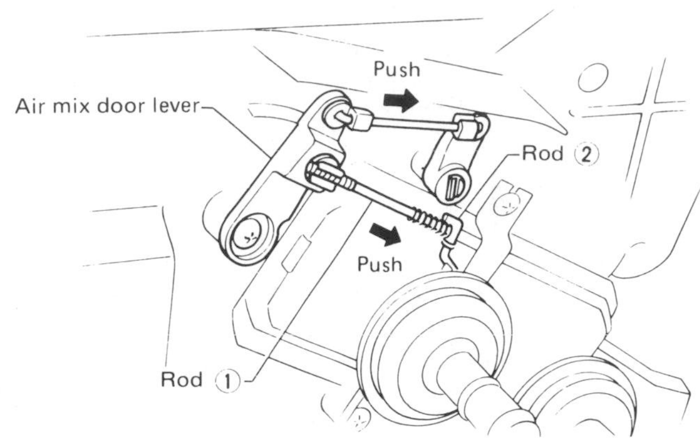

Fig. 11.27 Water cock control rod adjustment (Sec 36)

Chapter 12 Electrical system

Contents

Specifications

General

System type	12 volt negative earth, battery, alternator, and pre-engaged starter motor
Battery capacity	60 Ah

Alternator

Output	60 A
Regulated output voltage:	
Non-Turbo models	14.4 to 15.0 volts
Turbo models	14.1 to 14.7 volts
Minimum brush length:	
Non-Turbo models	5.5 mm (0.217 in)
Turbo models	8.0 mm (0.315 in)
Minimum slip ring diameter:	
Non-Turbo models	21.6 mm (0.850 in)
Turbo models	22.4 mm (0.882 in)
Alternator drivebelt tension deflection (power steering models):	
New belt	9 to 12 mm (0.35 to 0.47 in)
Used belt	11 to 14 mm (0.43 to 0.55 in)

Starter motor

No-load current:	
Standard type	60 A maximum
Reduction gear type	100 A maximum
Minimum commutator diameter:	
Standard type	32.0 mm (1.26 in)
Reduction gear type	29.0 mm (1.14 in)
Minimum brush length	11.0 mm (0.43 in)

Bulbs

	Wattage
Headlamp	60/55
Front parking lamp	5
Front direction indicator lamp	21
Side marker lamp	5
Rear direction indicator lamp	21
Stop/tail lamp	21/5
Reversing lamp	21
Rear fog lamp	21
Number plate lamp:	
Saloon	5
Estate	10
Interior lamp	10
Map reading lamp	2
Luggage compartment lamp:	
Saloon	3.4
Estate	10
Step illumination lamp	3.4
Glovebox lamp	3.4

Torque wrench settings

	Nm	lbf ft
Alternator:		
Mounting bolt	49	36
Pulley nut	59	44
Through-bolt	3.9	2.9
Starter motor:		
Mounting bolt	34	25
Through-bolt	6	4
Solenoid	7	5

1 General description

The system is of 12 volt negative earth type, with battery, alternator, and pre-engaged starter motor. The alternator is belt-driven from the crankshaft pulley and incorporates an integral voltage regulator.

Many of the electrical components incorporate micro-circuitry and it is important to connect the relevant wiring correctly to avoid damage. Disconnect the battery negative lead when working on these components. Disconnect the battery also when charging the battery or using electric arc-welding equipment.

2 Routine maintenance

Carry out the following procedures at the intervals given in *'Routine Maintenance'* at the beginning of the Manual.

Alternator drivebelt

1 On models *not* fitted with power steering, the alternator drivebelt also drives the water pump. Check and tension the drivebelt as for the water pump drivebelt described in Chapter 2 Section 2.

2 On power steering models the alternator is driven by a separate drivebelt. Examine the full length of the drivebelt for cracks, fraying, deterioration and oil contamination. Renew it if necessary, but if it is in good order check and if necessary adjust its tension as follows.

3 Depress the drivebelt with moderate thumb pressure midway between the alternator and crankshaft pulleys (photo). If the deflection is not as given in the Specifications, loosen the alternator pivot and adjustment bolts and swivel the alternator away from the engine until the tension is correct. On some models an adjustment stud is provided on the bottom of the alternator, and by turning the nut the correct tension can be achieved. On other models use a lever to move the alternator.

4 After making the adjustment tighten the pivot and adjustment bolts.

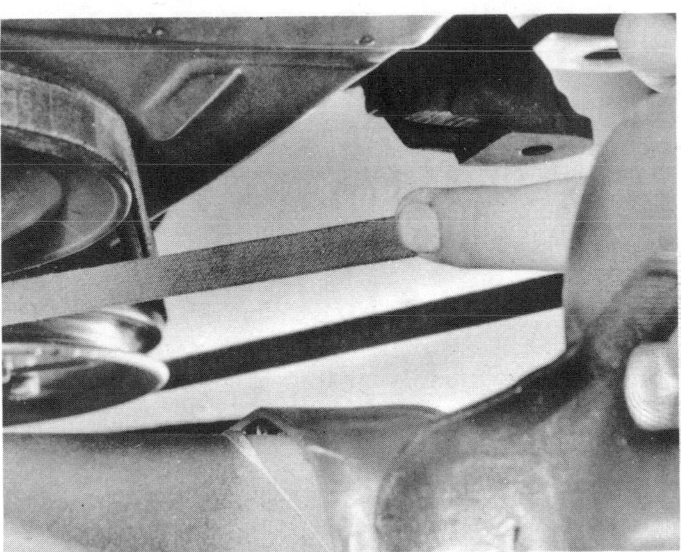

2.3 Checking the alternator drivebelt tension

3 Battery – general

1 The battery fitted as standard equipment is of maintenance-free type and under normal usage does not require checking of the electrolyte level. However the battery surfaces, particularly the top, should always be kept clean and dry to prevent possible discharging.

2 If the battery is used under severe conditions, the electrolyte level should be periodically checked. The battery case is translucent and

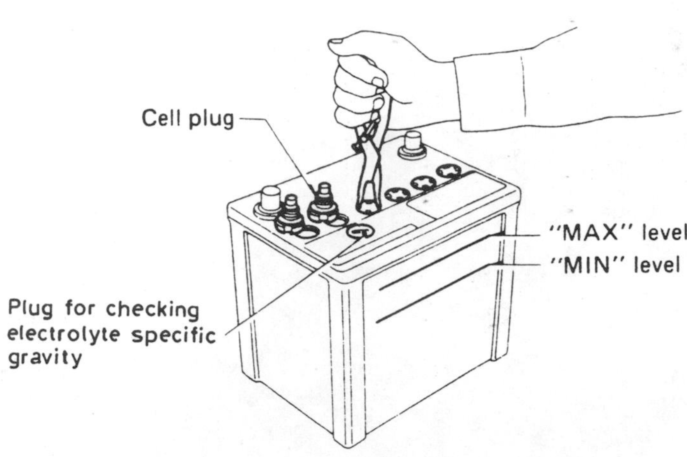

Fig. 12.1 Removing the battery cell plugs (Sec 3)

incorporates minimum and maximum level marks. If the level is low, remove the label where fitted and the cell plugs, and top up each cell with distilled water to the maximum level. Refit the cell plugs.

3 If required, the state of charge of the battery can be checked with a hydrometer. Remove the single plug from the top of the battery and draw some electroyte into the hydrometer. Compare the specific gravity readings with the following table, taking into consideration the electrolyte temperature.

Fully discharged	Electrolyte temperature	Fully charged
1.098	38°C (100°F)	1.268
1.102	32°C (90°F)	1.272
1.106	27°C (80°F)	1.276
1.110	21°C (70°F)	1.280
1.114	16°C (60°F)	1.284
1.118	10°C (50°F)	1.288
1.122	4°C (40°F)	1.292
1.126	-1.5°C (30°F)	1.296

4 If the battery requires charging, disconnect the negative lead followed by the positive lead, then connect a trickle charger and charge at 6 amps for two to five hours depending on the state of charge. When the specific gravity is in excess of 1.240, the battery is sufficiently charged for use on the car, and any additional charging will be made by the alternator.

4 Battery – removal and refitting

1 The battery is located on the left-hand side of the engine compartment (photo).

2 Pull back the covers, then disconnect the negative lead followed by the positive lead.

3 Unscrew the clamp nuts and remove the clamp.

4 Lift out the battery, keeping it level to avoid spillage of electrolyte.

5 Refitting is a reversal of removal, but clean the battery and tray, and connect the positive lead first followed by the negative lead.

5 Alternator – description and precautions

1 The alternator generates alternating current which is rectified by diodes into direct current which is needed to charge the battery.

2 Main components consist of a stator and a rotor with diode rectifier.

3 The current is generated in the stator windings with the rotor carrying the field.

4 The field brushes carry only a light current and run on slip rings.

5 The alternator is driven by a belt from the crankshaft pulley. A fan is located behind the alternator pulley for cooling purposes.

6 If there are indications that the charging system is malfunctioning in any way, care must be taken when diagnosing faults otherwise damage of a serious and expensive nature may occur to parts which are in fact quite serviceable. The following basic requirements must be observed at all times, therefore, if damage is to be prevented.

7 All alternator systems use a negative earth. Even the simple mistake of connecting the battery the wrong way round could burn out the alternator diodes quickly.

8 Before disconnecting any wires in the system the engine and ignition circuits should be switched off. This will minimise the risk of short-circuits in the system.

9 The engine must never be run with the alternator output wire (red wire on the positive terminal) disconnected.

10 Always disconnect the battery leads from the car's electrical system if an outside charging source is being used.

11 Do not use test wire connections that could move accidentally and short-circuit against nearby terminals. Short-circuits may not only blow fuses – they can also burn out diodes and transistors.

12 Always disconnect the battery cables and alternator output wires before any electric arc-welding work is done on the car body.

6 Alternator – testing

1 Ensure that the battery is fully charged. A 30v voltmeter must be available.

2 With the engine idling, place the positive probe of the voltmeter on the B terminal of the alternator and the negative probe on the L terminal. If more than 0.5v is indicated, then a fault (not in the voltage regulator circuit) is indicated in the alternator.

3 Increase the engine speed to 1500 rpm and check the voltage at the alternator 'B' terminal. If it exceeds 15.5 v, then the integral voltage regulator is faulty.

4 Remember that the ignition (charge warning) lamp must be on when the ignition is switched on and go out as soon as the engine is started. If this does not happen, check the bulb and drivebelt. If these are in order then the alternator must have an internal fault.

7 Alternator – removal and refitting

1 Disconnect the battery negative lead.

2 Disconnect the wiring from the alternator terminals (photos).

3 Loosen the pivot and adjustment bolts, swivel the alternator towards the engine and slip off the drivebelt (photo). Where applicable, loosen the adjuster nut.

4.1 Battery and clamp

7.2A Alternator with wiring attached

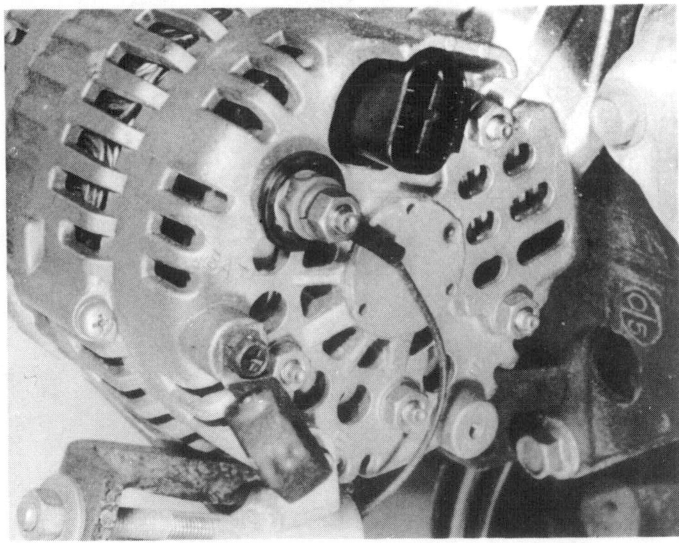
7.2B Alternator with wiring disconnected

7.3 Alternator pivot bolts (arrowed)

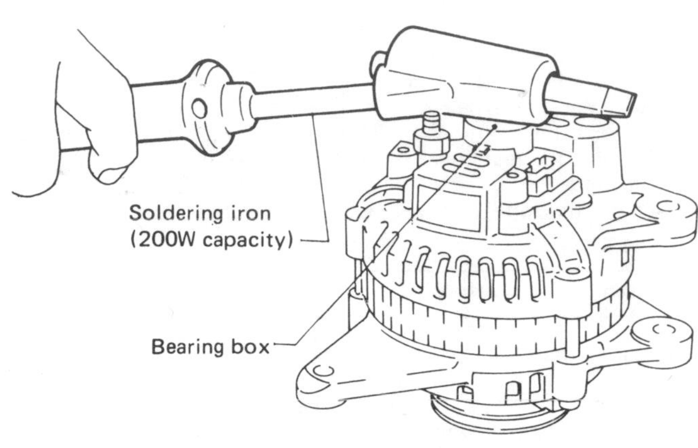

Fig. 12.2 Method of heating the alternator bearing box (Sec 8)

4 Remove the pivot and adjustment bolts and withdraw the alternator from the engine.
5 Refitting is a reversal of removal, but tension the drivebelt with reference to Section 2.

8 Alternator brushes – renewal

Note: *It is recommended that a new rear bearing is obtained before commencing work, as the original is likely to be damaged during the removal procedure.*
1 Remove the alternator as described in Section 7.
2 Mark the front and rear covers in relation to each other, then unscrew the through-bolts.
3 Using a 200 watt soldering iron, heat the rear cover in the vicinity of the bearing box (Fig. 12.2). Do not use a heat gun otherwise the diode assembly may be damaged.
4 Separate the rear cover from the front cover, allowing the brushes to ride over the rear bearing. If necessary, tap the front cover with a mallet in order to release the special half-ring retaining the rear bearing in the rear cover.
5 The brush holder is now accessible and the brush length can be checked for wear. A wear limit line is incorporated on each brush which corresponds to the minimum brush length given in the Specifications.

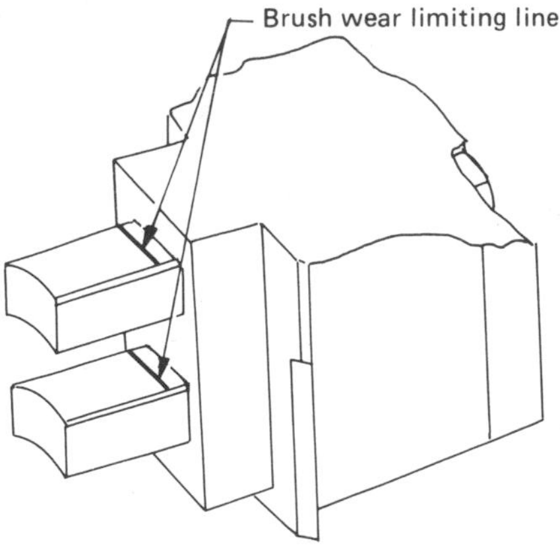

Fig. 12.3 Alternator brush wear limit line location (Sec 8)

6 Unbolt the brush holder, then unsolder the leads using the minimum amount of heat. Work quickly so that the heat from the soldering iron does not transfer to adjacent components.

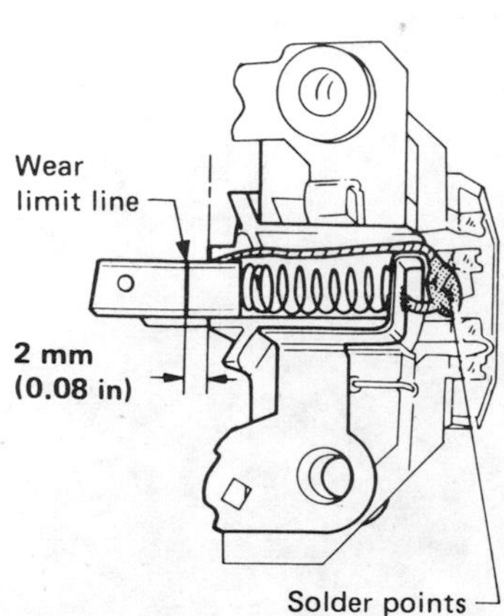

Fig. 12.4 Brush position when soldering leads (Sec 8)

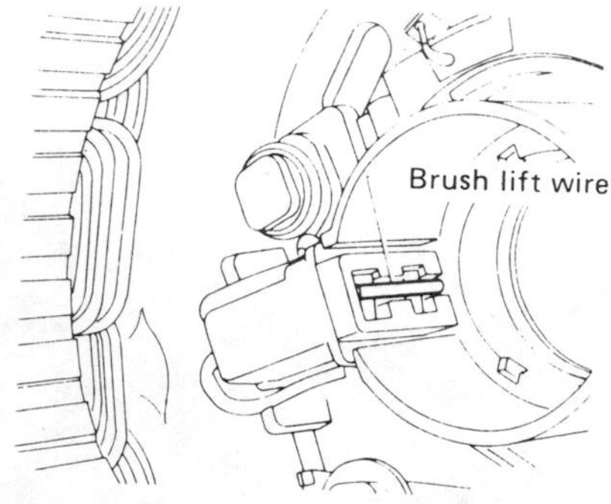

Fig. 12.5 Brush retaining wire in position before reassembling alternator (Sec 8)

7 Make sure that the new brushes slide freely in their holders, then solder the leads in position with the wear limit lines 2.0 mm (0.08 in) from the holder (Fig. 12.4). Tighten the bolts.
8 Push the brushes fully into their holders and retain while reassembling the alternator by inserting a length of soft wire through the special hole in the rear cover.
9 Locate the special half-ring in the rear bearing outer track eccentric groove, so that it protrudes by the minimum amount (Fig. 12.6).
10 Assemble the rear cover to the front cover. Insert and tighten the through-bolts.
11 Pull out the soft wire to allow the brushes to rest on the slip rings.

9 Alternator – overhaul

1 It will be found that renewal of the alternator brushes is really the only economical operation worth carrying out to an alternator. If anything more extensive requires dismantling, consider the purchase of a new or factory-reconditioned unit.

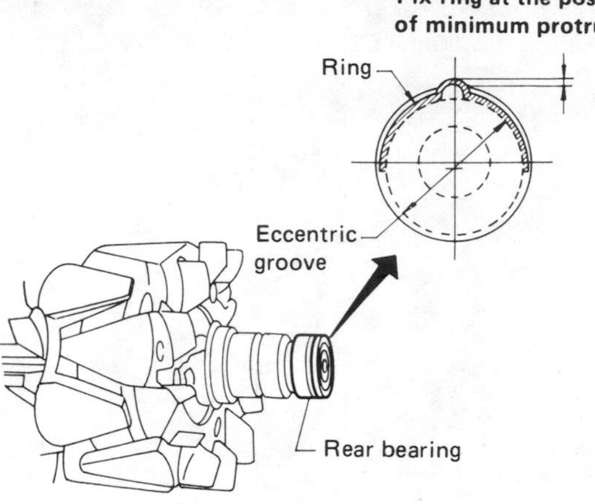

Fig. 12.6 Half-ring position before reassembling alternator (Sec 8)

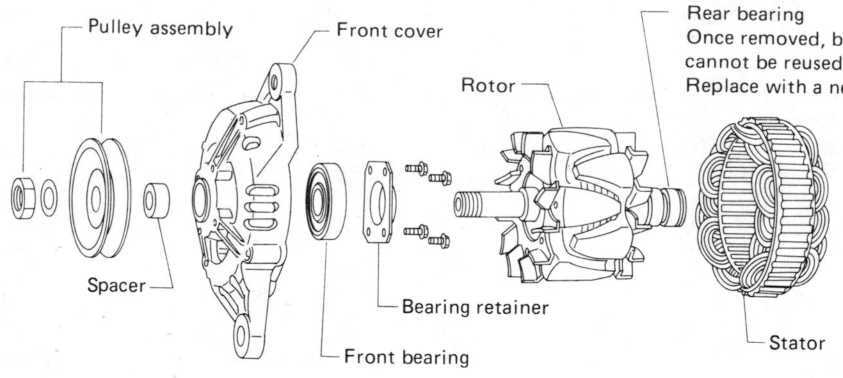

Fig. 12.7 Exploded view of the Hitachi alternator (Sec 9)

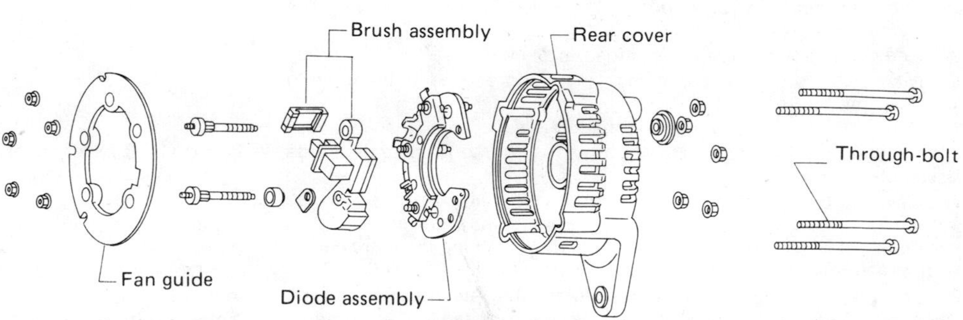

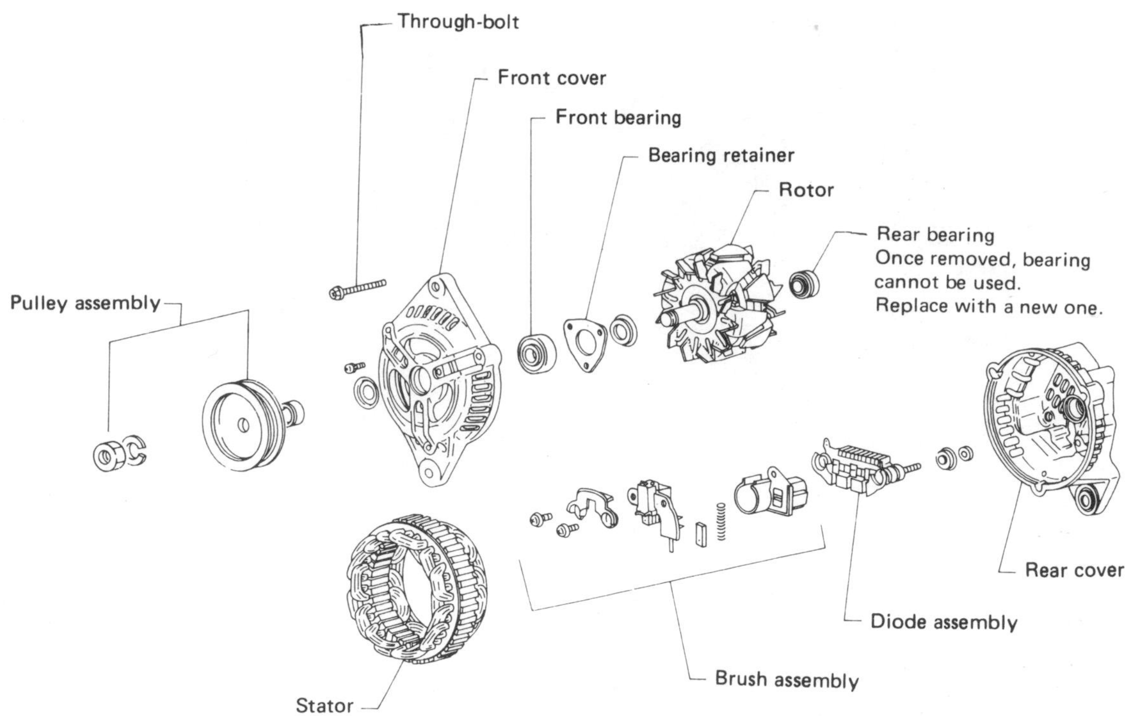

Fig. 12.8 Exploded view of the Mitsubishi alternator (Sec 9)

2 For those wishing to undertake complete dismantling, the sequence of operations is given in the following paragraphs.

3 Remove the brush holder as described in Section 8.

4 Unscrew the pulley nut. In order to prevent the rotor from rotating on some alternators, a socket is provided in the end of the rotor shaft. An Allen key can be inserted to hold the shaft still. If such a socket is not provided, place an old drivebelt in the pulley groove and grip its ends as close as possible to the pulley in the jaws of a vice, or alternatively grip the rotor in a soft-jawed vice.

5 Remove the pulley from the rotor shaft, then tap the shaft through the front cover and bearing.

6 Remove the front bearing retainer screws and withdraw the retainer and bearing.

7 Pull the rear bearing from the rotor.

8 Unscrew the nuts and separate the stator and diode assembly from the rear cover.

9 Using the minimum of heat, unsolder the diode assembly from the stator.

10 The rotor can be tested for continuity in the windings using an ohmmeter on the slip rings (Fig. 12.9). Check the windings for insulation by connecting the ohmmeter between either slip ring and the shaft (Fig. 12.10).

11 Using a micrometer, check that the diameter of the slip rings is not less than the amount given in the Specifications.

12 Similarly check the stator for continuity and insulation as shown in Figs. 12.11 and 12.12.

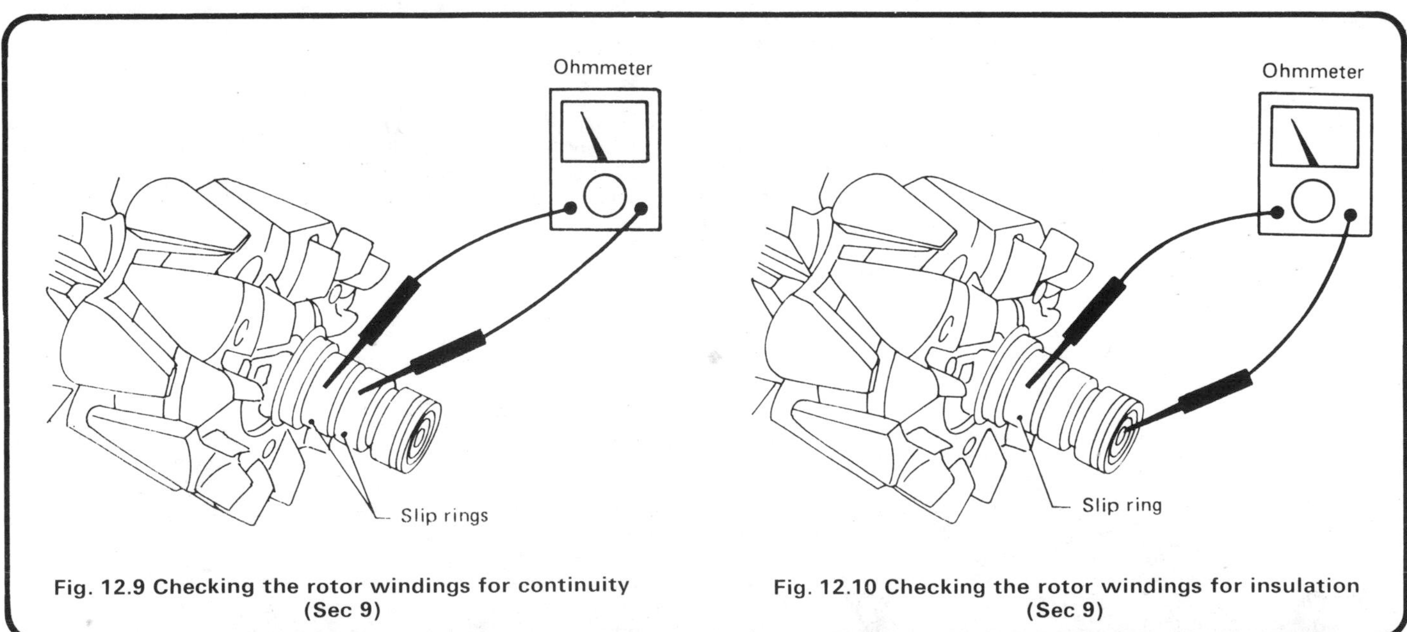

Fig. 12.9 Checking the rotor windings for continuity (Sec 9)

Fig. 12.10 Checking the rotor windings for insulation (Sec 9)

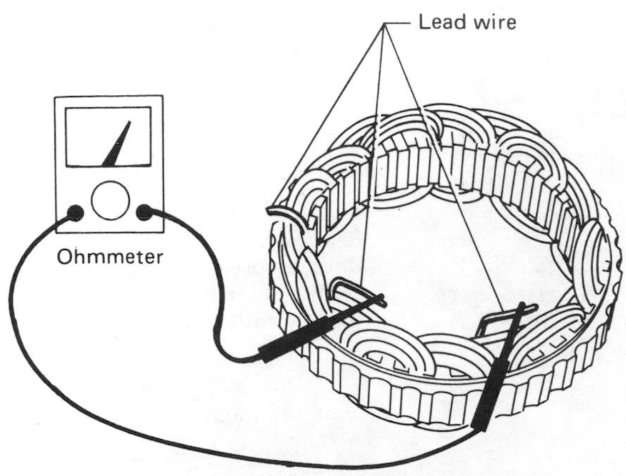

Fig. 12.11 Checking the stator windings for continuity (Sec 9)

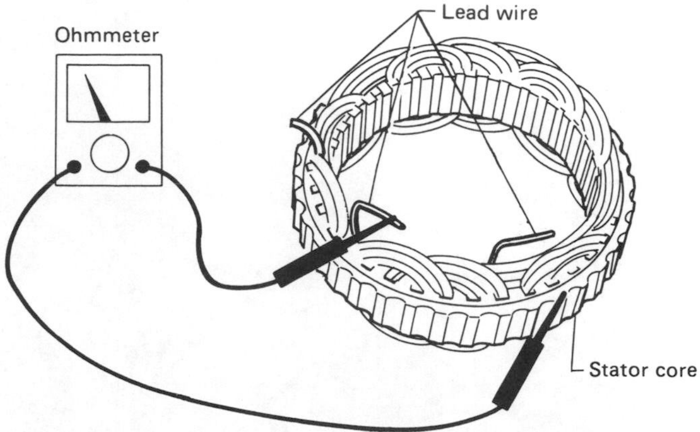

Fig. 12.12 Checking the stator windings for insulation (Sec 9)

13 Use the ohmmeter to check each diode – continuity must exist in one direction but not in the opposite direction.
14 Check the bearings for any roughness or obvious damage.
15 Renew defective or worn out components, then reassemble the alternator using a reversal of the dismantling procedure.

10 Starter motor – description and testing

1 The starter motor is of pre-engaged type, where the motor is energised after pinion engagement. Either a standard or reduction gear type is available.
2 If the starter motor does not operate, first use a voltmeter to check that battery voltage is available at the solenoid 'B' terminal. If not, faulty wiring exists between the battery and starter motor.
3 Disconnect the battery negative lead and the motor lead from the solenoid 'M' terminal.
4 Connect an ohmmeter between the solenoid 'S' terminal and the solenoid body. Continuity should exist.
5 Connect the ohmmeter between the solenoid 'S' and 'M' terminals. Continuity should exist.
6 Renew the solenoid if the tools in paragraphs 4 and 5 prove negative. If they prove positive but the starter motor still does not operate, remove the unit and carry out the overhaul procedure described in Section 12.

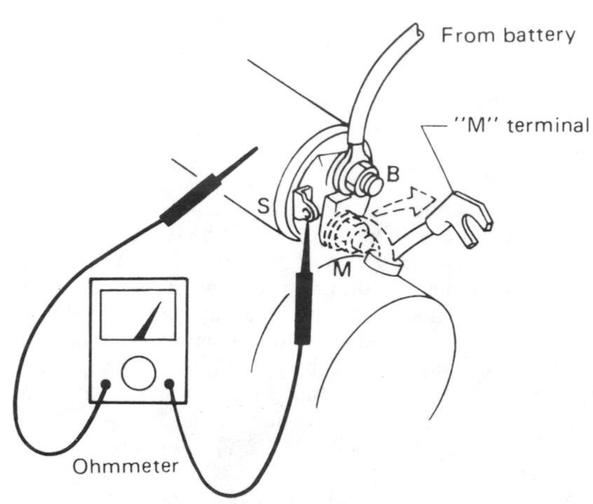

Fig. 12.13 Checking the starter solenoid windings for continuity (Sec 10)

11 Starter motor – removal and refitting

1 Disconnect the battery negative lead.
2 Remove the air cleaner and/or inlet ducting according to model.
3 Disconnect the battery and switch leads from the 'B' and 'S' terminals on the starter motor solenoid.
4 Unscrew the mounting bolts and withdraw the starter motor upwards from the transmission housing.
5 Refitting is a reversal of removal.

12 Starter motor – overhaul

1 With the unit removed from the vehicle, clean away external dirt.
2 Disconnect the lead from the solenoid 'M' terminal and then extract the two screws which hold the solenoid to the drive end housing. Withdraw the solenoid whilst unlocking it from the shift lever (photos).

Standard (non-reduction gear) type

3 Prise off the small centre cap from the rear cover (photo).
4 Prise off the E-ring and remove the thrust washers (photo).
5 Unscrew the through-bolts and the screws retaining the brush holder to the rear cover, then withdraw the rear cover (photo).
6 Lift the springs, release the two brushes from the yoke, and withdraw the brush holder from the armature.
7 Withdraw the yoke, armature and shift lever.
8 If the starter drive must be removed, tap the pinion stop collar down the shaft to expose the circlip. Remove the circlip, the stop collar and pull the drive assembly from the armature shaft.

Reduction gear type

9 Mark the gear case, yoke and rear cover in relation to each other.
10 Unscrew the through-bolts and withdraw the rear cover.
11 Separate the yoke, armature and brush holder from the gear case.
12 Disconnect the two brushes from the yoke, and remove the brush holder.
13 Lift the armature from the yoke.
14 Remove the shift lever and dust covers.
15 Unbolt the bearing retainer and remove the clutch assembly and shaft from the gear case.

12.2A Removing starter motor solenoid

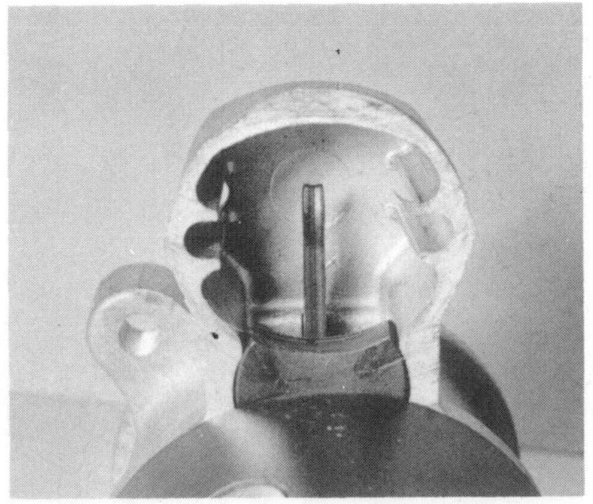

12.2B Starter motor shift lever

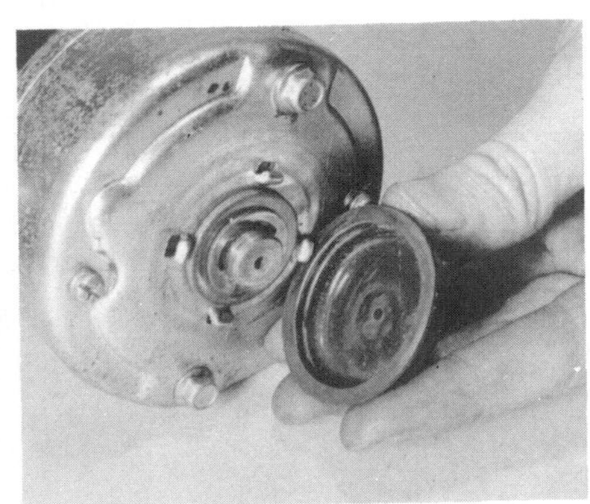

12.3 Removing rear cover cap

12.4 Starter motor E-ring and thrust washers

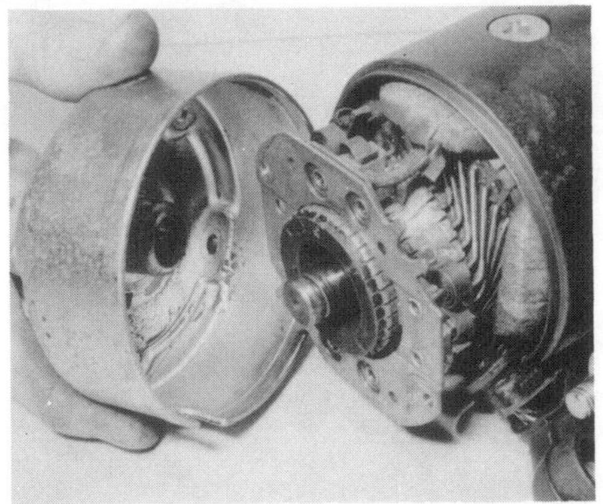

12.5 Removing starter motor rear cover

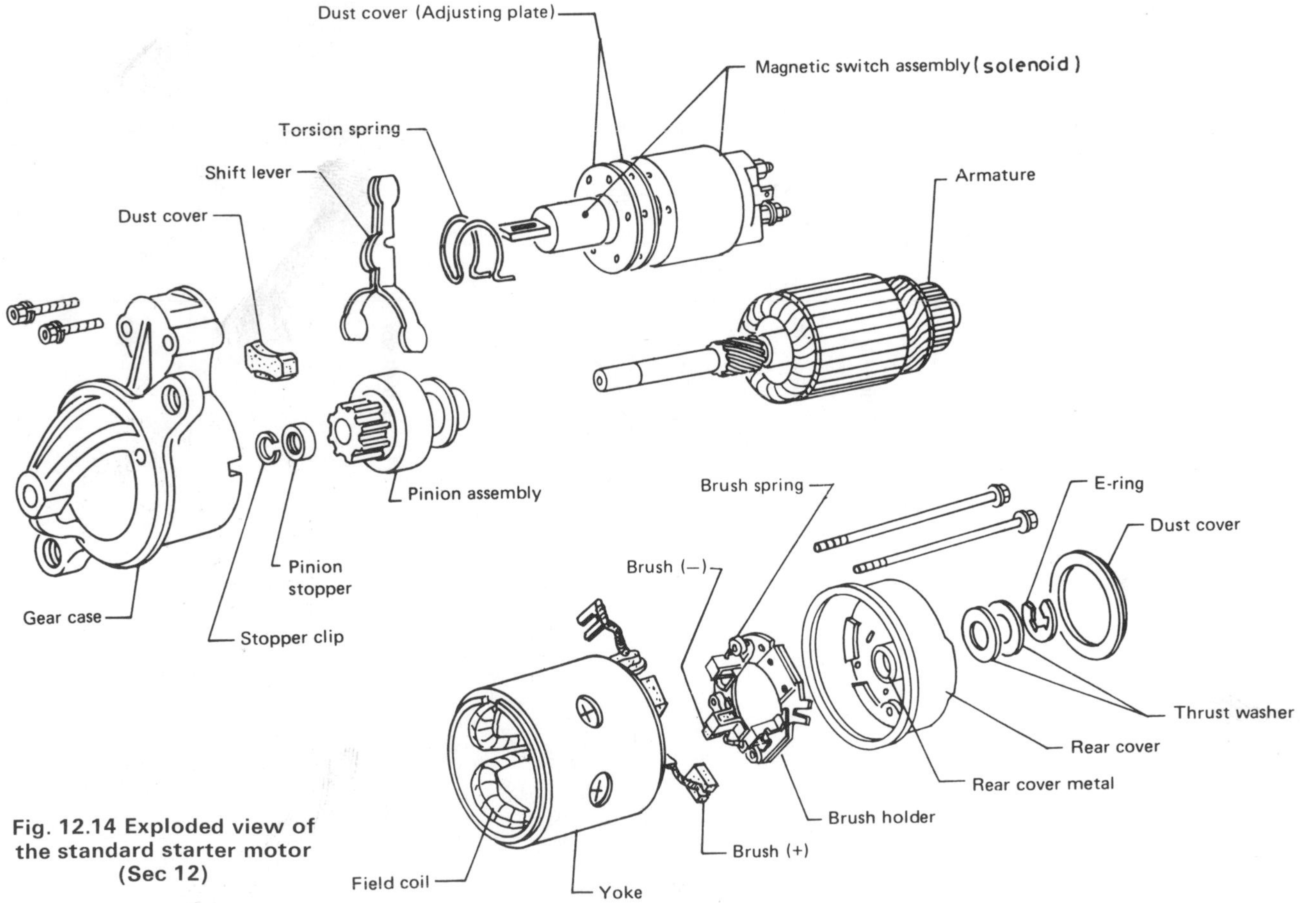

Dust cover (Adjusting plate)
Magnetic switch assembly (solenoid)
Torsion spring
Shift lever
Armature
Dust cover
Pinion assembly
Pinion stopper
Gear case
Stopper clip
Brush spring
E-ring
Dust cover
Brush (–)
Thrust washer
Rear cover
Rear cover metal
Brush holder
Brush (+)
Field coil
Yoke

Fig. 12.14 Exploded view of the standard starter motor (Sec 12)

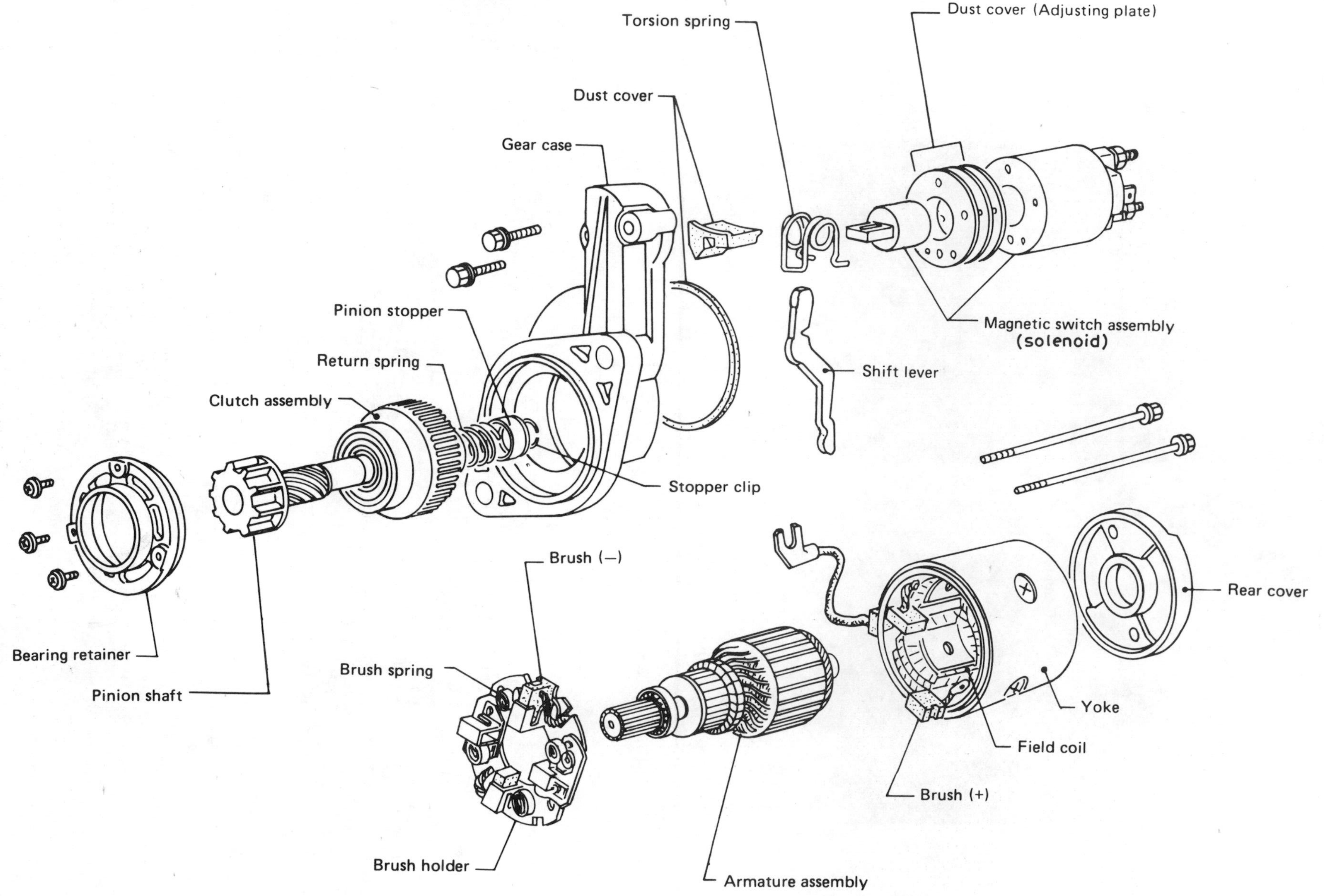

Fig. 12.15 Exploded view of the reduction gear type starter motor (Sec 12)

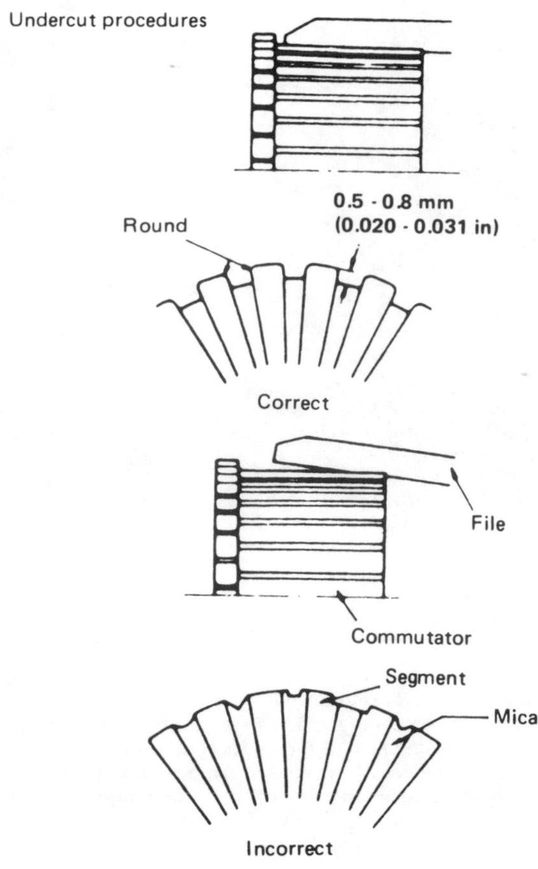

Fig. 12.16 Starter motor commutator undercutting diagram (Sec 12)

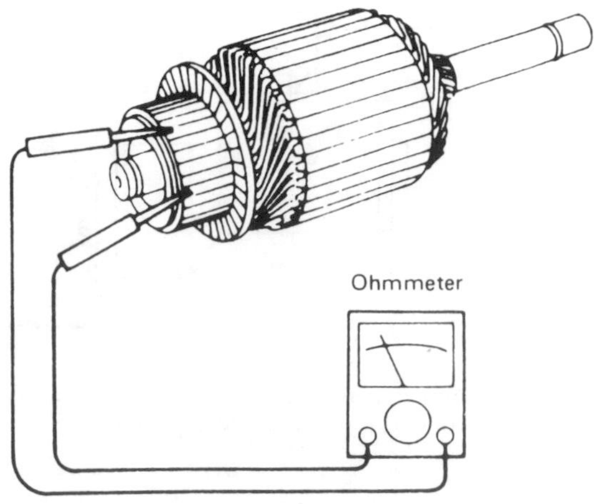

Fig. 12.17 Checking armature windings for continuity (Sec 12)

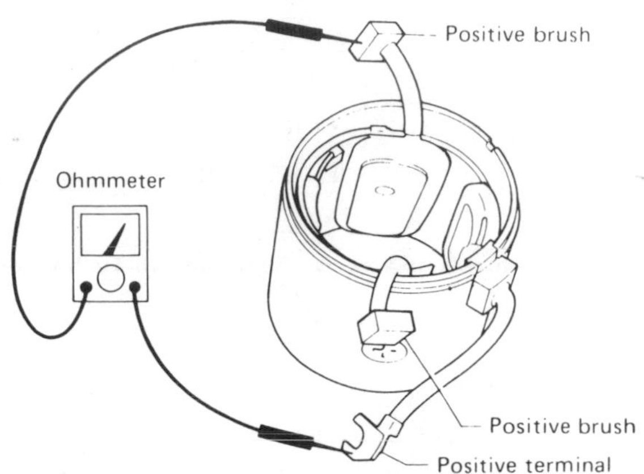

Fig. 12.18 Checking field coils for continuity (Sec 12)

All types

16 Inspect all components for wear and damage and renew as necessary.

17 If the commutator is discoloured, clean it with a fuel moistened rag or burnish with fine glasspaper.

18 If the mica separators of the commutator are not below the copper segments then they must be undercut as shown in Fig. 12.16 using a hacksaw or other suitable tool.

19 The armature may be tested if an ohmmeter is available by placing the probes on adjacent segments and working round the commutator. If there is no continuity, renew the armature.

20 Now check for insulation between each segment of the commutator in sequence and the armature shaft. Continuity here will indicate the need to renew the armature.

21 Check the brushes for wear. If they have worn down to 11.0 mm (0.43 in) or less then they must be renewed. When unsoldering the old brushes and soldering the new ones in place, work quickly and grip the brush lead with a pair of pliers to act as a heat sink and so prevent heat travelling down to the field coil. Take great care not to allow solder to run down the brush lead or its flexibility will be ruined.

22 The field coils can be checked if the ohmmeter is connected between the (+) terminal of the field coil and a positive brush. If there is no continuity, renew the field coil. This is a job best left to your dealer or auto-electrician as a pressure screwdriver will be needed.

23 Now check the insulation between the field coil positive terminal and the yoke. If continuity exists, then the field coils must be renewed.

24 Check that the drive pinion clutch is operating correctly. It should lock when turned against the drive direction and turn smoothly in the reverse direction.

25 Reassembly is a reversal of dismantling. Apply a smear of grease to the shift lever and drive pinion friction surfaces, to the armature shaft bushes and to the solenoid plunger.

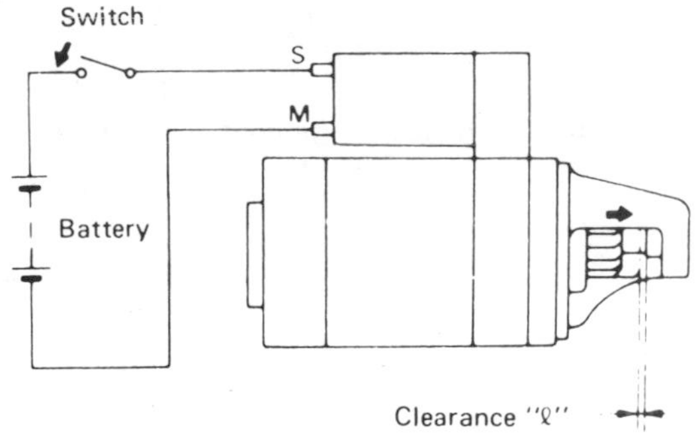

Fig. 12.19 Checking the pinion clearance dimension on the standard starter motor (Sec 12)

Clearances = 0.3 to 2.5 mm (0.012 to 0.098 in)

26 With the starter motor reassembled, but with the lead disconnected from the 'M' terminal, energise the solenoid by connecting a 12 volt supply to the 'S' and 'M' terminals. Check that the pinion clearance (standard type) or movement (reduction type) is as specified (Figs. 12.19 and 12.20). If not, change the thickness of the plates fitted between the solenoid and gear case as required.
Reconnect the lead to the 'M' terminal on completion.

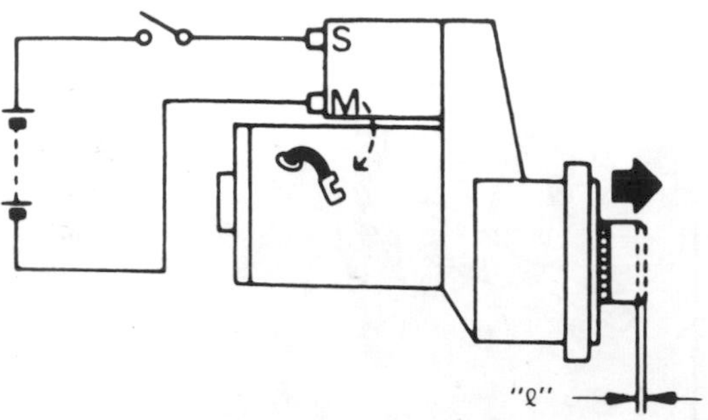

Fig. 12.20 Checking the pinion movement dimension on the reduction type startor motor (Sec 12)

Movement = 0.3 to 1.5 mm (0.012 to 0.059 in)

AIR CON	BLOWER	ROOM LAMP CLOCK	STOP LAMP	HAZARD	HORN	RAD FAN MOTOR	RR DEFOGGER	METER	TURN SIGNAL TRANSAXLE
15A	15A	10A	10A	10A	10A	20A	20A	10A	10A
ACCESSORY			LIGHT		BATTERY			IGNITION	
15A	15A	15A	10A	10A	10A	15A	15A	15A	
H/L CLEANAR	CIG LIGHTER	WIPER WASHER	AUDIO ANTENNA	TAIL LAMP RH	TAIL LAMP LH	HEAD LAMP RH	HEAD LAMP LH	ENG CONTROL	

USE SPECIFIED FUSES ONLY

Fig. 12.21 Typical fuse arrangement for non-Turbo models (Sec 13)

AIR CON	BLOWER	ROOM LAMP CLOCK	STOP LAMP	HAZARD	HORN	RAD FAN MOTOR	RR DEFOGGER	METER	TURN SIGNAL TRANSAXLE
15A	15A	10A	10A	10A	10A	20A	20A	10A	10A
ACCESSORY			LIGHT		BATTERY			IGNITION	
15A	15A	15A	10A	10A	10A	15A	15A	10A	10A
H/L CLEANER	CIG LIGHTER	WIPER WASHER	AUDIO ANTENNA	TAIL LAMP RH	TAIL LAMP LH	HEAD LAMP RH	HEAD LAMP LH	ENG CONTROL	FUEL PUMP

USE SPECIFIED FUSES ONLY

Fig. 12.22 Typical fuse arrangement for Turbo models (Sec 13)

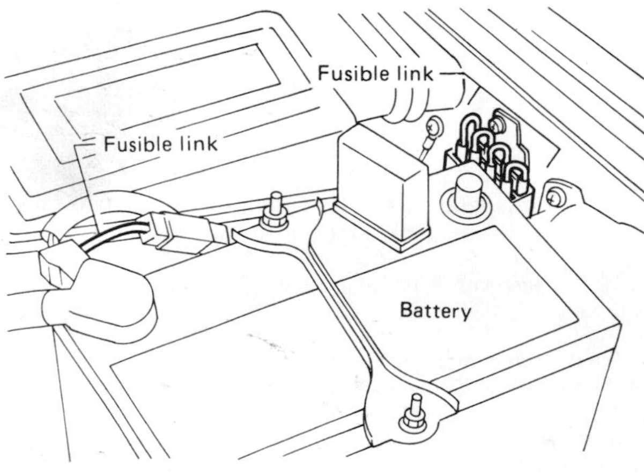

Fig. 12.23 Showing fusible link location (Sec 13)

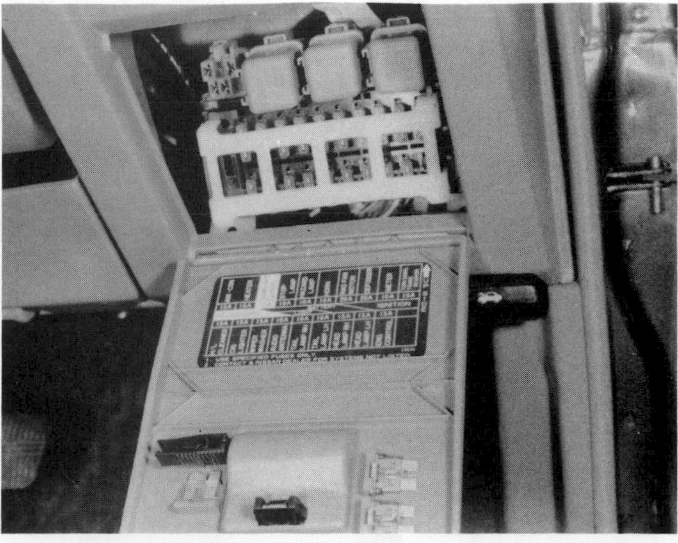

13.1 Fuse block location

13 Fuses and fusible links

Fuses

1 The fuse block is located on the right-hand side of the facia. Pull open the cover for access to the fuses – details of the circuits protected are given on the inside face of the cover (photo).

2 A plastic fuse holder is provided to remove and fit the fuses.

3 Always renew a fuse with one of the same rating, and if it blows again, trace the fault in the associated circuit.

4 Typical fuse arrangements are shown in Figs. 12.21 and 12.22.

Fusible links

5 The fusible links are located adjacent to the battery positive terminal, and the protected circuits can be determined from the wiring diagrams at the end of this Chapter according to model.

6 Should a fusible link melt this will probably be due to a major short circuit, rectify immediately. Never bind the leads of the fusible link with insulating tape or attempt a makeshift repair, only renew.

14 Relays and circuit breakers

1 The main relays are located on the right-hand side of the engine compartment or on the fuse box imside the car (Figs. 12.24 and

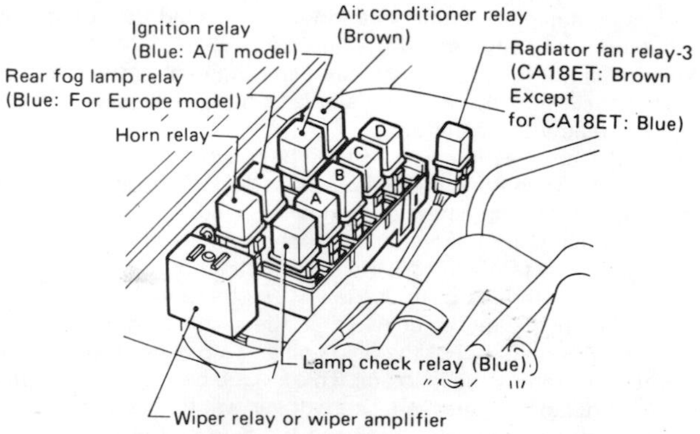

Fig. 12.24 Relays located in the engine compartment (Sec 14)

A Radiator fan relay (CA18ET) or emission relay (except CA18ET)
B Radiator fan relay
C EGI relay (CA18ET) or radiator fan relay (Except CA18ET)
D EGI relay (CA18ET)

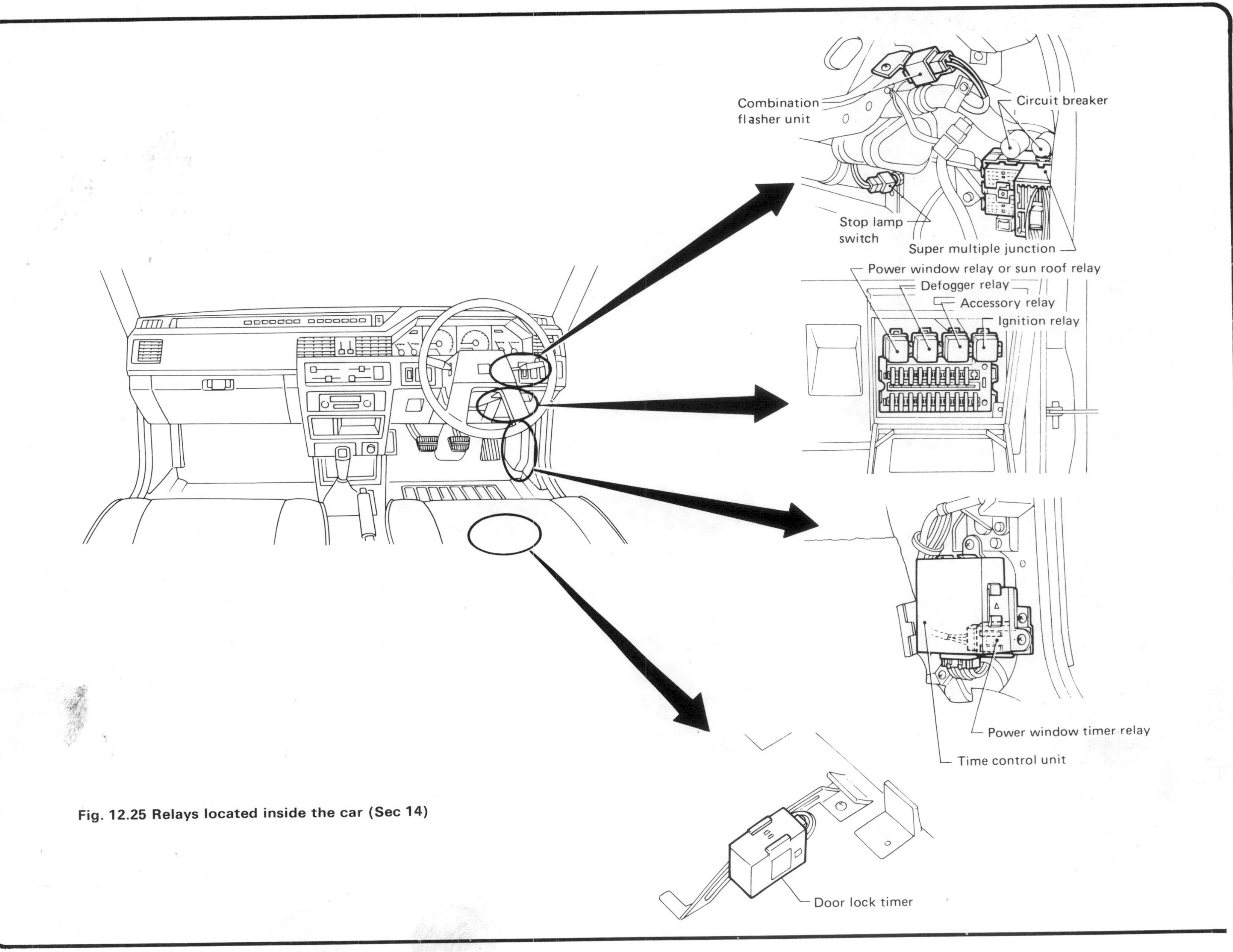

Fig. 12.25 Relays located inside the car (Sec 14)

14.1A Removing relay cover

14.1B Removing a relay

14.1C Wiper relay location

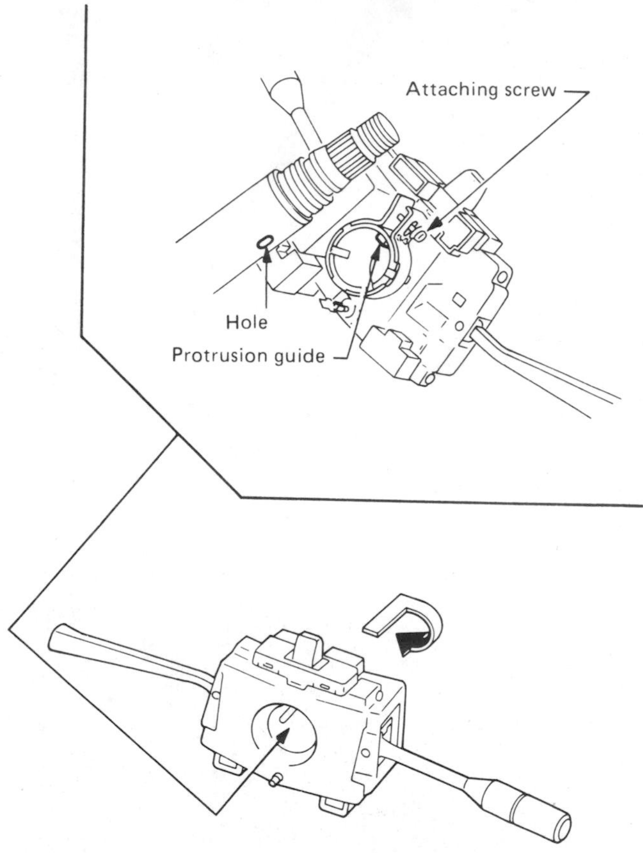

Fig. 12.26 Steering column combination switch removal (Sec 15)

12.25). The small relays are removed by pulling them from the multi-pin connector (photos).

2 On Turbo models, the boost sensor relay is located on the left-hand side of the bulkhead.

3 The combination flasher unit is located beneath the right-hand side of the facia.

4 The door lock relay is located beneath the driver's seat.

5 Circuit breakers are provided for the door lock, power window, and sun roof circuits.

6 A stop and tail lamp sensor is located within the luggage compartment.

15 Steering column combination switches – removal and refitting

1 Disconnect the battery negative lead.

2 Remove the screws and withdraw the top and bottom shrouds from the steering column.

3 The lighting or wiper and washer switches can be removed separately, however if it is required to remove the switch base, the steering wheel must first be removed (Chapter 10).

4 Disconnect the appropriate wiring, then remove the screws and withdraw the switch from the base (photos).

5 To remove the switch base, loosen the clamp screw, then push the base down, turn it half a turn, and withdraw it from the top of the steering column.

6 Refitting is a reversal of removal, but make sure that the pip on the base engages the hole in the column.

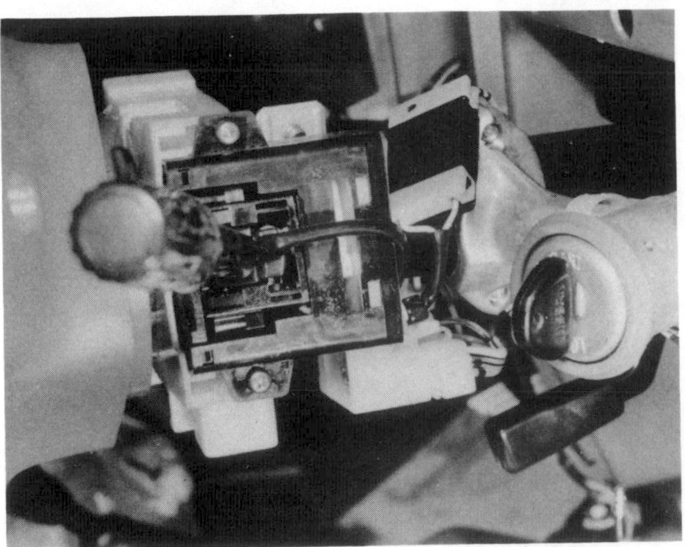
15.4A Light switch location

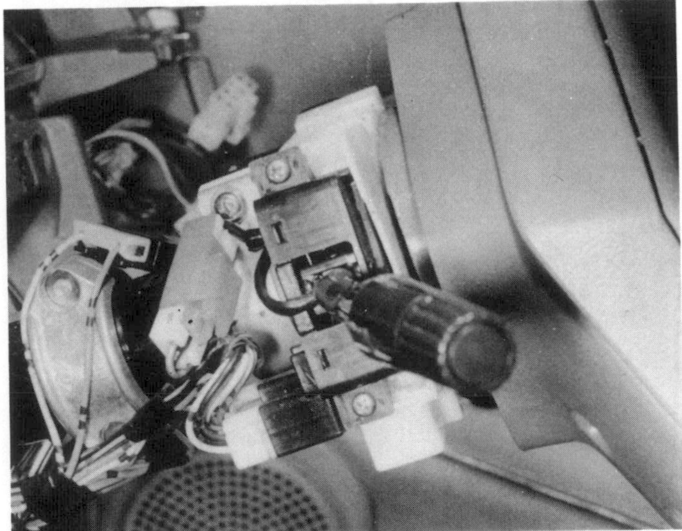
15.4B Wiper/washer switch location

16 Facia switches – removal and refitting

1 Disconnect the battery negative lead.
2 Prise out the switch (photo). If difficulty is experienced it will be necessary to push the switch from the rear, after removing the instrument panel or small facia panel.
3 Disconnect the wiring.
4 Refitting is a reversal of removal.

16.2 Removing a facia switch

17 Courtesy light switch – removal and refitting

1 These plunger type switches are located at the base of the centre pillar by means of a single screw.
2 Extract the screw and withdraw the switch (photos).
3 If the leads are to be disconnected from the switch, tape them to the bodywork to prevent them from slipping inside the pillar.
4 It is recommended that petroleum jelly is applied to the switch before fitting as a means of reducing corrosion.
5 A similar switch is used for the luggage compartment lamp.

17.2A Extract the screw ...

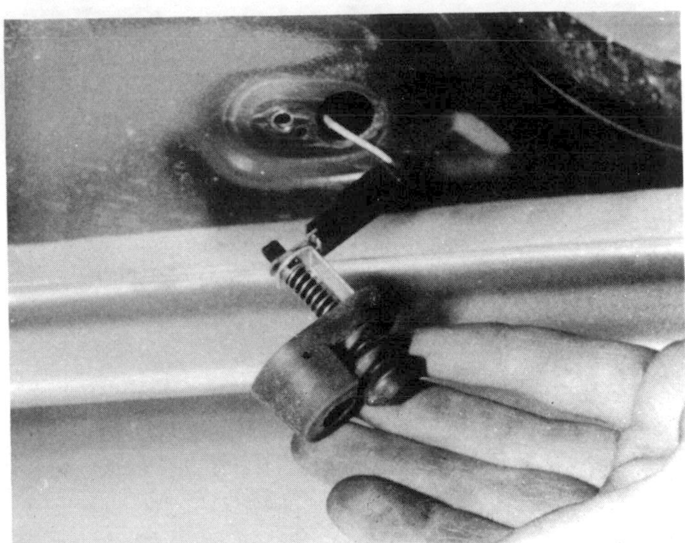
17.2B ... and withdraw the courtesy light switch

18 Handbrake warning switch – removal and refitting

1 Remove the centre console as described in Chapter 11.
2 Disconnect the wiring, then unbolt the switch from the handbrake base (photo).
3 Refitting is a reversal of removal.

19 Cigar lighter – removal and refitting

1 Disconnect the battery negative lead.
2 Remove the ash tray.
3 Remove the lower surround mounting screws and release the surround from the upper pawls. Withdraw the surround and disconnect the wiring from the cigar lighter and switches.
4 Detach the cigar lighter illumination lamp (photo).
5 Note the terminal position, then unscrew the nut and remove the terminal and cover (photos).
6 Withdraw the cigar lighter from the surround (photos).
7 Refitting is a reversal of removal.

18.2 Handbrake warning switch

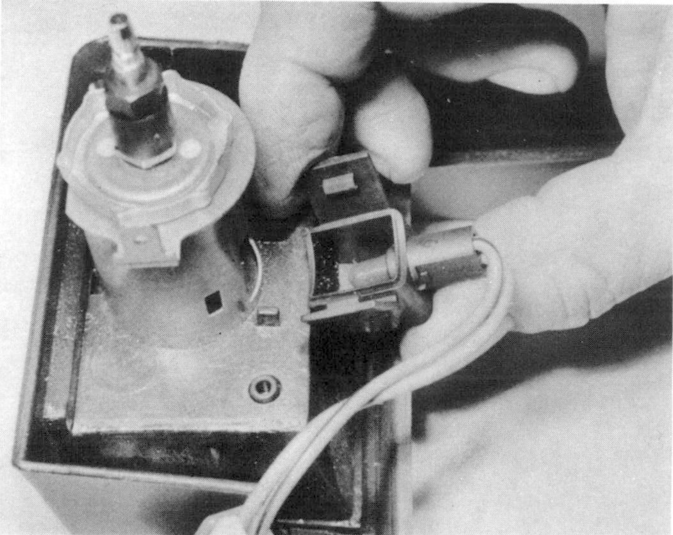

19.4 Cigar lighter illumination lamp

19.5A Showing nut and terminal on cigar lighter

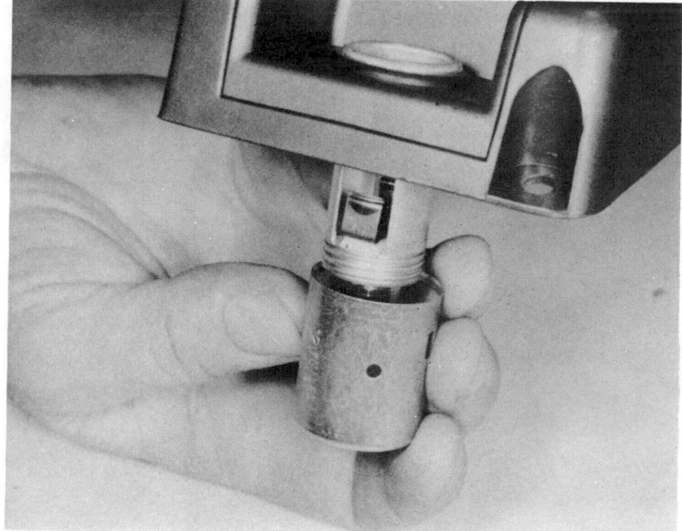

19.5B Removing the cover

19.6A Withdraw the cigar lighter from the surround

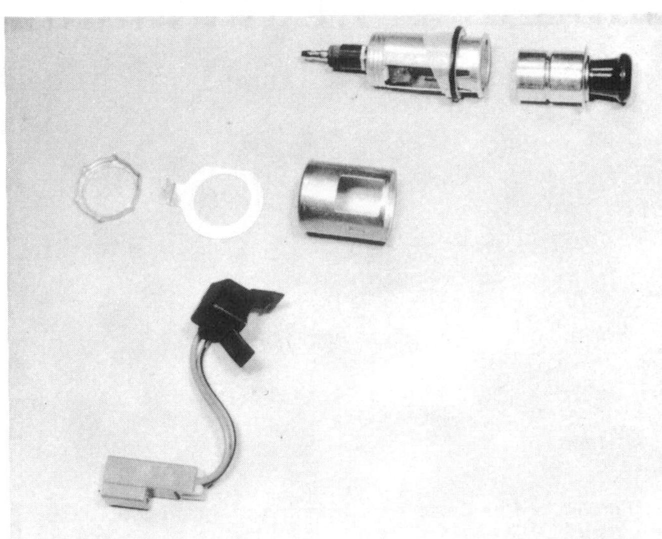
19.6B Cigar lighter components

20 Ignition switch – removal and refitting

The ignition switch forms an integral part of the steering column lock and cannot be removed separately. The procedure for removing and refitting the lock is given in Chapter 10, Section 18.

21 Headlamp bulb – renewal

1 Working in the engine compartment, disconnect the wiring from the rear of the headlamp bulb (photo).
2 Pull off the rubber cap, noting that the drain hole is at the bottom (photo).
3 Unhook and release the spring retainer (photo).
4 Withdraw the bulb and fit the new one without touching the glass (photo). If the glass is touched, carefully wipe clean with a soft cloth and methylated spirit.
5 Refit the spring retainer.
6 Refit the rubber cap with the word 'TOP' uppermost.
7 Reconnect the wiring.

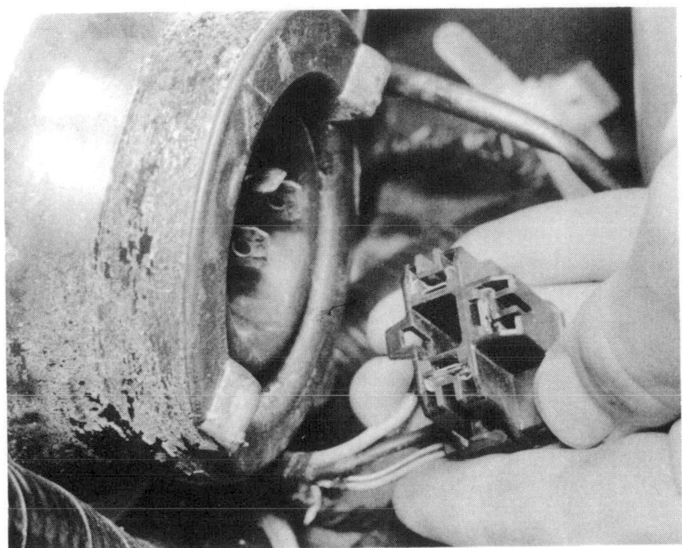
21.1 Disconnect the headlamp wiring ...

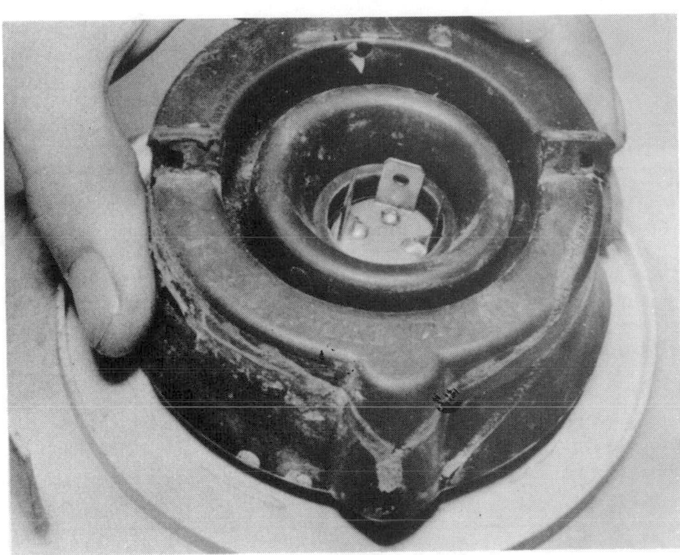
21.2 ... pull off the rubber cap ...

21.3 ... unhook the retainer ...

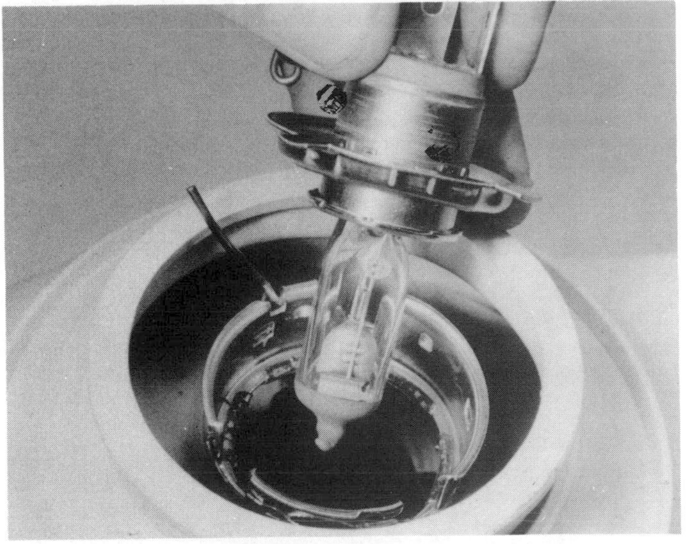
21.4 ... and remove the headlamp bulb

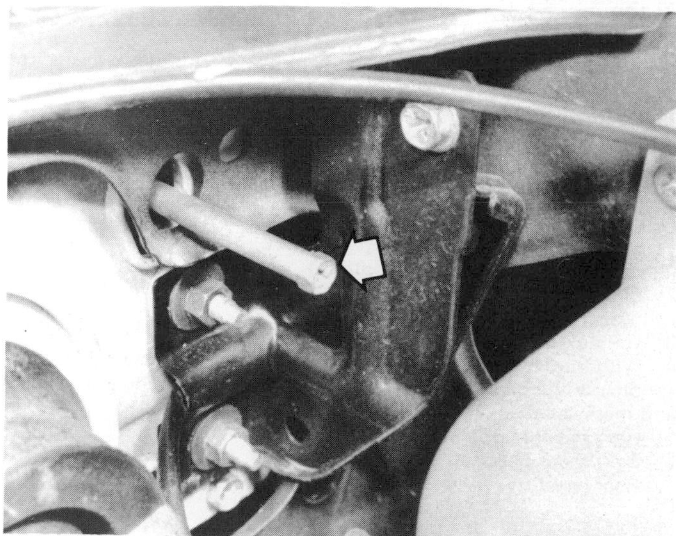

22.1 Long adjusting knob for headlamp beam

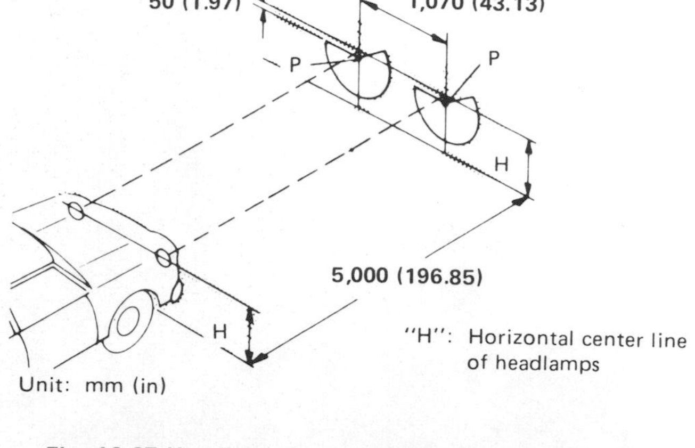

Fig. 12.27 Headlamp beam setting diagram (Sec 22)

22 Headlamp beam – adjustment

1 The headlamp beams are adjusted by the adjusting knobs on the rear of the headlamps. The long knobs are for horizontal adjustment, and the short knobs for vertical adjustment (photo).
2 It is recommended that headlamp adjustment is left to your dealer or service station where optical setting equipment will be available. In an emergency however, adjust in the following way.
3 During the hours of darkness set the vehicle square to, and 5.0 m (16.4 ft) from a wall or screen.
4 Mark the wall as shown in Fig. 12.27.
5 Switch the headlamps on main beam and adjust so that the brightest spots of the light pattern coincide with the marks made on the wall.

23 Exterior lamp bulbs – renewal

Front parking lamp

1 Remove the front headlamp unit (Section 25).
2 Twist and remove the bulbholder from the parking lamp (photo).
3 Pull out the wedge type bulb.

Front direction indicator lamp

4 Extract the two screws and remove the lens (photo).
5 Depress and twist the bayonet type bulb (photo).

Front side marker lamp

6 Twist the lamp anti-clockwise and remove it.
7 Twist and remove the bulbholder (photo).
8 Pull out the wedge type bulb.

Rear combination lamp (Saloon)

9 Release the clips and withdraw the lamp from inside the luggage compartment (photo).
10 Depress and twist the bayonet type bulb.

Rear combination lamp (Estate)

11 Extract the two screws and remove the lens.
12 Depress and twist the bayonet type bulb.

Number plate lamp (Saloon)

13 From inside the luggage compartment, twist the lamp anti-clockwise and remove it (photo).

23.2 Removing parking lamp bulbholder

23.4 Removing front direction indicator lamp lens

23.5 Removing front direction indicator lamp bulb

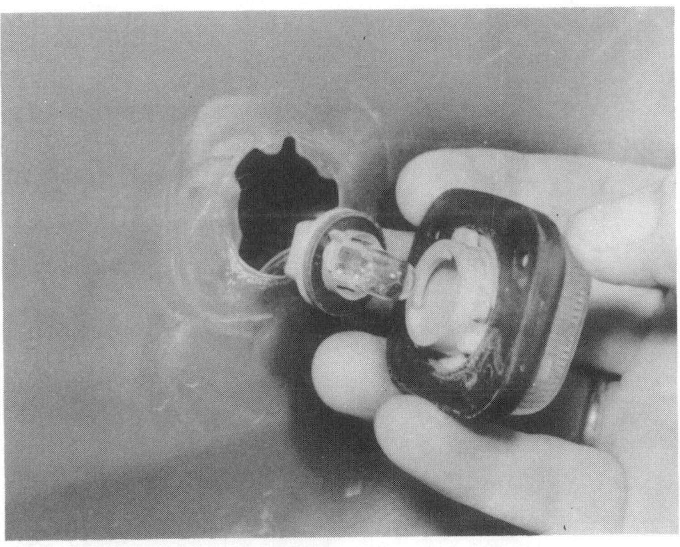

23.7 Removing front side marker lamp bulbholder

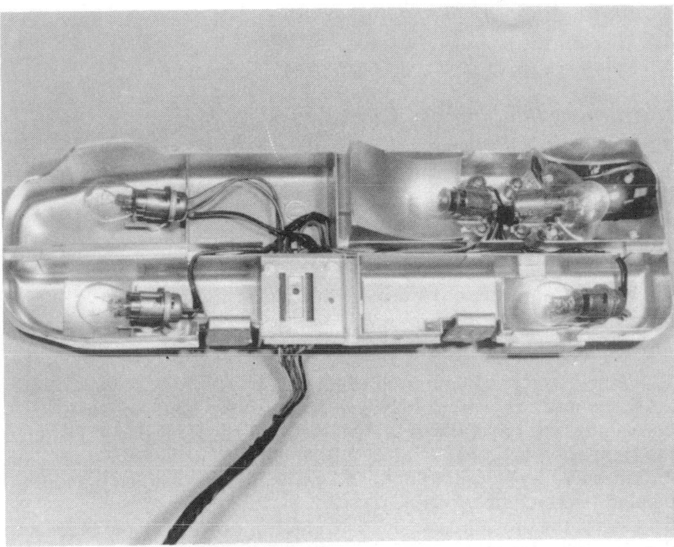

23.9 Rear combination lamp holder

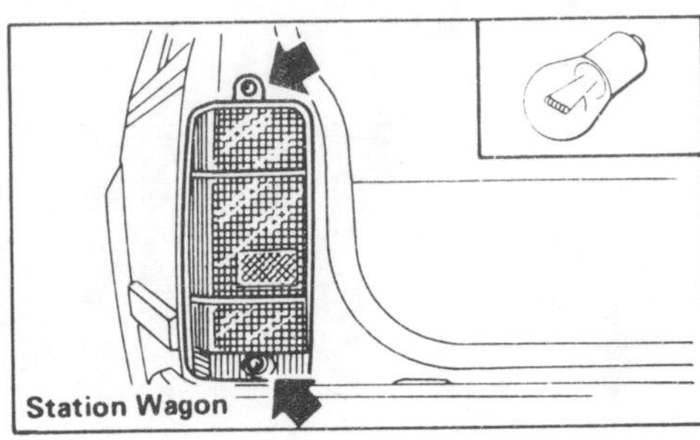

Fig. 12.28 Rear combination lamp bulb removal on Estate models (Sec 23)

14 Twist the bulbholder from the lamp and pull out the wedge type bulb (photo).

Number plate lamp (Estate)

15 Extract the two screws and remove the lens.
16 Depress and twist the bayonet type bulb.

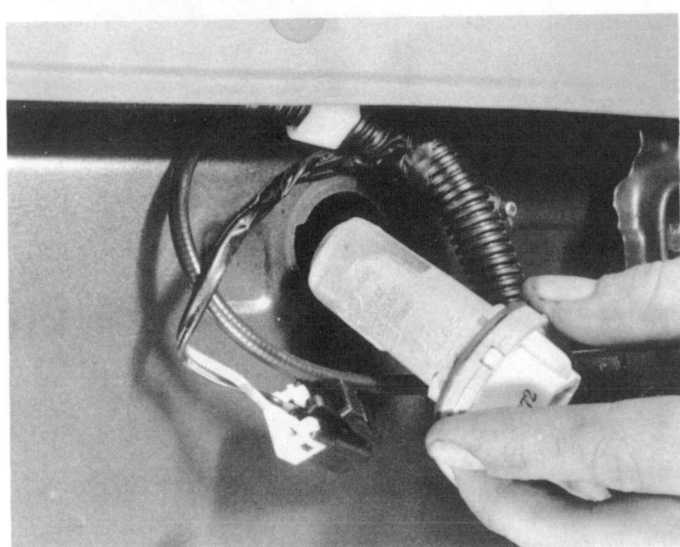

23.13 Remove the number plate lamp ...

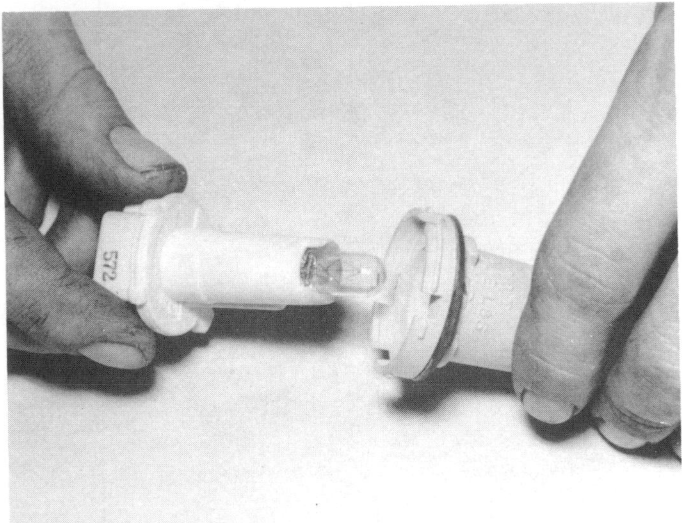

23.14 ... and twist off the bulbholder

Fig. 12.29 Number plate lamp bulb removal on Estate models (Sec 23)

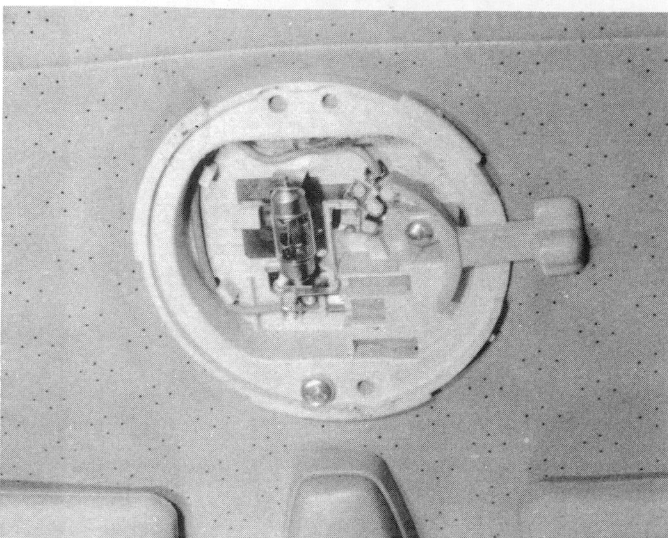

24.1 Interior lamp with lens removed

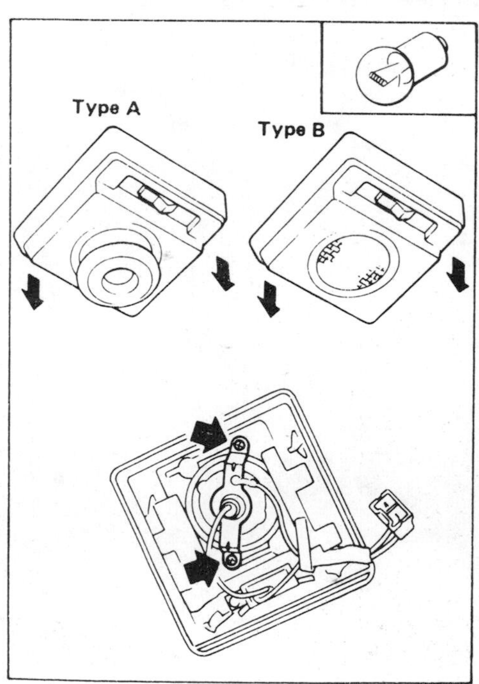

Fig. 12.30 Map reading lamp bulb removal (Sec 24)

Rear foglamp

17 Extract the two screws and remove the lens.
18 Depress and twist the bayonet type bulb.

24 Interior lamp bulbs – renewal

Interior lamp

1 Remove the lamp lens by twisting it anti-clockwise (round type) (photo) or prising it off (square type).
2 Pull the festoon type bulb from its spring contacts.

Map reading lamp

3 Prise the lamp from the roof.
4 Remove the two screws to release the bulbholder.
5 Depress and twist the bayonet type bulb.

Step illumination lamp

6 Extract the two screws and remove the lens.
7 Pull the festoon type bulb from its spring contacts.

Luggage compartment lamp (Saloon)

8 Twist the lens anti-clockwise from the bulbholder (photo).
9 Pull out the wedge type bulb.

Luggage compartment lamp (Estate)

10 Prise off the lamp lens.
11 Pull the festoon type bulb from its spring contacts.

Instrument illumination and warning lamps

12 Remove the instrument panel as described in Section 27.
13 Twist the bulbholder anti-clockwise from the rear of the instrument panel (photos).
14 Pull out the wedge type bulb.

25 Headlamp and rear lamp – removal and refitting

Headlamp

1 Remove the headlamp bulb (Section 21)
2 Disconnect the wiring from the front parking lamp (photo).
3 Remove the cross -head screws securing the front parking lamp to the front wing (photo).
4 Unscrew the mounting nuts and withdraw the headlamp and front parking lamp together (photo).
5 Extract the upper screws holding the front parking lamp bracket to the headlamp (photo).

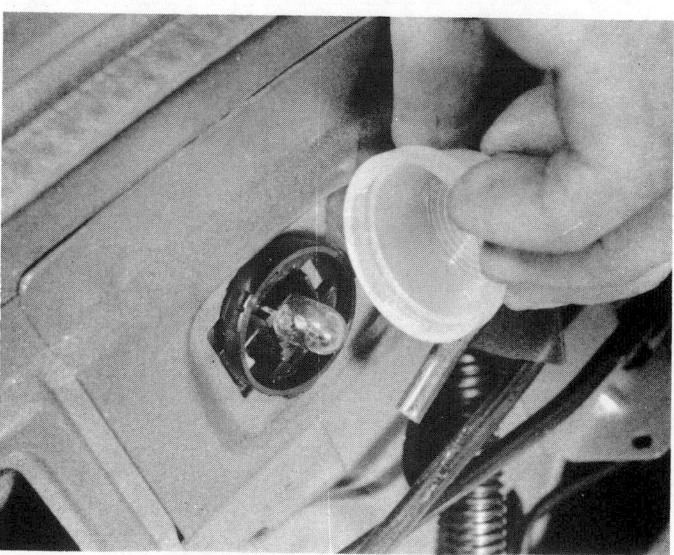

24.8 Removing luggage compartment lamp lens

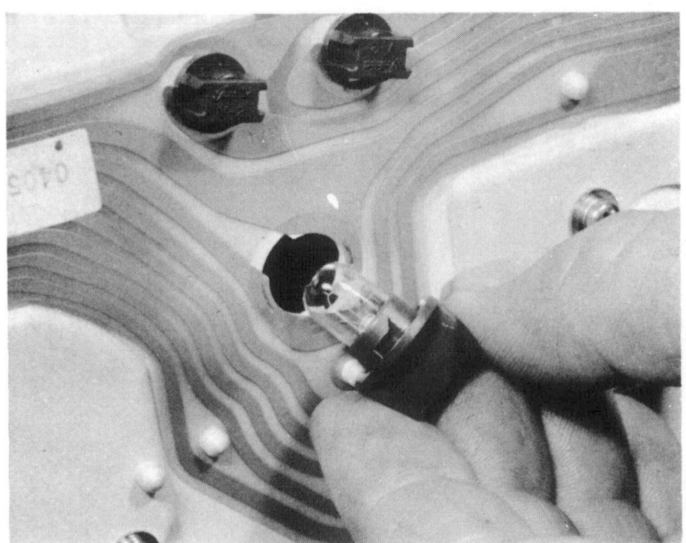
24.13A Large type instrument panel bulbholder

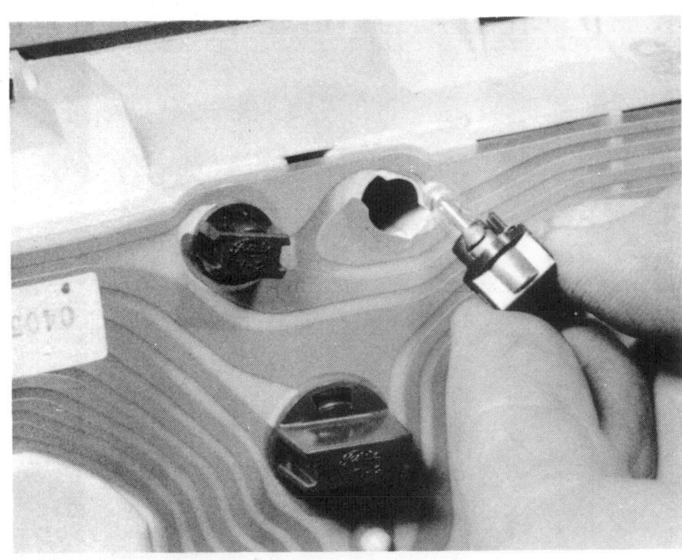
24.13B Small type instrument panel bulbholder

25.2 Disconnecting front parking lamp wiring

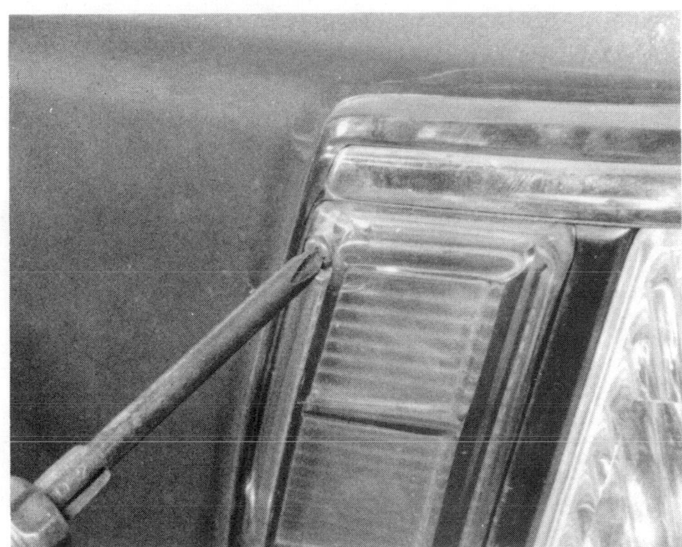
25.3 Front parking lamp securing screws

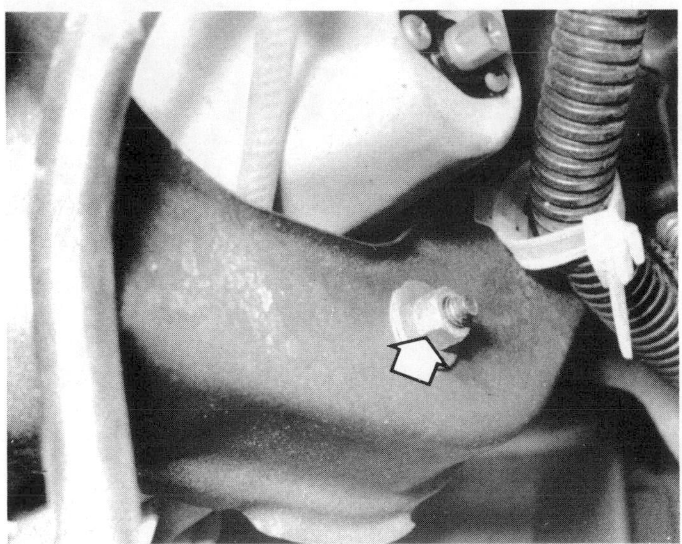
25.4 Headlamp mounting nut (arrowed)

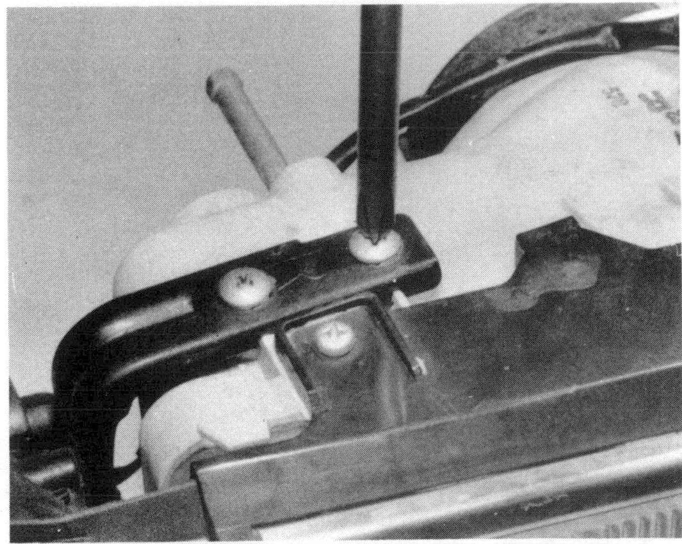
25.5 Front parking lamp upper bracket

25.6A Loosen the lower screw ...

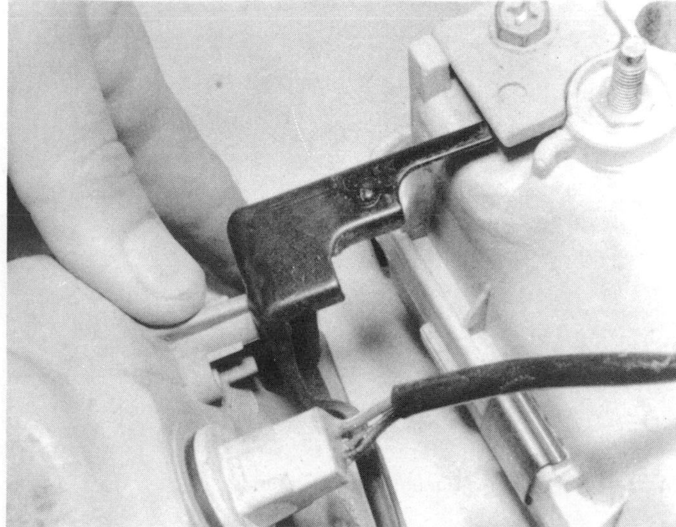
25.6B ... and separate the front parking lamp from the headlamp

6 Loosen the lower screw and separate the front parking lamp from the headlamp (photos).
7 If required, the lens can be separated from the body by removing the screws and clips (photo).
8 Refitting is a reversal of removal, but check and if necessary adjust the beam setting with reference to Section 22.

Rear lamp

9 The rear lamp is bonded to the rear panel and its removal and refitting should be entrusted to a Nissan dealer.

26 Front direction indicator lamp – removal and refitting

1 Remove the lamp bulb as described in Section 23.
2 Withdraw the lamp body from the front bumper and disconnect the wiring (photo).
3 Refitting is a reversal of removal.

27 Instrument panel – removal and refitting

1 Disconnect the battery negative lead.
2 Remove the ash tray.
3 Remove the surround mounting screws and release the surround from the upper pawls. Withdraw the surround and disconnect the wiring from the cigar lighter and switches.
4 Remove the screws above the heater control panel and the screws around the instrument panel location, then withdraw the surround and vent assembly.
5 Extract the instrument panel upper and lower mounting screws (photos).
6 Withdraw the instrument panel sufficiently to disconnect the wiring and the speedometer cable. Depress the serrated section on the outer cable to release it (photos).
7 The instrument panel can be dismantled to renew the individual gauges and meters by releasing the clips around its edge (photos).
8 Refitting is a reversal of removal.

25.7 Headlamp lens retaining screw and clip

26.2 Front direction indicator lamp wiring

27.5A Instrument panel upper mounting screw

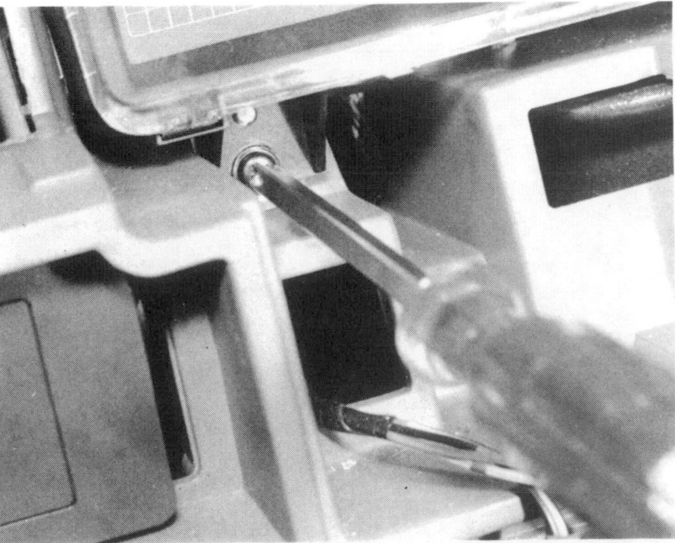
27.5B Instrument panel lower mounting screw

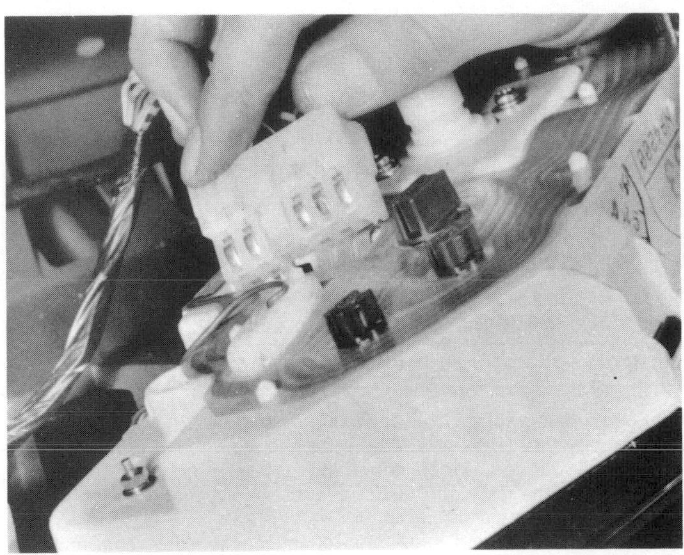
27.6A Disconnecting instrument panel wiring

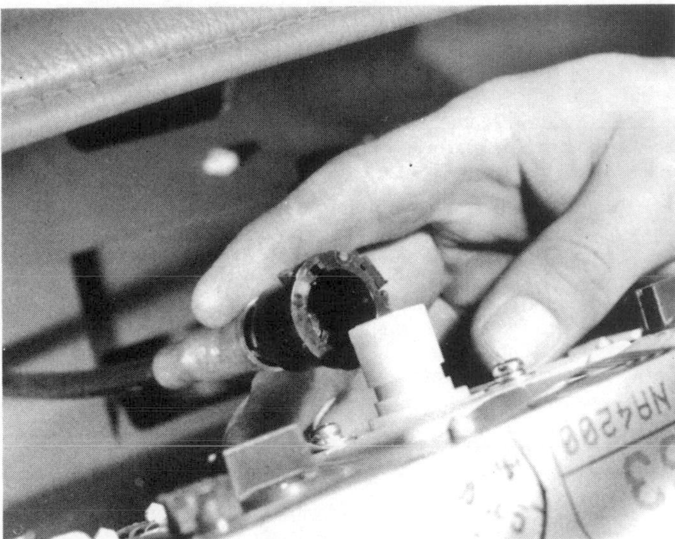
27.6B Disconnecting speedometer cable from instrument panel

27.7 Instrument panel section clips (arrowed)

28.2A Speedometer cable attached to transmission

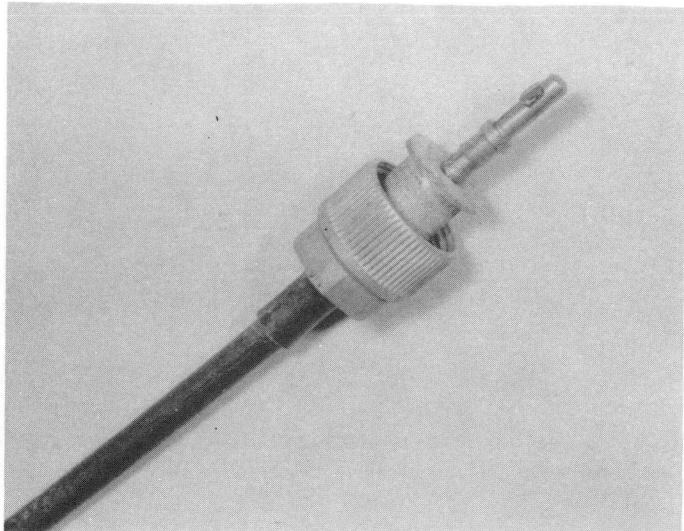

28.2B Transmission end of speedometer cable

28 Speedometer cable – renewal

1 Disconnect the cable from the speedometer with reference to Section 27.
2 Unscrew the knurled nut and disconnect the cable from the transmission (photos).
3 Release the cable from the clip and the bulkhead grommet and remove it from the engine compartment.
4 Fit the new cable by reversing the removal operations, but take care not to make any curves more acute than necessary.

29 Clock – removal and refitting

1 Disconnect the battery negative lead.
2 Remove the ash tray.
3 Remove the lower surround mounting screws and release the surround from the upper pawls. Withdraw the surround and disconnect the wiring from the cigar lighter and switches.
4 Extract the screws and remove the radio surround (photo).
5 Extract the screws and remove the coin box and clock surround (photo).
6 Extract the screws, withdraw the clock and disconnect the wiring (photos).
7 Refitting is a reversal of removal.

30 Radio – removal and refitting

1 Follow paragraphs 1 to 5 inclusive of Section 29.
2 Unscrew the radio lower mounting nuts (photo).
3 Unscrew the radio upper mounting screws (photo).
4 Withdraw the radio and disconnect the wiring and aerial (photos).
5 Refitting is a reversal of removal.
6 If the radio or aerial have been changed, then the aerial must be trimmed in the following way.
7 Fully extend the aerial and switch on the radio.
8 Tune in to a very weak station around 1400kHz.

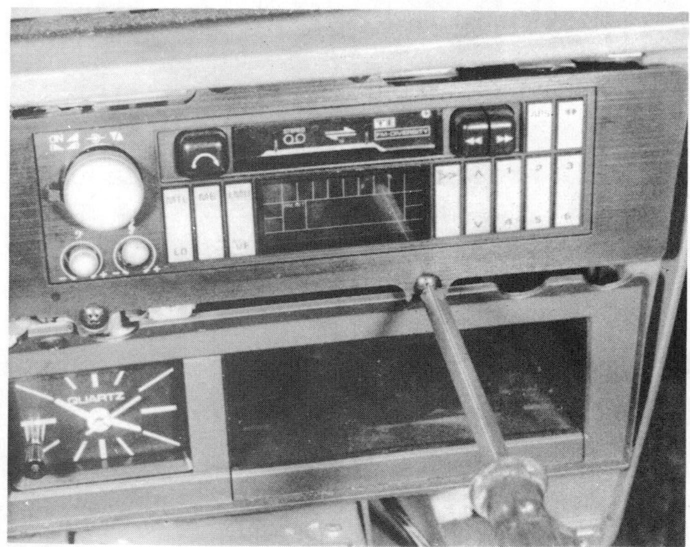

29.4 Removing radio surround

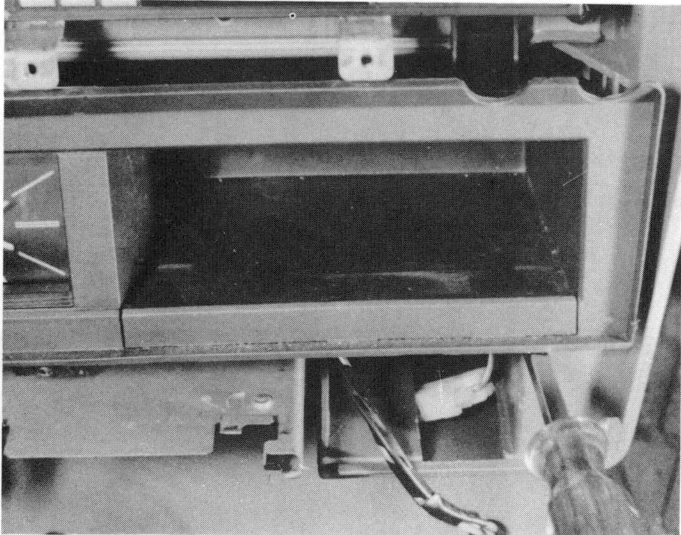

29.5 Removing coin box and clock surround

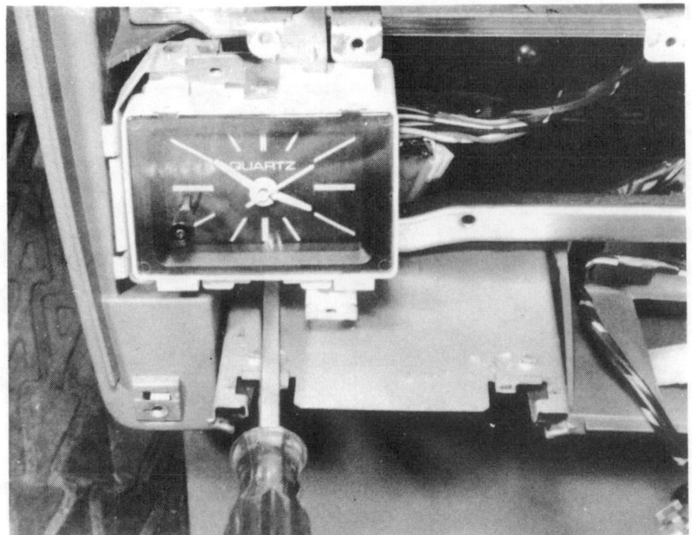

29.6A Extract the screws ...

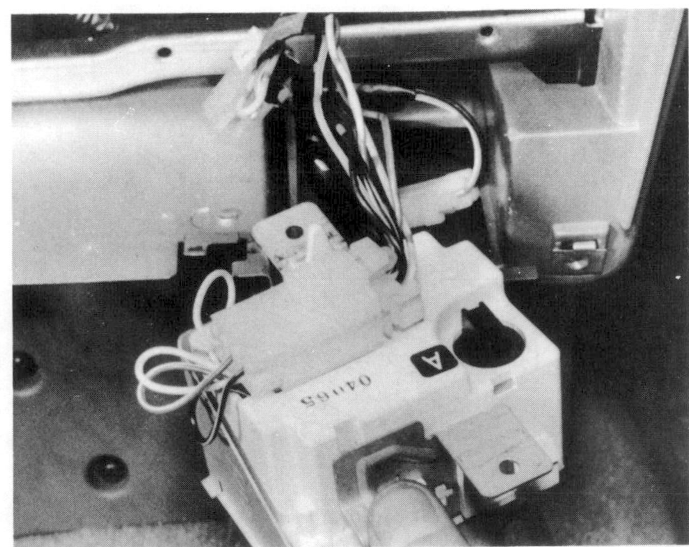

29.6B ... and remove the clock

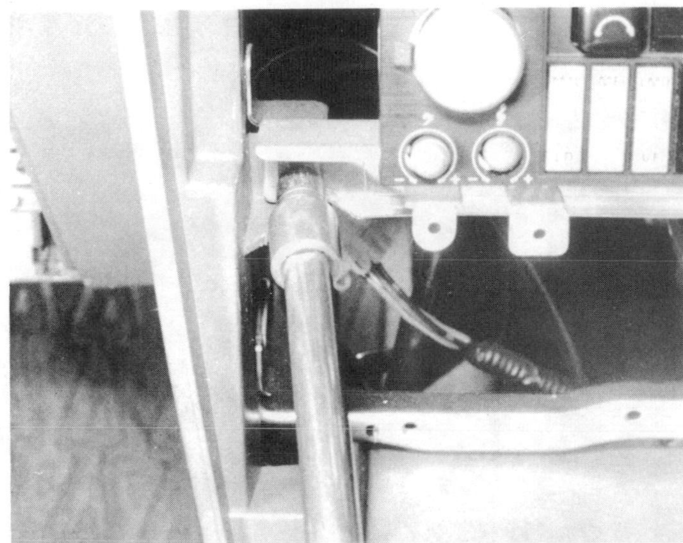

30.2 Unscrew the radio lower mounting nuts ...

30.3 ... the upper mounting screws ...

30.4A ... withdraw the radio ...

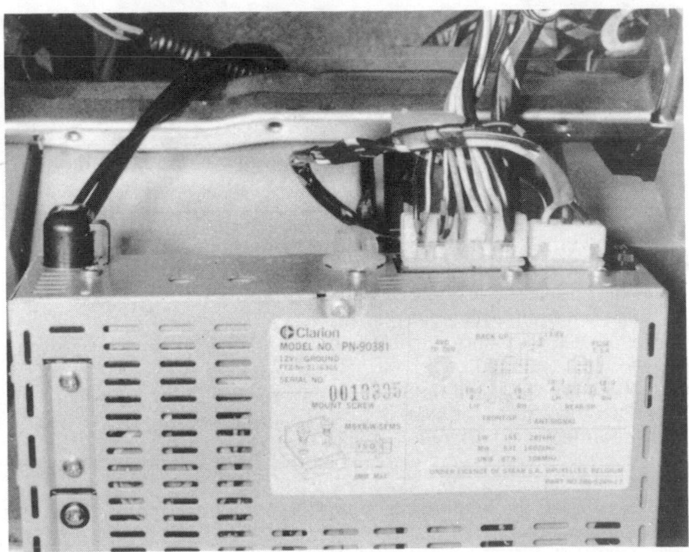

30.4B ... then disconnect the wiring and aerial

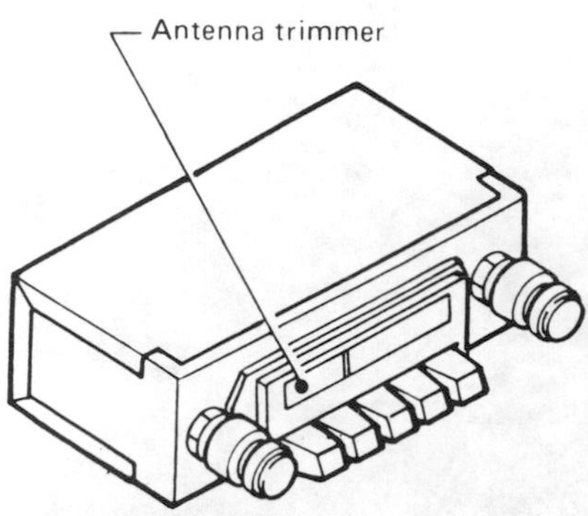

Fig. 12.31 Location of radio antenna trimmer (Sec 30)

9 Insert a thin screwdriver into the trim adjuster hole and turn the screw not more than half a turn in either direction until reception is at its best (loudest).

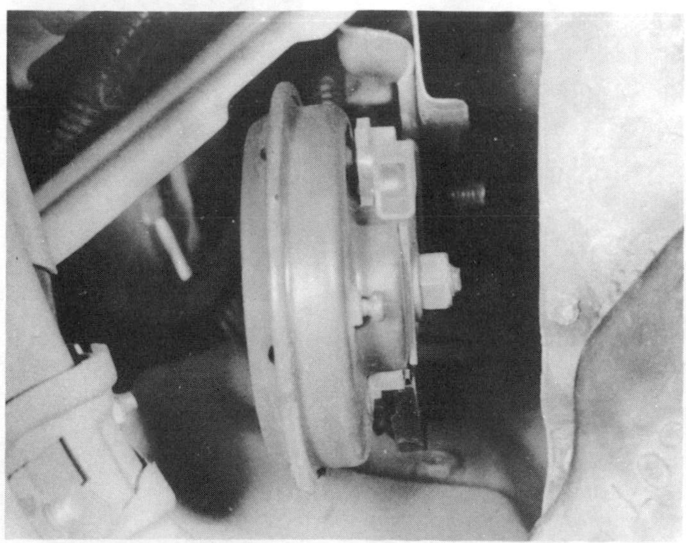

31.1 View of horn from under the car

31 Horn – removal and refitting

1 Either one or two horns are fitted according to model. They are located just below the headlamps (photo).
2 Apply the handbrake, then jack up the front of the car and support on axle stands.
3 Disconnect the battery negative lead.
4 Reach up behind the bumper and disconnect the wiring from the horn.
5 Unscrew the mounting bolt and withdraw the horn.
6 Refitting is a reversal of removal.

32 Wiper blades and arms – removal and refitting

1 The wiper blades should be renewed if they fail to wipe the glass clean.
2 Pull the arm and blade away from the glass and retain in this position by pulling out the lock on the base of the arm.
3 Depress the spring clip and slide the blade *down* the arm finally withdrawing it from the *top* of the arm (photo).
4 Complete blades or rubber inserts are available. Changing the rubber inserts only should be carried out in accordance with the manufacturer's instructions.
5 To remove the arm first note its position when 'parked'.
6 Unscrew the nut and pull the arm from the spindle (photo).
7 Refitting is a reversal of removal.

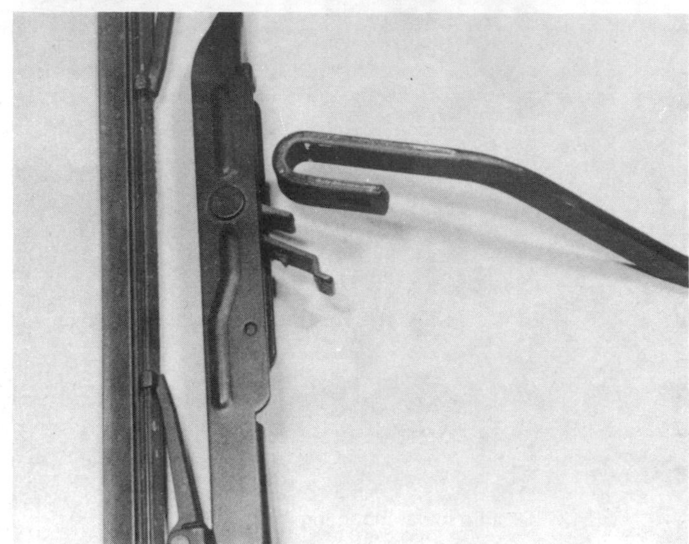

32.3 Showing windscreen wiper blade and arm connection

33 Windscreen wiper motor and linkage – removal and refitting

1 Remove the wiper blades and arms as described in Section 32.
2 Open the bonnet, then extract the screws and withdraw the scuttle cover from the base of the windscreen (photo).
3 Prise out the plastic vent grids.
4 Remove the sealing strip from the top of the bulkhead by prising out the clips (photo).
5 Extract the screws and withdraw the cover from the left-hand side of the vent chamber (photo).
6 Disconnect the battery negative lead.
7 Unscrew the nut and disconnect the crankarm from the wiper motor shaft (photo).
8 Disconnect the wiring, then unbolt the wiper motor from the bulkhead (photo).
9 Unscrew the spindle unit nuts and withdraw the linkage from the vent chamber (photo).
10 Refitting is a reversal of removal.

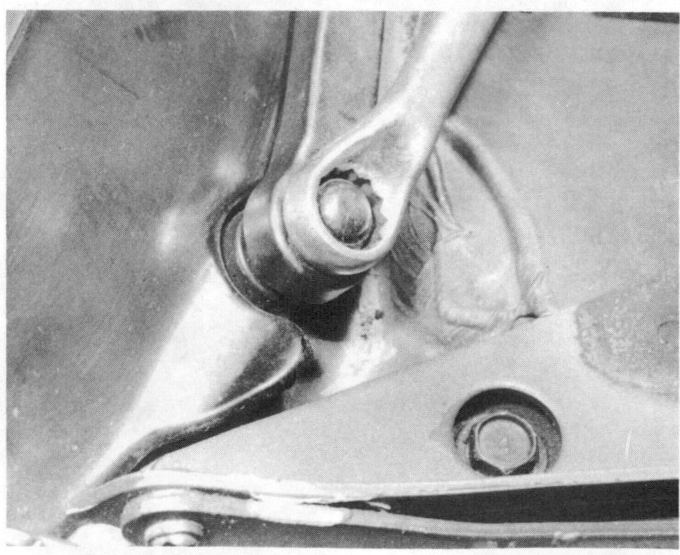

32.6 Removing wiper arm

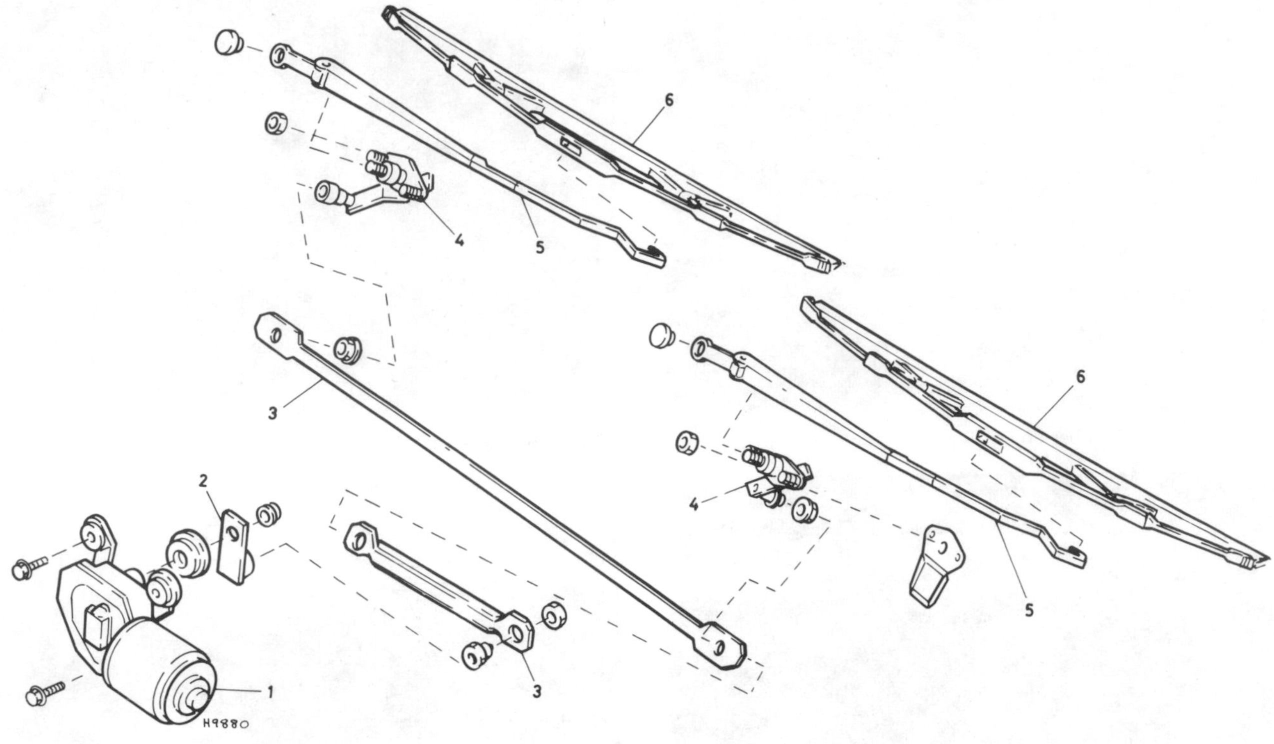

Fig. 12.32 Windscreen wiper motor and linkage components (Sec 33)

1 Wiper motor	*3 Linkage arms*	*5 Wiper arms*
2 Crank pin	*4 Spindle units*	*6 Wiper blades*

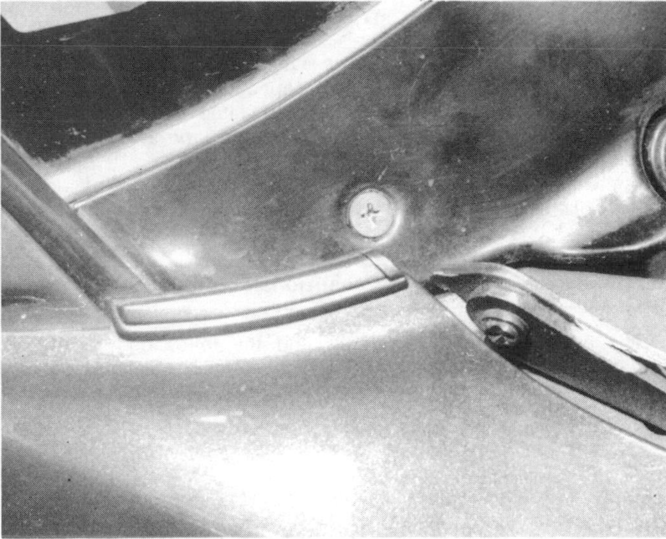

33.2 Scuttle cover and screw

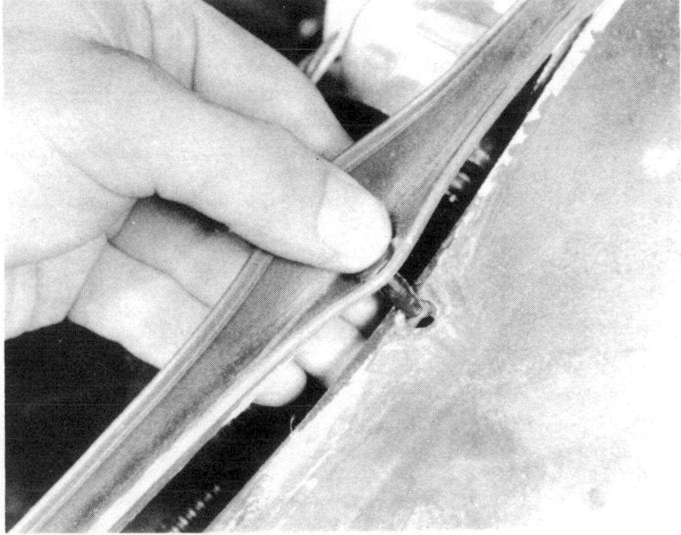

33.4 Removing bulkhead sealing strip

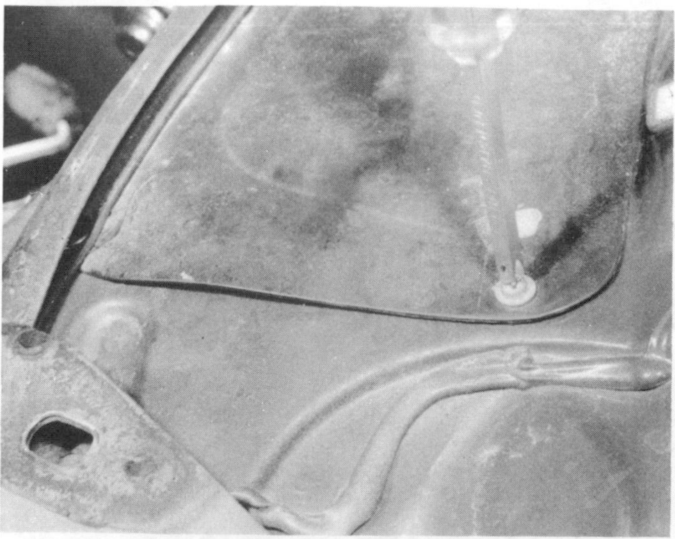
33.5 Removing vent chamber cover

33.7 Wiper motor crankarm

33.8 Wiper motor and wiring

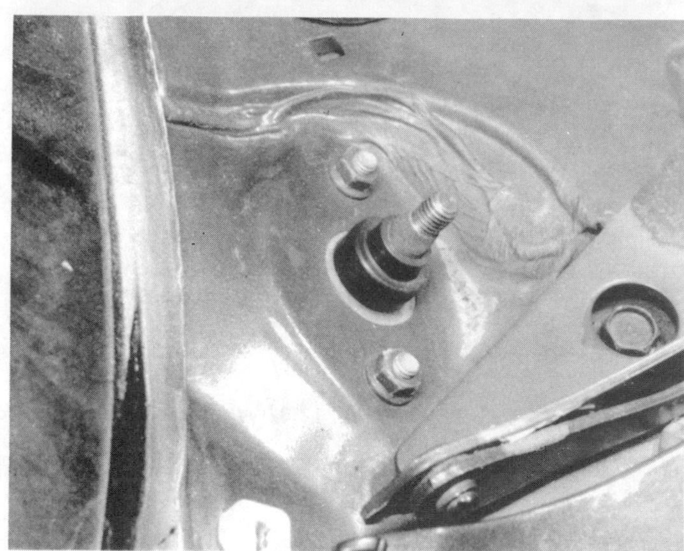
33.9 Wiper linkage spindle and retaining nuts

34 Tailgate wiper motor – removal and refitting

1 Disconnect the battery negative lead.
2 Remove the cover, unscrew the nut, and remove the wiper arm and blade complete from the tailgate.
3 Open the tailgate and remove the inner trim.
4 Disconnect the wiring, then unbolt and remove the wiper motor. Remove the seal from the spindle.
5 Refitting is a reversal of removal. Check that the wiper stroke is central on the rear window.

35 Washer systems

1 On all models, the windscreen washer reservoir is located next to the battery on the left-hand side of the engine compartment (photo).
2 On Estate models the tailgate washer reservoir is located on the left-hand side of the luggage compartment behind a small flap.
3 The headlamp washer reservoir is located on the right-hand side of the engine compartment. To check the fluid level, place the finger firmly over the vent hole, then remove the filler cap. The level will appear on the tube.
4 The electric pump for all systems is located on the reservoir outlet.
5 The washer reservoir should be topped up with special washer fluid. In very cold weather, add some methylated spirit to the fluid to prevent freezing. *Do not use cooling system antifreeze as this will damage the paintwork.*
6 The washer jets should be adjusted to aim at the central area of the wiper stroke using a suitable instrument.

36 Heated rear window – precautions and repair

1 The heater elements are fragile and the following precautions should be observed. Do not allow luggage or other items to rub against the inside surface of the glass.

Do not stick labels over the elements
Avoid scratching the elements when cleaning with rings on the fingers
Clean the glass with water and detergent only and rub in the direction of the elements

2 Should an element be damaged so that the current is interrupted, a repair can be made using one of the conductive silver paints available from motor accessory stores.

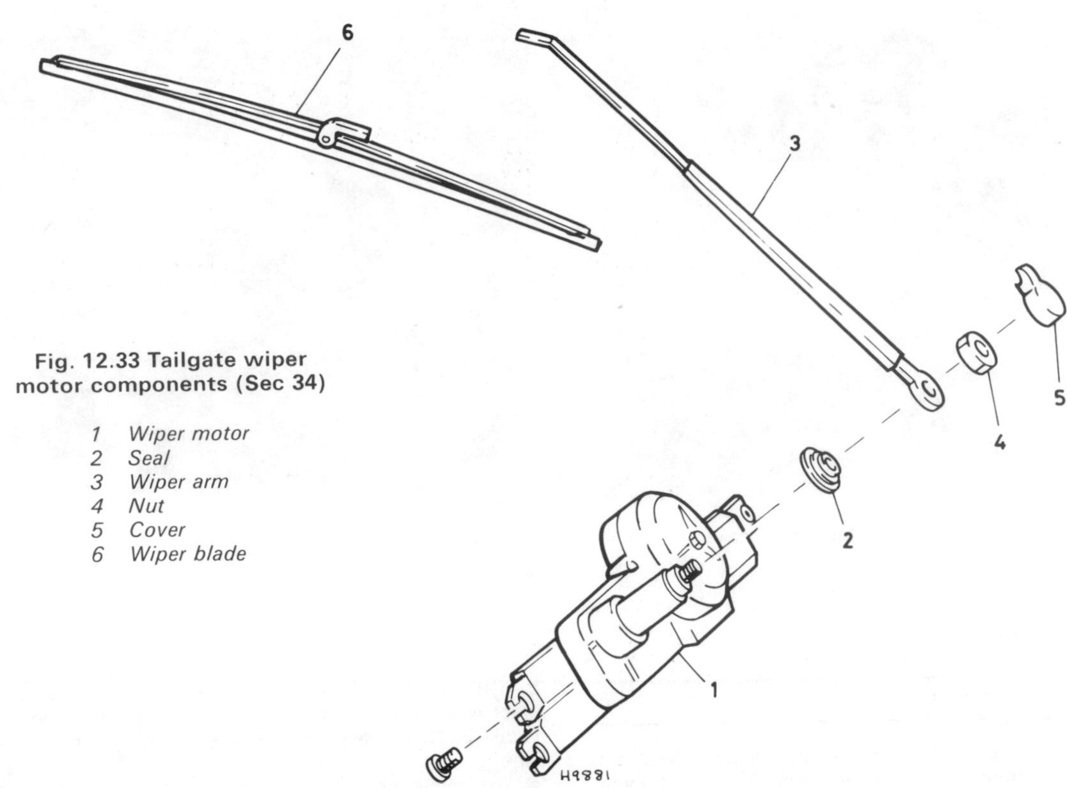

Fig. 12.33 Tailgate wiper motor components (Sec 34)

1 *Wiper motor*
2 *Seal*
3 *Wiper arm*
4 *Nut*
5 *Cover*
6 *Wiper blade*

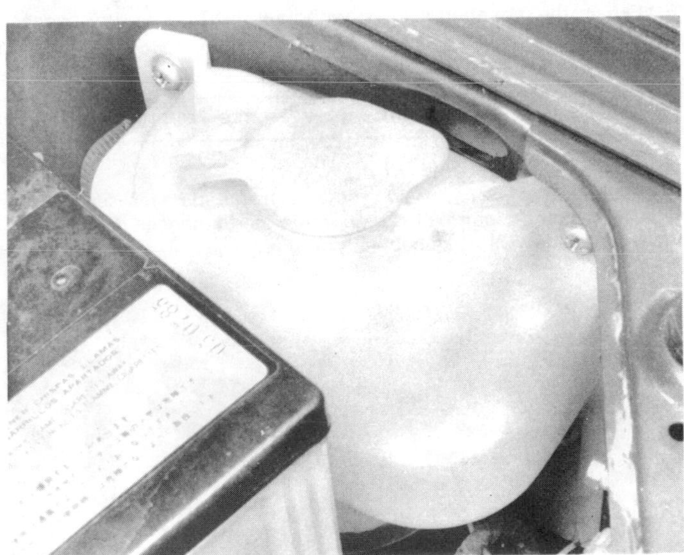

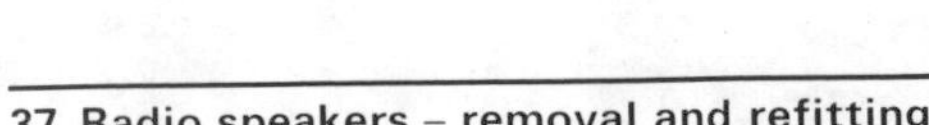
35.1 Windscreen washer reservoir location

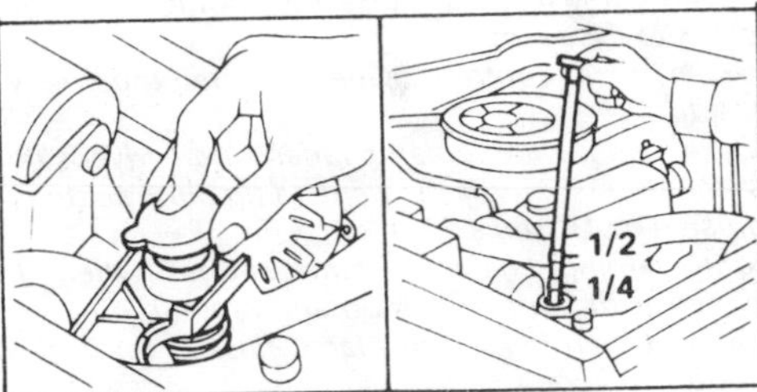

Fig. 12.34 Checking the headlamp washer fluid level (Sec 35)

37 Radio speakers – removal and refitting

1 The front speakers are located on the front door trim panels. To remove them, prise off the cover then remove the cross head screws. Withdraw the speaker and disconnect the wiring (photos). Refitting is a reversal of removal.

2 The rear speakers are located beneath the rear shelf. To remove them, remove the trim as necessary from the luggage compartment and disconnect the wiring. Extract the retaining screws and withdraw the speaker (photo). Refitting is a reversal of removal.

37.1A Extract the screws ...

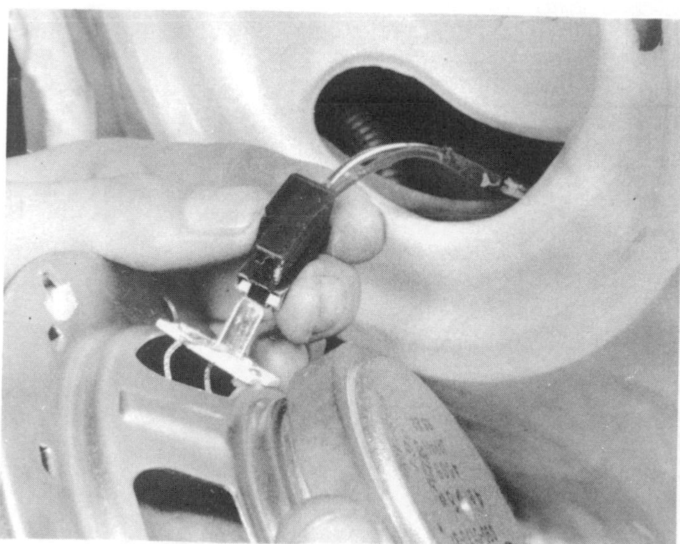
37.1B ... and disconnect the wiring from the front speaker

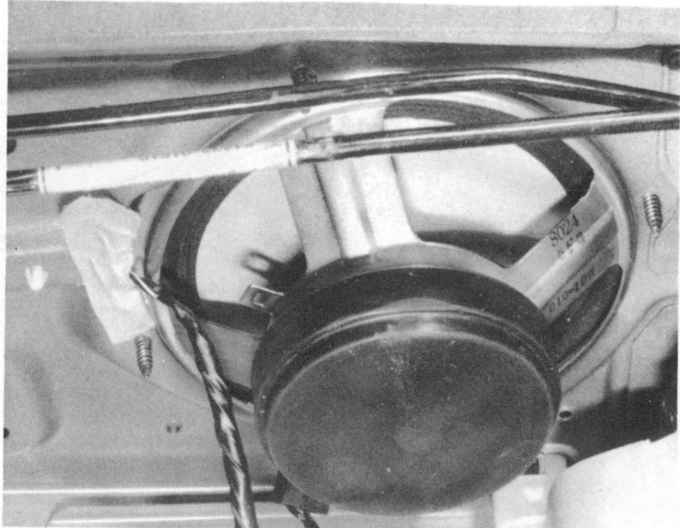
37.2 Rear speaker

38 Time control unit (TCU) – general

1 The time control unit is located on the right-hand side of the driver's footwell. Its function is to provide timing for the following items:

(a) *Intermittent wiper control – depending on setting of knob, from 3 to 12 seconds*
(b) *Washer/wiper control – wiper operated together with washer switch*
(c) *Interior lamp – interior lamp fades when driver's door is closed*
(d) *Illumination control – depending on setting, brightners adjusted in 16 steps*
(e) *Light warning chime – chime sounds when driver's door opened with light switch on and ignition off*
(f) *Seat belt warning lamp – lamp flashes for 7 seconds when ignition switched on*
(g) *Clock – pulse signal emitted to operate clock*

2 If the TCU develops a fault, check that the appropriate wiring is intact and correctly fitted. In-depth checking of the TCU should be made by a Nissan dealer or auto electrician with the unit installed in the car.
3 To remove the TCU, first disconnect the battery negative lead.
4 Take note that the TCU incorporates micro-circuitry and for this reason its terminals must never be touched with bare hands.
5 Extract the screws and withdraw the trim panel (photo).
6 Extract the mounting screws, withdraw the TCU, and disconnect the wiring (photos).
7 Refitting is a reversal of removal.

39 Mobile radio equipment – interference-free installation

Aerials – selection and fitting

The choice of aerials is now very wide. It should be realised that the quality has a profound effect on radio performance, and a poor, inefficient aerial can make suppression difficult.

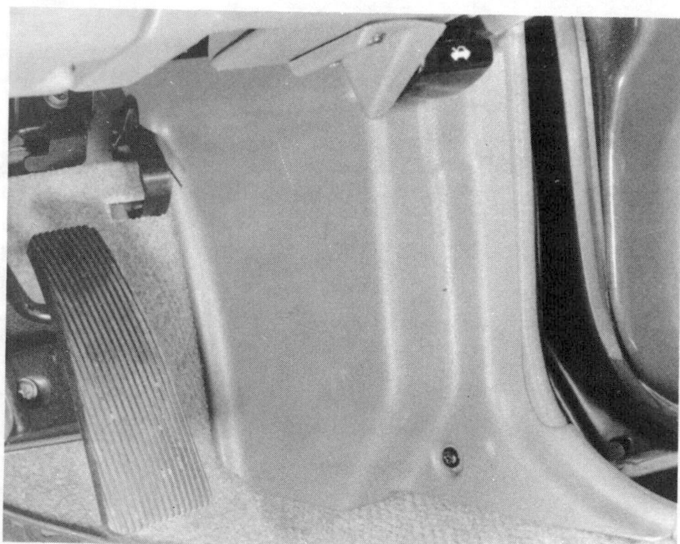
38.5 Footwell trim panel over TCU unit

38.6A TCU unit location and mounting screws

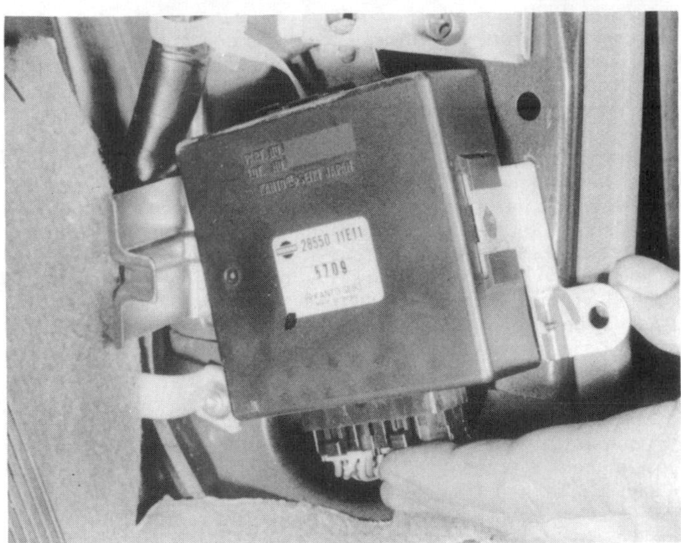

38.6B Removing the TCU unit

A wing-mounted aerial is regarded as probably the most efficient for signal collection, but a roof aerial is usually better for suppression purposes because it is away from most interference fields. Stick-on wire aerials are available for attachment to the inside of the windscreen, but are not always free from the interference field of the engine and some accessories.

Motorised automatic aerials rise when the equipment is switched on and retract at switch-off. They require more fitting space and supply leads, and can be a source of trouble.

There is no merit in choosing a very long aerial as, for example, the type about three metres in length which hooks or clips on to the rear of the car, since part of this aerial will inevitably be located in an interference field. For VHF/FM radios the best length of aerial is about one metre. Active aerials have a transistor amplifier mounted at the base and this serves to boost the received signal. The aerial rod is sometimes rather shorter than normal passive types.

A large loss of signal can occur in the aerial feeder cable, especially over the Very High Frequency (VHF) bands. The design of feeder cable is invariably in the co-axial form, ie a centre conductor surrounded by a flexible copper braid forming the outer (earth) conductor. Between the inner and outer conductors is an insulator material which can be in solid or stranded form. Apart from insulation, its purpose is to maintain the correct spacing and concentricity. Loss of signal occurs in this insulator, the loss usually being greater in a poor quality cable. The quality of cable used is reflected in the price of the aerial with the attached feeder cable.

The capacitance of the feeder should be within the range 65 to 75 picofarads (pF) approximately (95 to 100 pF for Japanese and American equipment), otherwise the adjustment of the car radio aerial trimmer may not be possible. An extension cable is necessary for a long run between aerial and receiver. If this adds capacitance in excess of the above limits, a connector containing a series capacitor will be required, or an extension which is labelled as 'capacity-compensated'.

Fitting the aerial will normally involve making a 7/8 in (22 mm) diameter hole in the bodywork, but read the instructions that come with the aerial kit. Once the hole position has been selected, use a centre punch to guide the drill. Use sticky masking tape around the area for this helps with marking out and drill location, and gives protection to the paintwork should the drill slip. Three methods of making the hole are in use:

(a) Use a hole saw in the electric drill. This is, in effect, a circular hacksaw blade wrapped round a former with a centre pilot drill.
(b) Use a tank cutter which also has cutting teeth, but is made to shear the metal by tightening with an Allen key.
(c) The hard way of drilling out the circle is using a small drill, say 1/8 in (3 mm), so that the holes overlap. The centre metal drops out and the hole is finished with round and half-round files.

Whichever method is used, the burr is removed from the body metal and paint removed from the underside. The aerial is fitted tightly ensuring that the earth fixing, usually a serrated washer, ring or clamp, is making a solid connection. *This earth connection is important in reducing interference.* Cover any bare metal with primer paint and topcoat, and follow by underseal if desired.

Aerial feeder cable routing should avoid the engine compartment and areas where stress might occur, eg under the carpet where feet will be located. Roof aerials require that the headlining be pulled back and that a path is available down the door pillar. It is wise to check with the vehicle dealer whether roof aerial fitting is recommended.

Loudspeakers

Speakers should be matched to the output stage of the equipment, particularly as regards the recommended impedance. Power transistors used for driving speakers are sensitive to the loading placed on them.

Before choosing a mounting position for speakers, check whether the vehicle manufacturer has provided a location for them. Generally door-mounted speakers give good stereophonic reproduction, but not all doors are able to accept them. The next best position is the rear parcel shelf, and in this case speaker apertures can be cut into the shelf, or pod units may be mounted.

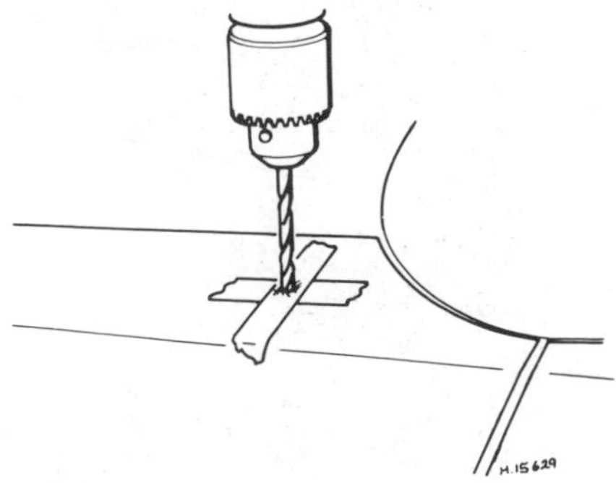

Fig. 12.35 Drilling the bodywork for aerial mounting (Sec 39)

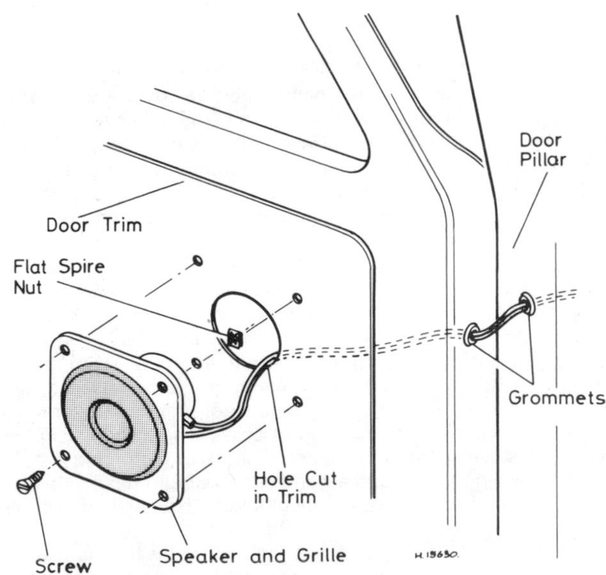

Fig. 12.36 Door-mounted speaker installation (Sec 39)

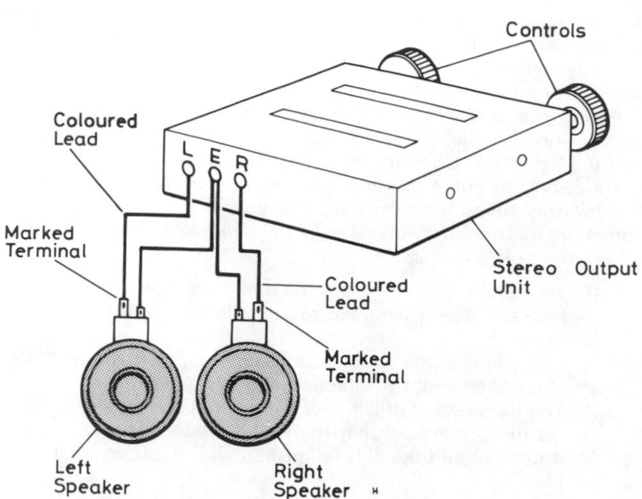

Fig. 12.37 Speaker connections must be correctly made as shown (Sec 39)

For door mounting, first remove the trim, which is often held on by 'poppers' or press studs, and then select a suitable gap in the inside door assembly. Check that the speaker would not obstruct glass or winder mechanism by winding the window up and down. A template is often provided for marking out the trim panel hole, and then the four fixing holes must be drilled through. Mark out with chalk and cut cleanly with a sharp knife or keyhole saw. Speaker leads are then threaded through the door and door pillar, if necessary drilling 10 mm diameter holes. Fit grommets in the holes and connect to the radio or tape unit correctly. Do not omit a waterproofing cover, usually supplied with door speakers. If the speaker has to be fixed into the metal of the door itself, use self-tapping screws, and if the fixing is to the door trim use self-tapping screws and flat spire nuts.

Rear shelf mounting is somewhat simpler but it is necessary to find gaps in the metalwork underneath the parcel shelf. However, remember that the speakers should be as far apart as possible to give a good stereo effect. Pod-mounted speakers can be screwed into position through the parcel shelf material, but it is worth testing for the best position. Sometimes good results are found by reflecting sound off the rear window.

Unit installation

Many vehicles have a dash panel aperture to take a radio/audio unit, a recognised international standard being 189.5 mm x 60 mm. Alternatively a console may be a feature of the car interior design and this, mounted below the dashboard, gives more room. If neither facility is available a unit may be mounted on the underside of the parcel shelf; these are frequently non-metallic and an earth wire from the case to a good earth point is necessary. A three-sided cover in the form of a cradle is obtainable from car radio dealers and this gives a professional appearance to the installation; in this case choose a position where the controls can be reached by a driver with his seat belt on.

Installation of the radio/audio unit is basically the same in all cases, and consists of offering it into the aperture after removal of the knobs (*not* push buttons) and the trim plate. In some cases a special mounting plate is required to which the unit is attached. It is worthwhile supporting the rear end in cases where sag or strain may occur, and it is usually possible to use a length of perforated metal strip attached between the unit and a good support point nearby. In general it is recommended that tape equipment should be installed at or nearly horizontal.

Connections to the aerial socket are simply by the standard plug terminating the aerial downlead or its extension cable. Speakers for a stereo system must be matched and correctly connected, as outlined previously.

Note: *While all work is carried out on the power side, it is wise to disconnect the battery earth lead.* Before connection is made to the vehicle electrical system, check that the polarity of the unit is correct. Most vehicles use a negative earth system, but radio/audio units often have a reversible plug to convert the set to either + or – earth. *Incorrect connection may cause serious damage.*

The power lead is often permanently connected inside the unit and terminates with one half of an in-line fuse carrier. The other half is fitted with a suitable fuse (3 or 5 amperes) and a wire which should go to a power point in the electrical system. This may be the accessory terminal on the ignition switch, giving the advantage of power feed with ignition or with the ignition key at the 'accessory' position. Power to the unit stops when the ignition key is removed. Alternatively, the lead may be taken to a live point at the fusebox with the consequence of having to remember to switch off at the unit before leaving the vehicle.

Before switching on for initial test, be sure that the speaker connections have been made, for running without load can damage the output transistors. Switch on next and tune through the bands to ensure that all sections are working, and check the tape unit if applicable. The aerial trimmer should be adjusted to give the strongest reception on a weak signal in the medium wave band, at say 200 metres.

Interference

In general, when electric current changes abruptly, unwanted electrical noise is produced. The motor vehicle is filled with electrical devices which change electric current rapidly, the most obvious being the contact breaker.

When the spark plugs operate, the sudden pulse of spark current causes the associated wiring to radiate. Since early radio transmitters used sparks as a basis of operation, it is not surprising that the car radio will pick up ignition spark noise unless steps are taken to reduce it to acceptable levels.

Interference reaches the car radio in two ways:

(a) by conduction through the wiring.
(b) by radiation to the receiving aerial.

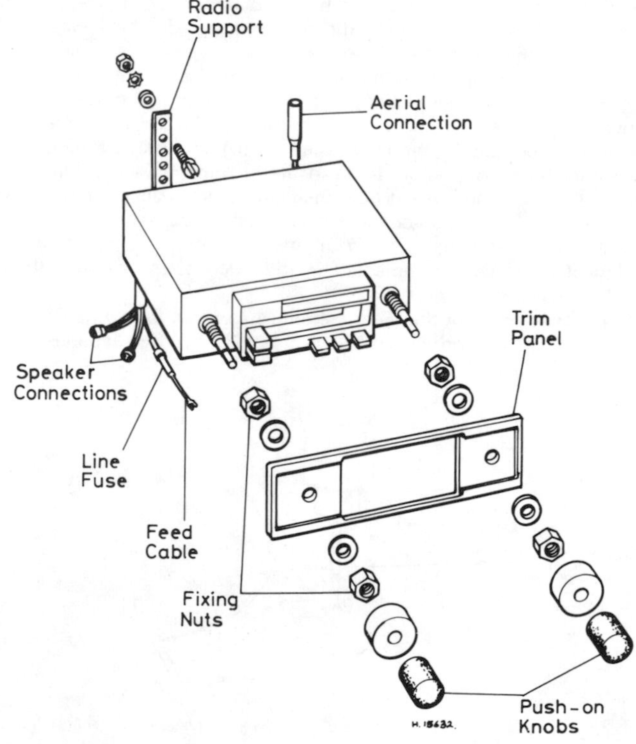

Fig. 12.38 Mounting component details for radio/cassette unit (Sec 39)

Initial checks presuppose that the bonnet is down and fastened, the radio unit has a good earth connection *(not* through the aerial downlead outer), no fluorescent tubes are working near the car, the aerial trimmer has been adjusted, and the vehicle is in a position to receive radio signals, ie not in a metal-clad building.

Switch on the radio and tune it to the middle of the medium wave (MW) band off-station with the volume (gain) control set fairly high. Switch on the ignition (but do not start the engine) and wait to see if irregular clicks or hash noise occurs. Tapping the facia panel may also produce the effects. If so, this will be due to the voltage stabiliser, which is an on-off thermal switch to control instrument voltage. It is located usually on the back of the instrument panel, often attached to the speedometer. Correction is by attachment of a capacitor and, if still troublesome, chokes in the supply wires.

Switch on the engine and listen for interference on the MW band. Depending on the type of interference, the indications are as follows.

A harsh crackle that drops out abruptly at low engine speed or when the headlights are switched on is probably due to a voltage regulator.

A whine varying with engine speed is due to the dynamo or alternator. Try temporarily taking off the fan belt – if the noise goes this is confirmation.

Regular ticking or crackle that varies in rate with the engine speed is due to the ignition system. With this trouble in particular and others in general, check to see if the noise is entering the receiver from the wiring or by radiation. To do this, pull out the aerial plug, (preferably shorting out the input socket or connecting a 62 pF capacitor across it). If the noise disappears it is coming in through the aerial and is *radiation noise*. If the noise persists it is reaching the receiver through the wiring and is said to be *line-borne*.

Interference from wipers, washers, heater blowers, turn-indicators, stop lamps, etc is usually taken to the receiver by wiring, and simple treatment using capacitors and possibly chokes will solve the problem. Switch on each one in turn (wet the screen first for running wipers!) and listen for possible interference with the aerial plug in place and again when removed.

Electric petrol pumps are now finding application again and give rise to an irregular clicking, often giving a burst of clicks when the ignition is on but the engine has not yet been started. It is also possible to receive whining or crackling from the pump.

Note that if most of the vehicle accessories are found to be creating interference all together, the probability is that poor aerial earthing is to blame.

Component terminal markings

Throughout the following sub-sections reference will be found to various terminal markings. These will vary depending on the manufacturer of the relevant component. If terminal markings differ from those mentioned, reference should be made to the following table, where the most commonly encountered variations are listed.

Alternator	*Alternator terminal (thick lead)*	*Exciting winding terminal*
DIN/Bosch	B+	DF
Delco Remy	+	EXC
Ducellier	+	EXC
Ford (US)	+	DF
Lucas	+	F
Marelli	+B	F
Ignition coil	*Ignition switch terminal*	*Contact breaker terminal*
DIN/Bosch	15	1
Delco Remy	+	–
Ducellier	BAT	RUP
Ford (US)	B/+	CB/–
Lucas	SW/+	–
Marelli	BAT/+B	D
Voltage regulator	*Voltage input terminal*	*Exciting winding terminal*
DIN/Bosch	B+/D+	DF
Delco Remy	BAT/+	EXC
Ducellier	BOB/BAT	EXC
Ford (US)	BAT	DF
Lucas	+/A	F
Marelli		F

Suppression methods – ignition

Suppressed HT cables are supplied as original equipment by manufacturers and will meet regulations as far as interference to neighbouring equipment is concerned. It is illegal to remove such suppression unless an alternative is provided, and this may take the form of resistive spark plug caps in conjunction with plain copper HT cable. For VHF purposes, these and 'in-line' resistors may not be effective, and resistive HT cable is preferred. Check that suppressed cables are actually fitted by observing cable identity lettering, or measuring with an ohmmeter – the value of each plug lead should be 5000 to 10 000 ohms.

A 1 microfarad capacitor connected from the LT supply side of the ignition coil to a good nearby earth point will complete basic ignition interference treatment. *NEVER fit a capacitor to the coil terminal to the contact breaker – the result would be burnt out points in a short time.*

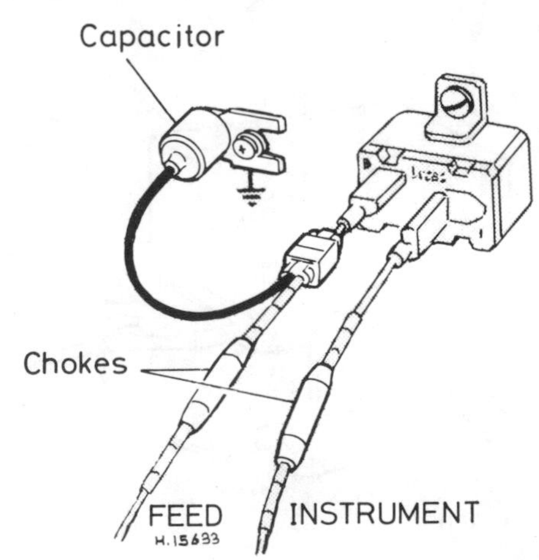

Fig. 12.39 Voltage stabiliser interference suppression (Sec 39)

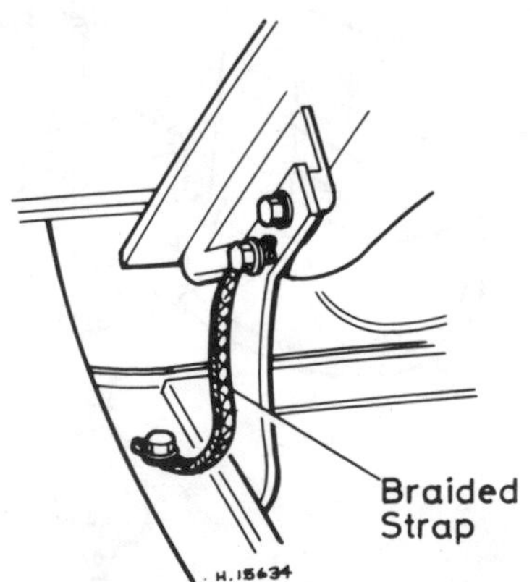

Fig. 12.40 Braided earth strap between bonnet and body (Sec 39)

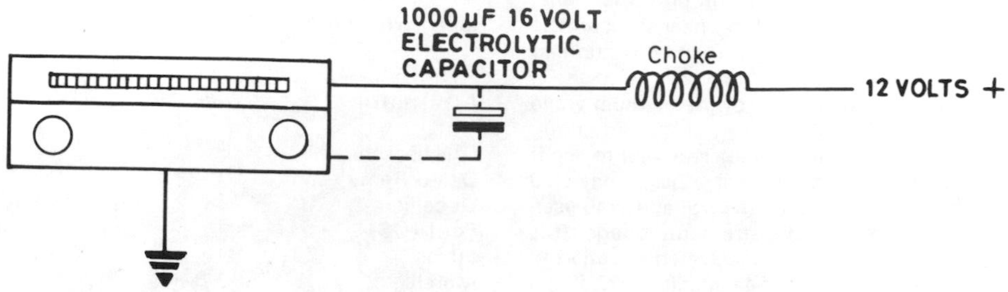

Fig. 12.41 Line-borne interference suppression (Sec 39)

If ignition noise persists despite the treatment above, the following sequence should be followed:

(a) Check the earthing of the ignition coil; remove paint from fixing clamp.
(b) If this does not work, lift the bonnet. Should there be no change in interference level, this may indicate that the bonnet is not electrically connected to the car body. Use a proprietary braided strap across a bonnet hinge ensuring a first class electrical connection. If, however, lifting the bonnet increases the interference, then fit resistive HT cables of a higher ohms-per-metre value.
(c) If all these measures fail, it is probable that re-radiation from metallic components is taking place. Using a braided strap between metallic points, go round the vehicle systematically – try the following: engine to body, exhaust system to body, front suspension to engine and to body, steering column to body (especially French and Italian cars), gear lever to engine and to body (again especially French and Italian cars), Bowden cable to body, metal parcel shelf to body. When an offending component is located it should be bonded with the strap permanently.
(d) As a next step, the fitting of distributor suppressors to each lead at the distributor end may help.
(e) Beyond this point is involved the possible screening of the distributor and fitting resistive spark plugs, but such advanced treatment is not usually required for vehicles with entertainment equipment.

Electronic ignition systems have built-in suppression components, but this does not relieve the need for using suppressed HT leads. In some cases it is permitted to connect a capacitor on the low tension supply side of the ignition coil, but not in every case. Makers' instructions should be followed carefully, otherwise damage to the ignition semiconductors may result.

Suppression methods – generators

For older vehicles with dynamos a 1 microfarad capacitor from the D (larger) terminal to earth will usually cure dynamo whine. Alternators should be fitted with a 3 microfarad capacitor from the B+ main output terminal (thick cable) to earth. Additional suppression may be obtained by the use of a filter in the supply line to the radio receiver.

It is most important that:

(a) Capacitors are never connected to the field terminals of either a dynamo or alternator.
(b) Alternators must not be run without connection to the battery.

Suppression methods – voltage regulators

Voltage regulators used with DC dynamos should be suppressed by connecting a 1 microfarad capacitor from the control box D terminal to earth.

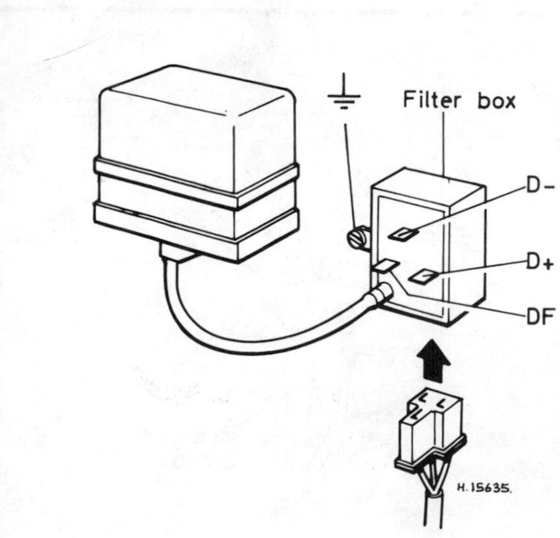

Fig. 12.42 Typical filter box for vibrating contact voltage regulator (alternator equipment) (Sec 39)

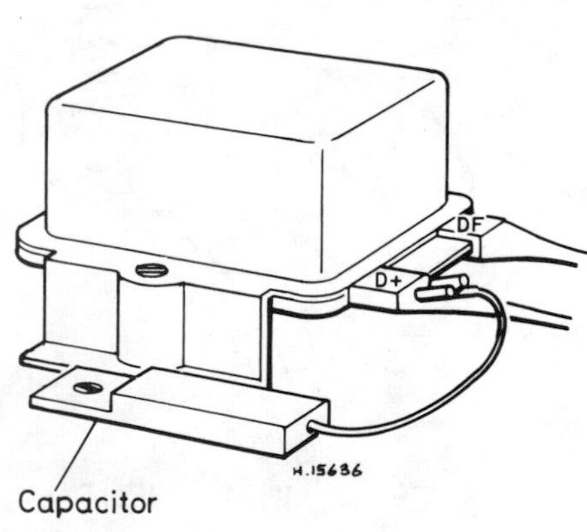

Fig. 12.43 Suppression of AM interference by vibrating contact voltage regulator (alternator equipment) (Sec 39)

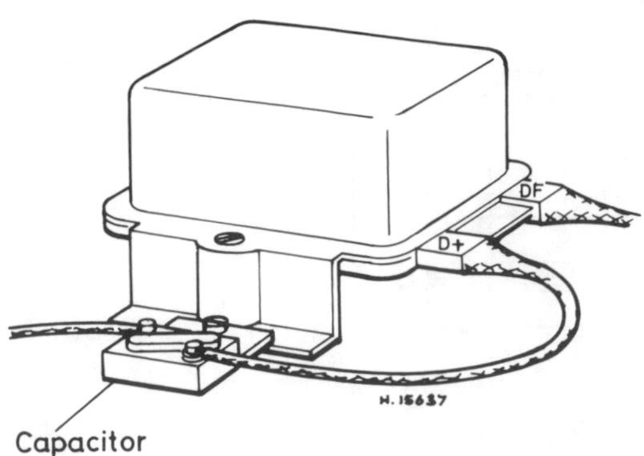

Fig. 12.44 Suppression of FM interference by vibrating contact voltage regulator (alternator equipment) (Sec 39)

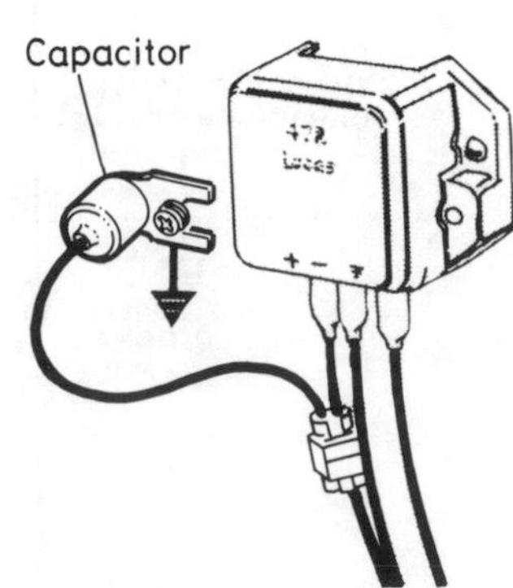

Fig. 12.45 Electronic voltage regulator suppression (Sec 39)

Alternator regulators come in three types:

(a) *Vibrating contact regulators separate from the alternator. Used extensively on continental vehicles.*
(b) *Electronic regulators separate from the alternator.*
(c) *Electronic regulators built-in to the alternator.*

In case (a) interference may be generated on the AM and FM (VHF) bands. For some cars a replacement suppressed regulator is available. Filter boxes may be used with non-suppressed regulators. But if not available, then for AM equipment a 2 microfarad or 3 microfarad capacitor may be mounted at the voltage terminal marked D+ or B+ of the regulator. FM bands may be treated by a feed-through capacitor of 2 or 3 microfarad.

Electronic voltage regulators are not always troublesome, but where necessary, a 1 microfarad capacitor from the regulator + terminal will help.

Integral electronic voltage regulators do not normally generate much interference, but when encountered this is in combination with alternator noise. A 1 microfarad or 2 microfarad capacitor from the warning lamp (IND) terminal to earth for Lucas ACR alternators and Femsa, Delco and Bosch equivalents should cure the problem.

Suppression methods – other equipment

Wiper motors – Connect the wiper body to earth with a bonding strap. For all motors use a 7 ampere choke assembly inserted in the leads to the motor.

Heater motors – Fit 7 ampere line chokes in both leads, assisted if necessary by a 1 microfarad capacitor to earth from both leads.

Electronic tachometer – The tachometer is a possible source of ignition noise – check by disconnecting at the ignition coil CB terminal. It usually feeds from ignition coil LT pulses at the contact breaker terminal. A 3 ampere line choke should be fitted in the tachometer lead at the coil CB terminal.

Horn – A capacitor and choke combination is effective if the horn is directly connected to the 12 volt supply. The use of a relay is an alternative remedy, as this will reduce the length of the interference-carrying leads.

Electrostatic noise – Characteristics are erratic crackling at the receiver, with disappearance of symptoms in wet weather. Often shocks may be given when touching bodywork. Part of the problem is the build-up of static electricity in non-driven wheels and the acquisition of charge on the body shell. It is possible to fit spring-loaded contacts at the wheels to give good conduction between the rotary wheel parts and the vehicle frame. Changing a tyre sometimes helps – because of tyres' varying resistances. In difficult cases a trailing flex which touches the ground will cure the problem. If this is not acceptable it is worth trying conductive paint on the tyre walls.

Fuel pump – Suppression requires a 1 microfarad capacitor between the supply wire to the pump and a nearby earth point. If this is insufficient a 7 ampere line choke connected in the supply wire near the pump is required.

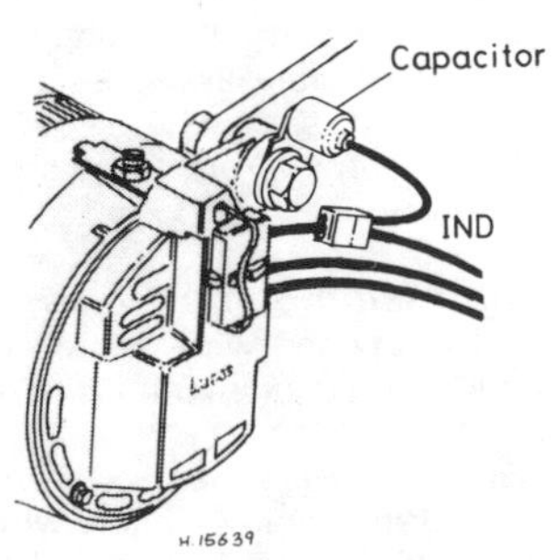

Fig. 12.46 Suppression of interference from electronic voltage regulator when integral with alternator (Sec 39)

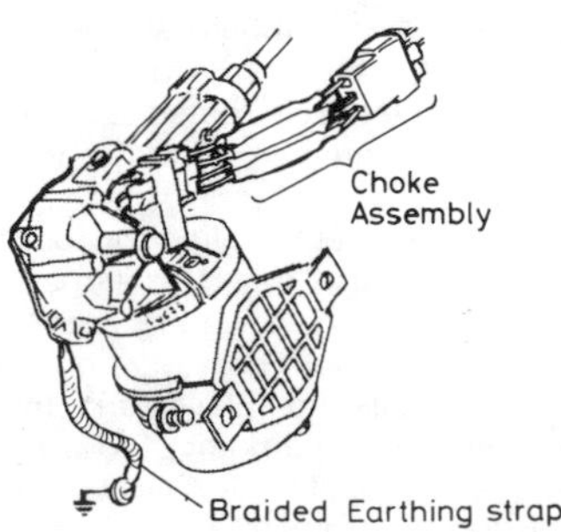

Fig. 12.47 Wiper motor suppression (Sec 39)

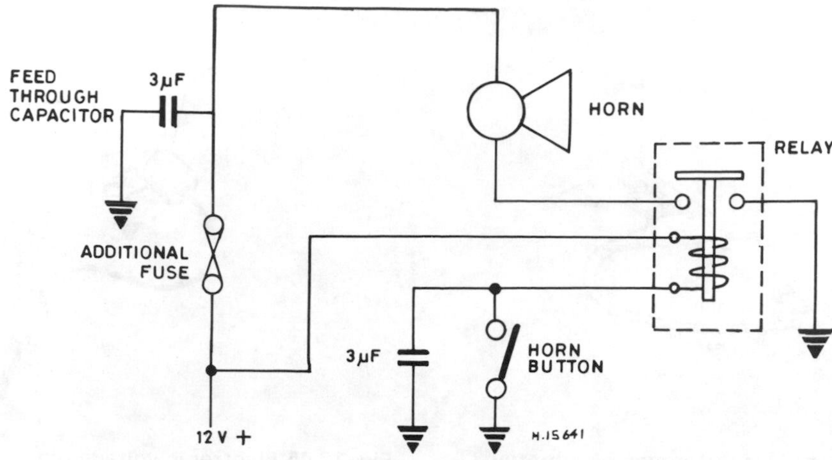

Fig. 12.48 Use of relay to reduce horn interference (Sec 39)

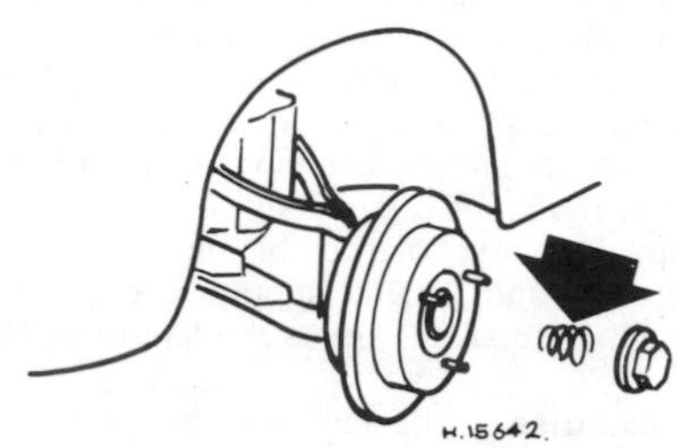

Fig. 12.49 Use of spring contacts at wheels (Sec 39)

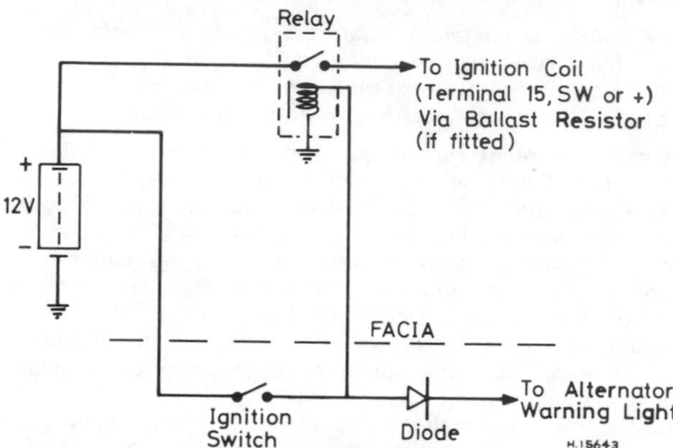

Fig. 12.50 Use of ignition coil relay to suppress case breakthrough (Sec 39)

Fluorescent tubes – Vehicles used for camping/caravanning frequently have fluorescent tube lighting. These tubes require a relatively high voltage for operation and this is provided by an inverter (a form of oscillator) which steps up the vehicle supply voltage. This can give rise to serious interference to radio reception, and the tubes themselves can contribute to this interference by the pulsating nature of the lamp discharge. In such situations it is important to mount the aerial as far away from a fluorescent tube as possible. The interference problem may be alleviated by screening the tube with fine wire turns spaced an inch (25 mm) apart and earthed to the chassis. Suitable chokes should be fitted in both supply wires close to the inverter.

Radio/cassette case breakthrough

Magnetic radiation from dashboard wiring may be sufficiently intense to break through the metal case of the radio/cassette player. Often this is due to a particular cable routed too close and shows up as ignition interference on AM and cassette play and/or alternator whine on cassette play.

The first point to check is that the clips and/or screws are fixing all parts of the radio/cassette case together properly. Assuming good earthing of the case, see if it is possible to re-route the offending cable – the chances of this are not good, however, in most cars.

Next release the radio/cassette player and locate it in different positions with temporary leads. If a point of low interference is found, then if possible fix the equipment in that area. This also confirms that local radiation is causing the trouble. If re-location is not feasible, fit the radio/cassette player back in the original position.

Alternator interference on cassette play is now caused by radiation from the main charging cable which goes from the battery to the output terminal of the alternator, usually via the + terminal of the starter motor relay. In some vehicles this cable is routed under the dashboard, so the solution is to provide a direct cable route. Detach the original cable from the alternator output terminal and make up a new cable of at least 6 mm^2 cross-sectional area to go from alternator to battery with the shortest possible route. *Remember – do not run the engine with the alternator disconnected from the battery.*

Ignition breakthrough on AM and/or cassette play can be a difficult problem. It is worth wrapping earthed foil round the offending cable run near the equipment, or making up a deflector plate well screwed down to a good earth. Another possibility is the use of a suitable relay to switch on the ignition coil. The relay should be mounted close to the ignition coil; with this arrangement the ignition coil primary current is not taken into the dashboard area and does not flow through the ignition switch. A suitable diode should be used since it is possible that at ignition switch-off the output from the warning lamp alternator terminal could hold the relay on.

Connectors for suppression components

Capacitors are usually supplied with tags on the end of the lead, while the capacitor body has a flange with a slot or hole to fit under a nut or screw with washer.

Connections to feed wires are best achieved by self-stripping connectors. These connectors employ a blade which, when squeezed down by pliers, cuts through cable insulation and makes connection to the copper conductors beneath.

Chokes sometimes come with bullet snap-in connectors fitted to the wires, and also with just bare copper wire. With connectors, suitable female cable connectors may be purchased from an auto-accessory shop together with any extra connectors required for the cable ends after being cut for the choke insertion. For chokes with bare wires, similar connectors may be employed together with insulation sleeving as required.

VHF/FM broadcasts

Reception of VHF/FM in an automobile is more prone to problems than the medium and long wavebands. Medium/long wave transmitters are capable of covering considerable distances, but VHF transmitters are restricted to line of sight, meaning ranges of 10 to 50 miles, depending upon the terrain, the effects of buildings and the transmitter power.

Because of the limited range it is necessary to retune on a long journey, and it may be better for those habitually travelling long distances or living in areas of poor provision of transmitters to use an AM radio working on medium/long wavebands.

When conditions are poor, interference can arise, and some of the suppression devices described previously fall off in performance at very high frequencies unless specifically designed for the VHF band. Available suppression devices include reactive HT cable, resistive distributor caps, screened plug caps, screened leads and resistive spark plugs.

For VHF/FM receiver installation the following points should be particularly noted:

(a) Earthing of the receiver chassis and the aerial mounting is important. Use a separate earthing wire at the radio, and scrape paint away at the aerial mounting.
(b) If possible, use a good quality roof aerial to obtain maximum height and distance from interference generating devices on the vehicle.
(c) Use of a high quality aerial downlead is important, since losses in cheap cable can be significant.
(d) The polarisation of FM transmissions may be horizontal, vertical, circular or slanted. Because of this the optimum mounting angle is at 45° to the vehicle roof.

Citizens' Band radio (CB)

In the UK, CB transmitter/receivers work within the 27 MHz and 934 MHz bands, using the FM mode. At present interest is concentrated on 27 MHz where the design and manufacture of equipment is less difficult. Maximum transmitted power is 4 watts, and 40 channels spaced 10 kHz apart within the range 27.60125 to 27.99125 MHz are available.

Aerials are the key to effective transmission and reception. Regulations limit the aerial length to 1.65 metres including the loading coil and any associated circuitry, so tuning the aerial is necessary to obtain optimum results. The choice of a CB aerial is dependent on whether it is to be permanently installed or removable, and the performance will hinge on correct tuning and the location point on the vehicle. Common practice is to clip the aerial to the roof gutter or to employ wing mounting where the aerial can be rapidly unscrewed. An alternative is to use the boot rim to render the aerial theftproof, but a popular solution is to use the 'magmount' – a type of mounting having a strong magnetic base clamping to the vehicle at any point, usually the roof.

Aerial location determines the signal distribution for both transmission and reception, but it is wise to choose a point away from the engine compartment to minimise interference from vehicle electrical equipment.

The aerial is subject to considerable wind and acceleration forces. Cheaper units will whip backwards and forwards and in so doing will alter the relationship with the metal surface of the vehicle with which it forms a ground plane aerial system. The radiation pattern will change correspondingly, giving rise to break-up of both incoming and outgoing signals.

Interference problems on the vehicle carrying CB equipment fall into two categories:

(a) Interference to nearby TV and radio receivers when transmitting.
(b) Interference to CB set reception due to electrical equipment on the vehicle.

Problems of break-through to TV and radio are not frequent, but can be difficult to solve. Mostly trouble is not detected or reported because the vehicle is moving and the symptoms rapidly disappear at the TV/radio receiver, but when the CB set is used as a base station any trouble with nearby receivers will soon result in a complaint.

It must not be assumed by the CB operator that his equipment is faultless, for much depends upon the design. Harmonics (that is, multiples) of 27 MHz may be transmitted unknowingly and these can fall into other user's bands. Where trouble of this nature occurs, low pass filters in the aerial or supply leads can help, and should be fitted in base station aerials as a matter of course. In stubborn cases it may be necessary to call for assistance from the licensing authority, or, if possible, to have the equipment checked by the manufacturers.

Interference received on the CB set from the vehicle equipment is, fortunately, not usually a severe problem. The precautions outlined previously for radio/cassette units apply, but there are some extra points worth noting.

It is common practice to use a slide-mount on CB equipment enabling the set to be easily removed for use as a base station, for example. Care must be taken that the slide mount fittings are properly earthed and that first class connection occurs between the set and slide-mount.

Vehicle manufacturers in the UK are required to provide suppression of electrical equipment to cover 40 to 250 MHz to protect TV and VHF radio bands. Such suppression appears to be adequately effective at 27 MHz, but suppression of individual items such as alternators/dynamos, clocks, stabilisers, flashers, wiper motors, etc, may still be necessary. The suppression capacitors and chokes available from auto-electrical suppliers for entertainment receivers will usually give the required results with CB equipment.

Other vehicle radio transmitters

Besides CB radio already mentioned, a considerable increase in the use of transceivers (ie combined transmitter and receiver units) has taken place in the last decade. Previously this type of equipment was fitted mainly to military, fire, ambulance and police vehicles, but a large business radio and radio telephone usage has developed.

Generally the suppression techniques described previously will suffice, with only a few difficult cases arising. Suppression is carried out to satisfy the 'receive mode', but care must be taken to use heavy duty chokes in the equipment supply cables since the loading on 'transmit' is relatively high.

Glass-fibre bodied vehicles

Such vehicles do not have the advantage of a metal box surrounding the engine as is the case, in effect, of conventional vehicles. It is usually necessary to line the bonnet, bulkhead and wing valances with metal foil, which could well be the aluminium foil available from builders merchants. Bonding of sheets one to another and the whole down to the chassis is essential.

Wiring harness may have to be wrapped in metal foil which again should be earthed to the vehicle chassis. The aerial base and radio chassis must be taken to the vehicle chassis by heavy metal braid. VHF radio suppression in glass-fibre cars may not be a feasible operation.

In addition to all the above, normal suppression components should be employed, but special attention paid to earth bonding. A screen enclosing the entire ignition system usually gives good improvement, and fabrication from fine mesh perforated metal is convenient. Good bonding of the screening boxes to several chassis points is essential.

40 Fault diagnosis – electrical system

Symptom	Reason(s)
No voltage at starter motor	Battery discharged Battery defective internally Battery terminals loose or earth lead not securely attached to body Loose or broken connections in starter motor circuit Starter motor switch or solenoid faulty
Voltage at starter motor – faulty motor	Starter brushes badly worn, sticking, or brush wires loose Commutator dirty, worn or burnt Starter motor armature faulty Field coils earthed
Electrical defects	Battery in discharged condition Starter brushes badly worn, sticking, or brush wires loose Loose wires in starter motor circuit
Starter motor noisy or rough in engagement	Pinion or flywheel gear teeth broken or worn Starter motor retaining bolts loose
Alternator not charging	Drivebelt loose and slipping, or broken Brushes worn, sticking, broken or dirty Brush springs weak or broken
Battery will not hold charge for more than a few days	Battery defective internally Electrolyte level too low or electrolyte too weak due to leakage Plate separators no longer fully effective Battery plates severely sulphated Drivebelt slipping Battery terminal connections loose or corroded Alternator not charging properly Short in lighting circuit causing continual battery drain Integral regulator unit not working correctly
Ignition light fails to go out, battery runs flat in a few days	Drivebelt loose and slipping, or broken Alternator faulty

Failure of individual electrical equipment to function correctly is dealt with alphabetically below

Symptom	Reason(s)
Fuel gauge gives no reading (refer also to Chapter 3)	Fuel tank empty! Electric cable between tank sender unit and gauge earthed or loose Fuel gauge case not earthed Fuel gauge supply cable interrupted Fuel gauge unit broken
Fuel gauge registers full all the time	Electric cable between tank unit and gauge broken or disconnected
Horn operates all the time	Horn push either earthed or stuck down Horn cable to horn push earthed
Horn fails to operate	Blown fuse Cable or cable connection loose, broken or disconnected Horn has an internal fault
Horn emits intermittent or unsatisfactory noise	Cable connections loose Horn incorrectly adjusted
Lights do not come on	If engine not running, battery discharged Light bulb filament burnt out or bulbs broken Wire connections loose, disconnected or broken Light switch shorting or otherwise faulty Fusible link melted
Lights come on but fade out	If engine not running, battery discharged
Lights give very poor illumination	Lamp glasses dirty Reflector tarnished or dirty Lamps badly out of adjustment Incorrect bulb with too low wattage fitted Existing bulbs old and badly discoloured
Lights work erratically, flashing on and off especially over bumps	Battery terminals or earth connections loose Lights not earthing properly Contacts in light switch faulty

Symptom	Reason(s)
Wiper motor fails to work	Blown fuse Wire connections loose, disconnected or broken Brushes badly worn Armature worn or faulty Field coils faulty
Wiper motor works very slowly and takes excessive current	Commutator dirty, greasy or burnt Drive to spindles too bent or unlubricated Drive spindle binding or damaged Armature bearings dry or unaligned Armature badly worn or faulty
Wiper motor works slowly and takes little current	Brushes badly worn Commutator dirty, greasy or burnt Armature badly worn or faulty
Wiper motor works but wiper blades remain static	Linkage disengaged or faulty Drive spindle damaged or worn Wiper motor gearbox parts badly worn
Heated rear window not operating	Blown fuse Broken filament Faulty relay

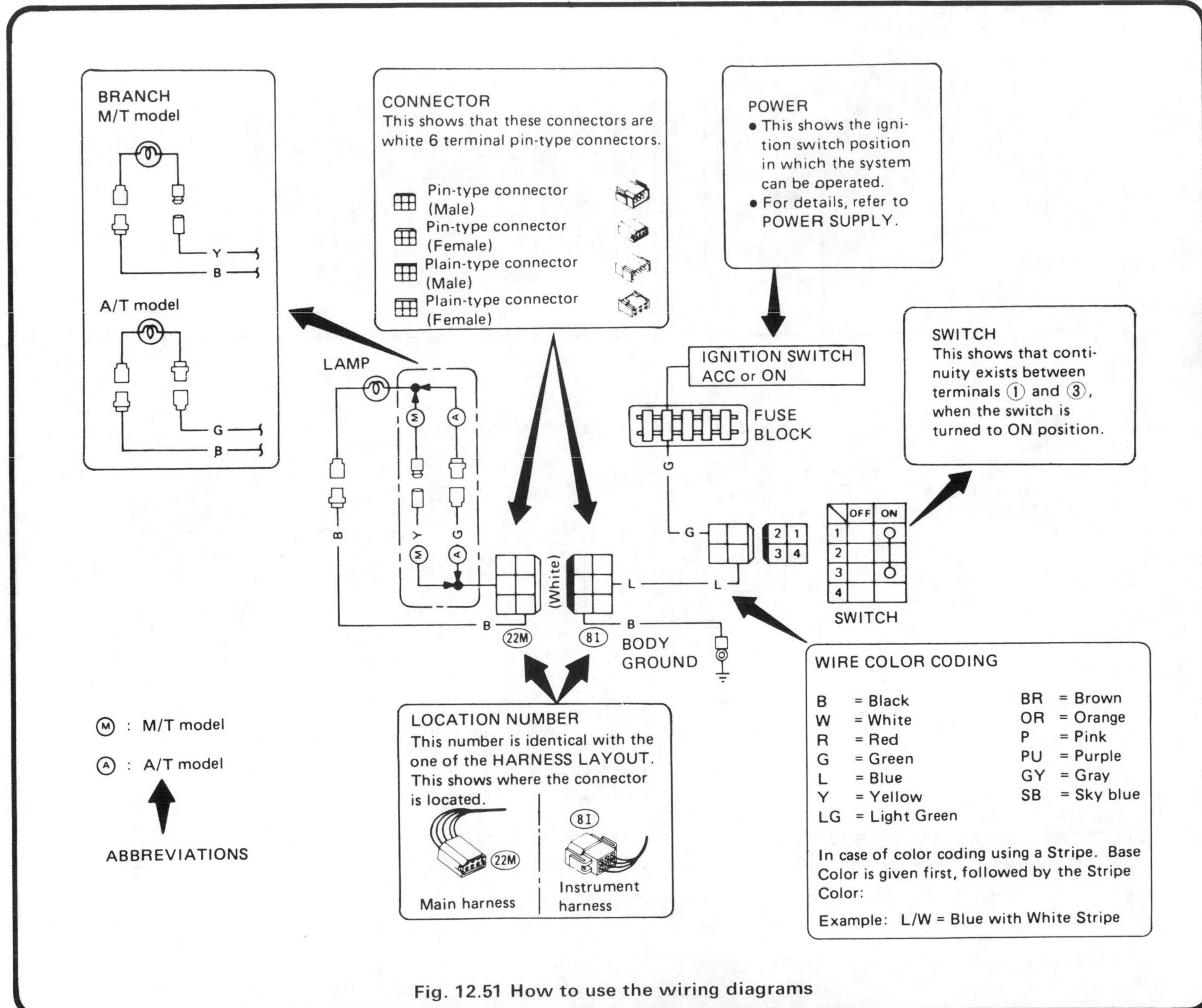

Fig. 12.51 How to use the wiring diagrams

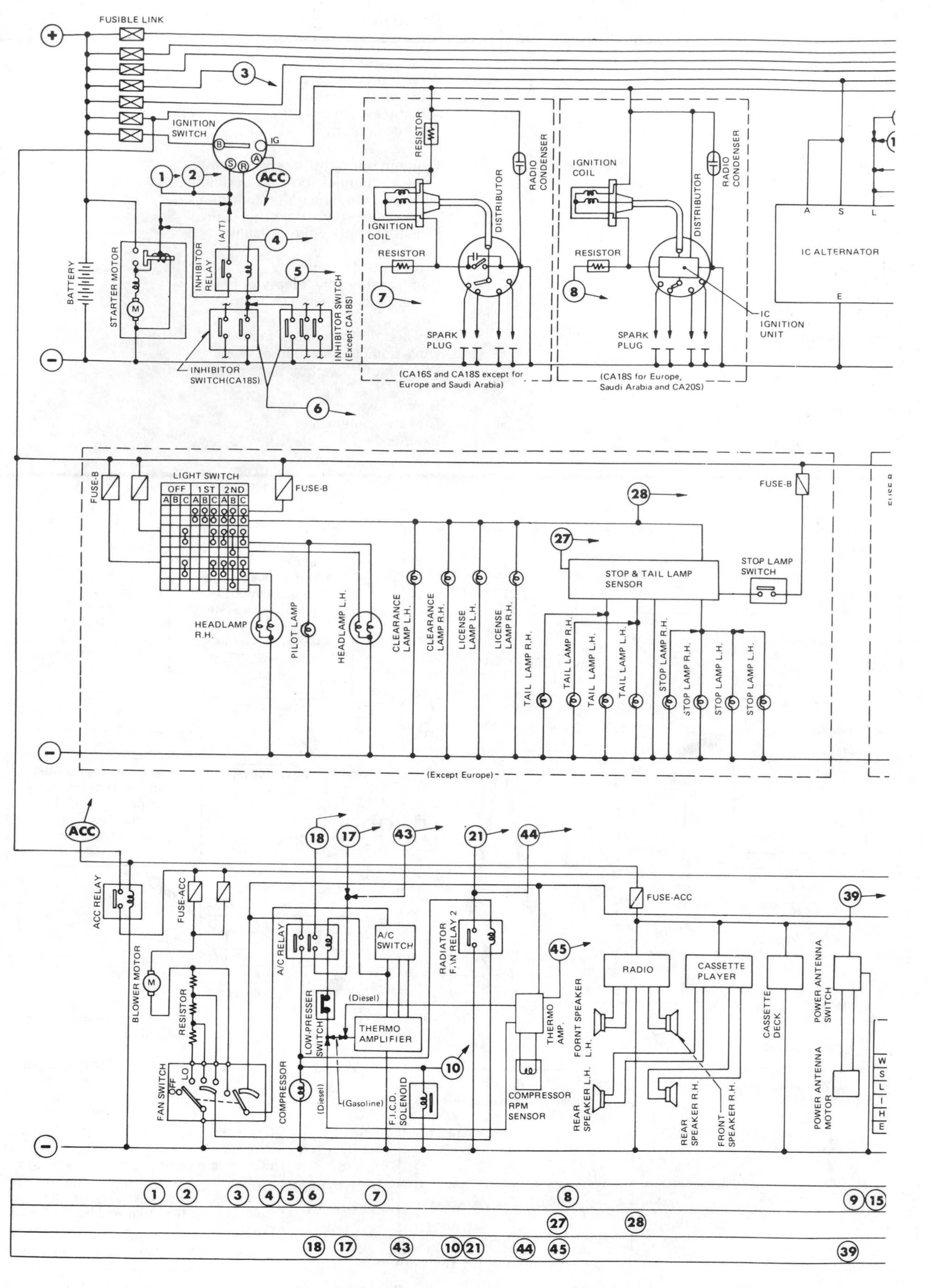

Fig. 12.52 Schematic wiring diagram (all models)

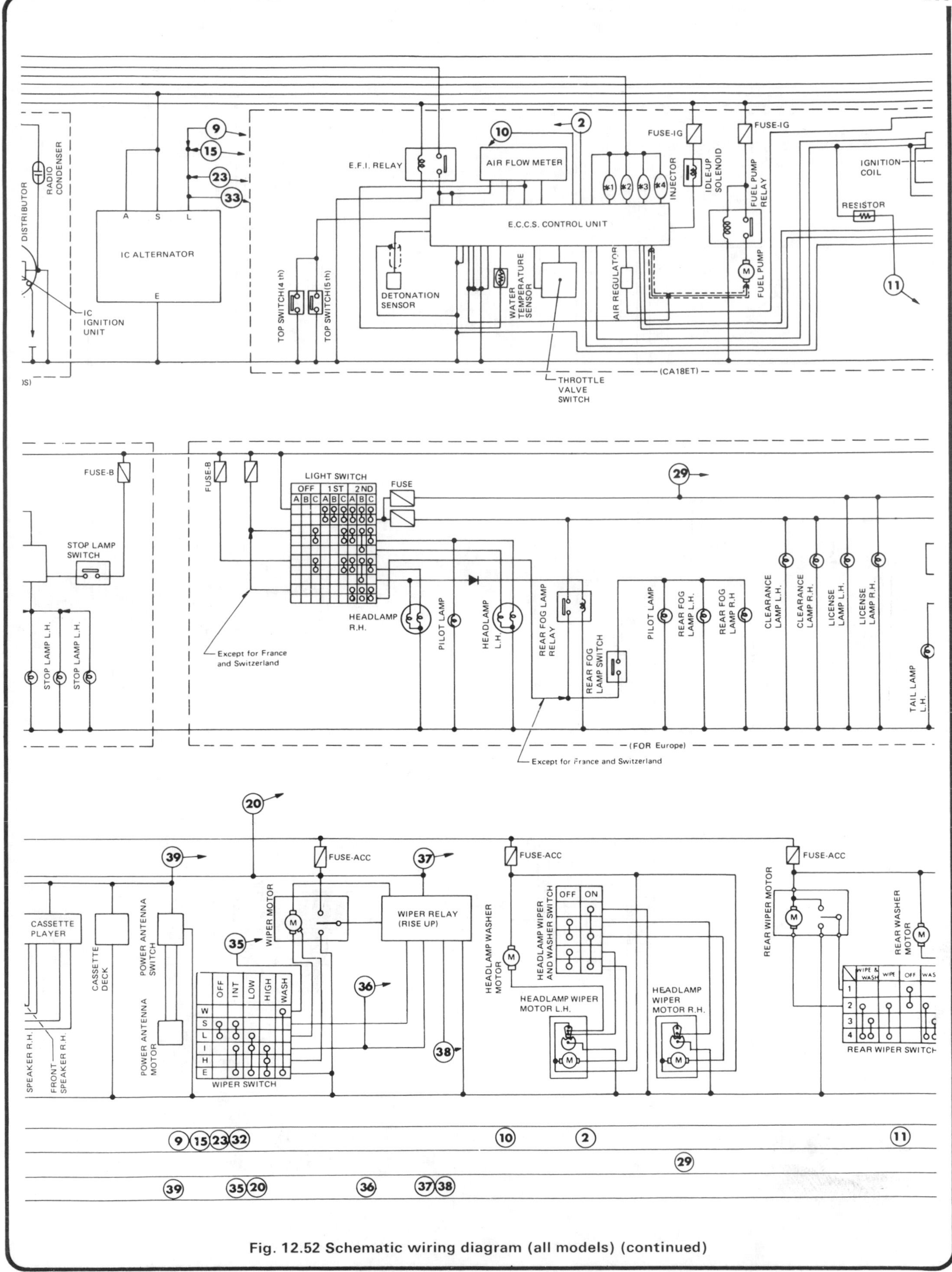

Fig. 12.52 Schematic wiring diagram (all models) (continued)

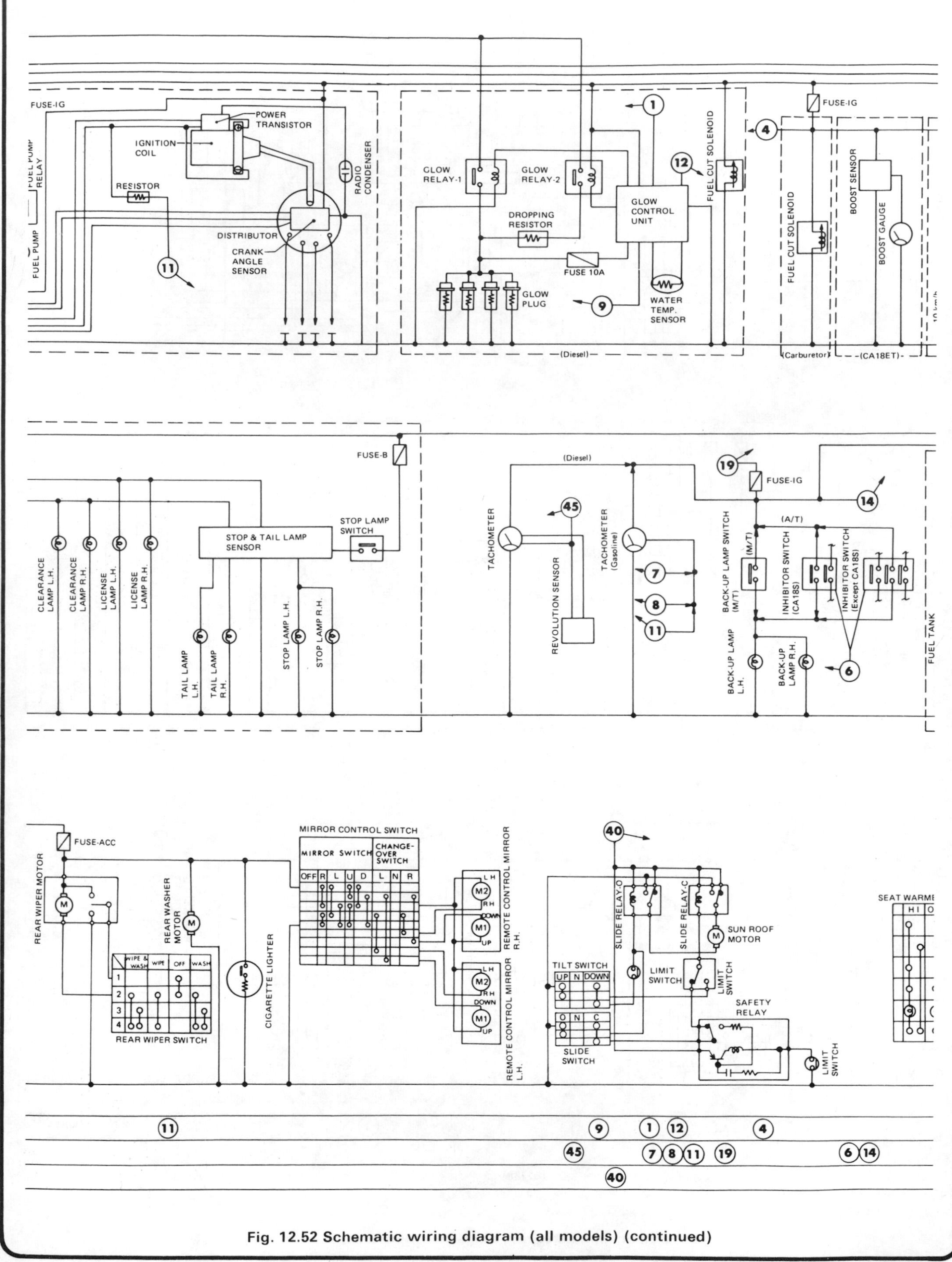

Fig. 12.52 Schematic wiring diagram (all models) (continued)

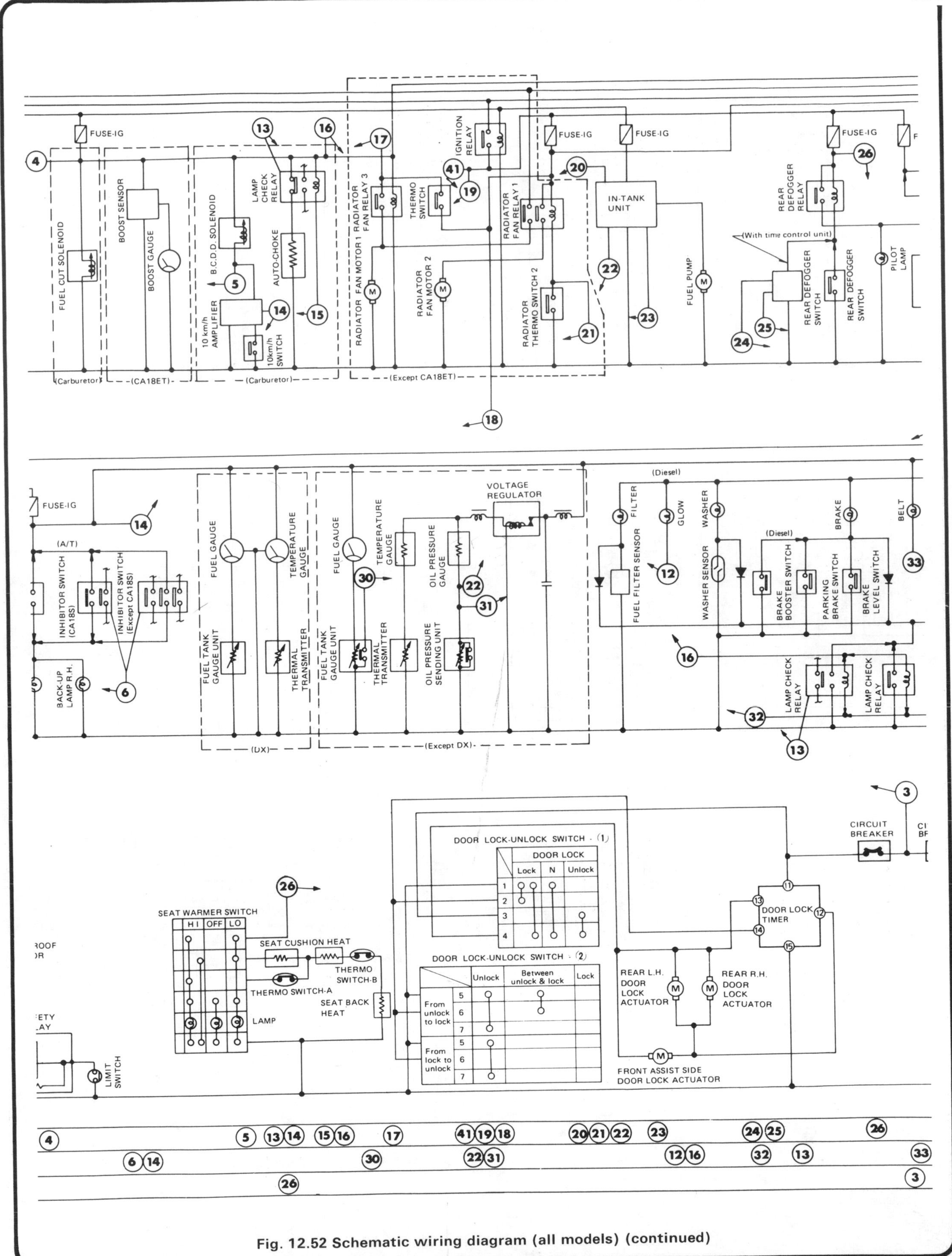

Fig. 12.52 Schematic wiring diagram (all models) (continued)

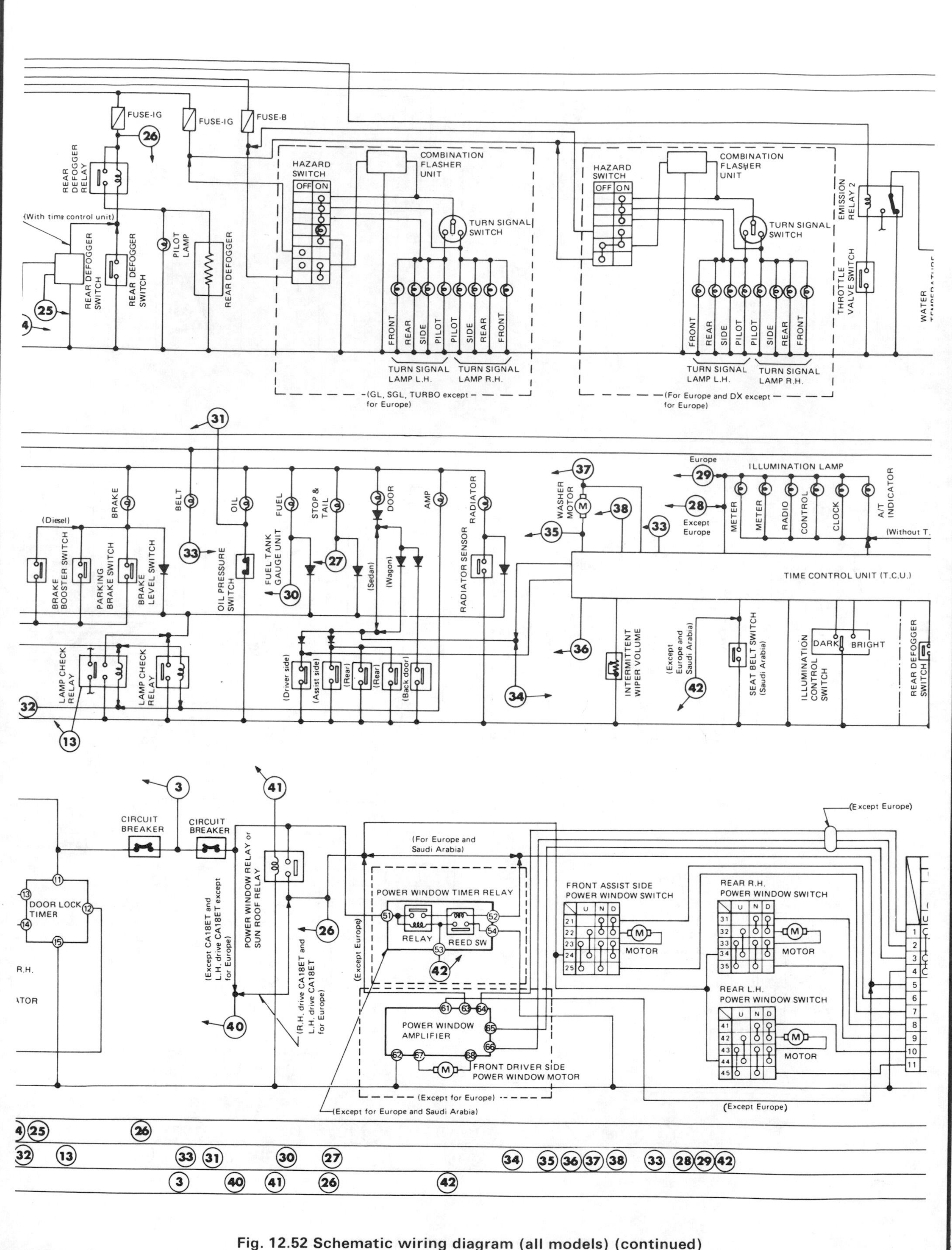

Fig. 12.52 Schematic wiring diagram (all models) (continued)

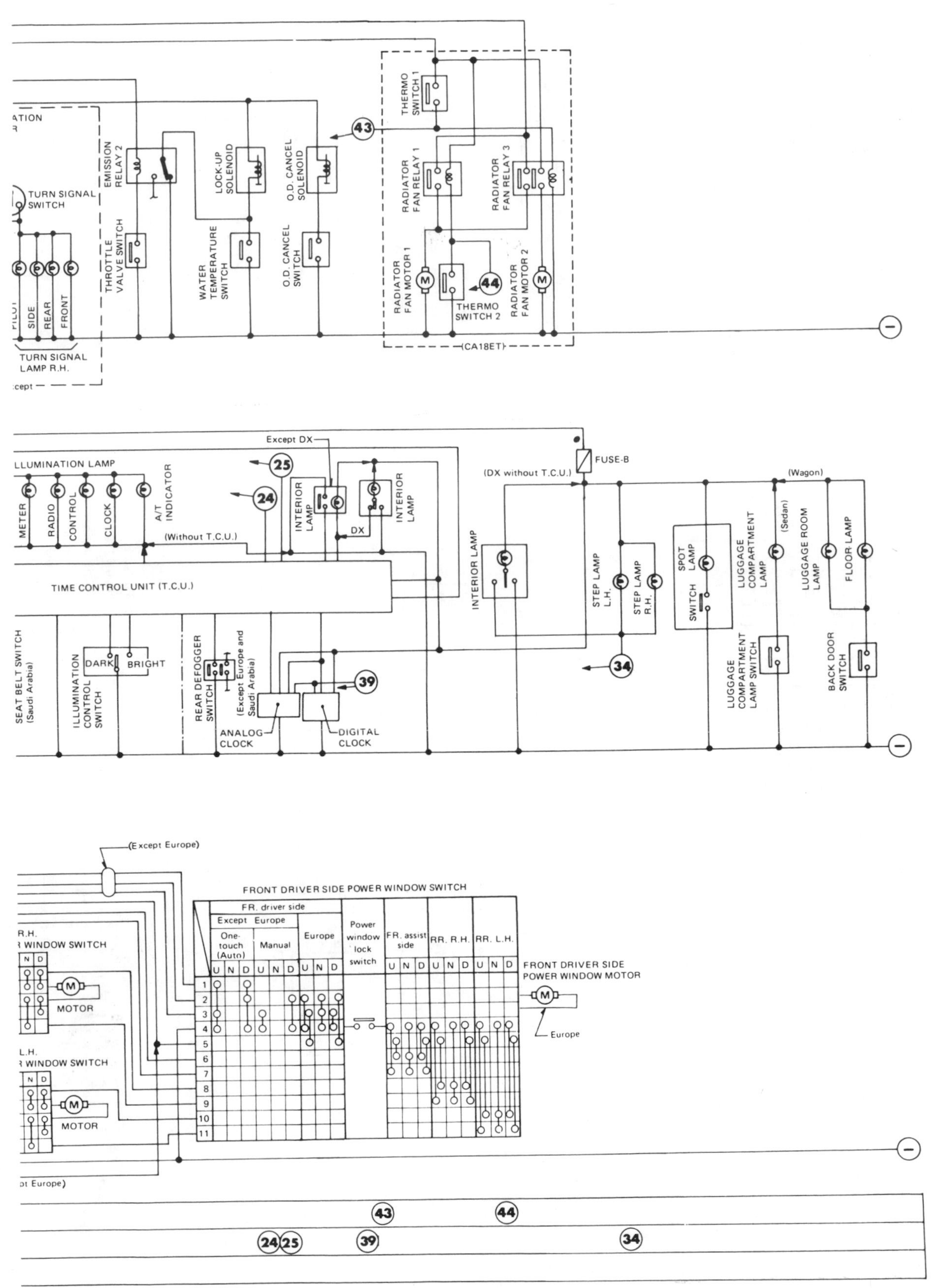

Fig. 12.52 Schematic wiring diagram (all models) (continued)

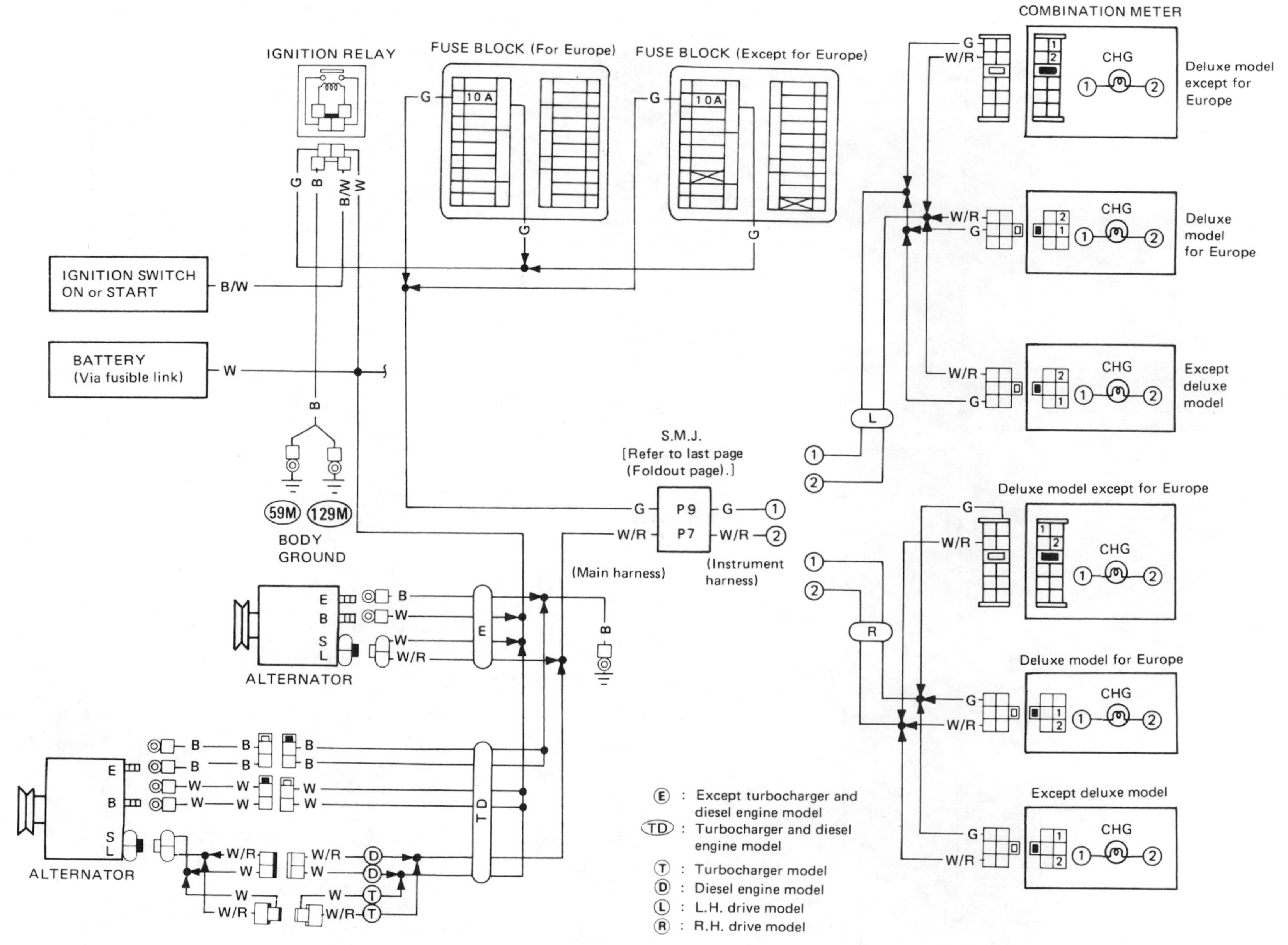

Fig. 12.53 Wiring diagram, charging circuit

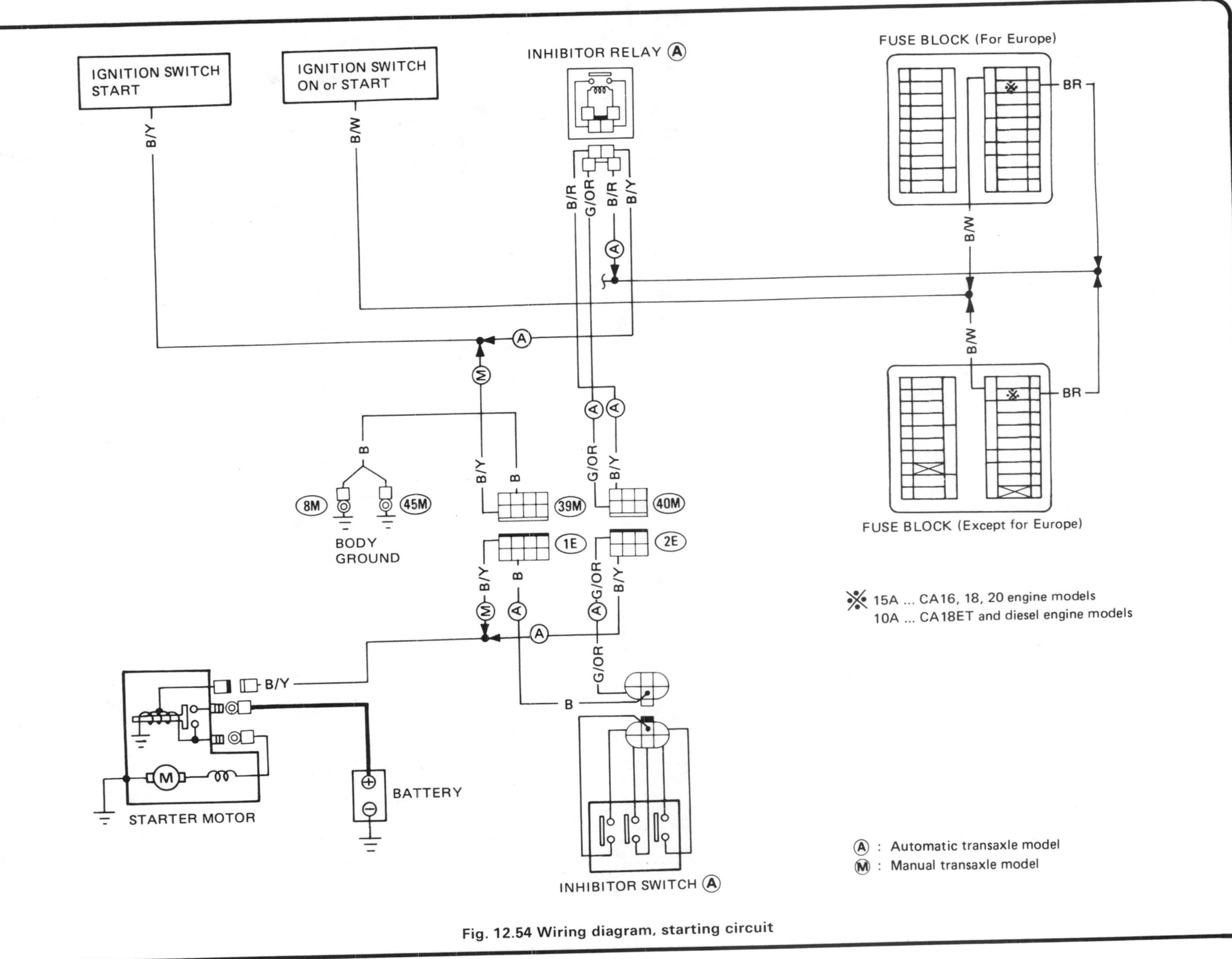

Fig. 12.54 Wiring diagram, starting circuit

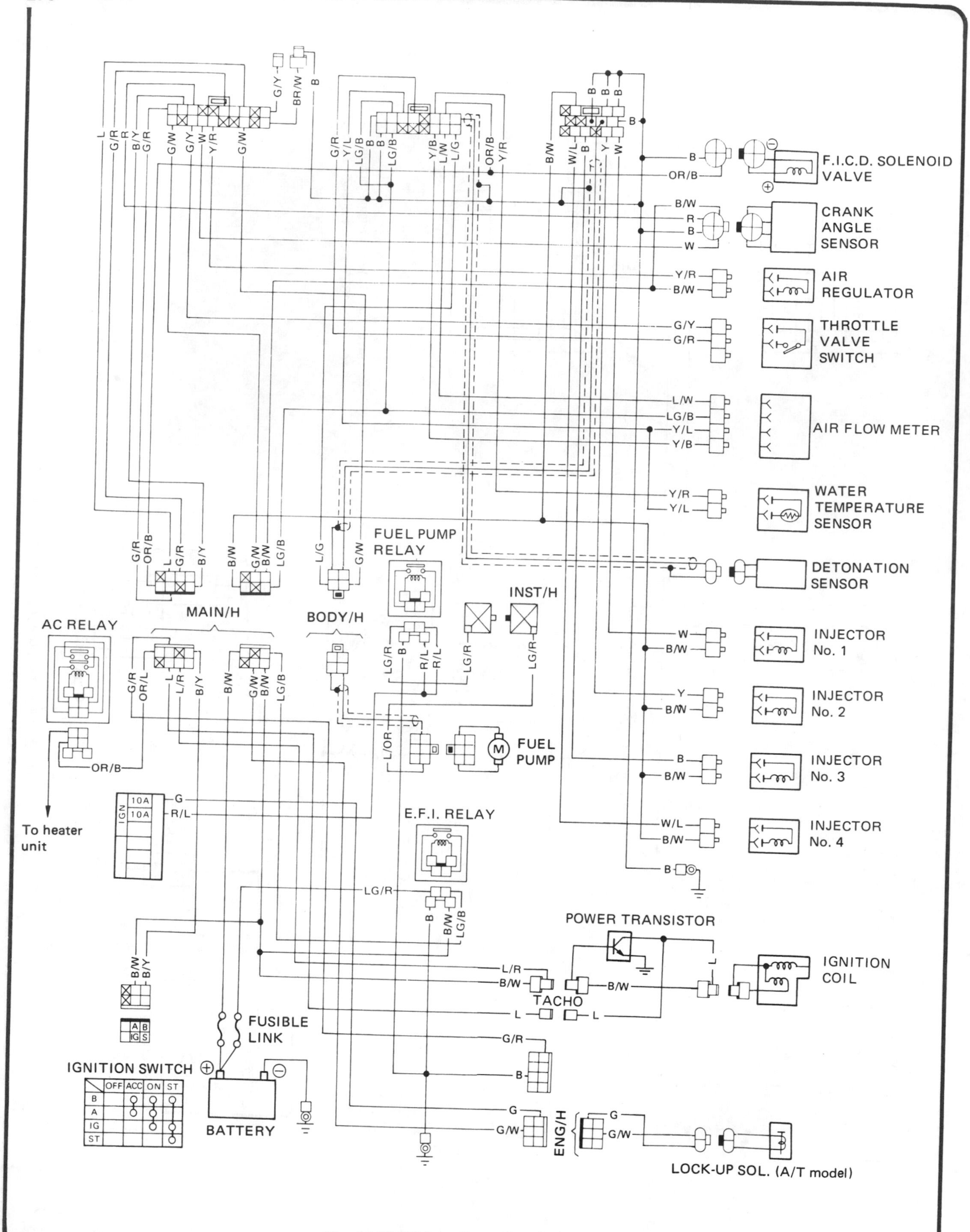

Fig. 12.55 Wiring diagram, ECCS circuit

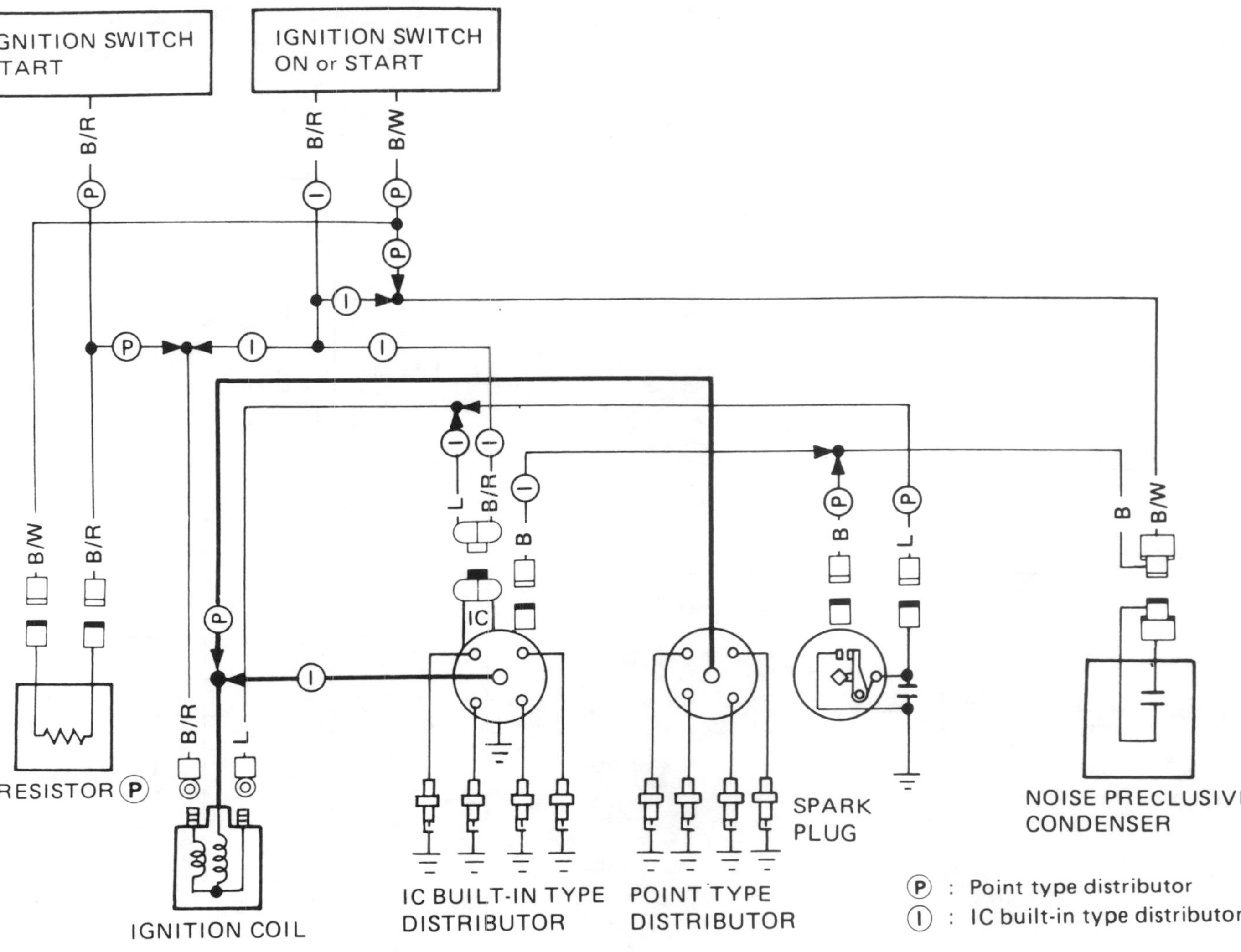

Fig. 12.56 Wiring diagram, ignition circuit (non-Turbo models)

Except for Europe turbo engine model:
(Twin cooling fan with a two speed motor equipped model)

THERMO SWITCH NO. 1
THERMO SWITCH NO. 2
MAIN FAN MOTOR
HI
LO
SUB-FAN MOTOR
RADIATOR FAN RELAY NO. 3
FUSE BLOCK
ACC
IG
Via fusible link
RADIATOR FAN RELAY NO. 2
To heater unit
RADIATOR FAN RELAY
AIR CONDITIONER LOW-PRESSURE SWITCH
AIR CONDITIONER COMPRESSOR
To air conditioner thermo switch

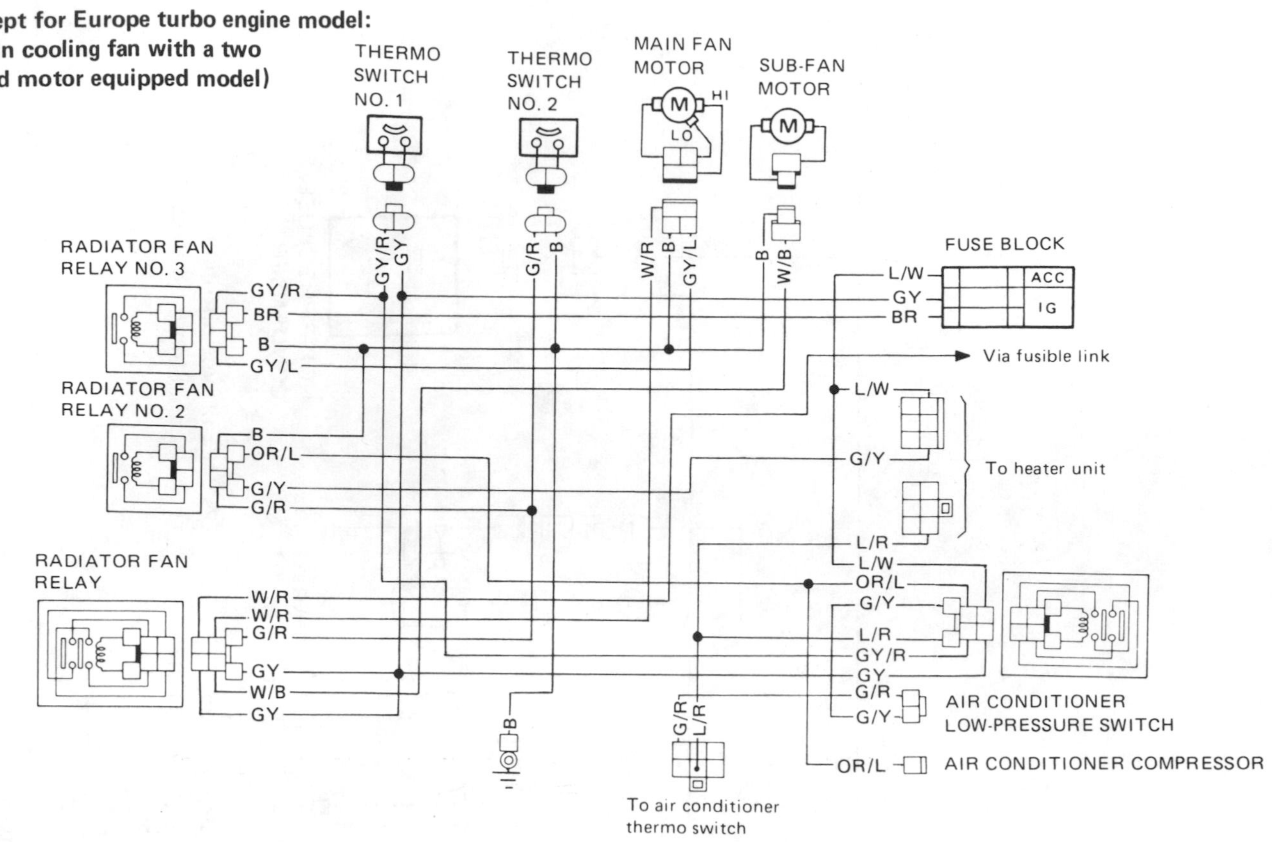

For Europe turbo

THERMO SWITCH NO.1
THERMO SWITCH NO.2
MAIN FAN MOTOR
HI
LO
SUB-FAN MOTOR
RADIATOR FAN RELAY
ACC
IG
Via fusible link
RADIATOR FAN RELAY NO.2
To heater unit
AIR CONDITIONER RELAY
RADIATOR FAN RELAY NO.3
AIR CONDITIONER LOW-PRESSURE SWITCH
AIR CONDITIONER COMPRESSOR
To air conditioner thermo switch

Fig. 12.57 Wiring diagram, cooling circuit

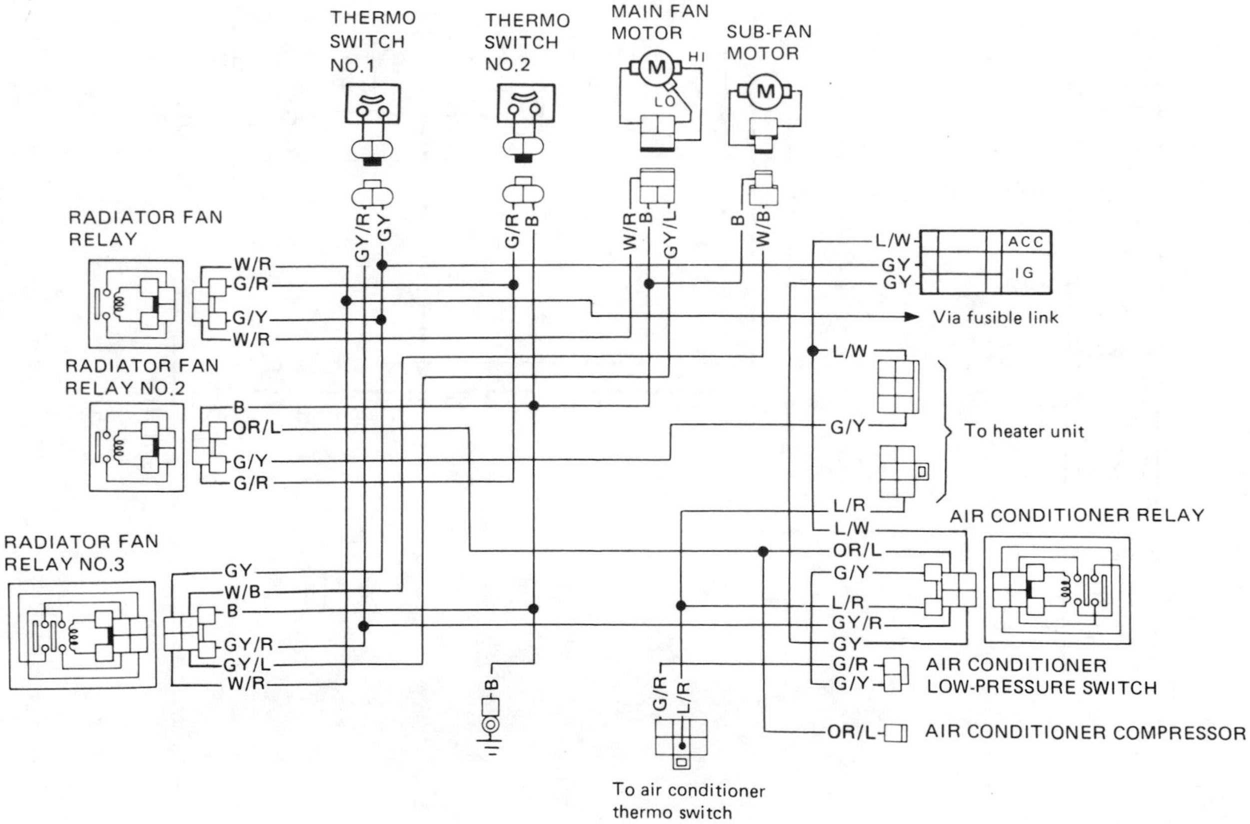

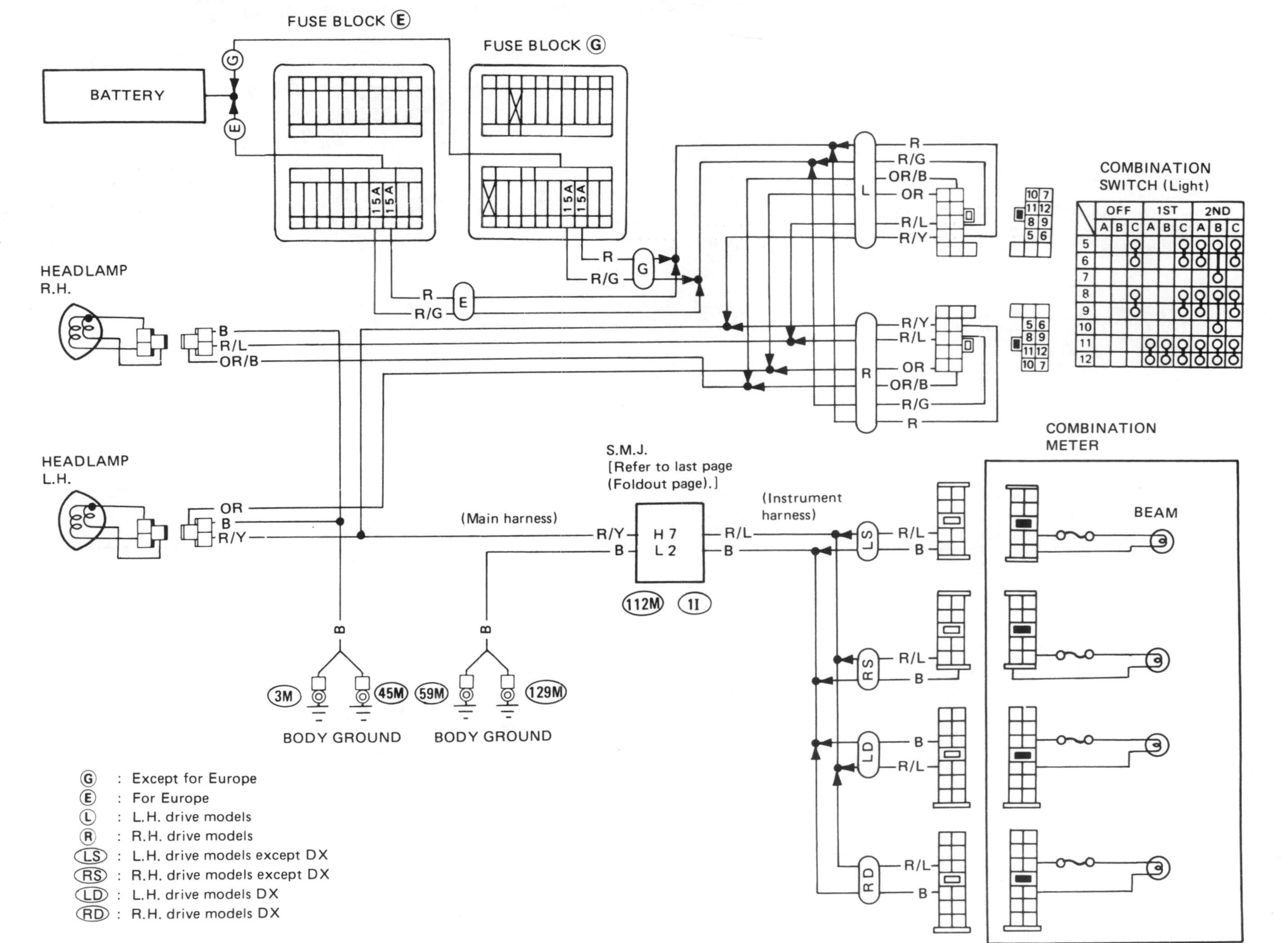

Fig. 12.58 Wiring diagram, headlamp circuit

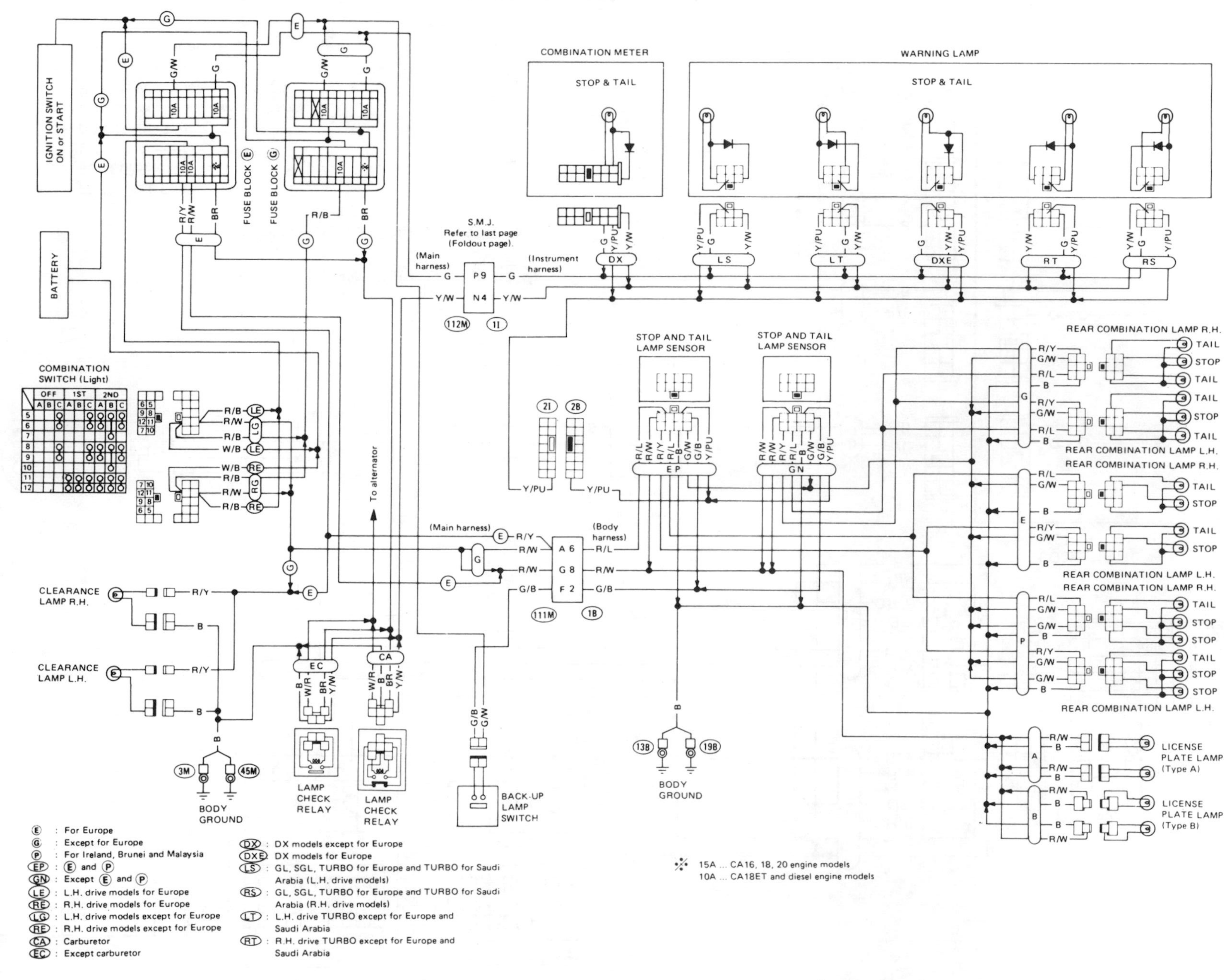

Fig. 12.59 Wiring diagram, side marker lamp, number plate lamp and stop/tail lamp circuits (Saloon)

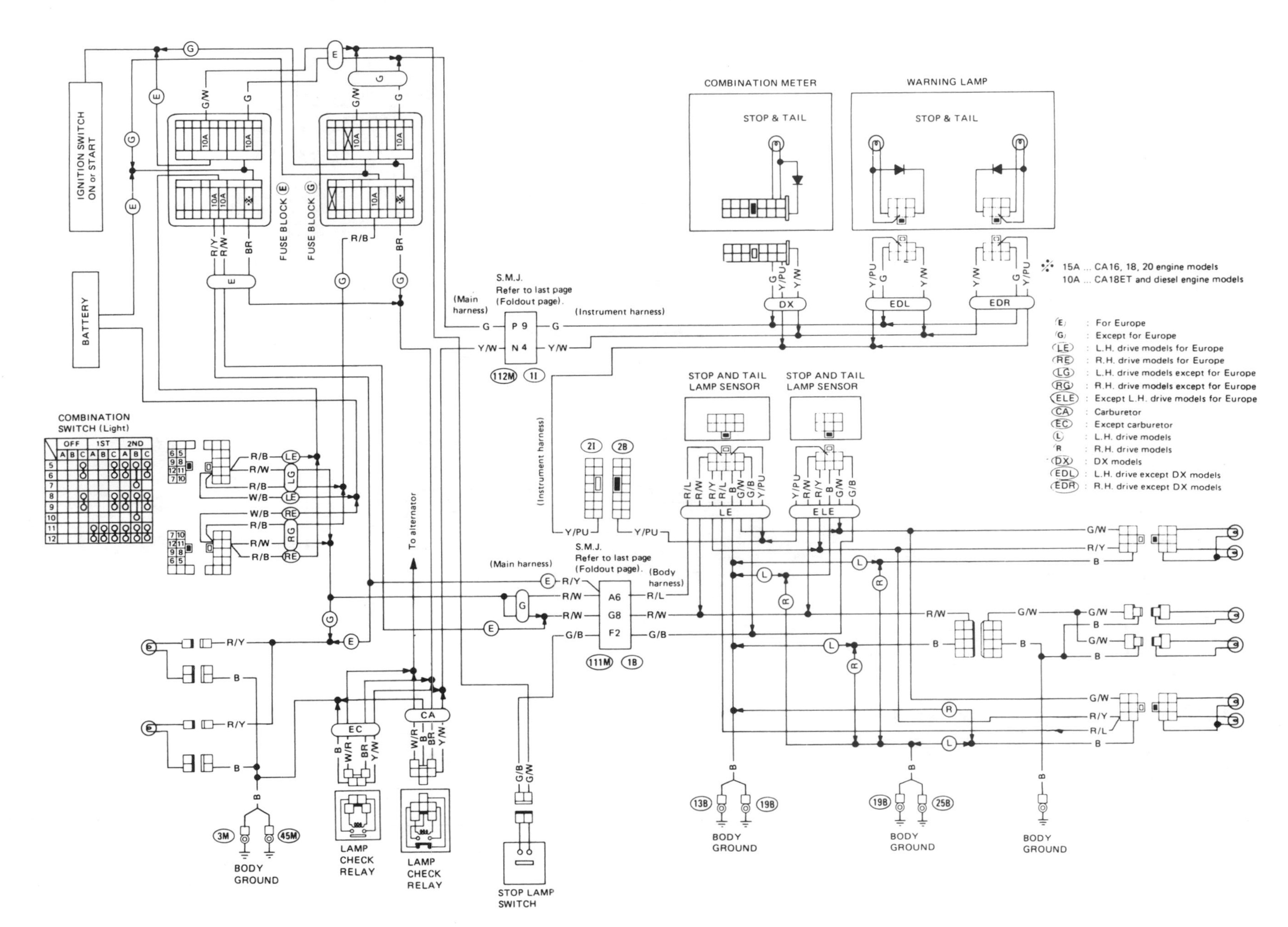

Fig. 12.60 Wiring diagram, side marker lamp, number plate lamp and stop/tail lamp circuits (Estate)

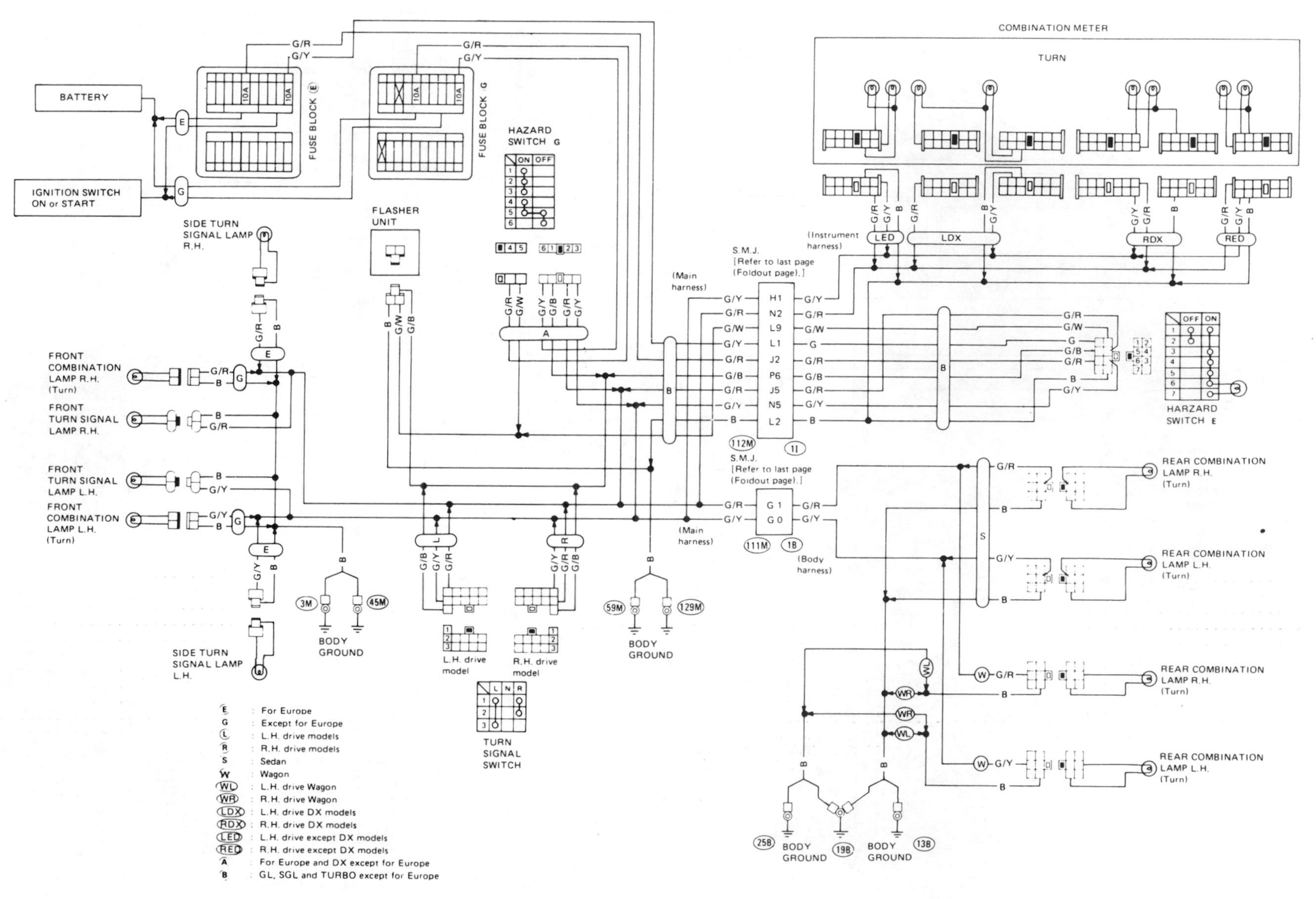

Fig. 12.61 Wiring diagram, direction indicator lamp and hazard warning lamp circuits

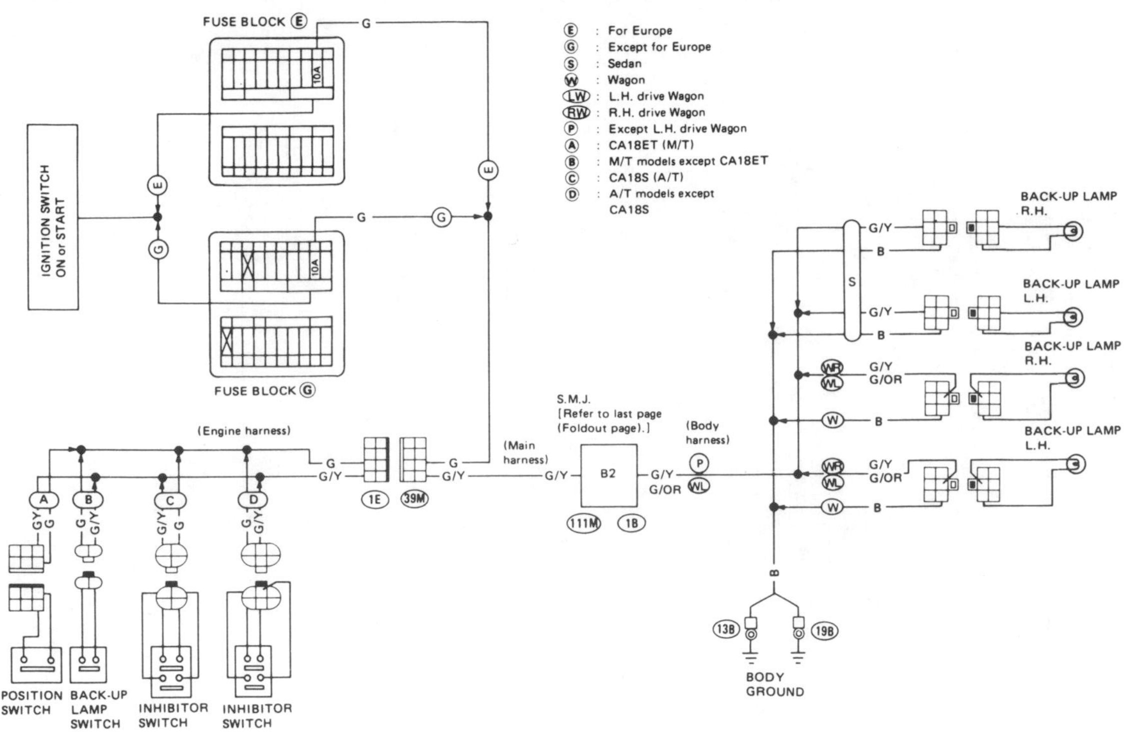

Fig. 12.62 Wiring diagram, reversing lamp circuit

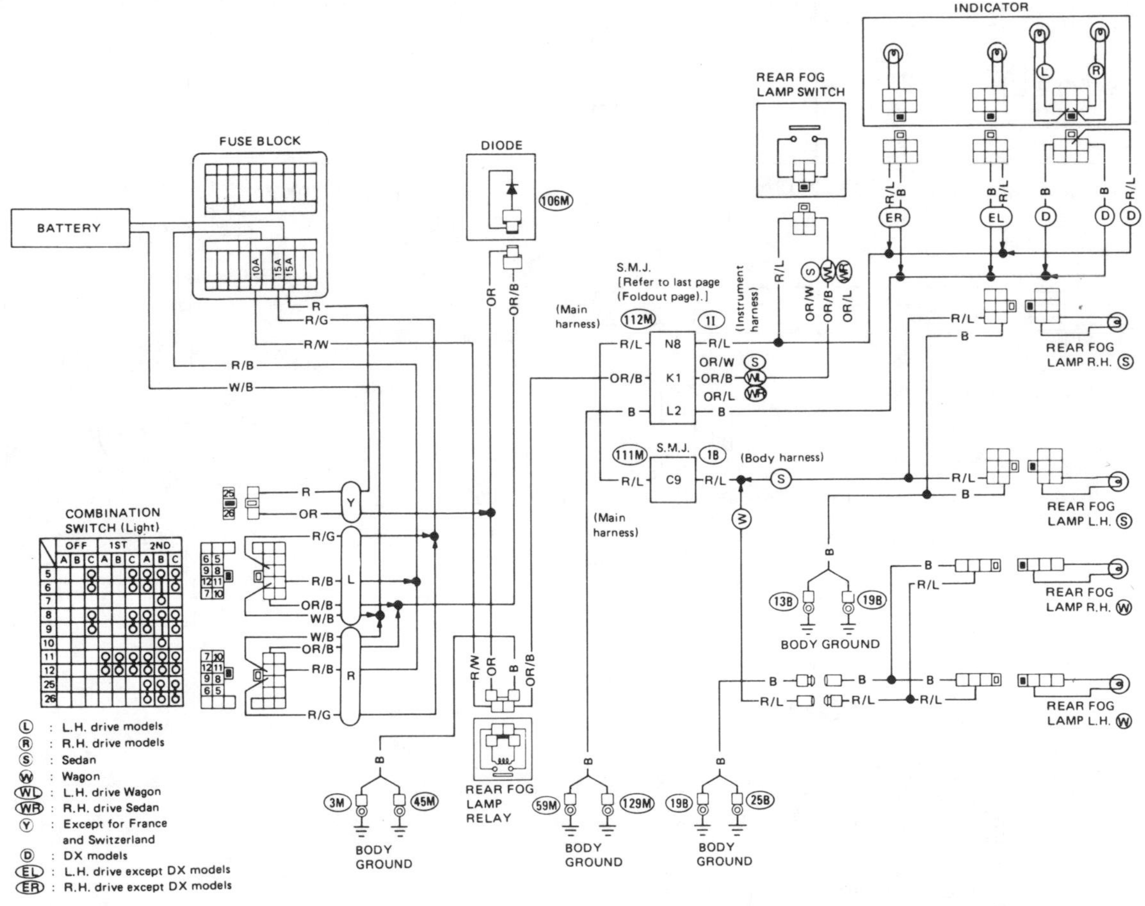

Fig. 12.63 Wiring diagram, rear fog lamp circuit

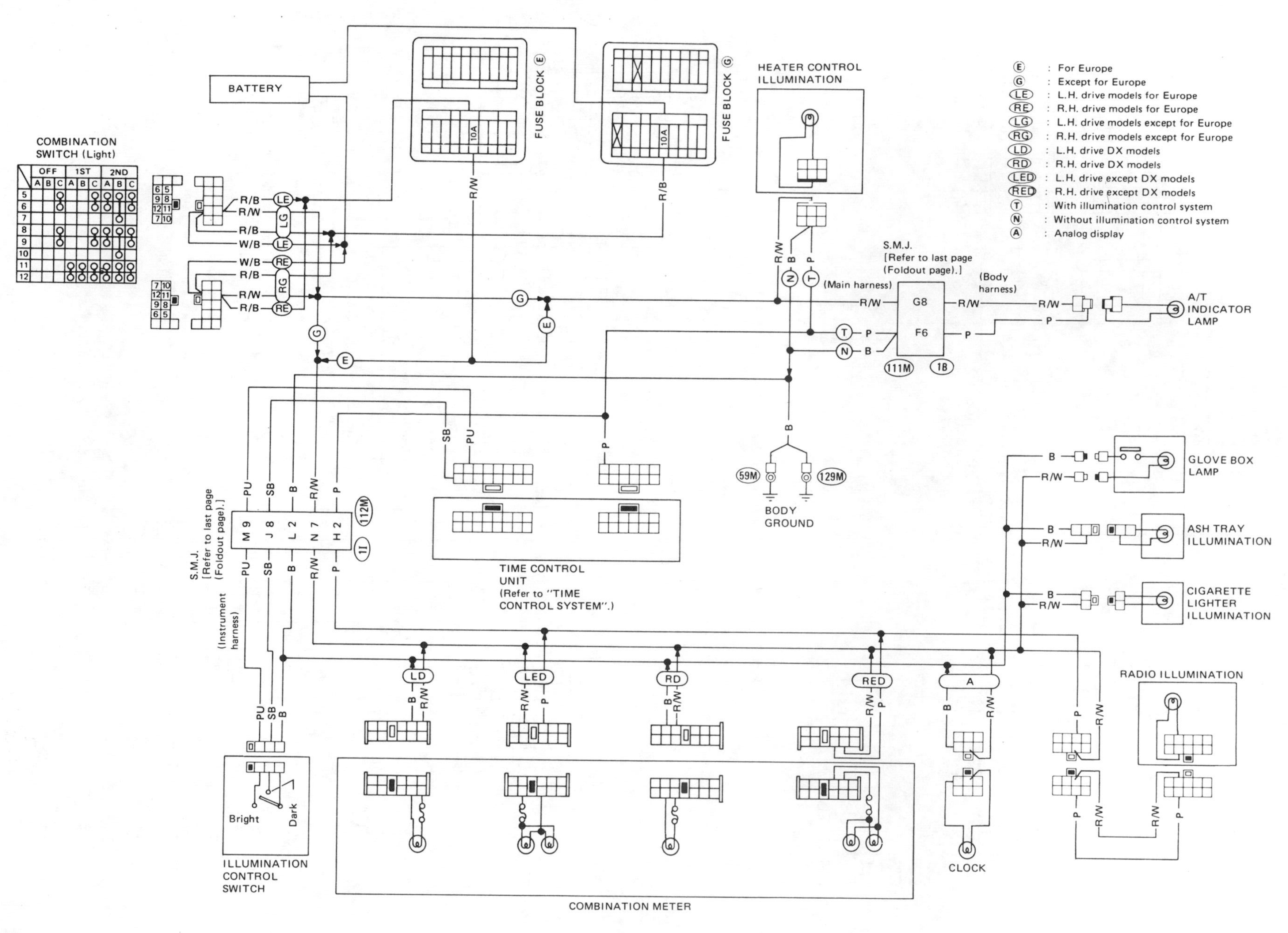

Fig. 12.64 Wiring diagram, interior illumination circuits

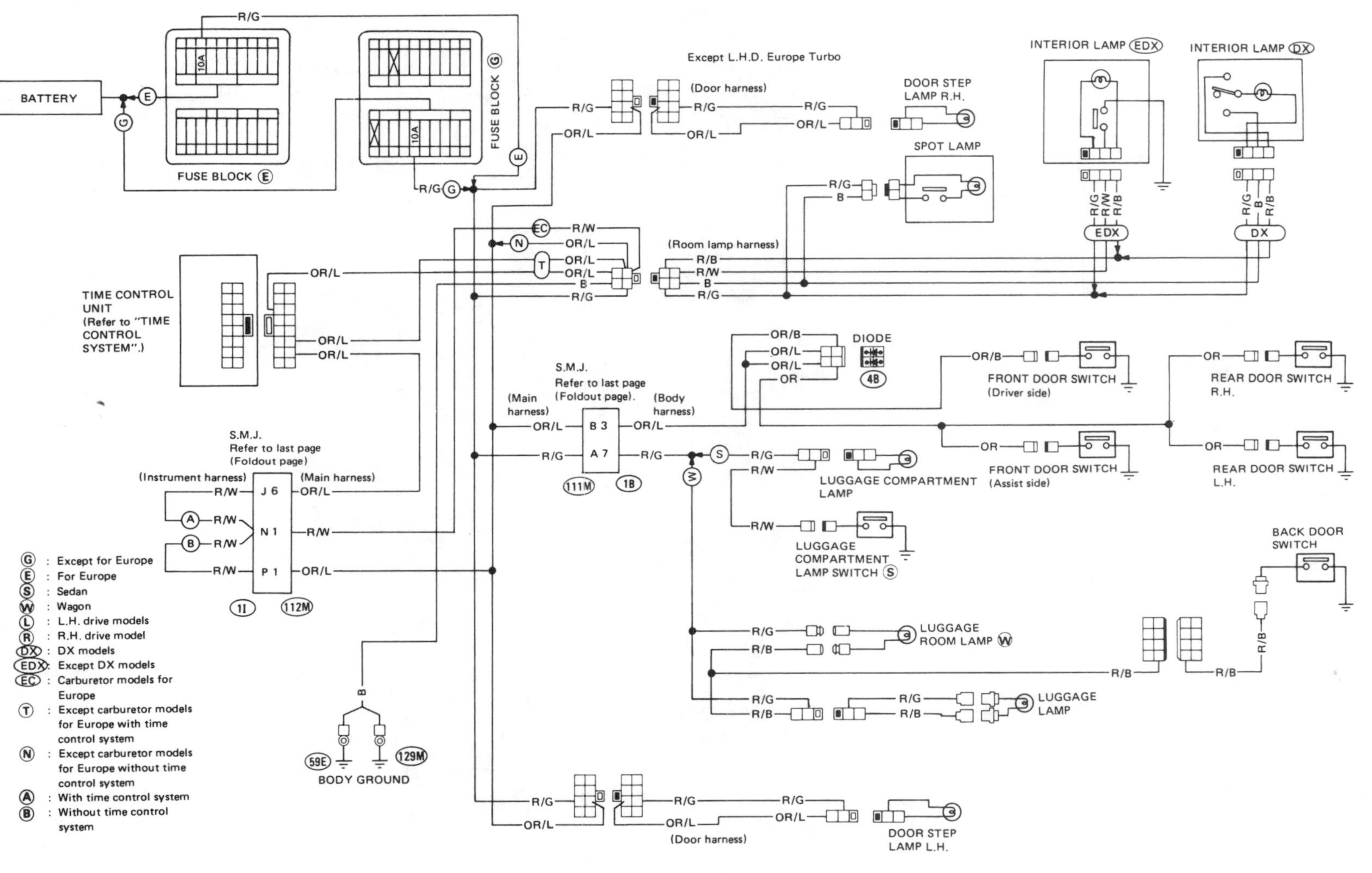

Fig. 12.65 Wiring diagram, interior lamp, boot lamp, map reading lamp and step illumination lamp circuits

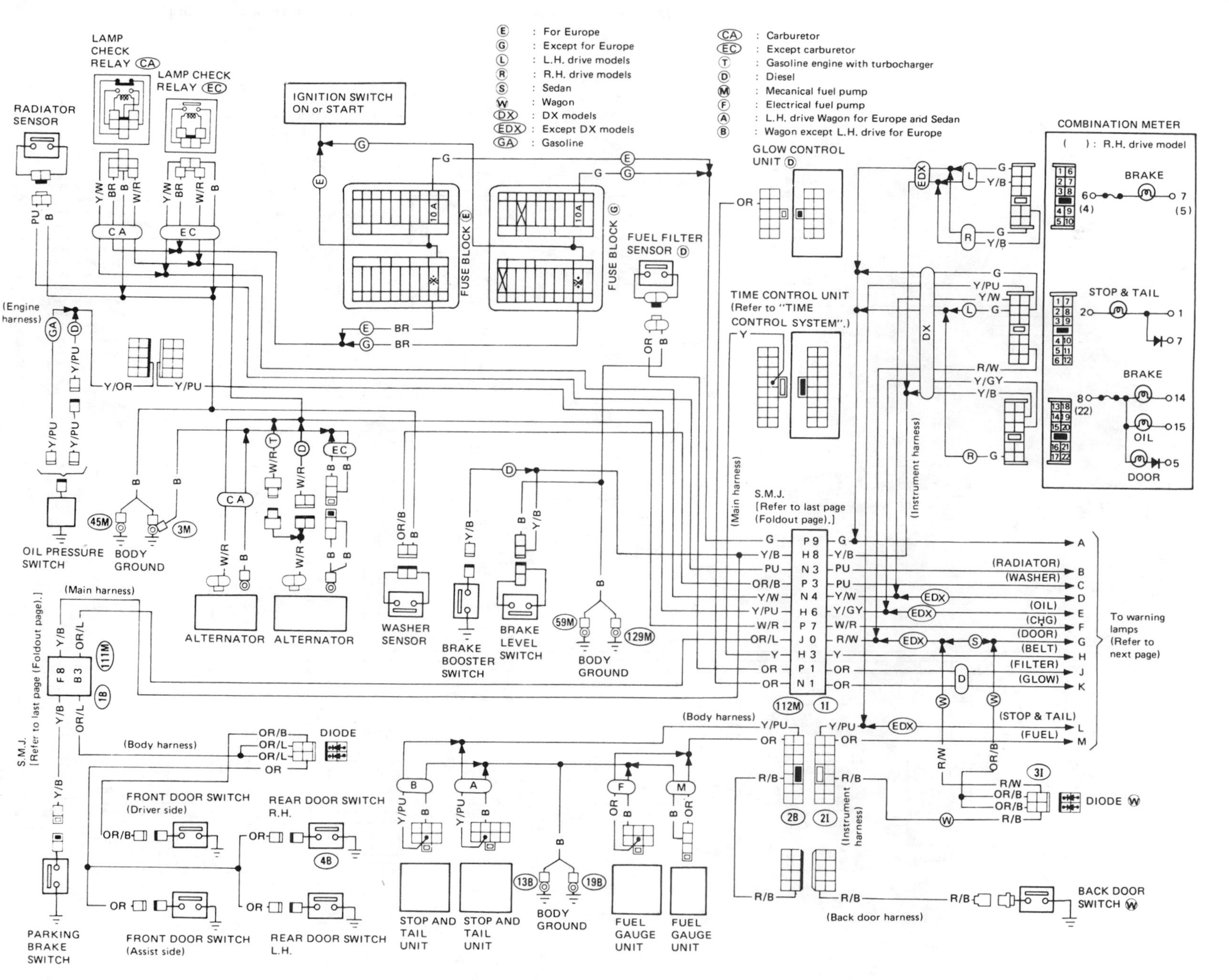

Fig. 12.66 Wiring diagram, warning lamp circuits

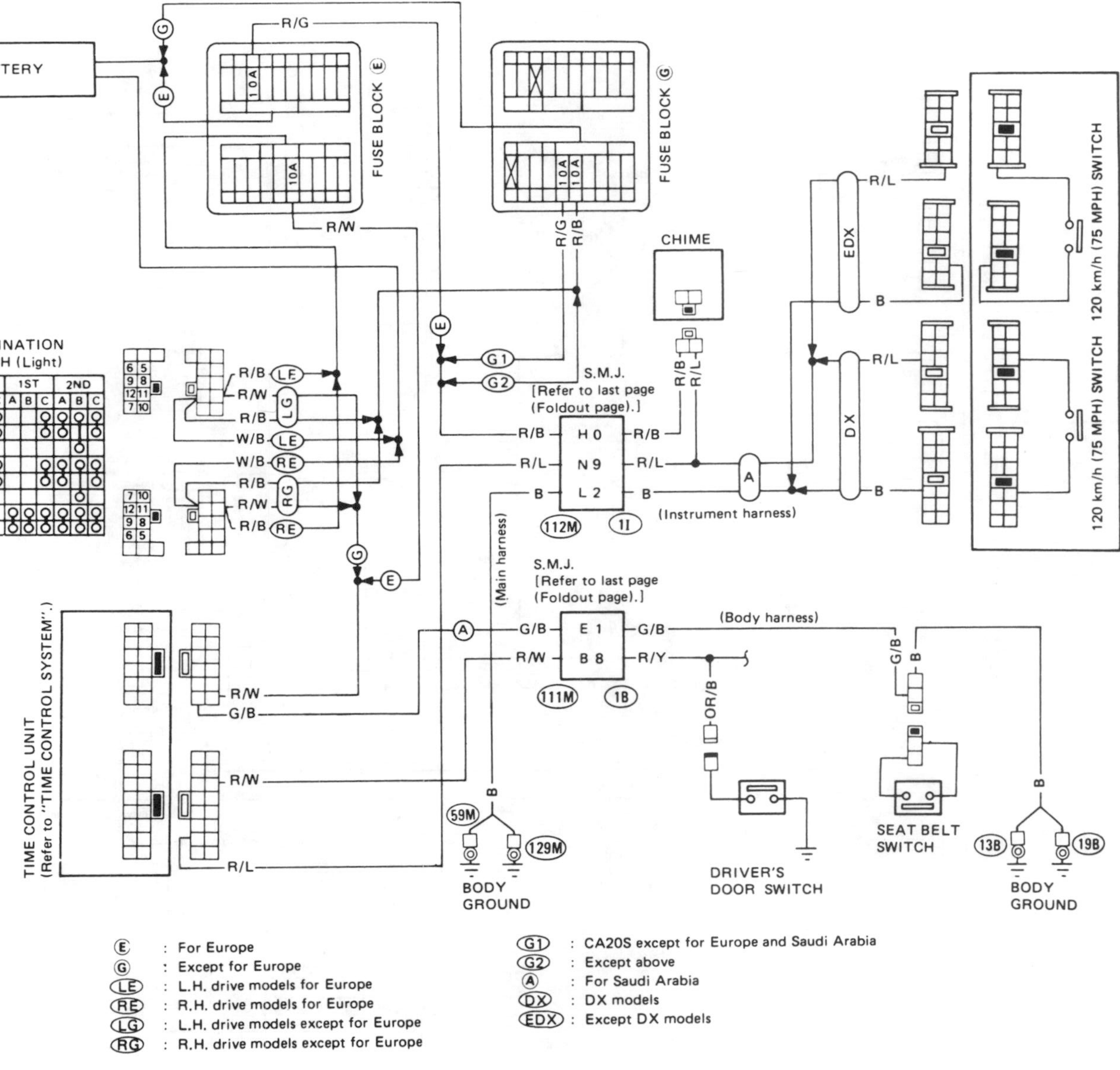

Ⓔ : For Europe
Ⓖ : Except for Europe
(LE) : L.H. drive models for Europe
(RE) : R.H. drive models for Europe
(LG) : L.H. drive models except for Europe
(RG) : R.H. drive models except for Europe
(G1) : CA20S except for Europe and Saudi Arabia
(G2) : Except above
Ⓐ : For Saudi Arabia
(DX) : DX models
(EDX) : Except DX models

Fig. 12.67 Wiring diagram, warning chime circuit

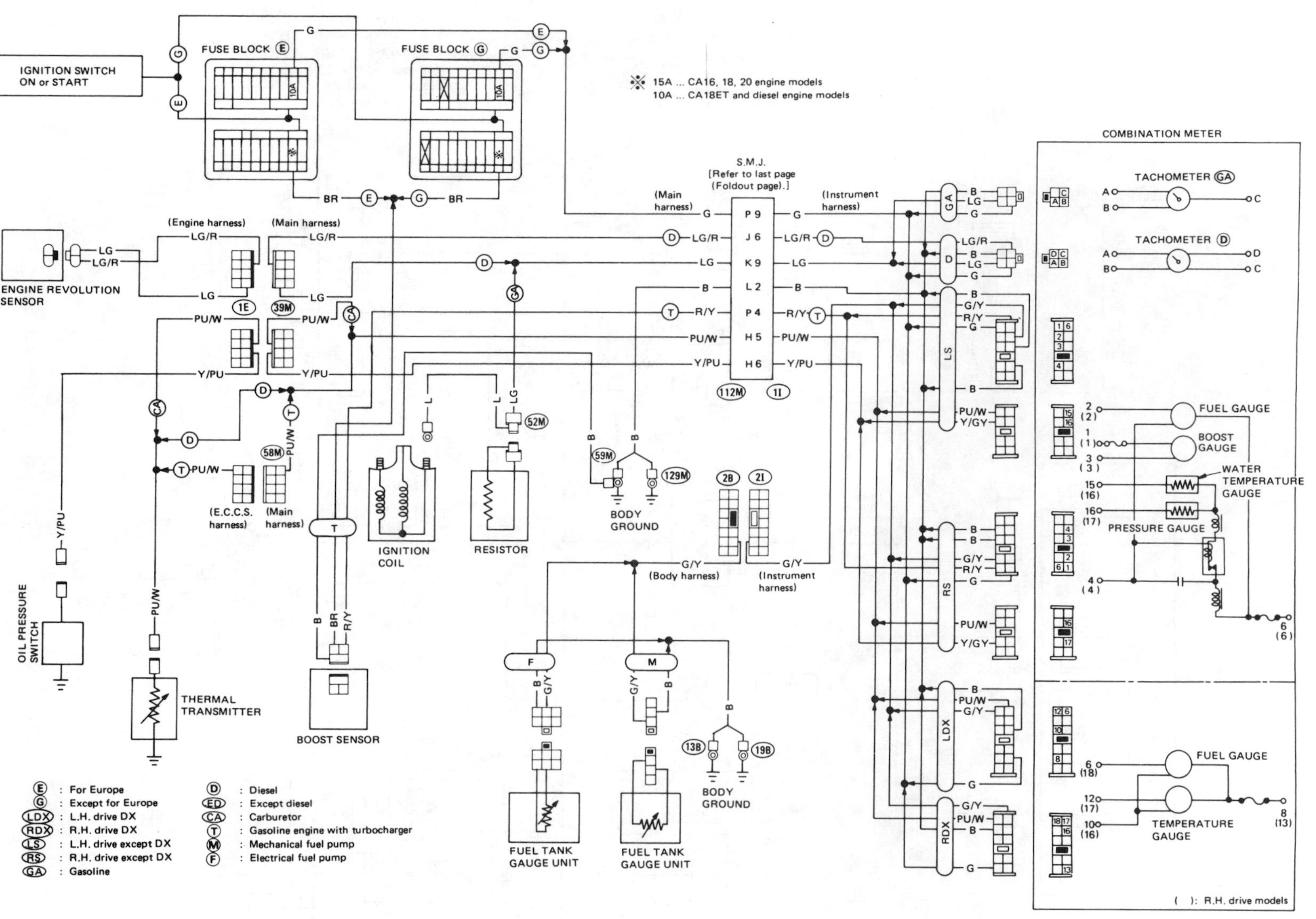

Fig. 12.68 Wiring diagram, tachometer, fuel gauge, boost gauge, oil pressure gauge and water temperature gauge circuits

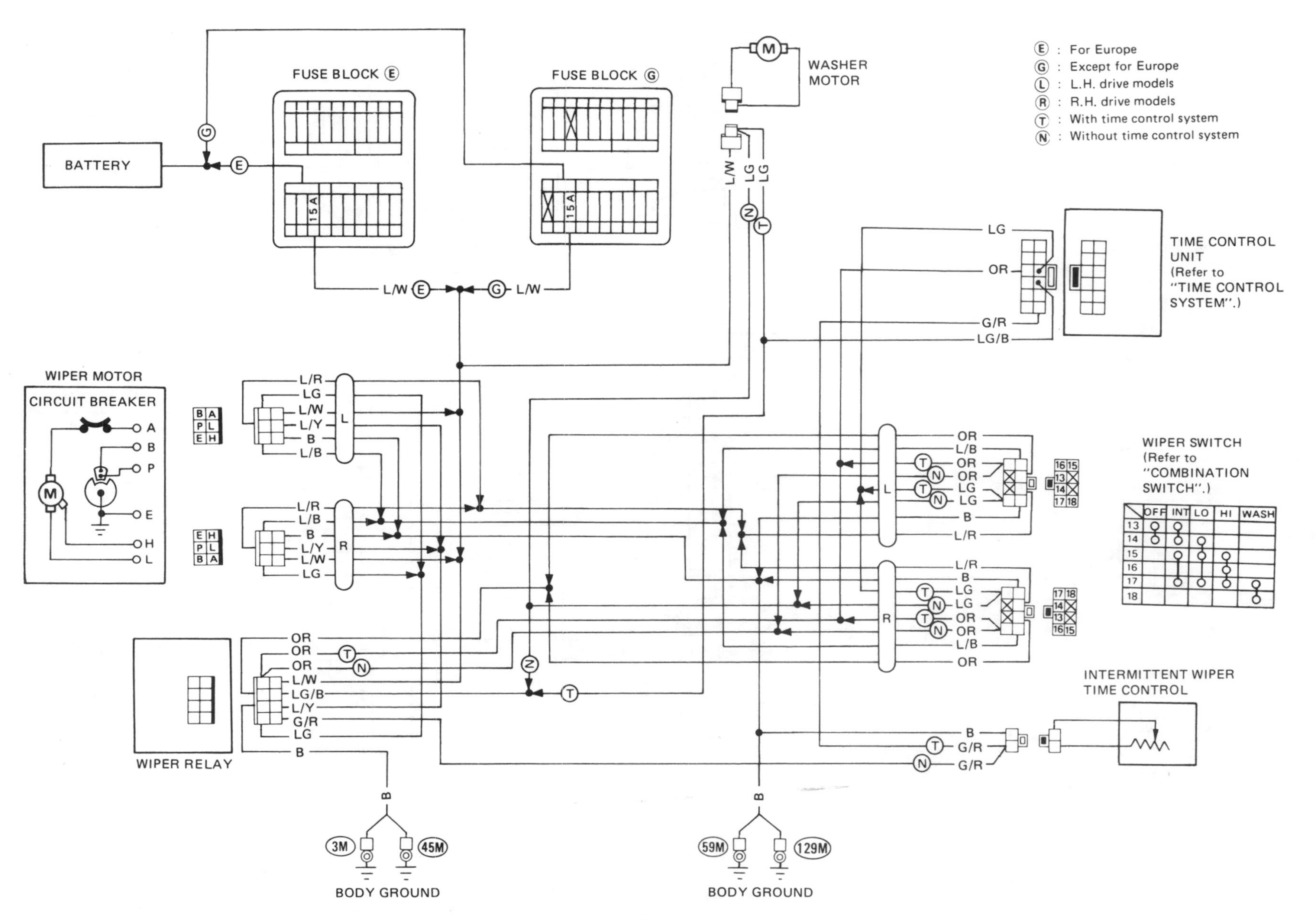

Fig. 12.69 Wiring diagram, windscreen wiper and washer circuits

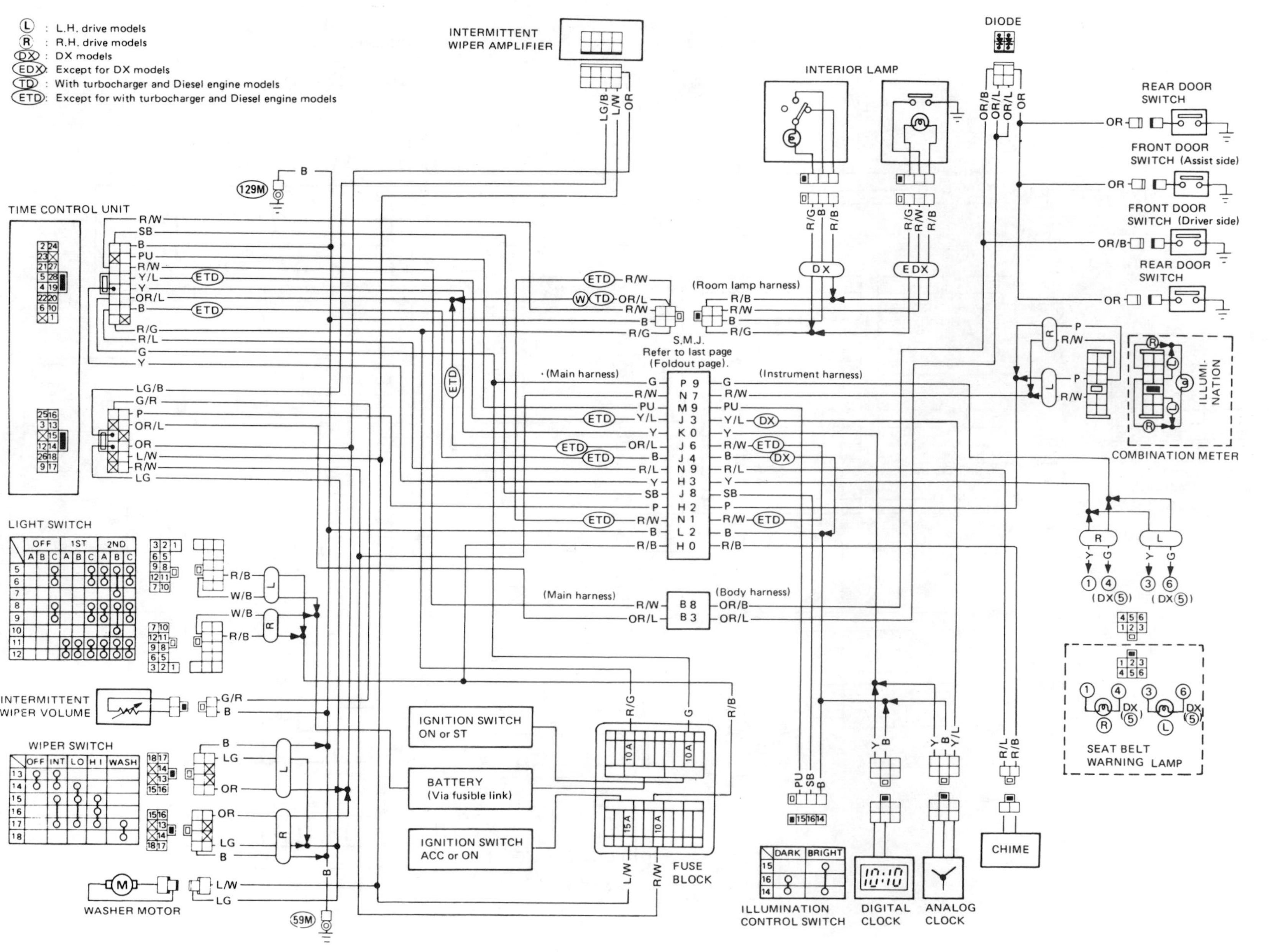

Fig. 12.70 Wiring diagram, time control circuit

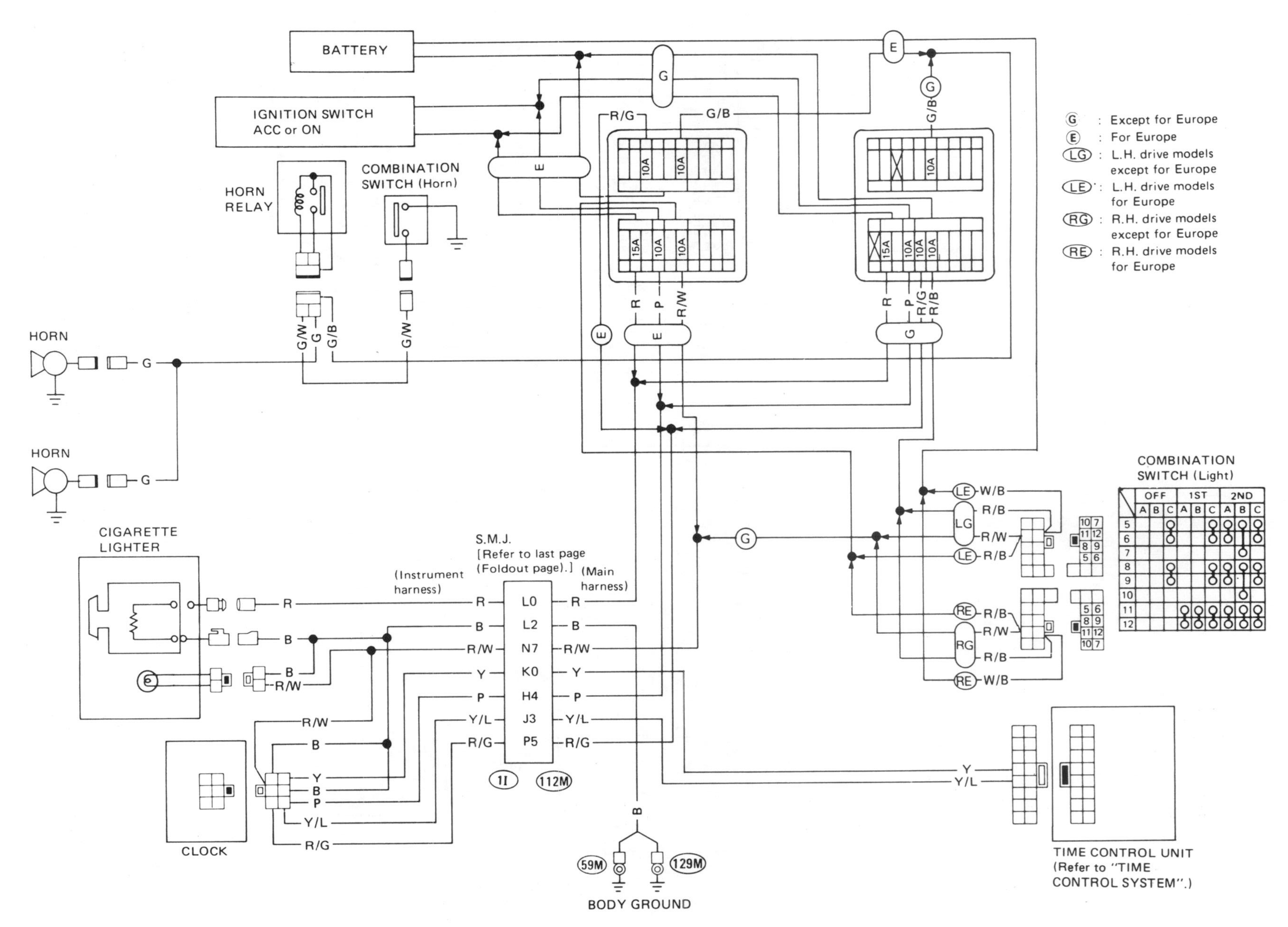

Fig. 12.71 Wiring diagram, horn, cigar lighter and clock circuits

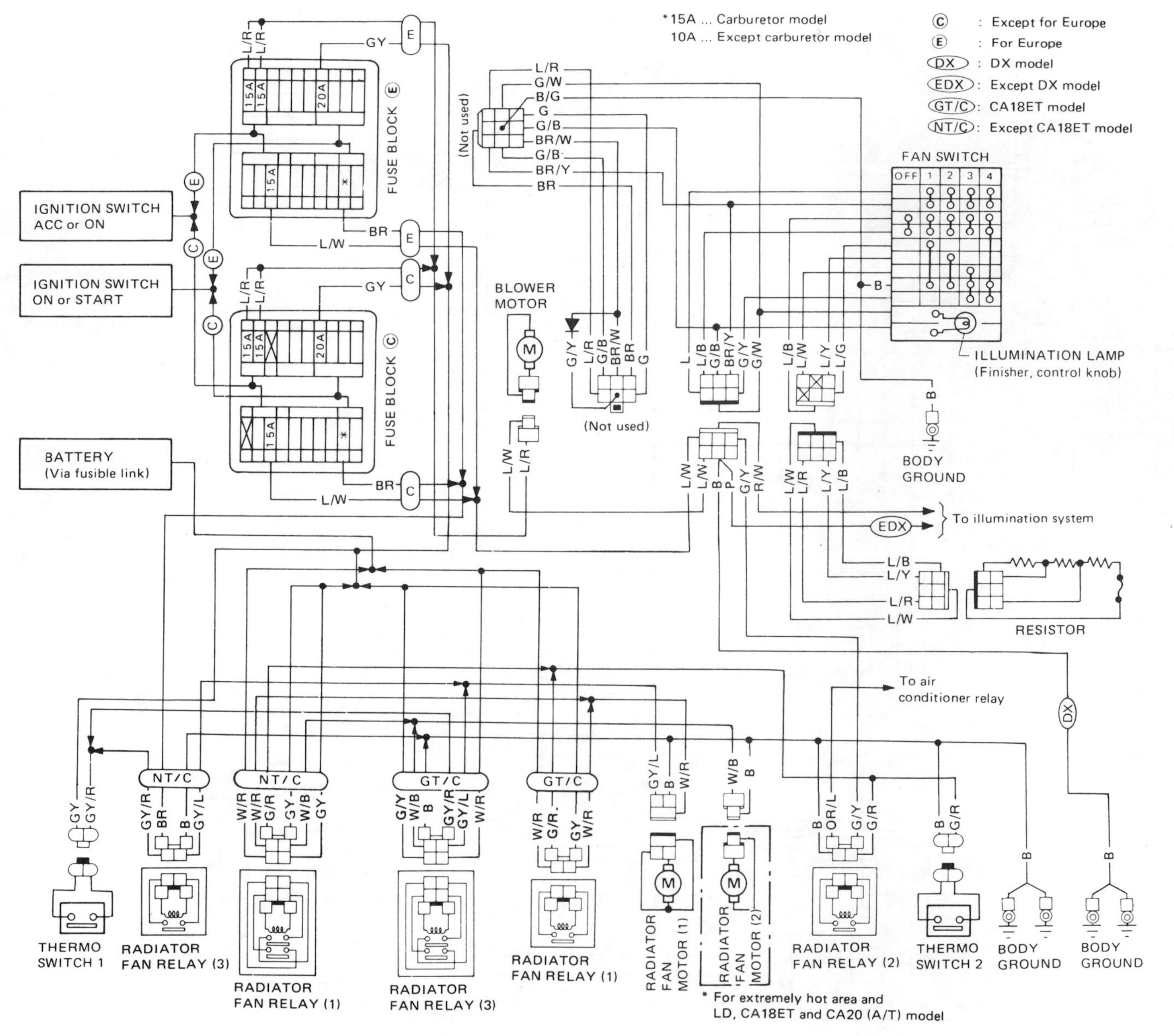

Fig. 12.72 Wiring diagram, heater circuit

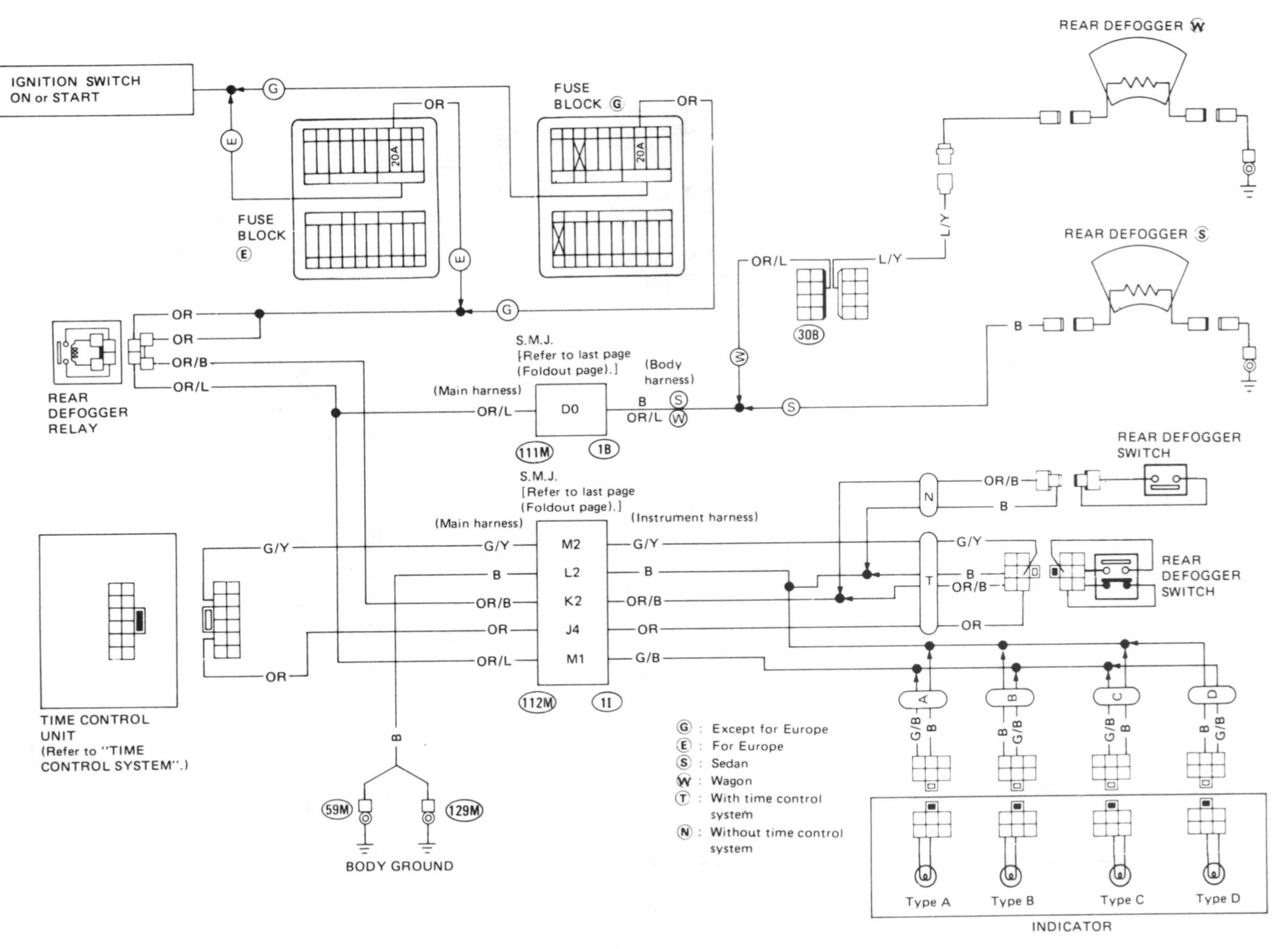

Fig. 12.73 Wiring diagram, heated rear window circuit

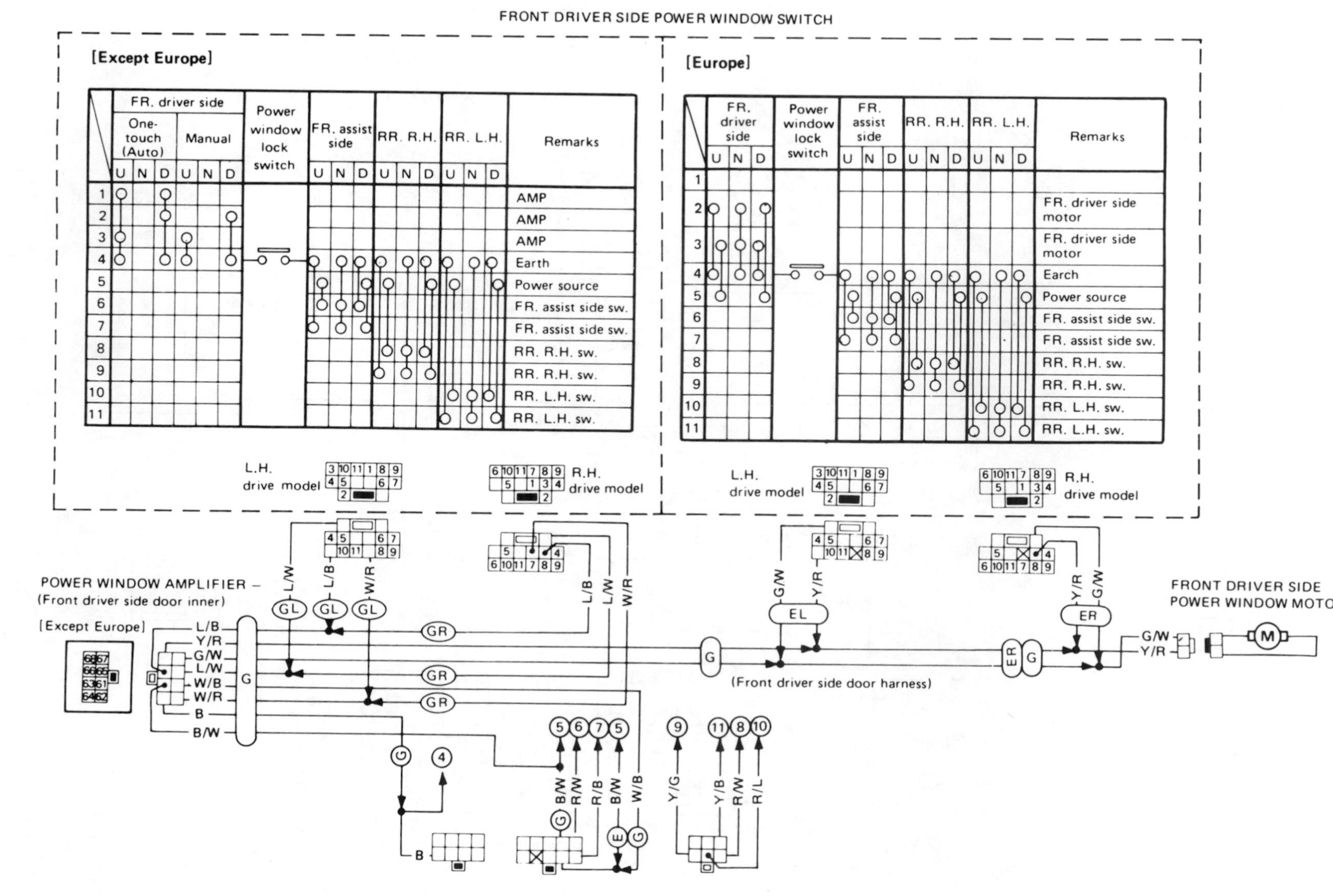

Fig. 12.74 Wiring diagram, power-operated window circuits

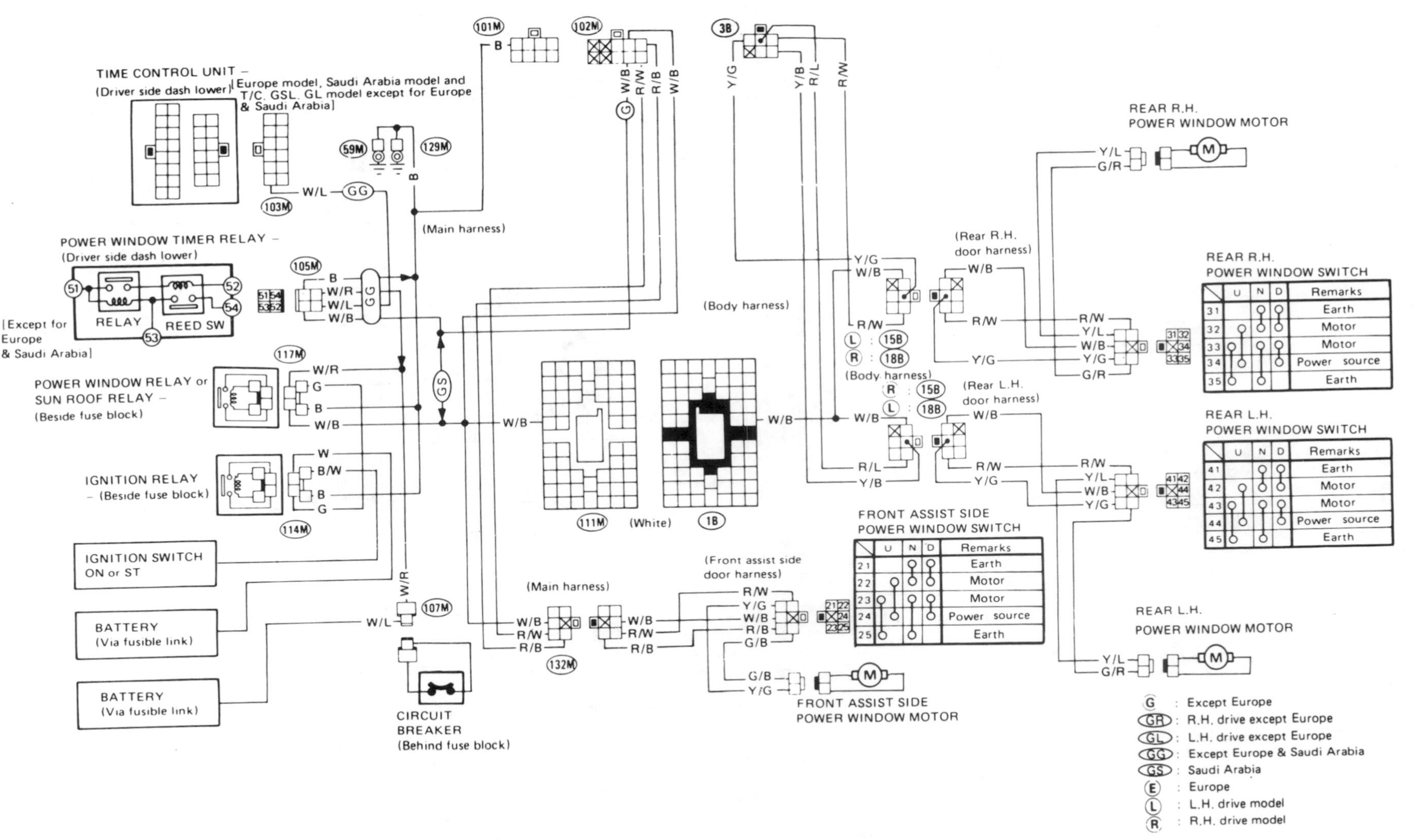

	U	N	D	Remarks
31				Earth
32				Motor
33				Motor
34				Power source
35				Earth

	U	N	D	Remarks
41				Earth
42				Motor
43				Motor
44				Power source
45				Earth

	U	N	D	Remarks
21				Earth
22				Motor
23				Motor
24				Power source
25				Earth

Fig. 12.74 Wiring diagram, power-operated window circuits (continued)

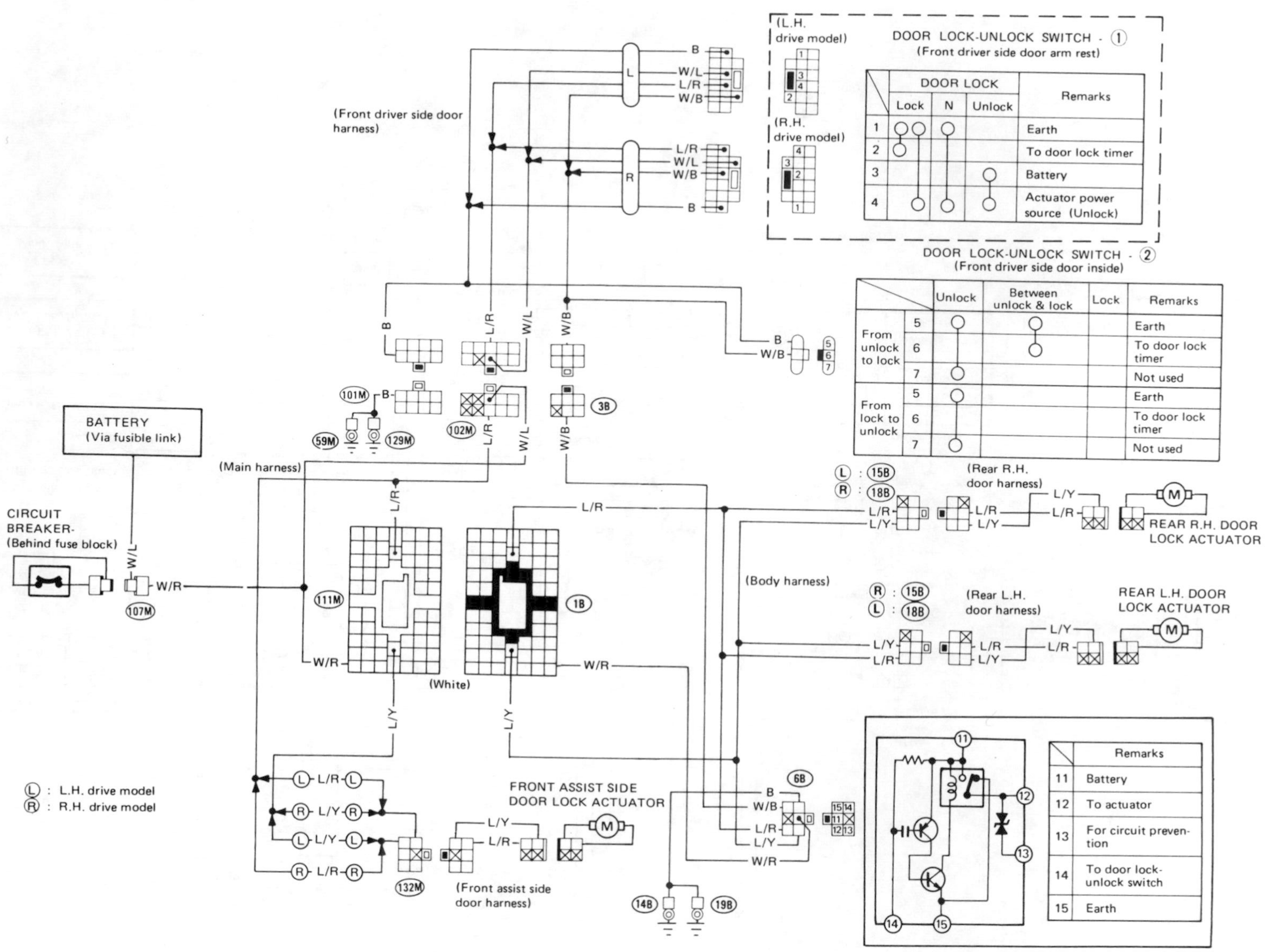

Fig. 12.75 Wiring diagram, central-locking circuits

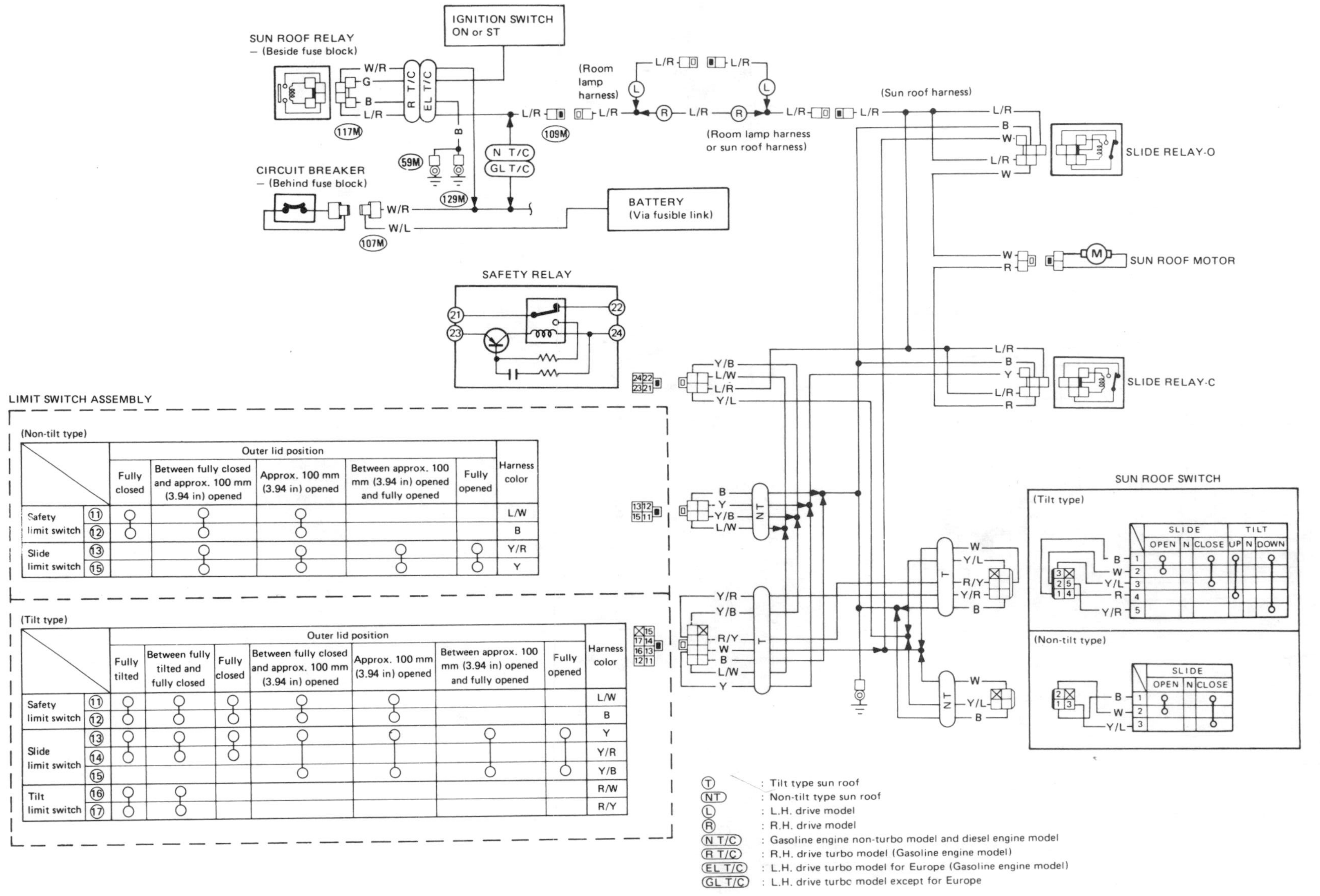

Sun roof switch (Tilt type)

Terminal	Harness	SLIDE OPEN	SLIDE N	SLIDE CLOSE	TILT UP	TILT N	TILT DOWN
1	B	O		O	O		O
2	W	O					
3	Y/L			O			
4	R				O		
5	Y/R						O

Sun roof switch (Non-tilt type)

Terminal	Harness	SLIDE OPEN	SLIDE N	SLIDE CLOSE
1	B	O		O
2	W	O		
3	Y/L			O

LIMIT SWITCH ASSEMBLY

(Non-tilt type)

		Outer lid position: Fully closed	Between fully closed and approx. 100 mm (3.94 in) opened	Approx. 100 mm (3.94 in) opened	Between approx. 100 mm (3.94 in) opened and fully opened	Fully opened	Harness color
Safety limit switch	⑪	O	O	O			L/W
	⑫	O	O	O			B
Slide limit switch	⑬		O	O	O	O	Y/R
	⑮		O	O	O	O	Y

(Tilt type)

		Outer lid position: Fully tilted	Between fully tilted and fully closed	Fully closed	Between fully closed and approx. 100 mm (3.94 in) opened	Approx. 100 mm (3.94 in) opened	Between approx. 100 mm (3.94 in) opened and fully opened	Fully opened	Harness color
Safety limit switch	⑪	O	O	O	O	O			L/W
	⑫	O	O	O	O	O			B
Slide limit switch	⑬	O	O	O	O	O	O	O	Y
	⑭	O	O	O					Y/R
	⑮				O	O	O	O	Y/B
Tilt limit switch	⑯	O	O						R/W
	⑰	O	O						R/Y

Fig. 12.76 Wiring diagram, sun roof circuit

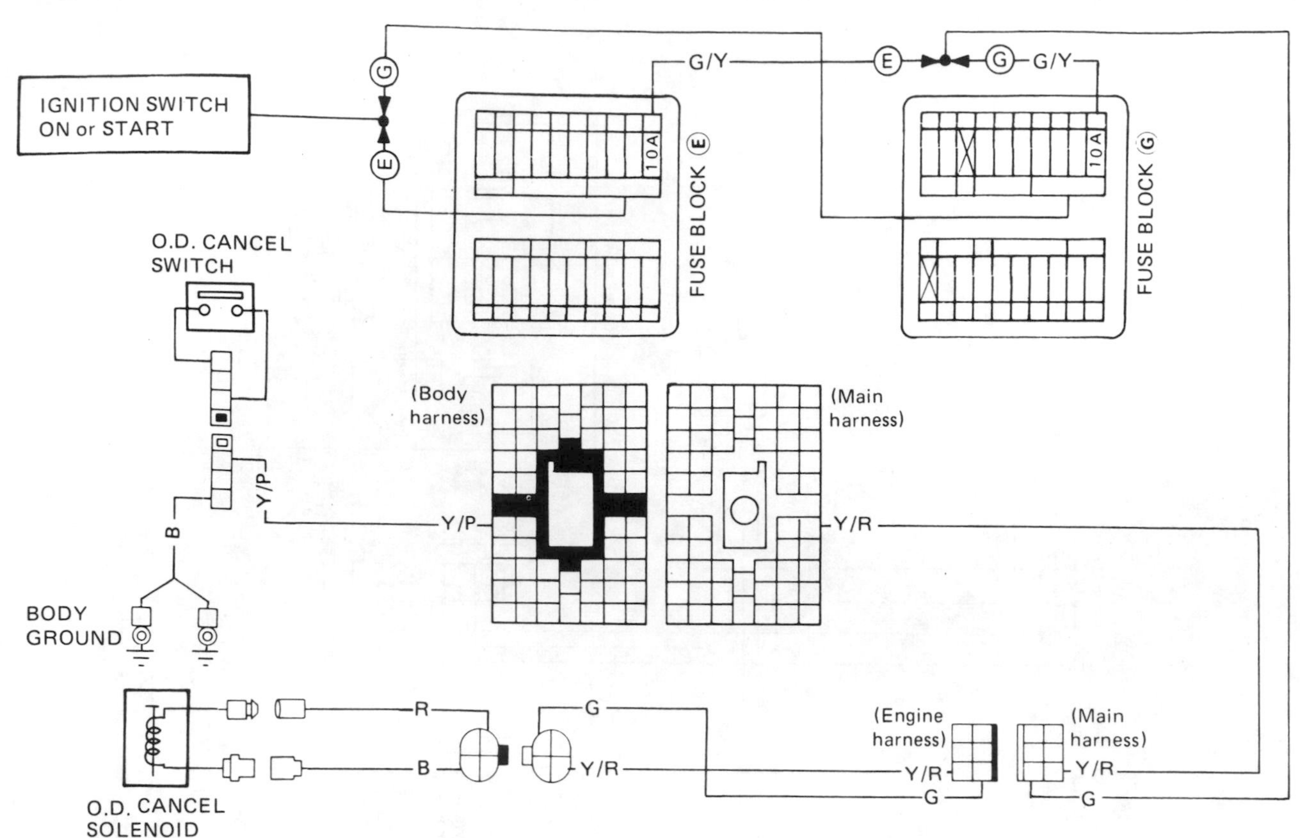

Fig. 12.77 Wiring diagram, overdrive control circuit

Index

C

D

E

I

L

M

O

P

R

S

T

U

V

W